MONETARY AND
BANKING THEORY

MONETARY

AND

BANKING THEORY

Edward Marcus

BROOKLYN COLLEGE

Mildred Rendl Marcus

PACE COLLEGE

PITMAN PUBLISHING CORPORATION

New York · Toronto · London

67- 9079

Monetary and Banking Theory is one
of a series of textbooks published in
cooperation with E. K. Georg Landsberger.

Preface

Although this book is intended primarily as an introduction to monetary and banking theory, it does not limit its coverage to just the elementary aspects. Throughout there has been the attempt to include the more advanced topics that currently trouble the field. For example, the impact of the nonbanking financial intermediary is discussed in several places, as well as the recent changes in the time deposit sector of the commercial banks.

There has been a deliberate minimization of the historical and institutional material, for the aim has been to concentrate on the understanding of monetary influences as they work through the banking system. Particular emphasis has been placed on liquidity and its manifestations through velocity. This, in turn, opens up other issues, such as the desire to hold money and the means whereby variations in this aim are reflected back on the activity of the major money suppliers. The relationship of the roles of other financial intermediaries, acting as both suppliers and demanders of such liquidity, are also explored.

Attention is also focused on major problems that have faced us over the past three decades. Greater emphasis is placed on those that it is felt will recur, such as the full-employment–inflation dilemma. On the other hand, bygone issues, such as bimetallism, have been omitted in order to give the work a more timely character.

We have also attempted to keep the language and style simple, designed for the student rather than for the professional. Based on some fifteen years' teaching, we have found that many textbooks are so obscurely written that the instructor has the added burden of explaining what the text really means. Through the use of elementary illustrations we hope to avoid this, thus freeing classroom time for use in exploring the broader questions of policy and the various implications of the current scene as assessed in light of the text material. Since our aim has been to avoid the more advanced fine points of monetary theory, we feel that this approach is feasible. It should be added, however, that some knowledge of the Keynesian (or macroeconomic) framework is of help in following the cyclical discussion, although a brief description is supplied in Chapter 2.

EDWARD MARCUS
MILDRED RENDL MARCUS

Contents

MONETARY AND
BANKING THEORY

Chapter I

MONETARY PROBLEMS AND THE ECONOMY

Our modern sophisticated economy is a dynamic and ever-changing one. Repeating this in an economics book is belaboring the obvious, but it may be worthwhile to point out one implicit point in this obvious remark: the problems facing our economy are also changing constantly. Some remain with us continually; some remain with us while their specific manifestations change; some disappear and are replaced with new problems. To cope with those that come within the scope of monetary theory is the role of the money-and-banking analyst. The implementation of his studies is the task of our monetary authorities— in particular, the Federal Reserve System and the Treasury.

Stability and Growth

Essentially, these problems can be subdivided into two categories: *stability* and *growth*. More complex issues include aspects of both. Viewed another way, our *growth* problems are essentially the longer-run tendencies of the economy, whereas the *stability* concern is more short-run. However, here "short-run" usually extends for a period of several years—the length of one business cycle—whereas "long-run" reaches ahead twenty, fifty, or more years. Often the *stability* topics are summarized by the conflict of full employment versus inflation, while *growth* assesses the possibilities of maximization of per-capita living standards and productive capacity.

Assessing the relative importance of these two categories has varied even within the lifetimes of many analysts still active today. In the 1930's, the severity of the depression made the stability problem paramount. Unemployment then enveloped about 25 percent of the labor force, and excess capacity characterized almost every industry. International trade was being strangled by the imposition of devices to protect the home producer. Today, however, emphasis has switched to growth. The United States and Western Europe have enjoyed two decades of peak production, and the recessions have been mainly interruptions to the expansionary forces. Unemployment at its worst has been relatively low by pre–1939 standards. Today we are confronted by comparisons with the rapid expansion of output in the Communist Bloc. This group of countries claims that in raising its production faster than we raise ours, it will eventually have more than enough to match our living standards, and also provide surpluses for the underdeveloped, poorer two-thirds of the world.

To a certain extent the two problems also intermingle. When a country experiences great instability, its income undergoes wide fluctuations, the business outlook becomes less certain, and it is more difficult to plan ahead. Hence, business is less likely to invest as much for expansion until it can project future sales with accuracy. Aggregate investment is therefore less, and future output is reduced more than it would have been had the planning horizon been more favorable. Growth, then, is reduced because of this short-run instability. And, as growth slows down, the future market outlets become that much less, and plant expansion is further inhibited, all this giving a cumulative character to this negative influence. Even the psychological impact is adverse, for the less optimistic atmosphere that accompanies a more slowly expanding economy also tends to inhibit the vigor so essential for its success.

An Ideal Economy

The nature of the problems we face can be best summarized by creating a hypothetical economy. In this economy growth is attained without cyclical disturbances. The conditions necessary to achieve this goal will explain the complexities that monetary and fiscal authorities must deal with in order to accomplish their objectives. It should also be emphasized here that the model economy postulated is a highly simplified one and far removed from the complex American society in which we live. Hence, the actual difficulties are far greater in practice than our example will imply.

In our model two basic and simplifying assumptions are necessary. First is the ratio of consumption to income. In our model we shall assume that individuals always spend three-fourths of their income while one-fourth is saved. Any addition to one's income is also to be divided in the same proportion: the marginal consumption-savings ratio is also 3:1.

Second, it is assumed that for every $5 invested in plant, equipment, and inventories, output expands by $1. This means the capital-output ratio is 5:1. And, since all output is assumed to be sold to final buyers, its value is therefore equal to income, since the proceeds are distributed in the form of wages, profits, rent, taxes, and so on. Every $5 invested adds $1 to both annual output and annual income; the latter, as already indicated, is then divided between consumption and savings, a 3:1 ratio. As a necessary simplification at this point we shall ignore depreciation.

TABLE I
Growth with Short-Term Equilibrium

	YEAR ONE	YEAR TWO	YEAR THREE
Capital Stock: TOTAL	2000	2100	2205
Capital*	500	525	551¼
Consumers**	1500	1575	1653¾

* Capital goods used to produce more capital goods
** Capital goods used to produce consumers' goods

Output: TOTAL	400	420	441
Consumers' Goods	300	315	330¾
Capital Goods: Total	100	105	110¼
Capital†	25	26¼	27⁹⁄₁₆
Consumers††	75	78¾	82¹¹⁄₁₆

† This year's output of capital goods that can produce more capital goods
†† This year's output of capital goods that can produce more consumers' goods

Income: TOTAL (= Output)	400	420	441
Consumption	300	315	330¾
Savings	100	105	110¼

Consumption: *Income* = 3:4
Savings: *Income* = 1:4
Capital: *Output* = 5:1

Figures are gross (before depreciation)

In our initial model year, Year One, we shall assume that the total stock of capital is $2000 billion. Of this stock, $500 billion represents various types of machine tools and other equipment for producing still more capital goods. The remaining $1500 billion represents equipment used by industries producing consumers' goods. Note that the ratio of the two sectors also reflects the 3:1 consumption–savings ratio.

Given this stock, we can easily deduce output (and income). Total output is then 20 per cent ($\frac{1}{5}$) of the capital stock, or $400 billion. Of this, $100 billion, or 20 per cent of the $500 billion, is the output of additional capital goods. Also being turned out are $300 billion in consumers' goods, again a figure equal to 20 per cent of the capital stock in this sector.

However, to maintain this crucial ratio of 3:1 between the consumers'-goods industries and the producers of capital goods, the additions to the stock of capital—the $100 billion of capital goods produced this year—must also be in a 3:1 ratio. Thus, $25 billion of these capital goods must be used for expansion of the capital-goods sector; $75 billion must be used for expansion of consumers' goods. Expressed another way, $25 billion of the capital goods produced must be of those items that can produce still more capital goods, whereas the $75 billion of capital goods produced for the consumption sector can produce only additional consumers' goods. Our capital-goods stock consists of equipment that produces *more* equipment for the production of still more equipment—the $25-billion subsector. Capital-goods stock also has equipment to produce equipment to turn out consumers' goods—the $75-billion subsector—and it has equipment that produces consumers' goods.

Phrased differently, suppose we have an economy with $2000 billion in all sorts of machinery. Some of this machinery, some $1500 billion, turns out $300 billion worth of consumers' goods, such as shoes, newspapers, and books. Other machinery, some $500 billion, turns out more machines, such as machine tools, printing presses, and boilers. Items such as the machine tools, of which $25 billion were produced in Year One, can produce still more machinery. The remaining $75 billion of capital goods turned out in Year One can produce more consumers' goods. At the end of one year our capital stock has increased to $2100 billion, of which $525 billion can produce more capital goods, and $1575 billion can produce more consumers' goods. The difference between these figures and those at the beginning of the one-year period is the $100-billion capital-stock addition.

Since output equals income in our model economy, income in Year One is also $400 billion. Three-fourths of this is spent on consumption, ($300 billion) while the remaining one-fourth ($100 billion) is saved and invested. These savings become the financing source for additional capital goods, the companies that purchase these machines obtaining the required $100 billion from the savers. So here savings and investment are equal. It is possible that some of the capital-goods purchasers saved the money themselves. If so, the saver and borrower have merged into one person. This could also be true for a company that made profits and then used these profits for the acquisition of additional equipment. Other companies, however, may have required more funds than were generated internally, and thus had to resort to borrowing from outside sources. Note, however, that whether these funds came from their own sources or from external suppliers, they were still savings.

In Year Two the expanded capital stock will result in an increased output of $420 billion, of which $315 billion will be consumers' goods, and $105 billion capital goods. This last figure, in turn, consists of $26¼ billion of capital goods to make more capital goods, and $78¾ billion of capital goods to make more consumers' goods. As for Year One, these figures reflect the ratios that have developed in our model. But now, thanks to the investment in Year One of $100 billion in capital goods, Year Two's output of its various sectors is that much greater—greater by one-fifth of this investment, or $20 billion. In turn this can be broken down into an increased output of $15 billion in consumers' goods, thanks to the $75 billion additional machines in the consumers'-goods industries installed in Year One, and $5 billion more output in the capital-goods industries coming from the $25 billion addition in Year One to the capital-goods industries. The $5 billion, in turn, was the sum of the increased output of capital goods to make capital goods (one-fourth of $5 billion, or $1¼ billion) and additional capital goods to make consumers' goods (the remainder, or $3¾ billion).

This increase in output would also result in a rise in income to $420 billion. Since we are assuming the continuance of our savings/consumption ratios, the former rises to $105 billion, the latter to $315 billion. The rise in savings here is matched exactly by the rise in investment in still more capital goods. The rise in consumption is exactly equal to the expansion of output in the consumers'-goods industries.

The analysis of Year Three is similar to that of Year Two. Additional capital goods increase output in the various sectors. (See Table 1.) Income also rises, and with it savings and consumption. And again, thanks to our previously established ratios, the increased output of consumers' goods is exactly equal to the demand—330¾ billion—and the additional investment in capital goods is matched by the savings forthcoming at this higher income level ($110¼ billion).

It is also of interest to note that the annual rise in incomes, and in savings and consumption, is at the rate of 5 per cent. If we multiply this by 5, the ratio of capital to output, we get 25 per cent, which in turn is the ratio of savings to income. We can generalize here. Any increase in output requires a savings ratio equal to a multiple of the desired output increase, the multiplier being the capital-output ratio. Rephrasing this in terms of our model, the percentage annual increase in output (5 per cent) requires a savings ratio (25 per cent) equal to a multiple (5) of the desired output increase (5 per cent), the multiplier being the capital-output ratio (5).

If we wished to reduce these figures to a per-capita basis to study the well-being of the average individual, then all of these figures would have to be reduced by the population factor. Expanding investment would still raise aggregate output, but the per-capita effect would be modified to the extent that the total population had also increased. In our model the 5-per-cent annual rise in output would mean a smaller rise in per-capita income if the population were also increasing.

Stability Conditions

Our model has now achieved both growth and stability. Each year saw the same increase (5 per cent) over the preceding year; thus the expansion path was a smooth one. Now, the assumptions that resulted in this ideal should be examined.

Probably most important was the constancy of the various ratios. Each additional invested dollar produced the same amount (one-fifth) in additional output. Each extra dollar of output yielded an equivalent increase in income, thus fixing the proportion of added consumption (three-fourths) and added savings (one-fourth). If, for example, the additional income had resulted in a different proportion consumed and saved, then the added output of consumers' goods would not equal the added demand for this output. Disequilibrium would ensue. Alternatively, the shift in the consumption-income ratio would have had to be correctly anticipated by entrepreneurs, who then would have had to shift their allocation of additional investment between the various subsectors of capital goods.

To illustrate this, assume that in Year Two consumers saved half of their additional income, or 10, spending only 10 more on consumption. If this had not been anticipated, then the consumers'-goods production of 315 would exceed demand of 310 by 5, and the probable result would be a cutback in production.

If, however, this shift had been anticipated correctly, then entrepreneurs in Year One would have added only 50 in capital goods, instead of the 100 that were added in our model, to produce the added consumers' goods (5 times 10). But this reduction would mean a decline in the output of capital goods in two ways: less machinery to produce consumers' goods, and fewer capital goods to turn out this reduced demand for machinery. Both capital-goods sectors would have to cut back. If this happened, aggregate output in the capital-goods sector would be below 100 in Year One, or less than the productive capabilities. We would thus have excess capacity in the capital-goods sectors, this further curtailing the incentive to invest. This would imply a decline in the demand for savings to finance investment just when the supply is rising more than would be expected. We would now see an excess of savings, downward pressure on the interest rate, and still further repercussions. These ramifications will be developed in subsequent chapters. In short, once we have a shift in the consumption ratio or, for that matter, any important relationship postulated, the odds are that we shall get disequilibria whether or not the shift had been anticipated correctly.

Now, if we allow for such shifts, we must also allow for incorrect anticipations. For example, it is possible for entrepreneurs to expect a rise in the savings-income rate, but in doing so, to misjudge the extent. Suppose the expectation was for a rise from 25 per cent of additional income to 35 per cent, whereas in fact it rose to 50 per cent. Then the added income of 20 is expected to be divided between added savings of 7 and the added consumption of 13. Hence, plans would be made to step up the output of consumers' goods from 300 to 313. But, as already mentioned, the savings rate was much higher, so consumption rose to only 310. Thus we have overproduction in the consumers'-goods sector, and in addition, cutbacks in the capital-goods sectors.

Even an unexpectedly high consumption would be of little help. Suppose the additional income was accompanied by 80 per cent consumption—16 more for consumers' goods and 4 more for savings. If unanticipated, we get excess demand for consumers' goods (316, against an output of 315), and a savings rise to only 104, against a demand for funds for investment amounting to 105. The consumers'-goods industries then are under an expansionary pressure, while investors may turn to the banks to fill the gap left by inadequate savings. This could be an inflationary problem, one that will recur often in this book.

If the shift were correctly anticipated, and consumers'-goods output were to expand in Year Two to 316, then the capital-goods stock in the consumers'-goods industry must be raised to 1580 (316 × 5). To effect this, the purchase of capital goods to make consumers' goods—investment in Year One—should be 80, not 75. But then the aggregate demand for savings (105) exceeds the savings (100), and the aggregate demand for capital goods (105) exceeds available output (100). Again we have what could be an inflationary pressure regardless of the accuracy of the anticipations.

To sum up our point, one source of instability could arise from the shifting of savings-income ratios as incomes change.

Another difficulty is the anticipations aspect. Assuming the stability of the savings-income ratio, our model requires that this stability be correctly anticipated, and in the right proportion. If the Year Two expectation were different from that postulated, production of consumers' goods and capital equipment would differ from the amounts actually desired. And again we would have a supply-demand imbalance. When we realize that investment decisions reflect the outlook of the individual companies, and these, in turn, number in the thousands, it is clear why the sum of all these individually made decisions should produce a total different from the planned distribution of aggregate income between consumption and savings. In fact, it would be a remarkable coincidence for these two totals to agree.

In our model we had no difficulty in passing the savings over to those who needed them to finance the purchase of capital goods. In reality this is a most complex task and is often unsuccessful. Much of the subject centering around liquidity preference is actually an analysis of the obstacles that stand in the way of this apparently simple transfer.

Shifts in the capital-output ratio would have effects comparable with those changes already discussed concerning the savings-income ratio. If, for example, in Year Two the extra output of consumers' goods were forthcoming at only a 6:1 ratio, then the investment during Year One would result in a smaller addition to output in Year Two. Consumers'-goods production would rise $12\frac{1}{2}$, instead of 15. Capital-goods production would still rise 5. Aggregate output in Year Two would then be only $17\frac{1}{2}$ higher than in Year One, not 20 higher, and the increase in income would be correspondingly less. Assuming that the savings-income ratio remains at $\frac{1}{4}$, then in Year Two the income of $417\frac{1}{2}$ would be split between consumption of $313\frac{1}{8}$ (more than the output of consumers' goods), and savings of $104\frac{3}{8}$ would be less than the demand for investment to purchase the 105 capital goods. Again we have a disequilibrium. When we consider that research and inventions could easily change the capital-output ratio of new processes, we can see how easily these various inequalities can result.

We have also assumed that if aggregate supply equals aggregate demand, the consumers wish to buy the amounts produced of the various consumers' goods, and the investors want the various capital items being turned out. It could well be, however, that while the aggregate output of capital equipment equals aggregate investment, the companies produce more textile machinery than is wanted and not enough boilers. Industry disequilibria could easily occur. Similarly, total production of consumers' goods could equal total demand, but the components may be in disequilibrium. Suppose more shoes are produced than people wish to buy, whereas the output of television sets is insufficient. The inequalities of supply and demand could produce cutbacks of production where supply was in excess. There would be accompanying unemployment, loss of incomes and purchasing power. Where demand was greater, the shortages of goods might induce price rises and excessive expansion to make up the deficiency.

The conditions essential to stability so far described are only illustrative of the many problems of equilibrium inherent in our complex economy. The list could be endless as we added more and more detail. But enough has been said to indicate the nature of the problem —the numerous decisions that go to make up the total, with the probability of agreement being so remote that instability is almost inherent in an economy such as ours. All we can hope for is a reduction in the degree of instability—more particularly, a mitigation of the repercussions of any instability to avoid the cumulative stresses of inflation and deflation with their inhibiting effect on long-run growth.

Growth and the Money Supply

Intimately related to the problem of smoothness of growth is adequacy of the money supply. If, for example, an economy grows and produces more goods for sale, the tendency of this increase in output is to depress prices. This decline, in turn, would narrow and perhaps eliminate the producers' profit margins, thus putting an end to the production expansion. If, on the other hand, the demand for these goods were to rise proportionately to the increase in supply, we would not have this inhibiting deflationary effect. But to expand purchases calls for either a rise in the total amount of money or increased efficiency in its use. The latter aspect is treated when we discuss the Velocity concept.

The inadequacy of the money supply can be reflected in either an insufficiency or an excess. Not enough money—including an inadequate improvement in the efficiency with which the existing stock is being employed—results in a deficiency of demand. Deflation follows. Too much money, including too efficient use of the existing stock, would cause an excessive growth in demand, outrunning supply, and perhaps causing an unwanted inflation. Both deflation and inflation, then, are manifestations of our stability problem.

The efficiency concept encompasses aspects of the liquidity subject referred to previously. If money is kept idle, it is not being used efficiently. Often this idleness reflects a desire to hold on to purchasing power for eventual use when prices are more favorable, or when business conditions are more hopeful. But while this period of idleness lasts, the money so segregated is withdrawn from the purchasing stream, and this action reflects itself in a reduction in demand. Once again we may be faced with a supply in excess of demand with its deflationary consequences. So, we must examine the forces that provoke a desire to be liquid, including changes in this desire, as well as means of influencing it in a way that is favorable for the economy. Both monetary and nonmonetary banking organizations must be considered in this study, for their liquidity influences may have differing impacts on the working of the economy and the movements of the various spending streams.

In terms of the framework outlined, we can also see how monetary policy can try to influence the growth trends in order to move the economy closer to the ideal. If, for example, in Table I, Year One, banks were not lending all the savings entrusted to them, so that planned investment threatened to exceed the amount of loanable funds, the monetary authorities might induce a rise in interest rates and so make it that much more attractive to lend. On the other hand, this increased cost of borrowing might reduce the demand for loanable funds and so curtail capital expenditures. Perhaps without such intervention, only $50 billion of the $100 billion would be lent; with intervention, demand may drop to $95 billion, but loanable funds would rise to that amount. We thus fall short of the desired amount—$100 billion—but this is still an improvement in the absence of any effort to influence the flow of savings.

Or perhaps in Year Three, pessimism arises among entrepreneurs and they do not want to acquire $110¼ billion of capital goods. If the monetary authorities are able to lower existing interest rates, the reduced cost of borrowing—and thus the enhanced profit margin— might change the minds of these people. Perhaps this lower rate might reduce the willingness of the banks to lend by only a small amount. Again the savings-investment amounts realized would diverge from the ideal, but by much less than in the absence of intervention. Hence, although the authorities may not be able to achieve the ideal growth pattern, we see that they may be able to thrust the country closer to it, thereby reducing possible disequilibrium. In what follows, we shall be concentrating our attention on the various ways in which the authorities can influence the many growth subsectors. We shall also examine some of the difficulties involved in estimating the reactions of the affected groups.

Summary

In this chapter we pointed out certain instabilities that arise from the long-run growth of our economy. Because of variations in both the marginal propensity to consume, and the ratio of additional output coming from new capital formation, it is virtually impossible to achieve a smoothly expanding system. In addition, there could be discrepancies between the output of, and demand for, specific industries, or the output mix of capital and consumers' goods as compared with the division of income between savings and consumption. We can thus get oversupply or excess demand in the various sectors, which can then lead either to production and income cutbacks, or to inflationary price rises and undue expansion. These tendencies could be further complicated by poor guesswork in regard to future trends, such as erroneous anticipations and expectations. To all these problems add the possibility of the money supply increasing at a rate different from the volume of business activity and we see the difficult framework within which monetary authorities function.

Chapter 2

THE FRAMEWORK
OF A MONEY ECONOMY

The sophisticated economy, such as that of the United States or the major Western European countries, is so complex to analyze that economists have been forced to use two different approaches. One is known as *micro*economics. It tends to concentrate on individual sectors such as the price of wheat or the output of an automobile plant. This method is associated with the traditional tools of supply and demand. The second conceptual framework is encompassed within the world of *macro*economics or macroanalysis. This attempts to study the movement of the economy as a whole, or, if more refined in its attack, stops at the important aggregates such as investment, income and employment. It is this second approach, macroeconomics, that will be studied in this chapter.

Income and Output

In order to study macroeconomics it is necessary to understand some fundamental identities. Perhaps the most basic is the equality of income and output, if both are defined appropriately.

As a first approach, we can select a typical manufacturing concern —for example, a producer of shoes. We shall assume that the annual value of its output is $1 million. For the moment we shall also assume that all of its output is sold for this amount, and that the volume of shoes produced is the same as the volume sold.

As a result of the year's operations, our firm had both an output and sales of $1 million. What happened to this money? Some was paid out in wages, thus becoming income to the employees. Some went for the purchase of raw materials, thus becoming income to the various suppliers. Still other funds were paid out in rent. This became part of the landlord's income. Taxes also accounted for a portion. This is used by the government to pay its employees, suppliers, and the like. If the firm borrowed money, it must also pay interest. This becomes income to its creditors. And, finally, if a profit remains, this becomes the owners' income. If a loss occurred, the net income is negative for both the company and its owners. But whatever the result, all of the output becomes someone's income.

The reader with financial curiosity may raise several questions. Suppose some of the money had been used to redeem an outstanding debt? This would not affect our analysis. Such capital transactions do not enter into an income statement. This would be simply an exchange of capital items, cash and liabilities both being reduced. To obtain the necessary cash, the firm must first have an excess of receipts over expenses, and thus a profit. In this illustration, the owners had decided not to take their profits in cash, but instead used them to reduce their indebtedness.

An alternative to the preceding illustration would be the use of cash to purchase capital equipment. Here one asset (cash) is exchanged for another asset (machinery), but the reasoning of the previous paragraph would still hold: profits had to be made to produce the cash surplus. These profits were then employed for the capital acquisition. (Alternatively, in this and the preceding illustration the cash could have come from depreciation, as illustrated below.)

What about inventory additions? Goods produced and not sold are stored in the warehouse. This inventory adds to the firm's working capital. But since there was no sale, there would be no cash receipt. However, we did have output. To produce this, we did pay out wages, buy raw materials, and so forth. The value of this output, translated into inventory, would be the sum of these various costs resulting in income to the recipient.

What about depreciation? This is a charge to cover the decline in value of the fixed equipment. This is a cost, and the money to pay it may then be set aside to provide a fund for the replacement of items when they wear out. This replacement purchase then becomes income for the seller of the new equipment. Only when the depreciation reserve is not used in the current period would we have a discrepancy; the value of output, as measured by sales, would exceed the income received (by the various employees and suppliers) by the amount added to the depreciation reserve and not utilized. Here would be an exception to our thinking; in practice this would not be significant for the economy as a whole. For any one year, some companies might add more to depreciation reserves than they use. Others might use more of the reserve than they add. The latter, in effect, would be spending several years' accumulations in this one year.

To illustrate: suppose a machine worth $5,000 is expected to last five years. Each year the firm sets aside $1,000 as a replacement fund. For four years it is adding more to its fund than it is utilizing, but in the fifth year it then uses the accumulated $5,000 to buy a new machine. In that last year it added only $1,000 to the reserve—just as it had done in each of the previous years—but it spent $5,000. So, in terms of our income-output discussion, it had an excess of output over income for four years, each year's excess amounting to $1,000.

But in the fifth year it added more to income (the $5,000 machinery purchase) than the $1,000 of output allowed for replacement. The excess of income over output in the fifth year ($4,000) is exactly equal to the previous four years' excesses of output over income.

While many companies are in the position of this hypothetical firm during the first four years—output being in excess of income because the company utilizes less than its depreciation charge—other companies would be in the same position as the hypothetical company in its fifth year; that is, incomes would be in excess of output because of their replacement purchases. We can usually assume that these two groups cancel each other, and for the economy as a whole, the depreciation charges approximate the replacement purchases, even though this may not be true for each individual company.

To summarize here, we can say that output and income are always equal. But the difference between the two terms is only a different way of examining the same item. Output views the process from the point of view of the payer. Income views the process from the point of view of the recipient. From the company position, money is being paid out to call forth production. From the employees' and suppliers' position, income is being earned for goods and services used to turn out production. This income, as we shall see, may then become an expenditure—a demand—and thus might well end up as a purchase of the very goods produced. We will show that variations in these two subdivisions account for much of the instability in our economy.

The Consumption Function

In addition to the equality of income and output, there is another relationship fundamental to an understanding of the economy's operation—the consumption function. This relates changes in consumption and spending to changes in income; its short-run reactions probably differ significantly enough from the long-run trend to warrant separate discussion.

Briefly, the belief is that people's spending habits, or their purchase of consumers' goods (including durables), display a certain slowness to change when conditions alter. As a result, if incomes rise, consumption will also rise, but more slowly. Arithmetically, not only will this change—the marginal propensity to consume—result in consumption changing less than income, but the proportion of these two shifts will be less than the prior relationship of consumption to income (the propensity to consume). For example, if a man earns $150 a week, he may spend $135, or 90 per cent, and save the remainder, or 10 per cent. If his income should rise to $160, his consumption would also rise, by less than $10, and probably less than $9. If he is to spend only $7 of this increase, his marginal propensity to consume would be 70 per cent, less than his previous average propensity (90 per cent); note that the actual additional amount spent is less than the income increase.

Implicit in the foregoing is the relationship of the propensity to save. Since the difference between income and consumption is savings, this, obviously, is the remainder from the previous calculations. In our illustration, the propensity to save, at $150, had been 10 per cent. The additional income of $10 added $3 to savings, or a marginal propensity to save of 30 per cent. The marginal propensity to save is therefore higher than the average: its proportionate change is greater than the previous savings-income relationship. If income were to decline, the short-run reactions would be analogous, but opposite. If our hypothetical worker had his income cut to $140, his consumption would decline, but not by $10. Probably not even by $9, or 90 per cent, the average propensity to consume. Assume that it declined by $8, to $127 from $135. Here the marginal propensity to consume is 80 per cent. Savings decline by $2: the income cut ($10) exceeded the spending cut ($8), and thus had to come out of savings. Total savings are now only $13. As before, the marginal propensity to save (20 per cent) is higher than the average (10 per cent).

A summary of the previous relationships can be expressed somewhat differently. If income rises, both consumption and savings rise in absolute amounts. But proportionately, savings rise faster than income, whereas consumption rises more slowly. If income declines, both consumption and savings decline absolutely. But proportionately, consumption declines more slowly and savings more quickly than did income. If income declines very much, the more rapid decline in savings may depress total savings to zero, or even to a negative figure: to sustain consumption, the people may not only spend all their current income, but also use prior accumulations of savings to sustain living standards. This extreme, of course, would occur only in a severe depression, such as we experienced the decade after the 1929 stock-market crash.

If incomes are deflated to extremely low levels, as might occur in a severe depression, it is possible for savings to become negative. People would be spending more than their incomes, drawing money from their bank accounts to meet this need. If, at the same time, industry is drawing down its inventories[1]—the decline in stocks matching the drawing down of past savings—we could have negative investment of just enough to offset the negative savings, and thus a new, low-level equilibrium. At some point, it is true, the decline in inventories would have to stop, for there are certain minimum quantities that businesses must keep on hand to operate, but that may be only after quite a deflationary spell. This absolute minimum in some recessions might put a stop to the downward spiral, as savings utilization is matched by new output. Then the upturn—or at least end of the downturn—is reached. This is examined when we discuss the graphic presentation of the macroeconomic system.

In the long run, however, the relationship of the two income components appears to be more stable. Once the income has changed and its new level appears to be more than temporary, then the individual starts adjusting his spending pattern. In our example, if the worker's income rose to $160 and remained there for some time, then consumption would rise even more, probably to $144, while savings would drop back to $16 (from $18). Consumption is once again 90 per cent of income, and savings 10 per cent of income. Similarly, if the worker's income were cut to $140, and were expected to remain there, he would slowly economize on some of his expenditures, reducing consumption further from its previous level of $127 to $126. Savings would thus rise from $13 to $14. Once again we are back at our 90-per-cent consumption and 10-per-cent savings ratios.

The apparent explanation of this long-run persistence appears to reflect almost a class bias. Within any community there is unequal distribution of income. People's spending habits determine their relative position in this income pyramid. If there is a general rise in income, the relative positions remain unchanged, and spending habits are resumed. This relatively stable position is not realized in the short run,

---

[1] That is, if sales exceed output.

when the income rise appears to be a windfall for a particular individual. But gradually he realizes that others have also obtained increased incomes, and the various social forces then reassert themselves. His previous spending relationships are reestablished.

If, on the other hand, his relative position has improved, then others' have gone down relatively. Hence, as his spending habits reflect his move upward on the pyramid, others' spending habits reflect their relative decline, and so for the group there has been no change. In the long run, therefore, it is not the absolute amount of income that determines a person's spending, but his relative position in his community.

The community, incidentally, need not be identical with the geographic environment in which the person lives. It really is the society in which he moves. Thus, rural areas, which generally have lower incomes than urban areas, reflect the same proportionate effects. A farmer midway in the rural income pyramid probably saves the same proportion of his income as a city dweller midway in the urban income pyramid, even though in absolute amounts the city dweller's income may be considerably higher. The position of an urban Negro midway in the income pyramid may mean more in relation to the urban Negro group than to the urban income pyramid dominated by white people and their spending habits. As a consequence of this relative influence, the society's aggregate consumption and savings relative to incomes tend to show amazing stability over long periods. The average propensities to consume and save apparently change little, if at all, over long periods of time.

A word of caution should be added here. Statistics are far from perfect, and their reliability diminishes as we go back in time. To say that incomes in 1790 were distributed between consumption and savings in the same ratio as they are currently is to ask too much of the current state of our economic knowledge. The data are simply not that accurate or reliable. More intensive research could alter these propositions.

Another qualification affecting the flexibility of the savings component is the implication that savings are a residual. When incomes change, the decision affects the spending pattern, and savings then become simply the arithmetic difference between these two figures. But in practice savings may not be so flexible. Many individuals, for example, have insurance policies through which they save by contracting to pay the premium regularly. When incomes decline, the first reaction is to continue paying the premium and reduce other savings, if available, or consumption, when other savings cannot be cut. In our example, if a man had committed $5 weekly for insurance, the decline in his income from $150 to $140 could have been met as before, by reducing other savings from $10 to $8. But if he had contracted to pay

$14 weekly and did not wish to drop or reduce his insurance, then the income decline would compel him to cut consumption by the full amount, so that at the lower income he still saved $14, paying it over to the insurance company.[2] In such a case, savings are most rigid, and the changes in consumption are then the residual.

Obviously, what we have said for insurance premiums holds for any contractual payment the individual wishes to keep paying. Installment credit, mortgages, mutual-funds purchase programs—all commit set amounts of money and are designed to compel the person to save. Subsequently, if he experiences an income decline, he must either reduce his consumption or curtail his savings plans. Often, however, the ending of such payments involves a penalty: the sales charges are usually taken out of the initial payments, so that termination of the contract results in the return of little or none of the money paid in. This creates an incentive to maintain payments, and so either non-contractual savings must be reduced that much more, or consumption must go down. Only when the decline seriously threatens the previous standard of living does the individual finally decide to modify or end his savings plans.

The extent of contractual saving methods varies among individuals. Poorer people may not have much insurance, but they may be indebted on installment contracts and mortgages. In the upper income brackets the insurance component becomes quite large. Often there are also mutual-fund contracts by which the contributor sends in a regular amount that the receiving company reinvests in a group of securities. On these contracts, as indicated, there is a sales charge, and the charge is usually related to the entire life value of the plan. But the deduction for this sales charge is often almost entirely from the first payments. Thus, little actually accrues as savings in the earlier period, since so much of the amount turned over to the company has gone for selling costs. It is only in the later years, when the sales-cost deduction is negligible, that the amounts contributed begin to provide a significant addition to the saver's assets. In effect, the contract "locks in" the individual, for once started, it requires continued payments to attain the objective—a fund in excess of those monies paid in, the additional income from the reinvestment of the amounts so received.

The Equality of Savings and Investment

Fundamental to an understanding of the cyclical process is the relationship of savings and investment. Savings can be defined quite

---

[2] Note that his other (voluntary) savings dropped by 100 per cent, and are now zero.

simply: the difference between income and consumption. Investment is employed only in its real, tangible form—additions to the stock of capital goods, including equipment, buildings, and inventories. (Net investment would be this figure less depreciation.) Excluded would be financial investment that merely transfers title without altering the stock of real investment. An example is the purchase of an outstanding security, the seller holding the proceeds idle.

With these definitions it can be shown that savings must equal investment. Total output consists of either consumers' goods produced and sold for consumption purposes, or capital goods, and additions to inventories of either. The production of consumers' goods that are not sold for consumption would be added to inventories—either by the manufacturers or the distributors—and thus included in investment (similarly for unsold capital goods). Hence, investment is the difference between aggregate output and the consumption of consumers' goods. Income, which is equal to output, minus consumption equals savings. Therefore, savings and investment are equal.

Expressed algebraically, using I for capital goods and In for additions to inventories, Y for income, O for output, C for consumption, and S for savings, we have:

$$(1) \quad O = Y$$

This is our basic equality of output (O) and income (Y).

$$(2) \quad O = C + I + In$$

Output consists of those goods bought by consumers (C) plus those capital goods that have been produced (I) plus changes in inventories of these two (In).

$$(3) \quad Y = C + S$$

Income (Y) is used either for the purchase of consumers' goods (C) or is saved (S).

$$(4) \quad O - C = Y - C$$

Here we simply subtract the consumers' goods bought from both output and income.

$$(5) \quad O - C = I + In = \text{Investment}$$

Having subtracted the output of consumers' goods sold to consumers from our output, the remainder is the output of capital goods plus changes in inventories.

$$(6) \quad Y - C = S = O - C$$

From equation (3) we see that income minus consumption leaves savings. From equation (4) we get the equality of $Y - C$ and $O - C$. Therefore, since things equal to the same thing are equal to each other, these two equal savings (S).

$$(7) \quad S = I + In$$

From equation (5) we see that $O - C$ equals the investment total, $I + In$. By substituting this component into equation (6) we get equation (7).

Keynes first put this equality forth in his book, *The General Theory of Employment Interest and Money* (1936). Needless controversy was engendered, but it was not realized that the furor resulted from a simple arithmetic relationship based on actual data. Using the above equations when studying a community's national accounts covering one year, we would be able to get the total output for that period, broken down by our three subsectors. Similarly, we would get the income total and its breakdown. Assuming for the moment that there are no foreign transactions,[3] then the above equations must hold. What the critics failed to distinguish was the arithmetic identities of the actual data and the possible divergences if the expectations element is present. That is, it is possible for the sum of the country's planned investments to diverge from planned savings,[4] but the amounts actually realized (or *ex post*, to use the Swedish phrase) had to be equal. One could thus talk of *divergences* between the two when considering the future, but of *equality* of the two when viewing an historical period. We shall see that it is the difference between the two *ex ante* which accounts for much of the cyclical characteristics of our economy.

Inventories

The role of inventories also proved troublesome in Keynes' formulation, but this, too, can be reconciled. If, for example, producers plan to turn out $100 billion of consumers' goods and $20 billion of capital goods, planned investment is then $20 billion. Suppose consumers plan to buy $90 billion worth of goods and save $30 billion. (Output and income are both $120 billion.) Then planned investment is obviously less than planned savings. Consumers' goods equalling $10 billion will be unsold, and therefore added to inventories. So, here unplanned investment in inventories turns out to be $10 billion. Total actual or realized investment is $30 billion—the planned investment of $20 billion in capital goods plus the unplanned investment of $10 billion in inventories of consumers' goods—or the same as planned savings. In this illustration, inventories reacted to bring about the necessary equality.

A similar arithmetic would work if consumers had planned to consume $110 billion of consumers' goods and to save only $10 billion. The excess of consumption over output of consumers' goods would have drawn down inventories by $10 billion. That is, unplanned

---

[3] See Chapter 24.

[4] The Swedish economists used the phrase *ex ante* for planned or anticipated decisions.

disinvestment of inventories was $10 billion, so that net investment was only $10 billion—the planned investment in capital goods of $20 billion and the unplanned disinvestment of inventories of $10 billion. Again we have equality of realized savings and investment. However, it must be added that the achieving of this equality need not be through the unplanned changes in inventories; it is also possible for output—and thus incomes—to vary when it is realized that the various plans do not appear capable of fulfillment, thus changing our basic figures again. This possibility will be explored later.

The Cyclical Process

The cyclical process can now be described in outline. Essentially, it is a reformulation of the equilibrium type of analysis common in economics—that is, when a disturbance sets up new forces that bring about another equilibrium, the new position then becomes stable until some other outside, unsettling factor enters to begin a new reaction to produce a new equilibrium.

In the cyclical analysis the significant factor is the marginal propensity to consume: as incomes rise, consumption rises, but less proportionately; and, as incomes decline, consumption drops off, but less proportionately. Consequently, the rise in income, reflected in an increase in supply, is more in absolute amount than the accompanying rise in demand (or consumption). Conversely, on the way down, the income (or supply) decline is greater than the consumption (or demand) drop. Hence, if it is excess demand that is pushing up income, the resulting faster rise in supply closes this gap. The effect of the consumption propensity is to reduce the pressure by adding more to supply than to demand. In a deflation, such as occurs when supply exceeds demand, the drop in income reduces supply faster than demand as a result of the decline in savings; this, in turn, reduces the excess supply gap.

In this section we shall limit the discussion to the major elements. Much of the remainder of this book is devoted to a more detailed analysis of the various threads that make up the system. It will also be assumed in what follows that there are enough unused capacity and enough idle resources (including manpower) to permit supply to expand as indicated.

If we assume that the system is for the moment in equilibrium, we would thus have the various equalities—income and output, savings and investment, and stability of inventories. Suppose there is a shift—for example, the government income-tax law is changed. This alters the take-home pay of many individuals. It will also alter previous savings-income and consumption-income ratios. Here we shall assume that the net effect is to lower the savings-income ratio for the economy, and consequently raise the consumption-income ratio. As a result, the previous equalities are disturbed, the demand for consumers' goods will rise, and the supply of savings will decline.

Initially, this rise in demand for consumers' goods will draw down stocks, thus reestablishing equality, as described previously. But this type of equality is only temporary. It, too, sets in motion forces that will create further shifts.

As manufacturers and retailers see their stocks of commodities declining, they will tend to step up production. Declining inventories are the signal that demand exceeds the supply currently coming from production. And, as output is stepped up, income, in turn, is increased. This income increase again raises consumption and savings, but the consumption rise is less than the income rise. This, of course, means that the added output of goods (equal to income) is greater than the added demand coming from this output because of the effect on increased incomes. The additional supply now is more than the additional demand. And since our original disturbance created demand in excess of current output, the secondary reaction is working to close this gap by adding more to output than to demand. But if output rises enough, it will add more to supply than the accompanying income increase adds to demand. And the supply-demand equality is reestablished. At this point inventories become stable again, and there is no longer any reason to continue to expand output. A new equilibrium has been attained.

The extent of this upward shift depends on the reaction of consumption to income increases. It must lag behind by enough to produce this net excess of output, thereby eliminating the demand excess. Hence, the lower the marginal propensity to consume, the greater the excess of the supply addition over the demand addition, and the quicker the gap is closed.

It is also possible that the demand increase might stimulate plant expansion, but only if the existing plant capacity is inadequate to supply the extra demand that initiated the upward movement. If so, then we have new investment plans, a new increased demand for capital goods, still more output and income, and a still greater demand for consumers' goods. Thus, to the original expansionary force we have now added this investment reaction. The *acceleration* principle details this further. Note that the addition of this capital-goods expansion—by adding further to demand—increases the supply-demand gap, thus making it necessary to expand output that much more in order to produce a still greater excess of additions to supply.

The downward process can be similarly depicted. Assume that the international situation deteriorates. The community gets worried, reduces its consumption and steps up its planned savings. The output of consumers' goods now exceeds demand, and inventories start increasing. Realizing that they are now overproducing, manufacturers curtail production. Incomes are thus reduced. Consumption declines further as a result of this loss of income, but the decline in demand is less than the decline in income. This means that the output (supply) reduction is greater than the secondary demand drop. The process which started this adjustment was the excess of supply; now we are eliminating it by reducing output faster than demand. Once we have reduced output and incomes sufficiently to end this supply excess, and once we have cut back supply more than the demand reduction that the supply cut provokes, we restore the equality of supply and demand and end the drawing down of inventories. We reestablish equilibrium, although at a lower level than before the process started.

The Multiplier

The change in incomes as a result of the initial disparity between aggregate supply and demand is contained within the concept of the multiplier. This is an attempt to measure more precisely the necessary multiple of the gap that will produce a new equilibrium. An exact figure cannot be arrived at, for, as already indicated, the marginal propensity to consume is somewhat variable, especially during the short-term change in incomes. Since this propensity, in effect, is the determinant of the difference between changes in output and changes in demand—the difference being the marginal change in savings—we get a somewhat fuzzy value for the multiplier. And, as already indicated, it is this gap and the rate at which it is closed that influences so significantly the final change in income.

To illustrate the multiplier computation by use of a somewhat simplified arithmetic example, assume for the moment that the marginal propensity to consume is 80 per cent. Assume that it remains constant as income changes. Assume further that demand shifts upward. Now it exceeds the supply of goods by $10 billion.[5] As the preceding section indicated, this will be reflected at first in a drawing down of inventories, but then production runs will be adjusted upward to replenish stocks. And for each upward move in output of $1 billion, demand will rise by 80 per cent, or $800 million. Hence, each $1-billion rise in output will reduce excess demand by only $200 million—the excess of the additional output over the additional consumption.

---

[5] This change could be due to any autonomous factor. For example, the government might pay out a new bonus to war veterans, thus adding to demand. The financing of such an expenditure will be discussed in Chapter 22.

Since the initial excess is $10 billion, it is clear that total output must expand by $50 billion in order to close the original gap. Of this, $40 billion will spill over into still more demand, leaving the excess additional supply at $10 billion, or just enough to fill the original gap. Our multiplier is thus 5—$10 billion, the original gap, multiplied by 5, to give $50 billion, or the total expansion as a result of the initial gap. Note that the marginal propensity to save—20 per cent, or one-fifth—is the reciprocal of this multiplier. (If we were to assume that investment also increased as a result of this large rise in output—the *acceleration* principle—the total rise would be still more, and would measure the multiplying effect of this investment stimulus.)

If we were to become more realistic now and build in a changing marginal propensity to consume, the final value would become more complicated. If, for example, with each rise of output and incomes of $10 billion the marginal propensity to consume dropped 5 per cent, we would have to calculate the equilibrium path in steps. The first $10-billion rise in output would raise spending by $8 billion, closing the supply-demand gap by $2 billion. The next 10-billion step would raise consumption by only $7½ billion, closing the gap by an additional $2½ billion. The third step of $10 billion would close the remaining gap by an additional $3 billion, and the final step would require about an additional $7 billion in output, because the associated marginal propensity to consume would be only 65 per cent. This would result in an excess additional supply of about $2½ billion, which, when added to the previous amounts would yield $10 billion. More complicated changes in the marginal propensity to consume would require more complicated formulas to calculate the multiplier.

If supply exceeds demand, such as in the deflationary illustration, the multiplier then works in a negative direction. Assuming a constant marginal propensity to consume of 80 per cent, the necessary output and income deflation would then be 5 times the original excess supply. As can be seen, the multiplier—the reciprocal of the marginal propensity to save—thus gives rise to wide swings in the economic level of activity. Note that the greater the marginal propensity to save, the smaller the magnitude of the resulting reactions of output and income. A marginal propensity to save of 33⅓ per cent (marginal propensity to consume of two-thirds) would yield a multiplier of 3, whereas a marginal propensity to save of only 10 per cent (a marginal propensity to consume of 90 per cent) would result in a multiplier of 10.

Note also that shifts in demand from a given income are not the only way for these movements to take place. If investment were to step up (if bank lending were to rise) so that the output of capital goods were to increase, thereby raising incomes and demand, we

FIGURE I

Income Determination

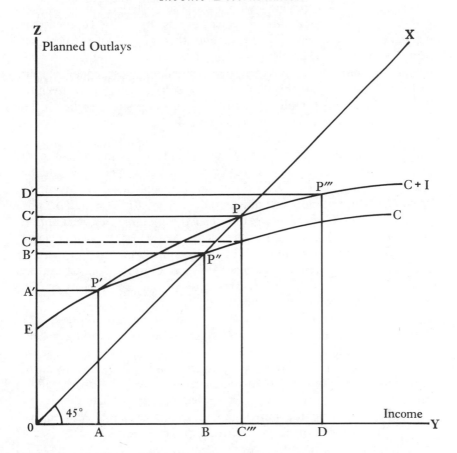

would again have a supply-demand gap. A rise in such bank-financed investment of $10 billion would expand output and incomes by $10 billion, which, assuming the 80-per-cent marginal propensity to consume, would raise the demand for consumers' goods by $8 billion. For the moment, then, we have not altered the output of consumers' goods, and we have an excess demand as before. Thus the expansionary process starts. This is also true, in reverse, if we cut back on investment.

The Graphic Presentation

The adjustment process already described can be depicted graphically. The accompanying graph (Figure I), illustrates this approach.

Essential to its understanding is the 45° line, OX. Every point on this line is equidistant from the two axes OY, along which we measure income, and OZ, along which we measure the planned (or intended) outlays on consumption and investment goods. It will be recalled that output and income must be equal, and that every dollar spent on output becomes someone else's income. Therefore, in equilibrium output and income must be equal, and spending must equal output must equal income. (In this explanation we shall assume that inventories do not change.) Graphically, the equilibrium point must lie on the 45° line, since that point represents equality of income and output (measured horizontally) and spending (measured vertically).

The C curve indicates how much would be consumed out of a given income. Thus, P′ means that, at income AO, people would be willing to spend AP′ (or OA′) on consumers' goods. Were income to rise to OB, consumption spending would rise to BP″ (= OB′). The increase in income of AB is greater than the increase in consumption because of the rising savings component. Note that at income level OA (or less) there is no investment. As income rises past OA, investment rises—the difference between C+I and C—and rises faster than income. This reflects the greater response of this component to the higher levels of income and output.

At zero income (the origin) there is still some consumption, OE. This would be financed out of past savings. But the spending would then require output to meet this demand, thus generating incomes. And so, income and output move to the right. But this, in turn, would raise consumption still further, although by less than the additional output. The extra supply is increasing faster than the added demand, thus closing the initial gap of excess demand. And so we would see continued expansion until the gap is eliminated.

Although there is some investment at incomes to the right of OA, there is no planned saving. Until we reach income OB, consumption exceeds income. Only to the right of income OB do we see savings emerge. This is measured by the vertical distance between the consumption curve and the 45° line. At income OC‴ this difference also equals the difference between the C+I and C curves—the volume of investment—and here savings equal investment. As we proceed further to the right, the savings begin to exceed investment as the distance between the C curve and the 45° line exceeds the distance between the C and C+I curves. Thus, only our equilibrium income (OC‴) produces both an equality of income and output, and of savings and investment.

Total planned spending is read vertically, to the C+I curve. Investment is the vertical distance between the C and C+I curves. At very low levels of income, such as at *P'*, investment is zero; output is so depressed that it does not pay to expand capacity or even replace worn out machines. (To avoid the complexities associated with the depreciation of capital equipment, the investment curve is gross outlays, uncorrected for machines that are discarded or decline in value because of use. Correspondingly, income and savings are also gross.)

The point *P* is an example of equilibrium. At that level of income (*OC'''*), consumption (*OC''*) plus investment (*C''C'*) equal *OC'*, which in turn is equal to *OC'''*. Planned outlays now equal income. At *P'* consumption would be *OA'*, greater than income of *OA*; since consumption of *OA'* means that the sellers are gaining incomes of *OA'*, which is greater than *OA*, such a point cannot be an equilibrium. Similarly, at *P'''* income is *OD*. This is greater than the combined spending on consumption and investment (*OD'*). Since the incomes generated by the spending of *OD'* cannot be less than the incomes received—whatever is paid out becomes someone's income—at *P'''* we have a situation where the income received (*OD*) is greater than that paid out (*OD'*). This is impossible, so again we cannot have an equilibrium point. *P''* would be an equilibrium point if there were no investment, for then total income of *OB* would be equal to total spending on consumers' goods of *OB'*. Because here there is the additional spending on investment, incomes are pushed higher, toward *OC'''*.

Shifts in the various propensities can be depicted in similar graphic fashion. For example, Figure II shows a situation where the consumption-plus-investment function is depicted by the line *C+I*. Our equilibrium point is *P*; at this level, consumption (*AA'*) plus investment (*A'P*) equals *AP*. In turn, this is equal to income *OA*. Assume here that for some reason people spend more out of each income. Out of income *OA* they now wish to spend *AB*, which is more than *AA'*. With each income, consumption would be higher than previously; hence, at each point we push up the consumption curve from its previous level (*C*) to a new, higher level (*C'*).

It is possible that with this higher propensity to consume, business would spend more on investment at each income level, and if this is so, the distance between the consumption and the total *C+I* curve would widen. If, however, each absolute amount of income calls forth the same amount of investment as before, the difference between the two curves would remain the same. But in either case, as each income yields a higher consumption, each total of *C+I* must also be higher than before. A new curve, *C'+I'*, is now our total planned outlay curve. To repeat, if each income level calls forth a greater amount of investment, then the distance between each point on *C'* and *C'+I'* is greater than the corresponding difference between *C* and *C+I*.

FIGURE II

Shifts in Macroeconomic Equilibrium

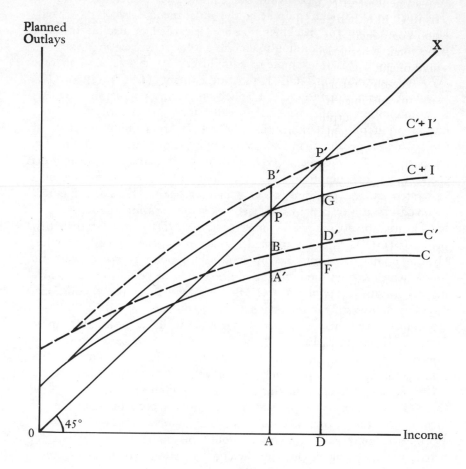

To illustrate the graphic shifts, let us examine the previous equilibrium point *P*. At that level, income was *OA*, and associated with
that income was consumption of *AA′*. That level of consumption
called forth investment equal to *A′P*. After the shift in the consumption propensity, the income of *OA* was associated with consumption of
AB. Investment can now react in two ways. It may continue in the
same relation to income so that the income of *OA* still calls forth
investment of *A′P*. Then our new *C′+I′* curve would be as far from
the new *C′* curve as the old *C+I* curve had been from the old *C* curve.
BB′, then, would equal *A′P*. Or, since consumption is higher, investment may be stimulated, and the investment associated with OA would

now be greater. In that case, the amount of investment associated with the new consumption curve C' (BB') is greater than the previous investment of $A'P$, and so $C'+I'$ lies further from C' than $C+I$ did from C. In either case, B' would have to be above P, for the consumption component has risen from AA' to AB. Alone this would push up the total, whether or not we add a constant investment or a greater investment.

We now return to the analytical impact of the shift in the propensity to consume. If consumption at income level OA rises, the total payments for output also rise. This total, AB', is now greater than the old total, AP, which in turn equaled income OA. Hence, the new output is now greater than the old income. This, of course, cannot remain, for the rise in spending must push up income. And as income rises, consumption and investment will also rise. Now, at this higher level of income there will emerge a still greater amount of consumption and investment, pushing incomes still higher. However, the output rise will tend to exceed the demand rise because of the savings propensity, so that the income push is slowing down. At income OD, consumption will have risen to DD', higher than its initial jump to AB. Investment will be $D'P'$, and the total output DP' ($DD' + D'P'$) will equal income (OD). Expressed differently, the initial rise in consumption from AA' to AB caused the demand at income level OA to exceed output by PB'. This generated further output and income of AD. Demand rose still further, from AB' to DD', but this rise was less than the aforementioned rise in output, AD. This excess output eliminated the original excess demand of PB'.

A similar approach could be used for the deflationary phase. Assume that we are at P' and consumers become worried. At each level of income the consumers decide to spend less on consumption. As a result, the old relation of consumption to income (C') is replaced by one indicating a lower propensity to consume, or C. At the moment this change occurs, total demand associated with income OD drops to DG, consumption having gone down from DD' to DF, and investment goes down from $D'P'$ to FG.[6] Output DP' now exceeds demand, and cutbacks begin. As output drops, income drops; demand also drops, but more slowly. If we deflate output from DP' to AP, deflating income from OD to OA, we cut total demand from DG to AP. The drop in output and income (AD) was greater than the secondary drop in demand—the difference between DG and AP—by enough to eliminate the original excess supply of GP'.

---

[6] As already explained, this may be equal to or less than $D'P'$, depending on the reaction of investment plans to this consumption shift.

The Interrelationship of Income and Demand

It will be recalled that the shifts in the level of the economy occurred because demand and supply were thrown out of equilibrium. The path to a new level, higher or lower, then worked through changes in output and income (changes exceeding the resultant change in demand) thus eliminating the initiating difference. But note that there were further shifts in demand arising from the change in income. That is, when output and income rose, demand rose less—but it did rise. When output and income dropped, demand declined by less—but it did decline. From this apparently obvious relationship many observers have drawn a policy conclusion, a generalization with much validity—namely, the implications for wage policy.

Wages are the most important component of total income within the economy. Often wages account for two-thirds to three-quarters of all income received. If there is a general shift in wages, we can assume that there will be a corresponding movement in total income since this sector is so large. Further, we can then deduce that the relationship of demand to income—the propensity to consume—will result in similar changes in spending. Spending, in turn, reacts on output, inasmuch as a change in spending tends to change output in the same direction. As output changes, employment and wage incomes will change, and with this we have completed the circle. We are saying that a cut in wages will generally reduce total incomes,[7] and this will reduce total demand. This will reduce output, employment will then decline, reducing wages still more, and so on.

The significance of this chain reaction arises particularly in a depression. Individual businessmen, during a recession, reason that sales can be stimulated if prices are reduced. Reducing prices requires lower costs. Since the only important cost element within management's control is labor, they argue that a wage cut would lead to lower prices, this leading to increased sales, and thus more employment. If everyone were to follow this policy, all business concerns would expand employment, and the recession would end.

Obviously, what has been overlooked is the depressing impact on incomes and demand. As each employer cuts wages, he also cuts the

---

[7] One exception can be noted. It is possible for a wage rate to be so high that the resultant cost makes it impossible to produce at a profit, the demand for the particular product not being sufficient to bring about enough sales. If the wages were lowered, the cost decline could then produce a profit margin, and so production would start up. Here, a wage cut would add to output and employment, since in this case both were zero; the wage cut did not reduce (nonexisting) income.

workers' incomes. As incomes decline, spending drops. The price cut that follows the wage cut may not be enough of a sales stimulant to offset the depressing effect of the income reduction. And thus this policy is unsuccessful.

Trade unionists go to the other extreme. Rather than reducing wages, they argue that we should raise wages in a recession. This will expand incomes and spending, stimulating the economy. But they, too, overlook certain aspects. When wages rise, individual employers see costs rising, and they may cut back even further on employment and output. As wage increases expand incomes, the accompanying cutbacks defeat this expansion, and again we arrive at a stalemate.

Of course, the relationships are not as simple as we have outlined. For example, if wages account for 70 per cent of total incomes, and the marginal propensity to consume is 80 per cent, a 10-per-cent reduction in wages would reduce total income by only 7 per cent. This, in turn, would reduce spending by 5.6 per cent (7 per cent $\times$ 80 per cent). The repercussions of the initial wage reduction on spending are thus somewhat less. There are also certain monetary aspects such as the effect on the amount of money used for transactions and liquidity.[8]

Summary

The equilibrium analysis for an economy as a whole works through the greater change in output than in consumption, so that rises in output generate additions to supply more than additions to demand, and declines result in cutbacks in supply greater than those in consumption. Since such rises are usually initiated by an excess demand, and since deflations tend to arise because of excess supply, we have a reaction that tends to eliminate the initiating disturbance. The explanation for this movement was contained in the analysis of the propensities to consume and save. More detailed study requires an examination of both these decisions (to save or consume) and the opposite paired decisions (to invest in capital goods and to produce consumers' goods). Divergences between these pairs—planned savings and investment, and planned output and demand for consumers' goods—help to explain shifts in aggregate business activity.

Some clues were also given to enable us to predict how great the eventual change in output and income would be if we know the size of

---

[8] The reduction in wages and prices would reduce the monetary value of the existing volume of production and so release some money from its previous transactions use. This surplus might then go into additional purchases, thus expanding the volume of output and employment. However, this possibility involves many points not yet covered.

the initiating gap. This tied in with our consumption-function analysis, and the multiplier relationships are its application. Since these various ratios are still not known precisely, and are not completely stable in value, there is still room for error in estimating the absolute amount of the final changes in the various components. However, these concepts even now can serve for some general policy conclusions, particularly those regarding wage policy in a recession. The close tie of this important income sector to aggregate demand and output now can be seen more clearly. Fluctuations in one are closely tied to similar changes in the other.

Chapter 3

THE CYCLICAL PHASES

Although we use the word *cycle* in connection with the movement of the economy, it must be understood that its regularity is not as precise as the word suggests. Fluctuations show an up-and-down characteristic, and must include an upper and lower turning point, but the timing is variable. Cycles need not be the same length, and each of the component phases may also differ in length. In reality the economy does not often show so distinct an up-and-down swing. At times its decline is really only a slowing down in its growth. At other times some sectors of the economy are rising while others are either declining or moving more slowly. Later the pattern may be reversed: the former group slows down, while the latter begins to rise again more rapidly. Finally, even the amplitude may vary. Sometimes the cyclical change may be measured in percentage shifts as small as 1 or 2 per cent. Sometimes the change may be 20 per cent or more. But usually the rising phase is greater in extent than the previous decline, thus imparting a long-run upward movement to the indices. Nevertheless, there is merit in using the cyclical approach, and for our purposes, the four phases to be explored will be the upswing, the upper turning point, the downswing, and the lower turning point. We shall discuss these four in terms of a typical or hypothetical cycle, remembering that any actual phase may still differ in terms of the variables mentioned so far.

The Upswing

As its name implies, the upswing is the recovery from a previously depressed level of business activity. Output and employment are rising, and with them, incomes and demand. Usually, new investment to expand plant capacity also increases, although this may not occur until the pickup in output has reached the point where it is approaching full capacity. Inventories are also being increased to handle the increased volume of production and sales. The improvement in people's incomes aids their credit standing, and so installment credit also rises, this supplementing the demand coming from increasing incomes. Bank financing is also on the rise. This helps meet the increased need for working capital, home mortgages, and new plant capacity.

The improvement in the business climate also influences the psychology of the businessmen and consumers. Increasingly the people become more optimistic. Each rise gives the feeling that still more will come. But then the extent of the expected upturn becomes exaggerated, and plans for further expansion are based on these excessive estimates. Investors start increasing stock prices; the boom in Wall Street makes still more funds come in, these investors hoping to participate before the boom has run its course. Since the economy is so complex, it is difficult to estimate accurately the magnitude of these increasing orders, and the boom atmosphere generates within the individual entrepreneur the expectation that he will gain a disproportionate share of the addition. As a result, production plans start to outrace the anticipated sales. At first these plans are merely feeding the boom at a faster rate, the added expenditures stimulating incomes and sales. The cumulative effect of these excesses at one point or another begins to show up in output, which is rising faster than demand. The upper turning point is approaching.

The Upper Turning Point

After the upswing movement has proceeded for a time, the various industrial sectors start to expand their rate of operations at different speeds. Those for whom the demand has responded more strongly are likely to expand more rapidly. Companies closer to full capacity are induced to add to their equipment in order to raise output in the future. Many will increase production to feed the rising demand and to add to inventories, so that they will have a better stock of goods with which to serve customers. Because of these various influences, the extent and amplitude of the expansion becomes less clear, and the different components now are moving at different rates.

The imbalance generated can be illustrated by examining two of the sectors. In this particular expansion we shall assume that people expand their demand for clothing, but at a somewhat smaller proportion than the rise in their incomes. To refer to our earlier terminology, the marginal propensity to consume clothing is much less. In contrast, individuals step up their purchase of television sets, perhaps much more, proportionately, than the rise enjoyed in incomes. As a result of this demand pattern, the clothing manufacturers may be pushed close to capacity operations, but if so, their demand for more machines to expand their productive capabilities will be muted by the smaller rise in clothing demand. Clothing-machinery makers, therefore, may experience some rise in sales, but this, too, will be relatively small. Television-set production, by contrast, is booming, and so probably will the demand for more machines to manufacture still more sets.

This sudden sharp rise in orders for the television equipment, as the booming demand for television sets spills over, encourages these producers to expand capacity, and so an additional step-up in the demand for other capital goods emerges, activating those companies that produce the equipment used to make the machines for television production. This booming demand spreads, and more and more workers must be found. To attract these needed workers, wages must be stepped up. Generally the wage level starts to rise when other workers, seeing this favored group gaining, press for similar concessions themselves.

The general rise in wages can be absorbed by the booming television sector and its auxiliary feeder concerns. But perhaps the rise is more than can be accommodated by the clothing sector, for here the demand is much weaker. Hence, it is possible for a cost squeeze to emerge, for if prices are raised, demand may be choked off. We may see now that what had previously been a generalized boom is thus becoming somewhat fragmented. The more affluent sectors are still expanding, while the less fortunate ones are being faced with restrictive pressures. The general feeling of confidence is now diminishing. A few danger signals are beginning to rise. It is even possible for the expanding sectors to suffer a shortage of employees, while at the same time some unemployment begins to emerge as a result of cutbacks in those industries unable to sustain the impact of the cost squeeze. Employees in the clothing business may not have the desired skills that the expanding industries require, and pockets of unemployment begin to emerge.

The banking system now is also feeling the pressure of the continuing boom. As more and more orders come in (output must be expanded), many businesses feel a need for more funds to pay for additional labor and materials, and to finance the growing volume of credit sales. Bank loans increase rapidly, and the demand for funds tends to encroach on the banks' liquidity. At some point, therefore, the banks raise their interest charges. They feel this will discourage some borrowers, and thus reduce the demand for funds. It is even possible that the banks are under a double pressure if their depositors start withdrawing cash to help carry on the larger volume of business. Retailers may feel that they need more money in their cash registers to handle the larger volume of sales. Individuals whose incomes have been rising may now reflect this increased affluence in a desire to carry a greater amount of cash. Because the banks now see funds going out from two sources, they must conserve their remaining funds that much more.

But the impact of rising interest rates, if successful, may also contribute further to the upper turning point. We have already seen how some industries may start to drop out of the expansion phase (the clothing-business illustration). Now, borrowing by some industries will also drop off, and as they obtain less money, they may be forced to cut back on output. More companies have now been compelled to stop their expansion move.

Reinforcing this tendency will be the pressures from the money market. Both the banks and the affected individuals may start to sell securities in order to obtain more funds—the banks, to enable them to continue their lending, the individuals, to replace the funds no longer available from the banks. As a result of this, pressures on securities' prices build up.

Now, as these various forces spread, and more and more firms and individuals are affected, tensions begin to emerge. If enough factors are influenced, business conditions may actually start to waver. Doubts may begin to spread regarding the permanency of the boom. At some subtle psychological moment these increasing doubts may avalanche, producing a stock market crash. Usually this occurs after business in general has ended its upward motion. The decline in stock prices merely directs the public's attention to what had already happened—the upper turning point.

The upswing, it should be noted, may well have masked other unwelcome tendencies. Many businesses find it profitable to sell only in an expanding market; the general buoyancy of demand allows their inferior products to enter the market. But once the boom atmosphere fades, their basic vulnerability then stands out, for the weakened competition in the boom has hidden the fact that these manufacturers' costs were too high, or their products less satisfactory. Moreover, many producers may have overborrowed on the strength of this flimsy position, so that the tighter economy to emerge in the downswing will force them into either financial difficulties or bankruptcy. Note here that borrowings to finance speculative securities and commodity positions grew as the boom boosted prices in these sectors. Profits were to come from continued expected price rises; but once the boom ends, this may result in declining prices. If the drop is sharp enough, the speculator may be forced to default on his loan, thus carrying down with him the financial houses that had been his creditors.

The Downswing

Now we shall examine the moving picture running in reverse. Output and employment are shrinking. Each shrinkage reduces income, spending, and thus demand. This activity reinforces the deflationary pressures. Bank loans shrink because banks become increasingly cautious in lending, and would-be borrowers hesitate to ask for funds in the face of declining needs. Inventories are cut back because firms reduce their purchases faster than their sales in order to conserve their liquid working capital. This decline in incomes and employment harms the credit rating of the individuals affected, and their ability to make installment purchases declines. Our business climate is becoming steadily worse.

The psychological reactions reinforce the other pressures. There appears now a more pessimistic tone. Talk of the severity of the downswing is more common. Fewer people can see ahead to the next turning point—that is, when the *upswing* resumes. Stock prices also drift in value as the once seemingly endless prosperity begins to be displaced by what now appears to be a bottomless recession.

The extent of the downswing is important in affecting policies which follow. If the drop is relatively mild—usually called a recession —then the downswing is often short-lived, and the pessimism reinforcing the downward pressures is less likely to make itself evident. But if the drop in business activity is so severe that it results in a cumulative feeling in which each decline sets in motion still more pressure for a further decline, the severity then becomes so great that it can be called a depression. In this more extreme manifestation, doubts arise about the solvency of many businesses, and as losses mount, creditors become less willing to extend or maintain their previous lending policies. At this point the debtor is forced to liquidate more rapidly so he can obtain funds to repay his previous loans. This means that he must increase both his selling activity and his efforts to reduce other payments, such as wages and materials purchases. More goods are now forced on the markets, and the incomes from which such purchases could be made are shrinking even faster. Should he fail, he reduces the solvency of his creditors as well. But if he manages to pay off the loan, the funds then may remain idle, as the would-be lender hesitates to re-commit his funds in the face of so dismal an outlook. More and more purchasing power is thus frozen, and the spending ability of the community is correspondingly reduced. This reduction feeds the deflation even more, and still other debtors are forced into this liquidating position.

As incomes drop off, the likelihood is that spending will decline somewhat. People usually try to maintain living standards, and as their incomes decline, they try to reduce savings by a disproportionately greater amount. Consumption, then, need drop that much less. So, as supply is reduced, reducing incomes paid out, demand may not decline by as much, since people reduce their savings rather than spending. Here there gradually emerges a situation wherein supply is reduced, so much relative to demand, that the downward pressures become less powerful as time passes.

At the same time, reflecting the growing surplus of funds—the drop-off in the demand for bank loans—the interest rate begins to decline. Banks may use their otherwise idle funds to purchase bonds. This boosts bond prices, making it easier to float new loans. Easy money conditions now become more evident.

The Lower Turning Point

Although the economy has always recovered from past downturns, the reasons why this must be so are less clear. In the 1930's the upturn did not come until the government intervened. The subsequent return to a relatively full employment status did not occur until after the situations emanating from World War II had generated enough of a demand.

One of the determining factors is the severity of the preceding downturn. We can label the more mild downturns "recessions," designating the word "depression" to mean the more severe setbacks. If there has been a recession, the reduction in spending tends to decline more slowly than the drop in output. This is because of the greater decline in savings. Here demand is sustained, and there is less incentive to liquidate inventories. As will be shown, the inventory factor alone can bring about an end to this decline. For as capital equipment continues to wear out, purchases of such goods must be maintained. Since the drop in sales has been mild, there is every incentive to maintain capacity. New machines must be purchased to replace the old ones. And as enough of these purchases are made, incomes pick up, demand picks up, and sales pick up. As a result, output is stepped up, and the multiplying effects of these additions further contribute to the expansionary forces. The upward phase then begins.

However, if we are experiencing a depression, then the decline in output and incomes is matched by correspondingly large declines in purchases. In addition, financial solvency becomes an issue for many individuals and companies. The outlook becomes even more pessimistic. Retrenchment becomes the policy, and the lower level of sales curtails business purchases of machinery to replace the older equipment. In effect, businesses reason that the drop in output will last for quite some time and that they will not require as much capacity to turn out the expected lower volume. It follows that fewer machines will be needed, and this reduction can be effected simply by not replacing the machinery no longer usable. Of course if sales volume is shrinking, there is no incentive to build up inventories or even maintain them.

The downward phase has been heightened now by the rising number of failures. Creditors then liquidate seized assets to realize whatever funds can be salvaged. These forced sales add even more to the supply, and drive prices down still further. Once we are in this cumulatively downward cycle, the cycle itself becomes almost self-enforcing. Except for governmental efforts to pump purchasing power into the economy, or a sudden jump in external demand (such as a foreign boom stepping up the demand for products of the country currently depressed), it is difficult to visualize exactly what can turn the cycle. The best that can be hoped for is an end to the downturn. The shrinkage in savings, it will be recalled, reduces demand less rapidly than output; at some point, if savings reach zero, output and demand become equal. While this may be enough to stop any further deflationary measures, it does not produce an upswing. What could easily follow is a low-level stability, the reduced output generating such a low volume of income that nothing is saved. If this is true, all the current supply can be disposed of. But there is nothing to stimulate producers to raise production, and so we achieve what can be known as an underemployment equilibrium.

Inventories

The movement of inventories throughout the cycle helps to explain the up-and-down character of the economy. In effect, a rise in inventories is output that produces incomes but no addition to supplies.

The goods are deposited in warehouses or placed on retailers' shelves. A decline in inventories is therefore an addition to supply that is not accompanied by income and demand. Goods are taken out of the warehouses or off the shelves without generating incomes in the process. (Remember that production is accompanied by income—wages, payments to the raw-material suppliers, profits, rent, and so forth.) Furthermore, the volume of inventories tends to vary with output and sales. If volumes are rising, manufacturers hold larger stocks of raw materials and finished goods to service the larger volume of production. Retailers carry more goods to handle the increased volume of sales. As output and sales drop off, inventories decline. Therefore, under normal conditions, inventories move in the same direction as these other two factors.

In the upswing, producers expand output by more than just sales. The excess goes into inventories, either in the manufacturers' own warehouses or to the retailers. Later the inventory increases taper off, and production need not continue in excess of sales. But when this happens, it generates reverse trends that lead to a downswing. Output is then cut back more than the decline in sales. The difference comes out of inventories. Once these have been drawn down, output then revives. Again it fills the gap that had been temporarily filled by the drawing down of inventories. And now we are stimulating the economy—that is, raising output (and thereby income). Now we have returned to the upswing.

Again an arithmetic example can illustrate the point. We shall assume that inventories are equal to one month's sales. A 10-per-cent rise in sales calls for a 10-per-cent rise in inventories. Now, we shall assume that an inventory adjustment takes a month and that this month's level of inventories is measurably equal to last month's sales. We shall also assume that the marginal propensity to consume is 50 per cent, a simplification necessary until we explore the concept of liquidity preference in a later chapter. In order to organize our illustrative cycle, we shall also assume that the upswing has already started, that sales have risen above the desired inventory level (see Table II).

For example, in Month One output is 100, sales 100, and inventory 90 (sales in the preceding month had also been 90). For Month Two the desired inventory is 100, so we must order 10. We add that amount to output to bring our inventories to the desired level of 100. This would raise output to 110. Since we have now assumed a marginal propensity to consume of 50 per cent, sales will rise by 5. So, with an output of 110 and sales of 105, inventories can rise to only 95. In Month Three, therefore, we must order 10, to bring our stocks to the desired level (105, or last month's sales), plus the 105 to meet the expected sales volume. Output, therefore, rises to 115, an increase of 5 over Month Two. But this rise in output will raise incomes *and* sales, the latter moving up by 2½, to 107½. Output therefore exceeds sales by 7½, rather than 10, and so inventories rise by a bit less than planned, reaching 102½, not 105.

TABLE II

Simplified Hypothetical Inventory Cycle

MONTH	OUTPUT (= *Orders*)	INVENTORIES *Actual*	*Planned*	SALES
ONE	100	90	100	100
TWO	110	95	100	105
THREE	115	102½	105	107½
FOUR	112½	108¾	107½	106¼
FIVE	103¾	110½	106¼	102
SIX	93½	107	102	97
SEVEN	87	100¼	97	93¾
EIGHT	87¼	93¾	93¾	93¾
NINE	93¾	90½	93¾	97

Orders = Sales of previous period + (planned inventories for current period—actual inventories of previous period).
Planned inventories equal last month's sales.

Since sales are now (last month) 107½, we raise our desired inventory goal correspondingly. We must now order 5 for inventory and 107½ for current expected sales. This would be a total of 112½. This is now 2½ less than the previous month; the slowing down in the rate at which sales plus inventory accumulations have been moving now results in a drop in output. The nearer we come to the attainment of our desired inventory level the more we dampen output. Note that at first we had 10 less than desired, then 5. This rise of 10 slowed to a rise of 5, and now it becomes a drop of 2½, or a total output of 112½.

Now, as output drops off, incomes drop off, and sales will react also. Sales will fall to 106¼, down 1¼, or 50 per cent of the output drop. Output exceeds sales by 6¼, so inventories rise from 102½ to 108¾. Now inventories exceed sales, and all that we need is a level of 106¼. So, we wish to draw down inventories by 2½. We do this by planning to order 2½ less than expected sales. Since last month's sales were 106¼, we therefore would order only 103¾. Output thus drops further, and so do income and spending, the latter going to 101⅞. Now, to get away from complicated fractions, let us assume that sales went to 102. This is 1¾ less than output, and so inventories rose still more, to 110½. And with this lower level of sales we want even less inventories—102, not 106¼, as previously planned. We must therefore order 8½ less than we plan to sell, or 93½.

An output of only 93½ will cut incomes and sales even more sharply. Although incomes have dropped by 10¼, sales will drop only half, or about 5. So, rather than cut their standard of living too drastically, consumers are starting to use prior savings, so spending falls to only 97, or 5 less than the prior month's 102. Since output and income are only 93½, 3½ must be drawn from prior savings. Now sales exceed output—as desired, in order to draw down inventories—so inventories drop by 3½, or to 107. They are still 10 more than sales, so we now order only 87. The drop in output by 6½ cuts sales by only 3¼ (one-half), to 93¾, thus drawing down inventories by 6¾ to 100¼. There is still too much in inventory, so we must reduce it by 6½—the difference between last month's sales (93¾) and current levels of stocks of 100¼. So we order only 87¼.

Note that we have stopped reducing output. But there is a minute rise of ¼. We shall assume, for simplicity, that so small an output-and-income rise does not alter sales, and further assume that these continue at 93¾. Hence, inventories fall to 93¾. These are now down to the desired level, one month's sales, so we no longer have to alter their amount. We can now order 93¾, just enough to match the previous month's sales. But if we do this, we are also stepping up our output appreciably. Sales will thus rise accordingly, to about 97.

Once again, sales exceed inventories, and our cycle can now recommence. The increase in sales results in an excess over output, so inventories drop to 90½. Now we must order 97 to take care of expected sales, plus 6½ to rebuild inventories. The motion picture of the inventory cycle is beginning again.

Starting our cycle, we can make it virtually self-generating. The initial imbalance made for an upturn, but this peters out, and is followed by a recession, which in turn is ended.

We might add here one comment regarding the electronic computer. This instrument is being employed more and more to speed up information and decision-making. Business can operate with smaller inventories because of better planning. It can change purchases more rapidly, key them in more intelligently with shifts in sales. A consequence of this is that the variation in the inventory component becomes less disturbing as these controls are perfected and as they become more widely used. Because of the computer, the influence of the inventory cycle could diminish in importance, but whether or not the computer can completely eliminate this unstable element is still uncertain.

The Accelerator

A major contributor to cyclical instability is the wide swing in purchases of capital equipment. If business is slack, new purchases can be postponed; the existing equipment can be used a while longer. When conditions improve, purchases can again be made. As a result, the boom is fed by a large increase in orders, while the decline in incomes (characteristic of a recession) is reinforced by the drop (or postponement) in output of capital goods.

Associated with this characteristic is the relationship known as the accelerator. This concept measures the heightened reaction of new investment in capital goods to changes in the demand for the output coming from this equipment. Changes in sales, in brief, set in motion exaggerated changes in the sale of machines to make the final products, particularly at rates of operation close to capacity. A rise in demand could result because consumers shift from a competing product, or because incomes rose and so pushed up aggregate spending. If sales rise, and the higher level is expected to be for only a short time, the producer is likely to work his men overtime, or perhaps introduce a new shift to run the existing machines more intensively. Thus, while output expands to meet the temporary rise in demand, his need for equipment manifests itself in the more intensive use of the existing stock. But this is not the most profitable reaction in many cases. Night labor is more costly and less efficient. Overtime means tired and perhaps less careful workers. Overworked and misused machines start to break down. A better reaction would be to expand capacity, and continue production at the more optimum work rate.

But to expand capacity implies a continued high volume of sales. If, as already mentioned, the sales boom is temporary, the subsequent decline can be met by ending overtime and nightwork. But if additional machines are used, the carrying cost of such equipment continues even if the sales drop off. Only if a sales rise is expected to last for a reasonably long term do we have some assurance that the purchase of additional machines will pay off.

Moreover, the rise in sales must be great enough to encroach on the existing capacity. If, for example, with the present working hours the machines can turn out 100 units daily, and orders rise from 50 to 75, there is no need for more equipment. But if the rise is from 90 to 115—25 more in each case—then we have a possible case for capacity expansion. We recognize here that rising sales in themselves do not make for rising machine orders. Only when the rise brings operations close to full capacity (if it is expected that this increased volume of sales will continue) do we step up our purchases of new machines. Incidentally, at this stage profits will also probably be high, thus facilitating the financing of these acquisitions.

In the absence of this sales stimulant there would still be some ordering of machines. As old ones wear out, or as new types are designed, the company would still place orders. For example, if the company had ten machines, and the average life of each was ten years, it is possible that each year one becomes too old for continued use, so each year a new one is ordered. But if sales rise so much that we need eleven machines to meet the higher demand, then we may order two—one to replace the worn-out unit, one to meet the higher sales volume.

Arithmetic at this point becomes significant in order to understand the accelerator. What has happened is that sales rose 10 per cent, from 100 to 110, and thus our need for machines rose from 10 to 11. But normally we order only one machine, the replacement requirement. Now, to bring our total stock to eleven, we must order two. Thus, a sales rise of 10 per cent produced a rise in orders for machines of 100 per cent—from 1 to 2. The sales rise accelerates in magnitude as it is reflected in the sales of machines to our firm. The relative swings in machine output, as a consequence, are of a greater magnitude than the sales swings of the goods they are to manufacture.

Suppose sales rise to 120. This requires us to have 12 machines. Again we order 2—one as a replacement, one to expand capacity. Here a sales rise results in only a continuance of our machinery orders. Suppose further that in the next period sales continue at 120. Then we need order only one machine for replacement purposes. A leveling out of sales results in a decline in machine orders. And if sales drop back to 110, which means we would need only 11 machines, we can cut back capacity from 12 to 11 by not ordering the current replacement. A small decline in sales, as in our last illustration, creates an enormous drop in machine orders.

These few highly simplified examples illustrate ways in which the swings in capital-goods output become magnified. Sales swings usually result in enlarged shifts in machine orders. Capacity considerations, the durability of the higher demand, the ability to work additional shifts or extend the life of machines—these factors tend to modify the swings in output in the capital-goods sector. Sometimes, as a result, the swing there is greater than in the customer industries, as illustrated in the accelerator example. The swing is sometimes less, as in our overtime-alternative illustration. But general experience indicates that the capital-goods sector will move more widely.

The Consumption Function as Equilibrator

The major influence in bringing the upward or downward movement of the cycle to an end was the slippage between income and spending. This was caused by the consumption function. As incomes were altered, this postulated a smaller change in consumer spending. There was less of a rise or decline in absolute amounts. And since income represented the other side of output, we can realize that in the upswing, demand will rise less than supply, and that in the downswing, demand drops less than supply. This cumulates in the upswing, until finally the increasingly excessive growth in supply stops the boom, or the slower fall in demand in the downswing finally cumulates sufficiently to act as a support to end the deflation.

On the other hand, this equilibrating force could be nullified by adverse movements in investment. In the upswing, sales expand, perhaps encroaching on current capacity. Orders for plant expansion add to the spending stream, and since these involve large amounts of money, the added demand could more than offset the rising supply excess. It is true that the composition of this supply might differ, more funds going into capital goods. But the impact would be the same. We would have rising output and rising income. Sales of consumers' goods would be rising, but by less than the income increase. Sales of capital goods would rise by perhaps enough to stimulate the economy still further, especially when added to the other expansionary forces. If such were to occur, we could spill over into an inflation in which the combined demands for both consumers' and capital goods outrun the ability of the economy to cope with these orders. If the inflation is sufficiently intense, we may see producers raising prices, and thereby profits. More investment may then be induced to participate in these enlarged gains, and so the demand for capital goods rises even further. Two different outcomes then become probable—even more inflation, and even more plant expansion. When this action is completed, too great an addition to supply may ensue, thereby precipitating a downturn. We see now that the investment aspect has not only intensified the upswing, but also helped to create overproduction and thus a downturn.

A similar reinforcing effect can occur in the recession. As mentioned, a downswing is characterized by supply (output and incomes) declining more rapidly than consumption, this behavior reducing the previous excess supply until it becomes equal to a now shrunken demand. But if this shrinkage in sales sets off a wholesale reduction in the normal capital outlays—for example, postponed replacement of old and obsolescent equipment—then the demand decline in the consumer sector is made still worse by this shrinkage in the capital-goods sector. If enough replacement purchases are postponed, we can get a drop in demand even faster than output, thus deepening the recession still further. Each drop could result in the postponement of still more potential machinery orders, thereby shrinking output and demand still further. Only when this capital-goods sector has dropped to absolute zero might this depressing influence come to an end. But that would indicate a catastrophic decline in business activity comparable with the 1932 disaster. Fortunately, recession does not usually reach such extremes.

The Cost of the Business Cycle

The social and economic costs of fluctuations in business activity are enormous. Some may be incalculable. In the downswing, people lose their jobs, machines stand idle or they work at less than full production. The country is turning out fewer goods and services than it is capable of doing. And with less being produced, less is being consumed. Living standards are thereby lowered. And no country is so affluent—not even our fabulous American society—that it has eradicated poverty for all its inhabitants. Even if such were to be attained, there is still the poverty throughout most of the world, and these idle productive facilities might have been used to reduce life's miseries for those less fortunate millions.

Furthermore, unemployment has social repercussions. Skills acquired during the employment period become rusty if not continually used. When a need for these skills returns, the jobless often can no longer fill the requirement. Our efficiency as a country is thereby impaired. Retraining becomes necessary, and this becomes an added cost to be charged to the previous recession. In addition, the morale of men out of work is impaired. In effect, society seems to be saying that they are no longer necessary. The home environment reflects this depressing psychological state, and often the children acquire attitudes toward society that increase this despair. Much of the yearning for security among people currently in their thirties and forties is the haunting memory of poverty they knew as youngsters during the 1930's. Hence, even society's long-run potential is diminished, as fewer people are willing to take chances on new ideas and processes.

If the downturn lasts too long and injures too many people, even greater desperation may emerge. People out of work begin to question the worth of the existing economic order. They turn to reforms, perhaps to extreme manifestations of this urge for change—revolution. It is no coincidence that the rise of Hitlerism in pre–1933 Germany coincided with the worst downturn that country had ever suffered. Disgusted with the results of their system, people turned to the hopes held out by the National Socialists (Nazis), and the road led inevitably to internal discriminations, then to World War II.

The upswing, especially if it carries over to inflation, also has its costs. As prices rise, people on fixed incomes suffer a decline in their living standards. Fixed receipts in dollars now buy less. Those who can, struggle for a higher income. Strikes and domestic conflict increase. Production is interrupted. Many individuals are unable to offset the higher prices, and suffer more permanent declines in living standards. In particular, this group is composed of the aged, the maimed, and the many who live on pensions. No longer employed, people find it impossible to readjust their income arrangements, and their already difficult lives become even more so.

Inflation also leads to maladjustments of the productive capacity. With rising prices it is much easier to make a profit. Inefficient industries can mask their high costs as they sell in a rising market. Hence, more and more inefficiencies creep in, protected by this additional boost. The economy functions less efficiently. Then, when the inflationary boom ends, the offset to inefficiency ends, and losses mount. Soon this becomes bankruptcy, because the resources at man's command are no longer used. In the hands of the more efficient firms, men and equipment might have functioned in both phases of the cycle. But in the hands of the less efficient, the machines are junked in the downturn and the men thrown out of work. A permanent loss to society results.

Inflation, as already mentioned, also leads to above-normal profits among the more efficient. These are the firms that would be making money even if prices were stable. With rising prices they earn even more. More and more firms are tempted to expand output, and excessive capacity and output results. It is here that the downturn begins. Now the losses of the recession must be charged to the excesses generated by the preceding inflation.

These ups and downs also lead to a long-run overcapacity. For example, a machine turns out 10 units monthly. The output is 100 a month, so we need 10 machines. If output rises each month by 10—to 110, 120, 130, and up—then each month we add a machine to our total capacity. But if we superimpose the business cycle, we get a somewhat different picture.

If output fluctuates around 100—sometimes dropping to 80, sometimes rising to 120—then we must have 12 machines for the peak period. But this, of course, results in idle capacity in the downturn. Note that we now need two more machines for the same average but fluctuating output. Analogously, if output rises 10 per month, but irregularly—say, from 100 to 120, back to 110, then up to 130—we must then add to our capacity at irregular rates. Sometimes we buy two more machines, sometimes none. As a result the new orders coming to the machinery producers fluctuate, and the producers, in turn, have the problem of excessive capacity. As a consequence, there is excessive capacity for the peak periods down the line, and, of course, overcapacity for all concerned when the recession strikes. With a smoother business activity everyone could have succeeded with less equipment, and so the entire society could have turned out the same volume of goods and services with a smaller amount of equipment. Less effort, in effect, would have been required for the same production—less effort in the capital-goods sectors. And the resources released from producing excessive capital equipment—or what would be excessive if the cycle were to be smoothed out—could then be used for turning out additional goods and services, thereby swelling the nation's income and standard of living.

Summary

Although the economy fluctuates, it does so without any precise regularity. However, as a generalization we can speak of an upturn, an upper turning point, a downturn, and a lower turning point. Each, with its characteristic features, produces forces that generally lead into the next phase, so that to a certain extent the cycle is self-propelled. Central to the analysis of the various phases is the influence of the propensity to consume, which causes the movement in output—up or down—to exceed the accompanying change in demand. This alters the supply-demand relationship. Special mention was also made of the instability of inventories, which alone can often account for much of the fluctuation in output and the acceleration impact of changes in sales on the demand for capital goods. The consequence of these various activities is the cyclical instability. This, in turn, results in costs to the economy, either in unrealized output, such as in a recession, or in excess capacity—that is, excess utilization of resources to produce a given output. It can also result in the terrible personal toll that arises from inflation and unemployment, the two extremes of instability.

Chapter 4

LIQUIDITY

The first three chapters established the essence of the problem of growth with stability. Now it is necessary to turn to a more intensive study of those aspects of our money-and-banking system that bear on this problem, either as the cause of it or as the cure. Most of the remainder of this book will be devoted to this aspect of the subject.

In order to approach the numerous factors that are relevant, it will be necessary to separate the main strands of the monetary system. We shall study each in isolation, then later weave them together to obtain a more complete and realistic picture of the economy. It may be necessary to repeat certain points as the context in which they are important changes, because their significance is such that repetition will also throw new light on a most complicated subject. Some economists claim that the money-and-banking mechanism is really understood by fewer people than the Einstein Theory of Relativity!

Foremost in our exposition, then, will be the concept of liquidity.

This theme is to recur frequently throughout the book, and so it is essential to outline its basic meaning at the outset of the analysis.

Liquidity and Money

For our purposes, we shall define an asset's *liquidity* as the nearness to which the asset approaches the major functions of money. But before spelling out this nearness, it would be better to define what we mean by money. Few people would believe that they do not know money when they see it. As can be quickly shown, there are some tricky aspects to this concept, so a brief explanation is in order.

While there have been exceptions in the past, a general definition of money would include any medium that is used to effect business transactions, to act as a store of value, and to be used to measure prices (sometimes referred to as a *numéraire*). It is quite obvious that for the United States the green paper that we call cash or currency—the dollar bill and silver and its various multiples—fulfills these functions completely. Currency is used when we make purchases, when we wish to hoard or save for some future need, or when we wish to express prices to a potential buyer. But there is also a close relative of currency that performs many of the same duties. Sometimes it does even better. This other form is the checking account, also known as the demand deposit. Virtually all such accounts are with commercial banks. Individuals with a sufficient balance at the bank can write checks and make purchases with almost the same ease as a person using currency. We say "almost," and will explain that qualification in a moment; however, in view of the large volume of transactions effected with checks—perhaps more than 80 per cent of all sales and purchases—it is now common to include this medium within the definition of money. In the United States the currency component is about $30 billion, the checking accounts $120 billion.

The differences and similarities between the two forms can be seen when we compare their treatment. Within the United States the dollar is accepted everywhere. This is not true of checks. A stranger in town might have difficulty in making a payment by check, whereas he would easily discharge his obligation with currency. To this extent checks are not perfect substitutes. On the other hand, the fact that use of a checking account requires some kind of identification makes it advantageous, too. If cash is lost, the finder can use it freely. It is virtually impossible for the loser to identify the money as having been his. But if a check is lost, it is often possible to trace it through its use, and thus reduce the possibility of its being employed by other than its rightful owner. This major protection is the requirement for endorsement; at the time it is used for effecting a payment, the owner must sign (endorse) the check, and normally the person receiving it will not accept the check if he does not know the payer and does not know that the signature is a bona-fide one. While such protection is not absolute—forgery can still be employed—there is less chance for misuse than in the case of currency. As a result, many people prefer to use checks even though cash is a more acceptable medium of exchange. This consideration is of particular importance where the amounts involved are quite large. Think of the security problems if a company were to make a payment of several hundred millions in cash! Not only would a check be preferable, but the number of pieces of paper necessary to make so large a transaction is miniscule if made by check, in comparison with the many pieces of currency necessary otherwise.

But what is it that makes money money? What gives it its "moneyness"? The simplest answer is that the owner can get full value for the asset instantly. If one has a $10 bill, he can buy something priced at $10 immediately. The seller will not say that he will allow only so much on the money. Were this a barter transaction, for example, and one wanted to swap a watch he owned, which he felt was worth as much as the lamp another was offering, both would haggle back and forth before establishing that the two were of equal value. Perhaps, if the owner of the lamp were a shrewder trader, he would end up by getting the watch and a little more—perhaps a pen—before effecting the transaction. But if the lamp were priced at $10, and if one were willing to pay that amount and also had the cash, then the transaction would take place quickly. The lamp buyer might still bargain if he felt that he could get the lamp for less, but there would be no bargaining regarding the value of the money itself.

This instant acceptance at full value is what has led to the inclusion of checking accounts in our definition. Once the need for identification is satisfied, and assuming that there is enough money in the account to pay the check, the check is usually accepted at the stated amount. It is true that under certain circumstances checks may be discounted, and check-cashing businesses charge a certain percentage for this service. Nevertheless, use of the check in so many of our dealings has led to its inclusion in the meaning of money.

Another minor qualification regarding checking accounts concerns the hours when the banks are open for business. If a person wishes to make a payment with cash, he can do so at any hour that the need arises. But if he wishes to pay by check, and if his creditor will not accept the check, the payer must then go to his bank to obtain the money. If this should occur at a time when the banks have closed (over the weekend), then the deal cannot go through. Note, incidentally, that if the check must be cashed—that is, if the creditor will not accept it in payment—then checking accounts are not serving the role of money. Just like any other asset, it must first be converted into money (cash). Had it been accepted in payment, it would serve the function of money since it obviated the need for cash. It happens, of course, that checking accounts can be converted into cash on demand, provided the banks are open and the drawer is near his bank, and has sufficient funds. It is necessary to make these certain qualifications for checks, but we do not have to do so for cash.

In effect, then, both cash and checks—the latter subject to the qualifications already indicated—have almost universal acceptability at full value instantly. This universality, incidentally, has peculiar variations. Some currencies are acceptable only within the country in which they are issued; others may have a more general area of acceptance. After World War II the United States dollar was so highly regarded that it could be offered for payment—and was accepted—almost anywhere in the Free World (and in the Soviet Bloc, too). On the other hand, a currency as sound as the English pound might not find acceptance if offered for payment in Reno, Nevada. The owner would probably have to go to a bank in order to exchange it for dollars; and he might find that the dollars he receives for his pounds are less than the amount he would get in Great Britain. By our definition, therefore, the pound would be money only within the geographical confines of the British economy, whereas the United States dollar might be money in the United States, Liberia, large Canadian cities, and so forth. The geographical scope might even vary with time. Before World War I, when the British were more important in world trade and finance, the pound probably had wider acceptability than it does now, since the past half-century's upheavals made people more wary of accepting foreign currencies.

The "moneyness," it should be noted, requires two qualities: acceptance at full value and immediacy. It is possible, for example, to have an asset that can be exchanged without a discount, but the process of finding such an acceptor takes a long time, perhaps even years. But since the value may be required immediately, this delay renders its liquidity aspect that much less. Similarly, we may be able to dispose of an asset quickly, but only at a large discount. For example, we may own a stock that is traded on the New York Stock Exchange. If we need money during the hours the exchange is open, we can sell it; but we may not get full value, especially if our sale were to depress the stock's market price.[1] Hence, the other requirement for liquidity is

---

[1] Moreover, we would probably have to wait four business days for the cash.

absent: the asset's sale at full value. In effect, we can say that an asset's liquidity can be gauged by both the speed with which we can dispose of it, and the minimum reduction in its value that we must accept in so doing.

It is also possible for assets to have a greater value upon liquidation. If we are in a period of rising commodity prices, a $10 bill will still have a nominal value of $10. But if we have 5 bushels of wheat, the passage of time will act to increase its value. When we come to dispose of it, we receive more, and so long as the rising price trend continues, we know that we shall receive more. As we shall see in our study of inflation, at such periods certain commodities are actually more desirable than money as a form in which to hold our wealth. In general, however, no other asset meets our liquidity test. Even wheat fails in a time of uncertainty, for prices may move up or down. And it certainly fails in a time of falling prices, for then the ownership of wheat is almost a virtual guarantee that at the time of liquidation it will sell for less than we had expected. (This, incidentally, is a partial explanation of why people hoard money in a recession—its nominal value cannot fall.)

The reader may have noted that we have used the phrase "nominal value" at different times when referring to money. This was necessary to distinguish another method of measuring the value of money— namely, its purchasing power. Since money has the same nominal value, its command over goods and services will vary as their prices vary. If prices move up, a certain amount of money buys less, and conversely in a time of declining prices. Hence, the purchasing power of money falls in a time of rising prices, and rises in a time of declining prices. But the nominal value remains the same—a $10 bill is always a $10 bill.

In our wheat example, we said that we might prefer to hold wheat, rather than money, during the period when the purchasing power of money is falling. The nominal value of wheat at the time of sale would be greater than its nominal value at the time of purchase, while the nominal value of money would have remained the same over an equal amount of time. On the other hand, in a recession the nominal value of commodities is shrinking, and so the use of money as a store of value increases since its nominal value remains the same. As implied, in times of declining purchasing power of money, people will tend to move out of money into other commodities, since the latter's nominal value will be rising; and in times of rising purchasing power of money, people will tend to move out of commodities back into money, since the former will be going down in nominal value. The implications of these shifts are of immense cyclical significance, and will be explored at greater length.

Interest, the Price for Parting with Liquidity

Summarizing the preceding discussion, we can say that liquidity is the command over purchasing power in the form of either cash or checking-account money. In what follows we shall not continue to distinguish between these two forms of money; rather we will use *money* as a term encompassing both. Only when there is a specific need to make the distinction will we revert to the two subsidiary definitions. For most purposes, checking-account funds are as liquid as cash, but there are certain times and places when this is not so; thus our always combining the two is not accurate.

The value of liquidity is also implicit in our preceding analysis. The holder of purchasing power has instant command over anything he wishes to buy, provided his funds are adequate. Furthermore, he is protected against loss through depreciation in the nominal value of his purchasing power. Actually, he is even partially protected against theft if he has his funds in a checking account. Only forgery would enable another person to gain illegal possession of these funds. Provided with these various safety features, we can understand why there is a value in being liquid.

A good deal of this value arises from the probability that an individual will require the use of his funds instantly. But it is possible that such liquidity is of little use to an individual. Suppose our hypothetical individual has a daily receipt of funds, and that these are in excess of his daily needs. Then only some unforeseen emergency that would require a quick payment of more than his daily receipts would call for liquid funds. Hence, his having ready money would depend on how greatly he assessed the probability of such a need arising. If he is a cautious person, fearful that any kind of emergency can strike—for example, a sickness requiring a quick operation—then he will always want to have some money ready. On the other hand, if he feels that such a possibility arises rarely, and that he can always obtain some extension of the payment due the hospital, then his need for funds that are readily available is that much less.

On the other hand, if our person has both a fluctuating income and a fluctuating need for money, and if these two fluctuations do not coincide, then he must have some balance to tide him over. Note that if the fluctuations match, he may still be able to do without liquidity. Suppose he is paid regularly on the last day of the month. Suppose that all his bills fall due the first of the month, and that they are always less in total than his receipts. Then his monthly receipt comes in time for him to meet all his obligations. On the other days of the month his cash income falls off, but so do his cash expenses, both dropping to zero.

Then at the end of the month, receipts again rise, to be followed by a similar jump in expenditures, thus utilizing the cash.

Barring such an unlikely coincidence, the person will have periods when his money receipts outrun his disbursements, and other periods when outlays exceed receipts. For these latter periods he would need a balance to bridge the difference, and the balance must be liquid. His need for liquidity, in other words, is greater than that of the individual in the preceding paragraph. Note, incidentally, that by careful planning, he might be able to reduce his liquidity requirement. He could plan his purchases so that the payments come when his receipts also come in. If he is on a weekly pay basis, he can try to arrange to have his bills fall due weekly. If he had only monthly accounts, then each week his income would exceed his cash needs until the monthly accounts came in. At this time his outlays would then exceed his income. By staggering his payments, he would reduce the need for funds "humping" at one time. In effect, he would more closely resemble our first hypothetical individual whose daily receipts were sufficiently regular and ample to reduce his cash requirements virtually to zero.

In actuality, the need for liquidity is not as precise as the foregoing implies. There are numerous reasons and amounts that could be fitted into each person's considerations, so that the liquidity requirements form more of a schedule than any one absolute amount would. It is possible that he might feel he should have a minimum of $300 for unforeseen emergencies—the lowest amount he would allow his funds to fall to. Then, depending on his numerous receipts and payments, he would have rising amounts of required funds, depending on how carefully he matched the two flows. If his income is very large, he might be more careless of the matching possibilities, not even caring to bother with such calculations. If his income is low, he might be more exacting in the estimate of his needs. Also, the amount of money he kept would depend on the alternative uses to which it could be put. If there were some other outlet, he might be more willing to keep a lower balance than if there were no alternative.

Since liquidity does have a use, to part with it would mean that the holder would wish to be compensated. Under ordinary circumstances, a person would not part with something of value unless he received some equivalent in return. For most people this would be some form of interest. (Interest is paid for the use of funds, or the giving up of liquidity.) The lender turns over his purchasing power to the borrower, and now holds less in liquid funds. In return, he expects to receive regular payments, and at some future date, the return of his funds. It may be that he expects more than the amount originally given up, such as a stock purchase that is expected to show a capital appreciation. But what we are saying here is that his expected compensation for forgoing liquidity is in a different form.

While a lender would not be likely to give up liquidity for less than it is worth, it is always possible that he would obtain a higher return. One might value his liquidity at 3 per cent; for him to give up the purchasing power he now has, he will want in return an annual payment of 3 cents per dollar given up. But there may be many people desirous of obtaining his funds, each expecting that possession of the additional purchasing power would enable them to embark on ventures that would yield them far more than 3 per cent. Hence, they may bid for his funds, and perhaps he could get 6 per cent. Note that he would not entertain an offer of 2 per cent, for that is not sufficient compensation for giving up liquidity. But if the demand for funds is sufficiently intense, he might get more than he wanted. Liquidity, then, establishes a floor for the cost of loanable funds. The demand helps determine the ceiling.

Now, the possibility of a rate that was higher than his liquidity requirements might induce him to part with more of his purchasing power. Since he had varying needs for which he was holding the funds, he also would have varying prices at which he might give up command over the money. He might say that under no circumstances would he allow his holding to drop below $300. At present he has $1,000. For 3 per cent he would be willing to reduce his money to $800, the $200 given up having been held for a somewhat remote need. For 4 per cent he would plan his spending a bit more carefully, so that all he needed to hold would be $600. He would now be willing to give up $400, or $200 more than at 3 per cent. At 5 per cent he would plan still more carefully, so that he could manage on a balance of $400, or lend $600. At 6 per cent he would go down to his absolute minimum ($300) or a loan of $700. But no rate above 6 per cent would draw his balance any lower. It is possible, of course, that the demand for funds is so intense that borrowers offer him 7 per cent. In that case he would still lend no more than $700, getting 1 per cent more than was necessary for him to part with that amount. On the other hand, if he were offered only 2 per cent, he might refuse to lend any money; that is, the rate is too low to make it worth his while to plan his spending so that he could get along with less funds.

It should also be pointed out that all we have done in this lending mechanism is to move assets around. There has been no increase or decrease. To the extent that he loans funds, he has less, but the borrower has more. In return he has his IOU. On his books there has been an exchange of money for notes payable to him. On the other party's books there has been the receipt of money matched by the increase in the other party's liabilities to him. But altogether there is just as much money as before; only its distribution is somewhat different. The $1,000 is still there, except that with certain low-interest rates he retains (does not want to lend) that amount, whereas when we raise the rate, he has less but the borrower more, the two of them still having $1,000 between them. It is possible, of course, that the money in his hands might have remained unused, whereas in the borrower's hands it might be spent, say, for the acquisition of raw materials so that he could turn out finished goods. This is a step we shall look into later (Chapter 11).

The reader should also note another relationship. We indicated that if we raise the rate of interest, our individual is induced to carry a smaller balance. The converse is implicit in this relationship: if we lower the rate of interest, he would tend to hold a larger balance. If we run the analysis in reverse, lowering the rate of interest from 7 per cent to 6 per cent, he would still be willing to lend $700, or hold $300. But if the rate dropped further, to 5 per cent, he would then lend only $600, or desire to hold a balance of $400. At the still lower rate of 4 per cent, he would desire a balance of $600, or a reduction in his lending to $400. At 3 per cent he would want a balance of $800—be willing to lend only $200—and at any rate below 3 per cent he would not lend anything, or he would maintain a $1,000 balance. In brief, if we wish people to hold more money, one way would be to lower the rate of interest.

In passing, we mentioned another factor that might induce people to hold larger balances—namely, the size of their income. The richer the person, the more likely it is that his balance will grow. Both the rate of interest and the size of one's income helps determine the cash balance. Later we shall explore the implications of this additional consideration, relating it to the discussion in Chapter 2 regarding the propensities to consume and save.

It should also be noted that even if the saver has no use for liquidity, there still must be some rate of interest above zero per cent to obtain the funds. If we offer the saver zero per cent, we are saying that he will get back precisely as much as he lends. But he could achieve the same goal by holding his funds in cash or in a checking account. Since money never shrinks in nominal value, he would always have the same value. In addition, should he ever want to use it, he has instant access to it.

The only time he might be willing to part with his funds at zero per cent, or even at a negative rate, would be if the bank imposed a service charge. For example, if he has $500 and leaves it in his checking account, he might have to pay a monthly maintenance charge of 75¢, or $9 per year. In effect, the bank is *charging* him 1.8 per cent interest, so after one year his account will amount to only $491. He could hoard it in cash, but a safe-deposit vault costs $7, or the equivalent of 1.4 per cent interest. To keep his money elsewhere is too risky, for burglary is always possible. Hence, in such circumstances he might actually be willing to lend at a negative rate of interest, say 1 per cent—that is, pay the borrower $5 to accept his money. We can see now that the net cost is less than the alternatives. This is admittedly an extreme illustration, but practically speaking, we can say that interest must be positive —more than zero per cent—if lending is to occur.

Income and Cash Balance

There are several influences that the size of one's income exerts on the cash balance maintained. These are of varying significance, but the larger the income, the larger the absolute size of the balance associated with that income, although the proportionate shift may differ.

One factor that has been observed, especially in the United States and Western Europe, is the tendency for many people to alter the form in which they carry their liquid funds. People with higher incomes carry more in their checking accounts; those with very low incomes would carry their liquid funds in the form of currency. In view of the fact that checking accounts tend to require minimum balances, this changeover is probably also associated with a general rise in the average liquid balance. In other words, as people's incomes rise from relatively low levels, they not only carry more money, but more and more of it would be in checking-account balances. Until recently it was thought that the manual worker preferred cash, whereas the white-collar worker would favor checking accounts, but this thinking has become increasingly blurred. However, this changeover need not mean that all of one's funds are kept in the checking account, for there would still be a need for day-to-day requirements. But the bulk of the balance would no longer be that hoard of currency kept at home in a mattress or hidden in the family vase.

Another influence here is the declining marginal value of each dollar as one's income grows. At very low levels every dollar may have to be spent for subsistence, and an unspent dollar is precious, for it competes (by its "unspent" presence) with the desire to buy food, clothes, and other necessities and comforts. As incomes rise, however, more and more of these other wants can be satisfied, and a surplus can still remain. Each dollar is now going for desires that have a lower intensity. Hence, the unspent dollar no longer represents a high-intensity want unsatisfied, and it becomes much easier to accumulate a balance. This cash balance, then, represents an outlet for funds that compete with other uses. These other uses are felt to be less necessary than the uses to which the balance might be put—to facilitate the bridging of receipts and expenditures, or as a precaution against emergencies, or as a fund ready for any other unexpected need, and so on. As incomes rise, the more essential of these competing outlets are satisfied. The less essential remain. Of these, the less desirous might then be used to add to liquid funds.

Associated with this value concept is the nuisance of maintaining too low a balance. The more one spends of a given income, the smaller the remaining balance, and the better one must budget now to insure that there is always enough money to meet the day-to-day demands. If not, one must resort to postponing payments. This means trouble, effort, and annoyance. If the money being spent is going for relatively essential needs, then the trouble associated with maintenance of the low balance is worthwhile. But if one's income has risen sufficiently so that the low priority outlets are also being satisfied, one may feel that it just isn't worth the trouble associated with the careful management of one's funds. So, simply to avoid these minor irritations, we might reduce some of these very low-value purchases, preferring to maintain a much higher balance than normally necessary, simply to free one from the funds-management chore.

Larger incomes also tend to produce larger gaps between receipts and expenditures. This requires the carrying of a larger balance. For example, a man earning $600 per month (paid monthly) who spends $20 daily would perhaps start each month with a $600 balance. This drops steadily until the end of the month. On the average he has maintained a $300 balance—that is, if we were to average his daily balances. If his income is doubled, and his spending pattern remains the same, so that now he disburses $40 daily, his average balance doubles. It would then fluctuate between $1,200 at the start of the pay period, dropping to zero by the end of the month. This would be an average of $600.

It is also possible that larger incomes result in disproportionate increases in certain cash needs, causing disproportionately large jumps in one's balance. For example, with a $60 weekly income, all the money may go for daily necessities. These outlays for food, clothing, and shelter are fairly regular and are generally geared to one's income. It may well be that the maximum balance carried is the amount of the weekly pay check, so that the maximum never goes above $60. But for the man who earns $600 weekly, the day-to-day requirements may be no more than can be serviced by a $200 balance. Hence, for him there is a large surplus which he can then invest. Suppose this individual

were to accumulate several weeks' surpluses before making an investment. His balance might rise into the thousands as he waited for an
appropriate profit opportunity to arise. The poorer man, because he
lacked a surplus, could not afford to build up such a comparatively
large balance. So, only when the income rise was sufficiently in excess
of the living needs could this new influence become a determinant for
the balance.

Associated with this shift is the probability that the upper-income
individual, unlike his poorer counterpart, has other investments. There
will be times, then, when he is pessimistic about the market outlook,
and he sells some of the securities, keeping the proceeds in his checking
account. His balance would rise during this waiting period. The poorer
man, lacking such resources, cannot act in this manner, and so his
balance does not rise abnormally. This speculative motive will be studied at greater length in Chapter 13. It is one of the important components of our dynamic monetary analysis; for any period in which
people expect declining values in their non-monetary assets, efforts to
shift into the carrying of larger money balances would probably
occur. In terms of the discussion in the preceding section, we state
here that a fear exists that the giving up of liquidity may actually
yield a negative income.

The Liquidity of Financial Instruments

The reason for maintaining a balance in highly liquid form is
related to the expectation that at some point the need for such funds
will exceed the expected receipts. It is possible to relate investment
policy with these objectives. If the need for funds can be anticipated at
some precise date in the future, then an investment that will return the
funds before that date meets all the liquidity requirements. Yet, during
the interim, the funds are employed and thereby earn an income. Of
course, we must be fairly certain that the funds will be returned on
schedule. If for some reason the debtor cannot meet the payment date,
although eventually all the funds will be returned, his failure to do so,
circumscribes the liquidity expectation. Consequently, we must not
only assess his ability to repay, but also his ability to do so on time. An
incidental implication is that his ability to repay prior to the expected
date fulfills the liquidity function, although this prior payment may
result in the loss of income for the unused period. This may be a
consideration, for at the time of investment we may have had an alternative which would have been repaid on time—not before, and not
after—and so yielded an income for the full period. By preferring the
former—the one paid in advance—we may have *foregone income*, a

cost no different from income lost.[2] But a prior payment, for liquidity purposes, would be preferable to one that has been delayed.

Assuming that we can place our liquidity needs as precisely as the preceding paragraph implies, then we need not hesitate to hold non-liquid assets, provided they become liquid on the day we need the funds. Of course, if we have misjudged our liquidity needs, and we require the funds sooner than we had originally planned, then the nonliquid asset becomes a burden. By its very nature it cannot be easily turned into money quickly without a loss, and yet we must obtain the funds before its due date. Hence, we must not only assess the assurance about the repayment certainty, but we must also be accurate in fore-casting our own needs.

Similarly, if we have a good profit possibility in the purchase of numerous nonliquid assets, but their repayment dates differ, we may actually find that as a bundle they are most liquid. For example, asset A may not be realizable for six months. Should we have a need for funds before then, we would be in difficulty. But suppose we have enough money to buy dozens of such assets, each of which pays off on a different day over the next six months. Then, on any one day only one is really liquid—the one that matures that day. Hence, we can say that the overwhelming bulk of our holdings is nonliquid. Yet, if our need for funds is no greater than the daily maturities, we have a very liquid group of assets, since each day one segment does pay off and thus supplies us with the minimum desired liquidity. By selecting an appro-priate bundle of nonliquid assets, we have converted them into a liquid group; no one of them is sufficiently liquid to warrant its purchase, but all of them together then become attractive. This process of amalgam-ating such diverse assets is one of the features of banks, because banks are in a position to mobilize nonliquid assets and so make the bundle extremely liquid.

Fortunately for modern economies, especially those of the United States and Western Europe, there are enormous masses of investments with differing maturity intervals. As a consequence, there are also many that mature in relatively short periods, even though the time from the initial issuance may be many years. For example, there are securities issued 20 years ago that are today very close to maturity;

---

[2] For example, suppose A offers me \$1 a day for the use of my funds, and B offers \$1.10. Both promise to repay within 30 days, which happens to be when I must make a payment. I lend to B. As it turns out, B is able to repay me within 25 days, so that my income for the period is \$27.50. For the remaining 5 days my funds are idle, earning nothing; I cannot find anyone else willing to borrow for so short a time. Had I lent to A, as I later discovered, he would have been able to repay only on the 30th day, thus giving me a \$30 income. I thus lost \$2.50 in the form of *foregone income*.

others, issued 19 years ago, have one year to maturity; others, issued 18 years ago, have 2 years to maturity, and so forth. These include those just issued, with 20 years to run. Others have lives of more or less than this period, and there are some as short as only one day.[3] As a result, we can get almost any combination of desired bundles, all tailored to a particular investor's needs. The result, of course, is to produce an enormous volume of constantly maturing funds that are thus available either for reinvestment or for other needs of the investor. We thus gain a flexibility in the disposition of our liquid funds that would be missed if we thought exclusively in terms of one investment for a specified period of time, not realizable until the due date.

Moreover, even if our liquidity needs should unexpectedly shift adversely, we might still find that our asset is highly liquid if it fits into someone else's requirements. Suppose that originally we wanted $1,000 on January 15, 1964, and in 1962 purchased a security with that maturity date. Unexpectedly, in mid-1963, we find we need the $1,000. Happily there may be another investor now holding liquid funds who has no need for them until early 1964. He might be willing to take the security in question, thereby gaining the income for the interval, and with this we are able to meet our liquidity requirements. It is because there are usually investors now holding liquid funds who have just such future, rather than present, needs that so many apparently long-term securities can be handled efficiently. For example, there are British Government securities that never mature, and never pay off. Does that mean that no one would buy them, since no one lives forever, and so there must come a time when he must regain his funds? No, for an investor who does not need his funds today will still buy these issues, knowing that when he does have a need, there will be others at that future date who will also have funds that *they* do not need for the time being. At that time he sells the issue, and so passes on the holding for a while to them. Then, when they wish to liquidate, they, in turn, can usually count on finding still another investor who has liquid funds in excess of his needs, and so on, ad infinitum. So long as there are always such investors, the bond can be sold and resold. And although no one investor holds it for any length of time, investors as a body may be holding it indefinitely. Of course, if at some future date there should be some question about the soundness of this issue, or of the debtor, then the possibility of resale might end. But that *need* not happen and, for a government as well organized as the British, probably never will. It is true that over a period of time anything can happen, and the longer the time, the greater such an adverse possibility. Hence, with

---

[3] Federal Funds are treated in Chapter 17.

infinite life issues there is that much more possibility of such unwanted developments. But the odds have been judged so slight that these issues continue to receive a constant interest on the part of the British investing community.

Summary

Liquidity is the ability of an asset to realize its nominal value with a minimum loss in as rapid a period of time as its owner desires. Currency, almost by definition, meets this requirement perfectly, and checking-account balances are almost as good. This liquidity is desired for a number of reasons, such as a reserve for emergencies, the desire to have resources to buy other assets that may go lower in price, the need to meet anticipated requirements in excess of income, and so forth. Since these objectives are of varying importance, it is possible to induce a person to part with liquidity for a price, usually the rate of interest.

The amount of liquid assets also reflects the owner's income, partly because of the potential usefulness of funds kept idle compared with their being spent for commodities and services also desired. The greater the income, the easier it is to satisfy more of these wants, and the less important are the remaining unsatisfied ones.

With intelligent planning of one's requirements, it is possible to have liquid funds when they are needed, and yet earn income by parting with liquidity in the interim. Provided there are financial instruments that can be tied in with this arrangement, we will have a market that is matching the supply of and demand for funds.

Chapter 5

THE SAVINGS-INVESTMENT PROCESS

While this study is aimed primarily at an analysis of the monetary sector of the economy, there is need to look into those aspects of the system that could be called "real." These are also significant as aids to a more complete understanding. Foremost in this category is the motivation for saving and the forces that give rise to a desire to invest and, perhaps, borrow in order to attain this objective. Much of what follows summarizes the thinking of economists such as Böhm-Bawerk, an Austrian pioneer in this field, and the brilliant English writer John Maynard (later Lord) Keynes.

The Savings Motivation

In the preceding chapters we have indicated numerous factors that motivate people to save—not simply their desire to hold liquid funds, but their desire for the accumulation of assets, or the excess of income over consumption.

Numerous reasons can be listed. Perhaps one of the major ones is the precautionary motive. No one knows when an emergency will arise, and at such a time it is usually necessary to have money to pay its cost. This is most obvious if we think of a serious illness requiring hospitalization. While it is often possible to borrow to meet such a need, many people prefer to have the assets to finance such a requirement. Indeed, it may be that for certain needs borrowing cannot be arranged, or only on such onerous terms that the individual would prefer to avoid such an undertaking. The larger the need, the less likely all of it could be financed through some outside source, so there would still be the need for mobilizable assets. Or, the lender may want collateral—assets that could be pledged with him, so that in the event the borrower is unable to repay, the lender could then take over or sell the pledged assets to recover his money. This might entail the risk of the borrower losing his house or other investments.

Another significant factor is the desire to provide for one's old age. It is true that this pressure has been reduced in recent years due to the spread of pensions and social security legislation. But for many people these funds are not sufficient to maintain the standard of living that had prevailed during the working years, so an additional income supplement would be most helpful. If they had been able to accumulate a fund out of the income during their active life, they could then use the income on these assets, plus, perhaps, slowly liquidating the fund, thereby increasing the money available during their later years.

With both the precautionary and old-age motives the saver is, in effect, transferring spending. Rather than spend all his income during the period in which it is received, he decides to cut current consumption and thereby raise his current savings. Then, at some future date, when an emergency strikes or when he retires, he can consume more than current income by the utilization of his prior savings. (The fact that the size of the fund may be larger because of the accumulation of interest and dividends, or profits, is an aspect we shall examine later.) Incidentally, if the feared emergency never strikes, the funds so set aside need never be used, and, if desired, they can be added to an old-age fund, or simply left untouched as a permanent addition to one's fortune. Similarly, if the emergency is larger than the precautionary savings are capable of handling, it might be possible to transfer some funds from the old-age sector. This would reduce the amounts available upon retirement; but since the emergency may be of so serious a nature that it could mean life or death, the significance of the retirement aspect dwindles. A person not spending in such an emergency would be like the fabled miser who, when assaulted by a thief with the demand "your money or your life," replied that the assailant should take his life, since the funds were needed for his old age!

A third important factor, particularly for selective segments of the community, is the desire to build up a business. This ambition requires a great deal of capital for the capital goods, equipment, and working materials. The greater the size of the business, the greater the income of the owner, and the stronger his status, prestige, and power. While this drive for status is not exclusively a pecuniary one, it does require the generation of more and more funds to fulfill the goal. Assets must be accumulated in various forms, and again this can be done only through the generation of a sufficient income to permit a margin for savings, this margin increasing as business success continues. But here the desire for eventual consumption of what was originally saved may not exist. The entrepreneur may wish to start a business dynasty, which implies that the assets are never liquidated, either in his lifetime or in that of his descendants. Rather, he may hope for continual increases so that the small business becomes a large one, then a giant, perhaps entering the select group of worldwide colossi, such as General Motors or Standard Oil of New Jersey.

Perhaps equally significant for many is the squirrel-like or miserly motivation found in many of us. Many people just love to accumulate hoards, whether canned goods, stamps, masterworks of art, or money. The last-named, in particular, appear to get pleasure simply from the size of their assets, rather than from their utilization. Such people strive constantly to save, often reducing their living standards to ridiculously low levels, all the while accumulating fortunes that are the envy of higher-income neighbors. As mentioned, they do not have the desire to utilize the savings in their later years. They never plan to spend the money so saved, but prefer to hoard it or invest it. In some respects the hoarders are similar to the ambitious businessman in the preceding paragraph, except that the unambitious have less of the ability to control the resources to aid them in their own work. The businessman is directly concerned with the use of his savings, putting them into the expansion of his own company. The miser probably wants no control over the utilization of his funds. He prefers to place them in the hands of borrowers, as either bank deposits, stocks, bonds, or loans. A word that has sometimes been employed to distinguish this type of individual is *rentier*—a person who sustains himself on interest and dividends, but who does not himself direct the final disposition of the funds.

A final factor which cannot be overlooked is the influence of social attitudes. This is certainly true of many sectors of the American economy. People are expected to save if they have reached a certain income bracket. The desire to save is involuntary. One who doesn't save is regarded as a spendthrift, a term whose connotation in this case borders almost on immorality. In many upper-income groups it is quite common to talk about one's investments; obviously the nonsaver would be an outcast in such a group. To maintain status, he must accumulate savings.

There is another category of savings which differs from those already discussed. It is somewhat short-run; we might call this "target savings." For example, to make a large purchase, such as an automobile or a house, it is customary to make a down payment, even though much of the cost can be borrowed. Obviously, to meet the down payment there must first be savings. But these savings are then disbursed at the time of the purchase. However, for the community, savings can still be sizeable at any one time. At any moment, although some people are giving up their previous savings by making the purchase, others are still in the savings stage. Hence, for the economy there is always a larger fund in this prior stage—the building up of funds for the down payment—than is normally being used up in current outlays.

Associated with this type of purchase is a different type of savings. Having made the purchase with borrowed funds, the buyer must then save in order to repay this loan or mortgage. Savings now follow the purchase. Yet these are no less genuine savings; it is only the time pattern that has been altered, plus whatever additional amounts must be used for the payment of the interest and other service charges. Instead of first saving and then making the purchase, he has bought first (after accumulating the down payment) and then saved. Note that this reversal has pushed forward the utilization of the good; he can now enjoy the auto or house sooner than if he had had to save the purchase total before making the purchase. In return for this faster access to the product, he has an extra payment or charge to make—the interest and service costs.

Actually, the preceding illustrates a growing habit—contractual savings. Usually when we think of savings, there is a voluntary element in the decision to save. John has a certain income, and if he wishes to save, he then restricts his consumption. If his income declines, or if other wants appear, he is free to reduce his savings, freeing his funds for consumption. But with contractual savings this freedom is greatly diminished, if not ended. Having contracted to borrow, he must save in order to pay off the debt. If he does not, the lender may take away his boat or auto. Hence, if his income falls, he must restrict his consumption in order to maintain the surplus over spending to meet his loan payments. Or, if other wants appear—new goods that he is most eager to buy—he cannot reduce savings in order to get the funds for the purchase. He must either abstain from this additional outlay or restrict his spending on other consumables. The extent to which the savings can be drawn upon is reduced by the amount necessary to repay prior obligations.

These contractual savings are not to be used solely to repay past debts incurred. They can also be used to accumulate savings for any of the motives already discussed. Most obvious of these is the insurance contract. People take out insurance for various precautionary purposes, such as death, illness, and fire. But in many contracts there is also a savings element. If the contingency insured against never arises, the money paid in premiums often has been reinvested by the company and has grown in size. After a certain time these become the property of the insured. They form an addition to his assets. In effect, he has accumulated a fund just as though he had saved the money in the bank. The contractual nature of his saving, however, has forced him to continue to save. With a voluntary bank savings plan the saver can always stop saving without incurring a penalty. But the insurance contract is so arranged that there is always an incentive to continue the premiums, because ending a contract before its term usually involves a sizeable monetary sacrifice, although this sacrifice is not comparable to the repossession possibility if a loan is not paid. But there is still a loss. The insured would have been better off had he maintained the payments, receiving less of a gain if he breaks his payments pledge. As a result, most people continue to pay their premiums even if their income declines. If any income exists, they prefer to sacrifice either consumption or voluntary savings. Only if income drops drastically—to zero—will such contracts be ended.

The Meaning of Investment

One of the troublesome words for the student of economics is *investment*. The popular meaning differs so much from its more restricted sense for the economist that a discussion of this distinction will help the student understand the analytical process itself.

The popular understanding of *investment* is "any acquisition of an asset that is expected to yield a gain, either annually as income or over a period of time as a capital gain or both." And this can be taken as reasonably true for any individual. But we must distinguish this definition from the one that is applicable to an entire economy. In particular, we must eliminate transactions that cancel each other.

To illustrate this cancellation, suppose Henry purchases one hundred shares of General Motors. He can now say that he has invested in that stock. But obviously someone must have sold it to him. Assume that it was another stockholder, and that the number of shares of

General Motors outstanding is the same. This one hundred shares changed hands from the seller to Henry. So, whatever funds he put into his investment were matched by the funds withdrawn by the seller of these 100 shares (except for the commission costs of the transaction). In effect, the seller disinvested. For the community there has been no net change other than the small amount of transfer or commission costs, such as brokerage fees and taxes. Ignoring this small qualification, we can say that Henry now has more shares and less cash, while the seller has more cash and fewer shares. So, because there has been no change other than the redistribution, we can say that there has been *no* net investment.

A similar line of reasoning would apply to any such "paper" transfer. Wherever one person invests by buying an existing security, someone else—the seller—has reversed the transaction. The buyer gains securities but loses cash; the seller gives up securities but obtains cash.

What, then, do we mean by *investment for the community*? One definition is "any action that results in a net increase in the productive ability of the community." For example, if James buys a machine tool which is to help step up his company's output, he can say that he has invested. True, at first glance it would seem that we have only had another transfer. James gave up cash and obtained a machine; the machinery maker gave up a machine and obtained cash. But the difference is that in the hands of the machinery maker the machine tool in question was not being used to increase output.[1] In James' hands it is. His action has added to the effective stock of the economy's capital equipment. Incidentally, we must measure this net, for if at the same time James discards another machine of equal productive ability, then he has not added to the community's productive capacity. The new machine simply replaces the old one. Hence, in our definition we must adjust for this using up, or *depreciation*, of the old equipment.

Investment can take many forms. To raise output, James may need more materials—working capital. This is investment of a short-term nature. The purchase of a factory building is also investment. Obviously, it is difficult to manufacture goods if there is no place to house the machines. By convention, even the acquisition of a house by an individual is considered investment, since it does produce a flow of housing services, as well as the savings on rental payments. Even education is considered a form of investment. Money spent on one's schooling is supposed to raise one's productivity as a worker and citizen.

---

[1] However, in practice, additions to inventories are counted as investment, reductions as negative investment or disinvestment.

Another somewhat intangible form of investment is research and development. Out of the laboratory come new products and processes which will help to raise aggregate productivity. Some economists believe that the most significant influence in raising per-capita production is the combination of education and new technologies.

In measuring a country's wealth, similar corrections must be made. Every paper asset is someone else's liability. If James has a corporate bond as part of his wealth, offsetting this is the obligation of the issuing organization. His bank-deposit asset is the bank's liability. The mortgage owned by the bank is offset by the debt owed by the homeowner. Even the currency cannot be counted, since the government or issuing central bank is the debtor. Hence, in estimating the aggregate wealth, we need count only the physical forms—equipment, inventories, and such. We can ignore all the representations, the titles to these entities.[2]

Money and Investment

Since investment involves a net addition to the community's stock of capital goods, including both working capital and the various intangibles, in practice it can be seen that the usual procedure by which such an action occurs is the transfer of money for the particular form of capital desired. Someone must produce the capital, make the machine, grow or mine the raw material, or build the structure, but it is not until the item is transferred to the person or firm intending to use it for further production that we have an investment. But in a strict sense this is not true. A machinery maker might produce machines and add them to his inventories awaiting buyers; he has added to his working capital until a buyer acquires his machine as a fixed investment. If no one buys the machines—suppose he had produced the wrong items —then this machinery is of no further use in raising aggregate productivity. Analogous reasoning would apply to stocks of raw materials.

In the first illustration, the purchase of a machine tool, we had a clear-cut case of investment. Or did we? It was assumed that James must have saved the money in order to obtain the funds to make the purchase. If this was true, his savings equalled his investment over the period discussed. But suppose he borrowed the money? On his books it would appear that he had *not* made an investment, for the increase in his assets (the machine tool) was matched by the rise in his liabilities (the loan), and so his net worth is no greater than before. Yet, by our

---

[2] Foreign assets and liabilities would be counted for any one country, but would, of course, cancel out for the world.

definition we must have had an investment, for the stock of fixed equipment in the community has been raised by James' action.

It is here that we can begin to merge the popular meaning and the economist's meanings. For the economist the net investment was James' action in adding to his productive capacity by the purchase of the machine tool. Now, how can we balance this with the popular meaning—no net increase in investment? If we turn back to the transfer aspects, it can be done. Where did James get the loan? Assume that it was an individual who loaned him the funds. Where did this individual get the money? One possibility is through saving. He consumed less than his income, produced a money surplus, and then turned it over to James. His savings action, in a sense, matched James' investment action. Perhaps the individual obtained the money by selling some other asset—for example, the General Motors shares already mentioned. Then he has not saved. He has simply changed his asset disposition. He now has fewer General Motors shares and more in loans. But then we must ask where the share buyer got his funds. Maybe he was the true saver. Among the numerous possible alternatives we will trace, the possibility of a bank loan will be covered in Chapter 8.

The preceding paragraph also illustrates another point: the saver and the investor can be the same person, although often he is not. One saves in order to invest, and apropos of this we have two decisions: action that produces the savings, and action that produces the investment. Where these two decisions are made by two separate people (or firms), certain possible disturbing factors arise. We may have people deciding to save the same amount that investors want for the acquisition of capital goods. We may have savings decisions that tend to produce more savings than the investors want to use, or less savings than needed. Finally we have the problem of inducing the saver to turn over his funds to the would-be investor, even if the quantity saved equals the amount desired.

Where the two are different, we have several possibilities. In our loan illustration the saver made (*a*) the decision to save and (*b*) the decision to lend to the potential investor. But there could also have been an intermediary, a bank or a nonbanking financial institution. For example, the saver may decide to save by buying a life-insurance policy. The insurance company then may be the one to decide whether the would-be investor is worthy of the loan. Here we have three decision-makers, namely the saver, the intermediary, and the investor. Once again we can raise the possibility of the various confusions in this procedure, any one of which could snarl the smooth workings of our development. We are now quite removed from our earlier case, in which the saver wishes to invest in his own enterprise, taking all the decisive steps himself. In this case—reminiscent of the earlier days of modern capitalism—the desire to save was often intimately linked with the investment opportunity. When this opportunity existed, it acted as an incentive to save (in order to exploit it). But in our modern sophisticated economy the man with the investment possibility must more often seek the funds. However, these may not be forthcoming if (a) there are not enough savings, (b) the intermediary does not obtain the saver's funds, or (c) the intermediary thinks the investor is not worth the risk.

On the other hand, this rather cumbersome procedure could also widen the investor's horizon. If he had to depend on his own resources alone, then his investment outlays would be limited by his ability to save out of income. With the addition of outside funds (obtained directly from savers) he has broadened the potential volume to the aggregate available savings of his friends and acquaintances. If we add the intermediary, we open his potential source of funds to the host of strangers entrusting their savings to the financial institution. In contrast, what borrower knows any of the policyholders in the insurance firm from which he gets the loan? He does not have to know any. All he must do is satisfy the loan officer of the insurance company. But the raising of funds directly from savers means that the borrower has to satisfy each would-be lender.

Loans from the intermediary will tend to reflect his standards and his desires to conserve funds entrusted to him. He may avoid riskier opportunities that promise great profits—but also great risk of loss—whereas the individual savers, the decision being left up to them, might have taken the gamble. In all probability the net effect has been to channel funds into less risky situations, and more so to larger firms already having established reputations. A small, new company with an unknown potential is more likely to suffer a shortage of borrowing possibilities.

The Marginal Efficiency of Capital

So far in this chapter we have spoken mainly about the supply of savings. The other activity—the demand—we shall discuss now. What motivates the desire to borrow? To invest? What are the differences implied by separating these two activities?

Suppose we examine a hypothetical, but perhaps typical, business firm engaged in a profitable manufacturing operation. If it is aggressive (this feature characterizes much of American industry), it is anxious to grow in size, to expand the scale of its operations—in general, to become large if now small, or become a giant if now large. There is hardly a profitable concern that does not want to enlarge its scope. And the opportunity is there, for we have already seen that it is in a profitable sector of the economy. But just what does this profitableness mean? From where and from what does it arise?

To answer these questions fully would require an extensive excursion into capital theory and the mainsprings of entrepreneurial activity. Here we shall simplify our answer, limiting its scope mainly to those factors of interest to the monetary analyst. Yet even this can become complex, if we pursue its implications. There are still many strands that puzzle even the keenest of economists.

Presumably, the firm in our illustration can turn out a product at a cost less than its selling price. This is obviously inherent in the meaning of profit. Furthermore, the demand is such that an increase in output can also produce a profit. We shall assume that the firm is already producing within reasonable limits of its present capacity, so that any significant and enduring increase in output would require an increase in capacity—more machinery and/or plant.[3] Actually, investment in this company must be increased, so the firm introduces more funds into the business (purchases needed equipment to expand capacity) and earns an increase in annual profits. It must therefore weigh these two sides of its investment opportunity—the addition to its stock of productive facilities, against the additional return over their productiveness. Borrowing a Keynesian phrase, we can call this relationship the "marginal efficiency of capital." For an affirmative decision, of course, the expected extra returns over the life of the additional equipment must more than compensate for the funds spent for this addition. To measure this relationship, we must approach the task in several stages: (a) expectations, (b) the measurement of the returns, (c) the profits element, and (d) the relationship of profits to interest rates. We shall also consider, as subsidiary segments, the effect of the business cycle on (b), and some factors that help explain the emergence of (c).

EXPECTATIONS. Since most decisions of this nature are based on estimates of future operations, planning in general tends to be in terms of *expected* income and costs. If we are basing our estimates on the performance of the next five years, we are ignorant of what actually will occur during that period. Based on our past experience and ability to guess the future, we make our estimates. But that is all they are. True, some of these estimates may be contractually fixed, but these are often

---

[3] We say "enduring," for a temporary output increase may be possible by working overtime, or reducing idle machinery by postponing necessary maintenance. But such stratagems are short-term makeshifts, not feasible for any continued period of expanded production.

the exception. Very few contracts fix either selling prices, sales volumes, or costs for as long a period as five years. A wage contract may be for two or three years, but then we have the uncertainty for the period following. Experience may have taught us that usually wage costs (including fringe benefits) rise 3 per cent at each new contract period, and to that extent we can estimate the wage costs for the subsequent years. But we could be wrong; perhaps the union will become more militant, or perhaps other sectors of our economy will become so inflationary that workers demand greater increases to offset the higher cost of living. We may not expect these developments, but again that is all our estimate consists of—expected wage costs.

Similar influences apply to other elements in our calculations. Since materials' costs tend to fluctuate within a certain range, a war or severe depression could upset this figure considerably. Sales estimates, both as to price and volume, are based on our estimate of current demand and how long it may continue (or increase). Perhaps some new competitor will arise and throw these estimates out of line. People's tastes may change. There are any number of shifting influences. All may be unlikely, but such confidence is only an estimate, and since there is no way of foreseeing the future, we must base our planning on such shifty grounds.

The uncertainty factor is also influenced by the length of our planning horizon. Different people confronted with the same data might also present different expectations, depending on their temperament and training. This degree of change, of an erroneous estimate, is less likely if we are trying to plan for the next few months than for the next few years. Yet we may have to plan for what would seem an absurdly long period. Some projects require such vast amounts of capital that it takes many, many years of expected profits to pay it off. The aluminum industry often limits its new bauxite exploitations to those that are expected to have at least enough ore for the next hundred years of operation. Of course, if our industry is one that foresees unending growth, then to some extent we are safe in making so long an estimate. What we are saying here is that sales will grow and grow, so that at the end of the century the volume will be far greater than that currently sold, and so that our receipts can be estimated accordingly. There are few industries that can plan confidently for such long periods, and any projection of this nature is suspect. All we have to do is think back a century, and see what we could have estimated for the economy today!

To a certain extent we can compensate for the uncertainty factors by allowing a larger range where the unknown is so difficult to calculate. For example, if we have just signed a wage contract for three years, we have removed this unknown. At least we have reduced its uncertainty greatly. There might still be wildcat strikes that add to costs, but at least the major uncertainty of the wage level has been removed. But three years from now there will be uncertainty, when the contract comes up for renewal. If we estimate then that wage costs usually go up 3 per cent, we may, for the next period, estimate it at 5 per cent. Thus we have allowed for error, and if, even with this 5-per-cent wage rise, our operation still pays, then it should certainly pay if the expected wage-cost increase of 3 per cent should result. By adding this factor for uncertainty—higher costs than expected, lower receipts than hoped for—we provide ourselves with a margin for error. Of course, if the margin turns an otherwise profitable opportunity into an unprofitable one, we must then assess the likelihood that we shall have made an error by the estimated margin. Usually this reflects the temperament of the individual; some hopeful personalities will take the chance that the errors will be less than allowed for and will go ahead with the project. The more cautious will hold back. The sanguine expand; the cautious do not. When correct, the sanguine grow even larger and more successful, but if wrong, they may end up with a loss and perhaps bankruptcy. Such is the lottery of business operations.

Another way to provide for the expectational uncertainty is to compose our estimates as reasonably as we can, but then suppose that we must make more than a certain profit to warrant our embarking on the venture. We may set as our guide the requirement that any contemplated venture must show a promise of at least a 20-per-cent profit, even though our goal is only 10 per cent. If our estimates are correct, we make a large profit—larger than our 10-per-cent objective—but if wrong, and our costs are higher than we had planned, or our receipts less, we may still meet our goal of 10 per cent. As before, this means that the 15-per-cent prospect will not be undertaken, unless the uncertainty element is much less. At times we may even embark on what superficially seems contradictory. A very uncertain project with a hoped-for return of 30 per cent may not be enough to warrant our undertaking it because the uncertainty is so great, while one with a prospective profit of only 15 per cent may be undertaken because the uncertainty of our estimates is believed to be so small.

Uncertainty varies with the industry and the particular segment of our calculations. Minerals exploration is especially hazardous. We don't know how much is in the ground, or whether it is, or if it can be taken out of the ground without excessive costs. What will the market be like when we have finally started to sell the output? Perhaps this will occur a decade after the initial exploratory efforts. There are a host of other unknowns. In contrast, a hydroelectric plant built to service a nearby government factory may incur most of its costs at construction, such as excavation, dam building, purchase of generators and other equipment, plus the various other capital installations, while a long-term contract may set the price and volume for years into the future. Certain costs can be fixed for long periods, such as leases on land. Others, such as raw materials traded on the organized commodity exchanges may move from day to day. Some uncertainties may even cancel out. It is possible that textile prices move in the same direction as raw-cotton costs, so that an error in the sales price would be matched by a corresponding error in input expenses. If we overestimate future selling prices for our textile output, and the sales price declines relative to our planned price, we may have an offsetting saving, since this presumably occurs only when the cost of raw cotton has also declined. Hence, to some extent the smaller income per unit is balanced by a somewhat smaller cost per unit, and so the squeeze on expected profit margins is less than would be influenced by the movement of either price considered alone. (Those familiar with trading on commodity exchanges will recall that hedging to achieve just such a relationship is common—to move certain costs together so as to cancel out, or at least minimize, the price fluctuation of any one item.)

Some observers have attempted to quantify this expectational uncertainty. In effect they place a range on each estimate, the range growing as the uncertainty increases. Then they apply a statistical weighing to the uncertainty: the greater the uncertainty, the greater the weight. In this way the expected cost or price is adjusted for the degree of uncertainty, the former being increased, the latter decreased. If, after such statistical manipulations, we still come up with a "go-ahead" sign that despite the wide range of uncertainty our project will still show a profit, then we have that much more confidence in embarking on the venture. But, as previously remarked, this means that many other ventures that would be profitable must be bypassed because the uncertainty factor is too great. But suppose the uncertainty aspects did not result; then they would have been worthwhile investments.

THE MEASUREMENT OF THE RETURNS. Given the normal profit motivation, we can say that an investment over its lifetime should yield enough above operating costs to produce a sum equal to its original outlay, or cost plus some gain. But this may not always be the objective. Sometimes investments (expansions) are made for other purposes, such as "empire building," even though by the usual measures they show a loss. But for our purposes we shall assume that the major incentive is profit-seeking.

Some of the calculations in our previous paragraph can be quite specific. The original outlay is often known so well that it can be counted out to the exact dollar. But over a period of time the return of an equal number of dollars may not mean that we have recouped our initial outlay. Suppose during the period there has been a generally rising price level. Then the same number of dollars will buy less in commodities and services than it did at the time of our initial outlay. Some sort of replacement equivalent is necessary to correct for such changes in the purchasing power of money.

We should remember that this return of one's investment is *not* a profit. Generally accountants provide for this element through the allocation of depreciation expenses. As the machine wears out, its remaining value is that much less. Finally it is no longer used. At this point it has only scrap (resale) or even zero value. This physically useful life may be shortened through technological advances which make it advisable to "scrap" the equipment even sooner. In these cases the annual depreciation must be calculated for this shorter time. Now, depreciation is accounted for like any other expense, and if sales do cover at least all costs, they automatically cover depreciation. But unlike cash expenses (wages and raw materials), the depreciation cost does not require any disbursement. In most cases a part of income is paid out for wages, raw materials, rents, and the like, and a part is set aside as a reserve fund, a reserve for depreciation. In effect, depreciation is a cash-segregating expense, rather than a cash-disbursing item. Presumably, over the life of the equipment enough money will be set aside in this manner to equal the (original or replacement) cost of the equipment, so that there will be sufficient money to keep the plant going after the purchase of a new item to replace the discarded one.

In the interim, while this fund is being accumulated—but before it is used to buy the replacement item—the money could be employed for other purposes, such as buying other new machines. In this way depreciation provides one means of expanding, for the firm is enabled to purchase new equipment before the old wears out. Its gross fixed assets thus rise during the interim and are offset by the declining value of the existing equipment as its remaining useful life grows shorter. Often these new machines are so much more efficient that productive capacity actually may increase, even though the net value of the equipment shows the same value on the company's books.

In summary, then, part of the return on a machine is also the depreciation, an amount that rises as the value of the machine declines. These funds are a return in liquid form of the original investment, and can be used for maintaining the investment—through the purchase of new equipment—or they are free for use elsewhere if the profit outlook in this particular sector is not satisfactory. This is a method for a

firm to disinvest. All it need do is *not* reinvest the depreciation reserves, and as a result, its physical equipment slowly declines in value as
the remaining useful life gradually drains away. The total value of the
company is unchanged. The decline in the value of the equipment is
being matched by the rise in the money in the depreciation reserve.

But now the investment devoted to this particular productive
operation—the use to which the equipment in question has been put—
is slowly being reduced. Funds are being freed and can now be put in a
different project, even used for consumption. In this last possibility, we
have negative savings (dissavings) matching the decline in investment.
What we would see here is a decline in the physical value of the equipment but no rise in cash, the money that had been generated by depreciation having been consumed. This latter item is in excess of income,
and this consumption was not out of any income, but out of capital.
And so this is regarded as negative savings,[4] offsetting the negative
investment.

Ignoring the dissavings possibility, we can say that depreciation is
that part of cost that returns the original investment, perhaps corrected
for price-level changes. Hence, if a project just covers all of its costs, it
means that it generates just enough cash—the excess of income over
the other cash expenses—to return our original investment. Again we
shall avoid the knotty problem of price-level shifts, leaving some aspects of the discussion to the chapter on inflation. If we do this, we can
then isolate the profits element, the excess of income over all costs,
including depreciation.

This profit element, of course, will vary with the business cycle as
well as numerous other factors. In a boom the economy expands; a
given project will tend to have a greater volume of sales than in a
recession. Even if all costs remain the same, the likelihood is that profits
will be higher in a boom simply because the volume of operations is so
much greater. In a recession, on the contrary, the shrinkage in sales
volume will cut into profits and thus make a given investment less
profitable. During a prolonged period of boom or depression, the same
project would show different profit possibilities. A project planned to
start in 1931, with the ten-year depression in the future, would obviously show less of an expected return than a similar one started in 1947.
Consequently, the general outlook for investments is usually much
better in a boom—or more precisely, if a boom rather than a recession
is expected. Hence, in speaking of this profits potential—the marginal
efficiency of capital—we must correct for the cyclical outlook, or at
least take such fluctuations into consideration.

---

[4] Since savings equals income minus consumption, and income is zero, savings
equals minus consumption, or a negative figure.

Now, as compared with a recession, we would probably see two differences. Projects that would be profitable even in the depressed period are that much more profitable—that much more attractive—in a boom. And other projects which would not be profitable because of the shrunken volume of sales in a recession may become profitable in the boom. Hence, the former would probably be planned on a larger scale if boom periods were the expectation. The latter would come into being only if the boom is expected. Both tend to raise the aggregate possible volume of investment—the aggregate of investment opportunities. It is partly for these reasons that the boom in consumption is accompanied by a boom in investment. We need more capacity to turn out the larger volume of goods demanded in the boom. This high level of demand makes it profitable to invest to expand capacity, which improves the profits and market outlook for some projects, while for other projects it makes the outlook profitable where before it had not been so.

In practice, the cyclical influences are not so simple. To some extent, costs will tend to decline in the downturn and rise in the upturn. Hence, we see in this respect an offsetting influence: profit margins tend to be squeezed by rising costs in the boom, and improve in the recession. But sales prices can also be raised in the boom, perhaps offsetting the squeeze, while the intensified struggle for sales in a recession may result in price cuts, thus counteracting the drop in costs. We are saying that competitive pressures increase in a recession and decrease in the boom, perhaps nullifying the effects arising from shifts in costs. Our conclusion, therefore, is that when balanced, the profits outlook is generally better in the boom, and the desire to invest is correspondingly greater. Certainly the psychological elements are more favorable in the boom, for the generally expansionist mentality makes businessmen that much more receptive to new investment opportunities. In effect, as mentioned earlier, the cyclical phases tend to feed on themselves. Economic and psychological forces interact so as to prolong and intensify the move, until the offsetting elements make themselves felt sufficiently to reverse the movement. And, as already explained, the additional re-enforcement element is investment. It rises because of these various pressures in the boom and declines in the recession.

PROFITS. Mention has been made of the desire to obtain *more* over the lifetime of an investment than just the amount originally invested in the project. This "more" is the profit. We shall see that it must be there to justify borrowing. It is profits that enable the payment of interest, for only out of such an excess income can one make a payment in excess of the amount borrowed, without eating into the capital itself. To understand better the phenomenon that creates this profit process, we should first recall what an investment is, in its essence. It will be recalled that, for society as a whole, people must save if they wish to invest. This means that they must consume less than income in order to provide this excess for investment. This investment becomes an addition to the productive capacity, and can then be used to raise future output and income. In effect, to save and invest means reducing current consumption in order to produce the savings which, when invested, will then raise future income.

It will also be recalled that the output requires the using up of goods and services, such as labor and raw materials. If an investment just pays off, the difference in value between the aggregate output over the life of the investment, and the goods and services used up in producing this output, is the amount set aside as depreciation. This amount is equal to the value of the original investment (ignoring the price-level problem). So, the increase in value of the output, after netting out the input of goods and services used to produce this output, is the depreciation. This means, then, that the net increase resulting from an investment is exactly equal to the decrease necessary to produce the investment.

A simple arithmetic example may help clarify this relationship. If one earns $10,000 in one year and consumes goods amounting to $9,000, he has saved $1,000. He could have consumed the remaining $1,000 if he had not wished to save anything. But this $1,000 is used to purchase a machine expected to last four years and for every unit produced by this machine the owner must purchase labor and raw materials amounting to $6. If he wishes to get back his investment (without any profit), the output must also provide for a depreciation expense of $1,000. Assume that this item can be sold for $7. Then, over this period, 1,000 units must be sold. Total sales resulting will be $7,000, and in the process the owner will have used $6,000 ($6 × 1,000) worth of goods and services. Thus he has provided the economy with $7,000 worth of goods, but in so doing he had to absorb $6,000 worth; net, he provided $1,000 more to the community than it would have had if he had not purchased the machine. Over the four years, then, he can spend on consumption the amount of the depreciation funds, if he wishes. He can now spend $1,000 on consumption because of his investment's just paying off. But if he had not bought the machine, he would have had $1,000 free to do the same thing before the process started. So, he has not gained anything by cutting down his consumption and investing the savings. All he has done is postpone the consumption from the time he put the savings aside until the time the depreciation flow came in. Thus no incentive exists to make such an investment, unless the return over the period of time the machine is used is greater than $1,000—that is, unless there is a profit.

Fortunately, most such investments—most such acts of cutting down present consumption to enhance future income—result in profits. Thanks to the inventiveness of man, capital equipment does add enough to the value of output to provide more than depreciation. Usually this occurs through the savings on wages. With the machine our man can turn out his product with less labor per unit. But without the machine, labor, materials, and other services would cost $7 per unit. With the machine he can save on labor, so that his per-unit cost for these items drops to $5. Assuming the machine can produce only 1,000 items during its lifetime, we see an aggregate output of $7,000,[5] other costs are $5,000, depreciation is $1,000, and profit is $1,000, or about $250 per annum. We must qualify the $250 figure because we have to consider the interest effect before making a precise profits estimate.

It is possible now that the 1,000 items could be sold only if we were in a boom. In a recession we may be able to sell only 800. Our total sales—assuming that prices and costs per unit remain the same—would be only $5,600. Costs would be $4,000, depreciation $1,000, and profits only $600. This is 60 per cent of the boom estimate. If sales should drop below 500 (say 450), total receipts would be less than $3,500, actually $3,150. Costs would be $2,250, and depreciation would be only $900, or less than our original outlay. Depending on the cyclical situation, we would make a large profit, that is, if sales were 1,000. This would realize a fair profit (on sales of 800) or a loss (on sales below 500). We would have widely differing incentives to invest here, depending on which of these three outcomes was the expected one.

In this example we assumed that the machine reduced labor costs to such a degree that it produced a difference between receipts and costs, this difference equal to more than the depreciation. Obviously, any cost reduction would have moved in the same direction. We can conclude that any cost-reducing innovation, if the cost saving exceeds the investment outlay, will show a profit. The larger the profit, the larger the incentive to initiate this innovation. But we must remind ourselves of the expectations qualification. Profit may not be large enough to allow for any possible uncertainties in our estimates. We may want a large profit to allow for unforeseen and possibly adverse

---

[5] In this example we shall assume that selling price remains at $7 before and after the purchase of the machine.

variations. Note also that we have not determined here how large a profit is necessary to justify making the investment.

Not all investments arise from cost-reducing projects. A completely new product attracts investment funds if it finds a new and profitable market. The advent of the television set was not a cost reduction. Such an invention had never appeared before, but people were willing to buy sets at high-enough prices and in large-enough quantities to produce a profit on the investment. Not all new products do this. If there is too limited a sales volume, there may not be enough of a surplus over other expenses to absorb the depreciation. In such a case we would have a loss situation.

It is not to be concluded that there must be a profit throughout the life of an investment. There may be periods, sometimes years, when losses are incurred. What is hoped for is that profits will more than offset losses by so large an amount that it will be sufficiently attractive to undertake such a project. Prospective profit must be enough to offset the risk of failure.

PROFITS AND INTEREST RATES. The relationship between profits and the rate of interest arises from the separation of investor and saver. The investor must obtain funds from savers, and the interest rate then must enter into the calculations. Under normal profit considerations, an investor will not borrow funds unless the cost, the interest to be paid, is less than the return he anticipates from his action. Profits expectation establishes an upper limit on the interest he will pay. As we have already implied in another context, this does not establish an absolute limit. If a manufacturer is so anxious to expand—to build an empire, so to speak—that he is willing to lose money, then he might borrow for projects that will yield less than the added interest cost. He takes the difference from profits received in other operations. This would not be the normal business attitude, but we shall see that consumer and government borrowing tends to take on just this exceptional character.

In practice, the investor-borrower would expect to earn more in profits than he would pay in interest to the saver-lender. If the two were exactly equal, there would be no net gain for the investor, and in most cases he would not undertake such a venture unless there was to be a clear net gain. And by "clear net gain" we do not mean a simple arithmetic excess of profits over interest. We mean enough of an excess to compensate for the risks and uncertainties should his estimates go astray. A venture promising a 6-per-cent return annually,[6] measured

---

[6] Interest rates are usually on an annual basis. All quotations in this text are per annum.

against a borrowing cost of 5½ per cent per annum, is not worth undertaking if unforeseen variations could shift the return up to 8 per cent or down to 4 per cent. Confronted with such a range, the investor might not borrow unless the excess were 2 per cent or more. Thus our 6-per-cent return really means our investor-borrower may borrow at 5½ per cent and gain 8 per cent, to earn a net profit of 2½ per cent, if his greater expectation is realized. If a pessimistic outcome materializes, he can gain only 4 per cent, for a net loss of 1½ per cent. But if the average return was expected to be 7½ per cent—ranging between 5½ and 9½—then even at its worst our investor would still not show a loss. The 2-per-cent additional expected (average) gain would give him the necessary protection against the less desired outcome.

Often this expectational uncertainty is so great that the cost of interest becomes a minor concern with the investor. Suppose our venture is estimated to yield a 10-per-cent profit, but the possible range of error could be a gain of as much as 25 per cent, or a loss of 5 per cent. A cautious investor might refuse to borrow, fearing that the less hopeful outcome is too much to risk. Even 1-per-cent interest rates would not tempt this investor. Regardless of the rate offered on borrowed funds, he will not risk other people's money. The rate of interest does not influence him.

But suppose he has a 50-per-cent profits possibility, a range of profit outcomes that is certain to remain within a minimum gain of 25 per cent, perhaps as high as 75 per cent. Here we may find that the rate of interest does not influence his decision. It probably will not if he lives in a community where lenders seldom ask for more than 7 per cent. But regardless of the expected interest rate offered this attractive project, he will borrow. The difference between his return and any feasible interest charge will be more than enough to make it worthwhile.

We now have examples in which the rate charged is of no influence. It is the profits rate that is *the* determinant, and we shall develop this further.

With normal profits calculations, we would not expect an investor to borrow unless the expected gain were enough in excess of the rate of interest to offset the various risks of the undertaking. (In our previous two paragraphs, the first example did not have enough return to offset the risk; the second did.) So, if the risk consideration is dominant, then the normal range of possible interest rates is usually too small to be a consideration. It is the profits and the risk potential that become the determinants.

We must point out here that the excess of profits over interest need not hold for each period of time. There may be periods of slack business when the interest cost is expected to exceed the return. But during the life of the investment, these are expected to be outnumbered by the excess-profits periods. Keeping this in mind, our investor might still be willing to embark on the described venture. But if the periods of excess interest costs drain him of his liquid assets—suppose he must draw on his cash balances to meet the deficiency—it might threaten the success of his operations to a degree that he would not prefer to take such a risk. With this alternative present, he might not borrow unless every period promised an excess return over interest charges.

The above qualifications should not be considered extreme. The reader need not swing to the opposite, to say that the rate of interest is of no consequence because profits, risk, and finance considerations seem so paramount. We shall see that the interest rate *does* and *must* play a part in the flow of funds between saver-lender and borrower-investor. The interest rate is not the exclusive determinant. In many cases it may not be the most important influence. It is, however, one of the more important factors to be considered. We must remember that its importance varies with particular circumstances.

To the extent that the uncertainty and risk components are not so overwhelming, however, we can see some interesting relationships as a result of shifts in either the profits expectation or the interest rate charged by lenders. Assume for the sake of the discussion that investors will not borrow and embark on a new venture unless the prospective return is at least 2 per cent more than the cost of borrowed funds. Then any project that yields less than this differential will not be undertaken, and any that meets the minimum will be embarked upon.

If, for some reason, interest rates should rise, then some projects that would have been undertaken at the prior rate will not be undertaken now. For example, if a particular project is expected to yield 7 per cent, it will be undertaken if the rate is 5 per cent or lower, but not when the rate rises above 5 per cent. An 8-per-cent project would not drop out until the interest rate rose above 6 per cent. We can thus conceive of all such projects standing in a line, the lowest yield at the beginning, starting, say, at 1 per cent return, and rising to 10 per cent. Some just would not enter the market at any feasible rate of interest—even at zero per cent the required 2 per cent excess rules out those projects that are expected to return less than 2 per cent. As the interest rate is raised, fewer and fewer will show the necessary excess, until above 8 per cent none do. Or, if we start with 8½ per cent, at which no project qualifies, more and more will qualify as we lower the rate. We can thus conclude that rises in interest rates will reduce the demand for borrowed funds and declines will increase the demand.

We could also have affected the demand had we altered the profits expectations. Reverting to our illustration, in a recession profits possibilities generally shrink. We might even encounter projects that become net losers. In a boom these would be producers of net profits. Certainly no one would borrow money to throw away on a losing venture. But now even profitable ventures are not as attractive as before. Perhaps our line now starts with a 2-per-cent loss and graduates up through zero per cent to, say, 7 per cent.[7] If the going rate of interest has remained the same, fewer projects are now worth attempting. For example, assuming that it had remained at 5 per cent, then before (in the boom) the 7½-per-cent project might have been undertaken. But now, in the recession, this project promises to yield only 6 per cent. Since the margin over the interest cost has dropped from 2½ to 1 per cent, the project is not undertaken. Only if the interest charge were also to decline—at least to 4 per cent—would we embark on the project. In brief, a general decline in profits possibilities reduces the demand for funds if interest charges remain unchanged. Conversely, when there is a general improvement in the profits prospects, the demand for funds increases.

Summarizing our relationships, we can say that where the risk component is not too significant, rises in interest rates or declines in profits prospects would tend to reduce the demand for loanable funds; and declines in interest rates or a general rise in the profits outlook will step up the demand. In our earlier discussion on liquidity we remarked that the supply of loanable funds is also responsive to interest rates—rising when the latter move up, declining when the latter drop. We can thus see the foundation of our supply-and-demand approach to the equilibrium rate of interest. However, this cannot be attempted at this stage. To do so would be to leave out some other essential influences; a simple supply-demand picture is inadequate for so important an institution as the money market.

If business is so depressed that our profits prospects shrink drastically—for example, if the best that can be hoped for is an annual gain of 1 per cent—then the required 2-per-cent differential is not obtainable. We have seen that people will not part with funds unless

---

[7] The order of the projects may not be the same as in our previous example. It is quite possible for the 1-per-cent gain in the prior illustration to drop to only ½ per cent, while a 4-per-cent gain before becomes a 1-per-cent loss now. The latter would be those more subject to the cyclical swings. These would now be among the less desirable, whereas before they may have been the more desirable investment. Incidentally, in our allowance for risk, we would have included the degree of susceptibility to such swings. We are also assuming that the 2-per-cent margin for the borrower remains the same throughout the cycle; actually this might very well *increase* in the recession because of greater uncertainties.

they receive some return—that is, until there is a positive rate of interest. But any rate above zero per cent must mean that borrowers have less than the desired 2-per-cent differential to make it wothwhile to undertake the risk. Hence, there may be no lending, or very little. There may still be a few projects that yield more than the 2-per-cent differential, but not too many. No rate of interest would call forth enough of a demand to absorb the available volume of savings. Unless we can reduce the risk component or step up the profits prospects, we are in a dilemma. This is an aspect of the "liquidity trap" to be discussed later. It is also theoretically possible to subsidize the lender, so that he would accept a negative return. The government would compensate him for the difference. For example, if a lender wants ½ per cent, and the profits prospect is only 2 per cent, we do not have the necessary 2-per-cent excess. But if the government paid the lender the ½ per cent, provided he would lend at zero per cent, then we do meet our liquidity and risk requirements.

Internally Generated Funds

Not all investments are financed through borrowed funds. Many businesses and individuals also draw on their own sources of supply. For the business firm this is mainly profits not distributed as dividends, or retained profits. For the individual, it is savings out of current income. In addition, either may dispose of saleable assets.

At first glance it would appear that the interest rate on borrowed funds would be of no influence on this sector. If a profit opportunity appears and the potential investor has the money to finance it, so much the better. But some qualifications are necessary. After all, the investor could have loaned his funds to other would-be investors. If they were willing to pay a greater return than would be obtained from his own project (after correcting for risk and uncertainty), he might have been wiser to be a lender rather than an investor. To some extent, then, the going rate of interest does become a consideration. Similarly, if he is thinking of selling an asset to obtain the required funds, he will be giving up whatever income he had been getting from that asset (interest or dividends), and this income given up must be weighed against that to be obtained from the new project. Here he has two alternatives: (a) to invest in the new project or to retain the saleable assets, and (b) to invest in the project either through the sale of these assets or the borrowing of funds. As before, among the considerations would be the rate of interest—either that lost when the asset is sold, or that incurred when the funds are borrowed.

On the other hand, financing out of one's own resources does bring up certain differences. If we borrow, we must pay interest and

eventually repay the principal. If our project turns out to be a mistake
—if we had overestimated its income and/or underestimated costs—
these obligations could become heavy enough to force us into bankruptcy, or at least drain our other resources severely. It is true that if
we finance through our own resources, we suffer the loss. However,
there is no additional burden from servicing the borrowed funds.
Hence, the risk element is less if we avoid borrowing. And if the risk
element is less, more projects become attractive. Because of this bankruptcy fear, the investor may embark on a project only if it yields 2 per
cent more than the interest costs. But if he has his own resources, he
might undertake it so long as the going rate of interest—that which he
could obtain by lending his funds to others, instead of undertaking
this particular project—were no more than the potential profit.

An additional difference arises from the "line of credit" concept
common among lenders. Many people can borrow funds, but only in
limited amounts. Hence, if they have projects that promise to yield
more than the risk differential in excess of the interest cost, they may
still be unable to obtain sufficient funds simply because lenders will not
lend them so much. For example, A and B may both wish to undertake
a certain project with an expected profit of 12 per cent, costing $1
million. A is a large, wealthy corporation and has sufficient profits
currently to provide it with the funds. B is a small corporation and has
not yet become sufficiently profitable; it would have to borrow the
money. But the market will not lend it more than half its required
amount. As a result, only A can undertake the operation, although B
could also do the job, maybe even better! To the extent that a firm can
generate its own financing, it frees itself from dependence on the
outside market.

A somewhat similar restriction operates on the borrower. Many
firms do not wish to incur too great a debt for fear that an unforeseen,
but possible, severe downturn in business activity would produce so
little income as to make debt servicing burdensome. The less the debt,
the less the possible danger. Hence, if a profitable project would involve a firm in too great a borrowing operation, it might forego this
opportunity. On the other hand, if it happens to be generating sufficient profits, it will go through with the project, since the borrowing
would then be within the desired limits. Note that here, too, as in the
preceding paragraph, it is not the profit or interest rate that has influenced the decisions to borrow and invest, but the availability of internal
resources and credit attitudes of both the lender and borrower.

As a result of these factors, some observers feel that the company
that is able to generate its own needs out of profits and thus avoid the
borrowing is, in effect, freeing itself from the judgment of the market.
When Company B in the example was allowed to borrow only half a

million dollars, wasn't the market saying in effect that it could not be trusted with more—that its management was not yet judged to be good enough to qualify for such a large sum? The market may feel the same way toward Company A, but is helpless to stop A from entering into the investment simply because A had enough profits to free itself from this restraining influence. It could be even more extreme. Suppose we have an investment project that yields only 2 per cent. If the company in question generates sufficient profits, it can undertake such an unattractive proposition. Perhaps the stockholders would prefer to get that money as dividends, so that they could reinvest the funds elsewhere at 6 per cent. But being small in number and scattered, they cannot influence management. Nor can the would-be lenders stop management by charging a rate that would be higher than the 2-per-cent profits. Management is not seeking borrowed funds. Again the judgment of the market is rendered impotent.

If we carry this last point to the extreme, we can almost contradict our earlier remarks. Here, what determines investment is the supply of internally generated resources. So long as these can be invested profitably, our corporation—assuming that it is characterized by this empire-building mentality—will plough back these funds into these new projects. It would probably be influenced by the potential profit rate to some extent. Given the choice, it would undoubtedly select the higher profit projects from those available. But the aggregate amount invested would be determined by the flow of funds. The level of profits in the potential investments would not be the influence we had previously discussed. If, for example, the firm has $10 million to invest, and has three potential $5-million projects, yielding 4, 5, and 6 per cent, it would invest exactly the same as if it had three projects promising 10, 12, and 14 per cent. In the first case it would select only the 5- and 6-per-cent projects, and in the second alternative the 12- and 14-per-cent ones. But in either case it would invest $10 million. The level of potential profits did not influence the amount invested, but only the direction of the flows. And since we are assuming that the firm does not borrow, it would not step up its investing if the rate of interest on loanable funds shifted. In effect, then, here is a situation where neither the level of prospective profits nor the interest rate influences the amount invested.

It might be noted that profits do have some influence. To the extent that the firm makes profits, it has funds for reinvestment. The greater its profits, the more the flow of such available funds. But note that it is the profit from its current operations that influences investment, not the expected profit from the potential projects. Here is an analogy to savings: income, rather than interest, forms the main determinant of the volume saved.

Borrowing by Consumers and Governments

Another large volume of borrowing is undertaken by two non-business groups: consumers and governments. To some extent the dividing line between a business-type loan and a consumption loan is difficult to draw. If a consumer borrows to buy or build a house, presumably the rent saved will enable him to pay his mortgage. But with a business loan, the calculation is fairly precise: Will the expected profit exceed the interest charge? With the homeowner there may not be so careful an estimate. He may well buy a house that requires servicing costs in excess of his rental alternative; therefore, he is borrowing without a corresponding profit (saving on rentals) as his income source to pay for the charges. It is his other income, probably wages, that is expected to bear the burden. One characteristic of a consumer loan, the purpose to which the funds are put, does not produce enough income (or reduction of costs) to service the obligation. Other income must be relied on to do this. Prominent among the purposes for such borrowing is the acquisition, in addition to homes, of other consumer durables, such as automobiles, household accessories, and home improvements.

An analogous problem arises in the treatment of government borrowing. Some borrowings are similar to business loans—for example, a bond issue to finance a toll road. Others are more borderline, such as borrowing to stimulate the economy. The hoped-for upturn in activity then generates increased incomes and, consequently, taxes to pay for the loan. Other loans are similar to the consumer-type, such as borrowing to finance current operations. Any level of government—federal, state, or local—can be involved in any of these categories.

What distinguishes the bulk of these loans, consumer or government, is the relatively weak influence of the rate of interest on the borrower's desire to borrow. The interest rate is a consideration, since it measures the cost of the loan to the borrower. But unlike the business loan, it cannot often be related to the source of servicing the loan. The business borrower can easily measure the cost of his borrowed funds against the income generated by the project. But the consumer and government borrower do not have so easy a task. The interest rate may be high or low, but is it too high to justify the desired expenditure? Is it low enough to make it worthwhile? Does a 2-per-cent loan rate justify borrowing to pay a hospital bill? Is 7 per cent too high? Should the new city hall be built if we can borrow at 3 per cent, or postponed if we must pay 5 per cent?

The ineffectiveness of interest-rate changes is even more obvious with regard to borrowing by the central government. In the United States a budgetary deficit is usually a deliberate policy decision. It is absurd to think that its magnitude would be altered if the going rate on new debt issues were to vary by a fraction, or even more than 1 per cent. While the Treasury Department would like to minimize the debt cost, it would not be greatly influenced in view of these broader considerations. The only possible effect might be in the specific selection of the type of issue—whether to put out short-, medium-, or long-term issues. But the quantity of money to be raised would still be the same; only the sources might differ.

The Influence of the Interest Rate

Throughout this chapter there has been frequent reference to the rate of interest. Sometimes it appears to have been significant in explaining the flow of funds, sometimes only peripherally important. Here we shall attempt to assess its place in the financial mechanism. It must at this stage remain incomplete, for we have not yet discussed the banking system, of obvious importance in our picture. But we can pull together the various strands treated in the different places, trying to make a preliminary assessment of the function the rate of interest does perform.

Based on numerous empirical studies, we can say that the rate of interest does not have much influence on the desire to save. Most people are mainly influenced by their income level. If we raise their annual income, we increase savings. If we keep their income the same, a change in the rate of interest is not likely to greatly affect the volume of their savings.

This conclusion is not to be interpreted as absolute or for everyone. Some people may save more as rates rise, simply because the reward for so doing has increased. Other people may have contractual savings, and this amount may vary with the rate of interest. With insurance, for example, the greater the rate of interest—that is, the greater the income received from paid-in premiums—the less need be paid as premiums to attain a given amount of insurance. Higher interest rates thus might induce some people to reduce their annual premium payments, a form of savings already discussed. It should be noted that a higher rate called forth a smaller volume of savings; this in contrast to the reaction of those people motivated by the reward element.

It should also be noted that people might save either more or less in a recession than in a boom, since incomes change and the psychological temperament of the community is different. But since we are interested only in the influence of the rate of interest, these factors become irrelevant for our point.

On the other hand, the rate of interest may induce a greater flow of loanable funds. The higher the rate of interest, the greater the proportion of savings that will be loaned. Here the rate of interest does play a role, for, given the volume of savings, we could draw a supply curve indicating that at higher rates more money is available for loans. This we covered in our liquidity discussion earlier in Chapter 4 and need not be repeated. However, it should be noted that the higher rate made more funds available. Whether or not more is actually loaned depends on the demand.

Our conclusion so far is that the rate of interest has relatively little influence on the desire to save, but it does influence the disposition of these savings.

The demand for funds is more difficult to assess. For some firms, where expectations can be made within narrow margins of error, the greater the rate of interest, the less the demand for loanable funds, because the profits excess is being squeezed. On the other hand, where the risk and uncertainty elements become very large, the rate of interest plays only a minor role in influencing the demand. It also appears to be of limited influence on consumer and government borrowing.

Probably the two major would-be borrowers who might be most influenced by shifts in the rate of interest are public utilities and mortgage seekers. The former is a remarkably stable industry. Both revenues and costs can be predicted with amazing accuracy. Hence, as major examples of our expectational certainty, they would be able to calculate fairly exactly the interest costs relative to expected investment returns before deciding on the borrowing operation.

The home buyer is in a somewhat similar position. His income is fairly certain, although there is the possibility that he could lose his job. More important, a large part of the annual cost of owning a home is the interest on the mortgage. In some cases more than 90 per cent of the purchase price was borrowed. Perhaps then, more than half the cost of running the house goes for interest. Marked shifts in this rate affect monthly costs significantly. These shifts could make the difference for many whether to buy or not—whether to borrow for a mortgage or continue to rent. Since it is likely that more than half of all loans for more than one year fall within these two categories— borrowing by public utilities or on mortgages—we see that the rate of interest still plays some factor in the determination of the demand for loanable funds.[8]

---

[8] To some extent a rise in interest rates could be offset by spreading the mortgage repayments over a longer period. Each payment is thus less, so the monthly amount is no greater. More goes for interest, less for reduction of principal. The number of payments is correspondingly greater.

We have also mentioned that particular sector of the market where loanable funds may be of little or no influence—those investors who generate their own funds out of current operations. Here, too, the rate did play some role; these funds could have been lent out. But again it appears that this sector is only marginally affected in its actions, the current profits and the outlook for the prospective new projects being the more important considerations.

One group, consideration of which we shall have to postpone, is the intermediary, the organization that accepts funds from the saver and passes them on to the borrower. There we shall have to touch on the cost of his services and the effect of anticipated changes in the outlook for interest rates in assessing the influence of the rate of interest. Remember that the rate of interest does have an influence, although its technical ramifications create their own problems.

To sum up, we can see that there are elements of the economy that are greatly influenced by the rate of interest. Others are not. Even if only a part react, this part may be sufficiently large in absolute size to exert a marginally significant effect on the economy. It may turn out that the tail that wags this dog is so large that it may rival the dog in size! Hence, we can tentatively conclude that the rate of interest does play enough of a role to warrant its use in influencing business decisions, and it is worth our while to explore these ramifications in greater detail.

Summary

To analyze the flow of funds, we must study separately the desire to save, to lend, to borrow, and to invest (the purchase of capital equipment). Each step has different motivations, and each is often performed by different individuals or institutions. Some of these forces can be influenced by shifts in the rate of interest, others by income and profit levels. Still others may be insensitive to these factors. In the last sector, most notable is borrowing by the consumer and various governmental units. In all efforts to understand the mechanism, a prominent place must be given to expectations, even though these are the reflection of subtle psychological forces difficult to assess precisely. Implicit in this feeling is the element of uncertainty, the difficulty of seeing precisely into the future. From this springs risk, a return additional to the interest cost, or a subtraction from anticipated profits. In addition, we must also correct for changes that arise from the variations over the duration of business activity—the business cycle.

Chapter 6

THE FUNCTION
OF MONEY

Previous chapters outlined some of the characteristics of a money economy. We have not yet introduced the banking system. To understand the function that these financial institutions play, it is first desirable to examine certain aspects peculiar to the use of money. These will enable us to gain a more thorough familiarity with the monetary system as a whole. We shall now examine the reasons why we use money.

Barter

It is not absolutely necessary for every society to use money. Communities still exist that are able to get along without such a medium. This alternative method of effecting exchanges is known as barter. It illustrates in many respects not only the uses that money serves, but also why money is so preferred by most people.

Essentially, barter is exchanging through swapping. The usual examples are so many that it would be tedious to elaborate them. *A* produces shoes and wants a cotton jacket. If he can find someone who has a cotton jacket and who is willing to exchange it for *A*'s shoes, we have a meeting of minds, and a swap is accomplished. The coincidence that must be present is that both sides must each have a desired item; each must also want the other's item, and the two items must be of equal value.

A few modifications to the strictness of our coincidence can be easily fitted in. *A* might find someone who wants his shoes but has no jacket to offer. Perhaps *B* has food he could exchange with *A*, and which *A* could then use to get the desired jacket. We see here that food would be serving some of the same purposes as money serves.

It is also possible that a pair of shoes is worth two jackets, although *A* wants only one. He could exchange his shoes for the two jackets, then try to re-exchange the extra unwanted jacket for some other item. The exchange of shoes for two jackets gives us the coincidence of values, even though *A* did not want to use both items.

In most conceptions of barter we visualize individuals wandering about looking for these coincidences. *A* might go from house to house with his shoes looking for a particular individual who has a jacket and who needs the shoes. Actually, barter societies are not this itinerant. Market day normally occurs. Once a week everyone with something to sell meets at some common location. Those who want to buy are also there.[1] Here the haggling process can take place *en masse* and the numerous transfers arranged more quickly.

For a sophisticated community this is too inefficient a method of exchanging goods and services. The task of matching countless thousands of all these supplies and demands would be virtually impossible. Only when we adopt something akin to our use of the food would some of these problems be solved. Only if there were an item that everyone would accept in exchange for his offerings, knowing that he could then dispose of this particular item for the goods he really wanted, would the numerous exchanges be facilitated. This, through the evolution of history, is what money has become—the medium of exchange. But as we shall see, this is not its exclusive function.

Thanks to the existence of money, the exchange process can be greatly simplified. Because of money, the required number of coincidences is greatly reduced. Now all that is necessary for the seller is that he find someone who wants what he has to sell and who is willing to pay the desired amount of money. If the potential buyer does not have

---

[1] Actually, every buyer is a seller, and every seller a buyer. *A* is a seller of shoes and a buyer of a jacket.

the money, the sale cannot be consummated, for we need both desire for the item and the ability to pay for it. If the buyer has money, he automatically has what the seller desires. The buyer no longer needs the ultimate item that the seller desires. In our earlier illustration, B, the shoe buyer, no longer needs the jacket that A desires, if he has the money instead. A can now purchase the jacket with the money received from B. This transaction of business, it will be recalled, had been done earlier through the medium of food. It presumed that food was generally acceptable, and it could have developed that most people would accept food, although the jacket seller would not. He may have enough food. What is needed is a medium universally acceptable by the entire trading community. This is money.

Besides its widespread acceptability, money also facilitates exchange in other ways. We no longer need the coincidence of values—the shoes being offered just equaling the value of the jacket. Since money can be subdivided into almost any fraction, it is not difficult to make a precise calculation. One may question how to exchange 1¾ cows for 2⅞ goats. Nor could this problem be resolved by offering 2 cows, for that would be equivalent to a bit more than 3¼ goats. Exactly 3 goats is worth less than 2 cows. But if cows are priced at $40 apiece, and goats at $24.35, then we can do business.[2] We may still find it difficult to sell ⅞ of a goat, but now we can sell cows and goats, using money as our medium.

But it should be remembered that we are still bartering, although now it is money versus the commodity. Where before we traded shoes for jackets, we now trade shoes for money and money for jackets. In effect, every sale of a commodity is a demand for money, and every purchase of a commodity is a sale of money.

Money has many other conveniences. If one is wealthy, it may be awkward to carry one's shopping funds in the form of hundreds of cows, shoes, or jackets. But currency can be carried in efficient forms. One piece of paper, a $100 bill, could replace quite a few shoes. The storage problem is simplified. Checking accounts simplify this problem even more. We can write out the amount of money involved, and thus not have to carry the funds around in our pockets.

Many cultural and historical forces influence the selection of a specific commodity as the accepted medium of exchange. Currently in almost all countries, this physical representation has been replaced by paper of various denominations. Some countries back the commodity with some other specific commodity—usually gold—but in virtually all

---

[2] Our previous equivalency amounted to about $70 for the 1¾ cows and 2⅞ goats; we will ignore the slight rounding error.

cases the face value of the money supply outstanding exceeds the face value of this backing. Even the backing is often spurious; in the United States it is virtually impossible for an American to obtain the gold backing unless it is intended for use as payment to a foreigner. Some of the implications of these relationships will be explored later.

We can say now that the transactions function of money serves essentially as a lubricant to smooth the exchange process. It reduces many of the problems necessary to effect a transfer. But its usefulness is not limited to this one objective. It also serves as a store of value, and the implications of this are far-reaching for monetary theory. Before treating this aspect, however, we should add several comments to the transactions use of money.

The Bridge Between Receipts and Expenditures

The flow of cash for the average individual or business corporation is irregular. Receipts do not match expenditures, so there must be some means of bridging this gap. In a modern economy this can be achieved in several ways. One way is to try to reschedule either side of the cash flow to bring the two closer to each other, thus minimizing the gaps. The second possibility is the utilization of credit. For those periods when outgoing demands exceed inflow, the would-be recipient could agree to postpone receiving the cash until the payer has money to make the payment. In effect, the would-be recipient converts a cash receipt into an account receivable. He relies on the debtor's honesty to fulfill his obligation at some subsequent date. This credit substitution is to be examined later.

For our present discussion, however, the major means of bridging the gap is through the use of money. If receipts exceed disbursements, there is a net cash inflow, a net accumulation of cash.[3] If the outflow is greater than the inflow, we would draw on previous accumulations. Of course, if the excess cash inflow becomes so great that it exceeds all foreseeable future drains, we might then convert some of this excess into some income-earning alternative, disbursing the cash to buy, say, a security. Conversely, if the cash drain exhausts our previous accumulation, we may then resort to credit—that is, borrowing, if our credit standing is adequate and the source of such aid available.

In a barter economy this cash flow would not show up. A somewhat analogous situation could develop, one akin to a modern economy's inventory variations. If a farmer has grown a lot of wheat, and if

---

[3] At this stage we shall not distinguish between currency and other acceptable forms of the money supply, such as checks.

his current desire for other goods can be satisfied by trading off a fraction of this wheat, the excess can then be kept for future trades. This is similar to modern man's cash accumulation. If he wishes to buy more things than he can obtain by exchanging the wheat that he is currently producing, he can supplement his buying power by drawing on this previously accumulated wheat. In effect, he draws down his cash balance. Obviously, the exchangeability of money is more general than that of wheat. But in principle the two work similarly. Money performs the same function that would arise in a barter economy, but its more general acceptability, for the reasons already established, also makes it more general a medium with which the discrepancies between inflows and outflows can be bridged.

A comment should be added regarding the amplitude of this bridging problem. If a man is paid $20 daily and spends all his money that day, his cash balance is zero, except for those brief moments between his being paid and his making purchases. If we switch him to a weekly pay basis, six days of working and spending, he obtains $120 once each week and then each day draws $20 from this amount. At the end of the first day he has a balance of $100, the second day $80, until he reaches zero on the sixth day. His average balance throughout the week is $60.

Suppose we switch him to a monthly salary. For simplicity, we shall select February, with its 28 days, assuming we have 24 working and spending days. In this case the month begins with his receipt of $480, and this drops each day (except Sunday) by $20. His average cash balance now is $240. In brief, by enlarging our pay periods, by increasing the discrepancies between receipts and expenditures, we build up automatically the size of our balance, and thus the demand for money.

On the other hand, we can reduce the demand through similar intervention in the payments procedure. One has already been touched on: the use of credit. There are many others that can be cited, but we shall limit ourselves to a few illustrative cases. One that is influential in an economy such as ours is the tendency toward what is known as vertical integration. If *A* sells to *B*, then *B* must have cash to pay *A*, unless there is a credit arrangement to postpone such a payment. But if *A* and *B* then merge, the new corporation can simply switch the goods from Department *A* to Department *B* without using money. A simple bookkeeping entry will suffice.

Another economizing measure has been the spread of banks. In our monthly example our individual carried $460 at the end of the first day, $440 at the end of the second, and so on. But if a bank is handy, he could deposit much of the cash, keeping one or two days' requirements, then replenishing his holdings by withdrawals. The bank now has the bulk of the money, and in turn can lend it to others. Borrowers of these funds now can carry smaller balances since the bank is there to help bridge the gaps between such loans. During World War II the reverse of this process became evident when the internal migrations brought many more people to small communities without adequate banking facilities. As a result, people were forced to carry more cash, because this handy depository was not available for both deposits and withdrawals.

Individual affluence also influences the size of the balance. If our individual received a raise and increased his spending proportionately, then the figures on both sides of our example would be increased, and the average balance figure would rise.

Mobile and Immobile Money

In studying the characteristic influences of the money supply, we shall have to distinguish between immobile and mobile funds. This is what has been called the distinction between money sitting still and money on the wing. These differences become of extreme significance when we reach the analysis of velocity. In order to establish more completely the nature of the money function, it is just as well to distinguish certain aspects here. As before, we shall not bother to distinguish between currency and other monetary forms.

Money can function in two situations. It is either mobile (active) or immobile (inactive). The activity is somewhat subtle, even though it is seemingly obvious. Whenever money is employed to effect an exchange, it is active. Money passes from the buyer to the seller, and either goods or services pass from seller to buyer. Even a gift is a two-way exchange; presumably the donor receives gratitude or gratification in return. At other times, when money is not acting in its transactions function, it is idle, inactive, immobile. Currency, for example, may simply be dormant in our pockets, whiling away the time until called upon to perform. Then, when its owner decides to make a purchase, it comes alive for that moment, only to go back to sleep again in the seller's possession. There is a subtlety in the obviousness of the implications in this example. Periods of inactivity are those times when money is serving as a bridge between receipts and disbursements. These periods of inactivity account for the absorption of the money supply. By lengthening the time between pay periods, we might increase the size of the average cash balance. In terms of our current discussion, then, what we have done is to increase the periods during which money was inactive. And in so doing, we tied up a larger amount of money. We shall see that an increase in the supply of money need not increase spending, if we offset this with a rise in the periods of idleness.

If we interpret activity as literally as it was developed in this section (that it means those few moments while the transaction is being effected) then we can readily see that for the most part money is idle. At any moment of time in a country like the United States there are billions of dollars being carried in wallets, pocketbooks, cash drawers, and vaults. At any moment some individual is effecting a purchase or other type of exchange. At these instants, money is galvanized into becoming demand. At all other times it is dormant and of no influence on the market. What is important is the frequency with which these idle periods are punctuated with the interruptions of activity.

Suppose John has $10, and he is the only person in the community with any money, and also that people do not barter. Then, until John decides to make a purchase, or in some way give up his money, no one can do any business. Suppose that everyone in this community has the habit of waiting one week after receiving any money before they decide to spend it. Then a week from now John spends $10 with A. One week later A spends it buying something from B. A week later the money passes to C, and a week later to D. Over a four-week period, the same money has effected $40 worth of business.

Suppose now that everyone's spending becomes more sluggish, that it takes two weeks after the receipt of cash before we get the subsequent disbursement. Then D will buy from E two weeks from now, E from F in two weeks. In four weeks the same $10 has now given rise to only $20 worth of business. Simply by lengthening the time between the momentary interruptions of activity, we have reduced aggregate spending. Note that in both four-week periods the stock of money remained the same ($10).

But let us add another change: assume that at the end of the fourth week we injected an additional $10, giving it to G, but still kept our two-week period of waiting unchanged. Then, after two weeks, G buys from H and two weeks later H buys from J. In the four weeks we have effected another $20 worth of business. As compared with the preceding paragraph, doubling the amount of money in the community has given rise to twice as much business; but as compared with the first four weeks, doubling the quantity of money has given rise to the same volume of business, because the increase in the supply of cash was counteracted by the increased length of time between receipts of money and the later disbursement. Here in essence is the basis of much of modern monetary theory—the variations in the quantity of money, its rate of use, and the reasons that give rise to variations in both components over the business cycle.

Goods versus Money

While not all disbursements are outright purchases, most transactions are designed to acquire either goods, services, or securities of various types, including bank deposits and mortgages. Consequently, we can think of the decision to activate money as a decision to acquire one of these objects. At the moment money becomes active, therefore, the individual has decided that he prefers some other object. For whatever reason, this other object has a greater value than the money he is giving up. It may be that this value will arise from his own consumption. It may be that the value is the potential profit through a later resale. It might also be that the object is expected to retain its purchasing power better than money. Or it may simply be that because money does not yield any return and a security does, the latter is preferable for that reason, its yield being worth more than the liquidity that money offers. We can then regard all these alternatives as competitors for a given supply of money.

Now let us suppose the individual does part with money because he has decided that these other items have greater value for him. We are also implying that for the seller, the money has greater value than the object he is disposing of. For the buyer, the object out-competed the money; for the seller, money out-competed the object. This does not mean that someone must have lost. It could be that the buyer is hungry. He wants food more than money. The seller has grown so much food that he has more than enough to feed himself. Perhaps the buyer may need the income, but not need the liquidity, whereas the seller prefers liquidity because of expected future payments or uncertainties in his personal situation. If this is true, then it is probable that both have gained.

In this competition there is also cross-competition. Many goods, services, and securities are available. As a group, they all compete for the would-be buyer's money. But within the group, each item competes with the other. Should he buy a new car? A new home? More stock? A bond? A trip abroad? Any one of these may be preferable to money, but which of these many possibilities is the most preferred? The outcome can be quite different in impact. The purchase of a car stimulates the output of automobiles. A trip abroad will affect the balance of payments. The purchase of a new security issue adds liquid funds to the corporation's activities, perhaps enabling it to expand its productive capacity through the purchase of machinery. We thus get cross-currents in our repercussions, and some of these may influence the money markets, while others might affect the level of economic activity. Later we will examine a threefold grouping: money, securities, and goods and services. In greater detail we will follow the lines suggested above.

Let us recall here that an increased competitive need for objects would speed up the spending of money, cause the active periods to occur more frequently, and shorten the length of intervals of idleness. Conversely, an increased preference for money would reduce the frequency of the active moments and lengthen the average life of the idle periods. The liquidity discussion in the preceding chapter assessed the reasons why money might be preferred, the value in holding money being the need for its liquidity.

Store of Value

Money can also serve as a store of value. This is a standard of deferred payment. Since money is acceptable generally and will be for some time into the foreseeable future, we can depend on its being accepted in exchange for goods and services. If we have more money than we wish to spend at any one time, we can keep the excess, knowing that we could use it at some future date for the goods and services desired at that time. Money's value is measured by the goods and services it can command, and its future value would be measured by the bundle of goods and services it will command at a future date.

If we expect prices in general to decline in the future, we are saying that money will have a greater value, a command over a larger bundle, or increased purchasing power. Conversely, if we expect prices in general to go up in the future, then we expect money to have a lesser value, a command over a smaller bundle, or a decreased purchasing power. If we expect prices to go so far up that our money will buy only an infinitesimal part of the desired bundle, then we are saying that our money will become practically worthless. This happened many times in the past. One example is the German inflation after World War I. So we must also consider this extreme possibility.

If we expect prices to rise in the future, it might be worth our while to hold our store of value in terms of some commodity other than money. If we expect prices to double, wouldn't it be better to exchange our money now for wheat, and then hold the wheat? If wheat doubles in price, then its command over other goods and services will be the same as today, whereas money will command only half the bundle it does today. The question is: What commodity should be selected as the alternative to money? Wheat may double in price and hold its relative value in terms of the other commodities. Wheat might even go up more, thus enabling a given volume to purchase more of the other goods and services. It might go up less, so that still another commodity would have been better as our selection. It is even possible for it to go down in price, which would make it a worse store of value than money. In addition, there is the cost of storing wheat, in contrast to the ease with which money can be held. Hence, unless the expected price rise is to be enormous, so enormous that we can feel confident that our commodity will perform better than money—although perhaps not as successfully as some other commodity might have performed—it may be better to stay with money even though we know it will lose some of its purchasing power. This can occur simply because of the costs and uncertainties associated with any other item. In an extreme inflation, such as the aforementioned German one, there is no doubt that every commodity would rise enormously in price, so much so that, despite the costs, the holder would gain more than by continuing to hold onto the money. In such an extreme case people would abandon money as a store of value.

A simple example may illustrate the complexities facing the selection. Suppose it costs 10 per cent per annum for storage costs of any commodity other than money, since money can be held at little or no cost. (A safe-deposit vault charge would be minimal for any large amount of money placed in it.) If over the year prices in general rose 10 per cent, the holder of a representative commodity is no better off than if he had held money. After subtracting the storage cost, he has as much value as if he had stayed with money. If prices rise 20 per cent, but his particular commodity rose only 10 per cent, he is again no better off than had he stayed with money. If his commodity in either possibility rises in price by less than 10 per cent, he is worse off. After subtracting storage costs, he will end up with less money than he started with. Only if he is certain that the price of his commodity will rise by more than 10 per cent will he gain. Such a certainty would be present if prices are rising by thousands of per cent per annum; then he can be certain that his commodity will go up by more than the storage costs. Just how much more would still be a guess.

When prices are generally stable—some rising and some declining, but the bundle as a whole costing about the same—we have the ideal circumstance for using money as a store of value. At this point, only chance can determine which commodity will rise by more than its storage costs over the period. And at this point we then enter the realm of the commodity speculator. The cautious outsider interested only in conserving his purchasing power knows that money serves as the perfect medium. Money is the absolute assurance of safety.

Would a declining price level be better? It would, in one respect. In a period of falling prices the odds become greater that the selected commodity will go up less than its storage costs. Probably it will go down, thus adding to the loss. Obviously, money is safer than the commodity. But the danger of too serious a price decline is that a wave of bankruptcies and social instability may accompany it. If we get too drastic a deflation, we may run into revolution and repudiation. Perhaps the moneyholder may have to flee the country. More important, this holding onto money intensifies the downswing, and in our discussion of liquidity preference we shall have to explore this aspect at greater length.

Store of Value, and Barter

Some of the implications of the preceding paragraph can be better illustrated if we contrast the store-of-value problem in a barter economy with its effect on a money economy. Suppose John grows perishable vegetables, and has raised more than he needs to swap for the commodities he desires. He will have a surplus of produce. He now wishes to translate this surplus into some commodity that will keep until he desires some more goods and services. Perhaps John feels that copper will be ideal. Copper is always in demand. It will not deteriorate easily if properly warehoused, and it has a fairly high value relative to its bulk. So John trades the rest of his vegetables for copper, even though he personally has no use for copper. At some future date, when John wants some more goods and services, he can then barter the copper for what he desires. So here the store-of-value objective has been accomplished.

Assuming that events develop as anticipated, the desire for a store of value required a supply of goods with which to acquire this desired item, and it required a supply of the desired item. Not only must John have grown enough vegetables to trade for copper, but the copper mines must have produced copper for him. In addition, the individual disposing of the copper must have had a demand for John's produce. Otherwise he would not have given up his copper. (The copper man may want the produce for his own consumption, or for trading it with someone else who desired it; in either case there was a demand for John's produce.) Hence, the desire for a store of value required both a *supply* of produce and of copper, and a *demand* for produce and for copper.

Similarly, when our individual subsequently disposed of his store of value (the copper), there had to be commodities produced that he wanted and people willing to accept copper in exchange. There had to be two demands—the individual's demand for goods and services, their demand for copper—and two supplies of each. As before, the desire to utilize a store of value resulted in both a demand for, and supply of, commodities.

Some readers may question whether production was necessary in these cases. Couldn't the goods have come out of inventories? They could have, but inventories are only another example of a store of value. In our example, during the period the man held copper as a store of value, he had an inventory of copper. When he disposed of the copper, he added to the supply copper that he had not produced. Similar reasoning would apply to any other inventory. Because John produced perishable vegetables, he could not use his own output as a store of value. The copper producer could. By producing more than he needed to obtain his current demand for goods and services, he could have put the surplus directly into storage (inventories). Again the desire for a store of value would add to the supply of a commodity. Only here, both supply and demand are for the same commodity, and by the same person. That is, our copper producer wants a store of value in the form of copper. He has as equal a demand for copper as did John, who produced the perishables. Only our copper producer also produces the copper supply he desires. John did not. But still we have both a supply of and demand for copper.

If we introduce money into the preceding illustration, we see some sharp differences. John, our producer of perishables, would try to sell all his produce, as before, but the surplus would go into money. For this portion of his sales we have a supply of produce but no demand for commodities. Note that all John's vegetables were sold for money; then, some of the money earned was respent as a demand for other goods and services (that part that would have been bartered for perishables). Here the store-of-value component would not become a demand for any commodity, for the demand for copper has disappeared, to be replaced by a demand for money. So, to accumulate a store of value in the form of money, we need to have a supply of commodities, as under barter conditions, but no demand. Similarly, when we dispose of our store of value at some future date, we add to the demand for commodities, as under barter conditions, but we do not add to the supply. Even our copper producer might now wish to keep his store of value in the form of money. If so, he would then sell the copper that under barter conditions would have been added to inventories, thus increasing the marketable supplies over the quantity that would have been extant under barter.

The desire to add to one's store of value in a money economy exerts a depressing effect. We are trying to sell commodities and obtain cash, and in so doing we are adding to supply but not to demand.

Similarly, the desire to reduce the stock of money kept as a store of value is an expansionary force. We are adding to demand without an accompanying addition to supply. If there is an expectation of a price decline, and people decide to resort to money as a store of value, we are actually working to accentuate the expected decline. More commodities would be offered in order to obtain the desired money, supply would increase without any rise in demand, and the price decline would become even sharper.

Probably nothing is of greater economic significance in the distinction between a barter and a money economy than this store-of-value effect. In barter, every supply exercises a demand, and every demand must be matched by a supply. Nothing is offered unless some other good or service is desired; nothing is demanded unless some good or service can be given in exchange. Supply creates its own demand, or demand creates its own supply.[4] But in a money economy, such is not the case. Supply can exceed demand if there is the desire to increase one's total store of value. Similarly, we can get demand to increase relative to supply if we reduce this store of value. In essence, we have the story of one major aspect of the business cycle. Swings in the desire for storing up purchasing power, if sufficiently widespread, can exert enough of a force on the supply-demand equation to precipitate recessions (when we try to increase our store of value) or precipitate booms (when we decide to reduce it). This thread is important throughout much of the remainder of this text.

The Circular Flow of Money

Implicit in the preceding section is the circular flow of money. In a money economy, where virtually all transactions are through the medium of money, each purchase involves the transfer of money from the buyer to the seller, while the movement of goods or services is from the seller to the buyer. In a sense, we have another form of swap. The buyer has reduced his holding of money and increased his stock of goods and services. The seller has increased his monetary stock and reduced his inventory of goods and services. These goods or services may disappear as the buyer puts them to some use. For example, he may consume the food purchased, and thus destroy some of the community's total food stock. But at the time of transaction we have had only a simple exchange.

For the seller we have several possibilities. If he is a manufacturer, he may then spend the money (disburse it) for the services of labor, the purchase of raw materials, the rental of land and buildings, the

---

[4] In capsule form, this is the famous law associated with the early nineteenth-century French economist, Jean Baptiste Say.

payment of taxes, or pay profits (dividends). Whatever the particular channel, the money starts out again on another exchange step, or the money obtained through the sale of his production then breaks up into numerous streams, some feeding into each of the aforementioned possibilities. Here our cycle is repeated; now our seller becomes a buyer of services or goods, and once again at the point of payment we have another swap. The money in these possibilities returns to perform its transactions function over again.

It is also possible for the money received by the seller to be held as a store of value, to be reserved for future payments. In this possibility the money does not return to the spending stream. It does not perform another transaction, so we have what is known as hoarding. (When our holder does decide to disburse this accumulation, it would be dishoarding.) The money in this possibility has been taken out of the stream.

If we ignore this hoarding possibility, however, the circularity becomes quite evident from what has been said. Our manufacturer disburses funds for goods and services of various sorts. Laborers, landlords, raw-materials suppliers, and the like all have more money. The manufacturer has the various items he needs for his production. The money recipients then disburse their funds for what they need—various goods and services. This provides a demand. The producers meanwhile have used the goods and services purchased to turn out other goods and services desired by the market. This is the supply side of the equation. Now, in selling these desired items, they replenish the money originally disbursed for what they needed, while the various workers, landlords, and others, who now become the market, absorb the output while giving up their funds. If no one hoards, then whatever money is obtained through the sale of one's output or service re-enters the market as a demand for the goods and services one desires.

Although fairly obvious, it may be well to trace certain aspects of this process in greater detail. Assuming that there is no hoarding, every individual or firm would disburse as much money as he receives. This money he receives is in return for the goods he sold or the services he offered. A farmer could be in the former category, a hired hand in the latter. In either case, the man was paid presumably for the approximate worth of what he had to offer. (If either had been overpaid, the buyer's costs rose. This reduced his potential profit—or increased his loss—if he was a producer, or reduced the real value of his purchases if a consumer.) Overlooking for the moment the parenthetical qualification, we can say that the supply of goods or services was balanced by the demand as represented by the money received. And, unless there is some dishoarding, the farmer or laborer cannot spend any more money than he received, nor will he spend less—that is, unless there is some addition to his hoard. Since we are ruling out these two possibilities for the time being, we can then say that he disburses exactly as much as he receives.

Now, if he is spending this money so received for his own consumption needs, then we have a demand for goods matched by an equal supply of money. Originally he received the funds from some producer; now he returns this money to another producer—though obviously not the same one as the original buyer of his offering—while absorbing the latter's output. The same amount of money that was paid out originally thus returns to the producers as a group; in the process, the producers had acquired goods and services needed to turn out the things wanted by the consumers. In effect, our consumer had played two roles; as a factor of production he had offered his goods (the farmer) or services (the laborer) for money, and then as a consumer he had returned the money in exchange for consumables. And the cash position of the producers is unchanged; what they paid out to the factors of production now comes back through the sales office. This sale then enables the producer to start the process all over again, since he has replenished his money supply. We can thus have a continuing cycle of exchanges—goods and services against money—so long as we do not disrupt the mechanism through hoarding or dishoarding. Again we have a case of demand always being equal to supply.

Note that for any one producer or consumer the equality of funds replenishment may not occur. A manufacturer may disburse cash for the purchase of the goods and services offered by the productive factors, and then not rebuild his balance if his sales efforts fail. Provided no one is hoarding this money, what has happened is that some other producer was more successful, sold more than he anticipated, or sold the same volume of goods at higher prices. This latter manufacturer has received more cash than he had originally paid out, and so he is enabled to expand his scale of operations: he can buy more goods and services than in the prior stage, thereby stepping up output and sales. In this case one man's loss is another man's gain. But suppose the cash had been hoarded and the second producer did not receive more money than expected. Here we would have had a loss not offset by a gain, so that, net, we would have had a depressing influence. In summary, therefore, if there is no hoarding, we can get sectoral imbalances —some paying out more money than they ultimately get back, others acting in the reverse position. But for the economy as a whole, there is the same amount disbursed and received back.

Assuming there were no sectoral imbalances, could we still have profits? Yes, for these profits would be accumulated as earnings either retained by a company or paid out to the owners. If we continue our assumption of no hoarding, then in the first case the firm would pay out these profits for some form of expansion, returning the funds to the spending stream. Alternatively, instead of all the money being paid out to farmers, workers, landlords, and government, some is siphoned off to the owners. These then respend the money for the goods and services they need. A little bit less is paid out to these other factors, thus reducing their demand, but this little bit less is going to the owners, thereby raising their demand. The total demand is still there, but its distribution has been altered.

What about losses that are fairly widespread? At first glance this would seem to be simply the opposite of the preceding paragraph— that is, more being paid out to the various factors of production than is returned through sales, resulting in a reduction of what would other- wise have gone to the owners. But if the producing sector pays out more than it gets back, someone else must have received more than he disbursed—that is, he is hoarding. But such a possibility of widespread losses cannot occur unless we reintroduce this disturbing feature. If there were no hoarding, all the money paid out would be respent. Then it would flow back to the corporations. Here, though, we could have zero profits—all the money received as sales being paid out to the various factors of production other than to the owners. A decline in profits amounts, in effect, to a redistribution of the money payments. But its transition to an outright loss, which means that the owners as a group are paying out more funds than they are receiving—dishoard- ing, so to speak—can come about only if some other element is hoard- ing (or disinvesting through inadequate depreciation).

So far we have concerned ourselves with the exchange of goods or services against money. What about a gift? Here we have a monetary transfer not matched by a supply of goods or services, except the intangible possibility of gratitude. This aspect—the so-called unilateral —can be fitted into our picture by regarding it as strictly a transfer, rather than an exchange. To illustrate personally, suppose I have re- ceived money in return for the goods I sold. Some of this money I then turn over to someone as a gift; in effect, part of my sales proceeds go to someone else, rather than to me, and I have acted only as a conduit for the gift. I have reduced my ability to spend by the amount of the gift, but in so doing, I have raised the recipient's ability to spend. Hence, we can regard all acts that are one-way payments—acts not matched by a return flow of goods and services—as analogous to this gift illustration.

Investment can also be easily fitted into our picture. I may not respend for consumption all the money I receive. Some may be di- verted to the purchase of a capital good, a house, a bank deposit, or a loan. In the first two possibilities, the money has been disbursed, but the goods received will not disappear through consumption. The seller, however, has obtained money just as would the baker or the grocer. The character of the goods transferred is different, but not the effect on the flow of funds. If I buy a machine instead of bread, I pay less to the baker and more to a machinery producer. Less can then be paid out to workers in the bakeries or suppliers of goods and services to the bakers, but more can be paid out to machinery workers or suppliers to the machinery industry. Again there has been a sectoral shift, but over-all the same aggregates—the same amount paid out.

For the possibility of a bank deposit or a loan, we must rephrase our question. In the first case we have transferred the funds to a bank,[5] and if the bank does not hoard, we must ask what it does with the funds. Presumably it will lend them out. So we have a loan, made either by us or by the bank; our funds go out to the borrower either directly or via a bank. Presumably the borrower will use the funds— will disburse them. Why else would he have borrowed the money? If he uses the funds for buying goods and services, he then returns the funds to the spending stream. What we did not spend we turned over to the borrower, who then did the spending. If he uses the funds to repay a previous loan, then we have to start again: What does the creditor do with the funds returned? If he does not hoard them, he relends or spends the money himself, and here we are back where we were before. We can see that the process of lending alters the function of the person who actually does the spending—the borrower, rather than the original recipient.

Suppose a sale is made on credit and payment need not be made until some time in the future. Here the seller has postponed the receipt of cash from the buyer. The money paid out for the factors of production is not returned as soon. During this interval the seller has a lower cash balance, and in effect he has dishoarded. The buyer now has a larger cash balance than he would have if he had paid at the time of purchase. During this credit period the buyer can spend more than otherwise, the seller less. (This is an illustration of why sellers must have cash balances—to tide them over this credit period until the cash does come in.) For the credit period, then, we have a short-time dishoarding illustration.

We have repeated frequently that there is a continuous exchange of money against goods and services, unless there is hoarding or dishoarding. We can now see that the only way a person can hoard is to receive more money than he subsequently pays out. As a consequence, the rest of the community has paid out more money to him than he has returned. Hence, to the extent that he hoards, the rest of the

---

[5] Here it is assumed that the funds are actually currency, not checks. The effect of payments through check transfers is covered in the chapter on velocity.

community has that much less money. Hoarding, therefore, does not add to the total money supply. It merely redistributes it. Hoarding puts more in the hands of the hoarder, who will not respend the funds, and less in the hands of others, who have that much less to spend as a consequence. The active supply of money has been reduced, the inactive (hoarded) portion increased. Only if some outside body, such as the government, then replenishes the active portion, thereby increasing the total money available, would this potential deflationary action be offset. But if the total amount of money does not change, hoarding can only reduce the active portion.

Dishoarding, of course, is the opposite. Someone pays out more than he receives, so that the remainder of the community receives back more than it had originally paid to him. The total money supply is the same, but somewhat less money is now in the inactive part, somewhat more is in the active part. The total potential for spending has risen, and so we have an expansionary possibility. To counter this (if we wish to), we must reduce the active portion to offset this increase, and thus reduce the total money outstanding. This action thus counteracts the addition to the active money supply as a result of the dishoarding; the active money supply is no more than before, the return from hoards being balanced by our withdrawal. But the amount in hoards is less, and our total money supply—active plus inactive—is less by the amount withdrawn, this amount equal to the amount that the hoarded sector decreased by. If there were no intervention, then the total money supply would be the same as before the dishoarding, but less would be inactive, and more would be active.

In the hoarding illustration the remainder of the community was forced to dishoard. By not paying back as much as he received, the hoarder reduced the total amount of money in the hands of the rest of the community. Its money stock declined, just as it would if these people dishoarded. In the hoarding example, the community dishoarded involuntarily. In dishoarding, the decision to reduce one's cash stock is voluntary.

Can everyone hoard or dishoard? No, for if everyone hoards, then everyone is trying to obtain more cash than he pays out. As long as the total amount of money is the same, this is impossible. If A pays out less than he takes in, then the rest of the community is taking in less than it pays out. It can only pay out less if A receives less than he pays out. But we have just said that A received more, so here we have a contradiction. Probably what really happens is that A cuts down his purchases, thus reducing B's receipts. B then reduces his purchases, cutting C's receipts. As each tries to accumulate more of a hoard, he reduces someone else's income. This effort of everyone to build up a hoard will be examined in more detail in the chapter on velocity. Similarly, we cannot all dishoard. If John pays out more than he takes in, then the rest of the community has received more than it paid out to John. If the community tries to dishoard, it tries to pay out more than it takes in, which means that John takes in more than he pays out. But this contradicts what we said John was trying to do. What really happens is that *A* pays out more than he receives, raising *B*'s income. *B* then pays out more, raising *C*'s income, and so on. Again we shall leave the further discussion to the chapter on velocity.

In our circular-flow discussion, hoarding means that in some sector—the sector that decides to hoard—we have a receipt of cash in excess of a disbursement. The rest of the community pays out more than it receives, and its payments to the various factors exceed its receipts. Hence, some other group dishoards involuntarily. If this should be a corporation, what we have is insufficient sales (insufficient receipts); if it is a factor of production, we have insufficient income.

For example, producers may pay out to workers, suppliers, and the like. But the recipients hoard, so that they buy less from the corporations than originally paid out. A loss results equal to this difference, along with a decline in the corporation's cash balance equal to the rise in the hoarders' balance. If it is the corporation that hoards, its receipts of money from sales exceed what it pays out to the factors of production. It has reduced the amount flowing to these factors, thereby reducing their income. Hoarding always strikes at someone's income somewhere in the community.

As would be expected, dishoarding is the opposite. A dishoarding producer pays out more to the factors of production than it takes in as sales. This could occur during an expansionary period when a company pays out more for machinery to expand output; the money paid for the equipment adds to the receipt of cash by the sellers of the equipment, but there is no return flow of money to the corporation, since it has not as yet stepped up its output and thus cannot step up its receipt of cash. Some recipient of this money could then build up his hoard, since the added supplies on which to spend the extra income are not yet available.

If it is the consumers who are dishoarding, the incomes received by the factors of production are less than the subsequent disbursements, and the excess spent comes out of previously accumulated hoards. The corporations receive back from sales more than they pay out to produce the goods. Now they can build up their hoards if they so desire. If neither the recipients (previous paragraph) nor the corporations (this paragraph) decide to build up their hoards, then we have stepped up spending; in the preceding paragraph the demand outraces supply, and we could get a profits inflation, the owners absorbing more money. In this way we could get a stepped-up demand by corporations for the factors of production, this inflating the incomes of these factors. If these recipients of the added spending then hoard, we have stopped any further expansion. But if they respend the increase, the inflationary process continues. Because of the many implications of these added respendings, we shall leave this discussion until we treat inflation.

Of course, at any time in this cycle we could have inserted an outside force. The government could have injected additional money if the tendency was for hoarding. Conversely, it could pull out some of the money if a dishoarding force were at work. In effect, we have touched on the role of fiscal and central banking policy, which regulates the circular flow and tries to keep supply and demand running in balance—not necessarily at a static level, for expansion is feasible. This is true provided both supply and demand expand by the same degree, thus continuing the equality.

Summary

Money has several functions. To effect transactions, it serves as a more efficient way to make exchanges than would be possible in a barter economy. Money can also serve as a store of value for future needs. It helps bridge gaps between receipts and expenditures. It can be also a general stock of liquidity. Where money is used as a store of value, we get a significant difference from barter, because changes in the amount so held cause discrepancies between aggregate supply and demand.

Money is either held idle or, for a moment, used to effect transactions. The longer the interval between transactions, the fewer the transactions in a prescribed period of time; the converse is true if we speed up (shorten) the interval. As a result, the inactive and active aspects of money are two different ways of observing the same thing. Yet it is here—in variations between the two—that much of the explanation of our business cycle is to be found.

If there is no change in the stock of money held, and no change in its rate of activity, we can see the circular flow of goods-money-goods-money, both for those who produce and those who consume. With a constant stock of money, no one can change his holding without altering someone else's in the opposite direction. Hence, there can be no aggregate increase or decrease in hoarding—no hoarding or dishoarding—unless we change the total monetary supply. Otherwise such shifts would reflect only flows between the active and inactive monetary sectors.

Chapter 7

THE ROLE OF CREDIT

Until now discussion has been in terms of money—either currency, checking accounts, or both. Credit was touched on in the last chapter. Now it must be introduced into the main body of our thinking, and its basic features should be outlined. Much of its impact will be spelled out in greater detail in subsequent chapters, especially as it is affected by the operations of the banking system.

Credit Is Faith

Credit is faith on the part of the individual granting credit, and is reflected in the subsequent behavior of the person obtaining credit. If I lend to you, it is because I have faith that you will pay me back at the stipulated time. Or perhaps I agree to lend the money to you for an indefinite period, repayable when I need it. Again I have faith that you will fulfill the agreement. If I do not have faith, then either I would not lend to you, or else I would give the money to you as a gift, and this situation would transform what might have become a credit transaction into a charitable one. This may happen between close friends, relatives, and countries. The United States may lend to a poor country, realizing that the prospects of repayment are slight. And if we do not grant the loan, we would probably give the borrower the funds. In either case, we feel that we must extend aid. With a loan transaction the borrower feels less like a charitable ward, and there is always the prospect that he will become sufficiently prosperous to repay.

This faith takes on many different aspects. If we buy common stock, the issuing corporation is not obliged to pay us back. But we have faith that it will pay us sufficient dividends to make our purchase worthwhile, or perhaps the company's expected prosperity will enhance the value of our shares. Our faith is of a somewhat different kind from that in the previous paragraph, but it is still faith in the ability of the company to perform its operations profitably.

Most paper currency represents an act of faith. The American dollar is not redeemable in the ordinary sense. Yet the American public accepts it, because it feels that the currency can always be used for transaction purposes; moreover, its value as expressed in its purchasing power will be relatively constant, or will decrease so slowly that it will not be worthwhile to shift to commodities. If one examines the inscription on a typical bill—for example, a $10 Federal Reserve Note[1]—he will read, "This note is legal tender for all debts, public and private, and is redeemable in lawful money at the United States Treasury, or at any Federal Reserve Bank." The first part is straightforward: if you owe an American $10, you can discharge this debt with the Federal Reserve Note. But the redeemable portion is another matter. If by chance you should test this meaning, the odds are that you will go to a great deal of trouble for nothing. If you go to either the Treasury or one of the Federal Reserve Banks and ask to redeem your money, in all likelihood you will be given two $5 Federal Reserve Notes bearing the same promise. If you persisted, you might then be given $10 in silver coins (half-dollar pieces). But since the silver in the coins is worth less than $10, there is not much sense in melting them down. Since we have faith that the money will be usable in the foreseeable future for various transactions, we will continue to accept and trust it. In the section on the absorption of money, we shall examine this aspect of the subject.

We have stated that credit in general rests essentially on faith. Assuming that faith is present, a credit transaction means that the

---

[1] See Chapter 10.

lender or creditor has turned over some tangible item of value—money, goods, or services—and has received in return some document representing this point of faith. Thus, I may lend money and get an IOU in return. Or I may sell goods to a buyer and get his promise to pay at some future date. In fact, if I am a local grocer and have sold to one of my regular customers, I may not even have this in writing. With or without the written promise, the seller has faith that the buyer will pay at some future date, a date stipulated expressly or generally understood, for example, ten days after the first of the next month. Or I may work for a corporation all month, knowing that my paycheck will be forthcoming on the last business day. Of course, in many cases nonpayment can result in a court action compelling the debtor to pay. Faith does have some sanctions to enforce the agreement, but relatively few cases go to court; most such transactions either go through as agreed, or are settled out of court.

Of special interest to our subject are the financial intermediaries, such as banks and insurance companies. People turn over their money to these organizations, and the intermediaries then become debtors to their depositors and policyholders. But in turn the intermediaries relend the funds, so that they become creditors. The faith of the original supplier of funds is really a faith in the ability of the intermediary to judge his debtors' repayment ability.

If there were no private credit, everyone would have to pay cash (or barter) for each transaction. This is not an impossible situation, for many underdeveloped areas lack banks and other forms of credit-granting institutions, and operate virtually on a cash basis. If, in addition, only gold or some other acceptable metal serves as money—and is not redeemable in something else—we have a virtually credit-less economy. But any advanced economy must have credit. In our discussion of the role of the cash balance, it was pointed out that receipts and expenditures rarely match. To help bridge this gap, we could either carry cash balances or extend credit, thereby postponing the disbursement of cash until sufficient receipts were available. If I am paid at the end of the month but have daily expenses, I could either start each month with enough of a cash balance to cover all my outlays until the end of the month, or buy on credit and pay when my paycheck is received. Similarly, corporations could either carry large enough balances to bridge any excess of disbursements over receipts, or get credit to postpone the disbursement until the receipts come in.

The role of credit can be best described in terms of a long-run transaction. If a corporation plans to build a $10-million plant with an expected annual net profit of $1 million, it is faced with several alternatives. It could have accumulated enough cash from its other operations, and when it reached the $10-million level, the plant could be built. Failing this, it is faced with our familiar gap. Receipts will come in after a period of years has passed, while the disbursement must come first or else there will not be any receipts. So it must borrow in excess of any available cash, paying off this loan from future net profits. It could issue stock, in which case it could use the profits to pay dividends, the anticipated return presumably satisfying the stockholder sufficiently to warrant his parting with his funds. If this were a completely new venture, then the possibility of a prior accumulation of cash is impossible, since the company is not operating as yet. Only through some form of borrowing (including the issuance of stock) could the company ever come into existence. If we operate on a cash-only basis, this company cannot get started unless some wealthy individual with $10 million to spare undertakes the job himself.

Assuming that a loan does finance this venture, it would seem that credit has actually created capital. With credit, we have a $10-million corporation; without credit, we have none. But this is not actually true, at least not in the way it would seem. Whatever funds the new corporation obtained must have come from someone. Hence, the lender's purchasing power was reduced, having been transferred to the borrowing corporation. Credit merely served as the basis for a transfer of purchasing power. And the lender must have obtained his funds from somewhere; this source is his own excess of income over consumption—his own addition to supply greater than his demand for goods and services.[2] This excess supply is equal to his savings, which he has then turned over to the corporation, which in turn spends the funds for the goods and services to be used in the construction of the plant. In brief, the savings now become demand equal to the previous excess supply. Once again we have our equality of supply and demand. Thus it can be seen that credit did not create capital; it enabled a borrower to acquire some of the excess supplies that resulted from the savers' desires to reduce their consumption below their income. By so doing, they released supplies which were then turned over to the borrower through the medium of the funds that were lent.

Let us assume that there had been no borrower, and that the saver did not have the know-how or desire to undertake the venture himself. It is possible, then, for the excess supplies to bring about a price decline, thereby causing losses to the producers of these excess goods. In other words, the producers would have negative savings offsetting the positive savings of our thrifty sector. In this sense, credit does create capital. It mobilizes what would otherwise be idle purchasing power,

---

[2] This is not true for banks—a special case to be discussed later.

thereby attracting supplies to the group that wants to add to the economy's productive capacity. The capital stock is greater than if we did not have credit, for it forestalled losses, and thus negative savings. On the other hand, had the savers decided that, since no borrowers wanted their funds, they would undertake the venture themselves, then we would have just as much capital as if the borrowing operation had materialized, the buyers of the excess supplies now being the savers in their role of entrepreneur. Only if the savers could find no entrepreneur who could use their funds would the capital stock be less.

Printing-Press Money

We have already said that in modern-day economies, government money is paper accepted as valuable simply because of the faith in the continued relative stability of the currency's purchasing power. What happens when the government prints some money, thereby increasing the total supply? (If it borrows the money, then we have an act analogous to a private loan transaction: the lender gives up purchasing power, thus offsetting the increase in the hands of the government.) At the moment money is printed, we have an increase in government's purchasing power, but unlike so much of the discussion in the last chapter, we have not as yet reduced any other person's purchasing power. For illustrative purposes, we shall assume that the government budget is in balance, and that this extra money is to be used to pay for some extra expenditure—say, a new free road.

With increased money the government can now exercise a demand for goods and services needed to construct the road. Here it steps up aggregate demand, but it has not as yet stepped up supply. People connected with the new project now receive more cash, and they, too, can step up their spending. To the extent that some will step up their hoarding, the spending multiple is stopped, for the increase in the currency issue now is being matched by the increase in idle hoards. But the active part of the additional money supply will be spent and respent, so we have a generally expansionary influence. This may call forth a greater output, which may push up prices. Incomes in general will rise, and with them savings will rise. Now more funds may be hoarded.

In brief, there are only two possibilities: hoarding or respending. In the hoarding possibility the hoarders have added more to supply than to demand, the difference going into their hoard. Hence, offsetting the government's added demand is this excess supply. In addition, the government has obtained goods and services it would not have obtained without the additional currency. Thus there is less supply available for the remainder of the economy. (Some of this supply, as already mentioned, may be the excess resulting from the hoarding action.) To fill this gap—the diverted supplies—either output will expand, or prices must rise. As output expands, incomes will rise and so will demand. If output expands faster than demand—because of saving—we have still more excess supplies to help meet the added demand initiated by the government's action. Should demand rise as much as supply, the demand gap remains, and the price-rise alternative may then ensue. This price rise could then reduce demand, thereby freeing enough supplies to close the gap. These reactions, because of their relationship with the whole subject of inflation, will be studied further when we review the concept of forced savings and hyperinflation. But, as in the preceding section, it should be noted here that the currency issue did not add to capital—except indirectly if it stimulated output or used supplies for road-building that otherwise would not have been used.

Investment Financing

Some of the major points made so far include the influence of the various transactions mentioned and their effect on the relationship of demand to supply. If a net increase in supply or decrease in demand results, we have a deflationary force; the reverse is true if supply drops or demand rises; a cancellation of these opposite tendencies results if demand and supply shift equally in the same direction. So, in a study of these numerous influences, it is essential to ascertain just what the outcome of the supply-demand relationship is. This approach to a cursory study of fixed-investment outlays will illustrate our objective.

Assume that we decide to build some new capital installation, such as a power plant. During the construction period there will be disbursements for labor, raw materials, and various other goods and services. There will not be any output until the project is completed and begins to operate. During this period of construction (some economists call this period one of gestation) we are adding to demand but not to supply. Moreover, having paid out these various sums, the recipients now have more income. They, in turn, can spend more and pass on the purchasing power to still others, who can increase their spending. In short, we have a multiple addition to demand.

At first glance it would seem that investment in the construction stage is definitely inflationary. But this is not necessarily so, because the answer really depends on the financing method. If the investment funds were obtained from the savings of other individuals or corporations, what has also occurred is a negative offset to the investment multiplier. The savers have added to supply, for which they obtained income; but through consumption they have added a lesser amount to demand. Supply therefore exceeded demand by the amount saved. If the savings had been zero, demand would have equalled supply. But in order to save, consumption had to be cut below this equality point, thus reducing the income of those who would have supplied these extra goods. Their income being less, they in turn must cut their spending. When this occurs, we get the familiar, but negative, multiplier. Savings, in other words, set up a deflationary chain.

If these savings are passed over to our investment in the power plant, the two multipliers tend to cancel each other, the negative savings multiplier being offset by the .positive investment multiplier. Thus we have neither inflation nor deflation. It may be that the two do not equal each other, but we shall ignore this smaller inequality in practice. An explanation of this possibility might be that the saver, had he decided to spend all his income, would buy consumers' goods; the sellers, in turn, might also spend quickly all their money so obtained. In contrast, the recipients of the power-plant disbursements might spend more slowly the money so received. We might also have the reverse. It will be recalled from the discussion of the cash-balance management that the more rapid the respending, the greater the aggregate amount of spending; the slower the respending, the less the aggregate. Hence, by diverting the stream to the power plant, we may have shifted the funds to people with different rates of respending, thus altering the aggregate amount spent over the period. Since it is difficult in most cases to assess just how and where these differences might exist, we tend to ignore this possibility.

Suppose the investment were financed through the creation of new money, as in the roadbuilding case.[3] Then, as before, the investment sets up a positive multiplier, except that now there is no negative multiplier as an offset. We now have a clear case of expansion. If supplies were limited, we would then have an inflation. On the other hand, if there were hoarding going on, which alone would tend to be a deflationary force, then this type of investment would be an offset to the hoarding. As money seeps into the inactive hoard, more money is being pumped into the active stream to replace the hoarded addition. As can be seen, we have simply repeated the roadbuilding illustration in another form.

Absorption of Additional Money Supplies

We have already indicated some of the ways in which increases in the money supply can be absorbed. The additional money can add to demand and exert an expansionary influence on prices and/or output.

---

[3] As we shall see, bank financing may take on a similar character.

Or it can offset additions to the amounts people decide to hoard. If there is a long-run tendency to add to hoards, there can be an equal rise in the money supply without any pressure on supplies, the addition to the active portion just offsetting the seepage into hoards. Here a question may be asked. Does a long-run hoarding tendency exist?

It will be recalled from the discussion on cash balances that essentially all money is hoarded, except at the moment it is being spent. What really counts is how quickly the intervals between respending are. It will also be recalled that each transaction is only an exchange of goods and services against money; after that, the goods and services disappear, if consumed, or they are used to turn out more goods and services, if used for a productive operation. Let us focus on labor to qualify this difference.

Suppose we have a laborer who works for one day and is paid $5. Presumably he has helped turn out some commodity, and the labor cost, so far as his contribution is concerned, was $5. Ignoring any profit, we have added $5 to supply and $5 to his income; if he then decides to spend all this money, we add $5 to demand. Aggregate supply and demand each move up $5.

We now have two sets of transactions: (a) labor services for money, and (b) the consumable sold for money to our laborer. Presumably we could repeat these two every day, so each day $5 worth of goods would be produced in exchange for $5 worth of services offered; and $5 worth of goods would be consumed or paid for from the funds received for the services of the workman. There is also another possibility.

Suppose our worker produced a machine which would expand output. During the period he worked on the machine—investment gestation—he would receive income without adding to supply. Let us assume that he is financed by some saver whose consumption was reduced, thereby offsetting the additional demand of our laborer. Once the machine was in production, it could turn out more goods; now the amount of money needed to finance the transactions has grown. If output is doubled, the value of transactions may be doubled (assuming no change in prices), and so twice as much money passes to the producer. He, in turn, disburses twice as much for wages, raw materials, rent, and perhaps profits. So, as we expand the volume of our output (assuming that prices do not decline), we expand the value of transactions, and the points at which money becomes active have increased. We can service this need in two ways: we can shorten the intervals that money is at rest, so that in a given period of time we effect a greater number of transactions; or we can maintain the same resting period, but increase the amount of money that is in everyone's hands.

In the second alternative, as the volume of transactions rises, the money supply can rise without exerting too expansionary an influence. The additional money supply buys additional goods. It is spent and respent at the same rate as the money previously outstanding, thus expanding total spending proportionately. But since we have assumed that supply has also expanded by the same proportion, the rise in demand is just matched by the rise in supply. If, of course, the money supply rises faster, we get an expansionary force. If it rises more slowly, there is a net deflationary force because of the greater rise in supply.

Short-Term and Long-Term Capital

A special aspect in the study of money and credit is the distinction between short-term and long-term capital, especially the distinction between the "real" and "monetary" manifestations. Capital is made up of the already produced instruments that are used for further production. Capital can be machines or raw materials, for both are necessary in a modern economy if we wish to expand output. The essential difference is in the pay-off life—the length of time necessary to get back the original cost plus some profit. With raw materials, the period is relatively short—roughly, the time it takes to manufacture the finished product and then sell it. The sales price presumably includes the cost of the raw materials, so that the sale produces enough revenue to return the original outlay. With a long-life machine, the sales return only a portion of the machine's original cost—the amount allotted as depreciation expense. It may take ten, twenty, or more years of sales to produce enough of such allotments to repay the cost of the machine. We can therefore differentiate between these two by using the familiar economic labels *short-term* and *long-term*. For an arbitrary distinction, we shall call short-term capital those produced instruments whose costs are recovered within one year, and long-term capital those produced instruments whose costs take longer to recover. And, as already indicated, virtually all production requires both types.

Since we have these two different types of pay-off periods, we must also have two different types of lenders: those who wish to recover their funds within a short time, and those who are content to wait for several years (or who feel that if they should need their funds sooner, they can find someone to take over their loan). Matching the short-term and long-term capital, are the equivalent short-term and long-term lenders. The latter, however, are not rigid in this demarcation. A lender can be in the short-term area part of the time and, if he wishes, can then switch over to the long-term sector. Similarly, someone planning to lend in the long-term market can switch to the short-term sector if the return there is more attractive. However, once the funds are loaned, the lender must either await the pay-off period or find someone else with funds who will take the loan off his hands. In the short-term sector this is not a serious problem, since the money will be returned to the lender within one year. But in the long-term area there is a long wait. A long-term lender who does wish to recover his funds must, in effect, find someone else who is willing to wait for this long time. The latter will then pay over his funds to the former in exchange for the return on the long-term investment. A long-term lender cannot cut short his wait, unless he finds someone who is willing to be a long-term lender.[4]

Given this conceptual framework, we can now see how certain borrowing acts influence the economy. If a borrower has a need for short-term capital, such as inventories of raw materials, he can borrow short-term funds, since the relatively short time until he sells his finished goods will suffice to pay back the funds borrowed. Similarly, if he has a need for long-term funds—say, to buy machinery—he can borrow long-term funds and pay back the lender over the long pay-off period, since the lender is presumably willing to wait the required length of time (or has found someone else who is willing).

However, it may be that both sides are not matched. Suppose a firm has a continuing need for short-term capital. Every time it liquidates a previous loan, it needs a new one for the next productive operation. Since this continual need exists, the firm may borrow long-term funds, thus sparing itself the continued trips to the short-term market to repeat the process.

Or a firm may wish to acquire long-term capital but discover that it cannot get long-term funds, or that the price is too high (although it may come down in the future). So it may borrow short-term funds to tide itself over. But there is a risk here. By its nature, long-term capital has a long pay-off period. If the borrower can obtain a renewal of his short-term obligation, or an alternative source which enables him to repay the original lender, he can continue the operation. But he might face the prospect of having to repay the loan without finding an alternative source of funds to meet this demand. His own operations will not be providing the necessary amount, since the pay-off will take years before the total amount borrowed is realized. As a consequence, this liquidity crisis may force him into bankruptcy, even though he is not losing money. It is this contingency that makes short-term borrowing for long-term purposes such a risky affair.

---

[4] For ease of explanation, we have constantly referred to lenders. Similar logic would apply to equity investors—for example, long-term investors in common stocks.

When we convert short-term obligations to long-term—in the preceding paragraph the borrower would have avoided the liquidity squeeze had he been able to—we are in effect obtaining funds from people who are willing to wait a long time, and repaying those lenders who want to wait only a short time. Thus we have added to the demand for long-term funds, or we have reduced the supply available for other borrowers and increased the supply of short-term funds (released by the conversion).

Anyone borrowing short-term and lending long-term risks a liquidity crisis. This is essentially the position in which banks continually place themselves. Their deposits can be withdrawn on a moment's notice, but their loans will not be repaid for weeks, months, even years. What is hoped is either that the day-to-day call for funds by depositors does not exceed the repayments of loans maturing that day, or that new deposits, bringing in money, will offset the withdrawals on old deposits. Obviously, so nice a balancing cannot always be relied upon, so banks always keep a certain amount of money in their vaults to meet small adverse drains; in effect, they too carry a cash balance to bridge the difference between receipts and disbursements. In addition, they keep very liquid (saleable) assets, should this drain exceed their available cash. They keep assets on hand which, they feel fairly certain, others will be willing to take over. Banks reason that there will always be lenders willing to transfer their money to the bank in exchange for some of the obligations the bank now wishes to dispose of. Because of the nature of these obligations, usually very short-term, it is felt that there will always be people willing to wait this short period of time in return for the income to be received. The bank can always rely on finding such potential lenders to take over the remaining waiting period. The reader will see how this relates to our earlier discussion on liquidity. We are saying that a security is liquid if it can be sold to someone else who is willing to wait for the remaining pay-off time.

One danger inherent in any boom period is that an excessive amount of funds may be wanted for long-term investment. If this demand should outrun the available supply, people might resort to short-term borrowing to fill the gap. When the business outlook is good, such financing can be risked, since the borrower can count on either renewing his loan or finding another lender. But if the turning point is reached and the lender's desires for liquidity increase, we might then have a solvency problem. If carried to the extreme, the borrower might have to suspend operations. In this case both the short-term lender and short-term borrower suffer losses—the former, since he cannot get back his funds, and the latter since (or if) he, too, has helped finance part of his now bankrupt operation.

Similarly, if we use up inventories of raw materials to add to our fixed equipment, we are in effect converting short-term capital into long-term. Unless we then replace these inventories, we run into a shortage of short-term capital, for we would be lacking the raw materials necessary to produce current output. If we used our stocks of steel to make machines, we would still need steel to turn out steel products which the new machines were designed to manufacture. Excess conversion of our "real" short-term capital into "real" long-term capital leaves us short of the raw materials necessary to turn out finished products. Production would be forced to stop just as certainly as though demand had dropped off. It is true that in a normally operating economy there would rarely be no raw materials left. Rather, we would see a rise in price as a result of the available supply declining, this having been siphoned off for the construction of fixed capital. The higher price would then make it less profitable to turn out as much in finished products as before, so the surface obstacle would be the cost of raw materials. This excessive cost, then, is the reflection of too great a diversion of working capital inventories to the relatively frozen end uses.

Summary

Our modern economy functions on credit. This implies faith, on the part of the creditor, in the debtor's ability and willingness to fulfill his obligation. There may be faith in the government, as issuer of the currency, or in specific individuals and corporations to whom a loan has been extended, or from whom a short-term debt is due. The debtor, in turn, must hope that his operations will produce a net surplus of money enabling him to meet his obligation when it is due.

Since debt is transferable, many creditors enter into transactions of longer duration than is actually desirable, knowing, however, that they will usually be able to find someone to purchase the paper when needed. From this marketability arise the numerous types of debt—short- and long-term—designed to satisfy the borrower's, the lender's, or the general market's convenience.

Credit also affects purchasing power, causing it to be transferred from lender to borrower. A special type of credit, currency, may cause a permanent transfer of such power. In order for transactions to take place, money must stay out in use. This means that the issuer does not have to repay the debt. In this way the long-run growth in supplies (which would tend to outrun demand because of the propensity to save) can now be matched by this additional demand through the issuance of additional money.

Chapter 8

MONETARY MECHANICS I: THE COMMERCIAL BANKS

Central to any monetary system is the banking organization. This may differ in detail, especially between developed and less developed countries; the major features, however, are very similar. Generally, the public deals with commercial banks. These banks, in turn, deal with a central bank. Other banking institutions, such as savings banks and savings-and-loan associations, will be discussed in the chapter on non-banking financial intermediaries. What distinguishes banks in this and the following chapter is the ability to create or destroy demand deposits, thereby changing the volume of purchasing power. Here we shall deal with the American banking system; the commercial banks will be described in this chapter, and the central bank—the Federal Reserve—will be discussed in Chapter 10. Our description applies to most of the industrially advanced economies, as well as to many of the less developed, more agricultural ones.

The Banks and Liquidity

Like any other banks, commercial banks are deposit-accepting institutions, but they are virtually the only ones that hold checking
accounts. As we said earlier, demands on these accounts are payable
instantly. In practice this is true of many other deposits, but these
usually require the holder to come into the bank or mail in his request
for funds. With a checking account, the depositor can have his funds
instantly simply by writing a check to anyone. People will always be
demanding funds, either because of checks paid to them or because
of funds they have deposited with the bank. As a consequence, the
bank must have resources to meet these drains. The commercial bank
must be liquid also, because its depositors regard their deposits as their
own liquid assets.

The bank also expects funds to flow in. People make deposits or
deposit checks to their account. Hence, it is necessary for the bank
only to have funds to meet any anticipated excess outflow, and since
this cannot be forecast, the bank should carry more funds, depending
on its ability to quickly realize any other assets it may possess. The
more of these it can mobilize quickly, the less cash it need carry in
excess of anticipated requirements. A bank, like an individual, must
carry a cash balance to meet the differences between receipts and
expenditures.

To do this, banks carry cash in their vaults. In addition, if they are
members of the Federal Reserve System, they will also carry deposits
with the Federal Reserve Banks. Since these balances are also payable
on demand, the member bank can carry less cash, for it can quickly
replenish any drain by drawing on its Federal Reserve account. The
closer the bank is geographically to the Federal Reserve source, the
sooner this transfer can be effected. Banks located some distance away
from their Federal Reserve source tend to carry a greater proportion
of their liquid funds in cash and a lesser proportion with the Federal
Reserve. The bulk of commercial bank deposits (more than 80 per
cent) are with Federal Reserve member banks. We shall limit our discussion almost exclusively to this group.

These liquid funds—vault cash, plus balances with the Federal
Reserve—are commonly called *reserves*. Banks must carry reserves to
meet possible drains. Even if none are foreseen, regulations require
this; the Federal Reserve Board stipulates a minimum percentage that
must be held against the various deposits. At present (1965) banks in
the larger cities, known as "reserve city banks," must carry reserves
equal to at least 16½ per cent of demand deposits, and 4 per cent of
time deposits; other banks ("country banks") must keep reserves equal

to at least 12 per cent of demand deposits, and 4 per cent of time deposits. To facilitate arithmetic illustrations, we shall use a demand-deposit reserve ratio of 20 per cent. Note that this figure is higher than most banks have been required to maintain in more than a decade. (For our purposes we can ignore the rather technical differences between time and savings deposits, other than noting that only individuals —not corporations—may place their funds in the latter type.)

These reserves can be used to meet drains originating with the depositors, or to make payments due other banks or the Federal Reserve. Changes in these reserves alter the *total reserves* a bank has available. The reserves that are held against the deposits are known as *required reserves*. If total reserves exceed required reserves, the difference is known as *excess reserves*. Arithmetically, for any one bank, a rise or fall in deposits raises or lowers required reserves, unless there is a shift from demand to time deposits. If total reserves have remained unchanged while deposits rose or fell, then excess reserves—the difference—either decline or rise—that is, move opposite to required reserves. If total reserves rise or fall, and deposits have remained the same, then excess reserves rise or fall. Excess reserves are simply a residual. We shall learn to recognize this as a most significant indicator of bank activity.

Banks earn no income on their reserves. This required sector is established by law, but any funds in excess of required reserves earn nothing and also are unnecessary. As a result, the bank has every incentive to convert these excess reserves into an income-earning asset. As long as the risk of loss from such a move is minimal, the bank will always try to maintain excess reserves as close to zero as practicable. This way it will maximize those assets that bring in income.

The Nature of a Demand Deposit

The demand deposit, or checking account, is familiar to almost everyone. Yet we must describe some of its characteristics in order to clarify the nature of deposit creation, the factor that most distinguishes the commercial bank. For most Americans a checking account means that the owner has the right to make out checks in payment of his various requirements, provided the total of such payments does not exceed the amount in his account.[1] Each check, as it reaches his bank, results in a reduction in his balance equal to the amount of the check. The cumulative sum of these checks must be less than the original balance, or else the depositor will need to add to his account balance

---

[1] In England it is possible to draw checks in excess of one's balance. This is known as an overdraft, and is similar to a loan from the bank.

by depositing funds or obtaining a loan. When a check exceeds the remaining balance, it cannot be honored; payment will be refused. (If the bank stipulates that he should keep a minimum balance, he may be assessed a service charge if his checks draw down his balance below this point.)

What counts in the utilization of a checking account is the amount that the bank has recorded in the customer's balance. It does not matter how the balance was created—whether funds had been originally deposited out of the owner's own assets, or whether from money he borrowed. All that is necessary is for the bank to know that he has a sufficient balance. In effect, the bank says, "You have so many dollars now in your account—we're not interested in their origin—and you may continue to write checks." If the bank assesses a service charge of $1, it is informing the depositor that his balance has been reduced by that amount. If the individual deposits $100, then the bank takes his money and tells him he may draw checks up to $100. If the bank lends him $1,000, then the bank will indicate that he may now draw checks up to $1,000, unless the borrower-depositor wishes to have the loan in cash.

As long as the balance in the account is adequate, checks will be honored by the bank. Anyone accepting a check can now be paid in full, either in cash or through an increase in his (the receiver's) account. Checking-account balances can be increased if we deposit other people's checks (payable to us) in our checking account. The payer's checking-account balance goes down; ours goes up. The origin of the payer's balance is of no concern either to us or to our bank. We are interested in knowing only whether the balance is sufficient to cover our check. We do not care if the payer's balance came from a deposit of cash, deposits of other people's checks, or loans.

The reader should also be reminded that variations in this balance —the amount remaining still due the depositor—carry required reserves. When we write checks, we draw down our balance, and, assuming a 20-per-cent required reserve, the bank's required reserves drop by 20 per cent of the decrease in our balance. As we build up our balance, the bank must build up its required reserve by 20 per cent of this increase. Our balance, which is an asset to us—our purchasing power—is the amount the bank owes us, and so becomes a liability for the bank.

Loans and Deposit Creation

We now come to the making of a loan. As discussed previously, most payments are by check, and anyone wanting a loan will be satisfied with the subsequent increase in his checking-account balance. If he needs cash, he can then draw a check for the required amount. We shall treat this subject in terms of checking-account payments exclusively, recognizing that exceptions may occur.

Loans are for the purpose of boosting the borrower's demand-deposit balance, enabling him to increase the amount he can pay out. All that is necessary in such a transaction is for the bank to increase the borrower's balance. A $1,000 loan is effected by writing up the borrower's balance by $1,000.[2] The bank is now liable to honor payments on checks written by the borrower up to this additional $1,000. Offsetting this increase in its liabilities is the note that the borrower has made out—the loan itself, which the bank carries as an asset. It now owes the borrower more through the increase in his checking-account balance, and the borrower now owes the bank more in the form of the note, IOU, or loan. It is even possible that the borrower owes a bit more if the interest was added in advance; this is usually through the discount. Thus, if the loan was repayable in three months and the annual interest charge was 6 per cent, or 1½ per cent for three months, the bank may actually add only $985 to the borrower's balance, accepting in return a $1,000 obligation on the part of the borrower. The $15, of course, becomes part of the bank's gross income, out of which it then pays its operating expenses, interest paid to savings depositors or profits. (In the United States, demand deposits earn no interest, while savings deposits do.)

Note that no currency has been exchanged in this loan procedure. The bank agrees only to honor more checks. Currency would pass if the borrower then drew a check and cashed it, but at the moment the loan is made, no cash is exchanged. Indeed, if the depositor uses the extra money to pay others by drawing checks, and if they then deposit the checks in their demand-deposit accounts, no currency is exchanged, unless these accounts are kept at a different bank. Literally by a stroke of a pen, our bank has added to the borrower's purchasing power by the amount added to his checking-account balance. Before the loan there was less in his balance than after the loan. And by adding to his balance, the bank did not take funds from anyone else. Aggregate bank liabilities in the form of checking-account balances rose and were offset by an increase in aggregate bank assets (loans). Total purchasing power in the community is now higher. As this extra money is spent, other people's sales and income will rise, as will their checking-account balances. Now they, in turn, can spend more. So again our familiar multiplier process is in action.

---

[2] This is technically known as a derivative deposit. It is to be distinguished from increases resulting from an inflow of funds.

People who receive checks from the borrower are not concerned that the payment came out of "created" balances. So long as the check is honored, they are satisfied. Thus, balances arising from the loan are just as valid as those arising from a cash deposit.

The Effect on Bank Reserves

At the moment a loan is made, the bank's liabilities rose, because the amount was added to the borrower's balance. This is a demand deposit, so it must have a reserve against it. Assuming the required ratio is 20 per cent, our bank has to add 20 per cent of the increase to its required reserves. Assuming the loan was for $985, then required reserves must rise by $197; excess reserves will drop by that amount. Total reserves are the same, since we have not altered either the cash in the bank's vaults or the amount it has on deposit with the Federal Reserve. Should the bank not have the necessary excess reserves, it can obtain the required amount through means to be discussed later.

We remember here that this 20 per cent is only enough to meet the legal requirements. Suppose our borrower draws out the entire amount of the loan in cash. Suppose he makes out checks for the full amount to people who wish to obtain cash. As a result of either of these actions, our bank will lose $985 in reserves. Since this is a distinct possibility, it had better have that much in excess reserves, or else it will be forced below the required range. For example, suppose the bank had total demand deposits due its customers amounting to $10,000 before the loan, required reserves of $2,000, and excess reserves of $197. The loan boosts the deposits to $10,985, the required reserves to $2,197; excess reserves are now zero. (Total reserves in both stages were $2,197.) If either the borrower or the people to whom he makes out the checks draw out all the money, deposits drop back to the previous $10,000 (our borrower's $985 has now been spent). Required reserves are again $2,000, but total reserves are $2,197 minus $985, or $1,212—much less than the required 20 per cent. Our bank has loaned too much money.

How much should it have loaned? It knows that each dollar actually loaned calls for an addition to required reserves of 20 per cent of that amount. It also knows that every dollar drawn out in cash reduces deposits by the same amount, and reduces required reserves by 20 per cent of that amount. *But it reduces total reserves by 100 per cent of the amount drawn.* In other words, if a loan is fully drawn out, the created deposit drops back to zero; no additional required reserves are necessary, since there is no additional deposit remaining. But every dollar loaned has pulled out one dollar of reserves. Hence, it would be wiser to limit this new loan to the amount of excess reserves, for then if the full amount of the loan is drawn out in cash, the bank will have the excess reserves to meet this drain and still have enough reserves to meet the requirements on the remaining deposits.

We will return to our example. We began with $10,000 in deposits, $2,000 in required reserves, and $197 in excess reserves. Suppose we make a loan of only $197. Then deposits go up to $10,197 and required reserves to 20 per cent of this, or $2,039.40; excess reserves ($2,197 minus $2,039.40) drop to $157.60 (see Table III). Since the bank still has excess reserves, it would seem that it could still make another loan. But the bank (in this situation) realizes that this excess is only temporary, for we are assuming that the borrower or his payees will demand cash as the loan proceeds are spent. So, $197 will be drawn out. Deposits now return to the $10,000 with which we started; total reserves

TABLE III
Deposit Expansion

1. INITIAL POSITION
   BANK A

Required Reserves	$ 2,000.00	Demand Deposits	$10,000.00
Excess Reserves	197.00		
Loans	7,803.00		
	$10,000.00		

2. BANK A MAKES $197 LOAN

Required Reserves	$ 2,039.40*	Demand Deposits	$10,197.00
Excess Reserves	157.60*		
Loans	8,000.00		
	$10,197.00		

* Note that *total* reserves are still $2,197.00, as in the initial position.

3. UTILIZATION OF LOAN

   BANK A

Required Reserves	$ 2,000.00	Demand Deposits	$10,000.00
Excess Reserves	nil		
Loans	8,000.00		
	$10,000.00		

4. BANK B (BEFORE RECEIVING PROCEEDS)

Required Reserves	$5,000.00	Demand Deposits	$25,000.00
Excess Reserves	nil		
Loans	20,000.00		
	$25,000.00		

5. BANK B AFTER BORROWER FROM A SPENT PROCEEDS OF LOAN

Required Reserves	$ 5,039.40	Demand Deposits	$25,197.00
Excess Reserves	157.60		
Loans	20,000.00		
	$25,197.00†		

† Note that at start Bank *A* had $2,197 reserves, Bank *B* $5,000, a total of $7,197. Now Bank *A* has only $2,000, Bank *B* $5,197; the total for the two is still $7,197. Note, too, that Bank *B* can now make a new loan of $157.60.

6. BANK B NOW MAKES A LOAN OF $157.60

Required Reserves	$ 5,070.92‡	Demand Deposits	$25,354.60
Excess Reserves	126.08‡		
Loans	20,157.60		
	$25,354.60		

‡ Note that total reserves are $5,197.00, the same as in step 5, before making this new loan.

7. UTILIZATION OF SECOND LOAN

BANK B

Required Reserves	$ 5,039.40	Demand Deposits	$25,197.00
Excess Reserves	nil		
Loans	20,157.60		
	$25,197.00§		

§ The decline in Bank *B*'s total reserves by $157.60 now accrues to still other banks as an inflow of deposits and reserves of $157.60 each. Against these additional deposits only 20 per cent, or $31.52, must be kept as required reserves. The remainder, or $126.08, goes into excess reserves, and thus can serve as the basis for a new loan in that amount.

have dropped by $197, from $2,197 to $2,000; required reserves (20 per cent of $10,000) are also $2,000. We have just enough to meet our legal requirements. No further loan can be made unless once again we are in an excess-reserve position.

Suppose the payees do not demand cash, but instead deposit their checks in their accounts.[3] Even if these are carried at other banks, it will make no difference, for the receiving banks will forward the checks to our bank, which must then pay these others from reserves. Checks deposited with other banks will be cashed by these other banks. The logic is clear: the deposit of the check in another bank raised that bank's deposit liabilities. Therefore, it must obtain more reserves because its required reserves are also up. It can obtain these added reserves by sending the check back to the paying bank, receiving the reserves in return.

---

[3] We have assumed that the checks drawn are deposited in the payee's checking account. If the checks were deposited in a time deposit, the reserve effects would differ. This is treated further in the chapter on deposit shifts.

Suppose the payees have their demand deposits in the *same* bank as the borrower. Then the bank merely reduces the borrower's balance and increases the payee's balance. Aggregate deposits for our bank remain the same. The increase and decrease in the two accounts are equal and offset each other. Required reserves are unchanged. There is no reserve drain. To the extent that the borrower does confine his payments to other customers of the same (lending) bank, we avoid a reserve drain, and the excess reserves held in anticipation of that drain need not be called on. They can now be used for loans to others.

It is possible that this payee now has a larger balance than he would have had if the borrower had not received the loan. The payee has made a sale to the borrower that he would not have made if the loan had not been granted. The payee may now step up his payments, and the amount of the checks drawn on his account will rise. If these checks go to people with deposits at other banks, we would still get the reserve drain. But the time between the original loan and this subsequent drain would be a bit longer than if the first payee had his account at another bank. The period that the excess reserve remained with the lending bank would then be prolonged by the time interval between the first payee's receipt of the borrower's check and the subsequent additional payment to the third party.

The possibility of the borrower's payments coming back to the same bank depends on many variables. The most important is the size and location of the bank. A small bank in a small town can expect that most of the borrower's creditors and suppliers live elsewhere and carry their balances with other banks. A large bank in a city can count on a certain proportion of the borrower's checks being drawn to other customers of the same bank. It can depend on a certain portion of the original loan *not* resulting in a reserve drain, and can release these funds for other loans. This possibility becomes widespread in countries such as Great Britain and Canada, where the banks have nationwide branch offices.

The Effect on Other Banks

As a result of the first bank's making a loan, the borrower was enabled to step up his payments by $197. Others then received more funds than they would have otherwise. We shall assume that these payments are deposited in checking accounts maintained at banks other than the first. At this stage we shall assume that these banks are also required to maintain a 20-per-cent reserve.

These other banks will now expand their deposits by the $197 paid in. In return they will receive the checks drawn on the original borrower's account (See Table III). These checks are then forwarded to the paying bank, which in turn transfers $197 in reserves (cash or balances at the Federal Reserve) to these other banks. As a result of these transactions, the other banks' required reserves have risen by 20 per cent of $197, or $39.40. Total reserves are now up by $197. Excess reserves have risen by $157.60. If they wish, these banks could expand loans by this additional excess reserve, or by $157.60.

Assuming they do this, we can start the loan cycle again, but with diminished figures. The loan itself raises the borrower's balance by $157.60. At this point these lending banks' required reserves rise by 20 per cent, or $31.52, reducing the excess reserves to $126.08. But this continued excess reserve is only temporary. As the borrower spends the additional amount, checks flow to still other banks, and the deposit balances of these new borrowers decline. Assuming that they spend all the loan proceeds, and that these also end up in checking accounts maintained at other banks, in the second cycle the bank deposits would drop back to where they were before the loan was granted. Required reserves would drop back to the same pre-loan level, and total reserves would drop by $157.60, an amount equal to the additional reserves that began the loan process. The net effect on this second group of banks has been to raise loans by $157.60, and to raise deposits by $197 (the amount paid in as a result of the first bank's loan and spending). The action has raised both total and required reserves by $39.40. Note that the reserves lost, plus the net addition to total reserves, account for the $197 reserves originally received ($157.60 plus $39.40). Additional liabilities of $197 are just balanced by the rise in loans and retained reserves ($157.60 plus $39.40). If the loan amount is increased by the anticipated interest, we would have the offsetting profit as the balancer.

The second cycle resulted in a third group of banks gaining deposits and reserves of $157.60. Again assuming the 20-per-cent required reserve ratio, $31.52 must be retained against new deposits, leaving $126.08 for excess reserves. Again the loan cycle can be initiated.

At each successive stage, the receiving banks gained an amount equal to the loan made by the bank in the preceding stage. After setting aside the required reserves for this inflow, the receiving bank then had excess reserves equal to 80 per cent of this inflow, thereby establishing the amount it could loan. Eighty per cent of this inflow is also equal to 80 per cent of the excess reserves of the bank in the preceding stage, since in the preceding stage that bank's loan equalled this excess reserve. Using these figures, the bank in stage one had $197 in excess reserves. It made a loan of $197. It lost $197 in reserves to the stage-two banks. This resulted in the stage-two banks having additional excess reserves of $157.60. This $157.60 is equal to 80 per cent of both the inflow of $197 and the excess reserves ($197) of the bank in stage one. It is also the amount of loans the stage-two banks can make. Here each stage shows an amount of additional loans equal to 80 per cent of the previous stage. Thus we get more and more loans, but at a diminishing rate—$195, $157.60, $126.08, and so on. Each bank affected is allowed to expand its loans because of the lending activity of the banks in the prior stage (a spillover of spending drawing in deposits and reserves, including excess reserves), thus giving rise to still more lending and more spillovers.

Will this chain of spillovers and loan cycles end? Practically speaking, it can. We can demonstrate what amount it is tending to reach. At each stage, 20 per cent of the reserves gained are immobilized against the inflow of deposits. The deposits arising from the new loan do not immobilize reserves for more than a temporary period. They are spent and are thereby reduced to zero, ending the necessity to maintain reserves against these additional balances. Each bank immobilizes reserves only against the deposits flowing in as a result of the spending by the borrower in the preceding stage. The remaining excess reserves are all that can be used to make loans. Subsequently these are lost to the banks in the succeeding stage. As each bank immobilizes this 20-per-cent component, less and less in reserves remains for still newer loans. To illustrate, banks in stage two immobilized $39.40, banks in stage three $31.52, and so on. When these immobilizations add up to $197, there are no longer any excess reserves and no longer any additional loans.

An original inflow of $5 for each bank, as a result of the spending by the borrower in the preceding stage, meant $1 in additional required reserves and $4 in excess reserves. The former figure represents the 20 per cent that must be held against the $5 in additional deposits. This meant that this particular bank could raise loans by $4, which in turn would then raise other banks' deposits by $4. This occurs when this particular bank's borrower spends the proceeds. This spending will draw the $4 in excess reserves out of the lending bank. Now for every $5 of reserves originally received we have $1 retained by the receiving bank and $5 in new deposits by this second bank. For the next bank in line the figures will be 80¢ and $4. We can see that the net impact on deposits will be five times the immobilized reserves. Since eventually all $197 reserves will be immobilized by the various banks, we can see that the net impact on aggregate deposits will also be five times that amount, or $985. But no one bank could afford to expand loans by five times its excess reserves. As explained, this would place it below the required reserve level. But since each bank lends only its excess reserves, it enables other banks to expand. Thus we have a paradox: no one bank can lend more than its excess reserves, but banks as a group can lend five times this excess. Since the required ratio need not be 20 per cent, it would work out to a reciprocal of the fraction that must be held. A 20-per cent (1/5) reserve gives a collective multiplier of 5; a 10-per cent (1/10) reserve gives a multiplier of 10, and so forth.

Preparing to Repay a Bank Loan

Repayment of a bank loan in effect runs our picture in reverse.

In order to be able to repay a loan, the borrower must first accumulate funds equal to the maturity value of his obligation. His checking-account balance must be built up by this amount. Assuming that the bulk of his receipts are checks paid by his customers, he must make certain that the amount of these checks being deposited exceeds the amounts he draws upon for his various needs. To the extent that he is building up his account, the other checking accounts are drawn down. Suppose he reduces his raw-materials purchases, thus cutting down the amount paid to his suppliers and causing their checking-account balances to rise by less. Suppose he postpones a machinery purchase, thus reducing the size of that company's balance from what it would have been. Had he maintained the size of his balance, the reduction in balances (as a result of his customers' payments to him) would have been matched by the rise in the balances of those people from whom the borrower bought materials. Aggregate balances would remain the same, although the composition had changed. But by building up his balance, the second group (those receiving checks from the individual in question) receive less than they would have otherwise. Their balances rise less, but not enough to offset the decline in balances of the borrower's customers. This difference amounted to the increase in the borrower's own checking account.

Banking effects also differ. If the borrower's balance remains unchanged, a reshuffling of balances from his customers to his payees occurs. Similarly, banks in which customers keep their accounts suffer a loss of reserves, those holding the payees' balances gain reserves. Each cancels the other. But if the borrower decides to build up his balance, the latter group of banks, the payees' banks, do not gain as much as the customers' banks lose. Instead, the difference is a net gain in reserves for the bank in which the borrower keeps his balance.

It should be observed that whether or not our borrower decides to build up his checking-account balance, aggregate balances and aggregate bank reserves remain the same. Only distribution is altered. With an unchanged balance, the payees and their banks gain more than if the borrower builds up his balance. On the other hand, the borrower, by building up his balance, also draws more reserves into his bank than if he had maintained an unchanged level. Just as the disbursement of the proceeds of a loan drew down bank reserves in the borrowing bank and built them up in the payees' banks, so the preparation for repayment of a loan builds up the reserves of the borrower's bank and draws reserves from the other banks. Assuming all banks must keep a 20-percent required reserve, the different shifts in deposits still leave the same aggregate. The level of required, total, and excess reserves remains the same, but it is distributed differently.

Since the banks in which the borrower's customers keep their accounts are losing reserves to the borrower's bank, we would expect to see a loss in lending power analogous to the gain they enjoyed when the borrower's spending added to their reserves. As each customer pays a check to the borrower, the latter deposits that payment in his account. The customer's bank reduces the customer's deposit balance and also pays the amount (in reserves) to the borrower's bank. If a customer made out a $100 check to the borrower, the former's deposit balance would drop by $100, the latter's would rise by $100. Simultaneously, the former's bank would lose $100 in reserves, the latter's bank would gain $100 in reserves. But the deposit drop released only a fraction of that amount (20 per cent) from required reserves; hence, the payment would draw off $80 of excess reserves, which is the difference between the reserves paid over to the borrower's bank and the amount released from required reserves. The borrower's bank would gain $80 in excess reserves—the difference between the receipt of reserves and the 20 per cent that had to be held against the rise in the borrower's balance.

A consequence of this reshuffling means fewer excess reserves in the customers' banks and more in the borrower's banks. Because of this, other banks would have to curtail their lending activity, and fewer loans would be made since excess reserves were down. Fewer loans mean less payments by thwarted borrowers, and also means less flow to other banks—banks whose customers now suffer from reduced sales to these thwarted borrowers. As these last would-be sellers sell less, they receive less. Their banks gain less reserves. This reduces these banks' capacity to lend. Here we would have a contractionary cycle similar to the expansionary one following the loan made by the initial bank in our deposit-creation discussion.

Repayment of the Loan

As our borrower builds up his checking-account balance, he also increases the bank's deposit liability to him. His deposit is an asset in his books, but a liability of the bank, since the bank owes to him. Here we have the achievement of an equalization of liabilities. The borrower has his liability to the bank—the maturing loan. The bank has its liability to the borrower—the deposit balance he has accumulated. To repay the loan, all we need do is cancel these two liabilities. The borrower offsets the loss of his deposit asset with an equal reduction in loan liabilities to the bank. Simultaneously, the bank offsets the loss of its loan asset by the cancellation of its deposit liability. Note that at this stage no currency is exchanged, just as none was exchanged at the time the loan was first made. All that has occurred is a cancellation of other assets and liabilities.

Now, by reducing its deposits by this cancelled amount, the bank also reduces its required reserves by 20 per cent of this amount. Repayment of a $5,000 loan reduces its deposit liabilities by $5,000 and thus frees $1,000 from required reserves. We have already observed that in the cancellation procedure no currency was exchanged. The total reserves are the same after as before this transaction. Therefore, if total reserves are unchanged and required reserves drop, then excess reserves rise. Loan repayment, in fact, frees reserves, and thus enables the bank to make a new loan—equal to the excess reserves, not the cancelled loan.

We have also reduced the volume of demand deposits through the cancellation. In other words, we have reduced the total amount of purchasing power. The borrower gave up purchasing power in order to repay his loan, and unless this reduction is replaced by a new creation of bank deposits—a new loan, for example—the total amount of purchasing power has been reduced. So, just as making a loan added to the money supply (checking-account balances), repayment of the loan reduced the money supply in the form of checking-account balances. Just as the deposit creation reduced excess reserves and raised required reserves, but left total reserves unchanged, so the deposit cancellation raised excess reserves, reduced required reserves, but also left total reserves unchanged.

The confusion that many newcomers encounter, regarding this effect on reserves and the money supply, arises from the failure to separate the various steps. There are four distinct stages: (a) making the loan and creating the deposit (adding to the borrower's checking-account balance); (b) the spending of the loan proceeds; (c) building up the borrower's balance in preparation for the repayment of the loan; and (d) repaying the loan and the subsequent cancellation of the deposit. In (a) and (d), total reserves are unaffected, but the volume of bank deposits does change. It rises in stage (a) and declines in stage (d). Here there have been exchanges of loans against deposit balances. In stages (b) and (c) the total reserves of the lending bank are affected, but not the total reserves of the banking system, for here we have the redistribution process. In stage (b) the lending bank loses reserves and deposits, but the other banks gain both. In so doing, they obtain excess reserves to make still more loans and deposits. In stage (c) the process is reversed. Other banks lose reserves and deposits to the borrower's bank. Again we have the (reverse) redistribution effect, including a reduction in these other banks' ability to make loans and deposits. In all four stages the total reserves of the banking system remain the same, although the distribution is altered in the two middle stages. In the first two stages the volume of deposits rises as loans rise in the first bank [stage (a)] and then in the other banks [stage (b)], and conversely for the (c) and (d) stages. The lending bank's total reserves are not affected by the making or repayment of the loan, although the amount in required reserves does change. That which changes its total reserves is the spending of these proceeds, or the process preparatory to the loan repayment. But if some of these transactions are between depositors who also keep their balances in the same bank, even this reserve flow is unaffected.

A minor qualification about slippage should be added. The theoretical process established here implies complete reactions to each shift —that if there are any excess reserves, loans expand and are spent; if excess reserves drop off, lending drops off and spending declines. In practice, the banking wheels turn somewhat less precisely. Not all excess reserves will be utilized. Loan increases may be less than the excess reserve increases. As a consequence, any drop in excess reserves can thus be cushioned; for not having utilized all of them, the possible loss to other banks need not be matched by an immediate decline in lending, but rather by a reduction in the unused excess reserve amount. Similarly, borrowers may not immediately spend all their proceeds, thus slowing down the distribution effect on bank reserves. Certain amounts may go into accounts other than demand deposits. They may affect time deposits, deposits in banks that are not in the Federal Reserve, or they may involve cash. Each of these possible alternatives could change the details of our explanation.

Clearing Principle

Until now we have spoken in terms of one loan by the initiating bank, and then of the consequences for other banks as a result of this operation. We have traced the steps leading to the repayment of this one loan. Obviously banks make more than one loan, and banks also buy and sell other assets, such as bonds and mortgages. These, too, must be fitted into the picture.

A loan is only one characteristic form of many operations. Bonds are loans to an issuing corporation. If a bank buys a newly issued bond, it is making a long-term loan to a company. If it subsequently sells this bond, then its buyer is taking over the loan—that is, paying the bank for this security. If a bank buys an already outstanding bond, then it is taking over the loan, or bond, from the seller. Similarly, mortgages are also loans used to buy or build a house or office building. While the time duration may differ, loans tend to be relatively short-lived. Bonds and mortgages endure for many years. But the essence of these transactions is similar. When a bank acquires any of these assets—loans, bonds, or mortgages—the seller receives the bank's check. For most loans, this means that the balance in the borrower's checking account at the lending bank is increased. For any other asset acquisition, the odds are that the seller will not have his account at the buying bank, so that his check goes into his account at a different bank. Reserves are then transferred from the buying bank to the seller's bank. The borrower in the loan example pays checks over to others, who then deposit these checks in their accounts at other banks. Similarly, when a bank acquires some asset, a check is paid to someone who deposits it in his account at another bank. What distinguishes a loan from other asset acquisitions is timing. There is usually some delay between the making of the loan and the subsequent loss of reserves, whereas with the bond or mortgage purchase the loss of reserves is almost immediate, for the preliminary step of deposit creation and then disbursement has been eliminated. Since there will almost certainly be this loss of reserves—unless the seller does happen to keep his account with the buying bank—acquisition of this asset, as in the loan example, will result in a loss of reserves equal to the amount paid. Hence, such purchases are limited by the available excess reserves that a bank can afford to lose. Incidentally, if the seller does keep his account with the buying bank, he would then deposit the check to his account. The net result of this possibility is a rise in the bank's assets (bond or mortgage), a rise in deposit liabilities (increased balance due the seller), and, of course, a rise in required reserves equal to 20 per cent of this. A corresponding drop in excess reserves would follow. In brief, we would have here the exact duplicate of the first stage of a new loan; assets and deposits rise equally. There would be no effect on total reserves, and there would be a decline in excess reserves (rise in required reserves) equal to 20 per cent of the deposit rise.

Where the seller does keep his account with another bank, we would then have the rise in this bank's reserves and deposits; a rise in its required reserves by 20 per cent of this; a rise in excess reserves equal to the remaining 80 per cent, and as a result, an increased capacity to make more loans. We are repeating here the repercussions of the second stage of a new loan—that is, after its subsequent use and disbursement among other banks. The effects are exactly the same. Any asset acquired by a bank from the public expands the deposits of the entire banking system.[4] In so doing, it uses up the excess reserves that enabled the first bank to acquire the asset, for the deposit expansion is a multiple of this excess equal to the reciprocal of the reserve ratio. And among banks there is a redistribution of existing reserves, the asset-acquiring bank losing reserves, the others gaining.

Every asset acquisition results in a loss of reserves to other banks, other than the small probability that some payees might keep their accounts at the bank acquiring the asset. We can see that the rate at which a bank acquires assets determines the rate at which it loses reserves. This rate is related to the prior position of its excess reserves. A result of this is that other banks will be gaining these reserves. But as a result of their asset acquisitions, they will also be losing reserves. So, for each bank there are two flows: reserve losses as a result of its acquisition of assets, and reserve gains as a result of other banks acquiring assets. Just how much of another bank's asset acquisition will result in any one other bank acquiring reserves cannot be stated precisely. This would depend on just which payees maintain accounts with the remaining banks. Suppose a building contractor in Manhattan makes most of his payments to New York City workmen and materials suppliers. Then most of his payments are lodged with other New York City banks. Perhaps an electronics manufacturer in the same city spends most of his money on purchases from out-of-town suppliers, this causing reserve gains to accrue in banks in other cities. In either case any payment going out in check form will end up in some checking account with some other bank. The reserves lost by the paying bank will end up as a reserve gain in another bank.[5]

Suppose we ignore these criss-crossing streams, and assume that they tend to balance out. Then we can say that on the average, banks will gain reserves at a rate determined by the asset-acquiring activities of other banks. Banks lose reserves at the rate that they acquire assets. We can see now that the two will offset each other if a particular bank is expanding at about the same rate as other banks; it will gain reserves

---

[4] Assets acquired from other banks would not affect deposits. A buying bank would give up reserves to the selling bank and in return receive the asset so acquired. In effect, we have a reshuffling of assets; both banks have the same amount in assets, but the composition of these assets has been changed. The buying bank has more income-earning assets, but less reserves; the selling bank has less income-earning assets, but more reserves.

[5] It is possible for reserves to end up outside the banks. This will be discussed when we treat the cash drain.

if it is expanding more slowly, since its loss of reserves will be at a slower rate than its reserve gain from the more rapidly expanding banks. And it would follow that it will lose reserves if it expands more rapidly than the other banks.

It will be recalled that as borrowers prepare to repay a loan, they build up their balances, thereby draining reserves from other banks. So, in the reduction of assets—the repayment of a loan not followed by the granting of a new one, or the sale of a bond or mortgage—reserves are pulled into the contracting bank. Similarly, other banks' contracting activities pull reserves out. If our bank contracts just as quickly as the others, it will neither gain nor lose reserves. But if it contracts more quickly, it will gain reserves. If it contracts less quickly, it will lose reserves. If a bank contracts while others expand, it will gain reserves; if it expands while others are contracting, it will lose reserves.

Because of these relationships, banks tend to move together. If, for example, some banks are sluggish during an expansion, they will start to gain reserves. As excess reserves pile up, banks are in a better position to make loans or to buy securities, so now they can step up their expansion rate. Soon they catch up with the others, because this new rate then drains off added excess reserves. Similarly, if they fail to contract along with the others, their reserves will start to flow out, and they will be forced to get back in step by starting to contract.

Cash Flows

Up to now we have discussed payments that return to the banking system, either to the paying bank or to another member bank. But this is not always the case. Some payments are in cash; some receipts are in cash. How does this factor modify our discussion?

First, we will discuss the nature of such movements. Cash responds to many influences. People need more currency when they travel, when Christmas comes around, when long weekends step up the number of days that banks are closed. Conversely, after such periods, cash needs decline. The banks tend to lose reserves as depositors draw money out in the first group of possibilities, then the reserves are replenished during the second group. These flows are so seasonal and regular in character that both the timing and the amounts are fairly predictable.

Over somewhat longer periods the cash flows reflect changes in income. As business improves, incomes rise and people tend to carry more money on their persons. Retail establishments do more business, and their cash registers have more currency in them. The opposite tendency rules during recessions. Cash tends to flow out of the banks during boom periods, then back to them during business declines. (In the last possibility, when people start to mistrust the banks' solvency, as they did during the depression of the 1930's, cash would flow out even in recession periods.)

Note that both the seasonal and cyclical forces are not easily influenced directly by banks. If Christmas is coming, it is unlikely that the banks could discourage people from drawing out cash to buy presents. In a boom it is difficult to persuade people who feel richer to carry less money with them. To some extent this could be done, of course; greater emphasis on thrift and savings accounts might counter this tendency. But as a general rule there is little that the banks can do to interfere with these outside forces. In summary, we can argue that the cash flows reflect the spending habits of the people as influenced by seasonal and cyclical variations. For all practical purposes, banks play a purely passive role in this movement, feeding out currency when the people demand it, drawing on their deposits, and piling up currency as surplus cash periods come around, the corresponding offset of this activity being the rise in the deposit liabilities of those bringing in the currency. Over the long run the growth in our economy has produced a gradual rise in cash in circulation.

The cash inflow can be easily analyzed. If some depositor is paid in cash, or if someone with cash deposits it in his account, we get an immediate increase in the volume of deposits and reserves, since cash is one of the reserve components. In this case the depositor has not enhanced his purchasing power, for the rise in his deposit is exactly equal to the decline in his cash holding. Assuming the money went into a checking account, the money supply in the hands of the public is unchanged, checking-account funds having replaced money in the form of currency. Against the deposit, the bank will set aside the 20 per cent required for reserves, and the remaining 80 per cent is an addition to excess reserves. And now the loan-deposit expansionary process can begin.

Suppose, in contrast, that one of the depositors has to make a payment in cash. Or suppose that one of the recipients of a check cashes it. One thing is clear: the paying out of cash will deplete the bank's reserves. Furthermore, there will be the reduction in deposits. With this decline goes a decline in required reserves equal to 20 per cent of the drop. The remaining 80 per cent—the difference between the cash paid out and that released from required reserves—must therefore come from the excess reserves.

But what if our bank has no excess reserves and cannot get them from some other source—for example, the possible sale of an asset to another bank that does have excess reserves. Then our bank must dig into its required reserves. But if it does, it will then have less than required. And since we have indicated that it cannot add to reserves, it must adopt an alternative—namely, bring down deposits, thus reducing the required reserves to the level it can fulfill.

For example, suppose we have a small bank with $100,000 in checking-account balances, $20,000 in required reserves, no excess reserves, and $80,000 in other assets.[6] (For simplicity, we are ignoring other accounts in the statement.) A depositor then draws out $2,000 in cash, reducing deposits to $98,000 and reserves to $18,000. If our bank cannot sell any of its other assets—perhaps they are loans to local merchants, and other banks do not feel they know the credit rating well enough to risk acquiring their notes—then our bank must reduce deposits to $90,000, for 20 per cent of this amount is $18,000, or the reserves now remaining. Hence, loans must be called in and not renewed, for this process will reduce demand deposits. In brief, a cash outflow beyond excess reserves leads to contraction, the reverse effect of a cash inflow.

It will be recalled here that preparations to repay a loan will draw in reserves, as debtors build up their balances. But this only means that some other banks are losing reserves. Thus, while this inflow will lessen the pressure on our first bank, it passes on the pressures of a reserve loss to these others. And so the contraction continues. Since as a group the banks have lost $2,000 in reserves (and assuming that none has excess reserves), then as a group they must contract until deposits have been drawn down by $10,000—the $2,000 originally drawn out, plus an additional $8,000 through the calling in of loans.

Of course, so small a bank could not cause this kind of deflation. But suppose there is a general withdrawing of cash throughout the country, such as might occur in a severe recession. Then many banks are losing reserves, and most likely these losses will exceed the amounts in the excess-reserve sector. Hence, banks as a group must now contract. They must bring their deposits down to the now lower level of reserves. For any one bank to resist this trend, as we have seen, the result would simply be a sharper loss of reserves to the contracting banks. But then the resultant pressure would force it to join in anyway.

It is in such a situation that the banks would also be unlikely to find a market for their assets. If any one bank is short of reserves, it could probably sell some asset—say, a marketable bond—to another bank that had excess reserves. This would be the most probable out-

---

[6] In practice, a bank this small would probably not be required to carry so high a reserve ratio, for it would be located in some small rural sector, which would classify it as a country bank. Thus it would bear a lower ratio.

come for the small bank. It would probably sell a $2,000 bond.[7] But if all banks are in trouble, none has excess reserves, and so none is anxious to buy assets from the other banks. This possibility of a wholesale liquidation of bank assets will be studied further.

Minimum Balances

Most banks require the maintenance of minimum balances, especially on larger checking accounts. This means that in practice most checking accounts will not go to zero, but will hover around this stipulated minimum. As a result, there is less of a potential drain of reserves. Suppose a loan of $25,000 is granted to the borrower, but a minimum balance of $5,000 is required. Then our borrower really has only $20,000 to spend, although he is paying interest on the whole amount. (The effective interest charge—interest divided by the usable portion—would thus be one-quarter more.) Hence, the bank can count on a reserve outflow of no more than 80 per cent of the loan. With excess reserves of $20,000, it could grant loans up to $25,000. So now our yardstick for new loans would be 1.25 times excess reserves.

But to the extent that this minimum-balance requirement is used generally, we also reduce the subsequent reserve gain of the other banks. This, in turn, would cut down their lending ability, in contrast to the stretching provided by our previous paragraph. Assuming that all banks use this approach, then all banks are virtually assured[8] that their deposits will not go below certain levels.

As a group, the banks would still have the same volume of reserves; all we are doing is guaranteeing that some reserves will not be lost to other banks. Hence, as a group, the volume of demand deposits can be no higher, since these are a fixed multiple of the reserve ratio (assuming no excess reserves). But instead of all these deposits being usable for spending, only that part in excess of the minimum can be effectively disbursed. Depositors as a group have less spendable money, or less usable purchasing power. In effect, we have stopped the spending of the minimum portion. If some borrowers then step up their loan request to compensate for that part that cannot be drawn on, then other, less fortunate borrowers will get less, for the aggregate of all deposits has been fixed by the volume of reserves.

Moreover, since the bank knows that most depositors will observe the minimum, it therefore knows that this money will never be drawn

---

[7] More precisely, it needed $1,600—20 per cent of $98,000, which equals $19,600 required reserves, as compared with $18,000 actually on hand. The withdrawing of $2,000, by cutting deposits, reduced (set free) required reserves of $400.

[8] A bank would not stop a depositor from dropping below the minimum, but if he did, it would then assess a service charge. This income could offset any cost incurred in obtaining the extra reserves to meet this unexpected drain.

out. This means that reserves need never be lost to other banks through utilization of the minimum. Twenty per cent of this minimum must be kept in required reserves, but the other 80 per cent is free to be invested as the bank wishes. Were it faced with a possible drain of this portion, it would have to keep enough saleable (liquid) assets ready so that an excessive drain could be met by the sale of these mobilizable assets. But now that there is no longer such a fear, these other assets can be less liquid and higher earning. Since the deposits will not be drawn down below this minimum, the potential need to obtain reserves is reduced, and correspondingly the possible need to sell assets is reduced. The liquidity of the bank can be reduced, and since part of this liquidity can be given up, earnings can rise. As a result, the minimum balance enhances bank earnings at the expense of deposit flexibility. Also, as more of the total thus becomes subject to the minimum, the more funds are thereby immobilized, and the less liquid the banks need be, enjoying now a corresponding lift to their income. In brief, the minimum balance results in part of the banks' deposits becoming less liquid; as a result, the banks' assets can be correspondingly less liquid.

To illustrate this point further, we shall employ an extremely simplified example. Assume that we have a bank with $1,000,000 in checking accounts and total reserves of $221,000; excess reserves are $21,000. It then makes a loan equal to its excess reserves, boosting deposits to $1,021,000. If it does not require a minimum balance, it must expect to lose all its excess reserves as the borrowed funds are spent. Furthermore, the other deposits—the initial $1,000,000—may also be spent in such a way as to drain it of reserves; if so, then it may have to sell off some of its assets to obtain the necessary money. To play safe, it puts part of its assets into highly liquid but low-yielding securities.

Suppose it now goes over to a minimum-balance requirement. Then the potential drain of reserves, as a result of the activity of its $1,000,000 sector, is reduced. Now, since there is less of a danger that it will lose reserves as a result of that sector's activity, there is less of a danger that it will have to liquidate some of its paper to raise cash. So, some of its low-yielding paper can be sold and replaced by better-income, less liquid assets.

Furthermore, it knows that the minimum-balance requirement will reduce the drain arising from new loans. Assume that this balance is one-fifth of the loan. Then our bank can extend $25,000 in loans— $4,000 more than without a minimum balance—and thus earn that much more. The initial loan will raise deposits to $1,025,000, while total reserves are still $221,000. Then four-fifths of this loan is spent, drawing out $20,000 in reserves (and deposits). So, reserves drop to

$201,000 and deposits to $1,005,000—$5,000 more than when we started, this being the minimum balance on the borrower's account. Twenty per cent of this $1,005,000 deposit total is $201,000 in required reserves, or exactly the amount remaining in the bank's reserve account. We thus see that the bank is not only able to earn more interest on its assets (because of its switch of some part from highly liquid to less liquid paper), but its aggregate loans are more—here by $4,000— thus further boosting its income. Note, too, that without a minimum balance the other banks gained $21,000 in reserves from our bank's lending activity; with a minimum balance they gained only $20,000. Their lending power is thus a bit less because our bank imposed the minimum requirement.

Summary

Commercial banks, as the only place where checking accounts are carried, are in a position to influence total purchasing power through the creation and repayment of loans and the acquisition and sale of other assets. So long as the reserve requirements are met, excess reserves give rise to deposit expansion, at first equal to this excess at the initial bank, but then equal to a multiple as the proceeds are disbursed among the other banks. Loan repayment has a corresponding but opposite effect on the reserve-deposit relationship. In effect, reserves may be lost by any one bank, but not by banks as a whole; they may be gained by any one bank, but not by the banking system as a whole. An exception to this statement would arise if depositors paid in or drew out currency. In general, banks lose reserves if they expand more rapidly than other banks, or when they contract more slowly. They gain reserves if they expand more slowly, or contract more rapidly.

Cash flows, as already indicated, upset these generalizations. Unlike the acquisition and sale of assets, in which total reserves of the system remain unaffected, cash does change this total. Hence, its movements tend to have a multiple effect on the ability of the banks to expand or contract. This multiplier is the result of the fractional reserve that must be kept against the deposit, the movement of which accompanies the cash flow. The difference between the required reserve and the cash flow affects excess reserves, which then affects the banks' ability to alter total assets and deposits.

To some extent a bank can reduce the reserve impact of its loan activity by requiring a minimum balance. This, however, is offset through its repercussions on other banks. For the entire system, such requirements merely raise bank earnings and borrower costs without affecting significantly the over-all total of assets and deposit liabilities.

Chapter 9

MONETARY MECHANICS II: DEPOSIT SHIFTS

In the United States the reserve requirements against deposits are not as uniform as we have assumed so far. One difference arises from the geography of the country, while another is inherent in the nature of the different deposits. Since shifts among these different segments are, at times, of monetary significance, we shall devote this chapter to examining the repercussions of such changes.

Reserve-Requirement Variations

The geographical difference arises from the division of the commercial banks that are members of the Federal Reserve System into either reserve city banks or country banks. For demand deposits, the Federal Reserve Board can vary the required ratio for reserve city banks between 10 and 22 per cent, whereas the country banks' ratio can range between 7 and 14 per cent. On time deposits, the ratio for both groups can move between 3 and 6 per cent. Normally, the time-deposit ratio is the same for both, whereas the demand-deposit ratio is higher for the reserve city banks. (A third category—central reserve city banks—with demand-deposit ratios ranging still higher than for reserve city banks, was ended on July 28, 1962.[1])

The justification for the lower ratio against time deposits reflects their lesser activity. Time deposits were felt to be more like savings accounts, with a very low rate of utilization. With less prospect of withdrawal, there was less need for reserves to meet such diminished drains. Demand deposits were expected to be drawn on frequently, and so banks were required to hold larger reserves to meet such requirements.

A later addition to this logic recognized the different spending implications of this variance in activity. The more active a deposit, the greater the amount spent; the greater this amount, the greater the demand for goods and services. Hence, the more active checking accounts were the major source of demand, in effect, and so a high ratio was justified to control this aspect. A dollar of reserves could back up a greater volume of time deposits, but offsetting this was their relatively lesser impact on demand, so that the latter canceled out the former influence.

A similar line of reasoning lay behind the geographical differentiation. City banks were believed to hold the more active deposits. This is characteristic of industry, commerce, and finance, so a given volume of deposits in the city banks would give rise to a greater volume of spending (of demand) than an equal volume of deposits would in the country banks. So, a dollar of reserves in the country banks would be permitted by the Federal Reserve to support a greater volume of deposits, since these deposits would be more sluggish than the smaller volume of deposits in the city banks that the same volume of reserves would support.

Theoretically, if all the banks were fully loaned up—if there were no excess reserves anywhere—then a payment out of a reserve city-demand deposit to a country-demand deposit would transfer an equal amount of reserves and deposits. But since the deposits now require less reserves, there would be an increase in excess reserves at the country banks. A rise in aggregate deposits could ensue. Similarly, if under the same fully loaned-up situation, there were a payment out of a country-demand deposit to a reserve city-demand deposit, there would be a need for higher reserves. Implicit in this logic was that the expansion in deposits in the first possibility was to offset the lower spending rate now that the deposits were in the hands of country people; con-

---

[1] These were mainly the large banks in New York City and Chicago.

traction in the latter possibility was to offset the greater rate of use the city folk would put the funds to. Note that in the switch to the country banks, the loss of reserves by the city banks would force a contraction there, but the equal gain of reserves by the country banks would allow a deposit rise greater than the shrinkage in the city. Conversely, the loss of reserves by the country banks would compel a contraction of deposits greater than the amount by which the same reserves would allow the city banks to expand their deposits. Net, as already indicated, the movement of reserves to the country banks would expand aggregate deposits of all the banks (more in the country, less in the city, but the former would rise by more than the latter would decline); the movement of reserves to the city banks would contract aggregate deposits of all banks (less in the country, more in the city, but the decline in the former would exceed the rise in the latter).

Analogous arithmetic results would arise if someone receiving a check deposits it in his time deposit. The paying bank loses in reserves what the receiving bank gains, and the decline in demand deposits is equal to the rise in time deposits. But the required reserves against the time deposits are less. Hence, for the same volume of deposits, less reserves need be kept, and aggregate deposits can rise. The converse holds for the time depositor who makes a payment by drawing money from his account and handing it over to someone who deposits it in his checking account. In terms of our macroeconomic model, a rise in the propensity to save might be reflected in a shift from demand to time deposits, thus releasing reserves and leading eventually to a rise in aggregate deposits.

Geographical Shifts

The significance of the differences in reserve ratios for country as against city banks becomes clearer when we view the geographical shifts that have been taking place in the United States since the start of World War II. As a broad generalization, there have been two relative movements. One has been an over-all growth in the American economy, but faster in the Far West and Southwest, notably in California and Texas. The other factor has been a greater decentralization of industry and a population shift to the suburbs. But the bulk of the major financing has continued to be sought from the larger financial centers, such as New York City and Chicago.

The influence of the different ratios on the geographic changes would not be significant if the moves were between banks in the same categories. For example, if the greater relative expansion in the California area raised the reserves of the Los Angeles and San Francisco banks, and attracted reserves from the New York and Boston banks, there would be no change in the banking system's ability to support deposits. The same volume of reserves would exist, although differently distributed. In both groups of banks, the required reserve ratio would be the same, so the same volume of deposits could result. True, the ability of the eastern banks to expand deposits would have been reduced, but this would be only a reflection of the slower demand and the rate of growth there. Compensating for this lag would be the enhanced ability of the western banks to grant loans and create deposits, to service the larger demand arising from the area's more rapid growth.

But the trek from the larger urban centers has also resulted in a relatively greater growth in the country banks at the expense of the city banks. Here we *do* run into impacts and repercussions that may alter the over-all picture, for we are shifting from banks with a higher required reserve ratio to those with lower requirements. The same volume of reserves can now support a greater volume of deposits.

As an illustration of how such a shift may occur, we shall assume that a large industrial corporation has decided to build a plant in Countrytown, reducing its manufacturing runs in New York City. Before this, it had been borrowing in New York to buy raw materials and to pay workers engaged in producing the output. Now it needs about the same amount of money, but less will be spent in the New York plant, more in the new Countrytown plant. In all likelihood, it will continue to borrow from the same large New York City banks, since the small Countrytown banks do not have the resources to make such large commitments.

As before, the corporation deposits are increased by the amount of the loan. The money paid out to the New York City workers will undoubtedly return to New York City banks, either as deposits or as funds spent with local retailers, who in turn will add the funds to their bank accounts. Although the lending bank may not receive back the funds, New York City banks will, and only that part of the loan spent with out-of-town suppliers will drain off reserves. Hence, as a group, to the extent that reserves remain in the city, the banks as a group need not curtail loans and deposits.

But with the opening of the plant in Countrytown, more will be paid to workers in that center and less in New York City. More of the funds loaned by the New York City banks will be paid to people in Countrytown, who, of course, keep their deposits locally, or alternatively spend their funds with stores that keep their deposits with the Countrytown banks. There is a greater outflow of reserves from the

New York City banks, much of it (that part going to the Countrytown depositors) ending up with the Countrytown banks. Had the corporation financed its Countrytown needs locally, instead of in New York, there would not have been this geographical shift. But as it is, the New York City banks, in effect, are financing the rise in the Countrytown banks' reserves.

Since a greater proportion of the loan proceeds will now be lost to the lending bank, and to the New York City banks in general, the net result will be that the volume of reserves in the New York City banks will be less as a result of the corporation's new plant in Countrytown. Thus, New York City banks will be compelled to maintain a lower volume of deposits, and correspondingly their lending ability will be curtailed. In contrast, the Countrytown banks will be gaining reserves, and their deposit-creating basis will be expanded, both because of the additional reserves and because of the lower required ratio.

Arithmetically, it would seem that the net effect should be an overall growth in deposits because the ratios differ. But in practice, the demand for funds in Countrytown may not be sufficient to absorb all these additional reserves. These banks are generally smaller than the city banks, so that they have great difficulty in financing the larger borrowers. These major demanders must go to city banks that have the resources. But these city banks are being strapped because of this drain of reserves arising from decentralization. Hence, the country banks tend to utilize their reserves less completely, and so the resulting rise in deposits is less than we would expect. As a consequence, greater excess reserves tend to be characteristic of these banks. The efficiency of the banking system has been reduced as a result. One of the changes emerging in the recent period has been that many of the larger country banks lend some of these excess reserves back to the larger city banks. We shall explore this new development when we discuss Federal Funds.

The Utilization of a Time Deposit

It will be recalled that the required reserve ratio against time deposits is considerably less than against demand deposits. As a consequence, the volume of time deposits that a given reserve may support is considerably greater than the alternative volume of demand deposits permissible. The justification had been originally that time deposits give rise to so much less spending that the increased volume would balance the greater activity of the small volume of demand deposits.

Whether or not this rationalization is correct is increasing in importance as a subject of debate. Do depositors leave their funds in time deposits if they do not expect to need them? Do they put them in demand deposits if they do expect to need them? Since time deposits pay interest, whereas demand deposits do not, may this not also be a factor in the decision?

The two sides of this argument can be easily illustrated. Assume that one has $5,000 in cash, and that he expects to spend about $1,000 over the next three months. That means that about $4,000 of this total will not be required. He would then decide to put $1,000 or more into his checking account, drawing on it as needed. The remainder would go into a time deposit to draw interest. If he has forecast his spending correctly, the time deposit will not give rise to any demand for goods over the period, since it will lie dormant. Of course, he may have made an error. Perhaps he spent $500 more than anticipated. In that case he could draw out this amount from his time deposit, and if he does so, this gives rise to some demand. But relatively it has been much less active. The $1,000 in his demand deposit gave rise to $1,000 in demand, or 100 per cent utilization. But the $4,000 in his time deposit gave rise to only $500 in demand, or 12½ per cent utilization. If his original forecast had been correct, the latter utilization ratio would be zero. Hence, since a dollar of time deposits calls forth a much less potential drain than a dollar of demand deposits, the banks need carry much less reserves against time deposits.

There is another way of looking at this situation. Suppose the forecast for $1,000 disbursements over the period really meant this: He thought he would need $1,000; but he might need as much as $1,500, or it could be as little as $500. In the previous example we had settled for $1,000, and it developed that it might have been $1,500. He could also have responded differently. He might have decided to put only $500 in his checking account, for this much spending is certain to be incurred. Then, as remaining needs arise—which may be as little as zero, but could be as much as $1000—he would then replenish his checking account by transfers from the time deposit.

If one acts on this pattern he can carry a much smaller volume of demand deposits on which he receives no income, and a much higher volume of time deposits that will pay interest. At the same time, he can spend just as much as before, simply making up any deficiency through the transfers. If he finally does need the $1,500, which means that he will have to transfer $1,000 from his time deposit, his time-deposit utilization actually shows a much greater figure. In brief, one can carry much less in his checking account if he can always look to his time deposit to make up any insufficient balance that may arise. In so doing, he will obtain more income, or the interest on his higher time-deposit balance.

If many people did this, there would be less funds carried as demand deposits and more as time deposits. Then banks as a group would need less reserves, because of the difference in required ratios. Expressed another way, the same volume of reserves could support a greater volume of deposits. Moreover, this switch to time deposits does not reflect a switch from active to inactive money; we have the same amount of spending, but a closer figuring in the management of the checking account. In both illustrations the individual spent $1,500, but by relying more on his time deposit, he was able to carry a smaller checking-account balance. At the same time, the banks needed less reserves against his combined deposits, and so set free some of their existing reserves for other uses, such as asset acquisitions, with the attendant rise in deposits. Banks as a group can now expand their activities because of the improved skill with which he managed his bank accounts.

The Effect on the Commercial Banks

At first glance, it would seem that the commercial banks benefit if their depositors shift to time deposits, since doing so frees reserves and permits them to expand their income-earning assets. But at the same time it also raises their expenses, for now interest must be paid out. Such a shift can always be reversed, thus recreating the need for reserves that had been released by the initial shift. The problem is further complicated if we view the situation from the vantage point of a single bank or banks as a group, since there is always the problem of the reserve drain to other banks if any one bank does start acquiring more assets.

To simplify here, we shall assume that the required reserve ratio against time deposits is 4 per cent, and for demand deposits 20 per cent. We shall also assume that the banks do not have excess reserves. As a consequence, if $1,000 is shifted from demand to time deposits, the required reserve drops from $200 to $40, resulting in excess reserves of $160. This bank can now expand income-earning assets by $160. Obviously, it cannot earn enough from so small an addition to assets to compensate for so great a rise in interest-bearing deposits. (We shall ignore the loss of income from checking account service charges.)

But if all the banks experience such a shift, we have a different picture. In the first stage, every bank obtains $160 in excess reserves for each $1,000 that moves. Each bank then adds $160 to its assets, and experiences a loss of reserves in the same amount. But each bank also gains what the others are losing. Our clearing mechanism is now in operation. The recipients of the $160, as they disburse the amount, will be turning the funds over to others; some of these will deposit the proceeds in their time-deposit accounts, others in their demand deposits. If the former occurs, of course, the receiving bank must set aside much less of the inflow as required reserves, and can thus, in stage two, initiate a larger asset acquisition than if the inflow is to demand deposits. Since there are many possible proportions, we shall limit our discussion to the two extremes: *all* funds flow into demand deposits, or they flow into time deposits.

If the former, then reserves set free are gradually absorbed by the rising volume of demand deposits. With a 20-per-cent ratio, this means an ultimate expansion in bank deposits, and assets of $800. That is, in stage one we reduced demand deposits by $1,000 and raised time deposits by $1,000. In stage two, we raised demand deposits by $800, for a net combined decline of $200 in demand deposits. Net, we need $40 less in required reserves in this sector, an amount just equal to the additional required reserves against the time deposit. Over-all, our deposits rose $800—the $1,000 rise in time deposits less the net drop in demand deposits of $200. And, matching this rise in demand deposits was a rise in income-earning assets ($800). If the average rate of return on these additional assets is one-quarter more than the interest rate paid on time deposits, the banks then earn just enough to offset the added costs. A 4-per-cent rate on time deposits, for example, would add $40 to costs; a 5-per-cent yield on these additional assets would be just enough compensation (ignoring any additional operating costs that might accompany the expansion in activity). Incidentally, this parenthetical qualification cannot be ignored in practice, and so the income yield would have to be more than 5 per cent; we ignore it since we have no basis to estimate this additional cost element. Note that the banks are forced into very high-income assets, which, as we shall see, are also the more risky ones.

If all the funds flow into time deposits, then the $160 set free in reserves could support $4,000 in additional liabilities, or a total rise in time deposits of $5,000. The accompanying asset expansion of $4,000 would, as before, require a return equal to at least one-quarter more than that payable on time deposits.

Banks could also expand earnings in another move. Before the shift, when the funds had been in demand deposits, the $1,000 liability had been matched by $200 in reserves and $800 in assets. These assets did not have to yield as much as if the $1,000 were in time deposits, since there was no interest expense to worry about. With the switch from demand to time deposits, the banks could also switch the $800 to higher-income assets, this being in line with the trend in the additional assets. This somewhat higher return would thus reduce the additional income required from the additional assets. If, for example, the original $800 asset were to be exchanged for another earning 1 per cent more, this $8 additional income would mean that the remaining $4,000 assets could yield 0.2 per cent less. In this way there would be a slight reduction in the risky character of these $4,000 in assets, but a rise in the risky character of the original $800. To repeat, no allowance has been made in these calculations for any additional operating expenses as a result of the expansion in activity—an expansion that would be particularly large if all the funds were to flow into time deposits.

Most banks feel that competition for funds has been forcing them to raise the interest on time deposits. Competition from the savings-and-loan associations, in particular, has resulted in a relatively greater growth for these institutions, and their edge has been gained mainly through the offering of more attractive interest rates on deposits. To offset this attraction, the commercial banks have also raised their interest rates. But this has been even less beneficial than would be implied by this discussion. In evaluating the net gain, we have weighed the added interest obtained from the expansion in assets and the shift toward higher-yielding returns as a result of the movement of funds from demand to time deposits. But when the interest rate is raised, all time deposits benefit, including those already lodged with the bank. The interest cost on all time deposits goes up, whereas the major contribution to income comes only from those demand deposits that are induced to change over. As a result, there are many observers who feel that the banks are worse off, from an operating profit point of view, although, as already indicated, they might be hurt more if the interest rates had been kept down and funds then flowed out to the other competing organizations.

Time Certificates of Deposit

Because time deposits can be drawn out when required, raising the liquidity problem, banks have started issuing a new form of this medium which is less of a liquidity risk. These are the time certificates of deposit.[2] Essentially they are issued for specific periods—say, three months—bearing interest rates comparable with time deposits. At maturity they are paid off. But during the interval between the date of issue and date of maturity, the holder cannot go to the bank for his funds. Instead he must sell them on the open market to any other buyer interested in purchasing them. Thus the issuing bank is spared the possibility of a drain until the maturing date. These certificates are traded by specialized securities dealers, and have been issued by both the larger and smaller banks. In general, the yields are somewhat higher on the obligations of the smaller, lesser-known institutions. Many large

---

[2] Banks maintain the same required reserves against these as for time deposits.

corporations with temporary excess cash have been the main purchasers. Another large segment of the demand has come from foreigners with large amounts of dollars accumulated as a result of our
balance-of-payments deficit (see Chapter 24). Most issues are for six to
nine months, which postpones the liquidity problem for some time.
An additional attraction is that the rates paid on the certificates can be
varied each time there is a new issue—more easily than on time deposits, whose rates are much more rigid.

However, these certificates do not obviate liquidity considerations. At maturity, it is probably feasible to issue a new series of
certificates to pay off the old ones. Either the existing holders or other
investors will take them up. But since the large corporate investor
forms so significant a portion of the demand side, certain dangers lurk
in this new financial area. Presumably, the funds invested were surplus
to the existing needs of the corporation. But if economic activity
should improve greatly—and the periods during which these certificates gained greater popularity were those characterized by less than
full-capacity operations—there might be a step-up in the corporate
needs for cash, such as for new capital outlays. Or, even if not all such
investors experienced the need, the general rise in activity would stimulate a demand for funds, thereby pushing up interest rates on competing securities. In either event, the corporate holders would then
demand repayment. True, the banks could meet this obligation by
increasing the demand-deposit balances of their creditors; that is, they
could pay off by adding to the holder's demand deposit an amount
equal to the maturing value of the certificate. But in so doing, they
would reduce their low required reserve liabilities (the time certificate
of deposit) and raise their high required reserve liabilities (the new
demand deposit balances), thereby adding to required reserves. Moreover, there is no assurance that their creditors will simply leave these
newly acquired liquid funds as idle deposits. They may very well pull
them out for investment elsewhere—perhaps abroad—and so put even
more pressure on the banks' reserve position. An analogous liquidity
problem could arise for the banks either if their time depositors were
faced with a rising need for funds—that is, a need to switch back to
demand deposits because of increased disbursements—or if they found
alternative investment outlets more lucrative.

To make matters worse, these demands could occur at a time
when the banks' assets are falling in value—this tends to be the case
in boom periods—so that any forced sale of these holdings in order to
offset the reserve drain could result in book losses as market prices
decline below original cost. Indeed, it is just those risky assets into
which the banks moved in order to gain the additional income that are
most vulnerable to price declines during periods of rising interest rates.

While no implication of a banking crisis is intended in this warning, the difficulties could be great enough to offset all the advantages that such encouragement for time deposits was presumed to yield.

In the foregoing, it was presumed that the banks could not obtain reserves except from other banks—which left the total for the banks as a group unchanged, such a transfer merely redistributing the reserves —or else through the inflow of cash, a possibility that is generally beyond the power of the commercial banks to influence in any significant quantities. But in practice there is a way for them to gain reserves, especially if they are really in need. Such a source is the central bank. In the United States it is the Federal Reserve banks. It is very possible, for example, that if there should occur a cashing in of maturing certificates of deposit, or a wholesale switching of time into demand deposits, the consequent need for greatly increased reserves would be met by the Federal Reserve. These semigovernmental institutions are looked on by the banks as a source of help, exactly as the average individual looks on his bank for aid if he gets into liquidity difficulties.

Summary

In the United States, reserves required against deposits are not uniform. Demand and time deposits have different required ratios, and these, too, are different according to a bank's location. As a result, shifts among these categories do not change total reserves, but they do alter the volume of required reserves, and thus excess reserves, the difference between the two. This, in turn, can affect both the asset and deposit volumes at the various banks, and also the totals for the banking system. To some extent, these variations in required ratios reflect differences in deposit activity, so that those sectors whose activity was regarded as likely to be smaller were characterized by greater ratios of deposits per dollar of reserves. But there is a great question as to whether or not these assumptions are true. In view of the shifts our economy has experienced over the past quarter-century, these reserve differences may have impaired the efficiency of our monetary machine. A particular area of doubt has been the recent tendency of demand deposits to move into various forms of time accounts. These have reduced reserve requirements, but interest must be paid on them. As a result, the banks have been moving into higher-yielding, but more risky, assets to service this added cost. Should reviving business activity induce the depositors to reverse this trend, then the commercial banks could be caught in an unpleasant squeeze, both on reserves and assets.

Chapter 10

MONETARY MECHANICS III: THE FEDERAL RESERVE SYSTEM

The Federal Reserve banks—the American equivalent of a central bank—are known as "bankers' banks." Their relations with those commercial banks that are members of the Federal Reserve System are similar to the relations the commercial banks have with the public. Just as the public keeps its liquid funds either as cash in its pocket or in checking accounts with the commercial banks, so the commercial banks keep their liquid funds either as cash in the vault or as demand deposits with the Federal Reserve. The commercial banks can borrow from the Federal Reserve, just as the public can borrow from the banks, and the deposit creation and extinction upon repayment work similarly. And just as the commercial banks' acquisition or sale of assets in general tend to expand or contract the volume of the public's demand deposits, so the Federal Reserve purchases and sales of securities have the same effect on commercial bank balances with the Federal Reserve.

The Federal Reserve System

Briefly, the Federal Reserve System consists of a supervisory Board of Governors in Washington, D.C. Its seven members are appointed by the President of the United States, with the approval of Congress, and usually serve for fourteen years. It is equivalent to other agencies of the government that are independent of particular cabinet departments. Its employees are recruited directly by the Board, although their tenure and working arrangements are similar to those of the Federal Civil Service.

There are also twelve Federal Reserve banks. Each covers a designated geographical section (called a district) of the United States (including Hawaii and Alaska, which are assigned to the San Francisco district). They are usually known by the city in which the head office is located. All but the Boston and Philadelphia banks have branches. These banks are private enterprises; their capital is subscribed by the commercial banks in their districts that have elected to join the Federal Reserve System (as member banks), paying in half the amount due when they join. They are subject to the control of the Board of Governors. Each bank recruits its own staff, although certain of the officers and directors are appointed either by or with the approval of the Board. Although they put up the capital, the member banks really have very little say in running the various Federal Reserve banks, other than the election of six of the nine directors. Even the dividends that may be distributed to the stockholding banks are limited, so that a profit motive rarely figures in Federal Reserve decisions.[1]

The official title of the governing body is the Board of Governors of the Federal Reserve System. The Board is charged with examining the various Federal Reserve banks. It has power to fix the required reserve ratios of the member banks, and virtually determines the discount rate—the interest charged by the Federal Reserve banks on loans to the member banks. In addition, there is a Federal Open Market Committee, consisting of the seven members of the Board and five officials from the Federal Reserve banks, that determines the asset acquisition and disposition policies. (These various powers will be discussed in greater detail later in the chapter, for it is here that their influence over the economy is most significant.) In addition, there are various advisory committees consisting of officials from both the Board and the banks.

Both the Board and the banks have been noteworthy for the high

---

[1] Most of the System's profits are paid over to the United States Treasury as a tax.

intellectual quality of their staffs and the relative freedom from political and other opportunistic pressures. Their position in the economy is
greatly enchanced by the respect in which they are held. This inde-
pendence of judgment is jealously guarded both by the System itself
and its host of supporters throughout the community. Although
founded as late as 1913[2]—the first central bank since the Jacksonian
veto killed the second Bank of the United States in 1836—the expertise
has brought it to a commanding position both in the financial arena of
the United States and among the world's central banks. In particular, because of its size accounting for about one-quarter of the System's assets
the Federal Reserve Bank of New York has usually been looked to for
policy leadership, its president often sharing the number-one position
in public prestige with the chairman of the Board of Governors. The
open-market transactions are made through the New York bank, although the other eleven share in proportion to their relative financial
position within the System.

It should be added that the reason the American central banking
system appears so much more complex than the simpler centralized
organizations prevailing in most other countries is a reflection of both
our size and political heritage. Fear of Wall Street domination led to
the splintering of the system into a dozen components, with a Washington governing body. Decentralization, or shared decisions, also reflected the fear of too much power in one spot, a danger that was
believed to be the drawback of the first and second Banks of the United
States. Our immense diversity of industry and resources is also reflected in the use of districts, each with its own governing body drawn
from personnel familiar with each area. Even fear of banker domination entered into the organization complex, for, as already remarked,
although the System can be of help to the member banks, the latter
have little formal influence on System policies. Yet the presence of so
many centers of power has rarely led to conflict, thanks to both the
coordinating role of the Board of Governors, which is charged with
direct supervision, and the Open Market Committee, the main sector
where both the Board and the banks' representatives confer. While
there have been differences in policy advocated (such would occur
with any large group of willful and intelligent people), what is important is that these differences could always be compromised or subordi-
nated so as not to interfere with an effective execution of decisions.

Although the United States is one of the few countries where the
central bank is still privately owned,[3] this distinction is only a nominal

---

[2] Operations began in November 1914.
[3] Except for the government-appointed Board of Governors.

one. It is unlikely that government ownership would have much impact on the character of the System as long as its organizational diversity continued. It is theoretically possible, for example, for the Secretary of the Treasury and the chairman of the Federal Reserve Board to pursue different policies. But it is very likely that even if the two were separate agencies of the government, they could still oppose each other. It is this independent character, rather than the nominal title to its shares, that has counted in the performance of the central bank. Only a drastic revamping of the power relationships—making the Secretary of the Treasury also the Board Chairman—would alter the position that the System has come to enjoy.

The Discount Mechanism

In the discussion of commercial bank operations, much was made of the importance of the reserve position. Excess reserves, it will be recalled, tended to result in the bank's expanding its asset holdings, whereas inadequate reserves might result in a contraction, either through sale or non-renewal of loans. But the member bank has an alternative method of restoring its reserve position—namely, through borrowing from its Federal Reserve bank. While the specific details vary, depending on the exact procedure adopted, the activity is very similar to that of an individual borrowing from his own bank.

A member bank has two major approaches to obtain additional funds. It can either rediscount some of the notes on which its own loans were based, or borrow, using acceptable assets as collateral. The use of the word *rediscount* arises from the custom of deducting the interest in advance of the loan. For example, if a borrower wanted $1,000 for three months and the bank charged 6 per cent per annum, the end result would be for the note to be repaid in the amount of $1,000, but for the borrower to receive only $985. This latter figure is 1½ per cent less than the note's maturing value, the 1½ per cent representing one-fourth of the annual rate of interest or the fraction of the year for which the loan was made. If, then, the lending bank needed additional reserves, it would take this note and rediscount it at the Federal Reserve. If the rediscount rate were 3 per cent, or ¾ per cent for three months, then the commercial bank would obtain $992.50 if it brought the note in on the same day. If it had waited a month, so that only two months (one-sixth of a year) remained, then it would have received $995 ($1,000 less 1/6 of 3 per cent). In both discounting steps, it is the maturity value that is the basis of the calculations.

In practice, the banks do not rely very much on this approach. A simpler one is to pledge acceptable paper, including government securities, for the amount of its Federal Reserve loan, and the rate charged —the rediscount or discount rate—is then based on the face value of the loan rather than on the face value of each piece of supporting paper. In this way a bank can make one large loan rather than numerous smaller ones. These loans are also known as advances, and the total is reported weekly by each Federal Reserve.

At first glance it might seem that the borrowing bank would decide whether or not to resort to such borrowing by a simple arithmetic calculation. If it borrows, it must pay interest to the Federal Reserve. Its expenses are therefore increased, and its operating profit is correspondingly reduced. Alternatively, it could have disposed of some asset in its portfolio. Sale would mean less income, and again less profit. If this asset had been bringing in an income less than the cost of this loan, the sale would result in less of a decline in operating profit. The converse would be true if the asset yielded more. Expressed more concisely, the bank would borrow if its disposable asset yielded more than the discount rate; it would sell the asset if it yielded less.

But there are other considerations. One is a tradition among American banks to minimize borrowing from the Federal Reserve. If they do borrow, they will often try to pay off the loan as quickly as possible. This feeling is supplemented by very practical reasons. As a member bank borrows, it uses up some of the System's lending powers to help still other member banks. If the banks do not repay these loans quickly, they make it more difficult for others to be accommodated. By minimizing their reliance on this help, they make it that much easier for other banks to be aided. As a consequence, limitations upon the powers of the Federal Reserve to come to the assistance of reserve-short banks are rare.

Another reason for this attitude is associated with the capitalization of the banks. If a bank continually resorts to such borrowing, it is an indication that it continually has insufficient reserves. Hence, rather than relying on such short-term borrowing, it would be more advisable to issue stock—against which there are no required reserves—and the funds obtained from the sale could be added to its reserves and thus end this reliance on "the Fed." If the subscribers should pay out of demand deposits held at the issuing bank, there is still some gain. The bank has less in demand-deposit liabilities, and thus less of a need for required reserves; subscriptions have set free reserves equal to the required reserve ratio kept against the deposits used for payment. Again the bank's reserve position has been improved, although not as markedly as if the stock sale brought in completely new funds.

Practically speaking, the normal resort to the discount mechanism is at the decision of the borrowing bank. The Federal Reserve does not guarantee that it will always lend, or even that it will lend the full amount requested. But because of the restraint shown by the banks, in practice, the mechanism works almost automatically. Banks can always gain reserves if they so desire.

In making the loan, the accounting is similar to the loan procedure discussed earlier. The Federal Reserve adds the amount desired to the balance that the member bank has with it, so that the loan means an increase in Federal Reserve demand liabilities. These balances are counted as member-bank reserves, so the reserve position of the borrowing bank is simultaneously improved.[4] Similarly, when the loan is repaid, the note due the Federal Reserve is cancelled against the balance the borrowing bank is carrying with it. Here both assets and liabilities of the Federal Reserve drop.

In general, we can expect to see an increase in borrowings from the Federal Reserve when the member banks are running short of reserves—for example, when their deposit liabilities are climbing (as a result of loans and other asset acquisitions) at so rapid a pace as to use up all available reserves. Such borrowing could also occur if there is an outflow of cash to the public—a decline in reserves—to such an extent as to threaten to bring the amount remaining below the required ratio. Normally, it is at these two extremes, booming business and extreme depressions shaking confidence in the banks, that these borrowings reach their most active period. The cash flow is also subject to seasonal influences (already discussed), so there may be a similar seasonal movement in borrowings. For example, before Christmas, as cash is withdrawn, the member banks might borrow to offset this drain, and then, when the cash returns after the New Year, the funds received would be employed to repay the Federal Reserve. (Later, the relationship between the member bank's balance at the Federal Reserve and its treatment of cash will be spelled out in greater detail.)

Open-Market Operations

As with the commercial banks, changes in Federal Reserve assets tend to change liabilities in the same direction. This can be seen most obviously if the Federal Reserve buys or sells securities in which the other party is a commercial bank. Purchase of an asset from the commercial bank is paid for through an increase in the selling bank's balance at the Federal Reserve; sale is liquidated through reduction of the

---

[4] In contrast to the required reserves for deposits, the borrowing bank does not have to keep reserves against this obligation. The amount received is thus an addition to total reserves, and equally to excess reserves, since required reserves are unaffected.

member-bank balance. These changes in member-bank balances, of course, are regarded by the member banks as changes in their total reserves, so they react accordingly.

In practice, the Federal Reserve limits its transactions mainly to United States government securities, particularly the Treasury Bills with a life to maturity of only a few months. As the title of this activity implies, transactions are actually made in the open market, just as any buyer and seller would do. The Federal Reserve does not call up its potential customers or source of assets; instead, it contacts the dealers in government securities and places its orders through them. Because of the volume of its orders, it deals directly with the major traders, as would any large insurance company, pension fund, or bank. In placing these orders, the Federal Reserve manages to disguise its intentions sufficiently so that the market at that moment does not get a clue regarding policy objectives. Later, of course, when the data are made public, conclusions can be inferred, but this may not be for days or weeks after the event.

Since the trades are made in this manner, they are in a sense anonymous. The other party to this transaction often is unaware that it is the Federal Reserve on the other side. As a result, the transaction could be with either a member bank or any other large financial organization. Often it may be with a government bond dealer himself; at other times he may merely be the agent bringing the two together. The initiative for these transactions is with the Federal Reserve, unlike member-bank borrowing.

If the transaction is with a member bank, the accounting and banking changes can be established quite simply. An open-market purchase by the Federal Reserve raises its holdings of securities on the asset side and correspondingly increases its liabilities to the selling bank, which in turn has an increase in one asset (reserves at the Federal Reserve) and a decrease in another (the securities sold). The increase in total reserves, without any change in member-bank liabilities, is thus an increase in excess reserves of an equal amount, and so it can now expand its activities if it so desires. A sale by the Federal Reserve to a member bank would have the opposite result. Both the securities on the Federal Reserve's asset side and the liabilities to member banks would decline. For the buying bank, its reserves drop but its securities rise. Since its liabilities are unchanged, the reserve decline is all in the excess-reserve sector, and so the member bank is less free to expand further. In brief, open-market sales tend to restrict the ability of the member banks to expand their activities—loans and asset expansions, as well as the creation of demand deposits—while open-market purchases are expansionary in influence. (The phrase *open-market sales or pur-*

chases, is always understood to refer to the Federal Reserve; its open-market sales are someone else's purchases, of course, and its purchases are someone else's sales.)

Suppose an open-market purchase had been from other than a member bank. Then the seller would receive a check from the Federal Reserve, which would then probably be deposited in his demand-deposit account. Member banks still receive the extra reserves, but now there is an offsetting rise in liabilities. Hence, the rise in excess reserves is less than if the seller were a member bank, since a portion of these added reserves must be kept against the added deposits of the seller. For the Federal Reserve, however, the change in the nature of the seller is of no consequence, for its securities and its liabilities to the member banks have risen, as before.

If an open-market sale had been to other than a member bank, the buyer would pay by drawing a check on his account, which presumably would be kept with a member bank. The check would then be presented by the Federal Reserve for payment, thereby reducing member-bank reserves. But unlike a purchase by a member bank, here demand deposits also drop, thus reducing required reserves. Hence, the drop in excess reserves is somewhat less than the decline in total reserves. Again, the Federal Reserve is unaffected by the change in character of the buyer; both its securities and its liabilities to member banks decline. In brief, open-market transactions with other than member banks have the same general tendency as before, but the magnitude of impact through the change in excess reserves is somewhat less because of the influence on the public's deposits, and thus on required reserves.

The difference regarding the other party to the open-market transaction should not be exaggerated. If we assume that the non-banking buyer or seller drew on or added to his demand deposit with a member bank, then the effect on total member bank reserves is identical with that of a transaction with a member bank. If the member banks then operate with minimum excess reserves, we will have the same impact on demand deposits. To illustrate (assuming a 20 per cent required reserve ratio): (a) The Federal Reserve purchases $1 million in securities from a member bank: member bank reserves go up $1 million, excess reserves go up $1 million, and demand deposits for the banks as a group can now rise $5 million; (b) $1 million purchase from the public: member bank reserves go up $1 million (as before), demand deposits go up $1 million, excess reserves go up $800,000, and an additional rise in demand deposits could total $4 million, for a total rise of $5 million (as before); (c) Sale of $1 million to a member bank: reverse of (a); (d) sale of $1 million to the public: reverse of (b). Note further that in (a) and (b) the banking assets rose by the same amount;

in (a) there was an initial decline of $1 million in securities followed by a rise of $5 million in assets as the excess reserves were utilized, or a net rise of $4 million, while in (b) the $4 million rise resulted from utilizing the $800,000 in excess reserves arising from the inflow of funds from the selling public.

The ability of the Federal Reserve to effect its objectives stands out here. If the member banks did not have much excess reserves, and if the Federal Reserve wanted to curb member-bank activity, it would find it difficult to get a member bank to buy securities, since there would not be enough excess reserves to make payment feasible. It is even possible that the Federal Reserve could not find a bank to buy, no matter how tempting the price at which it offered the securities. But the member banks' customers are in a different position. So long as they have an adequate balance in their checking account, they can be induced to buy the offering by making the price sufficiently attractive. This would draw down total reserves, and excess reserves would also be pulled down, offset somewhat by the freeing of the required reserves against the diminished demand deposits. But the member banks would still suffer mostly in the loss of excess reserves. Not having them, they might now have even a reserve deficiency. This would then force them to borrow from the Federal Reserve. In either, even their lending ability will have been curtailed, although the member banks themselves were not willing to help the open-market operation directly. Thus, the objective will have been attained.

Incidentally, we have made or effected payments through the demand deposits. If it were the time deposits that were affected, the change in required reserves would be that much less, the change in excess reserves that much more. We are also ignoring the possibility that a non-member bank may be involved, since the effects here would vary with the regulations of the fifty state banking laws. In essence, the general impact would be similar to that discussed, especially since many non-member banks do carry balances with member banks as part of their reserves.

Although a matter of secondary importance, it should also be noted that the change in securities held by the respective parties alters their income, the interest on these assets. For the Federal Reserve, an open-market purchase adds to income, but does not add to costs. This is because the member-bank balances do not bear interest. Conversely, a sale reduces income but not expenses. However, the System has almost always—particularly in recent years—earned so much above its operating costs that these effects are ignored.

If a member bank buys or sells, of course, its earnings rise or fall. Its deposits are unchanged, and thus its expenses remain the same. But if it buys, it loses reserves. The added income from the acquired securities is countered by its reduced ability to acquire other income-earning assets. If it sells, it loses income, but acquires free reserves which could then be used to enhance income.

If the public is the buyer, member-bank deposits go up, but not the bank's income-earning assets. If these are time deposits, then the interest expenses payable have also risen. But it has also acquired additional excess reserves and so can add to its income-earning assets. This income boost is, of course, greater if the inflow is to demand deposits; while it must keep higher reserves, thus reducing the rise in excess reserves, it is spared the interest expense as well. The reverse logic rules if the public is the seller.

There are also repercussions on money-market conditions. Not only have we changed the reserve position of the member banks, but, as we shall see, the mere act of buying or selling securities can alter relative money-market rates. This aspect we shall postpone until we examine the ramifications of open-market operations further.

Variable Required Reserve Ratios

The Federal Reserve Board is also empowered to vary the required reserve ratios of the member banks. This range, set by Congress, is between 10 and 22 per cent for demand deposits with reserve city banks, 7 and 14 per cent for demand deposits in country banks, and 3 and 6 per cent on all time deposits. Often the actual ratios remain unchanged for months, sometimes for years.

Since the multiplier effect of reserves is inversely proportionate to the fraction required as backing, increasing the ratio lowers the potential multiplier, and lowering the ratio increases it. A 10-per-cent required ratio, for example, would allow demand deposits of ten times the reserve volume; a 20-per-cent ratio would reduce this to only five times. For any one bank, the incidence of such a change would show up in a different fashion, and its manifestation would vary with the excess-reserve position.

A lowering of the required ratio immediately adds to excess reserves. Total reserves are the same; the amount that must be kept in the required sector is reduced. The difference (excess reserves) is thereby increased. Loans (or other assets) and deposits would still be limited by the amount in excess reserves, but this amount has now been raised. Furthermore, any inflow of funds as a result of other banks' expansionary policies would now affect excess reserves even more. If, the required ratio were 20 per cent, then only 80 per cent of each inflow is added to excess reserves. If the ratio is reduced to 15 per cent, then

85 per cent can be added. A reduction not only adds to excess reserves immediately, but it also adds to the free reserves arising from the spillover activities of the other banks. And these added excess reserves would then permit even greater asset expansion. Reductions in required reserve ratios, therefore, tend to cause expansionary reactions among the banks.

Raising the required ratio, as would be expected, would have the opposite—deflationary—effect. In practice, the increase must be more carefully set out. If, for example, such an increase in required reserves were to bring them above the banks' total reserves, there might ensue such a scramble for liquidity as to precipitate a severe downturn in business activity. Banks might be selling assets and destroying deposits in order to reduce the required reserves to those on hand, thus forcing a severe contraction in the funds available to the public.

As a consequence, increases are aimed generally at soaking up much of the excess reserves. Banks will tend to expand, it will be recalled, when they have excess reserves. But to stop an expansion, we need only eliminate this excess portion. If the banks as a group had 2 per cent in excess reserves, the Board could then raise the required ratio by this figure and end excess reserves for the banking system.

Of course, not all banks would have exactly 2 per cent excess. Some might have more, and thus still be left with some excess reserves, whereas others might find themselves somewhat short. To iron out such individual discrepancies, the latter might borrow from the Federal Reserve to tide them over the adjustment period. During this subsequent period, they could liquidate some assets through sales to the surplus reserve banks or to their customers. This would enable the borrowing banks to repay the Federal Reserve while also draining the remaining excess reserves from the more fortunately situated banks. And, if the Federal Reserve had overshot the mark—if it developed that the rise in required reserves was somewhat more than could be met by this adjusting process—the Reserve could always supplement the banks' actions by buying enough securities in the open market to relieve the strain.

Since the change in ratios affects all banks in the classification, it is obviously impossible to foresee what the impact would be on each bank. Quite a few could be caught short as a result of such an action. This could then result in quite a bit of churning around in the money market as the various deficit banks scramble to offset their strained position, while the surplus banks may or may not be buyers to help them out. It is for this reason that reserve-ratio changes are regarded as a sort of "meat ax" approach, and resort to this control device is therefore relatively infrequent. Its smoothest application comes when excess reserves are so enormous that the probability of any one bank being caught with an insufficient volume of reserves is minimal.

The income effect should also be pointed out. Lowering the reserve ratio means that more of the banks' assets can be used for income-earning; raising the ratio reduces the income-earning proportion. On the other hand, lowered ratios usually occur in depressed times, when the objective is expansion; interest rates are then generally low, so that the increased proportion in income-earning assets tends to be countered by the generally low level of yields on these assets. Conversely, in times when it is desirable to raise the ratios, the reduction in income-earning assets is somewhat countered by their generally higher average-income yield. However, since a member bank can also elect to leave the Federal Reserve System, too great a proportion tied up in non-earning reserves might induce it to resign.[5] Then it could enjoy the high yield and also expand the proportion of assets earning income, since most states require reserves lower than those the Federal Reserve Board stipulates. The more banks that are not members, the less effective are the Federal Reserve activities.

Selective Controls

The Federal Reserve Board has one specific power. This is known as a selective control. It may regulate the credit extended on stock-market transactions. This is an aftermath of the 1929 speculative bubble, fed by easy bank credit. If a stock-market boom threatens to get out of hand, the Board could raise margin requirements—the amount the purchaser must put up. Presumably, by reducing the proportion that could be borrowed, this would lower the over-all demand, and thus put a brake on too hectic a market. Then, if conditions changed and stocks sold off sufficiently, the margin requirement could be reduced, thereby tending to increase aggregate demand for securities. Since the trends in the stock market often parallel similar movements in business activity, it is felt that in such cases control over the course of stock credit would be an additional lever in the ability of the Reserve to influence the economy.

There have been times when the Board had other selective controls—over mortgages and consumer (installment) credit. In general, this reflected the inability of its more broadly based approach to exercise the desired degree of influence. Open-market operations, the

---

[5] National banks are chartered by the Federal Government, and must be members of the Federal Reserve System. If they wish to leave, they must also arrange for a new charter to be issued by the state in which they are domiciled. For a state bank, membership is voluntary.

discount mechanism, and the reserve-ratio powers all influence the volume of bank reserves. This, in turn, affects the banks' lending policies. But it does not necessarily affect the specific areas that are being financed excessively by the banks. Thus, if the Reserve felt that a boom in consumer credit were getting out of hand, it could restrict total bank reserves. But whether this would result in a reduction in loans to consumers, or a reduction in other loans, would be up to the individual member banks. It could be quite possible for the banks to react by cutting back on, say, loans to business, rather than sacrifice the more lucrative installment line. Yet business in general might not have obtained enough funds previously, so that this reduction would only curtail activity in general, rather than just the unhealthy segment. If the Reserve had direct controls over consumer lending, it could restrict this one area without curtailing activity in the other sectors that were still proceeding at a satisfactory rate. The problem of selective, as against more general, controls has many implications for policy, and we shall explore this subject at greater length.

One further point should be touched on. The administrative requirements of selective controls are much greater than with general controls. Each broker, or each finance company, or almost every lender may come within the scope of this power. The number of organizations that must be policed is enormous when compared with the number of the member banks that would otherwise be of concern to the Reserve. There would be a need for a much larger staff to check on enforcement of its regulations. And with the proliferation of outlets would grow the ease of evasion. The integrity of the Board itself might be called into question, as the successful evaders were regarded as those having some "insider" influence. This, in turn, would impinge on the Board's position of impartiality, and call into question the very merits of its authority.

Moral Suasion

A less definable power of the Federal Reserve is moral suasion, or rule by the mouth. In speeches and reports, the System can express opinions about actions it would like to see done by the member banks and other organizations, or tendencies it feels are contrary to sound economic activity. Because of its prestige, it is felt that such statements have an influence, although just how great is difficult to judge. Critics charge that this so-called "jawbone technique" is completely ineffective, since there are no powers accompanying it for enforcement. Coupling such appeals with use of the other powers, such as open-market operations, they feel is unnecessary, for the only effects will be those arising from the securities operations, and so the additional impact of moral suasion would be nil. In a way these critics reflect the traditional feeling of most central bankers that the central bank should not explain its actions, but should merely act, cloaking its intentions with a thick veil of secrecy. On the other hand, public statements reflecting System thinking could be taken as first steps to later actions; thus the forewarning might be sufficiently corrective. If it felt that bank lending was expanding too rapidly, the Board could so indicate through its Board members' speeches. If enough of the major banks took the hint, they would slow down their activity and the objective would be accomplished. If not, the Board could then follow up more forcefully by engaging in open-market sales and perhaps increasing the discount rate. And knowing that such positive actions might be the outcome anyway, the banks, in anticipation, would cut back and avoid the necessity for the later decisions to intervene.

The System's Check-Clearing Operations

Since the member banks hold reserve balances with their respective Federal Reserve banks, this also facilitates check clearing. Each member bank forwards checks received from its customers which have been drawn on other member banks,[6] in effect depositing them in their accounts at the Federal Reserve. If the paying bank is in the same district, the Federal Reserve then reduces that bank's balance. If the bank is in another district, checks are then forwarded to the Federal Reserve bank for that area. The latter then charges the appropriate accounts. The over-all change in Federal Reserve liabilities is unaffected, since the checks credited to the receiving banks, which increase their balances, equal the checks charged the paying banks, which decrease their balances. However, there is a temporary imbalance because of the time consumed in clearing, a factor which gives rise to "float."

There is also an inter-Federal Reserve payment where checks are received that are drawn on banks in other districts. The district whose banks received the checks has increased its liabilities to these banks, while the district containing the banks on which the checks were drawn has a drop in its liabilities. To balance the accounts, the latter district then transfers funds to the former through the Interdistrict Settlement Fund maintained in Washington, D.C. These are gold certif-

---

[6] Some non-member banks maintain accounts with the Federal Reserve to participate in this operation. But not all checks are so cleared; in New York City local banks maintain their own clearing mechanism. Net balances, however, are settled by checks drawn on their Federal Reserve accounts.

icates (the reserves of the Federal Reserve banks) and are the offsetting assets that move to maintain a balance. Note that here the system is unaffected, for the loss by one bank just equals the gain by the other. In practice, such transfers are the net of balances due other Federal Reserve banks because of checks drawn on the district member banks and balances due from other Federal Reserve banks because of checks received payable by out-of-district member banks.

This clearing mechanism also reflects the repercussions of member-bank loans (or other asset activity). It will be recalled that a typical loan resulted in checks being drawn by the borrower, which were then deposited by the payee in his bank. These checks would be presented for payment, and the original bank's reserves would decline. The receiving bank would gain the reserves. In practice, what would have happened in a more typical case would have been, first, a deposit of the check by the receiving bank in its Federal Reserve account, thus gaining reserves, and second, through the clearing process a decline in the balance of the paying bank.

The clearing mechanism is also a great time-saver. Instead of the receiving bank being required to go to each bank whose checks it has received—which may amount to thousands for large city banks—it need only bundle them together and send them on to the Reserve. The Reserve staff then sorts them, bundling the out-of-district bank checks similarly. Then each district can sort the incoming checks by paying banks, and so the path ends. Otherwise there would be costly messenger service with possibilities of loss and theft, as each bank maintained a staff of runners to bring the numerous checks to the thousands of banks scattered over the country.

Currency Issues

Virtually all currency in the United States is issued by the Federal Reserve. This will become increasingly so as the silver certificates are replaced by the Federal Reserve's currency. But even before this change (1963) the Federal Reserve notes accounted for more than 80 per cent of the currency in circulation.

Usually Federal Reserve currency (called "notes") comes into existence when a member bank has need for it. In general, this reflects the demands of its depositors. If the member bank has been experiencing too many net withdrawals, it will simply call on the Federal Reserve Bank for currency. The Bank will issue to the member bank the amount requested, charging that bank's balance. At this point there is no change in the member bank's assets or reserves, the drop in its Federal Reserve balance being just equal to the rise in vault cash. (If the vault cash is subsequently paid out, then reserves *are* affected.) Similarly, the Federal Reserve liabilities are unaffected, the rise in currency outstanding being exactly balanced by the decline in liabilities to member banks. The reserve position of even the Federal Reserve is unchanged, although the legal requirements against these two liabilities are in the process of being altered.

The volume of currency declines when we have a reversal of the former drain. As depositors bring cash to the member banks, the vault cash begins to swell to excessive amounts. (At this point, member-bank reserves are rising, too.) The excess would then be deposited with the Federal Reserve. Here again there is no further change in member-bank reserves; the rise in its balance with the Reserve is just equal to the decline in its vault cash. And the total liabilities of the Reserve remain the same, the drop in outstanding currency matching exactly the rise in liabilities to member banks.

The Federal Reserve has kept gold certificates as reserves equal to at least 25 per cent of its demand liabilities—balances due member banks and other depositors as well as currency outstanding. We shall examine this component later.

Other Federal Reserve Functions

Two other operations of the Federal Reserve should be added here. One is its role as United States government fiscal agent. This means that the government carries its checking accounts with the Federal Reserve, making its disbursements from such balances. The government also carries balances with the commercial banks, but only temporarily (see Chapter 17). In addition, the Reserve handles new issues and redemptions of government securities, and even certain special loan programs enacted by Congress. This last is usually of an emergency nature, such as special war-financing programs. Certain of these functions are also performed for foreign and international agencies.

The Federal Reserve is also a research and information center. Each of the banks, as well as the Board, issues monthly publications and special studies. These may be comments on current developments, analyses of trends, descriptions of various sectors of the financial community—in short, anything of interest to the monetary economist. Valuable statistical series are also collected and published. Some of these are basic for any analysis of the economy. The Board has pioneered new fields of information. Among the more notable statements issued is the weekly condition statement, the importance of which is so great that we devote an entire chapter to it. But these publications are not limited to the banking sector. The Board's Index of Industrial Production is often looked to as the guide to economic and business trends, while its position as banker for both the government and foreign agencies makes it a significant factor in balance-of-payments work. Backed by research staffs of the highest caliber, the Board has earned for itself a reputation that any university might well emulate.

Summary

Commercial banks can look on the Federal Reserve System in somewhat the same way as individuals regard their commercial banks. Asset acquisitions by the Federal Reserve expand member-bank reserves, and sales draw down reserves. Member banks can borrow from the Reserve, thereby adding to their reserves, and loan repayments draw down reserves. Thus, reserves of the commercial banks can be changed at the initiative of either of the two banking groups. The major difference is motivation; unlike the commercial banks, profit enhancement is a minor consideration, public policy the major one. In addition, the Federal Reserve can alter the required reserve ratios, thereby varying the deposit multiple per dollar of reserves, as well as the amount of income-earning assets the commercial banks may have. In another category is the Reserves' selective controls, now limited to stock-market credit.

The Reserve also has other functions, such as check clearing, acting as fiscal agent for the Treasury, and currency issues, and performs various other tasks for non-member and foreign banks, and handles a few emergency loan programs. In all these areas the Federal Reserve has earned a reputation of impartiality and competency which has given it a prestige that few government agencies anywhere in the world can equal.

Chapter II

VELOCITY

So far, most of our attention has centered on the money supply. This includes the money in circulation—currency and coins—plus demand (or checking) accounts. We have also noted the influence of time (savings) deposits. In this chapter we shall focus on the activity of the money supply. Combined, they will explain the so-called money equation.

Velocity and Idle Balances

In our earlier discussion of the reasons for carrying a cash balance (Chapter 4), it was pointed out that essentially money can have two phases—either it is idle, or it is being spent. Upon this elementary fact economists have constructed two types of equations for use in monetary analyses: the Fisher, or quantity, equation, which emphasizes the points at which money is being spent; and the Cambridge, or cash-balance, equation, which centers its attention on the idle periods. As we shall see, the two are reacting to the same phenomena from somewhat different points of view, but together these differences help us to understand the money system much better.

Each time money is spent, it changes hands; the spender has a smaller balance, while the recipient enlarges his cash balance. Each disbursement thus allows the receiver to spend more. If during a period of time—say, a month—the frequency with which money is spent speeds up, the frequency with which the recipients gain increases in their balances also speeds up. This, in turn, allows them to spend more rapidly, and so the volume of spending during the month is greater than if the rate at which spending took place were somewhat slower.

To illustrate this (Table IV), we shall take several hypothetical months. At the beginning of the first month we shall assume that the opening balance is the amount that each depositor aims to maintain. If his balance falls below this amount, he will cut back his spending; if it rises above the level, he will step up his spending. The former curtailment, it is hoped, will enable him to rebuild his balance; the latter action eliminates the excess part of his balance. Only A is an exception; in the first month we shall assume that his balance is $20 more than he desires, which explains the initial transaction. To simplify the arithmetic, we shall also assume that our entire community consists of four individuals, and that all transactions are limited exclusively to these four. Our month will have only four weeks.

In stage one the total money supply starts with $300, distributed as indicated. In this stage we shall assume that each adjustment is made a week after the disturbance. That is, A, wishing to reduce his balance to the desired level of $60, spends $20 at the start of the month, buying from B. B's balance now rises to $140, $20 more than he wants. His reaction takes places a week later; in this case he buys $20 from C. C, in turn, reacts a week later, and also spends $20, to restore his balance to the opening (desired) $60. This gives an excess balance to D, who a week later buys $20 from A.

Note that each week the total money supply remained at $300, although its distribution was changing. The volume of transactions effected during the month was $80. One way to measure velocity is to divide this turnover by the money supply (80/300 equals 4/15).

In the second month we slowed down the rate of reaction to two weeks between the change in the cash balance and the spending response. Note that the second and third months duplicate the first month, but the time period is twice as long. In other words, the longer the period between expenditures, the less the total spending in any given period. Here, a doubling of the dormant intervals meant that the monthly spending was reduced by half (the reciprocal of the doubling

TABLE IV

Velocity

(*Italicized figures indicate those affected by week's transactions*)

I. The First Month. One Transaction a Week. *A* Wishes to Bring Balance to $60.

	1ST	8TH	15TH	22ND	29TH—1ST
A	80	*60*	60	60	*80*
B	120	*140*	*120*	120	120
C	60	60	*80*	*60*	60
D	40	40	40	*60*	*40*
TOTAL	300	300	300	300	300

Transactions: $80. Velocity: 80/300 = 4/15.

II. The Second Month. One Transaction Every Two Weeks.

	1ST	15TH	29TH—1ST
A	80	*60*	60
B	120	*140*	*120*
C	60	60	*80*
D	40	40	40
TOTAL	300	300	300

Transactions: $40. Velocity: 40/300 = 2/15.

III. The Third Month. II Continued.

	1ST	15TH	29TH—1ST
A	60	60	*80*
B	120	120	120
C	80	*60*	60
D	40	*60*	*40*
TOTAL	300	300	300

Transactions: $40. Velocity: 40/300 = 2/15.

IV. The Fourth Month. *A* Decides to Raise Desired Balance to $64.

	1ST	8TH	15TH	22ND	29TH—1ST
A	80	*64*	64	64	*80*
B	120	*136*	*120*	120	120
C	60	60	76	*60*	60
D	40	40	40	*56*	*40*
TOTAL	300	300	300	300	300

Transactions: $64. Velocity: 64/300 = 16/75.

V. The Fifth Month. All Wish to Raise the Desired Balance by $4 Each.

	1ST	8TH	15TH	22ND	29TH—1ST
A	80	*64*	64	64	*68*
B	120	*136*	*124*	124	124
C	60	60	72	*64*	64
D	40	40	40	*48*	*44*
TOTAL	300	300	300	300	300

Transactions: $40. Velocity: 40/300 = 2/15.

VI. The Sixth Month. All Wish to Carry Lower Balances, Equal to Original Objectives.

A	68	*60*	*60*	60	*80*
B	124	*132*	*120*	120	120
C	64	64	*76*	*60*	60
D	44	44	*44*	*60*	*40*
TOTAL	300	300	300	300	300

Transactions: $56. Velocity: 56/300 = 14/75.

VII. The Seventh Month. *A* Decides to Hold on To All His Money.

A	80	80	80	80	80
B	120	120	120	120	120
C	60	60	60	60	60
D	40	40	40	40	40
TOTAL	300	300	300	300	300

Transactions: 0. Velocity: 0.

in length of interval). As a consequence, the monthly velocity is only 2/15, compared with 4/15 in the previous example.

This example also may help to clear up one of the confusions associated with velocity. Despite the fact that each person spent the same amount as before, the rate at which he was spending his money altered (slowed down) and thus affected the general level of economic activity. Sales declined by 50 per cent as compared with the first month. In any given period of time, only half as much in goods and services was bought, and presumably only half as much would be produced. Hence, employment and activity is half as much. In effect, by slowing down the rate at which money is respent, we reduce the number of transactions that occur in any one period. That is, in the second month *C* and *D* did not spend, as they had in the first month, and in the third month *A* and *B* were eliminated, because of the slower pace of activity. To see what would happen if the rate sped up, we need only go back to the first month; reducing the interval by half, from two weeks to one, results in a doubling (the reciprocal) of the aggregate monthly spending.

In the fourth month we illustrate another possibility. Here *A* decides that he would prefer a somewhat higher balance—$64, instead of $60. To achieve this, he must spend $16, or $4 less. But if he does, then *B* sells less to him, and since *B's* cash balance now rises less than before, his spending must be correspondingly reduced if he wishes to keep the same balance of $120. If he spent at the same rate as previously ($20), then his balance would be only $116, less than he desired. Hence, as a result of *A's* trying to achieve a greater balance, *B* either must reduce his spending or be content with a smaller balance. This, in turn, affects C, who then reduces his purchases from D, and D, in turn, then cuts back his purchases from A. All incomes decline.

What we have illustrated is that attempts on the part of any one individual to raise his cash balance can come only at the expense of other people's balances, so long as the total money supply is unchanged (here, $300). They, in turn, must either reduce spending or be satisfied with lower balances, thus resulting in a redistribution of the existing supply in favor of those who started the chain. Assuming that each tries to maintain the same balance as before—as is done in the fourth month—then the only result is a cut in spending. In the fifth month we have repeated this same effort, except that now each one is trying to build up his balance. The result, as would be expected, is an even more intense deflation. In the fourth month spending dropped to $64, or four-fifths, as compared with the first month (velocity is down to $16/75$). In the fifth month each is attempting to raise his balance by a small amount: A, for example, now wishes only $64, as before, but B, C, and D also desire to raise their balances by $4. Hence, each must reduce his spending, to offset the decline in sales as a result of the previous person's effort to build up cash balances and also to enable his own cash balance to rise. Thus B, for example, cut his spending by $8—$4 to offset the reduction in sales to A, and $4 to help raise his own balance. But this, in turn, reduces the balance of the next recipient even more. He must then take even more drastic steps to achieve his objective. We thus get increasingly severe cuts, until A sells only $4 to D, as compared with the $20 in the first month. Note that the drop in sales and velocity is even more than in the fourth month.

What would probably put an end to this continued cutting of spending would be the associated declines in activity and incomes. As each sells less, his income is reduced, and so there is less desire to keep higher cash balances. More likely, to offset the income decline, the various individuals would try to maintain living standards by using up some of these balances. In our sixth month, for example, A now decides that the decline in his income from $20 to $4 is too severe; to supplement this, he decides to spend an additional $8 from his balance, reducing it to $60. But if he does this, he steps up B's income. Perhaps before, B also reacted as A did, and decided to supplement his reduced income with spending out of his cash balance; B, in other words, now also decides to reduce his average balance. Similarly for C and D. The reverse now occurs. As each decides to reduce his balance, he spends more. But as he spends more, others obtain more funds. If they, too, are trying to reduce their balances, their spending is increased correspondingly, and so the revival of incomes becomes even more intense. Note how both income and velocity in the sixth month are now greater than in the fifth, just as the desire for raising their balances in the fifth month reduced spending and velocity drastically.

In the seventh month we have illustrated an even more drastic possibility. *A* decides to hold on to his money, to hoard. This means that he does not spend any of his balance. Then *B*'s sales drop to zero. *B* in turn then decides to cut back his spending, since he has no need for more raw materials and labor, having no need for further production. *C* now has zero sales. He, in turn, cuts back, hurting *D*. And *D*'s cutback now reacts back on *A*.

The fourth, fifth, and seventh months show us different aspects of the same problem. Whether we call it hoarding, as in the seventh month, or saving, as in the other months, the objective was to maintain a higher balance. If we reduce our spending relative to income, we presumably are saving the difference. But what really results is that the boost to savings results in a reduction of receipts—income—by the others in the community. If they react similarly, cutting their spending to offset the decline in their receipts, we then get a general deflation which often reacts back on the incomes of those whose efforts are the cause of the downturn. In brief, an effort to increase savings with a constant money supply means only a deflation of incomes; the economy is slowed down—conversely, of course, for the decision to spend more, as in the sixth month.

More precisely, what has been happening is a decision in those selected months to vary the amount of savings kept in liquid form. Had *A*, for example, decided to save $4 more in the fourth month, but then loaned it to *E* (a new business undertaking), then *E* could spend $4 more, thereby offsetting the deflationary impact of *A*'s reduction in spending. Note that *A* would still carry the same balance ($60), only now he would have *E*'s bond or IOU for $4. *A* would have more assets than before, but not more money. It was the decision to save and to keep it in liquid form—money (here, checking-account balances)— that caused the decline to spread throughout the economy. Hence, we can say that any attempt to increase liquidity where the available total is unchanged will only result in a slowing down in activity and a decline in incomes. The reverse, of course, would hold when people decided to give up some of their liquidity.

In each example the aggregate money supply—checking-account balances—stayed at $300. As far as the banks were concerned, the variations in the monthly spending rates had no effect on their aggregate positions. Demand deposits remained the same. If, for example, the banks' required reserves were at the minimum, so that there were no excess reserves, then the various declines in spending could not be offset through increases in the money supply. The banks were helpless to counteract the deflationary forces unless somehow or other they obtained additional reserves, for example, through the Federal Reserve.

The decision to reduce spending—to save (or hoard) more—did not put more money in the banks, and so did not add to their reserves. All that happened was a change in the rate at which the existing volume of checking accounts changed hands. A's decision to save $4 in the fourth month, and so build up his balance by that amount, did not add $4 to the banks' reserves. All it did was to reduce B's balance by $4 as compared to what it would have been otherwise. Similarly for the various efforts to build balances in the fifth month.

We also have here the answer to a question that is very common in a recession. As incomes drop, people are puzzled as to where the money went. If we compare the first month with the second, third, fourth, fifth, sixth, or seventh, we see that in each of these later months there has been a decline in incomes, spending, and activity. Where did the money go? Obviously, it did not go anywhere, for there is still $300 in our hypothetical community. What has been happening is a slowing down in the rate at which this money is being spent. And each decline in spending means a decline in the would-be seller's income. He, in turn, cuts back on spending, and so, perhaps, spends less on raw materials, labor or other people's output. Each spending is someone's receipt; each reduction in spending reduces someone's receipt. In brief, much of the phenomena of a recession can be summarized quite simply by noting that it is the velocity decline that is so evident in such a period. This is most true if the recession is severe, such as we experienced from 1929 to 1933. Incidentally, the shrinkage in velocity may be reinforced by a shrinkage in the money supply as well. Banks may become more cautious and not renew loans—or else make few new ones—in the same volume as the maturities. In such a case, the deflationary consequences of the velocity drop are reinforced by the absolute decline in the money supply. But this added factor is not necessary to precipitate a downturn; all we must do is either slow down the rate at which money is being spent—as in the second and third months of our examples—or have a sufficiently widespread attempt to build up liquid balances, as in the fourth, fifth, and seventh months. Expansions would be the reverse of these movements.

It should also be noted that a velocity greater than one is possible. For example, if the first month's operations were repeated each month, D will have received and spent $60 in a quarter of a year. For that period his account's velocity would be greater than one; his spending during the three months would exceed his average balance. He would be able to do this because he is constantly replenishing his balance. But the outcome is what many observers at first glance view as a paradox—

the ability to spend more than is in the account. Obviously, if his receipts were zero, then he could spend no more than his beginning balance. But with the continual influx of new funds, he is able to maintain a higher rate of activity, and so "turn over" his money quite rapidly. His average balance per month is $40 for the first three weeks and $60 for the fourth week, or $45. His monthly velocity is 20/45, or 4/9, and his quarterly velocity is 60/45, or 1⅓. For the United States, the per-annum average velocity exceeds 25, even if we exclude the very active accounts carried in major financial centers.

Turnover and Economic Activity

The measurement of velocity, or the turnover of money, is limited to demand deposits, for it is virtually impossible to discover how active the currency portion of our money supply is. However, since most payments are made by check, this omission is not as serious as it sounds for the American economy. In the less developed areas, where checks are still a minor method of payment, such an omission is correspondingly more significant.

The most common measurement is to divide the value of checks drawn during the period by the average balance during *that* period, such as we did in the preceding section. But in practice this is a far from accurate measurement of our objective. If, for example, *A* draws a $50 check in order to get cash, the action registers in exactly the same way as if he drew a check of a similar amount to make a purchase. Yet clearly, it is of little economic consequence if *A* changes his money from one form (demand deposits) to another form (currency), other than the fact that it is drawn out of the bank, and thus depletes reserves. But so far as its impact on economic activity is concerned, there is little of interest in the check-cashing operation. Indeed, *A* might not even cash the check at a bank; often the neighborhood retailers are only too glad to accommodate customers, since they often carry more cash in their tills then they have need for, especially on busy shopping days and evenings.

Somewhat the same logic applies to the economic significance of payments for the transfer of existing titles to property, such as stocks and bonds. If *A* buys 100 shares of General Motors for $7,000, his checking account shows quite a bit of activity. But if the seller simply deposits the proceeds in his checking account, aggregate bank deposits are unaffected, and even reserves are unchanged. There might be some effect if the two banks are in different reserve classifications. Also, a small amount will be diverted to the brokers as commissions. But nothing has really happened to the underlying economic forces. One man has 100 shares less of General Motors and more of a balance in his deposit account; another man has a smaller deposit balance, but now owns 100 shares more of the stock. Taking the community as a whole, there are just as many shares of stock around, just as much in deposits —especially if we assume the funds came from and went into checking accounts carried with banks in the same reserve classification—and the banks have a few more entries to make. Paper has been shuffled around, but that is about all.

On the other hand, if *A* bought $7,000 of a new issue, the company then using these funds to purchase equipment, there is a significant impact on the economy. Actually, this is taken care of in the second stage, when the issuing corporation disburses the funds. That is the stage at which the flow of commodities is affected. Hence, although there is this subsequent repercussion, which makes such a security purchase different from our General Motors illustration, the spending figures covering the corporation account will take this into consideration. This economic effect shows up twice—in *A's* account when he buys the new issue, and in the corporation's account when it buys the equipment.

This emphasis on the security transfers should not be interpreted as a straining at gnats. In the United States, from one-third to one-half of all check payments are for such shifting about of paper. Often this shifting is duplicated. The stock buyer's account reflects his payment to the broker. Then his broker's account reflects the payment to the selling broker. The selling broker's account then reflects the final payment to the stock seller. One transfer has affected deposit turnover three times. When we realize that the New York Stock Exchange often accounts for more than $2 billion weekly in transactions of stocks alone, we can see what enormous payments are made that are really repeat performances of little economic impact.

Of real concern to us are those transactions that *do* implement the economic process. These are primarily payments for goods and services, either for final consumption or for the financing of production. Here there is a tangible transfer in return for the funds flow. Each payment gives rise to a demand for materials or services—in effect, employment. As these payments rise, incomes and jobs increase; as these payments decline, we get the reverse effect. It is true that variations in financial activity may induce people to vary their spending habits, but it is the flow of goods and services that is the measurement of economic activity. Ideally, therefore, we should exclude all those checks that are used for other than the purchase of goods and services. In practice this is impossible. So, as a compromise, we separate the activity of the major financial centers, whose turnover figures are dominated by these strictly financial operations, from the other cities where such operations are of less influence. Even in New York, some of the checking accounts are used to buy goods and services! And many a small town has its stock and bond buyers whose actions help confuse the turnover data. But given the available information, this is the most feasible compromise possible.

For many purposes, analysts also wish to distinguish payments for goods and services to be used for further production from those that are for final consumption. Here, too, the problem of double-counting enters. If, for example, consumers buy bread, this represents only the last stage in a stream of payments—to the baker for bread, to bakery labor, to the flour producer, and so on. For example, if *B* pays 30 cents for bread, the baker may use 10 cents for his laborers' pay and 20 cents for flour. The miller, in turn, may spend 5 cents for his laborers' pay and 15 cents to the grain dealer. The latter, in turn, may spend 5 cents on transportation and 10 cents for the wheat itself. Even in this example, as can be seen, gross payments amounted to almost $1 in order that less than one-third of that amount would be added to actual consumption. Hence, if we wish to concentrate on the actual income of the community and the uses to which it is put, we would have to limit our attention to those payments that are for consumption, or final use—here, the bread buyer. But, of course, no such data are available. The usual compromise is to resort to the national income accounts and infer from those statistics what we cannot arrive at directly.

Part of the reason for this further distinction arises from differences in the chain of production. A wholly integrated operation might effect the various transfers by entries on the corporate books for the different departments without any actual passing of money. If, for example, a giant retail establishment had its own captive farms and flour mills, it might have paid out only 10 cents to its wheat farmers, 5 cents for transportation, 5 cents for its flour mill employees, and 10 cents for its retail operations. The same operation now affects the money supply in a much smaller degree. Hence, such variations must be corrected, and it is partly to eliminate such factors that this "final use" approach is employed. In effect, we are measuring the income velocity of money rather than its over-all velocity, and thus we eliminate the financial transactions and the effects of double-counting.

The Impact of Velocity

The economic significance of the statistical problem just discussed can perhaps best be illustrated by a study of the impact on the system's operations. What is of importance is the effect on the output of goods and services, which, in turn, represents the reactions of employment, income, and ultimately profits or losses. In a broadly general way, we can say that the usual chain of decisions runs from sales to production rates to employment and the demand for raw materials. Another chain may run from rising sales to investment decisions to capital installations and then to employment and materials ordering. The rate of sales, in other words, is a prime determinant in the decision-making process. Consequently, those actions that result in sales become of primary interest to the analysts concentrating on business activity. It is for this reason that the strictly financial transfers are of only secondary interest. At best, they reflect only the accompanying stage of an investment decision, such as the illustration already used of a new capital issue. While this issue is a financial transaction, it is also an indicator of investment intentions, and so, at first glance, should be included. Note that this type of financial exchange differs from the purchase of an already outstanding security issue. But, as we have remarked, such a new issue will show up again in our velocity reaction, for the funds received from the new issue will be spent to purchase the actual capital goods to be added to the company's stock of equipment. If the new issue is to repay temporary financing that had been used initially to acquire the equipment, then the steps in the procedure would be the reverse; first there was the spending of these temporarily borrowed funds to acquire the capital goods, then the new issue to repay the loan.

If we limit our velocity study to those purchases of only goods or services, we can see why the velocity index is significant. As it rises, the money supply is being used more frequently in a given period of time. This means that business activity is increasing, as evidenced by the rising flow of funds for goods and services. As the index declines, a given amount of money is being spent less often, and the volume of business activity will tend to decline. This is not the whole story for we can also vary the amount of money. We shall study this later in our discussion of the quantity and cash-balance equations.

The velocity series *do* show movements which are quite similar to the major changes in business activity. This is not surprising, since the change in the cycle is an evidence of a change in aggregate spending. But the inference—that a good deal of the cyclical swings can be attributed to these changes in velocity—is less clear. For example, in the 1957–58 recession, velocity dropped some 5 per cent; this pulled down the volume of transactions, and so the economy in general experienced a downturn.

On the other hand, the longer-run movement in velocity has been showing an upward tendency since the end of the 1930's. People are managing their checking accounts more carefully, and so carrying on a greater volume of business and spending relative to the amount normally carried in their accounts. This upward drift has been particularly marked by the behavior of corporate deposits. Not only are these accounts more active than those of consumers—the average corporate dollar does four times as much work as the consumer's dollar—but the rate at which activity has been increasing is sharper than for the consumer's checking accounts. For example, in 1952, the ratio of quarterly spending to the average checking-account balance was four times as high for corporate accounts as for consumers' accounts. A decade later it was almost five times as active. During the period each sector had shown a rise in the ratio of spending to average balances—the consumer accounts by about one-third, the corporate accounts by one-half. Even if there had been no change in the total volume of checking accounts, the movement upward in the rate of use would have added more than 40 per cent to the total amount being spent. The actual amount spent changed somewhat more because of an accompanying rise in the total volume of checking-account money; this total rose 15 per cent. Expressed differently, during the decade the volume of transactions rose more than 50 per cent; more than two-thirds of this rise was attributable to the rising velocity of both corporate and consumer checking accounts. In fact, in some of the quarterly periods, the total volume of transactions rose despite a drop in average balances, the rising velocity more than offsetting this opposite movement.

Pressures on the Balance Management

Increasingly over the past few years, corporate financial officers in particular have been paying increasing attention to the management of their balances with an eye to improving the efficiency of utilization. Checking-account balances, it will be recalled, earn no interest. To the extent that a given volume of checks can be handled with a smaller balance, less funds need be tied up in a non-income-earning form. Freeing a part of the balance could raise income directly, by enabling the company to either purchase an income-earning security, or reduce borrowings and thus lessen the interest cost. Either way, such freeing will help to raise net income.

Response to such considerations becomes more intense in periods of high money market rates, for it is at such times that the cost of idle funds becomes most obvious, as the magnitude of foregone incomes rises. In addition, since such periods are normally associated with an active business climate, these are the times when demands on corporate funds are most intense. With a high rate of operations, there are all sorts of additional uses for this money. Sales are rising, and with this goes a rise in credit extended to customers. The increase in output to service these additional sales is causing a cash drain to pay for the added wages and raw materials, but the sale on credit is slowing down the receipt of cash. A corporation that can free some of its money from its checking account could more easily bridge this gap and thereby minimize the need to borrow.

Also associated with such periods of active business is the general tendency to expand capacity. More money is spent for new equipment and its installation, and again, to the extent that some of this drain can be met through a more economical use of the bank balance, the funds problem is reduced.

Actually, this drive to economize on the checking-account balance is more than just the consideration of additional income or savings on borrowed funds. When corporations borrow, they do more than just add to their interest-bearing commitments. They also reduce their future capacity to borrow. Many concerns have definite credit ratings in the eyes of the would-be lenders. This rating limits the amount a borrower can obtain. Even if it were willing to pay interest on amounts in excess of this limit, it would find that the supply is not forthcoming. A reduction in the average balance thus actually adds to the total amount of funds at the corporation's command. It has the amount that its credit rating permits. As an addition, it has as much as it can free from its bank accounts. Thus, the value of this money that is set free is the extra profit the corporation can earn as a result of the greater rate of operations permitted by these additional funds. If, for example, these funds can be put into a 15-per-cent profit opportunity, then the contribution is this 15 per cent—not the smaller rate saved on borrowed funds, because this latter amount might not have been obtainable. As a consequence, the incentive to economize grows with the increase in these alternative uses for additional money.

The effect can be easily summarized. A given volume of checks through better planning can now be serviced by a smaller balance. By more intelligent spacing of receipts and/or payments, the danger of an inadequate balance can be avoided, even though it is smaller than before. The velocity index shows a corresponding rise: the denominator (average balance) has declined, while the numerator (checks drawn) has remained the same. It is no surprise, therefore, to see a long-run rise in velocity since World War II, accompanying the rising profits opportunities for American industry, and a cyclical aspect—that is, the rise being more intense in high-prosperity and high-profit-and-interest periods, but less intense in recession or low-profits-and-interest periods. (Note that for the banks there is a rise in costs per dollar of deposits—

more transfers and so more expenses.) The demand for corporate cash balances, in other words, has not been increasing in proportion to the rise in the volume of corporate transactions.

While the details of such improved management of the corporate cash balance are beyond the scope of this text, some indication of the method by which this is carried out may be helpful. Suppose our corporation receives daily $1,000. Suppose each month it must pay $8,000 in wages ($2,000 every week), $10,000, for raw materials, and $2,000, for all other expenses. We shall assume a five-day week and a four-week month. Then, over the month it takes in $20,000 and pays out $20,000, so that its month-end balance is the same as its opening figure.

If it pays all its non-wage expenses on the first of the month, then it must have an opening balance of $12,000, plus some additional margin for error—say, $1,000—or a starting figure of $13,000. Its first day's payments draw this down to $1,000. During the first week, this rises to $6,000 as a result of receipts. At the end of the week it drops to $4,000 because of wage payments. During the second week it rises to $9,000, dropping at the end of the week to $7,000. The third week sees a rise to $12,000 and then a drop to $10,000. In the fourth week this balance then goes to $15,000, ending at $13,000—the same as the balance at the start of the month.

Suppose, however, that by a better scheduling of purchases, the raw materials can be paid for at the end of each week—$2,500 per payment. Suppose further that the other expenses can be postponed to the end of the second week. We shall assume that the minimum balance allowed is still $1,000. If we start with a balance as low as $2,000, then during the first week the receipts raise the balance to $7,000; but this is drawn down to $2,500 as a result of wage payments of $2,000 and raw-materials purchases of $2,500. The balance rises to $7,500 the second week, but then drops by $2,000 for wages, $2,500 for raw materials, and $2,000 for other expenses, to a net of $1,000. During the third and fourth weeks, $5,000 is received in each for sales, $4,500 is paid out for wages and raw materials, so that the balance rises to $1,500 at the end of the third week and to $2,000 at the end of the fourth week, or again the same as the opening balance.

What has been accomplished by these shifts? For one thing, we can now free $11,000 from our cash balance. Even if this earns no more than 6 per cent per annum, we have added $660 to income. In addition, we have continued to operate without endangering our solvency. In both illustrations the balance never dropped *below* $1,000, but in both there was a point at which it dipped that low. What has been avoided is the long period during which the balance was far in excess of our needs, such as we had in the first example. Assuming that the cost of better planning is not too great, the additional contribution to profit then becomes a meaningful sum.

Implicit in this economizing reaction is a weakening in the ability of the Federal Reserve to control business activity. When the economy threatens to expand at too great a rate, so that either inflation or an adverse balance of payments may result, the Federal Reserve tends to restrict bank lending through pressure on reserves—through open-market sales. At such times banks react in two ways: interest rates are raised to choke off some of the demand for funds, and in addition many borrowers are allowed less than they would have been able to obtain before the restrictive policy. Such an outcome is likely to intensify the corporate efforts to economize on the amounts carried in checking-account balances. Every dollar saved reduces interest costs, and this element has increased. And every dollar saved can be used as an offset to the reduced amounts now available from bank loans. This double incentive thus heightens the efforts to economize, and as a result we see sharp rises in corporate-account velocities during such tight-money periods. As a consequence, to the extent that these efforts succeed, the efforts of the Federal Reserve to apply a brake on corporate activity have failed. All that has happened is that better cash planning has been resorted to, and thus tightening of the available money supply is minimized. In practice, the corporations are not able to completely offset the greater restrictiveness of bank lending, so that there is still some net diminution in the freedom to operate. But the decline is much less than would have occurred if there had not also been the rising corporate velocity. It is difficult to say whether the Federal Reserve can take this corporate behavior into consideration. It would require some quantification of the expected shift in velocity, and while there are some clues to explain the magnitude of such a change, small errors in the estimate can make for sizeable differences in spending. For example, if the Federal Reserve misjudged the expected velocity by 0.1 per cent, it would mean a difference of $4 billion or more in annual transactions. Since the quarterly changes in velocity can be as much as 1 to 2 per cent, or more, it is not difficult to see how an error as small as this can occur. Yet each such mistake can cost billions of dollars, enough to throw off the resulting reaction of the economy quite appreciably. An error in one direction could mean an inadequate brake on expansion. Too great a price rise or too large a deficit in our balance of payments can result. An error in the other direction might put too much pressure on the economy and so precipitate a sharp downturn.

Moreover, in making such an estimate, the Federal Reserve has to take two subfactors into consideration. One is the longer-run upward movement in velocity. This force is presumably working currently regardless of the state of business activity, a reflection of the increased prosperity of the United States since World War II, as well as of a greater degree of sophistication among financial officials on the corporate level. Second, sometimes reinforcing, sometimes reversing, the longer trend is the cyclical shift. This is perhaps partly induced by the Federal Reserve's own intervention. Considering the limitations of statistical techniques, it would be remarkable indeed if the error in estimation were kept as low as 0.1 per cent. Or, in monetary terms, a $4 billion error would be an excellent forecast.

The Quantity Equation

The concept of velocity and an understanding of the nature and size of the money supply enable us to formulate the quantity equation of money. Often associated with the work of the late Irving Fisher of Yale, this is also called the equation of exchange. Although there are several methods of presentation, we shall limit ourselves to two.

As we have seen, money tends to be spent and respent over periods of time, and its measurement of turnover is an indication of activity. Each dollar multiplied by the number of times it is spent during the period (times its velocity) tells us how much spending it has given rise to. If we then add this total for each dollar, we arrive at the total amount spent. Ideally, if the information were available, we would do this for each dollar in the demand-deposit accounts and for each dollar of currency, as well as for our coinage. Arithmetically, we could then deduce the activity of the average dollar; this average-velocity figure multiplied by the total money supply would then yield the same figure for total spending. In what follows, it is this average-velocity figure that we refer to.

To distinguish between the two types of monies, we shall use M for the quantity of currency and coins and M' for the amount in demand deposits. Since each may have its own average velocity, we shall use the symbol V for the average velocity of currency and coins, and V' for the average velocity of demand deposits. MV would thus represent the total amount of spending during a period effected with currency and coins, $M'V'$ the amount spent by check, and the two together the total amount of money spent.

The money is being spent on a wide variety of goods and services and, to be all-inclusive, for all the numerous financial transactions. Here we shall assume that our data are good enough to separate out these financial transfers, so we shall limit the discussion to spending on only goods and services. Each such purchase involves an item with a price, and so the value of such a purchase would be the multiple of these two—price times quantity. Since services often cannot be quantified, we us T as a symbol for the physical volume of such transactions, and so the value of all such purchases would be the sum of all these transactions times their prices, or PT. Thus we get a simple algebraic equation: the quantity of money spent during a period equals the value of things (goods and services) purchased, or $MV + M'V' = PT$. The alternative form of this equation combines both types of monies and strikes a new average velocity for the two, simplified somewhat to $MV = PT$.

Elementary as this equation is, it does focus attention on the major forces that impinge directly on the monetary sector. It is here that the possible sources giving rise to business-cycle fluctuations exist. Referring to the second equation, aggregate demand can vary for one of two reasons: the amount of money outstanding changes, and/or the rate at which it is used can alter. Noting this, we then infer that the first variable is within the confines of the banking system—including in this the workings of Federal Reserve policy through the impact on bank reserves and thus bank deposits. The second variable—velocity—tells use to look for those forces that induce people to hoard or, alternatively, to manage their balances more efficiently.

Our study of M leads us into both bank lending policy and Federal Reserve activity; our study of V gets us into liquidity preference and the savings-investment problem. At times we may even have to differentiate between M and M', if the cash flows into or out of the banks become significant. Alternatively, we would have to study it separately in those economies where the use of bank checks is less developed than currently is the case within the United States.

But the right side of the equation is also variable. Prices can change, and thus alter the value of purchases. Quantities can change, and thus alter the value of purchases. Or both can change, either in the same or opposite directions. P, in effect, is our guide to inflation. T is our guide to business activity, since variations in the volume purchased will usually change the amount produced, and in turn will alter employment and incomes.

Because of its historical importance, a brief aside should be made at this juncture to discuss the quantity theory of money. Once economists felt that the V was a very stable factor, reflecting people's habits, which changed slowly. In the short run, this stability meant that V could be regarded as a constant. Similarly, it was felt that a competitive system always tended toward full employment, since any factor that was not employed would lower its price and so regain employment. If all our productive factors are at work, we have then fixed the quantity of goods and services that can be produced, the T in our equation. Over long periods of time technological progress might alter output rates, but in the short run this, too, could be ignored.

This left only two variables, M and P. Hence, it was deduced that any changes in the quantity of money would alter the price level in the same direction. As a consequence, inflation in particular could be attributed to excessive issues of money. To avoid such an outcome, it would be advisable to place rigid controls over the possible increases in the money supply.

As later critics pointed out, and as mentioned in previous and subsequent chapters, it is the changes in V and T that can often be far more important and of much greater interest. But vestiges of the quantity theory still linger, and we shall encounter aspects of it from time to time in this volume and also when discussing monetary matters with the average, uninformed citizen.

However, the quantity equation does serve a purpose, not only in understanding what monetary influences are at work, but also how to manipulate them to bring about desired economic reactions. If there is a recession, with production levels well below the full-employment point—in other words, if T is too small—then we should operate on either M or V (or both) to bring about a recovery in demand and thus in output. Or if inflation is a threat—if P is starting to climb too vigorously—then we should try to increase output (T), adding to supply and thus putting a brake on prices, or we should curtail the money supply (M) or its activity (V), or both. Now we are back with monetary policy and the role of the Federal Reserve.

In terms of the ability of the Federal Reserve to influence the economy, we can also use the quantity equation to highlight its limitations and sector of operation. The Reserve's major strength is the operations it effects on the volume of bank reserves—discounting and open-market purchases and sales. To the extent that these reserves are used fully, we can say that the Reserve can set M'. But if banks vary the amount they carry as excess reserves, being more loaned-up at some times and less at others, then there is some variation in the M' magnitude relative to this reserve volume. M, as we have seen, reflects the people's habits and is outside the direct influence of the Federal Reserve. V and V' are also the resultant of plans that the Reserve cannot influence significantly. T reflects industrial capacity and its rate of utilization. P, of course, is partly the resultant of the other equation components, and partly the impact of corporate pricing policies. Thus we see the tenuous thread that ties Federal Reserve policy to the objectives at which it aims—only through member-bank reserves, which may or may not determine one component in the equation. We should remember here that it is the various slippages between this reserve total and the results on these equation members that we must understand and work on so as to achieve our desired outcome.

The Cambridge Approach

An alternative formulation of the monetary relationships was evolved through concentration on the average balance carried by individuals and corporations. This equation was developed primarily by economists at Cambridge University; and while it covered the same forces, its different emphasis proved helpful in illuminating many of the phenomena which tended to be overlooked by other monetary theorists.

The quantity of money, as in the quantity equation, could be represented by M, the sum of both currency and checking-account balances; or it could be broken down into these two components. We shall combine them to simplify the explanation. This M was simply the sum of the balances held either as cash on hand or in the bank as demand deposits. The volume of goods and services, T in the quantity equation, was essentially the same concept in the cash-balance approach, although the symbol used was R. P, as before, represented the average price of all the things that constituted R (or T); in shorthand form, P was the average level of prices.

The new symbol was k, the ratio of balances held to the value of goods and services bought. Arithmetically, this was the reciprocal of V, for just as V measured the ratio of spending (equal to PT) over the average amount of money (M), k measured the average amount of money (M) relative to the amount of purchases (RP, or TP in the quantity equation). Expressed algebraically, $V=PT/M$ and $k=M/RP$, RP being equal to PT. Hence, $k=1/V$. (We have used purchases, rather than output, since the two could differ by additions to, or reductions of, inventories.)

The significance in this different way of expressing the relationships arises from the concept of k. People were thought to reason in the following manner: There is the expected amount of income to be received periodically—weekly, monthly, quarterly. This level determined the amount to be spent, the RP. In order to service this volume of spending, there would have to be a certain amount of money on hand, geared to the rate at which it was received and the speed of payments. This amount (M) was thus relative to the RP. The ratio of the two (k) was the proportion that people felt was necessary for sound management of their finances. For example, people might feel that they should have on the average half a week's spending in their balance—$k = \frac{1}{2}$. If the weekly spending were \$100, then M would be \$50. If they received a raise, so that spending went up to \$110, and if their attitudes toward the management of their finances remained unchanged—k still $\frac{1}{2}$—then their average balance would rise to \$55. In this way, attention concentrated on the factors that led to the determination of k. What forces would induce people to hold a higher proportion of their income and spending in cash? What forces might lead to their lowering the ratio? (We have already discussed this latter tendency among American corporations.)

How does this differ from the quantity equation? What appears to be the major difference is that the quantity equation emphasizes the decision to spend money, the determinants of the monetary stock's velocity. The cash balance looks at the factors that induce people to hold money, the cash balance. But as we have already seen, the two are essentially the same decisions. If John says that he will spend his money one week after he gets it, he is also saying that he will hold that amount as a cash balance for a week. If he changes his mind and decides to spend his money two weeks after he receives it, he is also saying that he will hold that amount as a cash balance for two weeks. The weekly velocity has dropped by one-half in this second decision; the ratio of his cash balance to weekly spending is twice what it was before. If we look back at the first two months in Table IV, we note that the second month has a velocity equal to half that of the first. In terms of k, the average cash balance was $15/4$ (\$300/80) in the first month and $15/2$, or twice as much, in the second month (\$300/\$40). People were spending their money only half as fast in the second month. Relative to their spending, they were holding twice as much money. The economists could ask (a) what induced people to slow down the rate at which they spent their funds, or (b) what induced them to carry so much money when they were spending so much less, and had need for less of a balance? Expressed more picturesquely, the cash-balance equation looks at money sitting; the quantity equation looks at money on the wing. But as already emphasized, the only time money is on the wing is when it is not sitting; the only time money is sitting is when it is not on the wing. If we know the moment money is spent, we also know the period in which it was being held. If we know how long a period that money is being held, we also know when it is spent. But while the decision to spend is a decision to stop holding money, the reason we spend may not be the same as the reason we hold money. More likely, the reason we spend, if we do so, is more important than the reason we hold money; if we do not spend, the reasons for holding money are more influential than the reasons for spending. Hence we have a need to study both sets of influences affecting cash balance decisions.

Velocity and the Multiplier

In the analysis of economic fluctuations an important key is the multiplier. Any change in spending affects the income of the recipients, who in turn change their spending, affecting still others, and so forth. In a sense, therefore, our discussion of velocity can be taken as the monetary reformulation of this mutliplier concept.

In the multiplier each change in receipts causes a change in the same direction, but in a somewhat smaller magnitude, the difference being accounted for by the marginal propensity to save. If we assume that people spend 80 per cent of any additional income—or reduce consumption by 80 per cent of any drop in income—then at each successive step the original change continues, but at a diminishing rate. A rise in spending of $1 billion will cause the sellers to step up their spending by $800 million. The next group of sellers would then spend 80 per cent of this, or $640 million, and so on, the eventual cumulative rise in spending amounting to $5 billion, or 5 times the initial shift. This 5 is the reciprocal of the marginal propensity to save—⅕, or 20 per cent.

In velocity terminology, each change in spending raises someone's balance by that amount, and he, in turn, spends 80 per cent of this amount, the other 20 per cent remaining idle in his account. The next stage retains 20 per cent of the remainder, spending the rest. In effect, with each rise in income—each rise in receipts—there goes a rise in each person's average cash balance equal to 20 per cent of this amount. The reverse would hold true for decreases in spending.

The length of time it takes the multiplier to work itself out is also related to our velocity discussion. If the velocity is sluggish, then the multiplier is stretched over a longer period of time. If, for example, people do not respend any additional money they may get until a month later, then the next stage of the multiplier does not takes its effect until a month later. If the additional funds are respent within a week, then the multiplier effect occurs a week later. The higher the velocity for a given period, therefore, the quicker the impetus obtained from the multiplier.

Summary

Velocity measures the rapidity with which the community spends its available money supply, and thus the use to which it puts this money to speed the flow of goods and services or output and income. Variations in this rapidity, or in the length of time between disbursements, account for much of the variation in economic activity. Changes in velocity reflect changes in the desire to be liquid; barring alterations in the money supply, such shifts simply change the distribution of existing balances. A desire to build up one's balance (or reduce it) has no influence on the banks' operations; it simply changes the bookkeeping entries. Thus it is necessary to distinguish between the desire to save merely to build up a balance, and the desire to save in order to turn over this balance to someone else to spend. In both cases, the money supply is the same, but velocity and activity are significantly higher in the second possibility.

While the measurement of velocity is a difficult statistical problem, our data are good enough to draw policy implications. For example, since World War II, both corporations and individuals have been managing their balances with greater efficiency, the former category raising its velocity more rapidly. As a result, the postwar shifts in *V* have tended to overshadow shifts in the supply of money as cyclical forces. Because of the magnitude that this velocity multiplier exerts, the problem of Federal Reserve policy is much more complicated, since the Federal Reserve works mainly through affecting total bank reserves; from this item to total spending, many points exist for variations to creep in. Since a change in velocity is akin to a change in the effective spending power the community has, its movements can influence spending in a relatively uncontrolled manner.

In order to analyze these forces, economists have evolved two types of equations: one, the quantity equation, which emphasizes the spending of money; the other, the cash-balance equation, which emphasizes the size of balances being held by the community. Both analyze the same phenomena from different points of view, but in doing so, they tend to raise different questions, reflecting different aspects of our spending and liquidity motivations.

Chapter 12

MONEY AND INSTABILITY

The factor of velocity gives rise to various kinds of stability problems which are associated peculiarly with the use of money. These bring in complications which would be either absent or of relatively less importance in a barter economy. It is here that we see why the presence of money results in more than just a "greasing" of the ways, a simple means of facilitating transactions. In fact, it may not be an exaggeration to say that the use of money gives rise to the peculiarity of velocity, and becomes the most important source of instability in the monetary system.

Commercial Loan Policy

One type of concern that velocity produces is associated with the impact of new loans on over-all demand and supply equilibrium. When a bank makes a loan, it expands the money supply (demand deposits) and thus adds to aggregate demand. To avoid imbalance, such an action should work to expand supply equally, so that as both supply and demand expand, we maintain the same equilibrium as previously existed. Our conclusion follows: banks should make loans only for "productive" purposes—for operations that result in additions to the supply of goods and services. A good example of such a loan would be one that enabled a company to produce more books for sale, the loan enabling the publisher to buy his paper stock and other supplies and to pay his workmen. When he sold the books, he could pay off the bank loan; when the supply is removed from the market, the accompanying purchasing power is also removed through the loan repayment and the consequent destruction of demand deposits. This type of self-liquidating loan would seem to be ideal in light of our reasoning so far.

In contrast, a loan for consumption purposes would be viewed as unwise. The loan adds to purchasing power, or demand, but the borrower is not using the funds to add to output. Demand has risen, but not supply, and if carried to extremes, inflation could result. Furthermore, there is no automatic destruction of the demand deposits created by this loan. So long as the borrower can service the loan, the demand deposits will be in existence, and so will the purchasing power.

But both approaches overlook the impact of velocity. From the discussion in the preceding chapter, we have seen that each dollar gives rise to a certain quantity of purchases, the amount being greater (in any period of time) if the velocity is greater. A velocity of one per period means that each dollar is spent once; a velocity of two means that each dollar gave rise to two dollars of purchases; a velocity of one-half means that it would take two periods before we had one dollar of spending. In terms of our commercial-loan discussion, if we limit the meaning of *period* to the time it takes from the borrowing to the addition of the supplies on the market—the period of production—and if we examine the velocity for that period, we can come up with quite divergent answers, depending on the nature of the actual velocity.

Suppose that our book publisher borrows $10,000 to produce $10,000 worth of books three months later. (We shall ignore the interest on the loan and the possible profits from the sale.) Then at the beginning of the quarter we add $10,000 to demand deposits, and at the end we add $10,000 to supply. If the velocity is one per quarter, that would mean the money spent by the borrower is spent only once during the period of three months. The sellers—either of goods or services—are then presumed to hold onto the funds received until the next quarter. At the end of the quarter, we have made our sale, and with the proceeds, retired the loan. We thus destroyed $10,000 in demand deposits. Our net effects at the end of three months, therefore, were an increase in deposits for those who sold materials to the publisher or worked in his plant, offset by a reduction of an equal amount in the deposits of the people who bought the books.

The next period now begins with exactly the same purchasing power as before, although it is somewhat differently distributed, and presumably exactly the same supply conditions exist, the first quarter's addition of books having now ended. So, total supply in the first period was greater than that of the period that preceded it by the amount of the books; it is also greater than supply in the period that follows, by the amount of the books. Hence, aggregate supply in the period following the sale of the books is equal to aggregate supply in the period preceding the publishing of the books. The volume of demand deposits in these same two periods is also equal. However, one in-between period was different, so both supply (the books) and demand (the $10,000 additional deposits) jumped. Now we are back to the pre-disturbed periods.

Suppose our velocity were two per period. Then not only would there be the $10,000 spent by the publisher, but there would also be the $10,000 spent by the recipients. Now we have additional aggregate spending during the period of $20,000, or twice what we are adding to supply. Demand now exceeds supply, as compared with the period before the loan, and so we may have a slight inflationary pressure, since the additional funds exceed the available supply of goods and services. At the end of the period the loan is repaid, so that in the next period we have once again restored the relationships that prevailed in the period before the loan was made. But during this period of the loan, we have created a slight expansionary influence.

Although the third possibility is unlikely, we may as well discuss it briefly. Suppose velocity were less than one—say, one-half. This could be true for spenders in general, although the possibility of it holding true for our publisher is doubtful. For example, perhaps he has plenty of paper in stock, so that he spends only $5,000 on labor in this period and waits until the next three-month period to order his paper. His cash balance will go up by $10,000 when he obtains the loan, drop $5,000 as he pays his workmen, rise to $15,000 as he sells his books at the end of the quarter, and then drop back to $5,000 above his opening balance as he pays off his loan. In the subsequent three months, this would slowly drop back to zero—more precisely, to the same level as it had been before he had obtained the loan—since he is now replenishing his paper supplies. At the end of the first three-month period, he ends with a balance of $5,000 more than he started with (before making the loan); his customers have $10,000 less, and his workers have $5,000 more. We have expanded aggregate supply by $10,000, but aggregate demand rose by only $5,000. We have thus exerted a deflationary influence by our loan!

Now it may be asked how such could occur. If we retrace our steps, ignoring complicating details, we can see what is happening to the economy as a whole. If our publisher decided against this venture, then the people who would otherwise have bought his books would buy other goods, perhaps clothing. Thus, the clothing sellers would now get income, which they in turn spend. But if our publisher decides to produce the books, his customers buy books instead of clothes, so the clothing makers have less income, and their customers, too, have less income. The publisher, in other words, has diverted purchasing power from one sector (clothing) to another (his own). But in our first illustration (velocity equal to one) we have an equal offset to this loss of clothing sales. The paper sellers and the publisher's workers get income they would not have received if our publisher had *not* produced the books. Hence, within the economy there is a shift in demand —less for clothes, more for books, less for whatever the clothing makers would have bought, more for paper, and so on. In total, the economy has just as much demand as it has supply, the only effect being the change in composition.

When velocity rose to two, we had the same distributional shifts as in the preceding paragraph, but in addition, there was the secondary spending by the people to whom the publisher paid incomes—his workers and his paper suppliers. They are now spending in this quarter and acquiring goods and services that they would not otherwise have obtained. And since we have done nothing to expand output, other than that of books, we do not have the additional supply to meet this demand, and so some other would-be buyers are denied the items bought by our group—or else they offer higher prices and so start the inflationary chain.

In our third possibility—velocity of one-half—we have depressed the clothing demand as buyers switched to books, but did not offset this downward pressure by an equal rise in demand elsewhere. All we had as an offset was the money spent for labor ($5,000), and so the loss of income by the clothing workers and materials suppliers was only partly compensated. If half the clothing costs are for workers, then the workers as a group are no worse off; the loss for the clothing employees being balanced by the gain for the publisher's labor force. But the clothing raw-material suppliers suffer a decline in income not matched by a gain to any other sector. And thus we get our net depressing effect. (In the next quarter, it is true, there will be a step-up in demand for paper supplies, but that is three months away; meanwhile we have the downward pressure in the current quarter.)

In our economy there are thousands of such influences at work, and many of them criss-cross. As clothing buyers switch to books, perhaps other people are induced to buy less film and more clothing.

As clothing sales drop and cut the demand for cotton, tire sales may have risen and so offset the cotton effects. Hence, in our aggregates, these sectoral influences can be assumed to cancel out.

Guidelines for Bank Lending

If we assume that our objective is to arrange bank loans so as to effect a stabilizing influence—that such credit should act to exert neither an inflationary nor a deflationary pressure—then the discussion in the preceding section has given us a guideline. The amount of a loan should be geared to the estimated velocity impact. We ignore those transactions that merely transfer title to financial claims—or, more positively, include only those transactions that actually affect demand and supply. Arithmetically, the loan should be a proportion of total eventual sales (or output) additions equal to the fraction that is the reciprocal of this meaningful measure of velocity. If velocity during the life of the loan is 2, then the loan should equal ½ the expected additional sales value arising from the borrower's operation; if velocity for the period is 3, then the loan should be only ⅓.

By using a simple numerical example, we can illustrate how this approach brings about our stability aim. If each dollar of demand deposits created is spent and respent four times during the period that our borrower is getting his additional output going, the velocity is 4. That is, during the period each dollar will give rise to a demand for goods and services equal to $4. The result of these created dollars will be the added output and sales coming from the borrower's efforts. If we wish to maintain the supply-demand relationship as before, we must increase both sides of the equation equally. Each dollar created adds $4 to demand; the final addition of the borrower's output affects supply. Since we want the added demand to equal this added supply, we need only make a simple equation: original amount of loan times velocity equals additional supply forthcoming. With a velocity of 4, we then see that the loan value should be no more than ¼ the expected supply addition.

If, however, the bank finances only a fraction of the operation, how would the borrower cover the remainder? And if he does, wouldn't this also exert an expansionary pressure just as would a bank loan for this remainder? Our answer points in two directions. Either the borrower could finance the remainder out of his other funds, or he could borrow the difference outside the banking system, from a friend or insurance company.

Suppose our bank loaned the full amount; and we shall assume, as before, that the end result is to be more books worth $10,000 in three months. Given a velocity of 4, as we have seen, demand during the quarter-year will rise by $40,000, supply by only $10,000. Our guideline has indicated that only $2,500 should have been loaned, and that $7,500 should have been obtained either from other funds or from non-banking sources.

Assume, first, that the borrower in question—the publisher—does have other resources. If he borrows $10,000, he is free to use these other resources for other production ventures. This means that he is free to spend these other resources for still other operations. His demand is thus the aggregate of the money he obtains from the bank, plus the spending of these other funds; these, in turn, will have a multiple demand effect because of the influence of velocity. But if the bank lends only $2,500, then our publisher must divert $7,500 to the book venture, and thus cut down his spending in other ventures. His total spending is now $2,500 of borrowed funds plus $7,500 of diverted funds; before, his total spending was $10,000 of borrowed funds, plus the $7,500 of other funds. His spending from his own funds remains the same in dollars, but the scale of operations has been reduced because of this diversion. Hence, aggregate spending has been cut down (with a fourfold effect), and now the net addition to spending exerts only an additional demand equal to the additional output.

If he had borrowed the funds from non-banking sources, our logic would have been the same. If the bank lends him $10,000, he does not need an insurance company. So the insurance company would be free to lend the $7,500 to still another borrower. So in this particular sector, then, the total new demand would be the $10,000 lent by the bank, plus the $7,500 lent by the insurance company, or $17,500. If the bank lends only $2,500 and the insurance company lends the remaining $7,500, we cut aggregate new loans to $10,000. The net addition to spending is only $10,000—$2,500 times 4—for the $7,500 diverted would have been spent anyway (and ultimately spent four times). The spending stream initiated by our publisher with the $7,500 obtained from the insurance company (ultimately adding $30,000 to demand) is balanced by the loss of spending, now that the alternative borrower from the insurance company is denied the funds; what the publisher obtained the other borrower lost. The insurance company's loans are the same, but the total lending is reduced because of the bank's smaller contribution. And so, once again, the net addition to demand equals the net addition to supply.

Several qualifications to this analysis should be added. One has already been indicated—the problem of ascertaining the value of the velocity. This, as we have seen, is a published figure that is a hodge-podge of financial and nonfinancial transactions; the figure we need for our guideline can only be inferred from this statistic, and could be in error by a factor of rather uncertain magnitude.

We have also assumed that any loan to add to output will also result in the output being sold. If, instead, the producer stores the product in his warehouse, hoarding the merchandise, so to speak, because he expects inflation (at which time he could sell his products at a higher price), then our objective is thwarted. The demand impact arising from the bank loan is still the same, but the accompanying supply effect is absent. We have added only to demand. This, in turn, could spill over into a price inflation, and so the very aim expected by our goods-hoarders is realized simply by their own actions.

A third qualification arises from our discussion of alternatives. We said that if the publisher obtained the $10,000, he could use his other resources for still another venture, or the insurance company would lend to someone else. By lending only $2,500, the bank thus kept the impact of the remaining $7,500 unchanged, merely diverting the spending either from the publisher's second venture or cutting down the spending of the alternative borrower. But suppose these alternatives did not exist; suppose our publisher would have kept his $7,500 idle, or that the insurance company would not have loaned it to someone else?

What we are saying here is that a bank loan of $10,000 would have resulted in the $7,500 remaining idle, its velocity being zero. The $10,000 loan, with a velocity of 4, would give rise to additional demand of $40,000. A loan of $2,500 would give rise to an additional demand of $10,000, and the $7,500 activated by the publisher from his own resources (or by the insurance company as a loan) adds $7,500 to the spending stream, this latter having a velocity of 4. So, by the bank's reducing its loan, it is raising the velocity of the funds called on to fill the gap. Either way, additional spending would be $40,000, for the alternative use was *zero* spending. In this special case—the activation of otherwise idle funds—the loan operation would be just as inflationary whether it was one-quarter of the borrower's needs or 100 percent. There is a minor offset to this conclusion which might be significant: with a 100-per-cent bank-financed operation, the borrower retains his $7,500 idle funds. Thus it is possible for him to change his mind at any time and reactivate the money. If so, then we would have the double effect discussed in the first part of this section. Similarly, if the alternative had been the loan from the insurance company, it could always change its policy and start lending again. In contrast, a $2,500 loan precludes such shifts, since otherwise idle funds are now absorbed in the operation. But if there are enough new loans, and business does start to revive enough, it is possible that the business atmosphere could change and so alter the character of this idle money, thus bringing into being the multiple expansion through this reactivation.

Incidentally, we have also explained by inference why traditional banking theory is opposed to long-term loans. A ten-year loan, for example, would give rise to an enormous increase in spending—the cumulative effect of velocity—while the additional supplies are spread out over a long period. If a hydroelectric plant were to be built, there would be no added supply for at least five years (during the construction phase) and then only small additional supplies as the annual electric power came on the market. Thus there would be an enormous imbalance between supply and demand. On the other hand, contrary to this logic, it must be observed that banks enter increasingly into such construction loans. When the project is complete and ready for operation, new securities are then issued (to an insurance company, for example), these proceeds then paying off the bank loan. We thus have the inflationary impact only during this construction phase, the added money lasting only until the destruction of those funds put up by the bond buyers through the repayment procedure. The funds used to pay off the loan may have originally been demand deposits transferred by the insured people to the insurance company in payment of their premiums. Then the insurance company transferred these demand deposits to the bond-issuing corporation. The latter, in turn, cancelled these acquired demand deposits against its construction loan from the bank. Hence, what we had was an addition to the money supply for only the duration of the construction period, and an addition to demand (unmatched by any added supply) equal to this amount, times the velocity, for the construction period.

Self-Liquidating Bank Loans

The criteria set out here also explain why banks feel so much safer with such short-term loans: they are virtually self-liquidating. The loan enables the borrower to produce saleable merchandise. By the end of the life of the loan—assuming that the production cycle is the same length—goods come on the market and are then sold. The funds received pay off the loan. The loan, in other words, finances an operation that automatically enables the borrower to repay. (Of course, we are assuming that the borrower was shrewd enough to produce what buyers want, and encounters no selling problems.)

From the bank's point of view, the shorter the life of the loan, the more liquid the asset. If the loan is for thirty days, then the bank knows that in all probability the rise in deposits and resultant loss in reserves which occurred when the loan was made will be reversed within the month. Should business conditions change during the period, and the bank come under pressures—from a cash drain—its reserves will be restored as repayment is effected. If the loan is for ninety days, then its liquidity position is somewhat weaker, for now it must wait two months longer; the period during which an adverse occurrence could appear is that much longer.

Were the bank to make a really long-term loan—say, payable in ten years—there is a long period during which its liquidity position could come under pressure. Yet for this entire length of time it could not look to this particular loan for aid; other than the interest payments, it receives nothing back on this particular asset, and so cannot call on this asset for aid, unless it could be sold. Here we see another reason for the traditional banking preference for short-term assets: the shorter the life of an asset, the quicker its maturity will bring in reserves or reduce deposits (and so free reserves), and so the quicker it is in a better position to meet any liquidity pressures. And, of course, if these pressures do not arise, the funds can always be used again. But at least the shortness of life gives the banks the alternative if the need arises.

We should not exaggerate the difference in liquidity between the two types of loans. Even short-term loans can become nonliquid—cannot be repaid. Perhaps business worsens, and so the borrower cannot sell his goods to obtain the funds for repayment. Suppose his customers cannot pay him, and this prevents him from repaying. Or perhaps business is so good that he reinvests the funds in still more production, and again does not have the money to repay the bank. At maturity, therefore, the bank is virtually compelled to renew the loan. In the first and second alternatives a demand for repayment might force the borrower into bankruptcy, and the bank still might not realize on its loan. In the last case it would appear foolish to press an expanding business when its sales are booming. But whatever the reason, the loan is generally renewed, the money supply stays up, and from now on there is no additional output forthcoming as a result of the loan. In effect, we have violated one of our prime rules—not to make any long-term loans. The bank had not done so when the loan was originally made—later it developed that it had. American experience has shown that not only are banks making longer-life loans, but that there has also been an increasing tendency for loans to be outstanding longer than originally intended. In other words, the theory has not been practiced as completely as implied.

The long-term loan is also more liquid than our discussion indicates. To a certain extent, such loans are usually amortized. Perhaps each quarter part of the amount is repaid, so that the outstanding (nonliquid) remaining amount is constantly diminishing. Such a loan is known as a term loan. In addition, if the borrower's credit rating is good, the bank can often find some other bank, or a non-banking lender (an insurance company), to take over the loan. Although from the borrower's point of view the loan is still outstanding, from the original lender's point of view it is just as liquid as a short-term loan, for it was disposed of just as readily and in just as short a period of time as though it had been a loan with a shorter life. Note that if it is sold to another bank, the original lending bank would usually gain reserves; if sold to a non-banking lender that carried its funds at another bank, the seller would again gain reserves; if sold to a non-banking lender that carried its account with the selling bank, the result is a decline in deposits and freeing of reserves. These three possibilities are the same as would occur with repayment of a loan.

Flexible Currency Issues

In line with the philosophy of bank lending developed so far, there is a companion school of thought with regard to the currency-issuing privilege. Throughout history there has been the fear of excessive activity on the part of the government printing presses, leading to inflation and eventual worthlessness of the money. Critics can cite numerous cases, such as the great inflation in Germany following World War I, or our own country's experience with the Continental currency. Because of this, theorists have tried to set up standards that would ensure that there was neither too much nor too little money, the latter reflecting the opposite worry about deflation.

To attain this objective, there had to be some connection between the volume of currency issued and the need for currency. While there are many ways for the latter to be registered, probably the most obvious would show up as a drain out of the banks into the public's hands. Reserves would thereby be depleted, and so the banks would have to turn to the central bank to replenish their holdings.

But such a drain could also arise from an excessive expansion that could be inflationary. As prices rose, people would need more cash to meet daily expenses, and business firms would need more money to pay for the more expensive raw materials and labor. Yet if such were the situation, we would want to check the money issue in order to put a brake on inflation. There must be some means of distinguishing between the two.

To do so, the suggestion was made that banks charged with the currency-issuing privilege should use as backing only short-term commercial paper. Presumably this would increase only as business activity rose, and the demand fed by the additional currency would be matched by the supply produced through the commercial loan. As in our demand-deposit cases, we would see a matching of additional demand with supply. Moreover, as the supply were sold, the loans would be repaid, the volume of commercial paper would decrease, and thus the backing for the currency would decline. This would compel a drop in the amount of currency outstanding. Once again we had linked changes in supply and demand with movements in the money supply.

It was argued that this arrangement would be effective in limiting currency issues to "legitimate" demands. Any other type of demand expansion, such as loans to finance consumer spending, would be ineligible as backing, and the money supply could not be expanded. Similarly, excessive long-term lending would not be permitted to operate on the currency supply. Only loans tied to supply additions would be eligible. Of course, there would still be the qualifications already mentioned—one, that the additional output was not put into inventory hoarding, and two, the problem of velocity. But basically, the currency issue would be managed in a fashion similar to that established for commercial bank-loan officials.

In practice, what worked to nullify much of the logic of this approach was the ability of money to flow in more directions than originally predicted. For example, a businessman could come in for a loan, stating that the proceeds were to be employed to further production. But instead, he might use it to hoard supplies. Or he might use the funds to speculate in stocks. There was no guarantee that the funds would be used for his stated purpose. And there was also the problem of velocity: what if the funds turned over more rapidly than had been predicted? Or less rapidly? The former would lead to inflation, the latter to deflation. Moreover, as already indicated, many short-term loans have a habit of becoming longer-term. At maturity, the borrower finds that he is not in a position to repay as scheduled. And so the currency remains outstanding.

There is also the deflationary extreme. In a recession there is insufficient money and insufficient demand. There is a need to increase purchasing, through either a rise in velocity or an increase in the money supply (or both). Since the business outlook is so gloomy, there is little likelihood that the corporations will be coming to the banks to borrow in order to expand output. If anything, they will be repaying loans, not renewing them, and perhaps selling their inventories in order to obtain funds for this repayment. Hence, the volume of commercial paper outstanding will not rise; it may shrink. Simultaneously, the money supply will not expand; it may contract. Using the commercial paper criterion as our yardstick would prevent us from expanding the money supply to combat the depression. We are, in effect, in a vicious circle. We cannot escape the recession unless there is more spending. There cannot be more spending unless the business outlook improves. Business will not get a better outlook unless there is more spending. And there cannot be more spending unless business is willing to borrow, a factor dependent on the improvement in economic activity. And so the depression drags on. Later, in our discussion of fiscal policy, we can see how to break through this impasse: by lending to the government. But that, of course, means breaking with the commercial-paper tradition, a change which did not occur on any large scale in this country until the Roosevelt Administration (1933–45).

There are other questions raised by the commercial-paper approach. Suppose all businesses finance themselves out of their own resources, without any bank borrowing. How would we get enough money to effect the transactions? How does any change in the money supply get absorbed? How does industrial progress, with the attendant increase in output, affect the economy if it is not accompanied by a loan-induced addition to demand?

Velocity and Monetary Absorption

The analysis of velocity helps to explain the method whereby any change in the money supply, especially an increase, is absorbed by the economy. The additional money gives the first recipient purchasing power he did not have. This could be through a bank loan or perhaps the printing of paper money by the government. The initial difference between these two is simply one of who obtains the purchasing power.

With this added purchasing power, the recipient now can exert a demand for goods and services he could not have before. Assume as a first possibility that this is a borrower intending to expand the output of books. He now exerts a demand for labor and raw materials in addition to what existed before the loan. The sellers of these goods and services thus receive income they would not have had in the absence of this added demand. They, in turn, can now step up their spending. Here we see the velocity aspect.

But there is also the opposite side of the coin—the time during which the money is at rest. The sellers do not spend these funds immediately. There is the interim period during which they hold these funds idle. During this period there is no additional demand, and so the new money exerts no further effect. Suppose they hold these funds until the borrower's output comes on the market. Then the second stage of spending and added demand coincides with the added supplies, and the aggregates are in balance, both sides of the equation now rising equally. It is true that these secondary spenders may not purchase these particular additional supplies. They may buy other goods, diverting supplies from still other buyers. For example, they may buy shoes, thus reducing the supply of shoes that would otherwise have been available to other buyers. But then these other buyers may decide that since the shoes have been bought by our secondary buyers, they may now decide to buy the available books being supplied by the borrower-publisher.

Expressed more succinctly, the people who sold goods and services to the borrower can now get something from the available pool of goods and services that they could not have obtained in the absence of the borrower's operations. Thanks to his borrowing, they can now buy. There is consequently less remaining for the rest of the community. But offsetting this diversion of supplies is the addition coming from the borrower's operations. Hence, so far as the remainder of the community is concerned, aggregate supply and demand are still the same as before, although the supply side has been somewhat changed —some being channeled to our borrower's suppliers, some new supplies coming from the borrower's operations. As a consequence, we may get some sectoral imbalances; there may be fewer shoes available, but more books. But in aggregate, we can even out these minor differences and say that the aggregates continue to be equal.

This continuing equality for the remainder of the community was the result of our velocity being one for the period, and of the accompanying rise in supplies. But if the velocity had been greater, or if the borrower did not add to the volume of saleable goods, what then? In either event the additional demand would exceed the additional supply; for ease of exposition, we shall use the latter possibility.

Suppose our borrower wanted to buy an automobile with the loan. Then the bank has added to his purchasing power, as before, except that this time it has not also made for a rise in available supplies. Our borrower now can purchase a car that he could not have before, and the car dealer has money he would not have had before. There is now less of a car supply available for other buyers. For simplicity, assume that before the loan the demand during the month just equalled the supply of cars being produced and delivered; now, since the loan, the demand exceeds supplies by one.

We are now faced with several possibilities. Again, for ease of exposition, we shall limit the alternatives to two. During the month, one car buyer must go unsatisfied. Perhaps he may decide not to buy, but simply to hold his funds. His active money becomes inactive, its velocity dropping. In terms of our quantity equation, M has risen (the loan to the new car buyer), but V has declined (the thwarted buyer's funds); the two have changed to offset each other, this resulting in the same volume of purchases as before, only by different persons. MV has remained constant, the rise in M being balanced by the decline in V.

Suppose our buyer insisted on buying a car? Demand, then, exceeds supply for cars. Obviously, our auto dealer has no more autos than before. So he may decide to take advantage of the situation and charge a somewhat higher price. If this does not discourage buyers—and induce them to hold their funds idle (again the possibility of a decline in V)—then his aggregate money income rises. In symbolic terms, V remains the same, but since M has risen because of the loan, MV goes up; T is the same, but P has risen.

Now we have absorbed the additional money supply through a larger holding on the part of the car dealer. So long as he continues to keep the money idle, there is no further impact. But once he decides to spend this—and now he can spend more than before because of this higher sales value—our analysis is repeated. Again we have a greater source of demand than before, so the same reactions would occur with whatever he decided to acquire. In other words, at each spending stage, the M is somewhat higher; if V remains the same—if people continue to spend at the same rate as before—then there is pressure on supplies. On the other hand, if the higher balance is compensated by a slower rate of spending—that is, if V drops off somewhat—then the added money supply is absorbed through the accompanying rise in average cash balances. If, for example, people had a habit of spending their funds monthly (V equals 1 per month), then our car dealer would step up his spending after a month. A month later those who sold to the car dealer would step up their spending, and so on. Each month there would be a bit more spending equal to the additional M. Now, if the greater amount of money acquired were to be accompanied by a slowing down in the rate of spending, then the average cash balance would be higher and the spending perhaps no greater, the rise in M being offset by the decline in V.

The details of an analysis such as we have been attempting are obviously far more complex than we have indicated. But then, the ramifications become so vast as to defy exposition. However, some pointers along the way may be relevant.

Suppose the dealer had quite a few cars in his inventory. Then, instead of selling as many as he received from the factory, thereby keeping total inventory unchanged, he could have reduced his stock by one. The excess of demand over supplies would now be bridged by a reduction in inventories. In effect, he has exchanged one asset (stock in trade) for another asset (money). For the first period, we have augmented T by reducing inventory, and so the rise in M is balanced. But there would still be the possible additional spending in the following period, as the dealer with his additional money then faced the decision of continuing his rate of spending—higher M and the same V—or reduced his rate of spending, the lower V then offsetting the higher M. In brief, drawing down inventories is only a short-term expedient.

Suppose our thwarted auto buyer had neither demanded a car this month nor decided to abandon his buying plans, but simply waited until next month. Then the excess demand for cars has been postponed only to this next month, and so the problem will recur. Of course, it is possible that next month the demand for autos declines relative to supply, and so there might have been an excess of supply. Then such a postponement really works to offset the deflationary impact. What would otherwise have been a decline in sales is lessened because of this shift in purchases by the thwarted buyer.

Our thwarted car buyer might also continue to buy, but might switch to something else, such as a motorboat. Again we have merely changed the words. The excess demand for autos disappears, but now we have an excess demand for motorboats. The area of pressure changes, but not the problem.

Finally, suppose the auto makers detected this excess demand and therefore stepped up auto output by one unit. In so doing, they would also step up their payments for labor and raw materials. As incomes rose for these factors of production, spending would also rise, tempered by the possibility that some of this added income would be held as higher cash balances. This last possibility is just another way of saying that V declines and thus reduces the effect on demand.

One final point: Suppose the government had printed extra currency. Our analysis would still be as before: either there would be extra pressure on supplies, or a rise in average cash balances (decline in V). But there is an additional factor to consider. People who obtained the extra cash might not wish to spend it; so far, V is down. Probably they would deposit the extra funds in their bank account, and now bank reserves rise. If the banks then respond by making new loans, we have set the stage for a multiple expansion in the money supply through the deposit-loan mechanism. And now we are back to our first problem, the impact of an expansion in bank-created funds. It is because currency can show up also as the basis for bank asset expansion, as in this paragraph, that it tends to have a more explosive influence as it varies in amounts outstanding.

Reductions in the money supply can be traced similarly. We shall not spell out the details, but merely indicate the general course. Normally, people buy goods from retailers, who in turn buy goods from manufacturers, who buy goods and services from their suppliers and workers, thereby replenishing purchasing power to start the cycle again. But if the retailers use the sales proceeds to retire a loan from the bank, and if the bank does not make a new loan, then we break the chain. Manufacturers make fewer sales and fewer purchases. Suppliers thus do not quite replenish their cash, and so now they must spend less. Only if somewhere along the way people were willing to carry smaller cash balances—raise V—could this decline in M be compensated.

To summarize, a rise in the money supply is absorbed in two ways: a rise in spending, a rise in average cash balances (decline in velocity), or some combination of the two. The extent of the impact on demand—the inflationary pressure—is dependent on the rapidity with which additional money is spent. If people are sluggish in their handling of funds—if every extra dollar received is held idle for a length of time—then the added impact on demand is very small. Indeed, in the extreme, if the people simply hold the funds idle indefinitely, then there is no impact on demand. But if the funds are spent and respent shortly after being received, we get a much enlarged addition to demand and a much greater expansionary pressure. It is the time period between receipt and disbursement that determines how the money is absorbed. There will be a rise in cash balances that is inevitable since there is now more money. What counts is how quickly the rise is reversed through spending; the slower this reversal, the less is velocity, and the greater the average cash balance. The less the impact on demand, the less on supply.

Long-Run Growth

In a somewhat similar fashion, we can trace parallel expansion over the long run in the economic growth of an economy and the rise in the money supply, such as the United States has experienced over the past centuries. As the country grew in population and productivity, more goods were offered on the market for sale. If the volume of money remained the same—if M were unchanged while T rose—then either V would have to speed up, or prices would fall drastically. In practice, however, there is a limit (especially in the short run) to the expansibility of velocity—to the extent that people can economize on their cash-balance utilization. The money supply can rise without creating any undue impact on demand, because much of it will be absorbed in these balances. In practice, it is true that there were periods when the money supply rose more rapidly, and there were periods of inflation, just as there were other times when the money supply rose too slowly, or even declined, and thereby created a downward pressure on the economy. But most of the rise in the money supply has been an offset to the rise in the demand.

If a farmer is a self-sufficient producer, he has no need for money. This was once the case for the pioneer far removed from trading centers. As the country grew, he found growing markets for his output, and he could sell his crops for cash. At the same time, if he succeeded, he could also buy new supplies that became available. But there would be a time period between his sales and purchase, and during this interval he would be holding money idle. Note that as far as he is concerned, he has absorbed some money, in contrast to his pioneer moneyless days. Hence, even if the buyer of his crop had been financed with newly issued money, there would be no excess demand since our pioneer-farmer has now raised his idle balance (from zero).

Later he would spend the newly acquired money for goods. But the seller is also probably experiencing a growing volume of activity. He, too, would now be in a position to hold a larger cash balance, reflecting his enlarged activity. And so, as this reaction becomes widespread (which is characteristic of an expanding country), more and more money is being held idle. As a result, more and more money can be issued without upsetting our demand-supply equilibrium.

Suppose we had held the money supply rigid. Then our pioneer-farmer would be trying to sell his crops (as before) as the new settlements opened a nearby market. As he absorbed more cash, he would draw down the buyer's balance. In our earlier case, this had not been too serious, for the bank had first built up the buyer's balance through a loan, either directly to him or indirectly through a loan to the buyer's customers. These, in turn, used the funds to purchase from the buyer, and thus added to his balance. That is, the banks had first increased the community's money supply through loans, and so the loss of some of this money into the pioneer's balance was only an offset to a prior rise. But if there had not been this rise, then the drain on the part of the pioneer would create a net decline in the balances held by the remainder of the community. There would now be inadequate purchasing power—our deflationary alternative.

By examining these two possibilities in detail, we can show how the money supply is absorbed and the consequences of an inadequate expansion—and, incidentally, the reason the frontier always felt that there was a chronic shortage of money. We shall now reverse the order of exposition and start with the rigid money supply.

Suppose initially that the community is self-sufficient, a community with four members, similar to our first month in Table IV. The money supply turns over among these four, financing sales of $80, but each ends with about the same balance as he began the period. Now our pioneer—whom we shall call *E*—sells $20 to one of the members. If he has the same respending habits as the other four—the one-week interval—then our total month's spending is still $80, but it also means that someone does not make it this month. Before, in the first month, *A*, *B*, *C*, and *D* each sold $20. If, say, *A* buys from *E* and *E* buys from *B*, then our month's transactions—still only four—would involve sales by *E*, *B*, *C*, and *D*. *A* loses out, because *B*'s sale occurred a week later—*E* has now intervened—and so *C* sold a week later. *D*'s sale to *C* is now postponed to the next week and *A*'s—to the next month. But then everyone else has a later sale; the second month would include *A*, *E*, *B*, and *C*, and so on. Over a five-month period, each sells only four times instead of five. If, however, each is producing as much as before, then he has five months' output for sale, but the value of these sales is equal to only four months' demand ($20 times 4). Hence, each has to either cut back his output or reduce prices by 20 per cent.

Note that *A*'s purchase from *E* precluded him from also buying from *B*. Had he made both purchases, he would have reduced his balance to $60 when he bought from *E*, then $40 when he bought from *B*. His sale was only to *D*, so that the end-of-the-month balance would be down to $60. Unless he decided to operate with a lower cash balance, this would be contrary to his objective, and so he would probably have reduced his purchases from *B* to offset the purchase from *E*.

Suppose, however, that he did want to buy from both to step up his rate of operations. If a bank would lend him the $20, he could buy from both *E* and *B* and still end with the desired $80 cash balance. Moreover, the loan would permit him to spend twice as much during the month, so both *E* and *B* would get the sales just as quickly as before *E* entered the picture. That is, if the loan were made at the beginning of the month, *A* could spend $40 during the period; *B* could get his $20 from *A* on the first, as before, and then *C*, *D*, and *A* could continue as before. For each month there could be five $20 transactions —*A*, *B*, *C*, *D*, and *E*—instead of four, with a corresponding rise in output (that supplied by *E*).

If the money supply does not expand sufficiently to absorb *E*'s output, then some of the funds are drained from the others in the community, and there occurs the depressing effect described. If the money supply is increased, then *E* avoided such a deflation by returning the funds when he bought from the community. Had *E* bought less than he sold, the rest of the community would still show a net decline in its money supply as this difference went to *E*. Historically, *E* represented the Atlantic Seaboard—the net excess of purchases by the West developing because of the slower rise in its sales to the East. We have here, in part, an explanation of the constant shortage of funds in the more rapidly developing sections of our country's economy.

Incidentally, we can also see the impact of a self-financed expansion in output. If a company expands its supplies without borrowing —in contrast with our earlier example of the publisher—it adds to aggregate supplies without causing a corresponding rise in M. As in our pioneer case, this will work to depress prices, unless at the same time people are able to offset this by carrying lower cash balances—by stepping up V. Note that if A were to buy from both E and B by using his own funds, he would reduce his balance from \$80 to \$60, but his volume of transactions has not gone down; indeed, in the first month it went up. Hence, V would have risen by enough to offset the additional supplies coming from E. Alternatively, the company that added to output could reduce its prices, so that a given amount of spending could acquire a greater volume of goods. This is analogous to the possibility of a 20-per-cent reduction in prices already cited earlier in this section. But such downward price pressures are usually deleterious to production, and most producers would then react by reducing output. In other words, we now would have an interruption to our expansion—a recession. Here is a simple example of an excessively fast rise in output, and it contains the germ of the explanation of many of our nineteenth-century cyclical downturns.

Another implication of the velocity discussion is the explanation of a currency retaining its value, even if it does not have any backing other than the people's faith. In order to effect business in a money economy, we must have a medium of exchange. If people are willing to accept government and bank money, then these can serve as the medium. People's own habits will determine how much they will wish to carry as cash balances and how rapidly they will spend this money —our V and k. The more money we have, the greater P and T can be. If T is rising, we can also raise M without necessarily increasing P. Hence, if we regulate our money supply with an eye to the avoidance of an over-issue, it can retain enough of its purchasing power—P will not go up excessively—so that people will continue to use it.

In the special case of currency, any excess issue would probably end up in the banks and so serve as the basis for deposit creation through the expansion of bank assets. Hence, the currency should be limited to that needed for day-to-day transactions, plus whatever vault cash is required by the banks in their reserves. In other words, the community's willingness to hold idle balances determines how much money there can be that is not necessarily backed by anything tangible. If we should issue too much, it would show up in a sharp rise in P. If we issue too little, then P and/or T suffer. And so we see why currencies having no backing (the precious metals) still retain a value; if the supply is managed properly, there need be neither an inflation nor a loss in faith by the public. Neither would there be any need for idle gold in such circumstances. Indeed, if every country managed its money cautiously, there might not be any need for gold anywhere in the world. All the resources now devoted to mining, shipping, storing, and guarding this precious metal could be transferred to more productive ends, ends more useful to the community. We shall examine later the implications of this statement.

Summary

Since bank lending adds to purchasing power, and thus to demand, its proceeds should also increase supply (ideally), and thus keep the goods equation in balance. But the impact of velocity tends to upset this simple relationship; and since V tends to be greater than one for the period of the life of the loan, the amount loaned should therefore be only a fraction of the final sales value, this fraction being the reciprocal of the velocity. At the time the sale is made, the loan should be repaid and should thus destroy the purchasing power as well as remove the supply from the market. In practice it is difficult to assess the velocity value and also the right proportion that should be loaned.

Our velocity analysis also helps explain absorption of the money supply. The rising volume of transactions generally means that people must carry, on the average, greater cash balances; and so, the money supply is absorbed into these increased balances. When spent, they exert additional demand, this balancing the rising supply of an expanding economy. However, too rapid a rise in the money supply outraces output and could generate inflation; too slow a rise could cause deflation.

Chapter 13

INTEREST RATES AND YIELDS

In order to understand the workings of liquidity preference and its relationship to the monetary system, we must first discuss the technical aspects of interest rates and yields. This chapter will serve as a bridge between monetary theory and the money markets, for it is in the latter arena that the manifestations of monetary theory show themselves. Surprising as it may seem, it is a rather specialized aspect of the subject that serves as the vehicle for much of the analysis—namely, the implications of movements in bond prices and the return on fixed-income securities. Indeed, it would not be an overstatement to say that a thorough understanding of this money-market topic would encompass almost all that underlies modern monetary analysis.

As in so many other areas of economics, terms and instruments have a rather fuzzy character about them; their meaning to some observers often differs from that understood by others. While we shall attempt to be more precise, in order to maintain some consistency in the exposition, the reader is warned that he will come across these same terms in other contexts which may not bear quite the same connotations that we are using. Indeed, even our own usage will often be somewhat cloudy, for this very imprecision is part of the subject matter; it is because these components are not clear-cut that much of the confusion in policy matters has arisen. No answers can be given, of course, especially to the more controversial subjects, but it is our hope that greater clarity in thinking will result.

Types of Securities

The securities that fall within the scope of this chapter are known as *marketable* securities and have special characteristics that distinguish them from all others. Furthermore, we are limiting the exposition to fixed-income paper, thereby excluding equities such as common stocks.

Most individuals are familiar with the *non-marketable* securities, such as the baby bonds issued by the United States government during and since World War II. These can be redeemed on demand at issue price plus accrued interest,[1] so that the holder never suffers a capital loss. He may get a lower rate of interest if he cashes the bond before maturity, but he will never receive less than his original purchase price (in dollars). Furthermore, he can always buy or sell them; his local bank, acting as a Treasury agent, will perform both functions for him. The price to be paid is stipulated in the bond, so that there is never any doubt about the amount. Finally, the security is not transferable to another buyer; transactions are always either purchases from, or sales to, the government (through its agents). Incidentally, these bonds are available in relatively small denominations, often as little as $18.75. In what follows, none of what we say pertains to these issues, although this is not to deny their importance; the outstanding amount is some $50 billion.

The most distinguishing feature of the marketable security is that it is traded between individuals, and so may vary in price. Hence, the holder is uncertain as to the amount he will receive should he wish to dispose of it. There are only two possible occasions when the price is fixed—redemption either at maturity or at the call date. At all other periods between issuance and redemption, it may have any value, and this is determined by the interplay of the numerous market forces.

Bonds are usually issued in $1,000 denominations and multiples thereof. They generally pay interest semiannually, the amount equal-

---

[1] There are slight variations among these securities, but the essence, as discussed in the text, covers all the major characteristics.

ling the interest (or coupon) rate times the par value. A 4-per-cent $1,000 bond, for example, might pay $20 interest every February 1 and August 1. The quotation is usually a percentage of par; 99½ would thus mean $995 for the aforementioned bond. It is also understood that the price includes an addition for accrued interest. If, for example, the 99½ were the price on May 1, which means that three months have elapsed since the last interest date (one-half the interest interval), then the buyer would pay the seller an additional $10, or half the interest for the period. He would also pay a broker's commission. Only on bonds in default, on which the interest can no longer be expected, or on income bonds, the interest on which is determined by earnings, would the security sell "flat" (without accrued interest). In what follows we shall assume that the bond interest is being met regularly.

The bond is issued by governments and corporations. The issuer pledges himself to a few simple but important acts: to pay the interest semiannually, to pay the holder at maturity, and to observe any of the rules laid down in the bond indenture. Most of these regulations can be found in any standard text on finance or investments, but for our purposes here, what is important is that the issuer does *not* have to redeem the bond at any time between issuance and the redemption date. At his option he may pay off the bond before maturity, if a call provision permits, and for this privilege he may pay the holder a small premium. But at other than maturity he is not required to do so. This makes it markedly different from the *non-marketable* United States bonds, which can be redeemed at set prices at the holder's volition. The only way the holder can get his funds is to dispose of the bond to someone who is willing to acquire it, and the price agreed upon is determined by market forces rather than by the corporation's financial ability to repay.[2] If the holder should sell, he would not lose any interest, because of the accrued-interest feature; if he held the bond for only one day, he would receive whatever proportionate interest had accrued.

There are several types of fixed-interest securities, but all have these features in common: redemption at set prices, an unchanging interest payment at set dates, and no obligation on the part of the issuer to redeem the bond before maturity. Whether the company's earnings rise or fall, the bond terms remain unchanged, provided these requirements are met. Improved earnings do not result in higher income, nor will income decline if earnings drop off. This differs from common stocks, where higher earnings may produce higher dividends, and lower earnings less or no dividend. Indeed, if the company's earnings

---

[2] Except to the extent that this capacity influences investor judgment of the bond's attractiveness.

dropped off so much that it was forced to reduce the interest payment, then we would consider it to be in default, if not bankrupt.

There is one important exception to the interest arrangement. Very short-lived securities, known as bills, are sold at a discount. Usually they have a life of only three months, but some are issued for longer periods, though less than one year. The difference between the sales price and maturing value then represents the interest income. For example, a $1,000 three-month bill, sold at $990, yields $10 income in three months, or about 1 per cent of purchase price. Since interest rates are calculated on an annual basis, we would multiply this figure by four, so that its yield would be about 4 per cent per annum. No other interest would be paid. In addition to bills and bonds there are issues having intermediate lives—one to five years normally—known as certificates and notes: since they have many of the characteristics of the bond, we shall not discuss them separately, but treat them as relatively short-lived bonds.

In determining the life of a security, we look at its remaining life. For example, on February 1 a three-month bill is issued, to mature May 1. On February 1 it has three months' life, on March 1, two months, and so on. Thus, an original forty-year bond now having only a year to maturity, is regarded as the equivalent of a one-year bond. That is, all 4-per-cent bonds maturing on February 1, 1968, would have the same remaining life whether they had been issued in 1800, 1900, or 1963. The only qualification concerns the call date, a technical point we shall discuss later.

The element of transferability means that the issuer has no real concern as to who the holder of its bonds may be. On interest payment day, it gives the amount to whoever holds it; on maturity day it gives the principal to whoever holds it. But at all other times, the security could be changing hands frequently or staying with the original buyer. Note that the only time the issuing unit receives any money is at the original date of issue. After that, all transactions are between buyer and seller, and the funds that pass from the former to the latter in no way affect the company's financial condition. But this is not literally true, for there are some factors of concern to the issuer. For example, a public utility might prefer that its bondholders be residents of the area it serves, for then it can build good will and perhaps even a pressure group that would oppose government efforts to reduce the rates charged for its service. Or a company might like widespread distribution of its bonds so that it is better known and thus can market a new issue more readily. But in the narrow financial-flow sense—in so far as its actual receipt of cash from a particular bond issue is concerned—it is in no way affected by the transactions subsequent to the issue, other than on interest days and at redemption time. And, as already re-marked, the bondholder has no claims on the issuer other than those implied in the terms of the contract.

A minor qualification should be stated regarding convertible bonds. These are exchangeable usually for a company's common stock, sometimes with an additional payment of cash to the company. The owner exercises this privilege, and if he does, he affects the company's capital structure. Because such a security is more like a common stock, it will not be discussed here, and the reader is referred to standard texts on the subject. However, a brief mention will be made in connection with bank portfolios.

Yields

Because bond prices do fluctuate, the stated interest rate is no guide to the proportionate return to a prospective buyer, and so we must bring in a new concept, that of bond yield. The interest that is payable on a bond, as stated, is figured on the bond's par value, which we shall take as $1,000. But if the buyer pays other than this amount, his rate of return is different from the stated interest rate, for the interest income now applies to his purchase price. A 4-per-cent bond means that it pays $40 annually. If a buyer paid $1,000, he would receive 4 per cent as his rate of return. But if he paid only $990 for the bond, then his rate of return is somewhat higher (40/990); if he paid $1,010 it would be somewhat lower (40/1010). To distinguish the rate of return on other than the par value, we use the term *yield*. However, in practice the two terms are often used interchangeably, and since it is clear from the context whether we mean the return figured on the par or the market value, such sloppiness is not serious. Incidentally, al-though a bond normally matures at its par value, it need not be issued at that figure. It may be issued at a premium, which means that the first buyer paid more than $1,000, or at a discount, which means that he paid less than $1,000. Similarly, after issuance it could sell above $1,000, at a premium, or below $1,000, at a discount.

Actually, the concept of yield is more complicated than the pre-ceding paragraph indicates. We must correct for the fact that there is a difference between the purchase price and the redemption value—a capital gain if the security is purchased at a discount, a capital loss if purchased at a premium. We must also take into consideration the time remaining between the purchase and redemption dates. To bring all these together, the discussion will proceed in stages, treating each point as a separate illustration. As will be shown, both the time factor and the capital differential can be calculated precisely. In fact, since interest rates and yields are always on a per-annum basis, we *must* make these adjustments, so that comparability results. It should also be remarked that an actual purchase or sale, such as we are discussing, is not really necessary in order to calculate the yield. So long as we know what price the bond could be sold for—or could be purchased at—then we can make our estimates as though the transaction actually occurred at that price. Thus, in our first illustration the price of $990.48 need not be an actual sale price; it could be an offer to sell or an offer to buy. But having been given that figure, we can make our yield estimates as though the transaction went through at that price. Then when we have arrived at the yield, we can decide whether it is satisfactory—whether we want to pay or accept that amount.

ONE-YEAR BOND AT A DISCOUNT. To introduce the subject, let us assume that the United States government had issued long-term bonds some time in the past at 4 per cent. These bonds mature one year from today, and although originally issued for a longer period, they can now be regarded as the equivalent of a new bond with a one-year life. Here we shall restrict ourselves to government issues in order to avoid the additional problem of risk of default. In the American financial community there is no security with greater safety than United States government obligations, and because of its taxing and monetary powers, we can regard this one segment of the money market as virtually riskless so far as the possibility of default is concerned. There are other risks, but none involve a mistrust of the government's ability to pay either the semi-annual interest requirements or the repayment of the principal at maturity.

We shall assume that the government is planning to issue a one-year bond. Simultaneously, business is prosperous, and there are many corporations anxious to issue ("float") bonds in order to obtain funds for expansion. Furthermore, there are also other eager would-be borrowers, such as prospective home buyers trying to obtain mortgages. All of these are willing to pay higher interest to the lender than the government will pay. This reflects the fact that such securities do have a risk of default, but in part this higher rate also reflects the intensity of demand for loanable funds. So, in order for the government to induce enough people to purchase *its* bond issue, we shall assume that it must offer the prospective buyer a 5-per-cent annual interest.

If such were the case, consider the owner of the 4-per-cent government bond who may wish to sell it today because he has some other use for his funds. His bond also has one year to run, and it, too, is a government obligation. Until now, its attractiveness parallels that of the new issue. But on his security, the new buyer will get only 4 per cent; on the new one he will receive 5 per cent. Therefore, if the present owner of the 4-per-cent issue wants to find a buyer, he must make it as attractive as the competing 5-per-cent issue.

The present owner cannot change either the interest to be paid on the 4-per-cent bond or that on the 5-per-cent security. The former was set at the time of issue and was determined by the United States government; hence, this aspect of bond income is fixed. Similarly, the 4-per-cent owner cannot influence the government to alter the 5-per-cent rate, for that was determined by the Treasury after studying the money-market conditions. Hence, the 4-per-cent holder has only one alternative, to offer the prospective buyer additional income to offset the 1-per-cent differential. This he can do by accepting a price below par, for then the buyer will obtain a capital gain which, if correctly calculated, will just compensate for the lower nominal income on the 4-per-cent bond. To simplify the arithmetic, we shall ignore the cost of the brokerage commissions.

Viewed from the buyer's position, what he would be faced with is that he can buy either the new bond from the government, paying $1,000 and obtaining $50 income over the year, or the 4-per-cent bond for somewhat less than $1,000 and earn $40 interest income plus a capital gain. His objective is to receive the same rate of return per dollar invested. That is, the ratio of his total income ($40 plus capital gain) to his investment (the purchase price) should come to 5 per cent—what he could otherwise obtain on the new issue. The unknowns in this 4-per-cent situation are the capital gain and the purchase price. Actually, there is only one unknown, for if we know the purchase price, we automatically know the capital gain, since it is simply the difference between $1,000 and the purchase price.

Our objective, then, is to earn 5 per cent on our investment in the 4-per-cent bond. Therefore, we must figure out how much capital gain is necessary, which, when added to $40, will give us a numerator that then gives us a 5-per-cent ratio. In practice, the student would find books on bond yields that give the answer. Otherwise, some trial-and-error arithmetic will be required. Shortcutting the latter, and rounding the figures for simplicity, let us try a purchase price of $990.48 (in market terms, a price of 99.048 per cent of par). As can be seen, this will give a capital gain of $9.52, or a total income over the year of $49.52. This $49.52/$990.48 equals 5 per cent (rounded slightly), which is our objective. This is the price the buyer should pay if he wishes to attain the same rate of return as on the new issue.

Suppose he paid more—perhaps $992. Then his total income would be only $48, and, per dollar of investment, he would be earning less than 5 per cent and so could do better by buying the new bond.

But what about a price of only $990? Here his return would be $50/$990, better than 5 per cent. But then the seller would be foolish to agree, for he would have made the 4-per-cent bond even more attractive than the new issue. At $990.48 he would have just about matched the attractiveness of the 5-per-cent bond, and so could count on the close calculation of the money market to shift enough buyers to his 4-per-cent issue; any lower price, such as $990, would produce a swarm of buyers, all eager to earn this return now made superior to the 5-per-cent issue. Such an enormous demand would then push the price of the 4-per-cent bond back to $990.48, at which point its equivalency with the 5-per-cent issue would reduce the demand sufficiently to create equality with the supply.

It might be argued that the $1,000 bond at 5 per cent would still be more attractive, for more money is earning this rate of return. Ten dollars more are at work, so to speak. But this is not so. There are enough investors with large amounts to dispose of, so that either alternative would absorb their funds. For example, suppose a large pension fund had $1,981,000 to invest. It could buy 1,981 bonds at $1,000 each, earning 1,981 times $50, or $99,050.00. Or it could buy 2,000 4-per-cent bonds, paying (2,000 times $990.48) $1,981,000 (rounded; it is actually $1,980,960). It would earn $80,000 interest income, plus $19,040 capital gain, or $99,040 (the $10 discrepancy is due to our rounding). That is, in either alternative it invests about the same amount, and receives in income about the same amount.

The reader should note that this seemingly technical discussion about the calculation of a bond price has implicitly answered two important points. One is the relationship of bond prices to interest-rate shifts. In this example, we have seen that if the market rate moves up, as it did on government bonds, the price of equivalent outstanding bonds will decline. That is, if a one-year bond paid 4 per cent, and now one-year bonds must pay 5 per cent if they are to find buyers, then one-year bonds with only a 4-per-cent interest will decline in price—a decline that can be figured precisely. We have also seen why bond prices might decline: the intensity of demand for funds is such that new borrowing must be at higher rates, so already outstanding bonds decline in price. Note, too, that even with a government bond there is an element of risk—fluctuations in the market value. Despite the fact that there is no suspicion of default, the 4-per-cent bond declined in value. This decline in no way reflected a lack of faith in the United States government. It was simply the response to changes in money market conditions (in the demand for, and supply of, funds) that brought about the shift in interest rates and, through them, the change in bond prices. Incidentally, since rising interest rates mean declining bond prices, we also see when the possibility of a capital loss could arise—namely, in boom times, when there is an enormous demand for money.

We can also now define our yield more precisely. It is the interest income, plus capital gain, divided by the purchase price and expressed as a percentage. This will differ from the original interest rate if the purchase price is at other than par, because of the capital gain or loss factor. (Even this must be corrected for time, which we shall do in the third and subsequent illustrations.)

ONE-YEAR BOND AT A PREMIUM. As before, we shall start with a United States government bond issued some time in the past at 4 per cent having now only one more year to maturity. Here, however, we shall assume that business is slack, that the demand for loanable funds is much less than in our first illustration. As a matter of fact, the demand is so little now that if the United States government wished to issue a one-year bond, investors would be willing to purchase it even if the interest rate were only 3 per cent. We now have the reverse of the preceding illustration, and, as we would expect, the 4-per-cent bond will go at a premium. This section will discuss its calculation, as well as some of the implications.

If a prospective investor were faced with just these two alternatives, he would see that his choice is either an annual income of $40 on the already outstanding bond, or only $30 on the new issue. Obviously, other things being equal, he would prefer the former, so much so that he would start bidding eagerly for it, as would many others. As a consequence, the price of the bond would rise until it reached a price that made it *no more* attractive than the newly issued 3-per-cent bond. As the price rises above par, the emerging premium means that the new buyer will obtain a capital loss, or the excess of the price paid over the maturing value. Once this loss offsets the additional interest income or once the interest minus this premium, divided by the purchase price, nets out to 3 per cent, the two bonds are equal in attractiveness, and so have brought about a new equilibrium.

As before, there are bond tables that give us this answer. But here we shall resort to simple arithmetic to illustrate our point; our price for the 4-per-cent bond would be about $1,009.71. By paying that much, our buyer nets $40.00 minus $9.71, or $30.29. Three per cent on an investment of $1,009.71 is $30.29, or the net income. Thus, whether he buys the 4-per-cent bond at this premium price or the new 3-per-cent bond at par, each dollar nets him 3 per cent. He is willing to pay a premium, even though he knows there will be a net capital loss, because the higher-interest income will compensate for it.

As before, we can now deduce certain relationships. Should interest rates tend to decline because of shifting money-market conditions, the price of bonds already issued will tend to move up, even though there has been no improvement in the underlying quality of the bond. The government is no safer than before. The risk of default is no less than before. But the supply-demand conditions have shifted. What results is an excess supply of funds at the higher rate, for now lenders are willing to accept a lower return. Holders who had bought earlier can now realize a capital gain. We have here one of the speculative aspects relative to even high-quality bonds: if we expect rising interest rates, we should sell bonds, since that expectation implies declining prices; if we expect declining interest rates, we should buy bonds, since that implies a rise in bond prices.

Incidentally, we have been using as our starting point the par value of a bond; in the first illustration, a $1,000 bond dropped to $990.48; in the second it rose to $1,009.71. Similar calculations could be made for any price. For example, suppose a one-year bond paying 4 per cent had been selling at $990.48. That indicates that its yield is now 5 per cent. If the going rates changed to 3 per cent, then we would refigure as before and see that it should now sell at $1,009.71. If it had only a 3-per-cent annual rate of interest, then it should sell at $1,000. If it had only a 2-per-cent annual rate of interest, then it should sell at a discount—a smaller discount if alternative equivalent bonds sell for 3 per cent than if they sell for 4 per cent.

Similarly, if we start with the price, we can estimate the yield. A 4-per-cent bond selling for $990.48 with one year to run yields 5 per cent; if we are told that it is selling for $1,009.71, we can figure that it yields 3 per cent. Fortunately, there are tables that do this for us, adjusting for changes in the remaining life, the interest payable, and the selling price, and relating all three.

To summarize the first two illustrations, we can say that a rise in interest rates will tend to lower bond prices; a decline in interest rates will tend to raise bond prices. Or, a decline in bond prices indicates that interest rates have risen; a rise in bond prices indicates that interest rates have fallen.

A TWO-YEAR BOND AT A DISCOUNT. When we pass beyond one year, we run into the compounding problem. This is similar to a deposit in a savings account. If money is left with the bank for more than one interest period, the interest is added to the total at the end of the first period, and then at the end of the second period the interest is calculated on this new sum, which is more than in the preceding period. Each interest period would then show a higher total because of this accumulation of interest being added to the previous total.

A similar approach is used in adjusting discount and premiums on bonds where the remaining life is more than one year. To simplify our arithmetic, we shall use an annual compounding approach. In effect, we shall say that the capital gain or loss to be realized on maturity is spread over the remaining life so that each year's share is added to (or subtracted from) the compounded total in such a way as to arrive at a yield that includes this compounded factor. This rather cumbersome statement can be better shown if we break down the arithmetic into several stages.

We shall start with a United States government bond with two years to run, paying 4 per cent per annum, $40 per year. We shall also assume that the government can issue a new two-year bond at par only if it pays 5 per cent. What should be the price of the outstanding issue?

As a first approximation, we know that the outstanding issue will pay $80 in interest over the next two years. The new bond will pay $100 during the same period. Hence, the apparent income differential is $20, and so we set the 4-per-cent bond at $980, since that will give a capital gain in dollars equal to the dollar difference in interest income.

But then we get a new discrepancy. To get $100 income, A could buy the new bond for $1,000. To get the same income from the 4-per-cent bond, A need pay only $980. Since the latter requires less capital for the same income, it is obviously more attractive. In other words, we have priced it too low.

Suppose we raise our price slightly, to $981.41. In the first year we should get 5 per cent, or $49.07. But all we actually receive is the $40 interest; we must obtain the remainder from the capital gain. So, at the end of the first year, the bond's theoretical value should go up by $9.07, or to $990.48. The second year we should also receive 5 per cent, but now it should be on this higher amount, to compensate for our not having received the full 5 per cent in the prior year. Hence, this year's return should be 5 per cent times $990.48, or $49.52. Forty dollars is received from the interest income, and since the bond matures at $1,000, we get the remaining $9.52 from the capital gain. And so we have earned our 5 per cent per annum if we pay only $981.41 for this 4-per-cent bond with a two-year life remaining.

As in our first illustration, the rise in the going rates of interest depressed the price of the bond under discussion. But there has been a difference. The bond in this section has twice as many years to run as the bond in the first section. But the decline in its price was not quite twice as much—$18.59, the discount of the two-year 4-per-cent bond from par, is not twice $9.52, the discount of the one-year 4-per-cent bond. Note that at the discounted prices, both 4-per-cent bonds are selling to yield 5 per cent. On the other hand, the discount for the two-year bond is considerably greater than for the one-year bond. Hence, we can conclude that for a given shift in yields, from 4 to 5 per cent, the capital impact will be greater for bonds with a greater length of life remaining, although proportionately this greater impact will be less than the relative increase in life.

A TWO-YEAR BOND AT A PREMIUM. Here we explain the reverse—a two-year bond paying 4 per cent interest in a market that experiences a decline for similar issues to 3 per cent. As in our second illustration, we would expect the 4-per-cent bond to go to a premium, greater in absolute amount than the rise in the one-year bond, but not quite twice as much. Our price is approximately $1,019.14.

If we have equilibrium, as already explained, this two-year 4-per-cent bond selling at the above price should yield only 3 per cent over the period. Three per cent for the first year, based on the purchase price, is $30.57; but actually we receive $40 in interest. The difference is thus set aside to offset the expected capital loss. Hence, we deduct the $9.43 excess income from our cost, so that its value at the end of one year is now only $1,009.71. Three per cent on this remaining amount is $30.29; we actually receive $40, or $9.71 in excess, just equal to the remaining capital loss as the maturing date brings in the $1,000 of capital. As before, in the third illustration, the two-year bond's premium is larger than the premium for the one-year bond, even though both yield 3 per cent, but the former is not quite twice as great, even though the number of years is twice as many.

This last point can be brought out more clearly if we discuss a twenty-year bond with a 4-per-cent interest rate selling in a 3-per-cent market. Such a bond would sell for approximately $1,150, a premium far greater in absolute amount than either of the two so far discussed, but not reflecting proportionately the greater life. That is, its premium is less than twenty times that for the one-year bond, and less than ten times the premium on the two-year bond. (A qualification must be made regarding the size of this premium, discussed later in connection with the call privilege.)

SHORT-TERM BILLS. Securities issued with a life of less than one year are sold and traded at a discount from the maturing value, the difference between the purchase price and the maturing value representing the income. The yield is computed by adjusting the return to an annual basis; income for a three-month period, for example, would be multiplied by four, whereas income for a two-month period would be mutliplied by six. Conversely, a stated yield is divided by the period covered to get the actual income. A 4-per-cent yield for three months really means 1 per cent; a 6-per-cent yield for two months is also 1 per cent. In this section we will limit the discussion to three-month United States Treasury bills with a maturity value of $1,000; other (short-term) lengths of life and amounts are also available, but the principle. of valuation would be the same.

A 4-per-cent bill, therefore, would be issued at about $990, since it has only a quarter of a year to go, and a quarter of 4 per cent here equals $10. Actually, there is a small discrepancy, for the buyer is earning $10 on an investment of $990, which is a bit more than 1 per cent. In what follows, we shall ignore these slight adjustments. If the yield at time of issue had been 5 per cent, the selling price would be somewhat lower, $987.50. As with bonds, a higher yield is associated with a lower price. But note how small the change is—a $2.50 differ-ence. In contrast, the difference becomes marked for long-term bonds. The difference between a 2-per-cent and a 4-per-cent bill is $995, compared with $990, or $5. But a 2-per-cent bond with twenty years to run, selling to yield 4 per cent, would sell for $726.50, more than one-quarter below par.

We can therefore see that large changes in the yield on bills have relatively small effects on their capital values, but large changes in bond yields have drastic effects on their capital values. Indeed, even a yield of 3 per cent for the aforementioned 2-per-cent bond would put it at about 85 per cent of par, or a discount of almost $150. That is, a yield difference of 1 per cent on the bond produced a capital drop thirty times as great as the yield difference of 2 per cent—twice as much—on the three-month bill. Hence, if we expect a rise in interest rates, it is the longer-term bonds that will decline most sharply in price. Conversely, if we expect yields to decline, it is the long-term sector that would show the best possibility for capital gain. In our example, if bond yields moved down from 3 to 2 per cent, our bond would rise from $850.50 to $1,000, whereas the bill would move up by only $5, even if its yield dropped in half, from 4 to 2 per cent.

BILLS AND THE PASSAGE OF TIME. Because of their extremely short life, another factor influences our assessment of bills—namely, the passage of time. For example, a 6-per-cent yield on a three-month bill means that it sells for $985. After one month, if it still yields 6 per cent, it would sell for $990; now we take one-sixth of the yield instead of one-fourth, and so deduct a smaller figure. Similarly, after two months, with but one-twelfth of a year remaining, it would sell for $995. Hence, if bill yields remain unchanged, the price of a bill will slowly rise, this rise being the income for the period.

If, however, during the period of its existence the yields should rise, then we have two different forces at work. The rise in yields tends to depress the price of the bill, but the passage of time between shifts in yields tends to raise the price. Suppose a bill were issued at 4 per cent, or $990. If yields remained the same, it would sell for 993⅓ after one month. But suppose that by the end of the month the going rate for two-month bills had moved up to 6 per cent. Our bill would then sell for $990. A three-month bill yielding 6 per cent would sell for $985. As can be seen, the net effect of the shift in yields was to depress bill prices in general; for the particular 4-per-cent bill under examination, the passage of one month tended to raise its price. The combined effect was a cancellation of these two opposite effects. As a 4-per-cent three-month bill, it sold for $990. As a 6-per-cent two-month bill, it sells for $990. Despite a rise in yields of one-half, there was no actual loss on this particular bill. And if yields had moved up somewhat less—to 5¾ per cent—the original buyer would still earn an income, although not as great as originally anticipated. In that event the bill would sell for $900.42, or a net gain of 42 cents for the month, compared with the expected income of $3.33, had yields remained unchanged.

If yields had moved down over the month to 2 per cent, then there would be a double gain. The three-month bill would now be a two-month bill selling for $996.67; the original holder would have gained $6.67, or twice as much as originally anticipated.

Because of this time factor, we have a strong cushion as protection against yield increases. With bonds, we could virtually count on a capital loss if yields rose. But with bills this might not be so, if the time factor is strong enough. In practice, yields change at a rate slow enough so that it is most unlikely for an actual loss to be experienced. Normally, the force of time pushing up bill prices is almost always sufficient to offset any depressing effect if yields do rise. As a result, we can say that the risk of capital loss is virtually absent with such short-term securities, in contrast to the wider swings in bonds. This heightens their attractiveness for those financial institutions that may have to liquidate on short notice, as is true for banks. If banks are forced to sell assets, the one that is almost certain not to cause them a capital loss, no matter how adverse the interest-rate conditions, is the Treasury bill. Hence, to the extent that unforeseen drains of cash could produce a need to liquidate assets, the safest (in the sense of capital protection) is the bill. It is for this reason that this particular security has come to occupy so important a position in any analysis of bank liquidity. And the most important of these short-term bills are the Treasury issues, for not only are they absolutely safe, but the daily volume of trades is enormous, thus making it easy for any one institution to buy or sell the desired amount.

POTENTIAL CAPITAL LOSSES AND BOND YIELDS. As we have seen, on extremely long-term bonds, a rise in yields can produce a sharp drop in
price and so bring about enormous capital losses. Many banks and
other financial institutions are reluctant to risk such losses, for they
would impair capital, or cause stockholders to doubt the ability of
management, perhaps impair confidence in the very solvency of the
organization. Hence, if yields rise too much—if bond prices fall too
much—sales may dry up, and the price may not fall as much as it
would otherwise if this "locked-in" effect did not exist. As a consequence, if prices do not fall as much, yields do not go up as much.
Therefore, while we might see a rise in bill yields from 2 to 4 per cent,
since there is little, if any, capital loss (sellers are not discouraged from
liquidating bills in view of the absence of this locked-in feeling), long-
term bond yields would not be as likely to show so great a swing.
Perhaps a rise from 2 to 3 per cent—about a 15-per-cent decline in
bond prices—is all that the holders will suffer. Sales then dry up, and
the price does not decline any further. We are thus likely to see bond
yields move within a narrower range than yields on bills. However,
capital values will swing much more widely for bonds than for bills. In
our illustration, bill yields might move between 2 and 4 per cent,
whereas bond yields might stay within the 2- to 3-per-cent range. But
that means bill prices range between $990 and $995 on three-month
issues, whereas twenty-year 2-per-cent bonds go from $1,000 to
$850.50.

The demand side also works to reinforce this difference. If bill
yields fall, little capital gain can be realized, since the price moves
within so narrow a range. But if bond yields fall, especially on a bond
as long as twenty years, there is a sizeable capital gain to be realized.
Speculators are more likely to step in and buy bonds rather than bills
after a substantial fall in price. This demand sustains the price, and that
means that it puts a brake on the upward movement in yields.

It might be thought that the same logic applies to premiums on
bonds if yields drop greatly. However, we run into another influence,
the call provision. This acts as a brake on any rise in bond prices, and
also on any decline in bond yields. This aspect holds only if the bond
rises above par. We shall discuss this in the next chapter.

Summary

We can summarize the yield-interest discussion as follows:

1. A rise in yields means a decline in bond prices. A decline in
yields means a rise in bond prices.

2. A rise in bond prices is a decline in yields; a decline in bond prices is a rise in yields.

3. The longer the life of a security, the greater the absolute amount of a change in value as a result of the change in yields.

4. With short-term issues, especially under a year, the mere passage of time will increase the bill's capital value.

5. Because of the time factor, there is little likelihood of a holder experiencing a capital loss on bills even if yields do move up.

6. Because of the impact on capital values, yields on bonds tend to move within a narrower range than yields on bills; however, the absolute value of the bond tends to move over a much wider range than that of the bill.

Chapter 14

INSTITUTIONAL FACTORS AND BOND MOVEMENTS

In the preceding chapter we discussed the basic influences governing the relationships of bond yields to bond prices, and the shifts in each. But in practice there are numerous institutional factors that tend to modify the relatively straightforward presentation of these forces. Aspects that pertain to the monetary analysis will be covered now in order to present a more complete picture of the money-market operation.

Call Date

Many bonds are issued with a call provision. At the issuer's option, this permits either partial or complete redemption of the issue, at a date before maturity. For example, a bond might be issued to mature in 1990, with interest payable on February 1 and August 1 of each year. In addition, the bond is callable on any interest date starting February

1, 1970. If less than the total outstanding is called, the selection of the particular bonds to be redeemed might be determined by lot.

Three major factors would determine the decision to call a bond before maturity. At the time it was issued, the debtor's financial position may have been clouded, so certain provisions surrounding the bond, such as a mortgage on all the property, may have been required. Now the issuer feels that its credit is so good that it wishes to remove these restrictions by calling in this bond issue and replacing it with a less onerous one. Or the flow of funds may have so exceeded estimates that the issuer is now able to pay off the debt, and so end the interest charge.

Probably most important is the shift in interest rates. If the bond had been issued when yields were high, then the interest charged the debtor would reflect this fact. Later, money-market conditions might change and rates would come down. The same debtor could now issue a bond with a much lower interest rate, using the funds to redeem the higher rate (the older debt) and thus reduce its expenses. This influence, it should be noted, is strictly one-way. If yields have risen since the bond was issued, there is no compulsion for the debtor to call in these bonds and replace them with a higher yield issue, thus helping the bondholder. The buyer, in other words, is faced with a "heads you win, tails I lose" choice: if yields rise, his bond drops in price; if yields decline, the bonds may be redeemed and he can either take the cash and reinvest it at the currently lower yields, or accept the new issue, also at a lower yield than the retired bond.

There is some compensation. Bonds called before maturity are generally redeemed at par, plus a small premium, the premium decreasing as the redemption is closer to maturity. For example, the bondholder might get an extra six months' interest. But this is a small offset for the loss of a high-yielding security. Hence, many large bond buyers insist on clauses that either forbid calling or postpone it for many years.

Since a bond may be called if yields decline, a prospective purchaser is faced with a problem. If yields go below the interest on the bond, the bond not only rises but goes above par. The greater the decline in yields, the more it goes above par. But the greater the decline in yields, the greater the chance that the bond will be called. Once the bond price exceeds the call price—assuming calling is permitted—there is a growing danger of a capital loss. Since the call is usually given only a few months in advance of redemption, the loss can be considerable. If we go back to the fourth illustration in the previous chapter, we see that a twenty-year 4-per-cent bond selling to yield 3 per cent would be priced at $1,150. This yield assumes that there will be twenty years to receive $40 income annually, or more than the 3 per cent on the principal ($1,150 times 3 per cent, or $34.50), the excess then being used to offset the $150 capital loss. But if the bond is called in six months, then we receive only $20 interest income; even if the call price were $1,050, there would still be a capital loss far in excess of the income received. The most that a buyer would probably pay in such circumstances would be $1,070—the call price plus the six months' interest (the remaining life, if the bond were to be called). He might pay more if he felt there was no likelihood of the bond being called. For any debtor whose credit rating is reasonably good, the call provision becomes an ever-present consideration. Its standing will always allow it to issue a new bond in order to obtain funds to pay off outstanding obligations.

If bonds are selling at a premium, bond yields are often figured as though they will be called at the earliest possible date. Thus, if our twenty-year bond could be called within one year, it would be treated as a one-year bond, although in actuality it could remain for twenty years. Its premium would then amount to only $9.71. On the other hand, if yields are higher than the stated interest rate, which means that the bonds would not be called, then the maturity date is selected in calculating yields. Hence, a rise in yields could push bond prices down quite far, whereas a decline in yields does not produce enormous premiums unless the bond is non-callable. Non-callability has a value in itself, since it removes the danger of a return of funds when yields are low; hence, bonds issued with this clause may bear a lower interest than one with a callability clause, simply because of the greater freedom to rise in times of low yields.

Income Taxes

In our discussion of yields, we were concerned solely with income, whether obtained as interest or capital gain (or loss). In the first illustration in Chapter 13, a 5-per-cent bond selling at par with one year to maturity, was equal to the 4-per-cent bond selling at $990.48. But this is not necessarily so. On the 5-per-cent bond, the entire return is treated as income and is therefore taxable. On the 4-per-cent bond, part of the return is a capital gain and is subject to a lower tax. Actually, the 4-per-cent bond may be giving a greater after-tax return. However, this does not hold true for all bonds, nor for all buyers, so the same two opportunities can be viewed differently, depending on both sides of the picture.

For example, if the prospective investor is a tax-exempt foundation, then the distinction is meaningless. It does not pay taxes on either kind of income so both alternatives are equal. If the investor is an individual in a very high income-tax bracket, then he is most concerned with maximizing income from capital gains. If the bond is a United States government obligation, then the income component is not subject to the state income tax. If the bond is a state or municipal obligation, then the capital component and not the interest income is subject to Federal income tax. Obviously, each example here alters the relative after-tax income of the two alternative issues, and each example must be considered. Since most investors are in the business to make money, those who deal in bonds are particularly shrewd. Purchases and sales may involve single transactions of $10 million or more; an error of even 0.1 per cent can amount to more than $10,000. Moreover, in a money-and-banking book we cannot ignore the fact that banks are subject to the corporate income tax, which can be as high as 52 per cent (before 1964); hence, in any discussion of bank portfolio decisions, these tax considerations are not likely to be ignored.

Actually, tax influence is more subtle than is implied here. With corporate taxes so high, the borrower often feels only half the cost, because the interest paid is treated as an expense and is deducted from income, thereby reducing the tax levy. In effect, a 4 per-cent bond costs only about 2 per cent net after tax considerations. A government unit, in contrast, must levy taxes to pay all its interest; it has no offset. So a 4-per-cent rate is much higher to the latter than to the corporation.

Commercial banks are in a more peculiar position, because tax treatment is different. Because of the special impact on their performance, we shall treat it separately.

Price-Level Changes

Some economists have believed that anticipated changes in the price levels also enter into interest-rate calculations. If *A* expects prices to rise 2 per cent over the year, then his money will have less purchasing power twelve months from now. If he decides to lend only if he nets 4 per cent, then he must actually charge 6 per cent in order to offset the loss through declining purchasing power. However, it is doubtful if this consideration really enters into the determination of rates. How would such an investor enforce his objective? If the borrower refused to pay so high a rate, the investor would have to hold his funds idle. These would decline in purchasing power by 2 per cent, and a year later would be equivalent to only 98 cents per dollar. Had *A* lent the funds out at 4 per cent, he would have had $1.04 after the year, but after correcting for rising prices, this would be equal to about $1.02. He has had a net gain in purchasing power of only 2 per cent, but, as compared with his alternative of holding funds idle, he is still better off by the 4 per cent he received as interest ($1.02 versus 98 cents).

The purchasing-power consideration probably shows up in two ways. If A expects prices to rise, he might prefer to acquire some asset that would also rise in value more rapidly as a result of this price movement—for example, real estate, common stocks, commodities. If the inflation is really enormous—as is true in some Latin American countries—then higher interest rates are accepted by both sides of the loan transaction, for alternative uses for investible funds compete with the would-be borrower for the available money. This inflationary aspect of our problem will be discussed later. Here we can say that for the normal price movements experienced by the United States in peacetime, it is very probable that the purchasing-power shifts do not affect the interest rate significantly, other than through the diversion of funds to other types of assets, such as those mentioned at the beginning of this paragraph.

Inflation, by raising prices, usually improves profit margins, since costs tend to lag. This might induce firms to expand operations; and to do so, they would probably have to borrow. With this increased demand for loans, there would probably be a rise in interest rates, and so, in this rather roundabout way, the lender does get a higher return as a result of the price rise. However, it is doubtful if the adjustments are offsetting, so we can say only that some benefit does accrue to the creditor, but probably not enough to compensate for the decline in the purchasing power of his funds.

Risky Securities

The element of default is always a consideration in assessing the wisdom of buying a fixed-interest security. There are organizations that rate bonds with this danger in mind. In general, the more remote such an eventuality is for the issuer, the better the grade of the bond. As a consequence, banks tend to confine themselves to the better grades. (In general, our discussion of bonds will be similarly limited.)

Within this category there are variances in the default possibility. To compensate for this risk, the yield is adjusted; the greater the risk, the higher the yield. So the safest security always sells for a lower yield than a risky one, after correction for the tax impact. But the spread between the various risk categories may vary. For our purposes we shall cover only the top four grades: *Aaa, Aa, A,* and *Baa.* These are the classifications used by Moody's, the best-known of the rating services, and, with slight variation, by Standard & Poor's, another leader in the field.

As we have seen, if the demand for funds drops off relative to the supply, there is a tendency for yields to go down. One way this occurs is that the demand for outstanding securities is increased, since funds are no longer demanded in as great an amount by new borrowings. In response, their prices rise, and this indicates declining yields.

Suppose the *Aaa* bonds are the first to feel this force. Their yields drop, thus widening the spread, as compared with the other categories. At some point the investor may feel this spread is excessive, and so starts buying *Aa* bonds. This then pushes up their price and depresses their yields, and demand then switches to the *A* category, and so on.

To illustrate, let us assume that at the moment the risk between categories is assessed at ¼ per cent. If *Aaa* bonds yield 3 per cent, *Aa* bonds would yield 3¼ per cent, *A* bonds 3½ per cent, and *Baa* bonds 3¾ per cent. If investment demand pushes *Aaa* bonds to 2¾ per cent, then the riskier *Aa* bond is being assessed a penalty of ½ per cent. But this is more than the market feels the risk is worth; it has felt that ¼ per cent was enough compensation. In other words, now the additional premium (½ per cent) obtainable from buying *Aa* bonds is greater than the risk cost (¼ per cent), and so investors switch. As they do, the *Aa* yields decline, and the spread against *A* bonds widens. And from there we go to *Baa*.

An analogous shift would occur if demand for funds had increased so much—for example, a sharp increase in the volume of new loans— that the price of *Aaa* bonds started to drop. If it dropped so much that *Aaa* yields rose to 3¼ per cent, the same as is obtainable on *Aa* bonds, no one would want the latter. Why buy a riskier issue that yields no more than the safer one? So *Aa* bonds are sold, depressing their price and raising their yield. But then the *A* bonds become less attractive; and then *Baa*.

Sometimes these shifts are also accompanied by changes in the assessment of the risk. Suppose the general decline in yields occurred in a recession. In such a period, people worry more about the default possibility. They see profits declining and some firms threatened with insolvency. Perhaps now they feel that each category should sell for ⅜ per cent more; the risk possibility is now evaluated somewhat higher. Then, as the *Aaa* bonds dropped from 3 to 2⅞ per cent, thus producing a ⅜-per-cent spread compared with the *Aa* issues, people would not switch out of the former. Only if *Aaa* yields went still lower—say, to 2½ per cent—so that the risk spread grew to ¾ per cent, would switching occur, bringing *Aa* yields down to 2⅞ per cent. In this latter possibility, both categories showed a yield decline, but the *Aaa* issues moved much more.

In our rising yield situation, the risk premium might narrow as improving business lessened the fear of bankruptcies. If *Aaa* yields rose to 3¼ per cent, *Aa* yields might move up only ⅛ per cent, to 3⅜ per cent. Both yields rose, but the riskier ones rose less because of the offsetting effect of the narrowing in the risk premium.[1]

In very extreme recessions and booms, it is possible for the categories to move in opposite directions because of changing risk premium evaluations. Suppose the recession produced such a plethora of funds that *Aaa* yields dropped to 2 per cent, but that the severity of the decline resulted in each category's risk premium rising to ¾ per cent. Then *Aa* bonds would drop to 2¾ per cent from 3¼ per cent, *A* bonds would remain at 3½ per cent, and *Baa* bond yields would actually rise to 4¼ per cent. If recovery came, narrowing our risk premium back to ¼ per cent, *Aaa* yields might rise to 3 per cent while *Baa* yields decline to 3¾ per cent. Such a diamond pattern—the riskier yields rising as the safest categories decline, then the former declining as the latter rise—occurred in the severe depression of the 1930's.

It should be added that ratings and assessment of risk premiums raise many questions. In fact, there is some evidence that the results sway investors toward the safest categories and away from the risky ones. The latter yield is more than justified by the underlying default possibility, while the very safest issues yield less than is justified. This, in turn, makes it more advantageous for the latter to borrow, thus channeling funds to the established companies and governmental units, while the newer, less experienced, more risky firms are starved for funds. Some alert investors willing to pursue this theme have been able to improve their income by putting more of their funds into those issues concerning which, it is felt, the risk spread is excessive. Incidentally, United States government issues are regarded as default-proof, and are not rated.

Short-Long Relationship

A most difficult problem to answer definitively is the relationship between short-term and long-term interest rates, other than for the default risk. In what follows we shall avoid such complications by discussing only high-grade security yields. In this way, the additional uncertainty of non-payment is eliminated.

There are people who want to borrow for a short time, and there

---

[1] Not all long-term yields move immediately. Mortgage rates tend to move less frequently and less quickly when the yields on marketable issues change. On bank loans to business, the rates in New York City have been persistently below those charged in the other northern and eastern centers, which in turn have been lower than those in the South and West.

are people who wish to lend for only a short period of time. These two form a demand and supply for short-term funds and so produce a short-term rate of interest. Similar remarks would be made for the long-term market, and thus we have two markets with two rates.

People and institutions on both sides of the market can and do move between the two, so that the rate in one influences the actions of many in the other. For example, commercial banks lend on both long and short term. The proportion of their funds divided between the two is not fixed; at times more may be in the short-term side; at other times it is the longer-term market that gets a larger share. Similarly, a long-term borrower may feel that at the moment the rate is too high, and that it is likely to come down in the not-too-distant future; if he needs the funds now, he may borrow for a short term and then pay off this loan through a long-term issue when the latter rate has declined. Consequently, it can be seen that there is some kind of linkage between the two markets; since both are money markets, the same commodity can be traded in either sector. It is difficult to sell aluminum to a steel consumer; it is not difficult to switch dollars from the long-term to the short-term borrower, or vice versa. In the latter case, both want the same commodity, so funds can move freely.

Before discussing the factors that link the two markets, we should point out that there are sectors that operate as though the two were walled off. In practice, a person wanting a mortgage to buy a house would not be likely to borrow short-term; for him, only the long-term market is effective. (However, a builder might obtain a short-term loan to finance the project until the final buyer, financed through the long-term market, appeared.) Many long-term borrowers are in practice precluded from moving into the short-term sectors by the nature of their needs. Similarly, many short-term borrowers need only temporary financing; their needs are seasonal, or endure only while the goods to be produced are in process. To tie themselves up with a long-term debt would be foolish no matter how attractive the rate might be, since their needs are relatively infrequent, and a long-term debt would require continual interest payments.

Similarly, there are lenders who do not cross over. A long-term lender, especially the small investor, does not want to be bothered with the trouble of a constantly maturing loan which then requires him to seek a new outlet. By investing in a long-term obligation, he can forget the selection problem for years. If the rate of return is satisfactory, he can then turn his energies to more important matters. Many large investors are in a similar position. They may be pension funds that must plan for requirements ten or twenty years in the future. They do not want to devote their energies and staff time to constantly seeking new outlets. If they can find a good long-term resting place for their money, they are most happy. And many banks, faced with the possibility of daily withdrawals, also need to have funds in relatively short-term assets so that the possible demand for money from their depositors can be met by the rapid maturity of the assets; hence, no matter how attractive the long-term rate may be, they still will not place more than a certain proportion of their funds in other than short-term outlets.

But there are enough lenders and borrowers who can and do move so that the linkage between the two is sufficiently strong to produce some sort of relationship, although it may not be a constant and unwavering one. We have already indicated the type of switches that might occur; here we shall examine them in greater detail, with the implications that lead us into liquidity considerations.

The borrowing side is somewhat easier to see. The long-term borrower might borrow short temporarily if he feels that long-term rates will soon come down. Or he might postpone the project and thus put off his demand for funds until a more favorable rate were available. He might even "roll over" (renew) his short-term loan if the long-term rate is persistently higher, thus saving on interest expense. However, reliance on this form of financing is risky, for monetary stringencies could occur where the short-term lender refuses to renew; at such a time the borrower may be in real trouble, for he may find both the short- and long-term markets frozen. The one advantage of a long-term loan is that the requirement of paying off the debt is postponed for many years, although sinking funds may require that a small part be paid off regularly.

There is less likelihood for the short-term borrower to switch to the other side. If he found that the short-term rate were high and that he was getting regularly into short-term debt, he might move. For example, suppose he always financed production through such borrowing. As soon as one batch was completed and the loan paid off, he would start another operation, raising a new loan. In effect, although each loan was liquidated upon completion of output, the firm would be continually in debt because it would be continually producing. In those circumstances, if the long-term rate were lower, it might be wiser to float one long-term loan and use the funds to finance the continual production needs. A similar consideration would influence consumer credit firms that borrowed short, since their need for funds was short; each such borrowing might be geared to specific installment contracts, but the continual issuance of such contracts results in the firm being constantly in debt.

Lenders, too, reason in somewhat the same way as debtors. If the short-term rate is persistently below the long-term rate, some may switch to the latter even though it means tying up funds for a longer period of time. If long-term rates are persistently lower than short, then some long-term lenders might enter the short-term market even though it means frequent reinvestment problems. But there are other, more subtle forces at work overshadowing these factors. To understand these forces, we must refer to our earlier discussion regarding expectations, in Chapter 5. Indeed, almost all investment decisions are really expectations as to outcome, rather than any certainty as to profit.

Suppose we believe that interest rates are likely to decline. We have seen that this would mean a rise in long-term bond prices, with the prospect of a significant capital gain. Short-term securities would also rise in price, but by a miniscule amount. Hence, people hovering between the two markets would be likely to invest in the long-term market to reap the expected capital gain. There would be less funds in the short-term market, and this decline in supply might actually reverse the previous tendency there, driving rates up rather than down, as had been the trend. Regardless of the expectations for short-term yields, the overwhelming influence is the expected marked rise in long-term bond prices, and so funds would flow to that sector.

Suppose we expected a general rise in yields. This indicates falling bond prices and capital losses. People would rush to sell their long-term securities and put the funds into short-term loans. Such a transfer (increasing the supply) might drive down the short-term yield. But since it is the fear of large capital losses in the long-term market that is dominant, any yield in the short-term market would suffice. It would be better than holding the money idle, earning nothing. Again, because of the nature of the short term security, there is virtually no worry about loss, and it is a haven while the long-term rate is expected to move adversely. Hence, we could say that if the two main yields move in opposite directions, it probably indicates an expectation of a shift in the general level of yields.

Now, the expectation of a change in the long-term rate does not necessarily set up the shifts indicated. If the long-term return is sufficient to offset the possible capital loss, so that the net return is still better than that obtainable in the short-term market, then funds will not shift as indicated. And we can lay down some general guidelines that would indicate under which conditions the two possibilities operate.

Historically, yields on long-term quality bonds move over fairly wide ranges, but there are certain limits. United States bonds, for example, never yield less than 1 per cent or more than 6 per cent—at least not in the relevant past periods. Let us take as our expected range 2 to 5 per cent. If the current yield on such bonds is close to 2 per cent, we can feel safe that yields will not go much lower—prices will not go much higher—and if there is any shift, it would be toward higher yields (lower prices). Hence, the closer the market yield gets to the lower end of the historic range, the greater the risk of a reversal and consequent capital loss. Furthermore, if we purchase at this point, our expected income is quite low—2 per cent per annum approximately. It would not take much of a rise in yields after we purchased the bond to produce a price decline that would wipe out any income we had as interest. A 2½-point decline within a year would mean that we had a net loss of ½—that we would have been better off had we kept our funds idle.

On the other hand, if yields are closer to 5 per cent, we know that there is not much chance of their going any higher. The possibility of a price decline and capital loss is quite small. Furthermore, even if the yield should inch up, we are getting a sizeable income to offset the loss. For example, suppose that over the next year bond prices drop another point after we make our purchase; then we still have a gain of 4 per cent (5 minus 1) for the year. If short-term yields are less than 4 per cent, then we are better off to buy the long-term issue, even if we know there will be this small decline, than to stay with the short sector.

Expressed another way, the lower the yield is now, the greater the possibility that it will move up. The greater the possibility of a capital loss, the less the interest income will be to offset this loss. The higher the yield is now, the greater the possibility that it will move down. The greater the possibility of a capital gain, the more the interest income to offset any loss. This would probably be small, if we have misjudged the market. There is thus a heightened incentive to get out of long-term bonds if their yield is low, and the reverse tendency when yields are high.

Dynamics of the Short-Long Relationship

The preceding section has to be examined further if we are to grasp the realities of the situation. We have indicated a major influence on expectations[2]—the relationship of long-term yields now to the historic range. This was established in the preceding three paragraphs. If

---

[2] There are also other influences on interest-rate expectations—a change in business outlook, shifts in the international political climate, and so forth—all of which may be expected to set up changes in the supply of, and demand for, loanable funds, and thus alter interest rates.

we *expect* the long-term yield to decline, we move out of short-term into long-term. This liquidation causes the short-term yield to rise, contrary to the expected move in long yields. If we *expect* long-term yields to rise, we move into the short end of the market, and the consequent buying is likely to depress short-term yields. In other words, if funds shift in sufficient amounts as a result of the expectations regarding long-term yields, the movement of the short-term rate is *opposite* to the expected movement in the long-term rate. As a consequence, when a change in long-term yields is expected, this may be signaled by the change of the short-term rate in the opposite direction.

As our earlier discussion indicated, borrowers, too, may be influenced. An expectation of a rise in long-term yields might speed up the demand for such funds in order to avoid the expected rise in costs. An expectation of a decline in yields might reduce current demand, as borrowers postpone their needs (or borrow short) to await the lower-loan costs. The effect on the long-term rate would be to accentuate the movements already discussed. The expectation of a rise has reduced the supply of, and raised the demand for, such funds, thus accentuating the move; the expectation of a decline has pushed up the supply of, and reduced the demand for, such funds, again accentuating the move. In the short-term market, however, there may be somewhat different effects. For example, if long-term rates are expected to decline, lenders may shift out of short-term issues and borrowers may demand more short-term funds, thereby accentuating the pressure in this sector. Alternatively, the borrowers may simply postpone their demand, and so the additional influence on short-term rates coming from the borrowing side is not present.

If these opposite movements are sharp enough, we could get quite a difference between the levels of the two rates. If long-term yields are quite high and business activity is slackening, this would be a hint that the demand for long-term funds may soon drop off, and so result in a decline in long-term yields. Investors would then move out of short-term funds, boosting the yield in that sector. Incidentally, as they do buy long-term bonds, they push up prices there, thus contributing to the expected downward move in yields. Hence, during this transitional period, short-term yields might move up so much as to rise above the long-term yield.

But suppose we are in a recession, with low long-term rates, and business starts to improve. This may be the signal that the demand for long-term funds will soon pick up, thereby boosting long-term rates and depressing bond prices. Investors would then switch to the short-term market, depressing rates there, and if enough funds move, the short-term rate could drop to a point well below the long-term rate. In such periods of change, the two rates could diverge by sizeable margins.

On the other hand, once the rate shifts had stabilized—once no further significant movement in long-term yields were foreseen—then investors would no longer be motivated by the prospect of capital gains or losses. Now they would measure the income obtainable from the two sectors and move into that one promising higher returns. If at that point the short-term rate were higher, funds would flow to that sector bringing down that rate; if the long-term rate were higher, funds would flow there bringing up the short-term rate. Implicit in the foregoing is the effect on the long-term market. If funds flow to the short-term market, it may mean sales of long-term bonds, and so there would still be some impact on yields there. And if funds flow to the long-term market, prices there would respond. In practice, therefore, if the short-term yield were higher, we would then see an adjusting rise in long-term yields, as some investors sold their long-term issues to take advantage of the higher short-term rate. The subsequent move into the short-term market would bring that rate down. The two rates, in other words, would be drawing together because of the movements in each. Similarly, if long-term rates were much higher than the short-term rate, investors would switch, drawing funds from the short-term sector and thereby raising yields there, and purchasing long-term issues and thus depressing yields there.

However, this is not to imply that even in stable periods the two rates must be the same. Under modern conditions, where liquidity considerations are so important, many investors, such as commercial banks, would prefer a short-term asset if its yield is no less than the long-term. As we have seen, there is a risk element in the long-term security—the possibility of loss if yields rise unexpectedly. Virtually no comparable risk exists with short-term holding. Because of this risk, these special investors will not buy long-term securities unless there is a somewhat higher yield, enough to compensate them for the risk of a possible adverse fluctuation. Normally we would expect the short-term rate to be somewhat lower, simply because of this added consideration. Our previous discussion, therefore, would be rephrased: if the short-term rate is very much below the long-term rate, and if no significant shift in long-term yields is expected, funds will flow from the short to the long market. If long-term yields are only a little above the short, or even if they are below, and if no significant shift in long-term yields is expected, then funds will move from long- to short-term securities.

In summary, therefore, expectations of changes in the long-term rate tend to push the two rates in opposite directions; an expected rise in the long yield will result in a decline in the short yield; an expected decline in the long yield will provoke a rise in the short yield. Expectations of stability in the long-term rate tend to move the short-term similarly to the prior move in the long-term rate; a long-term rate that rose, and is expected to remain high, will push up the short-term yield, and a long yield that had declined and is expected to stay low will depress short yields.

It might be argued that similar reasoning should be applied to expectations of change in the short range. Our argument has been turning exclusively on the long-term rate as the prime influence. The answer appears to be negative, though. If there is an expectation of change in the short-term rate, there is still little that can be done to take advantage of such a move. If, for example, a 4-per-cent three-month bill is expected to sell soon in a 3-per-cent market one month from now, then its $990 price will rise to $996.67 instead of $993.33— not an overwhelming change. This would be true conversely if the rate moved up. Moreover, it is doubtful that a potential borrower would switch out of shorts because of such a change. If he had expected to borrow at 4 per cent and now must pay 5 per cent, the total cost of his operation for three months has risen by $2.50 per thousand. True, some borrower may be deterred, and so the demand for short-term funds might decline. But he would not swing over to the long-term market; most likely, he simply would not go through with the transaction. As we have seen, there are few cases where a short-term borrower would want to tie himself up with a long-term debt. His choice is to borrow short or not to borrow at all. In contrast, the long-term borrower could borrow short if it were worth his while to postpone the long-term issue until the yields in that sector improved.

Indirectly, however, there may be some tie-in as a result of a change in short-term rates. As these rates change, the cost of borrowing to purchase long-term securities also varies. Those who operate on borrowed funds might borrow more if the short-term rate drops, since the cost of financing such an operation is less. The opposite is so if the short-term rate rises. For these people, a decline in short-term yields might raise their purchases of long-term bonds because of increased borrowings. These added purchases would then push up long-term prices and lower long-term yields. Conversely, when short-term yields rise, borrowings drop off. Demand for long-term securities declines, prices drop there, and yields rise. To the extent that these operators are important, we would get a reaction running from moves in short-term rates to changes in the long-term rate. (We shall return to this force in connection with new-securities underwritings.)

We should remember here that in discussing expectations, it cannot be assumed that everyone in the market has the same outlook. Some people may expect rising long-term yields. If so, they will sell long-term securities. Others may expect a decline in such yields and buy. The balance of these forces is important—whether on balance the market expects a rise or decline, or whether on balance the market is moving out of or into long-term securities.

Playing the Pattern of Rates

The character of the security is determined by its remaining life rather than by its original life. A twenty-year bond, with one year remaining, is no different from a one-year bond. And, as it gets even closer to redemption, it becomes a short-term security. True, unlike a bill, it still pays interest. But the market adjusts for this formal difference in its equilibrating role. As a consequence, particularly during periods when the rate structure is stable, there can be opportunities for special profits. Taking advantage of them is known as playing the pattern of interest rates.

We have indicated that under such stable conditions, the short-term yield would be less than the long-term yield because of the former's virtual absence of risk of fluctuation in capital value. Assume that, because of this difference, a two-year security sells to yield 4 per cent, and a three-month bill yields 3 per cent. Assume further that the interest on the two-year issue is also 4 per cent, so that it is selling at par. But in twenty-one months it passes into the short-term character, at which time it would yield 3 per cent, even if there were to be no change in going market rates. Hence, as it nears maturity, it would sell for a small premium, about ¼ per cent, since it is still a 4-per-cent issue but is now selling in the sector that yields only 3 per cent. If we bought the two-year bond at par and held it for twenty-one months, we would earn the interest (equal to 7 per cent for the 1¾ years) plus the ¼-per-cent capital gain, or a total of 7¼ per cent. If enough investors realized this, they would buy the two-year issue, pushing up its price slightly and thus lowering its yield slightly. This reacts a bit on three-year issues, and so on. In other words, given a stable interest-rate pattern, we see a gradually falling yield as we approach closer to maturity. Theoretically, if we charted the yield of varying maturities in such a market, short-term issues would have the lowest return. As we lengthened the remaining life, the yield would rise smoothly out to the longest life. Such a chart is known as a yield curve.

Such smoothness, of course, presupposes stability of the rate structure. If there is an expectation of change, as already described, then the calculations become upset by the adjustments to anticipate the various fluctuations. Hence, if at any time we were to make such a yield curve and see that its expected smoothness is not there, then we know that shifts are being anticipated. For example, in a period when long-term yields are expected to rise, the yield curve would show an abnormally low point for extremely short-term issues. If long-term yields are expected to decline, the short end of the curve would be boosted abnormally. Different shapes to the yield curve can thus be interpreted as guides to what the market expects, especially regarding the longer-term sector.

Variability of Rates

The market is in a constant state of flux. Every change in a bond price is a change in yields. But these may cancel out, a rise today being offset by an equal drop tomorrow. And if we look at almost any period, we see that rates do change, often drastically. The sharper changes come when the economy is shifting appreciably or abruptly, such as in the downturn to a recession or the swing into a vigorous boom. But even within the cyclical phase there are changes.

These changes are also within the family relationships. *Aaa* rates may be rising (or falling) along with *Aa* and *A* rates, but the relative spreads between them may be changing. All sorts of short-term disturbances can create still further variables. Perhaps this week some large foundation wishes to buy a tremendous amount of short-term bills; for this temporary period the short-term rate drops sharply, to recover once time has removed this influence. Or tax legislation changes the impact of capital gains versus interest income; this might disturb the relationship of the tax-free bonds relative to the taxable issues, or those issues selling at par compared with those with a lower interest rate selling at a discount. Or, perhaps the Federal Government has decided to refund large amounts of short-term obligation by issuing a long-term bond; this alters the demand for short-term funds (down) and for long-term funds (up), and thus affects the rates in the two sectors. This disturbance, by upsetting the previous equilibrium, brings about new reactions as the market adjustments get to work to reestablish a new equilibrium.

Some of these disturbances can almost be counted on regularly. For example, some large cities still have a tax on personal property (such as securities). However, United States government obligations are exempt from the tax. Hence, just before the taxable date, large investors sell their taxable assets and purchase Treasury bills, and then reverse the transactions after the tax date. As a consequence, short-

term yields are abnormally depressed on the first date, then rebound on
the latter; similar but opposite moves are going on in the long-term
area. Since the tax date is known in advance—say, April 1—the market
can always count on this disturbance, and so need not regard it as some
new influence come to alter previous estimates of the interest-rate
picture.

So far we have ignored the major possible source of disturbance
—Federal Reserve policy. As this organization influences bank reserves
and lending policies, it in turn alters the impact on the short- and
long-term market, thus affecting both expectations and the pattern of
rates. This subject is so important that we shall treat it at greater
length.

Summary

General remarks in Chapter 13 on the movement of bond yields
and prices must be modified because of numerous institutional details,
such as call dates, tax rates, and perhaps even anticipated price-level
changes. Risky securities must be distinguished as to relative default
possibilities, compared with the absolutely safe United States government obligation; the assessment of this risk quality varies over the
cycle, thus also altering relative yields.

Perhaps most important is the relationship between short- and
long-term rates. In general, the expected change in the latter will
dominate decisions because of the impact on capital gains and losses.
Expectation of a long-term yield rise will move people out of longs
into shorts; expectation of a decline will cause the reverse. As a consequence, the short-term rate could move in a direction opposite to that
expected of the long-term rate. On the other hand, if there is not much
expectation that the long-term yield will shift, then the short-term rate
will tend to be somewhat lower because of its superior protection
against capital loss. Disparities in this spread under such circumstances
would tend to draw the two yields closer to each other. Because of
variations in these various spreads, numerous opportunities to "play"
the rate structure arise.

Chapter 15

BANK ASSET
MANAGEMENT

Managing commercial-bank assets is not unlike walking a tightrope while juggling. Since a bank is run for profit, it tries to maximize its income while pursuing policies compatible with its other goals. It must also be sufficiently liquid to meet any drains—either cash being withdrawn by its depositors or checks being presented for payment by other banks. It must also comply with the reserve requirements; it cannot afford to meet a drain by an undue drawing down of its most liquid asset. Since these three forces are often opposed, the bank is pulled in several directions at once, and so must balance the various considerations to arrive at policy decisions.

Function of Reserves

We have already seen that the member banks are compelled to keep certain minimum reserves either in cash or with the Federal Reserve, the amount depending on the type of deposit and the classification of the bank. These are the bank's most liquid assets, but only in a sense. They are liquid in that they can be used immediately if the need arises. But if doing so will plunge the bank into a reserve deficiency, then remedial actions to remove the deficit must be taken quickly. Hence, the most liquid asset is really the excess reserve, for using it does not require any further action by the bank. It is for this reason that the excess reserve determines how much the bank can lend or invest. In practice, the large banks are extremely careful managers, and rarely have excess reserves for any length of time; small banks, in contrast, often carry an excess.

Many observers feel that the reserve requirement really operates to determine the volume of bank deposits, and through them the volume of bank assets. If the required ratio is 20 per cent against demand deposits and there are no time deposits, then a bank could have $5 in demand deposits for each dollar of reserves, which means $4 of income-earning assets. And since banks tend to utilize their reserves fully, we can be fairly certain that those figures will prevail. If some of the deposits are savings or time deposits, there is some slippage. Then the same reserves could support a greater volume of deposits, and thus a greater volume of income-earning assets. When we come to discuss Federal Reserve policy, we shall see the important position assigned to both total reserves and excess reserves (corrected for member-bank borrowings from the Federal Reserve).

In practice, our assumption of full usage of reserves is also somewhat incorrect. This gives rise to another type of slippage. We have already mentioned that the smaller banks are more likely to have excess reserves. Hence, a different distribution of reserves would give rise to a different volume of excess reserves. Also, in view of the different ratios required of country and city reserve banks, the same volume of deposits gives rise to differing volumes of required reserves, depending on the location.

It is because reserves earn nothing that banks try to minimize the volume of excess reserves. Yet there is the danger of an unexpected drain, a drawing down of reserves below the required amount. To meet this need, the banks could carry excess reserves, but that means foregoing income. To place them in profitable assets might mean tying up the funds when they are most needed. To meet the two objectives, banks have a category known as secondary reserves—highly liquid assets that can be sold readily if the need for funds arises, yet at the same time produce an income. In particular, the major form in which such assets are held is the Treasury bill, since the risk of capital loss is so small.

Because of the enormous volume of transactions daily, usually exceeding $250 million, the Treasury bill can be sold in any practical quantity without difficulty. Similarly, if the bank wishes to expand its secondary assets, it can acquire any normal volume of such bills without creating any disturbance in the market. Most banks look to this asset as the first line of defense in case there does arise a need to replenish reserves. While the relationship is not rigid, banks do tend to keep a certain proportion of such secondary reserves against deposits, especially the more volatile demand deposits. Expansion in deposits thus raises *required* reserves by the legal amount and *secondary* reserves by the bank's customary ratio. Hence, only a smaller portion is left for the loan-and-bond account. For example, if the required-reserve ratio is 20 per cent, and in addition the bank carries 10 per cent in secondary reserves, an inflow of cash through new deposits would result in only 70 per cent of the amount being put into new loans. Expressed another way, a part of excess reserves goes into Treasury bills, and only the remainder is utilized to meet the reserve drain from new loans.

Government Securities

In our discussion of bond prices and yields, it was pointed out that there is virtually no danger of capital loss in short-term securities of high quality, and no danger of default on United States government obligations. The Treasury bill, by combining these two features, is ideal as a secondary reserve. But the holding of other, longer-term governments is also a safety feature. While it is true that, if yields rise, the risk of capital loss remains, the danger of insolvency is completely absent, so that one of the two risks is thereby eliminated. To the extent that banks have increased their holdings of government securities, the danger of a drastic fall in the safety of their assets is reduced. And, partly as a result of the long depression of the 1930's and the enormously expensive financing of World War II, mainly through debt issues, banks hold far more in governments as compared with half a century ago. In so doing, they have thereby reduced the danger of their failing because their debtors are insolvent; one big debtor now in the portfolio cannot fail.

On the other hand, the presence of increased government activity has also worked to reduce the bank's liquidity. In order to qualify as a depositary for government funds, the bank must pledge government securities. To that extent, it is less able to utilize these assets for liquidity purposes. For many banks, more than 60 per cent of their government securities are thus tied up. About one-quarter of all commercial-bank assets are in governments.

The trend over the past thirty years has been toward increasing safety within the bank-asset composition. Reserve requirements have risen, and more assets are composed of government bonds. Since these two categories are absolutely safe against default, the proportion of such riskless assets (abstracting from price fluctuations) comes to almost 50 per cent of deposits for the typical member bank.

The presence of so large a government component has an additional stabilizing effect. In the old days, when banks were relying primarily on personal loans and corporate debt, signs of a serious depression raised the spectre of wholesale default and a subsequent insolvency for the bank. To protect themselves against such an eventuality, banks would start to call in loans and sell off assets. This would reduce the volume of demand deposits and thus the public's purchasing power, thereby further depressing the economy. If carried to extremes, as occurred from 1929 to 1933, it could create the very default that was so feared.

Now, however, banks have an alternative. First of all, a substantial part of their assets is free of the default fear. Second, if they do decide to cut down on loans, they need not hold the free reserves idle; they can now go out and add still further to their holdings of governments. Hence, as deposits shrink (reflecting the repayment of private loans), they could expand to reflect the purchase of governments. The aggregate volume of demand deposits would hold up much better, and so the downward pressure through curtailment of purchasing power would be mitigated. Of course, such an alternative presupposes that there is a large government debt outstanding so that the available bonds can be had. If there were little or no government debt, as was true before 1914, then we would not be able to sustain purchasing power so easily in a recession. It was not too far from the truth when a cartoonist remarked that the very size of the government debt gave one confidence! Any substantial reduction of the debt would actually impair the safety and liquidity of our banking system.

Liquidity Distribution of the Portfolio

Under usual banking conditions there are certain predictables that enable the bank's portfolio manager to plan for various needs. Barring a catastrophe, such as a run on the bank, with all its depositors demanding cash immediately, the bank can expect to experience both inflows and outflows of funds. If the two are equal, there is no need to liquidate other assets to obtain funds to replenish reserves, since none are being lost. If inflows exceed outflows, there is even less need to liquidate assets. The only contingency that might require sale of an asset is the possibility of an excess withdrawal of cash. It is this contingency that must be planned for, no matter how unlikely.

To a certain extent, such net drains can be predicted. People usually draw out money on Friday for weekend expenses, and also prior to holidays. Similar drains occur during the more important vacation periods, especially summer. Pre-Christmas shoppers are also in need of large amounts of cash. Indeed, these flows are so regular that a bank can count on their occurrence. Judging by past records, it can often predict how much will be drawn out. For such needs, the only risk is underestimation, and for this the bank could plan to have more liquid funds than it really believes is necessary. Or it could have a secondary reserve, such as a Treasury bill, that can be sold quickly if the drain is more than anticipated. The ready sale of such a security is sufficient protection.

Another type of drain reflects the business-cycle shifts. In a recession, people's incomes fall off—or at least this is true for a sizeable number. They may not wish to curtail consumption as much as the income decline calls for, and so they draw on past accumulations of bank deposits to make good the difference. This is also somewhat predictable, based on the impact of the cycle on the area served by the bank.

Other types of cash needs are less predictable for any individual, but they can be estimated for a large number. These are emergencies, such as hospital bills. A sudden need for cash to pay a doctor or any other large bill could force the person to draw funds from his account. Every day people fall ill, and every day some outflows for this requirement can be counted on. It may be that there is some seasonal pattern here, too; perhaps illness increases during the winter weather, and drops off during the middle of the year.

There is also the unpredictable. A severe downturn may shake people's confidence and so precipitate mass withdrawals. We shall discuss this possibility separately. But conversely, too hectic a boom could also cause mass withdrawals, as people rush to buy stocks, take more expensive trips abroad, or make any of a number of unusually large expenditures. There may be a large industrial shift away from the area in question, with many people moving. As they go, they draw out their bank funds in order to open an account in their new neighborhood. Or our bank may be extending loans at an active pace, and so reserves are drained as the proceeds are spent. Again, to a certain extent this, too, is predictable, but often the movement of funds cannot be estimated with any degree of precision.

Finally, on the other side, the bank can count on a certain proportion of its deposits staying put. These belong to people who are net savers during their entire life, who at death have a net estate which is passed onto their heirs, who then continue to leave the capital untouched. While such funds are usually in time deposits, to a limited extent the same can be said of the minimum balance of a demand deposit. Many checking accounts are managed in such a way that they never go below a certain amount. This figure can also be regarded as being held permanently in the bank.

Given these various possible outflows, our portfolio manager can now plan the distribution of assets to meet these various drains. Some assets would be kept in highly liquid Treasury bills. Any time the drain exceeds the estimate, these can be sold immediately with no loss, and so the reserve position is protected. However, since these are usually the lowest-yielding income source, the objective is to maintain them at a minimum consistent with the safety factor.

Next, our portfolio can contain somewhat longer life securities. For example, if this is January and the Christmas drain starts in November, we can safely hold securities maturing in nine to ten months, the funds flowing in from these maturities matching the outflow to the Christmas shoppers.

We could also hold medium-term securities, since the cyclical needs may not arise for several years. Even if the downturn comes a bit sooner and we do have to sell these securities, whatever loss may be necessary because the sale occurs at an adverse date would probably be compensated for by the higher income during the holding period.

Finally, since we can count on a sizeable portion of our deposits never going out of the bank, we can safely purchase long-term securities (including mortgages). We can be certain that the drain will never be so large that we would have to liquidate. And since they involve the greatest uncertainty, they will yield the greatest income. We have thus combined a liquid portfolio with one that gives maximum income.

These general principles need not be followed exactly. In certain circumstances numerous compromises are feasible that might actually help us attain our various objectives with even greater success. For example, a long-term loan is nonliquid. But suppose the borrower agrees to repay a portion every six months.[1] Then each half year we have converted part of a nonliquid asset into a liquid form. The income from such an operation could well yield more than if we had split the amount between a short-term asset and a rigidly fixed long-term asset.

Or suppose that because of the peculiarities of the yield curve, the bank would rather put more funds into very nonliquid assets, bringing

---

[1] These are known as *term*, or *installment*, loans.

in an unusually high return. But this would reduce the bank's liquidity. To compensate for this, other funds might be moved into Treasury bills. The bank might then hold a disproportionate amount of bills that are highly liquid, and so have less need for intermediate securities of less liquidity; the remainder can then be switched to the long-term nonliquid opportunities. In effect, the portfolio's average liquidity is the same, although differently distributed—more in the very liquid sector accompanied by more in the very nonliquid part. In so doing, the over-all income has been improved.

We have not discussed equities as investments since banks do not put much of their funds into such outlets. The main way by which they can participate in a stock-market rise is through the purchase of convertible securities (provided the securities meet investment quality requirements). These are bonds which can be converted into a fixed number of common shares of stock. If the price of the stock rises appreciably, the bond will follow it. On the other hand, if the stock falls, the bond may not follow it down, for its fixed income payment then gives it value as a bond. Thus, within certain ranges, the bond is a bond, mainly on the way down. On the way up, it can behave like a stock.

Recent Shift to Time Deposits

Earlier we discussed the shift from demand to time deposits. Commercial banks have encouraged this transfer by issuing certificates of indebtedness, which are, in effect, transferable time deposits. Such movements raise questions about the necessary composition of bank assets to reflect these changes.

We have already established the formal effects. Time deposits require smaller reserves per dollar of liability, and so a given volume of reserves can support a larger superstructure of deposits. Time deposits add to the interest expense of the bank, and so compel the bank to move into higher yield assets. Now the impact of liquidity starts to come in.

As we have seen, the higher the yield of an asset, the greater the risk associated with its ownership. This risk could be the more obvious one of possible default, or the more subtle fluctuation in market value of a long-term bond. It brings with it the possibility of a capital loss. Using risk in this broader sense, we can see that the change to time deposits pushes the bank into a more risky portfolio.

If the time deposits were genuine savings deposits, this would not be cause for concern. The true time deposit—the savings account—is money that the owner does not need soon. Indeed, he may be setting it aside for his old age. Barring some unexpected emergency, most such deposits are left untouched for years,[2] and so the need to have liquid funds for possible withdrawals is minimal. It is this stability that enables savings banks and savings-and-loan associations to concentrate so much of their assets in the long-term sector.

In recent years much of the so-called "time money" with commercial banks has been of a markedly different character. This is often excess checking-account balances that have been converted to take advantage of the income feature. These surplus balances may have been a reflection of lessened corporate activity, and the need for their utilization could subsequently compel a reverse shift.

To illustrate the problem, let us start with a corporation whose checking-account balance is just sufficient to handle its regular volume of transactions. Each month it sells $1 million worth of goods, each month it spends $1 million on wages, raw materials, taxes, and dividends. Then comes a recession. Sales and purchases decline to $750,000, and so the activity of the bank's checking account declines; less of a balance is required to handle this smaller activity. It is even possible that the firm might draw down inventories and thereby even increase its balance. This is accomplished through spending less on current production than it is taking in from sales, the excess demand being met through additional sales of goods in stock. Probably both will be going on, so the corporation checking account rises above its current needs.

Anxious to maximize income, especially since its regular source of earnings (sales) is contributing less, the treasurer decides to draw out the excess and place it in time deposits or a certificate of indebtedness, the interest income thus helping to offset the shrinkage in profits from operations. The bank now has less demand deposits but more time deposits, and aggregate required reserves are less, although its interest expense has risen. It therefore shifts some of its deposits from the high probability of a drain (the demand deposit) to the low probability of a drain (time deposits). To reflect this diminished need for liquidity, it then sells some of its highly liquid, low-yield assets and purchases less liquid, higher-yield assets. In addition, since it now has excess reserves, it also expands its aggregate assets.

But suppose business recovers. Sales pick up, and our corporation must increase its purchases of raw materials, labor services, and the like. Where will it get the extra money? It cannot draw down its checking account further, for it had already done so when it drew out the excess for its switch to time deposits. Probably it will be forced to sell its certificate of indebtedness; but if most corporations are in a similar position, there may not be a buyer. Upon maturity, the corpo-

---

[2] Estimated annual turnover is about ½, compared with a demand-deposit rate of 29 or more.

ration will demand repayment, and the funds so received will go back to the demand deposit. If the money had been in a time deposit, the company could have drawn out the funds and not waited at all. In either case, the bank is faced with a rise in demand deposits, a rise in required reserves, and a possible drain of reserves as these funds are spent by the corporation. How will it meet such a drain? It could sell some of the assets it had acquired when the original switch from demand deposits had occurred. But that had probably been when interest rates were low, reflecting the slack in business activity. But now that business is brisk, the demand for loanable funds is high, so interest rates are moving up. The longer-term securities acquired previously now are falling in value. The sharpness of this recovery and the consequent impact on bond yields will measure the severity of the capital loss the banks will undergo.

Recently some attempts to meet this danger have been made. A few banks have issued long-term securities, thus obtaining funds that would not be switched into demand deposits on short notice. How far this new approach will be used to reduce the dangers discussed in this section remains to be seen.

Loans and Liquidity

This tendency toward a decreased liquidity in bank portfolios, relative to the potential drains on assets, is not confined to the securities shifts. Over the past years loans also have become less liquid. The typical commercial loan assumed that it would enable the borrower to expand output, and with sales would come the funds to pay off the loan. Since the typical period of production was relatively short—usually a few months—the loan, too, would have a correspondingly limited life. While the bank might have difficulty in selling these loans before maturity (if it needed additional funds), at least it could count on a return flow in the not-too-distant future, and so regard such an asset as a supplement to its secondary reserves. (Actually, if the borrower were well known, the bank could resell, or discount, the paper with other lenders even before maturity, since many investors are anxious to invest funds in short-term paper.)

But time has brought certain changes and has revealed pitfalls in this type of paper. If a company does depend on such short-term borrowing to finance its operations, what happens after it has made the sale and paid off the loan? It needs another loan to finance the next cycle if it is to stay in business. Since most firms operate with continuous production runs, they would therefore need continuous financing. To stay in business, they must rely on the bank's making continual loans. If such is the case, the loan is not really liquid, except in a formal sense, since the bank is virtually committed to a continual loan. It can no longer regard the maturity as a return of funds, since it must immediately replace this with a new loan and a consequent drain.

A second development has been away from our simple production-sale operation. Firms now borrow for relatively long-term needs, such as the purchase of capital items. These will presumably produce a flow of funds over their lifetime to pay off the loan, but the life may be ten years or more. Hence, a three-month loan means that the firm may obtain only enough free funds from operations to pay off a small fraction of the principal, and so require a renewal. The bank has actually made a long-term loan despite its nominal appearance as a short-term asset. The bank's only hope for liquidity is if the borrower can find another bank to lend it the funds; but if the first bank's needs occur at a time when the system in general is under pressure, this is unlikely. To compound this danger, banks have been putting a rising proportion of their assets into such loans, so that we see a greater proportion of assets moving into less liquid form and becoming even less liquid than formerly. As a result, we see two offsetting tendencies: a higher proportion of safe and liquid government paper, but also a higher proportion of nonliquid longer-term loans. The seriousness of these opposite tendencies and their net effect on bank solvency have yet to be tested.

The reader may well ask why the bank is forced to renew the loan. After all, how can a debtor compel his creditor to do this, since it is the creditor who is traditionally regarded as having the upper hand. The answer is that there are all sorts of personal ties to weaken the creditor's position. Suppose the bank refuses to renew, and the borrower does not have sufficient liquid funds to pay. Then it must restrict its operations and in an extreme case go into bankruptcy. This means a loss of jobs and incomes in the area, and no bank needs this publicity. So it must be careful in pressing borrowers for fear of damaging its own position. In extreme possibilities such an attitude could rebound and affect the bank's own solvency. If the borrower is forced to close down, the bank may take a loss on its loan. Furthermore, the employees of the closed plant may be compelled to draw funds out of this very bank to make ends meet. The bank thus experiences a heightened drain, and if its assets are not sufficiently mobilizable, it may go bankrupt.

There are mutual obligations in loans. The rate structure varies all the time, and often the differences between various obligations also change. At times, many large borrowers could obtain lower rates from non-banking lenders (these will be discussed in the next chapter). But if the borrower deserted the bank on every such occasion, the bank would be faced constantly with fluctuations in the composition of its assets and earnings, and its reinvestment problem would become that much greater. Since loans usually earn more than other assets, this particular paper is most prized by the bank, which does not want to lose a borrower.

But if it expects a borrower to stay with it when there are cheaper alternative sources of funds, then it has an obligation, too. When money was easy, the borrower did not desert the bank. When money is tight, the bank should not desert the borrower. And so each comes to depend on the other, and thus liquidity diminishes. Moreover, the interest on such loans does not vary as much as on the more marketable types of security. If yields should decline, the bank may find that its bonds are being refunded for lower-interest issues, and so its income declines. But if it has a loan, the likelihood is that renewal will be made at the same rate, and so income is sustained. The corporate debtor is under no obligation to its bondholders *not* to take advantage of lower rates; the bank borrower *is* under this obligation, since it is his insurance that the bank will in turn supply him with funds when money is less readily available.

There is a further consideration that binds the borrower to his bank. Banks are in an excellent position to give valuable economic and financial information and advice to a steady borrower. This reflects their expertise in the area, one which most borrowers do not have. Hence, the slight extra interest cost is well worth the free help the bank offers. Moreover, with high corporate income taxes, much of the interest cost is offset through the savings on taxes; every dollar paid is a reduction in net income, and thus a reduction in the tax liability. The net effect on profits of this somewhat higher charge is thus quite small.

However, it should be added that not all corporations reason this way. For some, the appearance of cheaper alternative sources of funds will induce them to switch their borrowing from banks. They may feel that their own staff can supply the information as competently as the bank. Or they may feel their credit is sufficiently high so that they can always find a lender. If the volume of their borrowings is large, relative to their net profits, the interest differential then plays a more significant part. This could be the case for finance companies that relend for installment purchases, their major profit being the difference between the interest charged their customers and the rate they pay on their own borrowing.

Liquidity for the Banking System

Our discussion of an asset's liquidity has been in terms of a sale by one bank, implying there were numerous buyers around, some of whom could be induced to purchase if the price were made sufficiently attractive. And, as we have seen, the probable price concession would be minimal with short-term assets and perhaps quite large for long-dated maturities. But suppose most banks are faced with a need to sell; where, then, would there be the buyers? Such a situation need not be that of a panicky reaction; in a boom, for example, most banks experience an expanding demand for loans, and so may decide to sell other assets in order to preserve their required reserve position. In this section we shall assume that our situation is more akin to this one.

If we do have this rise in loan demand, and if it is being satisfied, then bank deposits are also rising. If excess reserves are available, there is no need to sell off assets. As we have already seen, banks might actually acquire secondary reserves, such as short-term Treasury bills, their higher liquidity balancing the increase in the less liquid loan sector. But if this process continues for any length of time, it is very likely to reach the point where reserves are inadequate to back the rising volume of deposit liabilities. When the bulk of the banks have reached this stage, our question regarding the liquidity of the entire banking system becomes germane.

First we shall dispose of certain alternatives that are not pertinent to this section. Reserves could be replenished by borrowing from the Federal Reserves. Or the Reserve itself could come to the assistance of the banks by buying securities in the open market, thereby supplying the wanted reserves. Since this ends the whole problem, we shall ignore this possibility for the time being; actually this topic brings us into the broader problem of Federal Reserve policy which is to be treated more fully later.

Therefore, if banks in general must protect their reserve position, their only remaining hope is to sell off assets, especially the more liquid ones. For any one bank the logic is obvious: by selling these assets it will obtain funds that can be added to reserves and thus meet its requirements. The paying bank, of course, loses reserves. But if banks as a whole are net sellers, then, for the most part, the selling bank cannot find another bank to buy.

In such a situation there is only one remaining possibility—namely, a sale to other than a bank. Assume that the New York bank and the Philadelphia bank are each encroaching on their reserve positions. Both wish to dispose of Treasury bills; therefore neither can look to the other for help. The New York bank offers its bills for sale. Let us assume the price is sufficiently attractive so that the Pennsylvania Manufacturing Company decides to buy them, drawing down its deposit with the Philadephia bank in payment. The result will be a rise in the New York bank's reserves and a decline in the Philadelphia bank's reserves, as well as a decline in the Philadelphia bank's deposits. Meanwhile, we shall also assume that the efforts of the Philadelphia bank to sell bills have attracted as buyer the New York Insurance Company, which will now pay by drawing on its deposit with the New York bank. This reverses the effect on the two banks' reserves, and for this simple illustration we shall assume that both banks sold the same amount of bills. The net effect has been to leave both banks' reserves unchanged, but it has reduced both banks' deposit liabilities, and thereby both banks' required reserves. With total reserves unchanged, and required reserves down, there are now excess reserves, so we can resume the loan-deposit expansion. In brief, a general liquidation of assets on the part of the banking system can produce only a decline in deposits as non-banking purchasers are attracted, paying through the drawing on their deposit accounts.

Suppose, however, we worsen the situation. Suppose we have a world condition as dismal as that of the 1930's, when people mistrusted the banks. In such a period people start to draw out their deposits, drawing down the banks' reserves. And if this is carried on sufficiently, these reserves fall below the required point. Again ignoring the possibility of resorting to the Federal Reserve, what would happen? The banks could try to sell off assets, as in the previous illustration, but with the public in so panicky a mood it is doubtful that buyers would appear in sufficient numbers. *The one-time liquid asset is no longer liquid*. It cannot be sold. It is for this reason that monetary observers refer to the *shiftability* of an asset; its liquidity actually rests on the ability of the seller to shift it to another buyer. If the latter cannot be found, the asset is no longer liquid. Hence, when we judge an asset's liquidity, we are really determining how saleable it is; and this may reflect the situation in the market as well as the character of the asset. In our illustrations, the same bill was shiftable in the first case, but not in the present one.

The banks could exert pressure, but obviously they cannot force anyone to buy their bills. However, there is another asset that can be disposed of through force—loans. The banks could call for payment those matured loans that have been unofficially allowed to run on. Or as other loans mature, they can refuse to renew them. This forces the borrowers to pay off, if they can, and so bank assets and deposits are reduced equally, again freeing reserves. The need to resort to this—the need to free reserves from the required component—will depend on how much is being drained by depositors clamoring for cash.

In practice, however, any such large-scale loan deflation would probably worsen the over-all situation. How could so many borrowers pay off their loans? They could stop operations, and the money that would otherwise go for raw materials and wages can now be used to pay back the banks. But if this occurs, the suppliers are worse off. Their sales are down, and now they cannot pay the banks. Workers now cut down purchases. Retailers cannot make sales, cannot get funds, cannot pay off their loans. And as retailers cut back, the manufacturers are forced into the same situation. More and more borrowers are compelled to default, so instead of loans being repaid, they are wiped out. The asset disappears, but there is *no* corresponding drop in deposits. Now even the banks are in trouble, and if this is carried far enough, they too fail. In this paragraph is the story of the 1930's.

Fortunately some safeguards now exist to help ward off a repetition of this drama. We now have a Federal Deposit Insurance Corporation, which will pay off most depositors (up to $10,000) if banks fail. Knowing this, the average depositor no longer worries about the bank's solvency, and so the likelihood of the panicky withdrawals of funds is much less. There have been virtually no bank failures since those pre–FDIC days. Today a greater component of bank assets is in government securities. These are safe, and so the loan-deposit contraction now covers a smaller proportion of bank assets, and a smaller proportionate impact of loan liquidation results.

The existence of the Federal Reserve is perhaps most important of all. True, it was in existence during the 1930's, but now experience has taught it how to act more wisely. In effect, it is the lender of last resort. If the banking system needs reserves, and if sale to the public would precipitate a liquidation squeeze comparable with that of the early 1930's, the Federal Reserve would undoubtedly step in. It would make rediscounting easier, thus allowing hard-pressed banks to obtain additional funds; the banks could pledge their assets as security and thus avoid the necessity for sale in the open market with the consequent destruction of deposits. And the Reserve would also pursue an aggressive open-market policy, supplying reserves to those banks that were trying to sell securities.

It is true that there are still some who doubt its effectiveness. Suppose the international situation darkened and depositors panicked. Suppose they demanded their $300 billion in cash. Would the "Fed" supply so much in reserves? Would the FDIC, with less than $3 billion in assets, suffice? Suppose all our qualifying remarks about the decline in bank liquidity came true—the rise in time deposits that may be called on demand, or the frozen part of apparently liquid short-term loans, or declining prices and rising yields on governments. Because of the catastrophic implications of these uncertainties, it is perhaps wiser not to ask the questions. The ostrich may be intelligent after all.

Bank Capital

From time to time we have indicated that a bank could face losses: securities decline in price, or loans are not paid when due. In general, profits on other operations are usually more than enough to absorb such incidents. But there may be times when the losses are so large as to exceed profits; such could occur in a period of rising yields when the bond portfolio undergoes a drastic decline in value. If the bank is a seller at such a time, in order to obtain funds to be used in its lending activities, it may well undergo this unpleasant experience. Or, as already covered, such may arise in a severe recession, the type of shock that the previous section described.

If a bank had only deposits, then any shrinkage in asset value would cause its liabilities to exceed its assets, and it would be faced with the prospect of insolvency. Hence, as a cushion against such danger, the commercial bank has capital stock contributed by its founders, supplemented by profits that are not all distributed as dividends. In addition, it sets aside some of its earnings as reserves against such contingencies. It thus has assets in excess of deposit liabilities equal to these three accounts. If losses should occur, the shrinkage would be reflected in a reduction in the size of these accounts, diminishing the difference between assets and deposit liabilities, but still leaving the former in excess. These three accounts, therefore, can be regarded as the depositors' protection against loss. Expressed another way, the relative magnitude of these three is a guide to the potential loss a bank could suffer without endangering the deposits. For most banks, this protective component is about 8 to 9 per cent of assets, or about 10 per cent of the public's demand and time deposits. A bank's insolvency will not cause loss for the average depositor, but it should be noted that the investor in bank stocks will still suffer. Moreover, insolvency, by reducing the number of banks, reduces competition for the borrower's needs, because the number of lenders he can turn to declines.

This proportion has tended to decline slightly, reflecting the greater growth in assets than in these protective accounts. In addition, it reflects the diminished possibility of loss. As government securities increased in importance, the default risk declined, of course, and so did the need for protection against such loss. Furthermore, the capital value decline applies with serious concern to only that portion of governments that are relatively long term. The generally buoyant economy characteristic of the United States over the past quarter century has also reduced the default danger. The greater reliance on monetary and fiscal policy, thereby reducing the fear of any serious depression, also helps to reduce the loss danger. Whether the decline in this protective margin has gone too far is difficult to say. Certainly, if banks did wish to build up these reserves by setting aside more of their earnings, the stockholders would complain as they experienced a decline in dividends. If the banks decided to sell more stock, stockholders would also be unhappy, for their profits would now be spread over a greater investment; per dollar of invested capital, the return would be less. But there is the worry that safety standards may have dropped so far that the lower proportion of this protective margin could prove to be inadequate if a somewhat more severe downturn were to be experienced than has been our luck so far. It need not be another 1929, but it could be a wider swing than the post–World War II period has had. What if recessions do increase in severity? Would we be back to where we ended the preceding section?

Summary

Banks must manage their assets within certain restrictions and be pulled by forces in different directions. They must keep adequate required reserves. They strive to maximize income, and so reduce low-yielding or non-income-earning assets to a minimum. They must be liquid, and so avoid risky assets. They must earn enough to pay the expenses of operating their business, to meet the interest costs of time deposits, and to earn enough to keep their stockholders happy. And in all this they must maintain sufficient flexibility to cope with the shifts in business activity and the turns in monetary policy.

Adding to their difficulties are the recent tendencies to counter even these many contradictory objectives. Demand deposits have been shifting into time accounts, yet may be pulled back at any time; no longer can these be regarded as genuinely long-term funds. Self-liquidating loans have become less so. In fact, the mirage of liquidity has become a feasible goal if only a few banks in the system strive for it. The banking system as a whole cannot be liquid, unless an outside force, such as the Federal Reserve, steps in to rescue it from the dilemma. Otherwise the efforts to attain liquidity will only make the economy worse, and so rebound on the banks themselves. At its extreme, such as from 1930 to 1933, this means bankruptcy for the banks and the economy.

As offsets to these alarming trends, there has been some minimization of risks. Deposit insurance (FDIC) has reduced the possibility of a wholesale run on the banks, the wholesale conversion of deposits into cash. More of the banks' assets are in government bonds, thus ending the liquidation pressure in a recession. In fact, these securities are an alternative outlet if the loan segment declines. In this way, the community's purchasing power can be better maintained, rather than be depressed and so reinforce the downturn. As a result, there has been a tendency to reduce the proportion of the bank's assets coming from capital, and thus a decline in the cushion against losses.

Chapter 16

NON-BANKING FINANCIAL
INSTITUTIONS

At first glance, the chapter heading would raise a question regarding its place in a money-and-banking book. After all, this is not a survey of the entire field of finance, and for a long time the subject would not be found, or would be barely touched upon, in standard works in the field. But, especially since World War II, these many non-banking organizations have been entrenching on, and competing with, much of the activities that are normally associated with banks, particularly commercial banks, our main concern. They are now so important that a chapter on their banking and monetary influences is necessary to complete the picture.

Who They Are

While drawing a line of demarcation in the field of finance is always arbitrary, we shall do so here, recognizing that any classification is open to question regarding detail. Since we are going to deal with only the broadest aspects of the field, these minor differences can be ignored, but only for purposes of our analysis.

First to be included in our category will be the noncommercial banks, such as the savings banks, credit unions, and savings-and-loan associations. The peculiarity that distinguishes the commercial bank from these other organizations is that they do not create demand deposits. Readers may quibble about the inclusion of banks in a chapter on non-banking institutions, but as will be shown, the effect of these banks' operations is more like that of the non-banking group than the commercial bank. Their combined assets are in excess of $100 billion, and we cannot ignore a figure that large.

Another important group is the life insurance companies, with their enormous reserves, plus the various retirement funds. Since a great deal of the funds of life insurance companies are for old-age use, we have combined the two here. Not counting the Social Security fund, this sector probably accounts for another $150 billion.

Next we have the numerous credit organizations that extend installment loans, charge-account credit, and personal loans. Much of this is done by the various banking groups so far referred to, and their activity is included in the figures already cited. Hence, the remaining lenders probably account for $15 to $20 billion.

Another large sum is accounted for by business firms lending to other business firms. Some of this is simply trade credit—merchandise sold to other customers, to be paid some time in the future. But some is actual lending, either for short-term or long-term, where money changes hands for use in purposes similar to that of any bank loan. This combined total is probably at least $100 billion, although it may well be more. The overwhelming bulk is in trade credits, but a significant amount is the financing of business by business, rather than by banks. In fact, this latter is particularly competitive with the commercial banks, for it is the short-term loan that is most prominent here.

These various segments thus account for at least $370 billion. Commercial banks account for perhaps an additional $210 billion, or roughly more than half the combined figure for these other institutions. It is this tremendous amount that has caused us to set aside this chapter in a money-and-banking text.

In addition—and to some extent included in the foregoing—is the role of the non-banking lender as a supplier of funds to the United States government. Insurance companies hold more than $10 billion in Federal obligations, while other corporations hold about twice as much. An equally large factor here are the state and local government funds, such as pension plans; these, too, own more than $20 billion in Federal securities. In addition, foreign ownership, particularly in the short-term sector, has increased markedly in the past decade as a result of our balance-of-payments deficit. Such holdings now exceed $15 billion. The significance of this last category will be discussed separately in the chapter on international economics. All together, exclusive of individuals, these various holders account for more than $75 billion,[1] one-fifth more than is held by the country's commercial banks.

Fluctuations in Non-Bank Funds

These various sources are not equally stable in their influence on the market. Some, such as the insurance companies, are quite stable. Others change their status from net suppliers to net demanders of funds even within the year. Others are steady but erratic suppliers. Each has its own peculiar fluctuation pattern.

The life insurance company is probably the most extreme in its stability. If it is large and growing, it receives a constantly rising stream of premium payments. In addition, it has its investment income, most of which is from fixed-interest assets. The offsetting stream of payments for death benefits and retirement policies reflects the activity of many years, and so is a much smaller volume than the present size of its insurance in force. That is, its new policies may be rising at a rate of 10 per cent per annum; in 1964 it probably sold new policies equal in value to perhaps ten times the volume sold in 1940. But the death and retirement payments are mostly on this earlier year's smaller volume. Its premium income is from its current year's enlarged volume. Since most people pay their premiums once the policy is contracted for, the company can fairly well count on the inflow of premiums; its mortality tables give it a fairly definite guide to its out-payments. So there is little probability of fluctuation in the amount available for lending.

Savings bank and savings and loan association activities reflect mainly their success in attracting deposits. Both these groups have registered steady gains, although the rate of growth of the latter has been more rapid. Over the past decade the assets of the former have increased by about two-thirds, whereas the latter showed a growth of more than 150 per cent.

Trade credit is somewhat more volatile. It tends to move with the volume of sales, and increases in volume in good times, and drops off in a recession. On the other hand, the credit aspects are fairly automatic: the buyer either gets the goods on credit, or he does not. Fluctuations in interest rates have virtually no impact on either the amount of credit or the trade terms. The seller has usually allowed for

---

[1] Savings banks and savings-and-loan associations are included in this total.

the credit cost in the price charged for the commodities; indeed, sales for cash are often at lower prices to reflect the absence of this cost.

Corporation purchases of securities are in a somewhat less tidy category. Some of these purchases do show some regularity. For example, each month a corporation may be making a profit, thus adding to its income-tax liabilities. However, the tax is not due immediately. Hence, the treasurer could use the funds to finance other operations, hoping that future sales will provide the funds needed when the tax date comes around. Or he could purchase a short-term security that matures when the taxes are due; he gets some income during the interval and also has the assurance that he will be sufficiently liquid to meet the tax bill. Any other future cash need could be treated similarly. If the company floats a $10 million issue to put up a building that takes five months to construct, it needs only $2 million the first month, $2 million the second, and so on. Rather than hold the funds idle in its bank account, it may buy $2 million worth of bills maturing in one month, $2 million more with a two months' life, and so forth. Or again, if it finds that its need for funds rises in the winter and Easter seasons, but drops off at the other times, it may invest the funds in bills for the slack periods.

Large corporations gear their investment policies to the internal net cash flow. The difference between what they receive from current operations (sales) and what they need for inventories, net capital equipment, and other expenses represents the net available for investment. In effect, this amounts to the excess of earnings, plus depreciation ("cash flow") over capital additions (fixed or working). If the excess is positive, the firm is a net buyer of securities. If the funds outflow is greater than the net inflow, then it would sell off some of its securities. So, through such portfolio management, it actually has open to it an alternative to borrowing; if there is this need for money, it would borrow if the interest charged is less than that earned on its investments. If not, it reduces its borrowings and obtains funds through liquidation of investments. In practice, the cash flow from depreciation is fairly regular, so that the main source of fluctuation of the inflow is the retained earnings, or the excess of net income over dividends. The combination of changes in net earnings and varying outflows for capital expansions determines whether the particular company will be a net supplier or demander of funds.

Some of the large lenders can tailor their loans to meet the specific needs of the borrower. The commercial bank, for example, is hampered in its flexibility by the constant worry about liquidity: deposits can always flow out, draining it of reserves and perhaps compelling it to sell some of its assets. The large insurance company has no such worry; it can count on a net inflow of funds all the time, and so need never sell an asset. (Only in the worst of the 1930's depression did the policyholders create net drains through borrowing on their policies or cashing in their insurance.) In its lending activity, the large industrial corporation has even less concern for liquidity since it lends mostly surplus funds. Hence, these two can often agree to unorthodox arrangements, and for this accommodation the borrower is often willing to pay better interest. For example, suppose a borrower wants funds for two months and seventeen days; it wants funds for that length of time because it expects a large payment on a contract on that date. Until then it needs financing; after that it won't. It might be difficult to float a loan or short-term issue for just that period. Any shorter period would not solve its problem; any longer period would require it to pay interest for a longer time than necessary. Hence, it might turn to the corporate lender for this "tailoring."

This so-called private placement is one evidence of this tendency. The corporate borrower can strike all sorts of agreements for large amounts with just one large lender, but if it resorted to a public issue, it would have to issue a bond that pleased many smaller lenders. In order to reach the latter, it would have to offer the more commonly accepted type of bond. With one lender it can sit down and work out just those payment terms and amounts that are most convenient for mutual benefit. As a result of such flexibility, the amount of new corporate bonds privately placed often exceeds that issued publicly.

The Effects of Non-Bank Lending

The impact of such lending, in effect, has been to raise the velocity of bank deposits. In part, this has been through the greater activation of the existing deposits; in part, it has been through the reduction in the use of deposits to perform a monetary function. Some examples will illustrate these two influences.

Suppose A has $1,000 normally in his bank deposit, and his pattern of income and spending causes it to fluctuate between $1,200 and $800. A local savings-and-loan association offers a new lamp if he opens an account. It offers interest as well. Succumbing to this lure A shifts $300 by depositing a check. His checking account now will average only $700, moving between $500 and $900, and the savings-and-loan association now has $300 more in its account with the commercial bank.

The velocity of A's funds has risen; the same volume of transactions goes on, but there is now a smaller average balance to handle it. And the $300 he transferred to the association will probably be reloaned to help someone build a house. Hence, it will be spent, and so the original $1,000 now is doing more work. Seven hundred dollars of it is handling all the transactions in his account that the $1,000 did before. And it has the extra volume of transactions arising from the savings-and-loan association's building loan.

A similar step-up in velocity arises if the corporation can function with a smaller average balance and thereby release funds for a loan to another corporation. It now has a smaller balance to handle the same volume of transactions, and in addition there are the additional transactions arising from the borrower's actions. Note that both here and in the preceding paragraph there was no change in the volume of money outstanding, as there would have been if a commercial bank had been the lender. And since M' (the amount in demand deposits) is the same, there is no change in required reserves.

Some of these non-bank financing devices reduce the demand for money; some of the PT is being removed from the equation, so that the existing volume of money now services a smaller volume of transactions. For example, suppose A buys from a department store on credit, payable at the end of the month. Suppose he makes all his purchases on a similar basis, so that all his bills fall due on that date. And suppose he is paid on that date, and that his paycheck just equals the amount of his bills. Then A need only endorse his check over to his creditors, and he would not need any money during the month. Had he bought the same items for cash, then for the same volume of transactions he would have had to maintain a cash balance between pay periods, and thus some of the community's cash would have been absorbed in his balance. As it is, A needs no cash, and so the rest of the community has that much more money. Its volume of transactions is the same, regardless of the way in which he pays, but its money supply is different. And, to the extent that A leaves it with more money, the money can be used for other spending, and so its velocity is that much higher than if he had absorbed some in idle balances.

Any form of book credit contributes to this freeing of money. Trade credit, Diner's Club accounts, open-book accounts—all these permit their users to reduce the holdings of money to effect a given volume of transactions and thus free it for spending elsewhere. As a result, the community is able to effect a greater volume of transactions —if we add in the portion removed from the direct impact of the money stream.

We have already indicated that these various non-bank lenders have been growing in importance. This implies, therefore, that the effective velocity of our money supply has been increasing. In effect, we have been learning to transact our business more efficiently; either we make the money supply work harder, or we find ways of avoiding the use of money. Either way we raise the proportion of transactions to the existing quantity of money, and so, implicitly, the effective velocity.

There are obviously many other ways of achieving this economy that do not reflect the activities of the non-banking corporation. We have already indicated the motives for economizing on the size of the bank balance even aside from the corporate lender's intent. In addition, even business integration reduces the need for funds, as intracorporate entries replace money transfers. But what makes this sector's lending impact so significant is that there is the direct relationship to the money market, and thus yields and, through it, business activity. We shall explore this further.

Commercial-Bank Pressures

Another aspect of the operations of non-banking institutions actually concerns the competitive impact of the noncommercial banks—the savings banks and savings-and-loan associations. Their deposit appeal is essentially to the same small depositor who might have his funds in a savings account with a commercial bank. By offering him a higher rate of interest, they may be able to induce him to transfer his funds.

Since the intent of these other banks is to relend the money, either as loans, mortgages, or investments, they will usually redeposit the funds received into their own checking accounts which they maintain with a commercial bank.[2] Then when they make their loan or investment, they simply draw a check payable to the borrower, who then may use the money received for still further expenditures. Once again we see idle funds become active.

But there is an additional impact. The original individual who has switched his funds has merely exchanged a savings account at a commercial bank for a savings account at one of these competing groups. So far as his spending is concerned, there has been no change, and his asset composition is the same, although the name of the debtor bank is different. But the commercial bank has experienced quite a change. It now owes more as demand deposits and less as savings deposits. Its reserve requirements have increased. And this could lead to a reduction in its ability to expand, since the additional required reserves must

---

[2] The reader will recall that only commercial banks hold checking accounts. Hence, even these other banks, if they wish to write checks, must have an account at some commercial bank. Since their disbursements for any asset acquisition are usually paid for by check, all liquid funds other than cash in the vaults are carried as demand deposits. Hence, the entry of the commercial bank into the picture.

come out of either excess reserves or borrowings from the Federal Reserve. Thus, any large-scale transfer of savings deposits out of the commercial banks puts this sector under pressure. This is another aspect of the problem of transfer between these two deposit categories already mentioned. We thus would see a curtailment of aggregate commercial-bank assets, but a rise in its more volatile deposit component. Once again, the over-all velocity will have risen.

Not all of this transfer effect is one way. In a boom, as businesses and individuals need more funds, there will be a tendency for some savers to draw out their money from the various savings institutions to help finance the increased activity. This could be small businessmen using their personal funds to expand their own operations, or savers subscribing to new securities issues. The funds drawn out by the investors are then usually redeposited in the debtor's checking accounts. As these funds are drawn out, there is an accompanying pressure on the savings institutions, which must either slow down their new lending or liquidate other assets.

In most cases, the reverse flow will probably not offset the inflow to the savings institutions, so that this counter-move merely diminishes the impact on the commercial banks. That is, we see two streams countering each other—some money flowing from the commercial banks' savings accounts through the savings institutions and into the latter's checking accounts. Other funds are flowing out of the checking account to the savings institutions' depositors, who are withdrawing their funds to finance business, and thence back to the commercial banks as the funds are put into the corporate demand deposits. Net, therefore, we see a move from commercial-bank savings deposits to demand deposits, just as would normally happen with any corporate surplus funds that had been kept in time accounts. In effect, this is a more complicated version of the movements already discussed.

Suppose, however, that the withdrawals by savings-institution depositors actually exceeded inflows, compelling them to liquidate assets to meet the net drain. Then we have various possibilities, and to explore them all would consume too much space. The purchaser might be still another saver with a savings institution; in that case, all we would have would in effect be an exchange of savings-institution assets for deposits—both dropping, but no more funds coming in to meet the drain. Or the buyer could be a commercial-bank depositor; then there would be a drain of funds out of the commercial bank to meet the net drain out of the savings institutions. These funds so obtained may then be redeposited in the commercial bank, as already indicated.

This last sentence may need further clarification. Assume that Jones withdraws $1,000 from his savings bank to buy a bond issued by

General Motors. To meet this drain, the savings bank sells United States government securities, and the buyer is Smith. (a) If Smith pays by drawing out money from a commercial-bank savings deposit, this money goes to the savings bank, then to Jones, then to General Motors, and then back into the commercial bank (General Motors' checking account). Net effects of (a): savings-bank assets and deposits down; commercial-bank savings deposits down, but demand deposits up; commercial-bank required reserves up. (b) Smith pays by drawing on his checking account. As before, this money goes to the savings bank, then to Jones, then to General Motors, and finally back as a General Motors checking-account deposit. Net effects of (b): as before, savings-bank assets and deposits down; commercial-bank demand deposits unchanged; required reserves unchanged. However, it is likely that General Motors will utilize these funds more rapidly than Smith would have, so there will still probably be some increase in velocity.

Money-Market Effects

There is no question that the presence of these numerous financial intermediaries introduces changes in the money patterns that would not have occurred if only the commercial bank were the important lender. We have already indicated that commercial banks tend to have a higher proportion of their funds in shorter-term assets; savings banks, savings-and-loan institutions, pension funds, and insurance companies tend to keep a higher proportion in longer-term assets. Hence, this shift would seem to favor the longer-term borrower.

Furthermore, these intermediaries may change the flow of savings in other ways. Some of these financial intermediaries offer almost liquid assets, since their savings accounts can be withdrawn on demand, yet pay interest if held through the quarter or half-year. In effect, these deposits are almost as liquid as demand deposits, yet produce an income while being kept idle. Perhaps this has induced some depositors to entrust funds with them. If these organizations did not exist, these individuals might have preferred to leave the money in their checking accounts. As a result, idle demand deposits have become active through this transfer. Commercial-bank short-term lending declines while the intermediaries add to the long-term supply.

An alternative possibility that these savers may have selected would be to lend directly to the ultimate borrower. In the absence of the intermediaries, such savers would then become lenders, and the outcome could be an addition to the supply of short- or long-term funds, depending on the type of asset preferred. But by entrusting the funds with these savings organizations, the money now goes into house mortgages as well as into corporate and government bonds. Again, we see shifts in both the life pattern and destination of savings as a result of these organizations.

Moreover, even within the long-term sector there may be differences. Funds going to commercial-bank savings accounts may result in a higher proportion going into corporate bonds, whereas funds with savings-and-loan associations might end up as mortgages. Pension funds tend to place more money in common stocks of already established companies; funds with insurance companies go more into fixed-interest assets.

Analogously, the competition of corporations for short-term assets to absorb temporary surpluses of funds may alter market relationships. More of these securities go to the corporate buyer, so less is left for the commercial bank. Perhaps this pushes the latter into longer-term assets, a more risky proposition than they would have wanted otherwise. Or, alternatively, with this increased demand for such paper, there is an increased supply;[3] companies that might have borrowed for somewhat longer terms now decide to use short-term issues to take advantage of the supply of such funds.

We must also keep in mind the impact on the flow of goods. If more goes into long-term investment, we may end up with more houses, machinery, and the like. Or if more goes into short-term paper, we may have more consumers' durables bought with shorter contract terms. And these shifts, in turn, alter future production, demand, and consumption patterns. In brief, the ramifications become endless, even if we were certain just how these numerous alterations in funds flows did reflect themselves. Unfortunately, we are still in the dark as to the specific data on which to base any conclusions.

Since the various savings institutions attract funds by offering a higher interest, commercial banks fight back by offering their own savers more, thus reducing the incentive to shift accounts. But this works to raise interest rates in general. As these competitors start raising the rates they are offering, they are also raising their own costs, and so must now attempt to charge more to borrowers in order to get additional income to meet the higher interest charge. Alternatively, the banks may move into more risky, higher-yield assets. Hence, to the extent that we get these reactions we may get a general moving up in yields or a rise in the less risky yields and a damper on more risky yields.[4] Or if the banks shift some funds from the lower yielding, short-term securities to the higher yielding, long-term issues, again we

---

[3] Lending by the commercial banks and the corporate surpluses.
[4] As banks switch from the safer to the less safe, higher yield securities.

get changes in the flows within the various money-market sectors. And this is traceable to this competition for savings by the banks.

The member banks are restricted somewhat by Federal Reserve regulations in this competition. The System sets maximum interest rates that these banks may pay, and so reduces their freedom to raise the attractiveness of their savings accounts. In general, rates on savings in the non-commercial banks exceed those paid by member banks, and so tend to divert some savings to the member banks' competitors.

We can see the difficulties in assessing the effects of these inter-mediaries even if we examine the picture in general terms. As a group, these institutions have large amounts of deposits and other liabilities payable virtually on demand. Even the insurance company policy is in this category, although in practice few policyholders exercise their right. If these intermediaries did not exist, then these liquid payables would not exist. Matching these payables are the assets held by these companies, most of which are long-term—bonds, mortgages, and others. If the intermediaries did not exist, are we to conclude that the many savers would have loaned directly to the home buyers or corporate borrowers? If so, the intermediaries would have placed themselves between the lender and borrower, substituting their own liabilities, which can be called for at any time; these intermediaries, in other words, borrowed short and loaned long, whereas in their absence the lenders would have had to be satisfied with lending long themselves. We have thus raised the liquidity of the individual lender, giving him a deposit or policy claim which he can exchange for cash virtually on demand, in **place** of a long-term asset which is either subject to capital fluctuation **or,** in the case of mortgages, not saleable easily under any circumstances. The risk of realization of these long-term assets has been assumed by the intermediaries, and perhaps the law of large numbers protects them; while some individuals may need to draw out their deposits, others will have surpluses. The inter-mediary balances these two, and so has no need to liquidate. If it were not there, then the former group of individuals would be trying to sell their long-term assets, and the latter would be buyers; but perhaps these latter would not want the assets offered by the former. It is possible, therefore, that the intermediary has made such demands and supplies of funds more interchangeable. Instead of the people with surpluses bidding for certain long-term assets, and others in need of funds trying to sell different types, now both groups either deposit or withdraw from a savings bank or savings-and-loan institution, and the aggregates balance.

But can we be certain that, in the absence of these intermediaries, the savers would lend to the ultimate borrowers—the homeowners, government units, and corporations? Perhaps they are so unsophisticated financially that they would not entrust their funds to these units. Then we do have a marked difference. In the absence of these financial intermediaries, there might be more idle funds, less actual loanable funds, and less investment. Thanks to the expertise of the intermediaries, the saver does entrust his funds to this group, and they in turn, with their specialized knowledge, can afford to take the risks associated with long-term lending. As a result, there is more lending, more investment, higher incomes, and more savings. Perhaps the intermediaries actually generate their own funds!

If this last paragraph is true, then we have a heightened demand for and supply of long-term money. In that case, the final impact on the rate of interest may be to push it higher or lower than it would be in the absence of the intermediaries. Indeed, perhaps even the risk premiums are changed, since the expertise of the intermediary may lead to a more careful assessment of the riskier outlets, whereas the individual might shy away from them and thus reduce the supply of funds so much as to boost the rate abnormally. In this way we can see that the very interrelationship of the various money-market segments is altered so much as to defy analysis.

If the reader is puzzled as to how so large a volume of financial transactions could take place outside the commercial banking system, a hypothetical illustration may indicate the essentials of the cycle. In the absence of any intermediaries, some people would have demand deposits with commercial banks. Corporations (or other would-be long-term borrowers) would then offer their securities at so attractive a rate that some of these depositors would subscribe to the new issue. The depositor now has the asset (bond or mortgage), and the borrower gets the demand deposit. This is then spent, and so other people get the demand deposits. Some of these, in turn, may be attracted to turn over their demand deposits to still other long-term borrowers, and so on. Gradually, as this process continues, more and more people come to hold long-term paper, and the volume of demand deposits keeps moving between the long-term borrowers, the people from whom they buy, and then to some security buyers who thus start the cycle all over again.

If we now introduce the financial intermediaries, there is really not much difference. People with demand deposits transfer their funds to the savings bank. The savings bank now has the demand deposit and lends it to a home buyer or corporate borrower. These, in turn, spend the money, and so still others get the demand deposits. Some of these then switch their funds to the savings-and-loan association, and this organization then relends the demand deposit received. And so our cycle continues. In the process, more and more savings-deposit liabilities are being created as funds move into the various savings organizations, and these in turn acquire more and more long-term paper. In the process, as before, the demand deposits are moving back and forth. In both cases we did not expand the volume of checking accounts, although in practice these would have expanded, too, as a result of the commercial banks' lending activities. But the velocity has risen appreciably.

It should be added that in the absence of the financial intermediaries, the original demand-deposit holder could have left his balance idle. Then no long-term borrower gets the money, and so our cycle is broken. M remains the same, but V is nil, whereas in the two processes just described, V is extremely high. This zero-velocity possibility is the one already referred to when we discussed the alternative of little or no lending and investment in the absence of the intermediaries' expertise.

If these various cyclical phases can be made to move rapidly enough, then we are really saying that velocity is being pushed higher. This, in turn, is boosting aggregate spending, and may be doing it so rapidly as to outrace supply. Here we enter another area—the danger that too successful an operation by these intermediaries could create an excess demand and lead to inflationary price rises. Once again we are back to our earlier point, that the essential factor of the operations of these various non-banking institutions turns on the reactions of velocity. Of course, if velocity had been too low before, the rise may simply activate otherwise idle productive facilities. But if the velocity goes too far in this direction and thus exceeds what full capacity can meet, then we have the inflationary spectre. Until we are able to balance the velocity-supply figures with and without these intermediaries, we cannot really say whether they work to add more to output or to the upward price spiral, or to both.

Interest-Rate Side Effects

There are some points regarding the effect of interest-rate shifts on the non-bank investor which should be kept in mind in assessing the impact of these groups on the money market. For one thing, as mentioned, some of these, especially the savings bank and savings-and-loan institution, are in direct competition with the savings department of the commercial bank for the same type of money—that coming from the small saver. Hence, one inducement to attract his patronage is to offer a higher return. This would not induce him to save more—as we have noted, it is mainly his over-all income that is the determinant of savings—but it could result in a switch in his existing savings from one bank to another.

If this occurs, then the total expenses of the banking organization rise. Furthermore, this rise in interest offered applies to all savers; no distinction can be made between the new deposit and those already in the bank. (Actually, the practice of some institutions in offering a higher rate for funds that have been in the bank for long periods of time works in the opposite direction.) Hence, total interest payments rise in order to attract a marginal supply of savings. The additional assets that the bank can now acquire must earn enough to support both the interest on the new deposits and the increased interest on the already existing deposits. Many question whether such a goal is feasible without acquiring unduly risky paper that could go into default or slow payment if a recession strikes.

However, there is some offsetting help in the direction of higher income. As loans and bonds mature, the funds so returned to the bank can then be reloaned or reinvested at higher yields. That is, the average return on the entire portfolio can be slowly raised as this maturity process proceeds. In this respect the commercial bank has an advantage over its competitors. The latter tend to concentrate their holdings in mortgages and long-term bonds; as a consequence, very little of this paper matures in any given period. In contrast, a higher proportion of the commercial bank assets are in short term and intermediary-life loans and investments, so that a greater proportion is falling due regularly. As a result, a greater proportion of the assets can be upgraded in income.

Mention was made earlier that much of the corporation's temporarily free funds arises from profits that are subject to income tax. During the interval, these could be put into bills that mature when the tax falls due and thus provide the necessary means to meet the tax charge. Indeed, the United States government has tailored some of its shorter-term issues to this specific need, the maturity coinciding with the tax-payment date. In this manner, the corporate investor can get some income while holding his funds available for the tax charge.

In effect, his net tax is somewhat reduced by this small, offsetting interest return from the so-called tax-anticipation securities. Hence, the higher the current yield on such issues, the less the net impact of the corporate income tax. The lower the yield, the higher the net corporate tax. Since yields tend to rise in boom periods and decline in the recession, we have in a small way a reduction in the effective tax rate for the corporate investor in good times, and a rise when business slackens. In the boom, the corporation's total profits tend to rise and the effective tax per dollar of profits drops off because of the offsetting rise in yields on tax-anticipation securities. In the recession, the corporate aggregate profit drops, and each dollar is taxed at a higher effective rate because of the decline in tax-anticipation yields. Thus, the aggregate after-tax return is improved in two ways in the upswing, and worsened in two ways in the decline.

Monetary Control

Does the presence of the non-banking investor weaken the ability of the monetary authorities to control the economy through the various devices described earlier—the discount rate, open-market operations, and variable required reserve ratios? One thing is clear: none of these controls affects institutions directly; only the member banks can be touched, since they alone have access to the Federal Reserve, and they alone must carry reserves subject to the System's control.

Critics who see a weakening in the System's influence point to the fact that none of these outside groups can be controlled. If, for example, there is excessive expansion and the Federal Reserve tightens up on the supply of bank reserves, only the member banks are hit. The others are free to expand, and so the commercial banks are put at a competitive disadvantage. Indeed, not only are they prevented from expanding equally with that of their competitors, but disappointed customers who now cannot borrow from the commercial bank may turn to these other sources for funds, and so lessen the remaining market for the commercial banks. Perhaps to offset this added expansion the Reserve then has to restrict the economy even more, putting a still greater hamper on the member banks.

In fact, these critics say that such an outcome is inevitable. Tight money produces higher yields. The noncommercial intermediary now raises the interest offered depositors and so draws funds from the commercial bank. With these funds it is able to attract the thwarted borrowers. We get just as much lending, only the other intermediaries are doing the work and getting the income. It is even possible that the pressure on reserves now facing the commercial banks as they lose savings deposits (which then return as checking-account deposits by the intermediary) would either further contract commercial-bank operations or force the Federal Reserve to reverse its tight-money policy simply to protect its members.

But the issue is not as clear-cut as the foregoing analysis implies. Tight money is tight money. Individuals and business firms are then forced to cut down their borrowing, and so both the commercial banks and the other lenders face some decline in demand for their funds. Furthermore, would-be borrowers then try to economize on their idle balances; perhaps some of the money in the savings outlets is then transferred back to the working balances in the checking accounts. Hence, there might even be a flow from the savings institutions to the commercial banks; earlier in this chapter we explored this process. It is thus likely that both M and V would rise, offset by a decline in the total volume of savings deposits. That is, aggregate deposits might drop, but there would be a reshuffling away from savings and into demand deposits.

Much of the answer to this problem depends on the assumptions regarding Federal Reserve reactions to any such thwarting that might result from the operations of these numerous intermediaries. We shall explore this subject further when we concentrate on monetary policy and Federal Reserve actions.

However, one aspect will be mentioned here. Suppose the corporate lenders—not savings organizations, but industrial companies—find that their own rising activity requires additional liquid funds. They could borrow, but the interest payable may be too high. Hence, they decide to cut down on their own investing, not renewing loans as they mature, and not reinvesting as their bill holdings mature. (To some extent, an analogous situation arose in 1929; at that time corporate lenders to stock-market investors cut back on such loans during the panicky price drops that year.)

Where would these borrowers now turn? If they go back to the commercial bank, then the latter is faced with a heightened demand for loans, and this could coincide with the period when the reserve position is under pressure. Unless the Federal Reserve reverses itself— changing its policy as a result of actions on the part of the non-financial lender—such an accommodation is impossible. Even if the banks lend to these new borrowers, other loans would then have to be curtailed. We thus get a concentration of the contracting forces on the commercial banks' customers. If carried to extremes, we would get a liquidity crisis as those who had been borrowing from corporations now struggle to raise enough liquid funds to pay off their obligations. This could result in a general contraction if these desperate borrowers cut back spending to conserve on the much-wanted cash. And, as these cut-backs ripple through the system, we would then get a general decline in business activity, and so the recession begins. Such an eventuality could be worrisome.

The implications of the preceding paragraph spread throughout the monetary system. For example, the commercial banks may decide to lend to these new borrowers in order to avoid such a contraction. In order to raise the funds, they start to sell short-term assets. This raises short-term yields, and other corporate borrowers are driven out of this end of the market. So now still more borrowers come to the banks. Or, would the Federal Reserve now start buying Treasury bills to avert too drastic a rise in their yields? If it does so, it is then easing up on the policy of restraint that it was trying to enforce. We are thus back with our question regarding the reactions of the monetary authorities.

Perhaps the commercial banks would dump long-term securities. But this would make it harder for the savings banks to sell and meet any drains they were experiencing. It would also make it difficult for corporations to raise funds through long-term issues. If they do need the funds, then they, too, might turn to the commercial bank for temporary help, and so the pressures on this one sector are increased even more. Meanwhile, this constant selling of securities would be forcing prices down and thus creating increased capital losses, this making the commercial banks more and more reluctant to sell. Yet, if they do not sell, they cannot make more loans. And it is just this pressure that causes all the trouble in the money market.

It is for this reason that we must keep returning to the position taken by the Federal Reserve. Here is the one organization that can do something about the situation if a panic is to be avoided, and we will now examine its policy and operation in greater detail.

Summary

A large part of the accepting and lending of money is done by financial institutions other than the commercial banks. In fact, the volume of their operations exceeds by more than one-half the assets of the business banks. Some of these others have very stable flows of funds; others are erratic. Some confine themselves to certain sectors of the investment areas; others compete with banks across the board. Often these outsiders can be more flexible, and so meet borrowers' wants more successfully.

In general, these other intermediaries' activities tend to raise velocity, although to some extent they may also reduce the aggregate volume of commercial-bank deposits if they induce savers to switch funds to these other groups. Hence, the commercial bank operates under a competitive handicap. It cannot expand beyond the degree permitted by its reserves. Yet it can lose reserve freedom as a result of its competition.

In addition, these intermediaries may be altering the flow of savings and lending from what they would be otherwise. They may affect the economy's division between short- and long-term, and within each of these categories they may alter the type of subsector that gains or loses. It is even possible—indeed, probable—that these shifts in turn alter aggregate output, incomes, savings, and the pattern of yields. Whether all these factors weaken the ability of the Federal Reserve to control the economy's direction is still a debatable issue, especially since we are not too clear about the impact of all this turbulence in the financial areas.

Chapter 17

THE FEDERAL RESERVE WEEKLY STATEMENT

As a prelude to the discussion of Federal Reserve policy, this chapter takes a long detour to examine its weekly statement affecting member-bank reserves. Since virtually all Federal Reserve policy actions of significance manifest themselves in some way by affecting member-bank reserves, this chapter examines the summary statement that discloses the data arising from such decisions. To understand its meaning is to obtain key clues to policy trends.

The Formalities of the Statement

The statement normally appears every Thursday evening and is carried in the major newspapers on Friday morning. Obviously, no one statement tells a complete story. Its meaning must be weighed in light of previous and subsequent statements. But when properly interpreted, it provides more hints about future economic tendencies than probably any other single source. In fact, it is not an exaggeration to say that the correct reading of these weekly releases can indicate appropriate action in much of the money-market sphere, including both banking decisions, fixed-interest securities, and stocks. References are to Table V, an illustrative statement.

The usual release contains four columns of figures for the major components of the Federal Reserve and Treasury activity. Combined, they include all items that change member-bank reserves. Comparisons are made with the week's changes and shifts over the year.

The first column is a weekly average of each component through the immediately preceding Wednesday. Thus, the statement for the week ending January 29, 1964, would average the daily figures for January 23 through January 29, and this average is entered in the first column. The figure for January 29 itself is entered in the fourth column. Hence the two differ, to the extent that the last Wednesday varies from the week's activity. On the other hand, if Wednesday were peculiarly out of line because of transient influences, and therefore not too trustworthy as a guide, the weekly average would give a more accurate picture of the item. Most readers of the statement, for that reason, prefer the weekly average.

The second column shows the change for each item from the week before—the change from the average for the week ending January 22, to the average for the week ending January 29. A "+" figure indicates that the weekly average for the particular item is greater in the current week than in the week before; a "—" means that it has declined. In the accompanying table United States government securities bought outright for system account show a —$205 million; the week before (the week ending January 22) the Reserve's average holding was $32,944 million, while for the week ending January 29, it averaged $32,739 million, or a decline of $205 million.

The third column indicates the change from the year before—in our table, from the week ending January 30, 1963, to the week ending January 29, 1964. In the week ending January 30, 1963, the Federal Reserve had owned $29,975 million United States government securities; over the year this had risen by $2,764 million, or to an average of $32,739 million during the week ending January 29, 1964. So we have + $2,764 million in the third column. In this way we get a quick picture of Federal Reserve activities over a longer period, for comparison with changes in the week immediately past.

The Reserve Level

Fundamental to an understanding of Federal Reserve policy and its manifestation in the weekly statement is the role played by the

TABLE V

*Factors Affecting Bank Reserves**

	AVERAGES OF DAILY FIGURES		
MEMBER-BANK RESERVES, RESERVE-BANK CREDIT, AND RELATED ITEMS	WEEK ENDED JAN. 29, 1964	CHANGE FROM WEEK ENDED JAN. 22, 1964	JAN. 30, 1963	WEDNES-DAY, JAN. 29, 1964

	(In millions of dollars)			
Reserve-Bank credit:				
U. S. Government securities—				
Bought outright—system account	32,739	—205	+2,764	32,721
Held under repurchase agreement	—	—	— 148	—
Acceptances—				
Bought outright	67	— 4	+ 6	66
Held under repurchase agreement	—	— 45	— 15	—
Discounts and advances—				
Member-bank borrowings	177	+ 13	+ 78	301
Other	32	— 1	+ 30	32
Float	1,764	—601	+ 149	1,347
Total Reserve-Bank credit	34,780	—843	+2,864	34,467
Gold stock	15,512	— 1	— 416	15,513
Treasury currency outstanding	5,582	— 4	+ 11	5,582
	55,873	—849	+2,458	55,562
Currency in circulation	36,364	—326	+2,284	36,310
Treasury cash holdings	410	— 6	— 22	427
Treasury deposits with Federal Reserve banks	869	—175	+ 32	847
Foreign deposits with Federal Reserve banks	141	— 7	— 79	130
Other deposits with Federal Reserve banks	208	— 8	— 89	197
Other Federal Reserve accounts (net)	1,041	— 18	+ 75	956
	39,034	—538	+2,202	38,867
Member-bank reserves:				
With Federal Reserve banks	16,840	—309	+ 257	16,696
Currency and coin (estimated)	3,316	+ 2	+ 288	3,628
Total reserves held	20,156	—307	+ 545	20,324
Required reserves (estimated)	19,892	—284	+ 712	19,867
Excess reserves (estimated)	264	— 23	— 167	457

* On January 29, 1964, United States government securities held in custody by the Federal Reserve banks for foreign account were $8,795 million, an increase of $152 million for the week and an increase of $1,688 million from the comparable date a year ago.

reserve level. As we have seen, the total volume of deposits determines the level of required reserves; conversely, the level of reserves sets a maximum to the total deposit superstructure. Changes in the latter's composition, such as between time and demand deposits, can alter the combined total, but it is still the available reserves that determine the maximum of this composite amount. If, however, the deposits are less than the allowable maximum, there exist excess reserves, and so, if the bank desires, asset expansion is feasible. Hence, both the total amount of reserves and the excess reserves are of significance. The former gives us a clue to the aggregate credit extended by the commercial banks; the latter indicates whether and how much additional credit can be supplied.

In particular, the analyst is interested in the remaining slack in the banking system, for if there is little, there would be little extra expansion; while if there is much, then a large addition to purchasing power could result through new loans and deposit creation. In short, if we want the economy to expand, we can help it by giving the banks excess reserves and so permit them to add to assets. If we want to put a check on the economy's growth, we reduce or keep low the volume of excess reserves, and thus put a damper on any further bank-credit increases.

However, there are some offsetting factors within the excess-reserve figure. For one thing, some banks may have excess reserves at the same time that others are indebted to the Federal Reserve. While the first group can still expand somewhat more, the second group cannot. It may actually be trying to contract operations. If we looked only at the excess-reserve figure, we would overlook the offsetting restraining influence of the latter banks. To correct for this, we have the concept of *net free reserves* or *net borrowed reserves*. The first is the net excess reserves after we have subtracted the total loans and discounts of member banks—the total of borrowed reserves. The latter is our figure if we subtract loans and discounts from excess reserves and find that we come up with a minus figure—that is, that the total of borrowed reserves exceeds the excess amount. Net free reserves are thus the same as though we amalgamated all the banks, hypothetically using the available excess reserves to pay off the borrowings of the debtor banks. Net borrowed reserves would be the same, only we find that the excess reserves are inadequate to pay off all such borrowings. If we assume that banks in debt to the Federal Reserve will try to contract operations in order to reduce deposits and thus produce excess reserves with which the borrowings can be paid back, then we are saying that a bank with $1 million in borrowings will exert a contracting influence exactly equal, but opposite in effect, to a bank with $1 million in excess reserves. Netting the two would give us a zero net figure, and thus indicate the zero net effect on total credit.

In practice, as we have noted elsewhere in this book, we cannot assume that the two banks will be acting so as to offset each other. The bank with excess reserves may be located in a stagnant area, and so may have little further demand for loans; its excess reserves do not produce any expansionary effects. Or the bank in debt to the Federal Reserve may not act quickly enough to contract its operations. Hence, equal amounts of excess and borrowed reserves could be offsetting, or they could still cause some expansion if the borrowing bank is slow to respond. Or they could cause some contraction if the excess reserves are not utilized. Hence, a more detailed analysis would be necessary to see where the excess and borrowed reserves were located, to see if some light could be thrown on these alternatives.

If we assume that banks always want a little slack, then we are assuming that they always maintain some excess reserves. Hence, only the excess above this level is truly excess in the sense that banks will then expand operations. Implicit in this statement is the recognition that we cannot normally change the level of excess reserves. Every time we add to total reserves, we raise excess reserves and thus the margin above the desired minimum excess reserves; banks then react to expand assets and deposits, thereby converting the surplus excess reserves to required reserves, and thus dropping the stated excess reserves back to the desired (slack) level.[1] Only if business were so poor that the banks could not or would not add to their assets would a rise in total reserves add to excess reserves; this did hold true for much of the later 1930's, when the extremely depressed American economy made the banks most cautious in extending loans or acquiring fixed-yield securities.

Even in the post–World War II years, the variability in utilization of free reserves was noticeable. At times, when yields were attractive, the banks would invest any additional reserves and so maintain free reserves at the same level, varying the total credit with this addition. At other times, especially when yields were less attractive, additional free reserves supplied by Reserve actions might not be used fully, thus adding to the level of free reserves. (The reverse observations would apply for reductions in free reserves.) Thus, there was no close connection between changes in the volume of free reserves and the resulting impact on bank credit. The remarks regarding the relationship of the two must therefore be read with a certain amount of leniency, since there was a slack in the reaction between the two, and even a variability in the extent of this slack. Because of the statistical difficulties in assessing the correctness of the free-reserve thesis, much remains to be studied before more definite conclusions can be made.

---

[1] Required reserves thus indicate the extent of the aggregate-deposit superstructure.

While reserves are non-income-earners and thus provide the incentive to expand assets in order to utilize them, this reaction does not necessarily hold true in the same degree for all banks. Earlier we mentioned the limitation on the bank located in a stagnant area. More generally, maximum utilization of reserves appears to be more true of the large urban banks and less true of the small country banks. Hence, the same volume of excess reserves, if concentrated in the former, will produce more expansion and a more rapid reaction than if concentrated in the latter. In view of the countrywide activities of so many American companies, such shifts among banking categories can happen quite easily, especially if there exist seasonal patterns to the flow of payments and receipts geographically.

In the past decade, when interest rates have been higher than in previous years, the cost of excess (idle) reserves has risen in the form of income foregone. There is pressure on bank management to minimize this loss, and so the excess reserve position has tended to decline. Offsetting this is a greater vulnerability to the Reserve's restrictive policies, since there is less slack to take up any loss of reserves that result from, say, open market sales.

Because of this tendency to utilize excess reserves as much as possible, the previously discussed guides may not be so obvious. For example, if a bank has excess reserves because of a decline in the demand for loans, it may very well turn to the purchase of securities as an alternative income source. As a consequence its excess reserves remain at the minimum level equivalent to that it would have had had an active loan demand existed. In this situation easier money would be reflected in a smaller proportion of assets in loans rather than in a rise in excess reserves. Similarly, a tightening of money would not necessarily show up in a declining excess reserve position, but rather in a drop in the proportion of assets in securities, as banks sold these assets and moved into loans.

We must therefore look at both the excess reserve position and the loans/securities ratio. If money is easier it can show up either in a decline in this ratio and a rise in excess reserves, as banks find that their reserves rise faster than they can utilize them, or in no change in excess reserves and a decline in the ratio, as banks switch from loans to securities. The converse is true for tighter money. It is even possible for the ratio to remain unchanged, if the banks utilize excess reserves in the same proportion. For example, if excess reserves rise banks may decide to expand both loans and securities in order to maintain some preferred "mix"; here the ratio could remain the same, the easier situation showing up as a drop in excess reserves. A tight money position might then be reflected not only in a decline in excess reserves, but also a drop in both loans and securities while the proportion of the two remains unchanged. Here the aggregates matter.

The Details of the Statement

UNITED STATES GOVERNMENT SECURITIES BOUGHT OUTRIGHT. This is the first and usually the most important entry in the statement. This item reflects the total amount of government securities owned by the Federal Reserve Banks. When we speak of open-market operations, it is in this account that such activities are mainly reflected. As the accompanying table shows, it is by far the most important asset account for the System. As explained earlier, purchases, whether from the banks or non-banking sellers, add to member-bank reserves, and sales reduce reserves. In the statement, a "+" indicates a purchase for the period, a "—" a sale.[2] Hence, the Federal Reserve was a net seller during the week ending January 20, 1964, but a buyer for the year as a whole. In fact, it was quite a sizeable seller in this most recent week; its sales were equal to four times the weekly average of the net purchases over the preceding twelve months.

Open-market purchases have a twofold effect. A purchase adds to member-bank reserves. But, in addition, the resulting demand for government securities on the part of the Federal Reserve pushes prices up—pushes yields down. Not only are banks in a somewhat better position to expand, but the general interest-rate structure has been lowered. Expressed differently, the purchase takes a certain amount of government securities off the market, thereby reducing the supply and thus forcing up prices. Open-market sales, in contrast, not only reduce member-bank reserves and thus put a damper on bank activity, but they also add to the available supply of securities, depressing prices, or raising yields. Note that the purchase not only makes it easier for banks to lend, but, by reducing yields, also makes it more attractive for borrowers to desire more loans; the sale not only makes it more difficult for banks to lend, but also less advantageous—more costly—to borrow. We thus have two aspects to the open-market operation, both working in the same direction. The subsequent reactions of the banks and borrowers add still further to the impact on the yield structure as the available amount of loans changes.

Some critics have contended that the use of open-market operations is a rather costly means of altering excess reserves. If we wish to reduce free reserves, why not increase required-reserve ratios? This

---

[2] A maturing bill not replaced by a new purchase would reduce total holdings, and so would be similar to a sale.

would mean that the existing volume of deposits would need more required reserves, and so part of the previous excess reserves at the lower ratio would now become required, and so thwart the unwanted expansion. Open-market sales, in contrast, while reducing excess reserves, also add to the banks' holdings of government securities, and thus cause an added payment of interest to the private banking system. (The Federal Reserve turns over most of its earnings to the federal government.) However, this variation in reserve ratios would also raise the non-income-earning portion of the banks' assets, and so, by reducing income, might induce them to cancel their Federal Reserve membership; as a non-member bank they become subject to much more lenient state reserve requirements, and thus would have less tied up in non-earning assets.

Furthermore, as we change the reserve ratio, we change the reserve-deposit multiplier; a change from 10 to 12½ per cent required reserves, for example, means that each additional dollar of reserves can now sustain eight times, rather than ten, in demand deposits. With open-market operations, we leave the multiplier factor unchanged, and so need not adjust our sights to take into account the further change in the "response coefficient."

UNITED STATES GOVERNMENT SECURITIES HELD UNDER REPURCHASE AGREEMENT. Sometimes sellers to the Federal Reserve sell with the understanding that they will repurchase the securities in a short while. In effect, they are obtaining a short-term loan for the period. This is especially convenient for dealers who specialize in government-securities trading, for they cannot borrow from the Reserve. The repurchase agreement is thus a route to the System's resources if they experience a temporary pinch. The prices at which the Reserve buys and sells in such a situation are so arranged that the dealer who is party to the agreement is usually charged the current discount rate. Normally these transactions are not a significant amount. It is only in times of temporary stringency, such as might occur during the Christmas season, that dealers are pressed for funds and find it difficult to gain accommodation from their normal sources, the commercial banks. The funds are used to finance the inventories of securities that a dealer must carry in order to service his customers; if the borrowing could not be arranged, the dealer would have to reduce his holdings in order to obtain the necessary funds, and so cut back on the scale of his dealings. This, in turn, would make the government-securities market less useful, for it is the ability to buy and sell large quantities quickly that makes the Treasury bill desirable as secondary reserves.

ACCEPTANCES. These are mostly short-term obligations issued by banks and purchased by the Federal Reserve in the open market. The monetary impact of such acquisitions is similar to that when securities are purchased, as well as to the effect on yields.

DISCOUNTS AND ADVANCES. As explained earlier, this may be either through rediscounting short-term loans made by the member bank, or through direct loans to the bank using the latter's acceptable assets as collateral; most such borrowings, however, are done through the latter procedure, and we shall not distinguish between the two approaches, especially since the impact on bank reserves is the same. It will be recalled that a loan by the Federal Reserve adds to the borrowing bank's total reserves, usually through an addition to its balance at the Reserve. Repayments of such borrowings operate in the reverse way. Member banks tend to repay their borrowings as rapidly as is feasible, since the Reserve frowns on too extensive a use of this availability, for it indicates that the member bank is overextending its operations, and so lacks sufficient capital to support its activities; it is thus supplementing its own funds with Reserve advances. The extent that Federal Reserve advances are tied down for any length of time by one bank lessens the available resources for other banks; in practice, however, in view of the Reserve's own ample resources and excess reserves, this has been a minor influence.

Member bank borrowing, it should be noted, adds to the reserves of the borrowing bank and to the reserves of the entire banking system. In contrast, were a bank to sell assets to another bank, its reserve gain would reduce the buying bank's reserves; reserves for the banking system would be unchanged. Were the sale to the public, reserves for the banking system would also remain unchanged, but there would be a decline in required reserves as the purchaser paid by drawing down (and thus destroying) his deposit balance.

If the discount rate is low relative to market yields on short-term paper, there would appear to be some incentive if the member bank needs more reserves to prefer to borrow, rather than sell off assets, since the extra interest cost on the loan is less than the income foregone through disposing of the asset. If the discount rate is high—as high as, or even higher than, short-term yields—then there is less incentive to borrow, since the added interest cost is great relative to the alternative of loss of income through the sale of assets. Hence, we would presumably see borrowings rise when the discount rate is well below short-term yields, and borrowings decline (or repayments rise) when the discount rate is relatively high. We can thus get a clue to Federal Reserve policy by comparing the relationship of these two rates. The closer the discount rate gets to market short-term yields, the more pressure there is on the member banks to cut down on their borrowing, and the less easy it will be for them to expand loans to customers, since reserves will be under pressure. When the discount rate is well below the market structure of short-term yields, then the Reserve is in effect giving the "go ahead" signal to borrow, add to reserves, and so expand assets.

Unfortunately, the logic is clearer than the practice. If the Reserve wants the banks to expand, it presumably reflects the depressed state of business activity. If business is depressed, the demand for funds is relatively low, and so yields drop off. Yields are low just when the Reserve wants the member banks to expand loans and securities purchases. But presumably, if business borrowing is insufficient, the member banks already have excess reserves, and so there is little incentive to borrow in order to obtain still more excess reserves. Indeed, if yields are low, how much lower can the Reserve put the discount rate in order to make borrowing attractive? Short-term yields in recession periods often sink to 1 per cent; would any lower discount rate provide enough of a margin to make it worthwhile to borrow?

Suppose we are in a boom that threatens to spill over into an inflation. The demand for loans is high, and yields are rising. Member-bank excess reserves are at a minimum. If the Reserve wishes to restrain the banks from still further expansion, it would raise the discount rate. But as this rate rises, and if it is effective, it results in still more pressure on borrowers and thus still higher yields in the market. Each hike in the discount rate could well push up short-term yields and thereby keep the margin between the two constant. Only if the rate were to go to extremely high levels might it so restrict borrowing as to become effective. But this rate may be so high as to be virtually punitive; a 7-per-cent rate, for example, is higher than allowed in usury legislation, although this particular rate is exempt from such legislation. Even this might not be high enough when the demand for loanable funds is brisk.

As a consequence, changes in the discount rate give rise to different interpretations that could often be erroneous. Traditional teaching has simplified the interpretation: a rise in the discount rate is a sign that the Reserve wants to curtail bank lending, while a drop in the discount rate is a sign that the Reserve wants to stimulate bank lending. But an increase could also indicate that business is so good that the Reserve must raise the rate; the boom is even stronger than we realized, so now business should really get going and expand. Or a decline in the discount rate could be interpreted to mean that the business outlook is so bad that the Reserve has to take steps to check the downturn. If so, then the economy is much worse than we had realized, so we had better cut back operations sharply. And a still different set of explanations could be possible: the discount rate had been raised simply because market yields were high and the Reserve wished to keep the two reasonably in line; or the discount had been dropped simply because market yields were coming down and the Reserve wished to maintain the same relationship. Both the rise and fall in yields—the cause of the shift in the discount rate—may have been due to extraneous influences not indicative of business activity at all; there may be a plethora of short-term funds because of foreign accumulations of dollar balances as a result of balance-of-payment swings. In this last set of possibilities, the discount-rate adjustment has been a technical move to reflect altered patterns of short-term rates.

However, the discount mechanism can be used effectively if coordinated with the Federal Reserve's open-market operations. Assume, for example, that the Reserve wishes to restrain the economy. It then sells some securities, thereby draining reserves from the member banks. If it wishes this restraint to be applied gently, it allows the resulting small rise in bond yields—reflecting the start of a tighter money market—to widen the margin relative to the discount rate, and so banks can adjust to the loss of reserves by borrowing from the Reserve. This replenishes the reserves lost through open-market operations. But as we have mentioned, the tendency is to repay borrowings as quickly as is feasible. Hence, the banks will now slowly start to restrain their own operations, thereby freeing reserves to repay the advance from the Federal Reserve. The transition to a tighter money policy has thus been slower and smoother. On the other hand, if the Reserve wished to exert a quicker and more severe restricting policy, it would increase its open-market sales and also raise the discount rate. There is now less incentive to borrow and more incentive for the member banks to restrict operations immediately. We thus accentuate the timetable for the adjustments to a tight-money policy; now the banks have to take rapid steps to cut down on lending and business spending.

By coordinating the discount mechanism with open-market operations, the Reserve can exert its pressure with a minimum of change in member-bank reserves. For example, assume that some restraint is desired, though not too much nor too rapidly. The Reserve then starts to sell Treasury bills in the open market, and these are purchased by pension funds and insurance companies, who pay by drawing down their deposits. This, in turn, reduces the reserves of the member banks where these funds keep their accounts. These banks then turn to the Reserve for an advance, and thus restore the necessary reserves. But since the banks do not wish to remain in debt, they now start to liquidate some of their assets. These are bought by purchasers with accounts in still a second set of banks. In paying, they bring reserves to the selling banks—which can then repay the Reserve—and reduce reserves at the second set of banks. Now these banks have to resort to borrowing from the Reserve, to be followed by their liquidating assets. in the open market. And so it goes. The tightness is gradually transmitted from bank to bank. As each bank is hit, it may resort to borrowing from the Reserve, but then this is followed by a liquidation of some of its assets. Thus, it cuts down its own expansion. But in so doing, it puts pressure on other banks' reserves. So now they must pull in their activities. Gradually the whole banking system feels the restrictive effects. In this way there is no need for the Reserve to sell so many securities that many banks lose reserves. So long as a significant number feel the impact, and if there is no hurry, the subsequent effects arising from the adjustments of the affected banks will transmit the pressures throughout the system.

Other advances include a miscellaneous group, too numerous and unimportant to be detailed. In general the movement of these advances affects reserves in a manner similar to that of other discounts and advances.

FLOAT. Because the week-to-week changes in float can amount to several hundred million dollars, often far more important in the impact on total reserves than any other item in the weekly statement, it deserves a separate section of explanation. But, as will be explained, its significance is really much less than the items so far discussed.

To explain float, we must first follow the course taken by a check. Assume that Smith in New York receives a bill from Jones in Sacramento, and mails a check in payment to the latter. (We shall assume that both maintain checking accounts with member banks.) Smith deducts the amount paid out from his account, but his bank is still unaware of the transaction; hence, on the books of his bank Smith has done nothing as yet. Similarly, neither Jones nor his bank is as yet aware that Smith's check is coming. Since the banking figures are as yet unaffected, this phase of the check's existence would not show up in the weekly statement.

Jones receives the check. Neither his nor Smith's bank is aware of this, and so we still do not record its impact in our statement. Even when Jones mails his check as a deposit in his bank, there is no change; although Jones now adds the amount to his balance, the bank does not, for it has yet to receive the check.

The check reaches Jones' Sacramento bank. Now we get the first banking action: the bank has a check to be collected from a New York bank and credits Jones' balance. However, the bank's reserves are unaffected; since only cash or money with the Reserve counts as reserves, the receipt of this check so far has changed neither of these two items.

Note that so far as the banking system is concerned, there has been a rise in demand deposits; the bank in Sacramento adds to Jones' balance, but the New York bank has yet to subtract the check from Smith's balance. Furthermore, since we have not yet altered either bank's reserves, we would not see the check's movements reflected in the weekly statement.

The Sacramento bank now forwards the check to its Federal Reserve bank (San Francisco), depositing it in its account and so adding to its reserves.[3] Now the weekly statement is changed; the Federal Reserve is aware of this check, and has made a change in its reserve accounts, increasing that of the Sacramento bank. At this point, the banking system's total reserves have been increased; the Sacramento bank's reserve is up, while we have yet to reduce the reserve balance of the New York bank. The check is in the process of collection, to be sent through for payment, but *in the interim between its being credited to the receiving bank and charged to the paying bank, we have float*. Float, then, means checks in the process of collection in which the funds are doing double duty—increasing the reserves of some banks and still being carried in the balances of the paying banks.

The Federal Reserve Bank of San Francisco forwards the check to the Federal Reserve Bank of New York. In exchange for the check it is now giving up, the San Francisco Reserve is given an additional amount of gold certificates—held in Washington—which is taken from that held for the New York Federal Reserve. That is, both Reserve banks have a change of assets; San Francisco swaps a check for gold certificates, whereas New York swaps gold certificates for the check.

When it receives the check, New York then charges it to the paying bank's balance, thereby reducing its reserves, and turns over the check to the bank, which then charges the Smith account. The New York Federal Reserve, in other words, cancels the check against its deposit liability to the New York member bank. The New York member bank cancels its reserve balance against the deposit due Smith. At the time the New York Federal Reserve reduces the reserve of the New York member bank, float disappears. At this point the check has now cancelled out its effect on member-bank reserves, the increase accruing to the Sacramento bank now being exactly offset by the decrease in the New York bank's reserves. This decline would also be recorded in our weekly statement. From then on, until the check finally reaches Smith, there is no further impact on bank reserves, and so no further effect shows up in the weekly statement.

By extending this explanation a bit, we can see how float rises and falls. To repeat: all deposits of checks by receiving banks in their Federal Reserve account add to their reserves and thus to float; all

---

[3] Because it is an out-of-district check, the reserve is not credited immediately.

checks that are cleared through to be charged to the paying banks reduce their reserves and thus reduce float. Hence, if in any week the amount of checks deposited exceeds the amount cleared, then we see a rise in float. If the amount cleared exceed the amount deposited, then float declines. Since there is the time lag to cover the process of collection, these two amounts could vary. For example, in the first week $1.5 billion could be deposited and $1 billion clear, adding $0.5 billion to float. Next week $1.6 billion is deposited; of this, $0.9 billion clears, plus the $0.5 billion of the preceding week. In the second week, therefore, total cleared checks amount to $1.4 billion, and so float rises by $0.2 billion. In the third week only $1.0 billion in checks is deposited; of this, $0.8 billion clears. In addition, the $0.7 billion not cleared the previous week is also cleared. Total cleared checks amount to $1.5 billion, and this excess over new checks deposited reduces float by $0.5 billion.

A rise in float is one indication of rising payments, for the new volume of checks deposited (reflecting current payments) exceeds the previous volume of payments now coming through to be charged to the paying banks. A rising volume of payments, as occurred in the previous example for the second week, thus tends to raise float; or, conversely, a rise in float may indicate a rising volume of payments. This could occur during the seasonal upswings in business activity or during the rising phase of the business cycle. In contrast, a declining figure for float could occur if current payments are lower than before, the new checks being deposited amounting to less than the amount of the old checks being cleared. Business activity, in other words, may be declining because of either seasonal or cyclical influences.

However, float is also subject to influences of only passing importance. Suppose there is a countrywide snowstorm. Many of the checks being routed through for collection are being delayed; if they do not clear this week, then float is not lowered as much. Again, suppose in our previous examples for the third week $1 billion in checks were deposited because they had been received before the storm. Some of the $0.8 billion of these checks being forwarded for payment are stalled en route, so that only $0.5 billion reach their destination. Hence, total checks cleared are only $0.5 billion plus the $0.7 billion of the previous week, or $1.2 billion. Float now drops by only $0.2 billion. Indeed, if all the $0.8 billion were stalled, then float would actually rise. Of course, in the following week, float would drop even more, as all these piled-up checks now came through along with the normal amount being cleared.

A similar delay could arise if the volume of checks being processed exceeds the capabilities of the clerks to handle them. If the checks reach the proper Reserve Banks but the staffs cannot process them, then the paying banks do not get charged right away. Some of the delayed checks then are carried over to the next period. This week's cleared checks are thus less than were actually received, and so the offsetting float aspect is less, just as happened during the snowstorm.

The Federal Reserve could reduce float by spending more on overtime work; this would speed up check clearing and so reduce the paying banks' reserves more quickly. But this additional pressure on the banks might then have to be offset by the purchase of securities in the open market to replenish the loss of reserves arising from the stepped-up collection rate. One may thus raise the question: which alternative movement of reserves is preferable? (It should also be noted that there is a cost involved for the Federal Reserve, too: labor costs are higher with overtime, and income is higher as the Reserve buys more securities.)

If such delays do occur, the paying banks retain their reserves a bit longer—a day or two, perhaps, and maybe even more. Since they know that these checks will be coming through shortly, they cannot afford to tie up their reserves in any long-range investment. But they could lend them out for a day or two. At such a period, extremely short-term money rates plummet, as this enormous temporary surplus of reserves is offered for loan. In the subsequent discussion of Federal Funds, these delays are one of the major disturbances to the more normal level of that rate, since such funds are essentially one-day money. However, such careful use of bank reserves is more applicable to the larger banks, where temporary surpluses can amount to the millions. The small rural and country banks would enjoy only a small amount of temporarily excess reserves arising from the delay in clearing, and it usually does not pay to bother with so short a loan. Hence, our remarks apply mainly to the large city banks.

To a certain extent, these apparently random variations in float are predictable. For example, the presence of a holiday raises float before the holiday and reduces it afterwards. This is most noticeable at Christmas, when the volume of checks soars in response to the seasonal upswing in business activity combined with the gift-giving propensities of the public. Then, as the post New Year's Day lull sets in, this move is reversed. Both the Federal Reserve and the commercial banks can plan fairly precisely for such changes, and they take the expected impact on reserves into consideration in their policy planning.

TOTAL RESERVE-BANK CREDIT. This item is a subtotal of those already discussed. It measures the effect on reserves arising from member-bank activities with the Federal Reserve—open-market operations, borrowings, and check clearing. The remaining items cover those activities that influence reserves but do not directly result from member-bank–Federal Reserve transactions with each other.

GOLD STOCK. Although this item is discussed at greater length in the balance-of-payments exposition, we shall capsule the major points insofar as they are relevant here. Essentially, any change in the gold stock causes an equal change in member-bank reserves. In effect, if gold is to be shipped to a foreign country, the money is first drawn out of the member bank, thereby reducing its reserves. Then it is presented to the Federal Reserve, where it is exchanged for gold certificates, thus reducing the System's reserves, and then exchanged at the Treasury for gold, thus reducing our gold stock. Inflows of gold are sold to the Treasury, payment being made from the Treasury's account with the Federal Reserve. The latter is then usually replenished by a deposit of gold certificates issued against the newly received gold. If the gold had been purchased from a domestic producer, the seller deposits the Treasury payment with his bank, thereby adding to deposits; the bank forwards the check to its Reserve account, thus raising its reserves. If the seller had been a foreign central banking institution, the credit is usually to the latter's account at the Reserve; and then, when utilized (presumably to pay an American creditor), member-bank reserves and deposits rise, as in our domestic sale.

These transactions in gold have altered the Federal Reserve's holdings of gold certificates, outflows reducing and inflows increasing the amount. The Federal Reserve has maintained a stock of gold certificates as its reserve equal to at least 25 per cent of its demand liabilities—deposits and currency outstanding. In practice, it has usually maintained a proportion well above this figure. It is very likely that if the stock of gold certificates were to get too low, if too much gold is drained out because of a balance-of-payments deficit, we would then see, as a further modification of this requirement, either a lower ratio or the complete abolition of the requirement. Although member-bank reserves serve as a check on aggregate member-bank deposit liabilities, gold certificates do not impose any barrier to the size of the System's liabilities. Thus it can feel free to expand member-bank reserves, and thus its own demand liabilities, in accordance with the broader questions of monetary policy, ignoring the formal restrictions that a reserve-ratio requirement would seem to impose. In summary, then, we can say that changes in the gold stock reflect our international-payments position rather than act as guides to the domestic monetary scene.

TREASURY CURRENCY OUTSTANDING. Under our monetary system, both the Treasury and the Federal Reserve issue currency. Currency put into circulation by the Treasury is first deposited with the member banks where the Treasury maintains most of its balances. (This is not strictly true; we shall discuss the accounting in somewhat more detail later in the chapter.) Hence, increases in Treasury currency outstanding tend to swell member-bank reserves. Similarly, currency withdrawn from circulation tends to come from the member banks, and thus reductions in the amount outstanding reduce member-bank reserves. This could happen, for example, if a taxpayer paid the Internal Revenue in currency; he would draw the amount out of his member-bank deposit account—or from a savings institution, which in turn would draw on its member-bank account—and the currency then received could be destroyed, if the Treasury were so inclined.

We have now reviewed the first group of accounts on the statement. The reader should note one aspect that these items have in common. If any of these various entries increase, then member-bank reserves increase. If any of these entries decrease, then member-bank reserves decrease. By summing each entry's change, we get the net impact of this group upon member-bank reserves; a net "+" raises reserves, a net "−" indicates that these have worked to lower reserves. The next group of entries, however, has an opposite arithmetic effect. Increases in these items tend to reduce member-bank reserves; decreases in these items tend to raise reserves. For this group, a net "+" is thus an indication of a source of drain on reserves; a net "−" is a guide to additions to member-bank reserves.

CURRENCY IN CIRCULATION. This item represents coin and dollar bills held by the public—specifically, by anyone except the government and the Federal Reserve. In practice, this amounts to what the public takes out of, or deposits with, the member banks. It will be recalled that vault cash—currency in the member banks—can be counted as reserves. Hence, if the public withdraws some currency—if, in other words, currency in circulation rises—what has probably occurred is their withdrawal of vault cash from the banks, whose reserves were thereby reduced. The banks then replenished this drain by drawing down their balance with the Federal Reserve; in effect, reserves at the Federal Reserve were exchanged for reserves in the vault, the cash drawn out of the Federal Reserve, which lowered reserves there, being balanced by the rise in vault cash, which raised reserves in this form.

Conversely, if the public deposits some of the currency it has carried in its pockets, thus raising the banks' vault cash and reserves, the banks then redeposit this additional cash with the Reserve, thus reducing reserves in the form of vault cash and raising reserves in the form of a Federal Reserve balance. Currency in circulation, as a result, has declined by the amount deposited. Note that the major impact of these cash flows is on the banks' balances with the Reserve, since they tend to keep their vault cash at a fairly constant level, reflecting the daily needs for over-the-counter transactions. Incidentally, a deposit of cash with a savings bank or savings-and-loan institution would not show up here. These organizations are included with the public, and their currency holding is regarded as still in circulation. Of course, member-bank reserves are unaffected by what happens to savings-bank holdings of currency. But if the savings bank then passes on the money to a member bank, depositing the funds in its account there, it does fall within our discussion; currency in circulation is now less.

As discussed in Chapter 8, there is also a fairly predictable pattern to changes in this item. People tend to draw out money—more goes into circulation—during vacation and holiday periods (flowing back afterward). Hence, these flows can be counted upon, and the banking system can plan for them. Sometimes, however, new forces come in to change the pattern. For example, during World War II many defense plants were set up in small communities not served by banks. People had to keep more cash handy, since it was more difficult to get funds quickly. Currency in circulation was therefore pushed up. In addition, people who understate their income for tax purposes prefer to hide their activities; checks can be traced, but currency cannot. And so the growth of illegal or tax-evasion income results in a rise in the use of currency, a rise in currency in circulation. (Sometimes even this can be detected; often the tendency is to concentrate such accumulations in large-denomination notes, for it is easier to conceal twenty $1,000 bills than twenty-thousand $1 bills. Hence, a scrutiny of the denominations of currency rising in circulation helps us in this investigation.)

The normal daily, or even monthly, variations in currency in circulation are not comparatively large. The change is rarely as much as 1 per cent over the month, although this could be well over $250 million. Over the long run it is true that this figure will tend to grow as our incomes rise, and so more money is needed to handle the increased retail transactions. Interestingly enough, there has recently occurred a somewhat sharper growth in this longer-run movement. As more and more teenagers become spenders, they carry more and more cash, for few will have been graduated to the use of checking accounts. The population boom is thus now showing up in a rising proportion of teenagers; financially, we see this as currency in circulation rising faster than incomes in general.

TREASURY CASH HOLDINGS. Since the Treasury also has cash on hand, we must take this figure into account. The example of the man who paid his taxes in cash will illustrate how this item could change. In drawing money out of the bank, he did not put it into circulation, and so it would not show up in the preceding entry. Hence, any addition to the

Treasury's holdings presumably came from a bank withdrawal or from currency in circulation. Its movement tends to reduce member-bank reserves (if the former), or to be offset by the opposite change in currency in circulation (if the latter).

TREASURY DEPOSITS WITH THE FEDERAL RESERVE BANKS. Normally this reflects money transferred from the Treasury's accounts with member banks. For much of its financing, the Treasury has a two-stage banking account. Most tax receipts and subscriptions to government securities are first deposited with member banks. Hence, member-bank reserves and deposits are unchanged, the deposit of the taxpayer or subscriber going down and that of the government going up. If the bank itself subscribes, then it merely adds to Treasury deposits, as it would if it made a loan to any borrower. Again total reserves are unchanged, although required reserves rise (and excess reserves drop).

But almost all Treasury disbursements are made from its Federal Reserve accounts. As it needs money, it transfers funds from its member-bank accounts, in effect drawing a check on the latter and depositing it with its Reserve account. The Reserve then charges the member bank's account, thereby reducing member-bank reserves. End result: Federal Reserve liabilities to the Treasury (the latter's deposit) rise by an amount equal to the decline in member-bank balances. There has been a reshuffling of Reserve deposit liabilities. Member-bank reserves are down, offset by an equal decline in Treasury deposits with the member banks. Some required reserves are released—the proportion required against these deposits—but, of course, this is much less than the loss of reserves. Hence, excess reserves decline.

When the Treasury spends the money, the recipients usually deposit it in their account with the member bank. We now reverse the transactions. Member-bank deposit liabilities rise, but so do their reserves, as the Treasury checks being paid in are then redeposited with the Reserve. It then charges the Treasury account and credits the member-bank account. Again we have just a reshuffling—in the opposite direction—of Reserve deposit liabilities, but also an expansion in both reserves and deposit liabilities for the member banks. The rise in required reserves against these additional deposits is less than the rise in total reserves, and so excess reserves are also increased.

Note that any net receipt of funds by the Treasury could be used to reduce member-bank reserves and thus curtail their operations; any disbursements by the government could work in the opposite direction. Thus a deficit is an excess of disbursements; surplus is an excess of receipts.

FOREIGN DEPOSITS WITH THE FEDERAL RESERVE. Many foreign banks, particularly central banks, as well as other foreign monetary authorities, keep some of their reserves in dollars, in order to meet possible balance-of-payment deficits. In addition, these balances are also used to finance foreign trade, the dollar being a currency more acceptable than their own. Some of these balances are kept with the Federal Reserve as deposits, while others are invested in short-term securities. The deposits tend to reflect the day-to-day activities. Normally, payments by Americans to foreigners are made by checks which end up at the American account of a foreign central bank. These checks might then be deposited in the Federal Reserve deposit account, and, upon receipt, the Reserve would then charge the paying member bank. The resulting rise in foreign deposits at the Reserve would thus decrease member-bank reserves. Conversely, payments made by foreigners to Americans would often be through checks drawn on these foreign deposits, the check being deposited by the American with his member bank. After the check had reached the Reserve, the foreign deposit would be reduced and the member-bank reserve account increased. Of course, if the foreign account were kept with a member bank, as many are, these payments would be transfers between American and foreign-owned deposits, and thus not affect the reserves.

OTHER DEPOSITS WITH THE FEDERAL RESERVE. These are a miscellaneous group of accounts, including some maintained by non-member banks to facilitate check clearings. Payments drawn on member banks that end up in this account reduce member-bank reserves; payments out of these accounts that end up with the member banks add to reserves. As was true of the other accounts in this group, increases in this item decrease member-bank reserves; decreases add to member-bank reserves.

OTHER FEDERAL RESERVE ACCOUNTS. This is the remainder (less important) of the items on the Federal Reserve balance sheet. Here, too, any payment that increases these accounts comes from some member bank, and so decreases reserves, whereas payments that reduce these accounts add to member-bank reserves. One such payment could be the dividends due on the member-bank stock in the Federal Reserve.

If we now combine the two groups of accounts to obtain a net figure, we get the final impact on member-bank reserves. The weekly statement breaks this down into its two components—that part held with the Reserve, and that part in the bank's vaults as currency and coin. The net figure of the items described in the Federal Reserve statement thus shows up as the net change in member-bank reserves held with the Reserve. The vault-cash component is estimated. Based on the estimated figures for bank deposits—both time and demand—

the statement also indicates how much of the reserves is required, and, of course, the residual then is the excess reserve. The effect on net free (or borrowed) reserves would then net out the change in excess reserves at the end of the statement, with the earlier entry for the change in discounts and advances to the member banks. We thus gain a composite picture for the entire Federal Reserve System and its member banks.

In addition, the weekly statement furnishes two other sets of figures. One gives a maturity distribution of the loans and securities held by the Federal Reserve as of the Wednesday reporting date, this furnishing a clue to the Reserve's operations in the different maturity sectors. The second set gives the amount of United States government securities held in custody for foreign accounts. These are mainly foreign balances of the various official monetary institutions. As already mentioned, many of these hold part of their reserves in dollars. Balances in excess of working needs are then invested in order to earn some income. The working balances, of course, were the aforementioned foreign deposits that do not earn interest. Much of the shift in this item reflects the net change in our balance of payments; this is that part of the payments flow that is not in gold. Hence, a better insight into the current state of our international position would be gained by combining the changes in the gold stock with that in foreign deposits and these securities in the Reserve's custody.

Some Accounting Points

In our explanation it was assumed that all changes in the various items were run through the member banks. But this need not be the case all the time. What about these exceptions? If we adopt the fiction that all items go through member banks, then any exception will be matched by an opposite and offsetting exception, thus canceling out.

For example, assume that the Treasury issued currency directly to the public. Then Treasury currency outstanding would show a "+", currency in circulation a "+", and member-bank reserves would be unchanged. Now, in our approach, the "+" for Treasury currency outstanding would also be a "+" for member-bank reserves, and the "+" for currency in circulation would be a "−" for member-bank reserves. The "+" and "−" for member-bank reserves cancel out, and so we arrive at the actual answer: no impact on member-bank reserves.

Or suppose the public pays currency that it has been carrying in its pockets to a foreign bank, which then deposits the sum in its Federal Reserve account; again member-bank reserves are unaffected. Currency in circulation is down, and foreign deposits with the Reserve are up. In our approach, the "—" for currency in circulation would make for a "+" in member-bank reserves, while the "+" in foreign deposits would make for a "—" in member-bank reserves, and again the effect on reserves nets to zero. So once again we have the actual impact.

Or again, suppose the Treasury prints currency, and deposits the money in its Federal Reserve account. Member-bank reserves are again unaffected. In our approach, the "+" in Treasury currency outstanding would register as a "+" for member-bank reserves, while the "+" for Treasury deposits would be a "—" for member-bank reserves. Again we have netted our reserve account to the actual effect of no change.

Suppose the Reserve bought government securities from a member bank, which then used the funds to repay a previous advance from the Reserve, thus leaving member-bank reserves unchanged. As before, the "+" for Reserve purchases indicates a "+" for member-bank reserves, while the "—" for discounts and advances yields a "—" for member-bank reserves. So once again our hypothetical approach yields the actual correct answer for the (zero) change in member-bank reserves.

Suppose a foreign central bank drew down its deposit with the Reserve, using the funds to obtain gold from the Treasury. Again we have bypassed the member banks, and so should not indicate any change in member-bank reserves. The "—" in gold stock indicates a "—" in member-bank reserves, while the "—" in foreign deposits with the Reserve indicates a "+" for member-bank reserves. Again our two hypothetical uses of the member banks have given us the correct (net) answer: no change in member-bank reserves.

These examples can be multiplied, of course, but the point would be the same. In our analysis of the weekly statement, we assume that each entry works through the member bank. If in fact this is not so, then we must have had at least two entries, each of which so reacts as to cancel out the erroneous impact of the other. To cite the illustration in the preceding paragraph again: when the foreign deposit was drawn down, the funds did not go to a member bank, as the earlier explanation implied. But since it did not, there must be some other entry that has a similar error in the opposite direction. That, of course, was the gold-stock item. The decline in the gold stock in our explanation is assumed to be caused by money being drawn out of a member bank and then brought to the Treasury. This did not happen. But by assuming it, we did get the entry that cancels the foreign deposit impact, and so our final figure, which is the sum of two wrong assumptions, gives us the correct effect on member-bank reserves.

Analysis of the Statement

If we look at all the items as a composite, we get some idea of what was happening to bank reserves as a result of Federal Reserve action, and what happened as a result of the public's activities. By examining each item's change, we can get some idea of where the banking system is heading.

However, not all items are equally important, nor are the same ones significant each week. As a rough guide, we could limit ourselves to those items that showed a large change, since presumably these would be the ones that would have the most effect on the total reserve picture. If, for example, we disregarded items that changed by less than $50 million in the week ending January 29, 1964, we would narrow our discussion to Reserve purchases of securities, float, currency in circulation, and Treasury deposits.

First, let us look at the totals for all the items. The first sector, we remarked, changes member-bank reserves in the same direction as their own change. This group, which registered a combined decline of $849 million, reduced member-bank reserves by that amount. The second group, whose signs are opposite to the impact on reserves, declined $538 million; as a result, this group *increased* member-bank reserves by that amount. Together they net out to a decline in member-bank reserves of $311 million; this differs from the reported decline in reserves by $2 million because of rounding. In addition, as a minor offset, vault cash rose $2 million, so that the net drop in reserves was $307 million. Of this amount, $284 million was a drop in required reserves and $23 million in excess reserves. Net free reserves—excess reserves, less discounts and advances—dropped $36 million, as excess reserves dropped $23 million and borrowed reserves rose $13 million.

As we can see, this particular week produced a tightening in the banks' position. Total reserves dropped. Required reserves dropped. While the statement does not tell us why the latter was less, in all probability this reflected a decline in deposits. It might, on the other hand, also indicate a shift from high reserve demand deposits to low reserve time deposits, or from high reserve demand deposits with banks in the reserve cities to lower reserve demand deposits with country banks. This could be checked from other Federal Reserve statements. In this particular week, it was the over-all drop in deposits that was the main reason for the drop in required reserves.

Why did this drop in reserves occur? While several explanations are possible, experience with this type of analysis, plus knowledge of the background of economic events, help piece together the story. We recall that currency flows back to the banks after the Christmas holiday; this would explain the drop in that item, and, incidentally, would probably raise deposits, thus adding to required reserves. We also note that the Treasury deposits dropped; this, presumably, reflects the excess spending of our government. In March and April we should see the reverse, as tax revenues start coming in. Together, these two alone would have added half a billion dollars to bank reserves, and presumably an equal amount to deposits, and a fraction of that amount to required reserves. Hence, the other forces making for a decrease must have been very strong to reverse such large amounts.

One large offsetting factor was float. As already discussed, there is usually a post-Christmas drop-off in spending, and thus a drop-off in checks in process of collection. This item alone drained the banks of more reserves than they had gained from the two items already discussed. But, in addition, the Reserve was selling securities—$205 million. In other words, the Reserve wanted to apply more pressure to the banks than was being exerted by float. Indeed, if we combine the operations in securities with the acceptances account, we see a net drain because of Reserve sales amounting to $254 million, or almost the entire final drop in member-bank reserves. Evidently, the Reserve wanted to keep the banks under a tight rein; had it stayed neutral, there would still have been a drop in reserves, but by no means in so great an amount as finally resulted.

We cannot say for certain just why the Reserve pursued this policy. If we believe that there is a normal post-Christmas business lull, during which many pre-Christmas borrowings are repaid, then we would expect a post-Christmas decline in demand deposits and the consequent freeing of reserves. These could be invested in short-term securities, thus depressing yields there. But this ran counter to Reserve policy, where, to protect our payments position, the objective was to keep short-term yields high. Hence, to forestall this flow of funds, the Reserve sold bills and acceptances, thereby absorbing the released reserves. Alternatively, the Reserve may have taken payment at maturity, rather than make an outright sale. Either way this would drain funds from the banks. Actually, it absorbed a bit more, thus forcing the banks to dig into their excess reserves as well; this may be because the Reserve erred in its estimate, or because of deliberate policy.

Is this absorption theory correct? Is the Reserve now trying to put a damper on member-bank activities by holding down their reserves? This one statement cannot give us the answer. But if we follow this for a period of several weeks, we can get a truer picture. If the first thesis is correct, then, when the seasonal pickup in loans comes, we would see the Federal Reserve feeding reserves into the system. This could be done either through outright purchases in the open market or by not offsetting other items that are net contributors to increasing member-bank reserves. On the other hand, if there is a tight-money policy in the making, then we would see this continued pressure on excess reserves, a continued rise in member-bank borrowings, and an upward shift in the interest-rate structure. In this way, we can also get some signals for action in the money market. If this is a tight-money story, then the gradual rise in yields will start depressing bond prices; hence, bank portfolio managers should steer clear of committing themselves to the purchase of additional long-term bonds, and perhaps even sell some they now have. On the other hand, if the absorption theory is correct, then there would be no need for apprehension regarding the bond market, and so securities operations can go on as planned

We might check our analysis in a very broad way by reviewing the third column, which summarizes the changes over the past twelve months. This is not as clear-cut, however, for there may have been a change in policy during the period which obscured the totals. But, still, it may be worthwhile to apply our analysis to the year just past. And here, three figures stand out: the loss of $416 million in reserves because of the gold outflow, the loss of $2,284 million in reserves as currency in circulation went up, and the offsetting increase in reserves as a result of Reserve purchases of some $2¾ billion in securities. In other words, the Reserve over the past twelve months has just about offset the pressures, so that there has been a small gain in reserves. Actually, the banks did utilize these reserves. They added so much to deposits as to draw down the excess reserves. It seems, therefore, that the Reserve did not want to stop bank activity, but it did want to keep it within bounds. The expansion that did ensue called for $712 million more in reserves, and the Reserve responded by allowing the reserve account to rise, but only by $545 million. Hence, it did exert some restraint. We can see this in the drop in excess reserves, as well as in the rise of $78 million in member-bank borrowings, but not so much as to cause a contraction. We can also see that there must have been an over-all expansion in business, because float did rise over the year by $149 million. This, too, accounts in part for the rise of currency in circulation, for as already remarked, this usually tends to vary with spending. As an interesting sidelight, most of the rise in deposits over the year was in the time segment; 1963 was a noteworthy year in the competition among banks, which raised interest rates to attract longer-term money, including the issue of certificates of indebtedness already discussed. Demand deposits were virtually unchanged, but velocity rose. Were businesses and individuals carrying lower checking-account balances, and putting excess funds into savings accounts, to be used as a reserve when needed? Or, was there a genuine increase in the desire to save? Current data cannot answer this. But if we watch the relevant figures for several weeks—even for as short a time as two months—a meaningful story does emerge.

Federal Funds

In order to understand the role of the discount mechanism, we must make another aside to explain the Federal Funds market. Since member-bank reserves must be either in vault cash or in balances with the Federal Reserve, any deficiency in required reserves must be made up through an increase in these two. One way is to borrow from the Reserve, but this is not the preferred way if an alternative is available. Hence, there has emerged another sector of the money market— dealings in Federal Reserve balances.

Suppose Bank *A* has $10 million in excess reserves, and has no foreseeable call on this amount for the coming banking day. Perhaps tomorrow it may use the money as a large loan to a corporate borrower, or there may be an attractive new issue on which subscription books open tomorrow; but today these funds are excess. As such, they earn nothing. But there may be Bank *B*, which starts the day with a deficiency in its reserves. Or it may have enough reserves, but a large loan application is coming through today, and the extra reserves for this need are lacking. It wants, let us assume, $5 million more in reserves. It could borrow from the Reserve, but it would rather not. Besides, by tomorrow the need will have passed, for $5 million of Treasury bills mature then, and so the reserves will rise. Actually, it needs this money for only one day. So it would be quite willing to borrow the amount from Bank *A*. And Bank *A* will be happy to lend the money, for it now gets some income—the interest on the one-day loan—and it will get back the loaned reserves by tomorrow, when it will have a need for them. So here we have a transaction. Bank *A* transfers $5 million from its balance at the Reserve to Bank *B's* balance, and on the next banking day Bank *B* returns the funds with interest. In this way, Bank *A's* excess reserves are put to work helping Bank *B*. Note that unlike borrowing from the Reserve, there is no net addition to bank reserves; rather, the existing volume of excess reserves is used more efficiently (by the borrowing bank). In brief, the market consists of banks with excess reserves willing to lend them for the day, and banks with insufficient reserves who wish to borrow.

The need to borrow does not necessarily arise because actual reserves are below the required amount. To meet this requirement, banks are allowed to average their figures over the week (for reserve city banks) or over two weeks (for other member banks). If Bank *B* expected to have excess reserves of $5 million the next day, it would not have had to borrow. But evidently it did not, and so it entered the Federal Funds market.

In addition to the banks with excess reserves, any institution with Federal Reserve money can enter as lender, and any in need of such money could borrow in this market. For example, foreign banks with United States agencies have large holdings of United States Treasury bills. At maturity these are paid off by the government with checks drawn on the Federal Reserve. Hence, these funds could be available for loan. Government-securities dealers are often on both sides of the market, receiving such funds when they are sellers, and requiring them when buyers. Corporations with large holdings of Treasury bills are another market element. Together, these often exceed $1 billion during any one day.

However, having such funds does not automatically mean that one can participate in this market. The usual individual transaction is $1 million, so that the smaller country banks are virtually excluded from this market. When excess reserves tend to be concentrated among these smaller banks, there is less of a supply in the Federal Funds market than when the larger city banks have these balances.

The rate for Federal Funds is fixed by the supply of, and demand for, such balances. When there is a relatively large excess-reserve position, the loanable supply jumps and the rate tends to decline. When reserves are running low and borrowers are very much in evidence, the rate climbs. However, it will not climb above the discount rate under normal conditions, for then it would be cheaper to borrow from the Federal Reserve. While the banks do not like to turn to this alternative, their reluctance can be overcome when the Federal Funds rate is higher. By watching the posted rate each day, the observer can get some idea of money-market conditions, a high rate equal to the discount rate (the possible effective maximum for Federal Funds) indicating tight reserve positions, and a lower-than-discount rate, indicating an easing of conditions. The lower the rate, the easier the situation.

Certain qualifications must be kept in mind. If tight money does push the rate to the discount rate, then Federal Funds can go no higher. Any further tightening of reserve positions would not be reflected in this area; instead, we would see a rise in member-bank borrowings. In other words, the Federal Funds rate is a better indicator when it is below the discount rate, or when it creeps up to meet it.

If Treasury-bill yields are above the Federal Funds and discount rates, then we also have some changes on the supply side. Banks with excess reserves may prefer to buy such bills because the return is higher than from lending in the Federal Funds market. The supply in this market thus drops off, pushing up the rate to the discount rate. Hence, what looks like tight money may really mean only the superior attractiveness of bill rates.

Recently, large New York banks have tended to adopt a policy of running with insufficient reserves and using the Federal Funds market to make up the deficiency through borrowing. In part, this reflects their willingness to extend a virtually unlimited amount of finance to the dealers in United States government bonds, the dealer loans occasionally resulting in a reserve deficiency for the bank, and so compelling it to turn to the Federal Funds market as borrower. We thus get an artificial demand for funds, a reflection of this new attitude rather than a genuine temporary shortage of funds. In effect, if enough large banks pursue this policy regularly, their demand for Federal Funds would be so great as to keep the rate at the discount point, regardless of underlying monetary conditions.

As a last caution, there is always the transient disturbing element. For example, in our discussion of float we pointed out that a slowdown of check collections could result in a temporary excess-reserve position for the paying banks. They know that this excess will last for only a day or so, and that their excess reserves are really a temporary condition. So they turn to the Federal Funds market as a means of earning money for this short time. Hence, a temporary large jump in supply occurs, and the rate plummets. Yet, this would not be an indicator of easy money. Once the checks cleared, the supply would dry up, and the rate would go right back to its previous level. By correlating the movements in the Federal Funds rate with the weekly float data, this could be spotted, and provision for this type of temporary fluctuation would be allowed.

Guides to the Money Market's Condition

This chapter has attempted to furnish the analyst with a means of learning what the state of the money market is (particularly the banking component) and what it means. But there is an additional point to be noted: the guides discussed in this chapter are available quickly. By Friday we know the condition of member-bank reserves as of two days before. Each morning we know what was happening to Federal Funds the day before. In contrast, most other statistical information is available a month, a quarter, or even a year after the event. Here we have an almost up-to-the-minute reflection of events. Properly interpreted, we can know not only what the current state of the market is, but also where it is tending. If, for example, the weekly statement indicates a decline in free reserves, we know there is some pressure being exerted on the banks. Perhaps this is affirmed by several days of the Federal Funds rate staying at the discount point. If this observation is repeated for several weeks, we begin to conclude that there is a policy of tight money, so we can expect a gradual liquidation of securities by the banks. This means falling bond prices. If we are correct, we know now what the probable trend in the bond market will be—downward—and therefore what action we should take with our portfolio. The reverse would hold if we saw rising excess reserves and a Federal Funds rate continually below the discount rate. Easy money may be on the way, bond prices will rise, and so we have a "buy" signal.

Obviously, the answers cannot be obtained quite as easily as we have described. We have pointed out that there are many possible transient and false influences that can also influence the various figures. It is only after following these statements for a long period that experience teaches us how to separate the true from the false. If we do learn, we have added a valuable tool to our understanding of current tendencies.

The aid to the portfolio manager has already been described. But how about the average individual who is not running a bank? He can benefit, although the aid is somewhat less. For example, quite often there is a lagging relationship between bond yields and stock prices. If there is a period of easy money, there will be a gradual decline in bond yields. Some investors will shift to stocks, to take advantage of the now enhanced relative yield of dividends. And so stocks may go up in price. Moreover, along with easy money there will usually go a rise in loans, a rise in spending, a rise in business activity, a rise in profits, and a rise in stock prices. Both forces work in the same direction. If the statements in this chapter show such a possibility, some time passes before its effects show up in the bond market. Still more time passes before the stock market reacts. And thus the astute individual has time to act—to get in before the market has changed significantly, and thus make a tidy profit. Similarly, if his weekly reading of the figures indicates that a tight-money policy is coming into force, he knows that bond yields will start to rise. Some investors attracted by this now higher income will move out of stocks into bonds. Furthermore, there may be some cutback in bank lending, and so a slowdown in spending, sales, and profits. Again both influences work in the same direction— lower stock prices. And again these influences will take time to make themselves felt. So, once more the astute investor can move quickly, sell his stocks before the decline, and so avoid losses. Of course, all this success is predicated on one assumption—a correct reading of the figures!

Summary

This chapter concerned itself with the most important source of currently and rapidly available information reflecting monetary conditions, the Federal Reserve's weekly statement. The impact on member-bank reserves was discussed for the more important items, as well as an approach to an analysis of these shifts as guides to future monetary trends. The importance of net free or borrowed reserves was stressed. The logic of the statement's accounting was also summarized. As a further aid to the student, the fundamentals of the Federal Funds market were explained. While this is even more rapid in its informational availability—daily, rather than weekly—it has many pitfalls and is subject to several unimportant transient influences.

No one statement gives much of a story, and all must be followed and analyzed closely for a period of several weeks if a trend is to be spotted. Furthermore, there are many technicalities that can mislead the unwary reader. Skill and experience are necessary to arrive at anything remotely resembling a correct interpretation. If such a goal is attained, there are rich rewards. Both bankers and outsiders can gain insights into planning their own financial programs through a better acquaintance with this new and powerful tool, for it can often furnish the necessary clues for a correct projection of bond prices and even stock-market moves.

Chapter 18

THE IMPLEMENTATION

OF MONETARY POLICY

In this chapter we shall give illustrative examples of Federal Reserve policies in different phases of the business cycle. Obviously, such an exposition does not pretend to be complete. Each situation has its own special characteristics. We will attempt to provide some insight into the Federal Reserve System's thinking, and how it coordinates the various monetary powers and influences in order to mitigate any unwanted repercussions in the economy.

A Policy of Monetary Restraint

We shall assume that the economy has been enjoying a vigorous upswing, and that both investment and consumption have been expanding rapidly. In addition, bank loans are also rising, and so is the creation of demand deposits. If this series of forces is permitted to continue, the rise in aggregate demand could be so great as to outrace the rising output of consumers' and capital goods. If such were to occur, then the excess demand would touch off a sharp rise in prices and thus profit margins. Rising profits would feed still more income to producers, thus inducing them to step up their demand for loans and spending on capital goods. Workers would press even more strongly for higher wages, thus pushing up production costs as well as their own incomes; the latter would probably supply the extra purchasing power to support price increases to offset the cost pressures, and so the cycle would become even more intensified.

Realizing this, the Reserve decides to take measures before this inflationary push takes hold. It has not yet started, but it is quite obvious that much more of this aggressive expansion could unleash forces that would be increasingly difficult to control. So it now decides to apply the brakes, gently but firmly enough to make its influence felt. Now it initiates a policy of selling off some of its Treasury bills in the open market, and thus begins to put a damper on bank reserves and lending.

In our discussion of open-market sales, we noted that some of these securities would be bought by those banks that still had ample reserves, and that others would be purchased by non-banking investors who, in paying, would draw down deposits and reserves. In either case, we do get some reduction in a few banks' liquidity, and so they now must react to this changed situation. Several paths are open, depending on the market outlook.

We have already covered one: the banks could replace the lost reserves with new reserves borrowed from the Federal Reserve. Then, since they would be anxious to repay this advance, they would take steps to reduce loans—perhaps not make as many new ones as the ones maturing—and so gradually reduce their deposit liabilities. This would permit some freeing of reserves which could then be used to liquidate the advance from the Reserve.

In addition, the banks could sell off securities that are producing less income than could be obtained through continued lending. In other words, the banks are reducing their assets by cutting down the portfolio sector. Buyers would probably be non-banking investors (pension funds and insurance companies) who would pay by drawing on their deposits. The sales by the banks would reduce their deposit liabilities and thus free reserves either to offset the drains already mentioned, or to allow more loans to be made than would otherwise be possible.

However, if too many banks follow this avenue, there are dangers ahead. We saw in our discussion of bond prices and yields that sales would depress prices, and so there would now arise the possibility of a capital loss. If such securities liquidation is great enough, then prices would fall so much that the potential capital loss could well be more than it was worth to continue to accommodate other borrowers. At that point, banks would reduce, or perhaps end, such securities sales, and thus end the decline in deposits arising from this operation.

A still alternative route might be to reduce lending somewhat. This could be done in several ways. Borrowers who were trying to increase their loans in order to increase their scope of operations might be accommodated, but not to the extent that they would wish. Perhaps a $50,000 request is being made; previously the borrower had been getting $35,000. If the reserve decline had not occurred, the bank might have granted the full amount. Now it may allow only $40,000, or perhaps no more than the previous $35,000. Or the $50,000 loan would be made, but the borrower must now maintain a higher balance on average; the effective amount loaned is reduced in this disguise. In any event, net borrowing is somewhat less than had been desired. Still other borrowers, those new to the banks, might even be denied loans. Since they are not regular customers, the bank feels less obligation to finance their needs. In effect, these become an unsatisfied fringe; if funds are ample, they get the loan, but if reserves are tight, they are refused.

It should be emphasized here that the Reserve has not been trying to cut back spending, but merely to put a check on its expansion—to keep the rise in spending in line with the rise in output coming from the various investments. In a sense, the Reserve is desirous of reducing the marginal addition to spending power—that extra bit that would produce the excess demand that could then spill over to initiate the inflationary spiral. We have seen that this has been accomplished. Some lenders got a little less; others have been denied completely. If this unsatisfied sector is cut down by just the right amount, then expansion continues, but it does so at a somewhat more moderate rate, and so we keep our expansionary path in equilibrium.

The reader will recall that securities sales have been depressing bond prices, thus raising their effective yields. Since these now promise a higher income than before, investors might now be induced to switch to these assets, and even some banks with excess reserves might prefer them to a new loan. To offset the pull of these now increased bond yields, borrowers may also be charged more. If this added interest cost is a significant consideration, it is possible that some borrowers will drop out of the market, and again we get a reduction in new loans. However, as we have already discussed, it is doubtful if many borrowers would be affected enough to change their plans. Since interest paid is deductible in estimating taxable income, the tax offset could easily reduce the net cost by half. If demand for the borrower's products is sufficiently strong, the higher cost of borrowed funds could easily be offset by inching up selling prices, thus leaving profit margins unaffected and thereby sustaining operating earnings.

However, there is one group of borrowers who might well be induced to cut back their activity and thus reinforce the aims of the Federal Reserve. These are the underwriters of new securities. A typical underwriting would require the borrowing of perhaps 95 per cent of the issue's amount; the subsequent sale of the securities then provides the funds to repay the loan, as well as covering the costs of flotation and profit to the intermediaries. The quicker the issue is sold, the shorter the life of the loan and the lower the carrying cost.

Suppose this tendency for banks to sell off securities prevails, thus forcing down bond prices. These new issues are encountering competition from the older issues now rising in yield. The underwriter is then faced with unpleasant alternatives. He could spend more money to attract buyers, thus raising his costs. Or he could sell over a longer period, hoping that time will uncover enough new buyers to replace those lost to older issues. Or he could shave his price. Any one of these decisions cuts into his profits, either by raising his selling or interest costs, or reducing his receipts. As a consequence, he will be less willing to float new issues; perhaps now he will handle only those that are certain to buck the trend. In short, he decides to reduce the volume of his operations. If the banks also raise their interest charges, they cut further into his profit margin, and again reinforce his decision to reduce operations.

If new issues now decline in volume, then corporate borrowing is less than it would have been otherwise. Less corporate borrowing means less corporate spending. And now we see again the desired check on demand. Since part of the potential threat of excess spending came from new investment, this decline will further contribute to the Reserve's efforts to ward off inflation.

It is possible, however, for some of these trends to be thwarted by the activities of the non-bank intermediaries, including the noncommercial bank. We have seen that a rising yield pattern has been in process. If these other lenders can now get a higher return on their assets, they can offer a higher interest rate to savers. Hence, funds could be attracted from the commercial bank. This could enable these other institutions to lend whatever was being denied by the commercial banks. As we have seen, much of this shift could be through commercial-bank time deposits moving back to demand, and thus putting pressure on their reserves. At this point the Reserve is faced with a real dilemma. If it maintains its hold on reserves, it tightens the pressures on the commercial banks even more, driving up yields still further in the process. But if it allows the reserves to rise to reflect the change in commercial-bank deposit characteristics, then it does not offset the stepped-up lending of the other financial intermediaries, and it may be that their stepped-up lending—in particular their impact on a rising velocity—could defeat the success of the Reserve's restrictive policy. Examining this another way, should we impose even further restrictions on commercial-bank lending because some of the previous restraints are being defeated by these other lenders? Clearly, our answer must be influenced by many considerations other than the cyclical-control worry. For what we are doing is placing a halter on one type of bank expansion and allowing its competitors to expand freely. It is no coincidence that the post–World War II boom decades have seen so much greater an expansion rate for these other institutions —and also so much of an increase in the velocity of demand deposits.

The Upper Turning Point

While the Federal Reserve may be successful in dampening the boom, it has yet to succeed sufficiently to keep the upward phase of the cycle going without interruption. At some point the outlook begins to darken. Business will stop rising, and change over to a declining rate of activity. There may be numerous causes for this reversal. Perhaps the Reserve put on the brakes too tightly. Or perhaps supply in some major sectors has outrun demand, and so their profits prospects have dimmed. Or a large firm may have overextended itself and been forced into bankruptcy, disrupting business and consumer confidence.

Quite often the change, especially in the securities markets, can come about so abruptly as to result in a drop of panic proportions. Suddenly realizing that the boom has ended, investors start selling their stocks and bonds, hoping to escape the expected debacle. These sales start prices down, and so still more are induced to sell. If carried far enough, we get wholesale selling—a wholesale attempt at liquidity— which, as we have already seen, is disastrous.

In times past, especially before the establishment of the Federal Reserve, this panic would soon spread to the banking system. Lenders would besiege the banks for financial aid, while creditors would be pressing debtors for repayment. Many people, to meet their debts, might then withdraw funds from the banks. The banks, faced with this widespread scramble for liquidity, would find that it was impossible to obtain enough resources to meet these various drains. Often this problem would have been aggravated by excessive lending in the boom for the purchase of securities; with prices dropping, the collateral for these loans would be shrinking in value. Banks, in their haste to protect their assets from inadequate coverage, would call the loans and so force the

borrowers to sell the underlying securities. This, of course, only made
the panic worse. Before long, the banks were faced with the inevitable
end of a cash drain that could not be met. They had to close their
doors. And now the public was virtually without a source of money
with which to carry on its daily business.

To meet such a crisis today, the Reserve normally would step in as
the lender of last resort. For example, member banks could meet the
drain by stepping up borrowing from their Federal Reserve Bank.
These additional reserves would enable them to accommodate the
more needy borrowers. Moreover, if the customers' drain of cash became serious, these reserves could then be drawn on for currency.
Only in 1933, when there was a virtually complete loss of confidence
in all the banks, did this intervention fail to stem the panic. (Some
critics attribute this failure to inadequate Federal Reserve assistance.)
On March 4, for the first time since its inauguration, the Reserve saw
the money system grind to a halt. To meet a crisis of this nature in the
future, reforms were instituted. One, the Federal Deposit Insurance
Corporation (FDIC), guaranteed most deposits, the hope being that
this guarantee would end runs on the bank. In addition, banks were
given greater leeway in their ability to borrow from the Reserve, thus
making the protection of their reserve position that much easier and
more certain. Now the Reserve will accept almost any kind of collateral as backing for its advances to member banks under pressure.
The latter now have the assurance that there is really a lender of last
resort.

The panic could be heightened if the non-banking lenders start to
curtail their operations. We have seen how the large corporation is
beginning to be a prominent source of funds in the short-term market.
Suppose, as the downturn strikes, that these investors refuse to renew
their advances. In most cases the borrowers would not have the funds
to pay them off in full. True, they would probably make every effort
to reduce spending in order to generate as much liquid funds as possible. Workers could be dismissed and raw-material purchases reduced
to a minimum, this reducing the outflow of funds for their normal
operations. This would lead to a still more intensified deflation as the
income declines ripple out. But no matter how severely such a policy
was followed, it is doubtful if it could produce enough free money to
pay off all the maturing paper. As a consequence, debtors would have
to run to some other source to bail them out—or face insolvency. The
obvious source is the commercial bank—the businessman's lender of
last resort. Hence, it would be essential for the Federal Reserve to
recognize the nature of this call on the banks' resources—that it was
not just an inflationary demand for money to be added to the spending

stream—and so the authorities should help by providing sufficient reserves. Indeed, it cannot be expected that the member banks would borrow reserves to meet this new need, for these loans would not be paid back so quickly. Additional reserves would have to be retained by the banks for quite some time. Therefore, the Reserve should help out through open-market operations. In this way, member banks could gain reserves without being under any pressure to repay them as soon as feasible.

The Recession

Once the period of tightness passes and the panic feelings subside, we see a reversal of the previous strained monetary conditions. With the decline in business activity, firms have a smaller need for funds; often they can now finance their current operations out of internally generated resources. With the falling off in spending on labor and raw materials, which is often at a more rapid pace than the decline in sales—drawing down inventories—there may even be a surplus of liquid funds. The demand for borrowed money drops off markedly, and often past loans are pared down. So far as this sector of the banking community's activities is concerned, there is a decline in the demands on the banking system combined with a dropping off in these loans and the accompanying fall in demand deposits. Required reserves are released, and excess reserves generated. In addition to this decline in the money supply (demand deposits), there is often also a corresponding drop in velocity as spending habits are curtailed and caution becomes the watchword.

It is here that the presence of a large government debt and an active government spending policy becomes an aid. In all probability the federal government will now begin to run a deficit. Declining incomes will cut into its tax revenues, and mounting unemployment and relief needs will be stepping up expenditures. Hence, the government will be entering the market as a borrower. One possible source of funds would be the commercial banks, since they now have ample reserves and so can acquire these new issues. In doing this, commercial banks reverse the downtrend in demand deposits, adding to the government's balances as they subscribe to these new bonds. The government then has the means to step up its own spending. Properly coordinated, this would not drain the banks of reserves. As the funds are transferred to the Treasury account with the Federal Reserve, they are promptly redeposited with the banks as a result of the spending of the various government activities. For the economy as a whole, the deflationary impact arising from the decline in demand deposits as business loans are repaid is being offset by the rise in demand deposits and spending as these government issues to the banks are financed and utilized.

Even if there is not this new issue to the commercial banks, the mere presence of a large debt will often suffice. The commercial banks, as we have remarked, are now faced with increasing excess reserves which earn nothing. In order to offset the loss of income resulting from the decline in loans, the banks will now start buying government bonds. Payment to the sellers will then expand the volume of deposits, and so again we have sustained the money supply. Of course, if these sellers then hold their newly acquired liquid funds idle—if the velocity is zero—then there will be no boost to spending. But if the sellers relend them, acquiring other bonds, then there may be a stimulus to the economy. These funds could be deposited with various savings outlets—either the commercial banks, savings banks, or savings-and-loan institutions. These, in turn, could then step up their mortgage lending, and so stimulate spending for new construction. Or perhaps some of the funds would be diverted to acquiring new issues by corporations. These latter may now decide to expand despite the recession, feeling that now that money is available, it would be wise to borrow rather than wait for the ensuing recovery and a possible tight-money era again. And so their spending could revive and help the depressed sectors.

Influencing the forces further in the directions already described would be a slowly declining interest-rate structure. As the banks start buying securities, they force up the price and thus reduce the effective yield. As yields on these securities decline, yields on others will drop, too; this is part of the stimulus to new corporate borrowing referred to in the previous paragraph. The banks will also react. As bond prices climb, their yields become less attractive. Hence, these various lending institutions will now be willing to offer borrowers loans at lower rates, too. If, for example, government bonds had been yielding 4 per cent and loans 6 per cent before the recession was under way, the movement of bank funds into governments may have brought government yields down to 2½ per cent. If the banks could get even 5 per cent from loans, it would be an attractive income alternative. Perhaps at 5 per cent borrowing will be stimulated, thus providing this alternative outlet. It is possible that the 1-per-cent decline may lower the monthly costs of a new home enough to stimulate such building. And so the entire economy is aided; the banks have more income, and the economy receives the stimulus of more spending. Banks would be only too willing to enter into such loan commitments, for they know that if there is a rise in demand, they can provide the necessary funds. Not only are reserves in excess, but they can always sell off the bonds if there is any shortage of reserves. With a rising bond market there is no worry about being locked in with capital losses, such as might occur in the boom phase. If reserves were used up, these bonds could always be sold without fear of loss. Knowing this, banks can tie themselves up without hesitation.

The Federal Reserve will be reinforcing this trend toward monetary ease, its intervention depending on the severity of the recession. More reserves could be pumped into the banks through open-market purchases. Not only will this add to the commercial banks' liquidity, but the buying will also push up security prices and so reduce yields. The discount rate would also be lowered, thus assuring banks that even if the revival should set in more strongly than had been anticipated, the Reserve would always be there to help. The low rate would mean that it would be cheaper to borrow to meet such a temporary strain, so there would be no pressure to sell off a more lucrative asset.

However, suppose the recession becomes severe. Then it is quite possible many of the stimuli able to reverse the downtrend would be absent. For example, as bonds are being sold to various banks, both Federal Reserve and commercial, there is a rise in deposits. If the sellers then leave their funds idle, there is no further spending boost. Suppose the corporate borrower also drops out, worrying more about the dismal outlook than the attractiveness of easy money. In this case, its borrowing does *not* pick up. Declining incomes may worry consumers so much that they do not feel confident enough to undertake the obligation of a new mortgage, so construction does not get the expected boost. This poses a problem.

Let us remember that easy money may not result in a pickup in lending and spending. But if such were the case, then further open-market purchases by the Reserve would be of little use. The only effect would be a still further rise in excess reserves and a still further decline in yields, but not a sufficient incentive to stimulate borrowing. Once again we must turn to the government as a possible source of additional spending, running a deficit and borrowing to finance expenditures. Since this gets us into the logic of fiscal policy, we shall postpone further discussion of it.

There is another task that the Federal Reserve might have. Suppose the downturn gets so severe that there is a general shattering of confidence in the financial system. People start to withdraw money from the banks, and these crucial sectors are now under pressure. If the Reserve now steps in with a vigorous open-market purchase policy, thereby supplying reserves to offset the drain by the public, the pressure is removed. The banks are further assured that if they must sell

off their assets, there will be no serious capital loss to worry about, and
they are more ready to resort to this means to meet any drain of funds.
Thus the financial stress could be met. In contrast, if the Reserve did
not help, then bank liquidation of other assets would drive prices down
even more. Losses would mount. Finally we would get back to the
danger already discussed—that of a wholesale closing of the banks, the
1933 tragedy. If necessary, the Reserve should be watchful that the
recession does not snowball into a financial panic; it is the added stress
of this latter force that probably accounted for the severity of the
1930's collapse.

The Recovery

In the recovery, especially in its early part, the Federal Reserve
has a relatively simple job. The commercial banks have ample reserves
as well as government short-term securities, which can be sold if additional reserves are necessary. Interest rates are comparatively low, and
with business revival there will come a gradual increase in the demand
for loanable funds. Since both the availability and cost are satisfactory,
there need be no hindrance to this effort to finance expanding operations. In addition, firms could perhaps work with somewhat smaller
balances, raising the velocity, thus further aiding the upturn. In short,
we are now in the phase where additional spending stimulates further
output. This, in turn, generates still more income and spending.

In such a situation, the Reserve has to keep its eyes open for any
excesses that might develop. This could be especially worrisome after
the recovery has been in progress for some time, when its continuance
might threaten to spill over into the boom that started the chapter. But
until then, its main concern is to see that the banks have ample resources to finance business requirements, realizing that the expansion in
demand deposits, and thus purchasing power, will be instrumental primarily in adding to output, so that both demand and supply will be
increasing. This will keep a lid on any price increases. Inflation at this
juncture is still a distant worry.

With the revival in economic activity will go a rise in the underwriting of new securities. Corporations are now in a borrowing frame
of mind. They see sales volume rising and profit possibilities increasing.
With the low interest rates current during this phase, the underwriters
have low carrying costs during the distributing period. Furthermore,
there is little concern with declining bond prices, for there is enough
money around to keep the demand for bonds sufficient, and so yields
will not move against them. The rising money supply will make it
easier to dispose of the new issues and at the same time reassure the

financial middlemen that any hitches during the time between their acquiring the securities from the issuer and their final sale to the investor need not develop. Hence, they are more eager to undertake such financing, and so the volume of corporate investing grows as they secure new funds from the public.

In the later months of the recovery, some pressure on the money supply may begin, but this would probably be relatively mild. Even if it does cause some decline in bond prices, this is likely to be limited, so any prospect of a capital loss would be in quite small dimensions. The banks would still not be deterred from selling if they desired to switch their assets from securities to loans. The underwriters would not find this mild pressure a significant factor in making it more difficult to dispose of their new issues. While there may be occasional losses on such underwritings, this is more likely to arise from the poor selection of borrowers, or an improper rate assigned to the new issue, rather than the general state of the money market.

It might also be added that the general improvement in the business outlook will also be reducing the risk assessment. Even if the high-quality issues start to show a yield increase, yields on the lesser-quality corporates may still move only slightly as the risk spread narrows. The relative ease with which such issues can be sold will be an encouragement for still more securities to be marketed.

The Effectiveness of Federal Reserve Policy

Probably the most serious problem facing implementation of policy is the need for the Federal Reserve to recognize economic conditions quickly enough. Normally, much of its judgment must be based on statistical material. But often these data are not collected until well after the event. It is quite possible, for example, for a cycle to be a boom phase in January, peak out in February or March, and be turning down by April or May. Yet, in March, the Federal Reserve may just be getting the January data indicating a boom. It then decides to apply the pressures on the banks, and by April this begins to take effect. But by April not only has the boom peaked out, but the country is actually in a recession. But the activities of the Reserve are still reflecting the boom fears that should really have been displayed in January! The result, of course, is to accentuate the early months of the downturn, and analogous reasoning would apply to other phases of the business cycle.

The Federal Reserve System cannot easily solve this problem. For one thing, the inflow of information is generally beyond its control. True, there may have been scanty signs in January—perhaps November figures—that the boom is threatening to get out of hand. But are these few indications sufficient for policy decisions? If the System does act, and these few signs turn out to be erroneous, then it implements the wrong policy. If it waits for more definite signs, it puts through the right policy but at the wrong time.

Furthermore, the System must try to distinguish its own influences from those of the economy whose movements it is trying to follow. For example, if we are in a recession, there is a general decline in the demand for loanable funds. The Board may try to initiate a recovery through open-market purchases. Because of the volume of its operations relative to the size of the market's activities, its buying will tend to raise prices and reduce yields. It now must figure out how much of the yield decline reflects its own operations, how much the response of the market is to its policy, how much the result of bank activity conditions the result of the infusion of new reserves, and how much should be attributed to the general decline in the demand for money. Because of its role as the center of monetary action, this difficulty—separating out its own movements, as reflected in the data, from the changes arising from shifts in the economy—becomes too difficult. Sometimes the Board is just not certain what actions are altering the statistics on which it must act. In effect, often the market is not responding freely to the competitive forces of supply and demand; it is being dominated by the moves of this one overwhelmingly important participant.

This problem is compounded by a time lag after policy has been initiated. First there is the decision to do something, such as open-market sales. Then slowly there is the reaction on member-bank reserves. The banks then react through borrowing from the Reserve, thus giving them time to adjust. Then slowly they adjust to the changed reserve picture. Gradually borrowers begin to feel the pinch. But they may be able to delay adjusting, for example, by running down their own bank balances, or perhaps getting more temporary help through trade credit. And then finally, perhaps, business firms that are affected change their own rate of production and spending. By that time the boom may well have passed. What is really desired now is an increased desire to spend, not a further contraction in demand.

But the System is also in danger if it tries to act in advance to adjust for these time lags. In our illustration at the beginning of this section, the time to stop the January boom may well have been in the preceding July. But in July business was far from the danger point. To start applying the brakes then might well discourage business quickly, and complete recovery may not be achieved. Yet, if the January spending is excessive, a six-month time lag would call for cuts as far back as the preceding summer, when the economic outlook is good but not threatening, implying excellent foresight.

Indeed, some spending might have to be cut back even sooner. Suppose it takes eighteen months to build a factory. Once funds are committed, the project must go through. Its spending effects thus spread out over a year and a half, and the associated multiplier impact for even a longer time. If enough such construction is underway, it could build up into a boom. But to cut down on such outlays a year and a half in advance would put the Reserve in the awkward position of checking a boom while the recession was still very much in evidence! Economic forecasting tools are still far too imperfect to justify such a long-range approach to policy actions.

Because of this problem, the Reserve has often been criticised for a policy that works in fits and starts. To return to our previous example, the Reserve would have taken restrictive action too late—in March, when the boom had already made its upward force felt throughout the system. Then the economy starts down and is jerked even harder as the March measures take effect. Realizing that the turning point had passed, the Federal Reserve would then reverse its tightening effects, again changing its course. Each time it overshot the necessary policy action—and this would be almost inevitable—it would then have to turn around almost completely. And so the stabilizing intent of its activities could well end up by making the economy more unstable. Picture a man on a horse that is running too fast; by the time the rider realizes this and pulls on the reins, the horse is already starting to slow down anyway. Its pace, however, is reduced even more sharply because of the rider's action. Then, realizing that the horse had slowed down, the rider spurs him on, but into a gallop, giving an uneven pace. And so the system would proceed.

On the other hand, no one really expects the economy to operate with perfect stability. It may well be that these System-induced shifts are minor in effect, so that whatever unevenness they do impart is no different from the normal month-to-month leaps and lags in our economy. Perhaps all it means is that we get a bit of a rise in activity where we might have had a dip. We could get a bit of a dip as the restraints are applied, where otherwise there would be a slight rise. Or if either the rise or the dip is reinforced by the Reserve's policies, how much more does it make this shift? If 1 per cent more, this is hardly a serious difference, if in the long run we have averted a 15-per-cent decline in business activity, or a 20-per-cent rise in the average prices paid by consumers. In assessing the success of the Federal Reserve, we must measure its results against what the performance of the economy would have been without any intervention. To compare it with some ideal yardstick is quite unfair to the officers of the Federal Reserve System who are charged with the difficult task of making decisions. They know all too well that if all goes smoothly, no one will send them a thankyou note, but if something goes wrong—even if the Reserve is not directly at fault—the blame would fall on the System for not having forestalled the unwanted development. Fortunately, central bankers have a long tradition behind them. They are accustomed to most of the arrows of outrageous fortune. Such an institution has never had to court political popularity, and so can well afford to take the buffeting, even if it is undeserved.

Actually, a more serious accusation is that the Reserve is deflationary-minded, that it sees inflation too quickly, but is too slow to see recession. If this is so, then its policies would tend to reduce activity on balance, as the length of the booms are reduced and the recessions are more frequent and longer. But whether this is so is difficult to judge, for bankers have always been overly cautious, and the Federal Reserve is, after all, a banker's bank, worried about the soundness of the country's money.

However, we should also point out that since the Federal Reserve must operate through the money market—or at least, as presently constituted, it must limit its activities to this sector—it is bound to introduce instability into this particular segment. Each time it buys or sells in the open market, it alters the demand or supply picture, and thus changes the rate picture from what it would have been if it had not intervened. And if it is true that the Reserve has had excessive fears of inflation, such reactions would lead to too frequent open-market sales, thereby raising the yield structure above what it would have been if the Reserve had taken a more balanced view. Moreover, the frequency of this intervention, or the greater instability it imparts to the government-securities market, also has its effect on bank policies. The latter now have a greater fear of being locked in as the rising yield causes declines in the capital value of their bond portfolios. Expressed differently, the accusation that the Reserve has been a too-frequent seller means that there have been too many periods when bond prices declined, exposing the banks to too many capital-loss experiences. It may well be, if this allegation is correct, that the banks are now somewhat more reluctant to purchase long-term securities, and that to induce them and offset this fear, the borrowers have to pay higher interest. The cost of raising new money rises for two reasons: the Reserve has been pushing up yields, and the banks are asking a greater risk premium. Whether this is true, and if so, whether it has reduced long-term borrowing and investment, is difficult to say. However, this much should be noted: over the past half-dozen years the economy has been continuously at less than a full-employment level, and much of this lag has been attributed to insufficient capital-goods purchases, the other side of the long-term investment picture.

Summary

In this chapter we gave illustrations of the way in which the Federal Reserve uses its various tools to influence the course of business activity through the monetary sector. When a boom threatens, it tries to tighten up on lending by applying pressure on reserves, either through open-market sales or a higher discount rate (or both). At the upper turning point, and in the subsequent downturn, it seeks to avert any liquidity scramble. Once the crisis is passed, it is most concerned with easing up on reserves, through lower discount rates and open-market purchases. However, in an extreme depression this may not stimulate borrowing and spending, and so fiscal policy must be called on as a supplement. Finally, once recovery is under way, its main task is to assure a sufficiency of funds and be on guard against excesses that could generate a new inflationary threat.

In instituting policy changes, the Reserve is forced to work with inadequate and outdated information. As a consequence, this may delay proper action and might even result in such moves being no longer appropriate for the current economic situation. Whether this leads to undue fits and starts in our economy is still a matter for debate. Moreover, there may be a Reserve bias against inflation that makes its policy excessively cautious, leading to a generally higher yield structure, with consequent adverse effects for borrowing and investment. Here, too, it is still difficult to come to a conclusive opinion, and we must not forget that Board members are human and should be judged by human standards, not by some abstract ideal yardstick.

Chapter 19

SPECIAL POLICY PROBLEMS

The experience of the Federal Reserve has demonstrated that model reactions to different cyclical phases (described in the preceding chapter) do not always work out in so stereotyped a form. In this chapter we shall discuss some of the major problems that provoke conflicts in the decision regarding the most desirable policy procedure to adopt. Sometimes these difficulties arise from economic cross-currents; at other times political overtones are quite evident.

One problem currently with us is so important that we have devoted Chapter 23 to it. This is the modern version of the stability and growth objectives discussed earlier. Essentially it concerns the difficulties that arise from a full-employment economy that does not want this high demand level to spill over into inflation, a dilemma that could plague the industrialized world for the remainder of this century.

War Finance

In any large-scale war, such as this nation underwent from 1941 to 1945, there is a tremendous strain on the economy. Output must expand, and its composition is drastically altered. Overnight the amount spent by the government must jump sharply and rapidly. The bulk of its spending is for items that do not go onto the consumer market. The production of war materials means that we are pouring out incomes, and thus raising potential demand, but without an accompanying rise in supply. With as much as one-half of total spending devoted to such output, the inflationary potential can be readily imagined. Its control becomes a major administrative problem.

To finance this spending the government can resort to four approaches. It can print the money; it can borrow from the banks; it can borrow from the public; or it can increase taxes. Assuming that we wish to avoid inflation, our hope is to offset the potential rise in demand by devices that reduce this potential and remove the threat. One obvious approach is to take the money out of the hands of those who are getting this excess purchasing power. Our last two approaches aim in this direction. If the public buys government bonds, it turns the purchasing power over to the government. Extra spending on munitions is now balanced by the reduction in spending by the public, since the latter no longer has the money in its own hands. The same result would occur if the government collected additional taxes, again taking the purchasing power out of the public's hands.

In practice, such an immaculate balancing cannot occur. People will not be induced to subscribe all their additional income for the purchase of bonds; they may buy more than they would in peacetime, but many other wants clamor for funds. As a result, much of the money will be retained for spending. To raise taxes sufficiently is also difficult in a democracy. The rates would be so high that many observers believe political reactions would be adverse. Indeed, too high an income tax could actually reduce output. If, for example, we find it necessary to raise rates to 80 per cent on the additional income in order to siphon off this purchasing power, many people might not work overtime. Out of each additional dollar they would be allowed to keep only 20 cents, and they may not feel that night work is worth it. Hence, the supply of labor does not expand, and production is kept down. This incentive worry is such a complicating factor that it often overrules the canons of sound public finance. Its discussion is beyond the scope of this book, but its importance cannot be overemphasized. Even in peacetime it is an ever-present concern, and much of the current debate over the size of the government budget is in part a dispute over the effect of the resulting tax structure on output and risk-taking.

All the necessary finance cannot be raised from the public, so how does the government meet its bills? We can cross out currency issues, for few modern governments with any degree of financial sophistication resort to this. The reason can be stated simply. If the government should spend, it would be putting new currency into the recipients' hands. They, in turn, would spend, and so incomes would rise. But most people would turn the currency into the banks, into their checking accounts. Most of the currency would become additions to bank reserves, and a multiple expansion can now begin. Extra spending by the government would now be reinforced through the tremendous push being generated by these bank-induced additions, making the inflation that much worse.

But, as we shall see, our remaining alternative differs little from this possible resort to the printing press. Should the government borrow from the banks, the latter must pay by creating deposits in favor of the government, which then spends these new funds for its various wartime requirements. Demand deposits now end up in the income recipients' hands, and are just as spendable as the currency alternative would be, the difference being that we do not get the flow of cash into the banks to serve as a base for multiple bank-asset expansion.

Actually, the effect on reserves of government borrowing from the banks is somewhat in reverse. As such borrowing goes on, the banks' demand deposits are rising. Hence, required reserves are rising. This may actually reduce the banks' other loans if the borrowing finally exhausts excess reserves. But in practice, the government would not want to stop all private borrowing. Many firms need funds to operate their war-production plants. To help finance these needed supplies, they would borrow from the banks. Some slack must be permitted in the banking system to service these equally necessary financing needs. As a result, the central bank would probably help out through open-market purchases. This would supply some reserves and permit a greater bank-asset expansion. Note here that part of the government deficit is now being financed as a result of the central bank's acquiring government securities. Consequently, some of the interest on this added debt does not accrue to the private sector. The banks' income is helped as a result of the deficit only to the extent that their holdings of government securities increase.

The effect of government borrowing, as we have seen, is to increase the volume of deposits. The more that can be raised through issues to the public and added taxes, the less must be borrowed from the banks. Consequently, the resulting increase in deposits is smaller. These additions, it must be remembered, are net additions to the public's money supply and also to its purchasing power. Much of the inflationary potential is supplemented here, perhaps, by the tendency of velocity to rise as wartime business activity steps up the call on business and personal spending.

Government deficits financed through the banking system put more money in the hands of the public. This new money is given in payment in return for the munitions produced for the government. But this new money can exert a demand pressure only if spent. Through appeals to patriotism the people can be induced to hold these funds idle, and with this, we reduce our inflationary threat. Reinforcing this could mean rationing; if the government can restrict spending, then people must hold on to their funds. They could break the ration laws by buying in the illegal (black) market, and this explains why such ugly phenomena thrive in a wartime atmosphere. In effect, spending that cannot be done legally is done illegally; the goods bought are diverted from law-abiding citizens to others. We thus anticipate even greater shortages and still more pressures to get the goods illegally.

But suppose most people are law-abiding. What happens then is that the money they are receiving from the government is not spent. It is held in idle deposits. Some of it might be used to buy government bonds, but we are assuming here that we have tapped this possibility to the maximum. As the war goes on, the public is holding more and more idle liquid funds. In effect, we have suppressed the inflation. The potential demand is there, but it is being withheld temporarily for both patriotic and rationing reasons. But once this compulsion ends, we could see this enormous spending power re-emerge on the market. Here we have given a capsule version of the financing during World War II and its inflationary aftermath. The various belligerents borrowed from the banks, thereby increasing the outstanding demand deposits. Then the funds were spent to pay for war materials, transferring these newly created deposits to the various factors in the industrial sectors. Some of these additions held idle, accumulated purchasing power without exerting a corresponding demand. Wartime inflation was consequently minimized. But once the war ended, all these accumulations of money could now be spent, and if they were unchecked, we would see a sudden enormous rise in demand, much more than could be supplied by wartorn economies. We know now that the actual evidence of inflation came after the war, although its origins developed during the preceding years.

Even in a country as productive as the United States, such a situation was inflationary. If we have a tremendous accumulation of purchasing power, releasing it steps up demand. As industry responds by increasing output, it also responds by paying more in wages and the purchases of raw materials to obtain these added supplies. As we add to supply to meet this enormous demand, we are also adding to demand. Thus, the new aggregate demand still outruns the added supplies, and we get the scramble for goods that makes it so easy to pass on price increases. Over a period of time, however, much of this added income will also produce added savings. As we increase output, we add more to supply than to demand, the difference representing this nonspending element. Supply, then, rises faster than this additional demand, and finally it may overcome the initial excess of demand arising from the war. Once this is achieved—if it is—we have brought the economy back into equilibrium. But this will not occur until we have gone through this intermediate inflationary experience.

Bond Pegging

As a means of assisting the efforts to sell bonds to the public during the war, the government announced a policy of stable yields for its bonds for the duration. This was in contrast to the World War I experience when subsequent issues had been floated at higher yields, thereby depressing the price of the earlier issues. To avoid this, and thereby remove the incentive to postpone purchases, the pegged-yield structure was virtually a guarantee that future issues would be at no higher yields than the current ones. This policy applied to the entire structure of government securities.

During the war period there was a minor, unwanted result of such a policy. The short-term issues were pegged at somewhat lower yields than the long-term. As a result, as the latter neared maturity, they rose to a small premium to reflect this lower-yield category. Hence, some additional gain could be obtained through playing the pattern of pegged rates.

The real seriousness of this policy became apparent after the war. With the conversion to peacetime output, an enormous demand for funds arose on the part of the private sector. Banks expanded loans and deposits, and as this expansion mounted, excess reserves disappeared. To obtain additional reserves, the banks then sold off government securities. If there were other buyers, such as pension funds and insurance companies, then the result was a destruction of deposits and freeing of required reserves. With this the loan expansion could continue. But these groups were also experiencing large demands for funds from the private borrower. Hence, the price of these government issues threatened to decline because of a lack of enough buyers. If this happened, the yields on governments would have gone up above the pegged level. This the Treasury was reluctant to see. But now that the war finance needs had ended, the Treasury still feared that since it had to refinance maturing issues, the rising market yields would compel it to refund these older, lower-yield issues with a higher-interest-bearing security. The cost of servicing the federal debt would thus be increased. And so the Federal Reserve was induced to continue its policy of pegging the securities.

But the peg meant that bonds could not be allowed to fall below the stated price (the yield could not go above the stated level). Then, as the banks continued to sell government issues, the Federal Reserve had to step in and buy to maintain its policy. This, in effect, amounted to an open-market purchase. Reserves were added to the banking system, and still more expansion went on. Whenever the banks needed more reserves, they could always get them through this easily assured liquidation, and without worry of capital loss.

This pegging policy could become most serious if the expansion threatened to spill over into an inflationary boom. At such a time, the Reserve would want to restrict bank lending. But how? Open-market sales would drive bond prices down. Note that the Reserve was not allowed to do this. Worse than that, the banks could always obtain reserves by selling off government securities in their own portfolio, which the Reserve would have to buy in order to preserve the price structure. Since the government had issued during the war many securities that the banks had acquired, enough were in their portfolio to take care of any foreseeable need for reserves through such sales.

Raising the discount rate was also a futile gesture. What need did the banks have to borrow when they could always obtain reserves through the outright sale? Since the assets they were acquiring were all yielding more than the bonds sold, there was every incentive to continue this route, and no incentive to resort to the discount window.

While pegging was limited to the government sector the entire money market was influenced. Since the other qualities of bonds—municipal, corporate, and others—were separated from the government yield by only the risk premium, the stability of the government component made for stability in the other yields. If the risk premium widened too much—if, say, corporate-bond yields rose excessively—then banks would simply sell governments and buy corporates, thereby pulling down the latter's yield. As a result, corporate yields were kept artificially low, and businesses had an added incentive to borrow still more to take advantage of such low costs. This added supply of bonds would always be absorbed, for it needed only a slight increase in yield to switch more investors out of governments and into corporates. With this, the business expansion was fed even more fuel. Conditions such as these made many regard the pegging policy as an engine of inflation.

At first, in mid-1947, the pegging of short-term yields was modified. Finally, by March 1951, the entire pegging policy was terminated. Now there was once again the factor of uncertainty about bond price movements, and slowly the bond sales forced down prices and forced up yields. To get reserves, the banks had to suffer a loss. Some returned to the practice of discounting, and gradually this instrument revived in importance. But while its relative importance is still not as great as in the 1920's, it is once again an effective Federal Reserve weapon.

The "Bills Only" Policy

In the period following the end of the pegging policy, the Federal Reserve intervened quite often through its open-market operations. For the most part, however, it limited its dealings to the short-term sector, the Treasury bills, and thus we have the "bills only" appellation. There were several reasons for this decision, and some of them became more and more questionable with the passage of years.

The Federal Reserve felt that one justification for this narrowness of operations was the marketability factor. The daily volume of trading in Treasury bills was enormous, so much so that a Reserve decision to buy or sell would not be a very disruptive influence, causing wide gyrations in prices. In contrast, if it were to attempt a similar volume of operations in the long-term sector, its daily transactions could exceed the normal volume of all other trades. With such proportions it feared that the price of long-term government bonds would move quite irregularly, causing misinterpretations among market observers and participants.

This latter point should be explored further, for it lies at the core of the argument. Suppose a danger of a boom appears, and suppose the Reserve decides to start a policy of open-market sales, ultimately amounting to $100 million. In order to make this policy effective, it does not want to stretch such sales over too long a period, and so decides to sell about $10 million daily. On certain days, however, it may refrain if other forces justify a delay. For example, an unexpectedly large drain of currency into circulation because of a holiday weekend might put a pinch on member-bank reserves, and if the Reserve added to this the pressures arising from sales of its securities, the combined drain might be more than desired; in such a situation the Reserve would hold off on its sales, and thus the cumulative selling policy would take a somewhat longer time. It was desired, let us suppose, to complete the sales in a three-week period; an average of $10 million per active day thus allows several days' leeway. Since the Reserve would need only ten actual selling days over the three weeks, this would still permit it to attain its goal within the allotted time.

Why did the Reserve select the $100-million figure? This probably reflects the feeling that by withdrawing that amount in reserves, it would probably drain off the equivalent in excess reserves and so reduce the potential expansion (through the multiplying effects) by, say, $600 million in loans and deposits. This would assume some spill-over into lower reserve time deposits. Then this, plus the more re-strained feeling that such a policy would engender, should be just enough to prevent the boom from getting out of hand. Note that here the Reserve is aiming at a reaction affecting the total amount of addi-tional bank assets and deposits; at this point it is not interested in affecting interest rates directly. Its aim is to control the volume of expected spending—the reduction in M' times the estimated velocity.

Having decided on a given volume of reserves to be taken from the banking system, one question remains: which securities should be sold? If the answer is Treasury bills, then this small addition to the daily supply will probably depress prices a bit, but, as we have seen, such small changes in bill yields are not highly significant. The mere passage of time will undoubtedly offset any possible losses arising from this decline, so that the banks' capital is in no way endangered. It is true that short-term yields will now inch up. It is also true that this may induce the marginal investor to switch from the longer issues to the shorter issues, and so long-term yields are also forced up—although probably this will be minute. But the objective has been accomplished —a reduction in member-bank reserves, and also their ability to fur-ther expand.

But suppose, instead, that the Reserve sold long-term issues. Here the addition of the supply is significant, for the volume of trading in this end of the market is quite light. The immediate impact of so great a relative increase in supply would cause a drastic drop in bond prices. It would also cause a sharp rise in long-term yields. Overnight, long-term investors, and in particular the long-term area of the commercial banks' portfolio, suddenly experience a drastic decline in values, a sud-den possibility of capital loss if they do decide to sell. New bond issuers suddenly face steeper interest rates, and must reassess whether they wish to incur such high borrowing costs. Many others may see these as bargain prices in the long-term area and switch out of compet-ing securities, thus causing declines in these other areas. In fact, such a change in bond prices could trigger off a wholesale uncertainty about future trends. It could turn a boom into a downturn. This is a far more drastic result than the Reserve had in mind.

But what has developed is only the immediate reactions. If the market does not panic and realizes that all that the Reserve is trying to do is to put a damper on the boom, then it begins to realize that this rise in long-term yields was excessive, simply reflecting the temporary enlargement of supply. So, funds begin to flow back to this market. Prices recover. Yields come down. Borrowers who had been caught in the transition period are now stuck with high-cost debt, while competitors who may have waited only a week or so come in with lower-cost issues. Government-bond dealers who suddenly saw their inventories of bonds drop in value—maybe they sold to protect themselves against still further losses—now see prices jumping again, and so they must buy back at still higher prices. Inasmuch as they usually carry over-all inventories some twenty times their own capital, any sizeable loss can jeopardize their continued operations. So, having been stung severely in this area, they may decide to confine their operations to the short-term sector. End result: a still narrower long-term market. In brief, operations in the long end of the market could trigger too many unwanted reactions that can endanger the various participants in a way unwanted by the Reserve. We can thus draw the conclusion that if the only objective of the Reserve is to alter the volume of bank reserves, then it would be wisest to confine its operations to bills. Needless to say, if the Reserve wanted to add to member-bank reserves as an expansionary incentive, its operations in long-term bonds would cause similar upsetting effects, but in the reverse direction from those described.

But the critics of the "bills only" policy are not quite satisfied with this argument. True, we may want to influence only the volume of reserves. But suppose we want to stimulate long-term borrowing, or to cut it down? Perhaps there is too much going into the acquisition of capital goods. How would the Federal Reserve stop that?

The defenders of the "bills only" policy would say that if such were the case, the Reserve would, as before, operate in Treasury bills and so alter the member-bank reserves and simultaneously the open-market yields on such bills. For example, if a restrictive policy were desired, the Reserve would sell bills, thus reducing member-bank reserves and raising short-term rates. The member banks would reduce their lending and also their purchases of securities, including long-term securities. This would force up the long-term yield, in addition to the upward pressures arising from people switching from the long to the short end of the market to take advantage of the higher yields in the latter. Thus, a general rise in long yields must ensue, although with a time lag long enough for these various reactions to occur. This higher-yield structure, accompanied by the reduction in bank purchases, would make it more difficult for long-term borrowers to obtain funds from new issues, and so the end objective has been accomplished.

Not so, answer the critics. Indeed, this tie between the short and long reactions is often exaggerated, and perhaps not even present. First of all, operations in bills affect member banks through their reserves, but it also affects the volume of secondary reserve assets. If the Reserve sells bills, it draws down the member banks' reserves, but it also adds to the availability of high-quality short-term assets in the market. If the member banks had been buyers, what probably happened is that they simply gave up non-income-earning excess reserves for the income on the newly acquired Treasury bills. And since these are so liquid, the decline in member-bank liquidity is quite small. After all, these bills can always be sold if the need arises. So, having made this swap, there is no further pressure on the member banks to make any further adjustments, and so the long end of the market is unaffected. True, there may be a long-run decline in the banks' acquisition of other assets, but how long will it take for this reduction in purchases to show up? Meanwhile, the capital-goods boom goes on unchecked. Moreover, even if there is a more rapid response on the part of the banks, how do we know that it will be the purchases of long-term securities that will be cut back? Suppose the banks reduce their mortgage purchases, or other loans. Again, the impact on the long-term corporate borrower is virtually nil.

But even if the critics grant that all the changes expected by the Reserve do occur, they still would be unhappy. As we remarked, the sale of bills reduces reserves; this reduces member-bank lending; this reduces, among other things, member-bank purchases of long-term securities. As a consequence, the reaction on the long-term sector is diluted by its being also transmitted to other areas. Loans and other assets also feel the restrictive effects. Thus, in order to curtail long-term corporate borrowing in the securities market, we must also reduce borrowing by all other market sectors. Everyone suffers in order to achieve our end goal of hitting the corporation. Would it not be simpler to sell a smaller amount of long-term securities? This would drain off much less bank reserves, and not cause as much restrictiveness for other borrowers. But at the same time, the long-term governments would show a sharp rise in yields. This would push up the yield on corporates, as the market adjusts to this change. And now we make it much more costly for the long-term borrower, hitting directly at the incentive to borrow.

Indeed, if the Reserve does try to influence long-term yields through the short end of the market, there is no fixed relationship between the two and no guarantee that a change in the bill rate will produce the desired shift in long yields. For example, if the short-term yield is close to the discount rate, then a rise in the latter may induce many banks to sell off bills to obtain reserves, rather than to resort to discounting at the Reserve. But if the market yields are well above the discount rate, they may prefer the cheaper alternative of borrowing. Hence, a given change in the discount rate may or may not produce a change in member-bank transactions in Treasury bills, and it may or may not produce a change in yields. Furthermore, even if short-term yields do move, how many people will be induced to switch between the short- and long-term sectors? If we wish to push up long-term yields, and do so by initiating a rise in the short end of the market, we then hope that some investors will sell long-term issues and buy short terms to take advantage of this higher return. But suppose very few do move—then what? There have been many periods when the short-term rate was even higher than the long-term; if that has been true, what assurance is there that a rise in the former will then produce the desired rise in the latter?

However, the Reserve resents this charge. It states that its aim is to govern the availability of bank funds, not the rate structure. It is interested in total spending, which is a reflection of the volume of demand deposits and changes in velocity. If, in operating on this availability, it incidentally alters rates, fine. But it is the availability, not the rate structure, that is its concern.

The problem came to a head with the emerging balance-of-payments deficit after 1958. Foreigners were beginning to accumulate large dollar holdings in excess of their needs to finance international trade. To induce them to keep their dollars and not exchange them for gold—thereby draining both member banks and the Reserve of their reserves—it was necessary to offer them high yields on short-term assets, thus making it worth their while to reinvest the dollars in the United States. To bring about this yield, it was necessary for the Reserve to sell short-term securities. But as it did, it also drained the member banks of reserves, thus cutting down on their ability to lend and acquire other assets. In addition, this tended to push up long-term yields, thus making it more difficult for the corporations to borrow and spend. As a result, the American economy experienced less than full employment and overcapacity, yet found that it could not stimulate the business community through the traditional resort to cheap money. For if the Reserve did pump reserves into the banks through open-market purchases, this would bring down bill yields, and foreigners would sell out, convert their dollars to gold, and so set in motion the drain of reserves. So long as the Federal Reserve pursued its "bills only" policy, this conflict would remain.

Gradually the realization grew that the major help, without endangering our gold stock, would be through assistance to the long-term borrower. It was felt that this sector was the main source of capital-goods purchases, and that much of our underemployment was in those industries dependent on such products. To reduce unemployment, we must step up output in the capital-goods industries. To raise this output, we must put more funds in the hands of the long-term borrower. To do this, we should bring down the long-term yields, and thus make it more attractive for this sector to borrow. At the same time, we should keep up the short-term rate—of minimal interest to the capital-goods buyer—and thus avoid the outflow of foreign funds. "Operation Twist" was the new policy now—designed to lower long-term and raise short-term yields. And this meant sales in the short-term sector accompanied by purchases in the long-term sector.

Some observers wondered whether the Reserve could pull off such a coup. After all, as we have already explained, a rise in one sector of the money market tends to communicate itself to the other, and a decline in one carries over to the other. If we raise short-term yields, the pressures would work to raise long-term yields—and this we did not want. If we focus on a reduction of the long-term yield, this would pull down the short-term yield—and this we did not want. How could the Reserve alter the short-long relationship?

Fortunately, at the same time as the Reserve was changing its policy, the market forces in these two areas were also shifting. There was the already discussed shift from demand to time deposits within the commercial banking structure. This, in turn, induced the banks to reduce their short-term assets, since the short-term liabilities were declining, and to raise their longer-term holdings as time obligations rose. In other words, the market as a whole was reducing its demand for short-term assets and raising its demand for long-term—pushing up former yields and reducing yields on the latter. Thus, the Reserve objective was being reinforced by this structural change within the deposit makeup, and so Operation Twist was seconded by the activities of the commercial banks.

The Cold War

The Cold War has generally been characterized by large United States defense expenditures, and this relatively rigid item has reduced the ability of the government to adjust disbursements to fluctuations in receipts. In particular, in recession periods there have been deficit years, in part a reflection of this rigidity, in part a reflection of fiscal policy versus cyclical considerations. Hence, there are frequent occasions when the government is forced to borrow, and this borrowing must be successful if defense and other needs are to be met. There cannot be a failure in financing, for such an interruption would be intolerable.

Normally there is no real worry. The government prices its securities to reflect the going rate in the market; the issue's life is subject to various considerations (to be discussed later). By appropriate pricing, it can depend on finding enough subscribers, and so the entire issue is sold. This means that the shortage of funds has now been bridged.

But let us assume that the deficit occurs during a boom—that, for some reason, spending on defense is raising budgetary outlays faster than revenues are coming in. Once again the Treasury has to go to the money market for funds. But meanwhile the Federal Reserve has become worried about the possibility of inflation. It has been engaging in open-market operations, selling bills to draw off some of the excess reserves. The policy has been fairly successful, for money has begun to harden, and yields are creeping up. The banks are now no longer in a position to add to their own bill holdings, and the private lender is being attracted by the rising yields into the riskier categories. Hence, the market for any new government issue is quite limited. If it is short-term, the banks already have their fill, thanks to the Reserve's sales. If it is long-term, most buyers are either shying away from bonds, fearing the expected price fall as money continues to tighten, or else they are moving into the other end of the risk spectrum, perhaps even into equities. As a result, the government issue cannot be marketed very easily, unless the interest rate on it is to be put up to an unrealistic level. And so the funds are not forthcoming.

Obviously, the government cannot be allowed to face such a failure. And the Reserve realizes this. So it must ensure that the market has enough reserves, that money is sufficiently easy to enable enough buyers to come through. But to do so means that its own anti-boom policies must be modified. So, because of the urgencies of the government, the economy must sustain a bit more of an inflation. The pressures of the Cold War have reduced the freedom of the Federal Reserve to follow through on its policies, compelling it to tailor its actions with an eye to the fiscal situation.

The problem is further complicated by artificial impediments. Legislation has limited the Treasury to a maximum of $4\frac{1}{4}$ per cent interest on its long-term issues. What this means, in practice, is that any booming demand for funds that would drive yields above that point forecloses the government's access to the long end of the market, even if the market would subscribe to, say, a $4\frac{1}{2}$-per-cent issue. Thus, in such a situation the Treasury would have to borrow short, which in all probability would be from the commercial banks. And this, in turn, means that the Reserve would have to engage in open-market purchases to add enough to excess reserves to enable subscriptions and additional deposits to go through.

Irrational Expectations

In all our discussion of policy implementation, an overriding qualification must be interjected regarding the market's—the public's—reactions to Reserve actions. In this text we have determined rational lines to follow once we observe certain Reserve shifts, or even the absence of shifts. But not everyone is a money-and-banking analyst. Many who are may not follow our method of reasoning. They may react differently, perhaps for rational reasons, but will be more worrisome for irrational reasons.

For example, the Treasury-bill rate has been hovering around 3½ per cent, while the Federal Reserve discount rate has been at 3 per cent. This has not been causing too much member-bank borrowing, but it has interfered with the smooth functioning of the Federal Funds market. Too many banks have preferred to put excess reserves into Treasury bills at the 3½-per-cent yield rather than into Federal Funds lending at the effective ceiling of 3 per cent. So, to allow greater scope to the Federal Funds market—to enable it to compete with the bill rates—the discount rate is raised to 3½ per cent, thus raising the ceiling for Federal Funds.

But observers who absorbed only a smattering of banking theory jump to hasty conclusions. They remember vaguely that a rise in the discount rate means that the Reserve wants tighter money. This is a signal that bond prices will fall, and so these observers decide that they had better get out of these securities before capital losses appear. And so a wholesale selling wave appears. Yet, this entire reaction was falsely based. The Reserve had not intended to influence the money market; all it did was make a technical adjustment to facilitate the movement of reserves from banks with an excess to banks with a temporary deficit. But in doing so, it triggered off a most unwanted reaction.

Borrowers could react equally irrationally. Seeing the rising discount rate, they interpret this as the ending of the boom. That means sales and profits are dropping off—or will in the not-too-distant future. So they refrain from borrowing for capital expansion, fearing that all they will have is overcapacity. So spending plans are postponed as profit expectations are marked down, all because of a misunderstood signal. This misunderstanding, if it results in enough cutbacks, can produce the very recession that was erroneously expected!

Or the borrowers may react in a different way. They could feel that the rise in the discount rate is the first of a series of tight-money moves, and so a period of gradually rising yields will occur. Hence, they had better borrow quickly before such funds become even more expensive. But if this reasoning leads to a quickened rate of borrowing, the same logic could lead to a slowdown in the lending rate. For if the investors also expect rising rates, they will be forecasting declining bond prices, and so they will be reluctant to commit their funds. We thus dry up the supply of loanable funds as we step up the demand. This may cause an immediate sharp jump in yields, thus creating the fear that was expected in error. Alternatively, to protect their capital, the lenders might decide to shift to the short-term market, thus altering the long-short relationship. Furthermore, by purchasing Treasury bills, they may draw off secondary reserves from the banks, thus upsetting their liquidity distribution. In short, the misunderstanding of a signal can set off a whole series of unwanted transactions that could transform both the money market and the level of economic activity in undesirable ways. Yet the Reserve had to make this discount-rate adjustment. If not, it would have hampered the Federal Funds sector. It is thus faced with the dilemma of acting correctly and perhaps being misunderstood, or acting incorrectly to avoid such misunderstandings. Either way, it may see the undesirable consequences that flow from the desired policy action.

To some extent, it could try to ward off the wrong behavior by making clearer explanations for any actions that it does take. In this way it can hope to educate the market and the public to a better comprehension of its role. But this sounds much easier to suggest than to put into practice. There will always be many concerned who will doubt the sincerity of the Reserve's intentions. In our illustration, they may not even comprehend the technicalities of the Federal Funds market, and so dismiss the Reserve's explanation as a camouflage for its real intentions. And so, even with the explanation, there is the same wrong interpretation—perhaps even more so, for now these doubters are convinced that the Reserve wants to tighten money. If not, why would they have given such an incomprehensible reason? And so the Reserve fails again in its efforts to achieve sanity.

Slippages

Although the problem of slippages has been mentioned throughout, the reader is reminded that this, too, constitutes a problem for monetary policy. The Reserve, as has been remarked, can control only the volume of member-bank reserves. But the resulting impact on deposits, and thus the money supply, can be quite variable. For one thing, the member banks might not use all these reserves, and so may carry excess reserves, thus altering the deposit-reserve ratio. Additions to reserves thus may or may not be fully utilized; withdrawals of reserves may or may not cut back a given amount of lending.

Indeed, we are not even certain how precisely the Reserve can fix member-bank reserve totals. Most of its operations are through the purchase and sale of government securities. Sometimes the other party is a member bank, and the effect is to change only member-bank reserves. Sometimes the other part is the public, using member-bank checking-account balances. If so, then there are equal changes in member-bank reserves and demand deposits. Or perhaps the transaction affects time deposits; this would have a still different result in the utilization of reserves as well as on activity of the deposits.

It is also possible that the funds will go to, or come from, a non-member bank. Perhaps it will be a foreign bank that is the partner to the transaction. Or maybe even the public's holding of cash will be the variable. All of these can vary the impact of a given operation, and all of these can be different at different times.

Furthermore, even the utilization of a given volume of demand deposits can vary. This, of course, is our velocity problem. A given amount of purchasing power, in the form of demand deposits, can give rise to varying spending totals, depending on who holds it, the secondary impacts through the non-banking intermediaries, the expectations and outlook of the public, and all the other considerations that enter into liquidity.

But the unknowns are not only on the monetary side. We do not know whether a given change in spending will affect prices or the volume of output. How will corporate price policies be affected by shifts in spending? In the availability of loanable funds? Are they the same when we have an expansion as when we have a contraction? Are they the same at different levels of capacity? Do expectations change if Federal Reserve policy operates through use of the discount mechanism rather than open-market operations? Or through a change in the required-reserve ratios? Does each of these different instruments, even though the reserve impact is the same, give rise to different, or the same, reactions, even though the ultimate policy aims are the same in each case?

In the face of all these uncertainties, the Reserve can operate only in a trial-and-error manner, making each move in small dimensions, so that it can assess how much power each step has exerted in practice. If it falls short of its goal with the first step, then it can attempt a second step, reassessing the situation after that has been accomplished. And then perhaps a third, if necessary. Obviously, if the time calls for immediate and far-reaching measures, it cannot use this slower approach. But then it opens itself to the danger of overreaching its goal and precipitating too extreme a reaction. Such has happened in the past, as in 1937, when the Reserve was trying to slow down the boom; instead, it went too far and caused a sharp slump, despite the fact that we were still far from a fully employed economy.

Summary

The Federal Reserve has been faced with many problems, some of which forced it to go counter to what it considered sound finance. This was most obvious in connection with the problems of World

War II and its aftermath. It had to insure that the government's war efforts were not impeded by inadequate finance, yet it also had to see that this did not cause excessive inflation. But it could not soak up all the excess purchasing power in the hands of the public, while the banks' enormous accumulation of government bonds gave them access to reserves as needed. Not until 1951 was this dilemma resolved, and once again the traditional Reserve controls have come back into use.

At first the Reserve used this freedom cautiously, limiting itself to operations in Treasury bills, supplemented by the discount mechanism. But this ran afoul of our current problem—a balance-of-payments deficit with an underemployed economy. The conflicts in interest-rate policies that this engendered led finally to modifications of "bills only."

But the Reserve's problems are not limited to these specific issues. There is still an enormous amount of variability in all the monetary relationships, so that it is not certain to what extent some specific action will finally work its effects on the economy. There is thus ample opportunity for misjudgments, and for either too little, too hasty, or too much intervention. As a result, the economy itself operates less smoothly than the ideal, but in view of our current abilities, this is, perhaps, the best we can hope for, although we can constantly strive to improve understanding of the System.

SOME INSTITUTIONAL INFLUENCES

In studying the monetary influences on the American economy—indeed, for any developed and sophisticated society—it is necessary to remember that a host of forces come into play which may modify or even alter the generalizations developed from any analysis. The proliferation of details that arise in tracing through even one strand of monetary theory can often obscure the whole; any advanced researcher soon finds these so distracting that it is often impossible to disentangle the basic movements from surface manifestations. In this chapter we shall explore the character of a few of the institutional factors that one must watch in order to understand the reactions of the affected sectors, and to help separate the possible superficial contradictions that too much concentration on details can cause.

Government Debt Management

The United States government has outstanding at any one time upwards of $300 billion in debt. Most of this is held by different sectors of the public—banks, insurance companies, industrial corporations, individuals, and others—all for a variety of reasons. Every debt has a maturity day, and this compels the government to make plans either to repay this debt or to arrange for new financing so that new debt replaces the expiring debt. In the management of this operation the government is thus compelled to deal with the state of market opinion regarding interest rates and the demand for new issues, and to tailor its plans accordingly.

Some of the debt matures on a definite date, but the holder need not present his claim for payment. These are the numerous non-marketable issues which most individuals purchase. They can cash in their bonds at any time, before, at, or after the stated maturity, and the rate of redemption reflects changing consumer attitudes. If there is a sudden upsurge in the desire to buy "big ticket" items, such as automobiles and other durables, cash-ins may rise as people need the required cash for the down payment. At other times, shifts in public spending may bring down this figure. Hence, about all the government can do is to watch these trends and make certain that it has the necessary funds as the redemption rate changes. To some extent, it can make continued holding more attractive. If the savings accounts with the various banks start paying a higher interest rate, there is some inducement for the small saver to shift from these bonds to the alternatives, either by cashing in his bond at or after maturity, or through the reduction in new purchases. If the government were to raise the interest rate payable on these issues, it would thus combat the tendency to shift and so reduce the demands it is receiving for repayment.

But by far the more troublesome and continuing problem is with the marketable debt. When any of these issues mature, they must be repaid; there is no option on the part of the holder to continue holding it. (More strictly, if a non-marketable issue is held after maturity, the holder continues to earn interest; if a marketable issue is held after maturity, the holder stops receiving interest income.) Hence, for all practical purposes, the government has to assume that it must raise the money to repay this maturing obligation. And since revenues rarely exceed disbursements by a sufficient amount, we can also ignore the unlikely probability that the surplus receipts will be enough to pay off the debt. For this section we can assume that each maturing debt must be paid off through the issuing of a new piece of debt. (In the chapter on fiscal policy there will be a discussion of debt repayment, however.)

At any moment of time, the government has all sorts of such marketable debt outstanding. Some may be maturing that day. Others —mainly Treasury bills—will be maturing every week over the next three months. Normally, each week there is a Treasury-bill issue maturing three months later, so that there are thirteen outstanding. And recently, longer-life bills have been issued, making for more outstanding issues. Still other securities may mature later in the year, next year, or in the years ahead, stretching into the future for perhaps forty years.

Looking back, at any moment of time some of the securities outstanding may have been just issued. Other bills were issued during the preceding three months. Still others may have been issued over the year before, several years back, perhaps as far back as forty years. At the time they were issued, they were short-, intermediate-, or long-term in expected life. But as they gradually approach maturity, their remaining life is growing shorter and shorter. So a long-term bond gradually becomes akin to an intermediate issue, then a short-term issue, then it expires.

On the supply side of this picture we also have diversity. Some investors want to be highly liquid, to hold securities that are very safe and can be easily realized in the market without danger of capital loss. They are primarily the ones who own Treasury bills. Others want a somewhat higher return with a minimal risk to capital—perhaps some fluctuation possibility, but limited to 1 to 2 per cent. These are usually the commercial banks which thus compromise between the drive for high income and the drive for liquidity by buying intermediate-life issues (three to five years). Then there are the many others who have minimal need for liquidity and yet want safety against default; for them it is the long-term government bond that most suits their requirements. Note that this diversity on the part of the suppliers of funds must be matched by a similar diversity among the types of government securities available if we wish to tap the potential source of financing to the maximum. And with a $300 billion debt it is quite obvious that the government cannot afford to ignore any important holder of liquid funds!

But a complication produced by the passage of time filters through this simple exposition of the debt structure. We have already remarked that every debt starts to get closer to maturity as soon as it is issued. For many issues this is not serious for much of their life; a forty-year issue is long-term when first issued, and it is still long-term three months later, when its remaining life is 39¾ years. Even a year or two later it is long-term. But as more and more years pass, it finally becomes an intermediate issue with respect to its remaining life, and so becomes attractive to new groups of investors—for example, the commercial banks. To them a new issue with only a three-year life, and a forty-year bond issued thirty-seven years ago, are similar: both are three years from maturity. As this latter gets close enough to maturity, it becomes subject to this additional demand, and its price may rise in response to the added purchases: its yield now declines from its former level. Hence, the long-term holder might now sell out, taking this capital gain as additional income. Now he can move his funds into another long-term issue.

A similar upward price movement could occur as this issue comes within a few months of maturity, when it takes on the characteristics of a short-term bill. This would mean that those who want the highest degree of liquidity would now be buyers. Those who prefer a some-what lesser liquidity and a somewhat higher yield, such as our com-mercial banks, would now sell out, taking the capital gain. Then they would move back to the intermediate market. In other words, as this forty-year bond moves along its life cycle, the pattern of its ownership has been changing, reflecting the altered character of its liquidity, of its possibility of appreciable change in capital value due to market changes in yields. We can now see why this constant churning occurs in the bond market as these different investors make their adjustments.

But let us look at the maturity day. Formally, the government is faced with the paying off of this long-term bond. To do so, it must issue new debt to obtain the funds to pay off the present holders. The simplest thing to do is to offer the present holders a new issue; thus, by a simple swap of old for new, the problem would be solved. But there is a catch. The present holders, for the most part, are those who want exceptionally short-term securities. Hence, they will not swap their maturing bond for another long-term bond. They probably would not accept anything other than a new three-month Treasury bill. And so, if we wanted to resort to this swap approach, we end up by replacing a long-term debt with a short-term Treasury bill.

It should be remembered here that this life cycle typifies all gov-ernment debt. At maturity virtually all the debt will be in the hands of these short-term investors. If we always resorted to this swap proce-dure, we would end up by replacing all our debt with Treasury bills. Technically, this type of short-term obligation is called a floating debt, and we shall examine the implications later. Note that such a short-term issue brings up the repayment problem in only three months.

What is the alternative? If feasible, it is to issue new debt with about the same characteristics as the old debt. If each long-term bond at maturity is replaced with a new long-term bond, then once again we end our repayment worries for many years. But the current holders do not want a longer-term issue. Hence, the government must now tap an alternative source of funds—the investor who has money to invest and who is interested in a less liquid, higher-income issue. It must make the new issue sufficiently attractive so that it gets enough money to meet its maturing needs. In practice, such nice equalization is not usually possible, and, as we shall see, a group of new issues is often selected.

Note that if we strive for the replacement of a maturing issue by about the same type of new issue, we keep the maturity distribution of the government debt about the same. Every day outstanding issues are getting closer to maturity; hence, every day the average life of these issues is getting shorter, and so the average life of the debt is becoming more and more short-term. But if we replace the maturing one with a long-term, then we raise the average life again and offset the shortening effect of the passage of time. So, just as each day makes the average issue a bit shorter in life, so the correct new issue would reestablish the average; in this way there would always be enough long-term bonds available for the long-term investor. As his present holdings come closer to maturity, he steps out of the picture, as we have already seen. But if we are also injecting new long-term debt, then he can switch to these bonds and so stay in the government debt picture. On the other hand, if we issue a Treasury bill, we do not offset the diminishing supply of long-term bonds and so lose the participation of this long-term investor. Hence, there is the need to put out a long-term bond when another is maturing, even though the present holders of the latter are essentially short-term investors.

An aside should be made at this point for the seasonality of the debt picture. The government normally collects its corporate income taxes at stated times. Its own cash needs have a different pattern, so there are times when revenues exceed disbursements—on the tax dates —and the other periods when disbursements exceed tax receipts. It would thus have a tendency to be a borrower at the latter times and a repayer around tax time. But the corporations are often incurring tax liabilities throughout the year. As they make profits, they are subject to tax, although the formal payment is made only on certain specific days. Since they know the taxes will have to be paid, they feel they may as well set aside the money as the profits accrue. To tap this source, the government then issues tax-anticipation bills during those periods when its own cash outflows exceed inflows and when the corporate tax liabilities and cash set aside are present. The corporation puts this tax-anticipation cash into the tax-anticipation bill, thus giving the government the money when it is needed. On the tax date the corporation simply turns in the tax-anticipation bill in payment of taxes, thus avoiding the need to accumulate and hold cash between the time the tax liability is incurred and the date it is due. In addition, it obtains an interest income, thus lowering the effective rate of its tax.

And, of course, the debt obligation of the government vanishes with the tax payment; no repayment or refunding is necessary. By properly tailoring the date and life of these tax issues, the gaps between periods of excess disbursements and excess receipts can be narrowed, and the seasonal variations in the former can be better matched to meet the latter. In our illustration, the purchase of the tax-anticipation bill reduces the cash inflow to the government at tax times, when normally it is receiving more cash than it has need for currently, and raises it during the time when its cash receipts from other sources are below its needs, the deficiency now being met by this corporate investment.

Timing the Issue

Since the money market is rarely static, an issue will be better received at certain times than at others. If the new issue can be properly timed, it will sell better, and the government could dispose of its securities with a lower interest charge. Not all issues can be spaced for this objective, of course; the Treasury bill issued weekly is almost a fixed operation, and goes on regardless of the immediate situation. While there is some freedom to vary the amount of the issue, in practice the weekly new issue usually matches the maturing old one. Then if the government wants to vary its short-term debt, it tends to vary the other types of paper—perhaps adding to a six-month issue or cutting down the new one below the amount of the maturing one.

Theoretically, therefore, the government might issue long-term securities when the demand for privately issued, long-term bonds is slack, and refrain when business is so active that the demand for long-term funds is driving up the yield structure. In this way, the excess of available long-term funds in the recession can be tapped more easily. But this fiscal objective runs into a countercyclical problem. In a recession we want to encourage the revival of long-term investment, which means, in part, that we wish to keep the long-term rate low, thereby encouraging industry to borrow and expand capacity. But if the government steps in with a long-term bond issue, it sustains the rate structure, lessens the decline in yields, and also removes part of the available supply. The result is to reduce the assistance to private industry.

From the countercyclical aspect, the government would be better advised to remove long-term funds in the boom. By reducing the supply available to private borrowers, it would reduce private spending on capital equipment and thus help take some of the pressure off the economy. But to do so would mean that its own demand for such funds would be added to the intense competition already existing among the private borrowers, and so the long-term rate would be driven up that much more. Considering the magnitude of such a government loan, the probable reaction on long-term yields and bond prices could be quite marked, so much so as to precipitate a liquidity problem for the existing long-term investor. In brief, it would seem that there is no time when the government can borrow long!

Fortunately, some of the long-term funds are virtually confined to government bonds. These are investors primarily concerned with the absolute safety of their money over the long run, with little worry about short-term liquidation. They plan to buy and hold the issue until maturity, so that intermediate price fluctuations are of little or no concern for them. As funds of this nature accumulate, the government could seize the opportunity and issue its long-term securities. Of course, the size of the issue would have to be smaller than the optimum desired for stretching out the over-all life of the debt, but it is the least disturbing way of entering the long-term market. In addition, there may be temporary financial lulls during the recovery from a recession when business activity is improving, yet the demand for long-term money has not picked up sufficiently to absorb all the available supply. At such a time the government could step in with its issue with a minimum of disturbance to the yield structure and long-term capital outlays.

Sometimes such opportunities occur before there is a maturity scheduled. To take advantage of the moment, however, the Treasury may engage in an advance refunding. For example, suppose a long-term issue is due to expire in 1966. In January 1964 there is a plethora of long-term funds, so that many existing holders of this 1966 issue would be happy to buy new government long-term bonds. The Treasury would then, in January 1964, offer the existing holders the opportunity to turn in their as yet unexpired bonds for the new issue, perhaps giving them a small bonus as an additional inducement. In this way, the acceleration of the maturity can be used to time the actual refunding with the propitiousness of the market receptivity. Of course, not all such holders of the 1966 issue might want the new, long-term bonds; for them the Treasury would probably offer as an alternative inducement a shorter-life lower-yield issue, perhaps in the three-to-five-year range; the additional life here is not much more than the issue being called in, which may be satisfactory to the investor, and yet it does have a somewhat longer life (one to three years more) than the called issue.

Problem of the Floating Debt

If the Treasury takes the easy way out and replaces each maturity with a new short-term issue, it gradually increases the volume of such short-term issues, which means that the frequency of maturities is increasing. Furthermore, as the proportion of short-term issues rises, more and more of the debt would be held by the commercial banks. This means that in payment the banks would be increasing the money supply through the accompanying creation of demand deposits. Here we see one of the inflationary aspects of the concentration of such issues.

In addition, since toleration of failure cannot exist, the Reserve must see to it that the commercial banks have enough reserves so that any of the newly issued bills not being taken up by the non-bank investor will be sought after by the commercial banks. If we have a boom period, when tight money is called for, the Reserve faces this obvious conflict: how to restrict bank reserves to curb the boom while leaving them ample enough to insure that each new Treasury-bill issue is fully subscribed? Inevitably it will have to give preference to the latter objective. This means that there will be less of a tendency to reduce reserves and less of a success in its efforts to check the impending inflation.

The problem has been further complicated as an offshoot of the cumulative deficits in our balance of payments. As foreign banks and other monetary institutions have been obtaining large accumulations of dollars, they have either withdrawn these by conversion to gold, or else left them here as short-term investments, mainly in Treasury bills. The latter decision was prompted in part by the satisfactory income thus obtainable. To continue to keep such funds here, the rate must be high enough to make it unprofitable to accept dollars at maturity and then exchange this money for gold. To maintain a high rate means putting pressure on the banks' reserves, thereby tightening the money market. But the tightness of the reserve position may reduce the banks' desire to buy the short-term issues. The more attractive we make it for the foreign investor, the less likely we will be to get funds from this important domestic investor. To solve this conflict, we should reduce the volume of short-term debt so that we do not need too many subscriptions from the banks; but that means resort to longer-term issues. Or we could increase the volume of short-term issues, thus adding to supply and depressing prices—raising yields.

Too many short-term issues also force the Treasury into the market too frequently and with too large an issue. It thus upsets the supply-demand relationships at such times. To reduce the frequency of such disturbances, it should plan for larger and fewer issues, but the larger the issue, the greater the disturbance when so large an amount is borrowed. To minimize the extent of this disturbance calls for smaller issues, but then the number of such new loans would be increased, and the frequency of these upsetting visits would rise. And to resort to the alternative long-term market means transferring the disturbing impact to another area. Truly, debt management is an art!

Treasury Aims

Often in the past the United States Treasury—and, indeed, treasuries in many other countries—took an extremely parochial view of debt management, akin to what the ordinary individual would do with regard to his own borrowings. The major concern was to minimize the cost of the debt and virtually ignore the impact of such financing on the money market and, through it, on the economy.

In order to achieve this objective, the Treasury resorted to various alternatives. One, already touched on, was the excessive use of short-term issues, since these are usually lower-yielding than the longer-term bonds. The fact that this issue appealed more to banks, and so contributed to excessive liquidity, was of little concern. In so doing, incidentally, the Treasury often missed opportunities to place more long-term issues with buyers who would hold them permanently in their portfolios, such as pension funds and insurance companies.

The Treasury in the immediate post–World War II years also froze long-term yields—or at least imposed a maximum—because of its influence on the Federal Reserve open-market policy. This episode was discussed in the previous chapter. Here we need add only a few comments. The Treasury did succeed in keeping down the nominal cost of the debt. But the cost was inflation, a rise in expenditures by the federal government, and a real burden on that part of the populace that suffered a decline in its real income or in the real value of its assets. For them the slightly lower tax burden because of the lower interest cost on the national debt was far outweighed by these other losses. On the other hand, many observers felt that the Treasury gained in two ways from this inflationary policy. As already mentioned, it kept down the nominal cost of the debt. In addition, the inflationary rise in incomes may have pushed up tax receipts faster than it increased government costs, thus making the budgetary position that much better. And, by diminishing the real burden of the debt—inflation, by boosting incomes, lowered the ratio of this debt to total income—the real cost of its servicing was thus made lighter. This last point, of course, was at the expense of the bondholders, including the many savers whose funds had been put into such securities by savings banks and insurance and pension funds. Whether the Treasury was really so calculating is still questionable.

It has also been suggested that the Treasury could lower the cost of the debt by creating a captive market. For example, if all banks were compelled to put a prescribed proportion of their assets in government bonds, the Treasury would be assured of a certain demand, and would not have to make this portion of its issues too attractive as an income source. This approach has been tried in several European countries, and is discussed further in Chapter 25.

Mention should also be made of the ability of the Treasury to shift between the short- and long-term markets in its borrowings. By thus altering the demand for funds in these sectors, it could exercise a significant influence on both the actual and expected rates of interest and the relationship between the two markets. The short-long relationships, discussed in Chapter 14, could be applied to this aspect, and it need not be repeated here.

Obviously, those interested in the wider problem of economic stability, and the use of monetary measures to help attain it, view with horror the points discussed in this section. The interest cost to the Treasury is a relatively insignificant concern compared with the impact of debt management on the country's economy. What matters is the general welfare, and the debt should be manipulated with an eye to that objective, not the household problems of the debt issuer. To such a person, all the problems in this section should never have arisen, since they were created to meet the narrow interests of a government department isolated from the more important trends.

Banks' Cyclical Income Pattern

From the banks' point of view, the growth in size of the government debt has had its pleasant aspects. In a recession, when the demand for loans declines, banks can now move into government bonds, thus sustaining their income and the money supply. We now see somewhat the following cyclical pattern: (a) recession—lower yields—higher bond prices—decline in bank loans—rise in bond holdings; (b) boom—rising yields—falling bond prices—rise in loans—decline in bond holdings. The banks' current income thus tends to rise in the boom as yields move up and they make more loans at this higher rate. Income tends to decline in the recession when more of income is from the lower-yield bonds. In addition, the boom period is usually characterized by a larger amount of total reserves and less excess reserves, so that the aggregate of income-earning assets is more, thus further helping income. In the recession there is a tendency for income-earning assets to decline in volume as well as in average return, thus further depressing income.

On the other hand, the capital performance shows an opposite picture. In the boom, as income is rising, bond prices are declining. To the extent that the banks must sell securities to offset the demand for funds from private borrowers, we may see a rising loss from such sales. Capital losses on portfolio transactions mount as a partial offset to the improving income picture. In contrast, in the recession, bond prices rise, and so the bonds that had been held through the period now show a rising market value. If sold, we get a capital-gains performance. This helps offset the deterioration in the income account, and thus mitigates the otherwise gloomy outlook for the stockholder. Combined, banks would now present a picture of much more stable earnings that would be true for most other companies. The boom sees a rising income from operations, but losses from portfolio transactions; a recession sees declining income from operations, but a rising return from portfolio transactions. Both together result in a relatively stable income over the cycle, and so, to the investing public, bank stocks become a good means of avoiding the ups and downs so common for the average stock.

This pattern is somewhat modified if we bring in the capital-gains tax impact. If a bank has a profit on its portfolio transactions on issues held for more than six months, it pays only half as much tax as if the same income were from operations; for the larger banks the latter rate can go as high as 52 per cent.[1] If, however, the bank has net (realized) losses in its portfolio account, it can write off the loss out of income and thus save the 52 per cent. By appropriate timing of gains and losses, the bank can actually make money on the tax law.

Let us assume that a bank has $1 million taxable income in 1962 and 1963, and that it has made no portfolio transactions other than those considered in this example. At the end of 1962, one of its long-term United States bonds has a market value $100,000 less than cost. It sells this bond and puts the money into another long-term United States issue. Next year yields decline, and both the issue it sold and the one it purchased rise by $100,000. Over the two years it would have had neither a gain nor a loss if it had held the first issue, so its income each year would be $1 million. By making these two transactions, it reduces 1962 income by $100,000, and thereby reduces its income tax by $52,000. Its 1963 gain is subject to only the capital-gains tax rate, or 25 per cent ($25,000). Thus, even though over the two years it again broke even—the 1962 loss equalling the 1963 gain—it has saved net $27,000 on its federal income tax. Since most long-term governments

---

[1] Before the 1964 tax changes. The new rates change the argument in the text by only 1 to 2 per cent.

will move together, it is not difficult to make such a move and thus save on taxes. (This example is somewhat simplified; it becomes more complicated in detail if we apply it to smaller banks whose income may not be in so high a bracket, or if there have been other capital gains and losses during the period.)

The commercial banks also have a tax leeway in another direction. Interest paid to depositors is treated as an expense and is thus deductible from income; this reduces the income tax payable. Income from state and local bonds is exempt from federal income tax. In a recession, when interest income tends to fall off, the banks may move into tax-exempts, so that although the average return on the portfolio is lower than from boomtime loans, the after-tax return does not drop as much because of this exemption privilege. As its interest income declines, it is also lowering its tax bill and so reducing the downward slump in after-tax earnings. Not all such recession purchases would be tax-exempts, for the bank must also consider its needs for liquidity (for secondary reserves). Hence, some of its purchases would still go into Treasury bills and other liquid taxable issues. Most tax-exempts have too narrow a market to permit ease in selling if the bank does wish to liquidate.

Because of this tax feature, banks may be somewhat more flexible in their portfolio management than is implied in the usual thinking about the effect of falling bond prices. That is, as a tight-money policy gathers momentum, the yields move up and bond prices slump. This means that sales to offset rising loans will result in capital losses. At some point the banks may decide to curtail loans to avoid the need to sell bonds. But if they happen to be in a favorable tax position—if in particular there have not been offsetting capital gains—then much of this loss can be offset through the tax switch described earlier in this section. Or a switch from taxable bonds to tax-exempts may produce an analogous saving. Hence, this "lock in" arising from falling prices should not be interpreted too rigidly.

As can be inferred, portfolio management that works within all these alternatives can often make tremendous differences in bank performance. If the manager foresees rising yields, he switches quickly from long to short issues and thereby cushions any capital-loss possibilities. Or if the yield picture changes, he moves back to longs to take advantage of the prospective capital gains. He takes portfolio losses in high-income periods, when his bank is in the upper corporate income-tax bracket, in order to maximize the tax savings. He switches into the appropriate alternative issues to capitalize on the long-term gains feature. He moves into tax-exempts at certain times and out of them at others. In short, he does not operate the portfolio with an eye solely to interest income, liquidity, or as a residual for the use of excess reserves.

True, all these elements must enter into his consideration. But even within these confines, he still has much flexibility to come up with a better or worse outcome. Since he may often have as much as a third of his income-earning assets in various investment possibilities, it becomes quite clear why astute management recognizes the many profits possibilities inherent in an active approach to the portfolio department.

Competition Among Banks

Much of our interest-rate analysis assumed a reasonable flexibility in the rate structure, so that variations would occur and be allowed to influence the economy. But, as in so many other sectors of the United States, there is a question regarding the degree of pricing freedom that actually exists. And banking is no exception; monopolistic and other forms of limited competition are present in varying degrees. However, just as the limited competitiveness of the steel industry is modified by aluminum and copper as potential alternatives for the consumer, so the presence of the non-banking lender offsets somewhat the restrictiveness of competition in the commercial banking sector.

The entire lending process is certainly much less mobile than the portfolio sector. Borrowers are more likely to remain with one source of funds on which they can rely, rather than to try moving when small-rate differentials appear. Indeed, many a small borrower is lucky to find even one source that will lend him enough money. Hence, there is probably very little crossing over of customers among these smaller units.

In the smaller centers a similar immobility is evident. Many of these have only one, two, or at most three banks. If one were to cut its lending rate, the others would be forced to follow. Realizing this, each maintains an almost invariant pattern, similar to that of the others, and thus without a formal agreement, price competition is absent. Moreover, the average borrower is helpless, for where else can he turn? The only ones who may be able to attempt to get funds from other cities are the large companies with scattered branches, or with area-wide reputations. But to be in this category means that the company is already fairly sizeable. In fact, it would not be too far from the facts to generalize and say that the larger the firm, the wider the area over which it can borrow, and so the more banks it can look to (the more competition for its business). And, as would be expected, the rates charged reflect in part this availability of alternatives; the larger the financial size of the borrower, the lower the average interest rate charged. However, it should also be remarked that the higher rates for loans to small borrowers often reflect in part the relatively greater costs of administration per dollar; the paperwork involved is frequently almost as much as that for loans of much larger amounts.

Competition is also limited because of the difficulty of entry. Legal restrictions on the formation of new banks work to protect local monopolies. Many states forbid branches outside the city or county, thus preventing the larger banks from entering the small underbanked communities. And the smaller volume of business in many of these one- and two-bank communities is often too small to make the profit possi- bilities high enough to attract a third independent. Often it is only because the rate structure is so high that even these local monopolies survive. (In part, this also reflects their inefficiencies; the cost of run- ning a small bank is much higher per dollar of assets than for the large bank with many branches.) This precarious profits position also militates against interest-rate reductions to extend the volume of busi- ness; the elasticity of demand is often so low that the net result may well be only a decline in income or a price-cutting war with other banks.

Branch banking, however, may not be the answer to attempts to increase the extent of competition. It is true that the branches of the same bank tend to charge the same rates, and if consistently followed this policy would result in the units in the smaller centers charging rates in line with those in effect at the head office. Since the latter would probably be in a more competitive large city we would see a tendency for rates in what would otherwise be high-rate sparsely com- petitive areas coming down toward the lower-rate urban market. On the other hand the growth in bank branches is often through the acqui- sition of previously independent banks. Thus, we would see fewer lenders than if the branch were a completely new unit, adding to those already supplying the funds sought.

Bank custom also keeps customers from switching. The large bor- rower might be willing to try the issuance of short-term commercial paper, but if such loans mature during a tight-money period and it does not have the cash for repayment, what then? Having broken its banking connection, it can no longer count on aid in times of stress. The fear of such a possible stringency keeps many a corporation wedded to its bank despite the higher cost of such loans. And from the banks' point of view they feel that this is not a higher cost, for the borrower is getting something for it—money, no matter how tight the market gets.

To a lesser degree, there are also imperfections in the money market itself. In our analysis of short- and long-term lending, it was pointed out that even if there are marked yield differences between these two sectors, there would be many investors who would not shift.

Tax considerations similarly reduce flexibility between state and municipals, on the one hand, and the taxable bonds on the other. Legal restrictions further impede freedom of movement; many government units restrict their pension funds for their own employees to United States government securities, or issues of the state in which they are located. However, there are enough investors who can move. These are supplemented by borrowers who are also willing to shift; together their combined influence is enough to keep these marketable securities fairly closely tied together so that we can regard this area as sufficiently mobile and competitive.

The effects of limited competition show up in a reduced influence for monetary policy. Tight money cannot be depended upon to drive up loan rates and thus curtail borrowings; nor can easy money be certain to lower rates and stimulate borrowing. Instead, by reducing reserves, the Reserve makes the over-all lending volume less, and then the banks restrict borrowers by a reduction in the amount available for the less reliable borrower—the unsatisfied fringe. Conversely, easier money leads to more reserves, and more would-be borrowers receive the funds they need. It is thus the banks' judgment rather than the cost of the loan that determines where the more (or less) limited supply of loanable funds is to go. And this may reflect past relationships, rather than the merit of the loan.

Summary

In applying our observations to actual cases, we must modify the findings for the numerous details that arise from the institutional setting within which the monetary system works. One such qualification applies to the management of the public debt, especially its handling of the maturities of marketable issues. The debt is constantly getting shorter in life, so that its ownership changes, reflecting this altered liquidity. As a consequence, at maturity the holders may not be those desirous of taking up the newly issued series to pay off this maturing one. There is a problem in tapping the right source of funds; it must be done in such a manner as to minimize the hardship for the private borrower that such a competition for funds might impose. It is thus a skill to know which type of issue and what life to maturity will appeal to the various segments of the market, and yet reflect the type of debt that also serves the government's purposes. All too readily resort is had to the easiest issue to float—the three-month Treasury bill. But this brings up monetary control problems and also has a tendency to encourage inflation.

Another important set of institutional considerations surrounds the management of the commercial banks' portfolios. Tax considerations and income offsets can often seriously change the handling of this segment of the banks' assets. Much of the calibre and quality of bank management can be deduced from the performance in handling this problem. Often, especially for the smaller banks, management has a semimonopolistic position with regard to its loan activities, so that its inefficiencies can be masked behind higher loan charges.

Chapter 21

LIQUIDITY PREFERENCE AND ECONOMIC FLUCTUATIONS

Throughout the discussion, the concept of liquidity has been an ever-recurring one. We have seen why it is desired and the major financial instruments that satisfy this objective with varying degrees of success. In this chapter we shall analyze the interaction of this preference for liquidity and changes in this feeling, and the impact resulting for money and other economic activities. It is this concept that lies at the core of all modern analytical work on monetary activity.

The Monetary Triangle

In our conceptual framework we can view the process in terms of a triangle—three angles that work on one another: liquidity preference, the interest rate, and money supply. A change in one necessitates a change in at least one of the remaining two, and a shift in any two will set in motion forces affecting the remainder of the economy.

Suppose people decide that they would like to be more liquid. This would reflect itself in a lessened desire to part with liquidity at the current price—the rate of interest. As a result, there are two alternatives present. To offset this heightened liquidity preference, borrowers could make lending more attractive by raising the interest rate. Or we could expand the money supply to satisfy the liquidity desire; in effect, as lending at the current rate of interest declines, the new supply comes into the market as replacement. If the banking system can be induced to step up its lending at the current rate of interest, the money supply rises. The bank loans replace the funds coming previously from private lenders but now being kept liquid because of the preference change.

The situation is similar if people's liquidity preference declines, and if, at the current rate of interest, they now w sh to lend more. This added supply of loanable funds at the going rate might then depress yields, and thus offset this shift away from liquidity, the now lower rate cutting back the loanable funds. In effect, the initial change meant that at each rate of interest people were now willing to lend more as compared with the amount before the change. The decline in yields that followed meant that less would be forthcoming than at the starting rate of interest. The change in liquidity thus shifted the loanable-funds curve, and then the drop in yields moved the supply down along this new curve.

Here a numerical example may clarify this (see Figure III). Suppose that at 4 per cent people are willing to lend $7 billion, and at 5 per cent they would lend $9 billion. At the moment the rate is 5 per cent, and so $9 billion is offered. Then liquidity feeling changes; now, at 5 per cent they would be willing to lend $12 billion, and at 4 per cent $9½ billion. At both rates more is now offered than before. However, the demand for such funds at 5 per cent is still only $9 billion. As a result, supply exceeds demand at 5 per cent, and the rate drops. As it drops, borrowers are willing to borrow more; assume that at 4 per cent they raise their demand to $9½ billion. We then get a new equilibrium at this lower rate. In summary, therefore, the liquidity shift increased the amount available at each yield. But the subsequent decline in yields lowered the amount *as compared with the higher rate after the shift*. Net, there is still more being loaned in our illustration—$9½ billion afterward (at 4 per cent), as compared with $9 billion before (at 5 per cent). But less is available at 4 per cent after the shift than at 5 per cent after the shift, although more is available at 4 per cent after the shift than at 4 per cent before the shift (and more at 5 per cent after the shift than at 5 per cent before the shift).

Alternatively, the central bank could offset the shift through open-market sales. If it wished to sustain the 5-per-cent rate, it could have sold $3 billion to the lenders, thus reducing to $9 billion the amount

FIGURE III

Loanable Funds Market

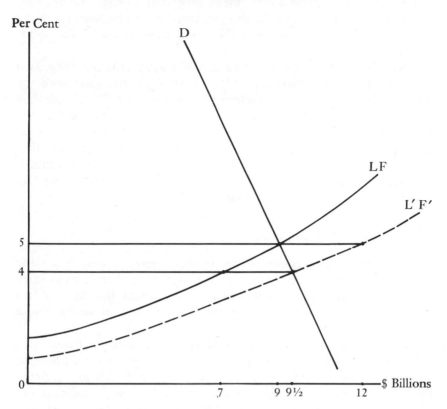

Per Cent

D

LF

L′ F′

5

4

0

.7   9 9½   12 $ Billions

available to other borrowers at 5 per cent, the same as before the shift. And so the rate continues as before.

But the initial shift need not be from the side of liquidity preference. A rising demand for loanable funds could push up interest rates. Now there is a greater return for parting with liquidity, and so more of a supply comes on the market. Or a reduced demand for loanable funds could lower yields, and the resulting diminished return for giving up liquidity reduces the supply of loanable funds.

Or again, open-market purchases could increase the supply of loanable funds; now the bondholders who sold have money to lend again. This addition to the available supply of loanable funds depresses the yield structure, and once again may dry up some other sources of funds, thereby restoring equilibrium. The added liquidity so depressed yields that it induced an offsetting rise in the desire for liquidity at this new lower rate of interest. Conversely, if we reduce the money supply, as through open-market sales, there is less of a supply of loanable funds, the previous amount having been reduced by the diversion to the purchase of these bonds. Yields now start to rise, and this may then coax more funds into the market; there would be less of a desire to continue to remain liquid now that the price of parting with liquidity has risen.

As before, in our discussion of the shift away from liquidity, two types of changes have occurred. Open-market purchases increased the supply of loanable funds. At each rate of interest more is available than before; the entire supply curve has moved. But this causes the new (enlarged) supply at the previous equilibrium rate of interest to exceed the demand for such funds. The rate of interest then declines, thus cutting back the supply of loanable funds until a new equilibrium is achieved. Our previous numerical illustration would apply here, too. And conversely for open-market sales.

A "Dynamic" Reformulation

The discussion presented so far in this chapter is actually a static one. The analysis has been worded as though there were a fixed stock of savings which would be either held idle or loaned. But this is only a partial story; at any one time we have both a stock of savings and a flow.

Let us imagine a hypothetical business day. Because of past efforts, people have a certain *stock* of savings distributed among cash, demand deposits, savings accounts, other financial assets, and perhaps real items, like goods in inventory, capital equipment, and so on. In addition, out of current income they are also adding to savings. This is the *flow* concept. These savings may be put into any of the various possibilities enumerated.

Suppose the rate of interest suddenly changes—perhaps upward. Then we get two areas of reactions. Some of the previous accumulation of savings can change; for example, some of the demand deposits held idle may now be offered in exchange for bonds whose yields are higher. And more of the current flow of savings could also go into such securities. The resulting rise in the demand for bonds could thus exceed the savings coming from current income because of the addition coming from the shift in past savings.

In this illustration the rate of interest has a double task to perform. It must equalize the flow of current savings with the demands made upon it—so much to new securities issued, so much into absorption of the expansion in the money supply, so much into additional real acquisitions, and so forth. And it must also maintain an equilibrium in the distribution of the stock of past savings among the various possible outlets. Any shift in this interest rate will then set in motion changes in both the composition of the stock of savings and the direction of the flow of new savings. In our analysis, therefore, we must constantly keep in mind that there are two aspects—stocks and flows—to the conceptual apparatus.

Furthermore, there are the longer-run repercussions associated with our macroeconomic framework discussed at the beginning of the text. If, for example, we change the rate of interest, we have presumably altered the equilibrium volume of investment. This in turn will change incomes, which then alters savings, and so changes the current flow. *The* equilibrium rate of interest, therefore, must include not only an equilibrium disposition of the stock of savings, but an income level that produces the flow of savings in equilibrium with the investment associated with that income level, all in such a relationship that there is no force or inducement for a still further change. This broader frame of analysis we have compressed, leaving its details to the more specialized books on macroanalysis. However, later in this chapter we shall give some brief examples of the process to illustrate its main workings and tendencies. These will omit many of the finer points, and in no way are they to be taken as the complete picture.

Before turning to this more detailed and longer-run view, we should also note that there is a competitor for liquidity. So far we have talked only in terms of money as the satisfier of this desire. But suppose we feel certain that the price of commodities is going to rise. Then if we wish to be liquid, we could also purchase these items, knowing that whenever we did want money, we could sell out at either our cost or perhaps even a profit. Hence, in such circumstances we could satisfy our liquidity desire—the ability to get cash immediately without capital loss—by moving out of money into these items. The more certain we feel that prices will rise—as in an inflationary period—the more the incentive is to make such a change. Conversely, if we feel that we are in for a period of declining prices, we would prefer money, since there is no danger of a capital loss. In practice, though, even if we do believe that prices will rise, we may still prefer money for our liquidity needs, since we cannot be certain whether the specific commodity we select would rise in price. It is quite possible for prices in general to rise 10 per cent, yet for wheat or cotton to drop during the same period. Since there is still the uncertainty of the actual selection, we might still prefer to avoid such a chance and remain with money. On the other hand, if the expected price rise is to be 100 per cent or more—such as could occur in some of the wilder inflations—then all commodities are virtually certain to rise in price, so that anyone we selected would be better than money. The only difference now is that some may go up only 50 per cent, whereas others might soar 200 per cent; but in either case we would be better off than if we had kept our resources as idle cash. We also see in this point that the greater the anticipated inflation, the greater the move into commodities, and thus the greater the upward pressure on prices. Simultaneously, there is a declining desire to hold money in cash balances, so that we see a rising velocity. The V rise thus helps produce the P rise.

To bring together the various considerations surrounding liquidity preference, we shall illustrate by describing two phases of the business cycle. We have already painted part of the picture in various chapters while describing the state of the economy as it moves through these different degrees and directions of fluctuations. Here we wish to use the same background, but focus attention on the liquidity problem. In doing so, we shall also draw on our discussion of the two monetary equations—the quantity and cash-balance expositions. In effect, we shall expand and integrate the earlier part of this section into the broader problem of cyclical stability. In doing so, we shall also bring in the broader series of repercussions, both the longer-run reactions that arise from the changing outlook for investment, and the other accompanying influences of importance that will be changed simultaneously with the shifts in the narrow area of the money market. We shall be running both a monetary and real exposition at the same time.

A Different Monetary Triangle

Another way of looking at an economy is to divide it into three parts—money, securities, and goods. People can move among these three. Inflation means that people are moving out of money;[1] deflation indicates a movement into money. Since inflation is a time of rising prices, people would move into goods; in a deflation, when prices are expected to decline, the movement would be out of goods.

The reaction on securities is not as easy to pin down. At first glance, if people are moving out of money, they should be moving into both goods and securities. If they are moving into money, they should be moving out of both goods and securities. But this need not always be so. For example, if the movement out of money is because of a reduced desire to be liquid, then it is true that they might move into securities because of the income to be obtained. They may just as well move into goods, where the price rise is an attraction. But if the inflation concern is paramount, then fixed-yield securities are not much better as a hedge than money is; both have a fixed value in dollars,

---

[1] However, some money will be absorbed for increased transactions needs as activity rises.

although securities yield some return as an offset to the price rise. Securities, in other words, are a slightly better hedge than money, for there is some income to be set against the decline in the real value of the currency. So, between the two, there would be a movement out of money and toward securities.

But between securities and commodities, the latter would often be a better hedge. Their expected appreciation might be more than enough to counterbalance the attraction of the income that can be obtained from securities. Hence, we can say that expectations of a mild inflation would not be likely to induce people to move from securities to commodities, but a marked inflation would see such a shift. An expected deflation, however mild, would move people out of goods and either into securities (if liquidity considerations were minor) or into money (if liquidity were a paramount factor).

A refinement should distinguish between fixed-income securities and equities. If inflation is expected to raise profits and dividends, and thus the capital value of equities, people might move out of money and fixed-income securities into equities and goods, the preference between the latter two reflecting relative expectations of gain. Similarly, if deflation were expected to reduce profits and dividends, and thus the market value of equities, people would move out of equities and goods into money and fixed-income securities. The division between money and fixed-income securities would reflect the relative weight of liquidity and income. On the other hand, if dividends and market prices were not to be greatly affected by inflation or deflation, then equities would be affected in a manner quite similar to that for fixed-income securities. The differentiation between the two would then be a matter of degree—mainly, the relative risks of the two categories.

The Upper Turning Point

We shall assume that a vigorous boom is under way and that the rising volume of sales and a generally favorable outlook is increasing the desire of many corporations to expand capacity. While much of this can be financed out of retained profits, an increasing amount must be through borrowed funds. Hence, this increased demand is causing a rise in yields in general, but particularly within the long-term category. At this point several outcomes are possible, and since there are numerous possibilities that could arise from each, we shall limit the discussion to only a few.

Again we must remind the reader of the problem of stocks and flows. At this moment the public has distributed a certain proportion of its savings between money (currency and demand deposits) and securities, and out of current savings some is being used to add to money holdings, some offered as loanable funds. The rising demand is for long-term funds—either to shift some existing holders from money to long-term securities, or to induce current savings to move less into the acquisition of additional money and more into the purchase of long-term securities. The pressure, in other words, is to reduce both the stock of savings held in money form, and the proportion of new savings going into money form. Phrased another way, the pressure is to reduce the volume of idle money and also reduce the proportion of current savings that would add still further to the holdings of idle money. Borrowers want to increase the proportion of active money to the total available by getting some of the idle money away from existing holders, and also by inducing other would-be holders (out of new savings) not to want more money, but to accept securities instead.

It is quite possible that the rise in interest rates releases so much money from cash balances (to take advantage of the increased return) that the volume of loanable funds rises to match the increased demand. The lenders are now able to operate with a smaller cash balance, and the velocity of their checking accounts rises. There may be even more of an inducement if the boom psychology makes people feel that prices in general will rise. If so, there will also be a movement into commodities and out of cash, as the desire for liquidity changes. In other words, the existing money holders reduce their average balance while maintaining their spending rate, and the funds so released are turned over to the corporate borrowers (and perhaps sellers of commodities), who now can spend that much more. For the entire community the aggregate spending out of the same money supply has risen, our V. In terms of the cash-balance equation, people are now holding a smaller proportion of their spending in cash form (k has declined).

At the same time, in terms of our flow concept, the rise in interest has induced those supplying new savings also to operate more economically, so that their need for cash is reduced. The combined effect is still to raise the volume of loanable funds.

To illustrate, assume that initially yields were 4 per cent. Total idle money was $75 billion, and active money $50 billion. (The reader need not be reminded that in a sense even this latter active money is also idle between transactions.) In addition, during the current period, savings are $5 billion, of which $4 billion will be used to buy long-term securities and $1 billion will become idle money. Implicitly, we are assuming that the commercial banks are expanding loans and demand deposits by $1 billion, which will end up as idle money—plus whatever additional amount will go into any rising transactions needs.

Suppose at 4 per cent the demand for funds by long-term borrowers rises to $7 billion, well in excess of the amount coming from current savings. The rate of interest therefore rises to 4½ per cent. This induces current savers to acquire more long-term securities—perhaps $4¼ billion, or $¼ billion more than at 4 per cent. It also induces other people—some of those holding the $75 billion idle money—to give up liquidity; perhaps $2½ billion now emerges. Also, since the cost of borrowed funds has risen, some of the demand drops out of the market —perhaps $¼ billion. At 4½ per cent, therefore, the total loanable funds for long-term securities is the $4 billion originally available at 4 per cent out of current savings, plus $¼ billion of current savings induced to become loanable when the rate was 4½ per cent, or a total of $4¼ billion available from current savings. We also have activated $2½ billion of otherwise idle funds, so that we have $6¾ billion available for loans; the higher rate reduced the demand for such funds from $7 billion to $6¾ billion, and now, at least for the moment, we have equilibrium.

This increased spending can raise either prices or output—either P or T. If there is sufficient unused capacity, it is possible that the added demand for goods will be accompanied by a rising output, and so the inflationary pressure on prices is reduced. If this occurs, we see rising output and incomes, additional spending now passing over the funds to these new factors of production. For example, suppose the corporate borrower buys machines from a previously under-utilized machine-tool industry. Unemployed machinists come back to work, and output rises. The funds borrowed now come into the hands of these workers as wages, and various other factors for raw materials, profits, and so on. Their income, in other words, will have risen. Now they, too, will spend more, but also they will save more. Their higher income means that more will be absorbed into cash balances. We thus see some of the cash balances originally released as loanable funds now ending up in the balances of the groups that benefitted from the resulting rise in incomes. This, of course, slows down the multiplier impact. The remainder that is spent—and the rapidity with which these funds reappear as demand—helps determine the ultimate effect on velocity of these shifts in spending and idle balances. The respending, of course, adds further to demand and incomes, and thus still again to a rise in this last group's ability to hold higher cash balances. Hence, it is quite possible for the initial shift toward lower cash balances to raise incomes for other groups in the community, thereby enabling the latter to hold more idle balances, as a reflection of their increased income. So once again we re-absorb all the funds, although differently distributed; in the process, as already remarked, aggregate output and income have risen.

However, not all of these additional savings will end up as idle funds. Much of these will also enter the loanable-funds market, either directly or through the financial intermediaries. This shifts our supply-demand relationship, and so may again change the rate of interest, starting us on a transition to still another temporary equilibrium. We shall not pursue this point further here, referring the interested reader to the more specialized works on macroanalysis.

It is also quite possible for the increased spending to run up against tight-output conditions, so that the result is to start the upward price trend. But this also raises incomes. Profit margins rise, which adds to the corporate owner's income. Workers might press more successfully for higher wages so as to share in this price boost, and so siphon off some of the profits as wages. Raw-material suppliers may boost their prices and thus also share in the rise. While the community's real income has not changed, since output is the same, the money income is rising, and so once again there may be a desire to hold increased cash balances to handle the higher money value of income and spending. As before, we have re-absorbed our cash into new balances. In the process we have raised money incomes, except that this time there has been little or no effect on output.

With output and prices rising in our two alternatives (in practice, probably both will occur), there is an increased incentive for corporations to expand capacity still more. Rising output reduces excess capacity, and so plant extensions are to be made. Rising prices clearly signal the shortage of supply, and again we try to step up output by increasing plant-expansion plans. And with increased profits we have the means to finance this new investment, either through retained profits or an enhanced ability to service the cost of any additional borrowing. In the latter case, of course, we have returned to our initial point—the step-up in the demand for loanable funds. And so the process could continue, the theme of rising output, prices, and profits running throughout the exposition.

This expansion, if unchecked, could soon spill over into a vigorous inflation. Capacity expansion would only feed spending power into the community, while the supply rise would not occur until months or years later, when these new plants were finally completed. We would thus see a rising V (declining k) not accompanied by a sufficient rise in T. Further, although not explicitly touched on, during this whole process we would also see a rising M as bank loans expanded, provided there were excess reserves to support this deposit rise. This, of course, would only accelerate the boom, for now there would be both M and V moving up, adding still further to the excess demand.

But more likely we would see steps by the Federal Reserve to check such a move. Reserves would be kept tight, so that the rise in the money supply was minimal. In fact, the generally rising yield structure that touched off the decline in liquidity and cash balances might eventually so depress bond prices as to lock in the banks, and so actually curtail further lending. Or it might discourage further underwriting in any large quantity, as brokers saw bond prices fall between time of purchase from the issuing corporation and sale to the ultimate investor. Or finally, some would-be borrowers might balk at the rising interest cost. Whatever the source, enough of these various restraints could bring about a concern that the upward movement cannot continue as vigorously as before. Or the profit margins may be squeezed as demand expansion is held down through these various influences, and thus the previous upward movement of profits starts to slow down.

The intervention by the monetary authorities would act mainly through curtailment in the availability of funds, particularly by reducing bank lending. This would tend to offset the rising availability coming from the decline in cash balances, and presumably it would act as enough of a check on over-all spending to prevent the boom from getting out of hand. Once these restrictions took effect, there would be a slowdown in economic activity; and the decline in profit opportunities—in particular, the end of the inflation-engendered rise in profit margins—could result in a significant cutback in new expansion plans. This, in turn, would decrease spending and incomes all around, and so the upward phase would soon be replaced by the recession. The severity of this reversal would depend on numerous factors, but reversal is almost certain to occur. Any cutback in plans that would be sufficient to stop the upward pressures inevitably spills over in its movement to become a reduction; so far we have never been able to level out the boom without pointing it in a downward direction. This art has yet to be learned.

The Recession

After the initial drop in business activity, there is often a tendency for the various economic indicators to level out. The downward force seems to be exhausted, but there is as yet no counter pressure to start the revival. Hence, the economy can bump along at this underemployment level—almost an equilibrium—without any appreciable shift one way or the other. At this point, some intervention could start the hoped-for revival.

While there could be many reasons for this low-level stability, one that most probably will be a part of the explanation lies in the stagnation of demand for capital goods. With output and demand well below the levels of the preceding prosperity, there is now more than ample capacity to meet current sales. It is true that there will still be some expansion plans; some companies may decide to add to capacity now to take advantage of the lower interest rate on new borrowing, or perhaps of the cheaper prices on machinery and equipment. But the total volume of such outlays is insufficient to produce the employment levels associated with full-capacity operations for the economy. One possible way to achieve this objective, therefore, is to make it more attractive for still more borrowing and plant expansion. (The reader might suggest as an alternative the stimulus to demand and consumption. This would increase the rate of operations, and thus perhaps provide an incentive to expand capacity to meet this stepped-up spending; this alternative will be discussed in the chapter on fiscal policy.)

To aid borrowing, interest rates must be brought down. At the current (recession) level they are undoubtedly below the boom rates —that is, when demand for loanable funds was much higher. But they have not come down sufficiently to create enough of a demand for such funds to be used for enough capital expenditures, thereby restarting the economy to full employment. A lower rate would make such borrowing even cheaper, and thus perhaps more attractive. Further, it would encourage underwriting, as the new issues were brought out in a rising market—the decline in yields creating the upward tendency in bond prices.

But there is often a serious hitch to this suggestion. As yields go down, there is less incentive to part with liquidity. Not only is such a return lower, but there is the prospect that if it succeeds, the demand for funds will pick up even more, yields will rise, and the securities bought in the recession when yields were low will then drop in price and thus create the certainty of capital losses. As a consequence, as interest rates drop—as bond prices rise—we would see two reactions. Some of the existing savings would shift from securities to idle money; in addition, a greater proportion of current savings would go into idle money, a smaller proportion into new securities acquisitions. Just as the demand for loanable funds is stepped up in response to the lower interest rate, we find the volume of loanable funds dropping off. In short, velocity drops off, as some of the funds that might have been turned over to corporate borrowers, and then spent, now remain with the savers as idle (demand or time) deposits. The lower yield has increased liquidity preference and so thwarted our expansionary attempts.

However, this obstacle can be met in many cases if the efforts to lower yields are effected through the Federal Reserve's engaging in open-market purchases. As the Reserve buys securities, the sellers are now left with liquid funds. If they reinvest them in other securities, we may see some of it going to new borrowers. Furthermore, the Reserve purchases will have lowered yields on the government portfolio, so now perhaps these investors will be satisfied with a lower yield on corporate issues, since the alternative interest opportunity has already declined.[2] If so, then we might see a revival of borrowing, new issues rising at this lower yield and the funds pushed out of governments going into these new issues.

Suppose, however, that some of these sellers to the Reserve hold on to their funds as idle deposits. Obviously, the funds received will then move into the bank, swelling both idle deposits and bank reserves. Now the banks have more funds that are not earning any income—the new reserves—and if the money came into time deposits, they have added interest costs. So, perhaps the banks will now ease up in their lending standards, accepting a somewhat lower rate on loans or investments just to keep their funds employed. As they follow through, still more deposits are created—those going to the borrower or new corporate issuer—and these funds presumably will be spent. The net result of this open-market purchase will then have been some rise in idle deposits, and the accompanying receipt of reserves then enables the banks to add to active deposits. The idle deposits satisfy the enhanced liquidity now that yields are lower, but in so doing, they enabled the banks to meet the additional demand for funds at this lower yield by expanding loans and investments and creating still more deposits.

Once the new spending gets under way and the multiplier effect gets to work, incomes will be rising throughout the economy. And, as incomes rise, more and more people will want to increase their average balance to handle the rising volume of transactions. Thus, more and more money will seep into these balances, lowering the velocity somewhat as compared with the initial jump when the deposits were first created. We will thus have a new equilibrium emerging, with a higher volume of M and, of course, the accompanying expansion in spending, probably resulting mainly in a rise in T. If it were not for this gradual rise in the size of balances, the money received by the first seller would be immediately respent, which would raise the next seller's balance, and since he has no desire to raise this amount he, in turn, will respend it, and so on. This would cause an enormous rise in spending. But instead, as incomes rise as a result of the additional spending, more and more is siphoned off to build up balances, which means that the rate of respending is slowing down, and so we get a brake on the expansion impact. However, as we have already seen, there will also be some

---

[2] Because of this lower rate of interest, some of the money received as income by current savers will now be held idle instead of being loaned to would-be borrowers. The total stock of idle funds is thus increased by this diversion of previously active money.

funds emerging from previously idle balances, and this now adds to the spending stream. If this happens, we get an additional upward impetus, and so the recovery continues; if not, the recovery dies, although at a somewhat higher level than when it began. (The reader should note here the similarity to our earlier discussion of the muliplier and investment acceleration.)

Again we must remember that our economy is in a dynamic phase. The change in incomes will change the volume of savings. The latter shift will alter the amount of loanable funds and the residual, if any, going into additional holdings of idle funds. These changes, in turn, may alter interest rates, the flow of funds, and so on. We are once again in the more complex macroeconomic world.

The Liquidity Trap

Suppose in the preceding example of recession economics the decline in yields did not stimulate borrowing too greatly. Or suppose it dried up the loanable funds so quickly that the demand could not be met. What then would be the best policy for the authorities?

In the first question, the business outlook is so gloomy that corporations do not want to borrow in any large amounts. Profits prospects are nil, and no matter how cheap the rate on borrowed funds, there is no incentive to expand. If such is the case, then we move over to fiscal policy (as in the next chapter), for what has happened is a virtual breakdown of monetary policy.

The second possibility could show up in the following form: in order to bring down yields, the Federal Reserve engages in an active open-market policy, perhaps buying both short- and long-term governments. Prices rise, yields decline. The sellers, however, simply deposit the proceeds with their banks. The banks, equally worried over the current situation, allow excess reserves to rise. The only expansion in the money supply is from deposits arising from the sale of securities, and these are being held idle, with a zero velocity. Moreover, the decline in yields on governments, by widening the spread relative to other securities, might induce some other holders to switch into the latter sector, but those sellers might also withdraw and hold their funds idle, so that we have not achieved any real step-up in lending. In addition, whatever savings are arising out of current income are also being held as idle money, reducing the active money total (reducing V).

It is easy to see why these sellers are holding their funds idle, even though this may mean zero income. The fear is that eventually there will be a turn-around in yields, a decline in bond prices, and so the expected capital loss would far outweigh any income received in the interim. This passion for liquidity would be most evident when yields reached extremely low levels—at the bottom of the historic range, so that any expected change would be upward. And such a possibility would be most likely in a severe depression when the demand for funds had already declined so much as to drive rates down toward this level. Then when we add the open-market purchases of the Reserve, and so bring yields down even lower, we have a perfect setting for this liquidity trap.

It is even possible that, try as it might, the Reserve could not drive the yields any lower. The more securities it bought, the more people decided to sell, fearing that any further price rise was certain to be followed by a decline. Hence, the supply of bonds becomes enormous above this critical price—below this critical yield level—and so the more the Reserve bought, the more was offered. The continual additional supply prevents prices from rising any further, or yields from falling any further. Theoretically, then, it is possible that a rate as low as 1 per cent might revive enough borrowing to bring about the recovery; yet the fear of capital loss would prevent such yields from going below 2 per cent. In other words, an interest rate that would produce enough capital outlays (through borrowing) to produce full employment would be impossible to achieve because of this strong liquidity urge. Again we have a case illustrating the possible breakdown of monetary policy. The only feasible way of meeting this problem might be through the government's lending directly to these borrowers at so low a rate, financing its operations through bonds issued to the Reserve. But this is not the monetary system we are examining in this book; rather, it is more akin to government intervention through fiscal policy.

The reader may raise a question regarding our discussion of liquidity in the recession. If investors shy away from the longer-term bonds for fear of a subsequent rise in yields and consequent capital loss, they need not move into idle funds. They could buy bills, which are almost as liquid as money, and yet furnish a return. This switch, of course, would lower short-term yields sharply, and indeed in periods of extreme liquidity such rates often drop close to zero. In other words, there is a gradual reshuffling of ownership which drives our short-term rates so low that, although the initial seller of long-term bonds may not move into money, some subsequent holder of short-term securities does so move; the latter's net sale thus balances the former's net purchase. Alternatively, the extremely low short-term yield might tempt some borrower to step up his demand for such funds, thus again absorbing the impact of the shift—in effect, the original long-term investor's desire for liquidity results in his receiving more short-term securities and the borrower receiving what would otherwise have been idle funds. (For the recovery the reverse would hold, of course, and need not be repeated.)

The Analytical Framework

It is now feasible to generalize from the monetary triangle outlined at the beginning of this chapter. Essentially, our path to a new equilibrium will be through the shifts in ownership and the activity of those balances affected by changes in the interest rate—the marginal-liquidity influence. The two relationships to be kept in mind are (a) the desire to hold money as the rate of interest changes, and (b) the desire to hold money as the volume of transactions changes.

Suppose that we have a certain level of interest rates. Presumably, this will be accompanied by a volume of lending and a volume of borrowing, which in turn will produce investment spending and so influence the level of incomes. Let us further assume that the economy is in equilibrium. Let us see what happens if we change the rate of interest, the volume of money, and the desire for borrowing. There could be many reasons why any of these might be changed from an existing equilibrium situation. Those mentioned here are solely for illustrative purposes.

Assume that the Reserve is worried about the current equilibrium getting out of hand; there may be too intense a demand building up into an inflation. It then takes steps to raise interest rates; we shall assume open-market sales which are all bought by the banks, thereby reducing excess reserves sufficiently. These sales have depressed securities prices and raised yields. Furthermore, the loss of excess reserves has induced the banks to charge more on new loans, in order to restrict the public's demand—to restrict any further growth in demand deposits.

One result could be to call forth *more* loanable funds. People who had held idle funds at the previous lower-yield structure are now attracted by the rise, and so offer some of their past savings. There is a greater incentive to lend; in effect, some of the existing money supply is transferred from the less active to the more active spenders. In addition, current savings might go less into additional idle deposits, if any had been so destined, thus further raising V.

In order to absorb this addition to the loanable-funds supply, there must also be an increased demand for borrowed funds, to match the rise in the supply. If the boom has gotten so strong as to raise profits expectations enough, we would see such an outcome—that is, the demand curve for loanable funds shifts to the right (see Figure III)—the

Reserve's step being interpreted as a warning sign rather than an active effort on its part to stop the boom. Hence, additional borrowing will result in additional spending, the existing money supply now effecting a greater volume of transactions. As a consequence, incomes will rise; and as this occurs, there will be an increased need for cash to carry on the now larger volume of activity. As a result, the initial spending is absorbed through the rising income into other people's balances.

On the other hand, if borrowers see this Reserve action as a sign that the boom is slowing down, then the loanable supply (which has increased) will be in excess of the demand. As a result of this excess, either yields will have to fall back, or the excess must be removed. We thus have a case for the Reserve's engaging in still more open-market sales; by so doing, it removes the excess supply of loanable funds and thereby sustains the now higher yield structure. Our money supply in the hands of the liquidity-conscious group has decreased; the excess, therefore, must either be absorbed through higher transactions balances as incomes rise, or else be removed if the increased yields that called forth this supply are to be sustained.

Suppose the banks had not used their excess reserves to purchase the securities offered by the Reserve, preferring to expand loans (and deposits) instead. If the Reserve still wished to restrain such lending, it would have to induce the public to buy the securities. To do this, it could offer them at a somewhat lower price (a somewhat higher yield) than that prevailing before the decision. This would tempt some of those with idle funds to buy the securities, as well as induce some of those currently adding to savings to buy these bonds instead of other securities (or instead of adding to idle cash). The funds then received by the Reserve would draw down bank reserves, and so check lending. In contrast with the previous possibility, the higher rate is necessary to attract the otherwise idle funds; at this higher rate, people wish to hold a smaller amount of their stock of savings as idle money, the difference going into the purchase of the securities offered by the Federal Reserve.

It is possible that the cutback in bank lending at the now higher prevailing yield structure is greater than the accompanying decline in the demand on the part of the borrowers; the latter may be relatively inelastic in their response to higher loan costs. If so, then at the new rate, the demand far exceeds the supply of loanable funds. This could force the rate still higher. As it climbs, some of the demand drops off, but probably not too much, in view of the aforementioned inelasticity. Instead, more funds will come out of the idle savings, as well as perhaps raising the proportion of current savings going into lending (reducing the proportion going into additions to idle money). We thus get an equilibrium at a rate higher than that initiated by the Reserve.

How would it work in a recession? Suppose yields decline. Some holders of securities decide they would rather be liquid, for the resultant rise in bond prices makes their current return too small to warrant tying up assets; they sell and wish to hold the proceeds idle. Presumably, some of the current savings is used to acquire these offerings, although, in addition, some current savings may go into idle funds, switching active to inactive money. To the extent that more purchasers buy existing offerings, we reduce the demand for new issues. This means less money for borrowers and less spending. This would tend to reduce incomes further.

As incomes decline, people need less money to carry on this reduced volume of transactions. So some of their now excess funds could be used to buy the securities being sold by those savers who now wish to acquire more liquid assets. Alternatively, as we have seen, the Federal Reserve System could step in through open-market purchases; as the lower yield induces present holders to sell off their securities, the Reserve buys, supplying the money that the sellers now want to hold idle. The resulting addition to total and excess reserves, plus the release of funds from excess cash balances, would thus permit the borrowers at the now lower level of interest rates to obtain accommodation. In summary, a decline in yields results in a greater holding of liquid funds. This can be achieved through either a release of funds from active balances as business activity declines, or through a rise in the money supply.

Suppose we now change the desire to borrow. For example, assume that the international situation improves and business firms become more optimistic. The future will see peace and prosperity. Profits expectations are better, even though as yet there has been no change in the actual volume of sales and output. So they wish to borrow more at each prospective interest rate in order to expand capacity. This rise in the demand for funds pushes up yields. This calls forth more funds from the liquidity group. Less is now held idle. As this added borrowing is spent, incomes rise, and there is a rising need for money to handle the increased transactions. Hence, the initial rise in investment prospects raised interest rates and so transferred funds from idle to active balances, thereby raising incomes in the process. If we had not wanted the interest rate to rise, we would have at the initial rate a rise in the demand for funds and the same supply. To prevent yields from rising would then require an increase in the money supply. For example, the Reserve could buy bonds and thus raise bank reserves; the banks could then step up their loans to satisfy the excess demand at the current yield levels and, in doing so, add to the money supply (the additional deposits created). These deposits, when spent, raise incomes, raise the demand for balances, and so find a new resting place. The additional money supply is thus absorbed through the rising incomes into the added balances to service this higher volume of transactions. In summary, therefore, if the demand for borrowed funds shifts upward, we either see yields rise, and so release idle funds to the active side, or see the money supply increase, to be absorbed as incomes respond upward.

Conversely, if the international scene darkens and business cuts back its borrowings, then we have an excess supply of loanable funds at the existing rate. The rate could drop off, thus inducing more would-be lenders to keep funds idle; the decline in the demand for funds by the borrowers is now offset by the rise in demand in order to be liquid. In addition, the drop in borrowing, and thus spending, will probably depress the economy, releasing cash from the transactions use, and thereby further depress yields in order to step up the demand for idle funds. That is, declining activity reduces the demand for money in the active sector, and to offset this, we step up the demand for funds in the idle sector by lowering yields—lowering the price for being liquid.

Alternatively, we may not want yields to drop off as borrowing decreases. Perhaps this drop would induce foreign investors to sell out and convert their funds into gold. So we must remove the excess supply of funds that emerges when the borrowers' demand declines. Moreover, as we have seen, this supply excess will be further increased as business activity declines and releases still more money from the active balances. Hence, the Reserve could step in with a policy of open-market sales, thereby removing the excess supply and so sustaining the yield structure. Once again we see how a change in one of our three key factors—here, the demand for borrowed funds—must result in a change in either the yield level or the quantity of money.

A comment regarding the longer-run effects should be added. To the extent that we alter the volume of borrowing for new capital outlays, we also alter the long-run total of capital facilities in the economy. For example, as we have seen, if yields rise, this could be due to more borrowing or a reduction in the money supply. If we select the former alternative, we add to our productive capacity; we have less if we select the drop in the money supply. Hence, the former type of decision raises long-run output more than would the latter. This, in turn, may affect our growth prospects. Continued infusions of new investment outlays could add to activity and capacity in the capital-goods industries, stimulating growth even more. Continual cutbacks in the money supply, by reducing the demand for capital goods, cuts back the long-run growth prospects. We thus have not only a short-run equilibrium problem to consider, but our solution to this short-run problem can also influence the nature of the economy's growth over the longer run. A succession of one type of equilibrium answers may mean a much larger gross national product over the years than a more restrictive approach to the short-run problems.

To repeat, in the preceding analysis we have spoken in terms of changing incomes. These shifts, in turn, change the flow of savings and the outlook for new investment, lining up still further forces for change. A more complete discussion would have to take into account these additional repercussions.

Equilibrium in the Savings Sectors

How do we know that the rate of interest that equates the supply of money with the amount of total savings that people wish to keep in liquid form, plus that used for transactions purposes, will also equate the flow of current savings with the demand for these funds for investment? Specifically, we have four possible disequilibrium situations: (a) the prevailing interest rate equates the available supply of money with the liquidity plus the transactions needs, but in so doing, the supply of current savings exceeds the demand; (b) same as (a), except that demand exceeds supply; (c) the prevailing interest rate equates the current savings with the demand for investment, but is so high that it tempts some previously idle funds to be offered for securities; (d) same as (c), except that the rate is so low that some existing holders of securities prefer to sell and hold idle funds.

In (a) not all the current savings can be absorbed. The rate must therefore drop. As it drops, some holders of securities will sell out and wish to hold idle funds. Some savers will decide not to lend. We thus have a step-up in the demand for idle funds; money that would have been loaned is now held idle. This drop in the transactions use will depress the economy, depress incomes, depress savings. We can reach an equilibrium only when enough money has been released from the transactions use to satisfy the increased desire for money on the part of those who had sold securities, plus that part of current savings that still goes into idle cash (unless the decline in savings dries up the desire to hold additional idle funds).

In (b) we have the reverse. The excess demand for funds raises yields, and so tempts previously idle money into the active stream. The subsequent expansion in the economy then absorbs this money in transactions uses. In both this and the preceding possibility, we have omitted the reactions of investment, both to the change in yields and the shift in income levels. We have assumed implicitly that in the first alternative, where the economy declined, investment at the new mix of lower yields and lower income levels adjusted to the changed saving flow; and similarly for the second case.

In (c) we have equality of savings and investment from current income, but now some idle funds are becoming active. Yields decline, and we can take care of these funds as follows: the lower yield reduces the amount of activated funds and, in addition, adds to absorption by inducing some current savers to hold part as idle funds; part is absorbed through a rise in investment and economic activity, a rise in the use for transactions purposes.

In (d) the reverse occurs. Savings equals investment, but some current securities holders are switching to money. Yields rise as these people sell their bonds. The rise in yields reduces the desire to sell, and also reduces the amount that would be sold as compared with the previously lower yield. The higher rate cuts investment and economic activity, cuts the use of funds for transactions purposes, releasing money for absorption by the bond sellers.

Note that in all four cases we worked toward a final rate that again gave an income level that produced equality of savings and investment and the distribution of the supply of money between transactions and liquidity uses in line with that desired by the people.

Money as a Cyclical Initiator

The monetary manifestation of liquidity preference has an interesting implication for business-cycle theorists and reformers. So long as the desire for liquidity can be expressed in monetary form, through variations in idle balances, we have an initiating factor for cyclical instability that is absent in the barter economy. In fact, it would not be too great an extension of this point to say that the phenomenon of the business cycle, as distinguished from supply-demand discrepancies for individual industries, is strictly a monetary phenomenon.

In our discussion of the barter economy in Chapter 6, we pointed out that if we wanted to save to store wealth for some future use, we still had to demand some commodity (say, copper), offering our wheat in exchange. That is, to get this storable wealth, we still had both a supply of, and demand for, commodities. Hence, the desire to store wealth does not reduce the demand for commodities. It simply alters the specific item desired.

With money we have a difference. There is still the supply of goods we must offer in order to get the money. But there is no demand for commodities on our part. In other words, in order to save in a money economy, we must reduce our demand for commodities in order to obtain a surplus to put into money form. If we translate this difference into cyclical terminology, we can see how money inflames the extent of fluctuation. For our barter exposition we shall assume that the persons in question produce wheat, but that the storable item desired for liquidity purposes is copper.

Suppose the general outlook gets worse; perhaps a war is in the offing. People become frightened and decide to hold their savings[3] in some form that can be kept over a period of time and then traded in the future. This would be copper in the barter economy, or idle deposits in a money economy. Or if there is a lack of faith in the banking system, this latter could be idle currency. In the barter economy the only way the objective can be accomplished is to produce more wheat, which is then swapped for copper. Alternatively, some of the existing output of wheat is no longer exchanged for consumables, but goes, instead, for copper. In the first possibility we get an increase in supply (wheat) and demand (copper); in the other, we get the same supply of wheat and the same demand (more copper, fewer consumables). There is thus a stimulus to the copper industry and, at worst, a decline in output of consumables. On balance there is no net deflationary impact.

But if the hoarding is in monetary form, we find a net decline in demand, as people reduce purchases in order to save money, or a net rise in supply, as people try to obtain more money. Either way, we cause an excess of supply, or insufficient demand. We thus have a net deflationary effect, and this can then trip a multiplier repercussion as the industries affected curtail output and incomes, which then affects others. In short, the desire for liquidity means a net deflationary impetus in a money economy, but not in a barter system, where hoarding must still create a demand for some commodity.[4]

Analogous reactions would ensue if the liquidity desire were reversed. In our barter economy, people would now offer their previously hoarded copper, raising the supply, but simultaneously they would be raising their demand for commodities—the items they now want in exchange for the copper. There is an expansionary impetus for the items they now demand, and a deflationary force for copper as marketable supplies rise. Here we can deduce that, net, the two opposite influences will probably tend to cancel each other. In a money economy, in contrast, dishoarding means that hitherto idle funds are now put back into the spending stream—people either spend these funds or lend them to others to spend—and so there is a net rise in demand unaccompanied by a contribution to supply. True, in response

---

[3] That is, current savings. In a barter economy, past accumulations of savings would be already in some real form, such as copper acquired in previous periods.

[4] If people wish to make their existing stock of assets more liquid, they might switch from bonds to money. Instead of deflation in the commodity market, as would occur if current savings were to be hoarded, we would have deflationary forces in the money market.

to this new demand, supply will rise. But then, so will the incomes of the people in these industries, and as these incomes rise, so will demand. So, net, there would still be a greater rise in demand than in supply as a result of the dishoarding of money. And once again we see a net change that is absent in the barter economy. In summary, therefore, hoarding in a money economy contributes to the downturn, while dishoarding in a money economy is a net expansionary factor. And if these liquidity shifts are of sufficient magnitude, we would have repercussions sizeable enough to cause the ups and downs in economic activity, especially when we add in the multiplier. And, of course, either of these liquidity changes could be reinforced by expectations of the change, which could then heighten the amplitude of the impact and so intensify the cyclical reaction.

What we see so far as monetary policy is concerned is the necessity to offset these shifts if they are unwanted. If, for example, the rise in the demand for liquid funds threatens to precipitate a depression, then we must take steps to satisfy this desire without curtailing borrowing and spending. Or if dishoarding threatens to spill over into excess demand and inflation, we must then remove the amount of money necessary to restore equilibrium. But such intervention, if calculated, will only neutralize the initial disturbance. In a barter economy such a problem would be absent; in a money economy we cannot eliminate it. We can only counter it.

Actually, as we have remarked, the combination of liquidity shifts and certain expectations assumptions could produce unusual outcomes. For example, if it appears that there is going to be a decline in liquidity —a rise in the demand for long-term securities—we then get the expectation of rising bond prices. If many investors expect this to happen, there would be a wholesale movement out of money and into securities; in an extreme case there could even be a negative preference for money! Or if the Reserve tries to check a boom by tightening money (by raising required reserves), the resulting rise in interest rates might call forth an *increase* in loanable funds; if profits prospects are sufficiently good, we thus might have more,[5] rather than less, investment. And it is even possible that the intervention by the Reserve could produce a step-up in the demand for funds, thereby absorbing the increased supply if corporations interpret the Reserve action as confirmation that the boom is really getting strong. The net outcome of such a combination would be an intensification, thanks to Reserve efforts to slow down activity. What may well result is a rise in velocity, as the liquid funds become active, and a corresponding improve-

---

[5] This is, the curve shifts to the right.

ment in expectations on the part of borrowers. It is because of such tricky outcome possibilities that the task of the Federal Reserve becomes so complex, since there is no way to foretell which expectation will be affected and how they will be affected when it does move. For this reason, it is necessary to indicate only possible paths of movement, rather than probable outcomes, in describing monetary actions.

Summary

Variations in economic activity can be analyzed in terms of movements among three monetary forces: liquidity preference, yields, and the money supply. A movement in one will induce at least one of the others to change in order to restore equilibrium; in so doing, it will usually change economic activity as well. In effect, various shifts are essentially movements between idle and active balances. The former reflect the reaction of liquility preference to the going yield structure, and the latter reflect the impact of business activity on incomes and thus the need to hold balances for transactions purposes. The two extremes are a flight from the currency—velocity (V) rising at astronomical rates—or the liquidity trap, a critical minimum yield below which the demand for money becomes virtually infinite.

If we wish to influence business activity—to stimulate it so as to absorb idle productive facilities, or to check demand in order to ward off a price inflation—we could work on the money supply. In effect, this is the path followed by the Federal Reserve when it resorts to open-market operations. Or we could try to influence expectations, perhaps altering the desire to borrow, and maybe even the willingness to lend. Incidental repercussions of these alternatives will influence interest rates. But it is also possible for the expected outcome to be different from that anticipated, especially if the businesses and individuals concerned misinterpret the policy actions.

Chapter 22

FISCAL POLICY

There are times when monetary policy cannot adequately cope with swings in the economy—for example, a liquidity trap, where any further lowering of interest rates pushes the securities sellers into idle balances, while borrowing cannot be stimulated except at lower interest rates. If boom conditions are raising profits expectations more than can be offset through tight money and rising yields, again the monetary authorities are stymied. Consequently, there is also a need to use the government's fiscal policies, either as a supplement or even, in extreme cases, as a replacement for monetary action.

The Government and Purchasing Power

Essentially, the federal government can be viewed as an intermediary marrying two streams of purchasing power. The community gives up purchasing power to this unit, either as taxes or as bond subscriptions. In return, purchasing power is returned in the form of expenditures, debt redemption, or outright grants. If the various receipts exceed disbursements, we have subtracted purchasing power from the remainder of the economy, and the converse is true if there is an excess of disbursements. (The special problem of bank borrowing and repayments will be discussed later.)

This is not meant to imply that a dollar of receipts balances a dollar of spending by the government. In a more detailed analysis, we would also have to examine the character of each. For example, if A pays taxes, A has less take-home pay. Therefore, basing his planning on this latter amount, he would spend less on consumption and also save less. If his total income is $10,000, he might spend $8,500 on consumption and save $1,500. But if taxes reduce this to a $9,000 take-home, he may then spend only $8,000 on consumption, and $1,000 would be for savings. On the other hand, were his tax bill only $500, and if in addition he bought $500 in government bonds, although the government still gets $1,000 from him—as in the alternative, where taxes were higher—his spending pattern might alter. A would then have a take-home pay of $9,500, of which $500 goes into government bonds. This he would regard as a net addition to his assets, unlike the tax payment. Hence, it *is* no different from any other savings, so far as A is concerned. A may then decide to spend $8,250 on consumption and save $1,250, of which $500 goes for government bonds. Note that he still turns over $1,000 to the government, but because in return he received $500 in bonds, his asset position is superior to the $1,000 tax alternative, and so it alters his remaining savings and consumption pattern. By changing a $500 tax into a bond purchase, A decided to spend more on consumption and save more; but savings, other than payments to the government, were less; with a $1,000 tax he saved only $1,000, but all of it was available for lending anywhere. With a $500 tax he saved $1,250, but only $750 was freely disposable, since $500 had already been tied up by his government-bond subscription. As can be seen, the method by which the government obtains the funds does make a difference.

Similar reasoning applies to the comparison of receipts and expenditures. If the government gets the funds from one sector of the economy and spends them in another sector, we may get analogous differences in over-all relationships. There are a multitude of possibilities, and we shall cite a few.

Money is paid in as taxes by the upper-income groups and used to aid the poor and unemployed. The former may offset the lower take-home pay by reducing savings and lending, thereby reducing corporate borrowing and thus the latter's purchase of capital equipment. The recipients are spending most of their additional receipts on food and clothing. The net result is a decline in sales of the capital-goods industries and a rise in the consumers'-goods sector. Note also that the decline in capital formation may also reduce our long-run production potential.

Or these taxpayers decide to economize by spending less on travel abroad, taking a cheaper vacation within the United States. Not only are our payments to foreigners reduced, which may induce them to cut back their purchases of our goods, but we have also stimulated the local tourist industry, as well as the consumers'-goods sales to the poor. The offset, if it does occur, is a loss of export sales.

But there is also the possibility that this is a recession, and the upper-income brackets are putting their savings into idle balances. By taxing them more, we may induce them to reduce this segment of their allocations. Thus we get both a stimulus to the consumers'-goods industries (as the poor spend more) and no loss in purchases from the wealthy, the money supply now having a higher velocity.

Suppose the government spent the funds on military expenses in a foreign country. Then the taxes collected may induce the taxpayers to reduce their spending, most of which would be on American goods and services, while the disbursement goes for the purchase of foreign goods and services needed by the armed forces. The net result here is to curtail the demand for our output and stimulate demand for foreign output. Unless this latter flow of purchasing power to foreigners induces them to buy more from the United States, we would see a net deflationary impact of the government's activities.

Or suppose the taxes received are used to build a new hydroelectric plant. The tax collections, by reducing take-home, may reduce the taxpayers' consumption. The government spending raises the demand for capital goods and the future productive capacity of the economy. We have thus reduced the community's aggregate consumption and raised its savings and investment—and, of course, switched demand from consumers' goods to capital goods at the same time.

Recognizing these many complexities, we shall have to ignore them in this chapter, since we are trying only to outline the problem. But despite what has just been said, we shall assume that a dollar subtracted from the community equals a dollar added to the community, unless specifically noted otherwise. Thus, if the government takes in as much as it pays out, then its net effect on the community's purchasing power is zero. If it takes in more than it pays out, it is subtracting (net) purchasing power from the community. If it pays out more than it takes in, it is adding (net) purchasing power to the community. In popular terminology, a balanced budget leaves the economy's purchasing power unchanged; a surplus reduces it, a deficit increases it.

The reader will note that we are speaking mainly in terms of the

federal government. It is true that any governmental level can be analyzed in terms of this framework. But for our policy purposes, there
are significant differences. For one thing, the credit rating of the federal government is such that it can always issue new bonds (or other
debt instruments), if it has a deficit. This is not true of the other
governmental units; there is a limit to the amount the market will
absorb. Furthermore, the federal government operates all over the
country and so can influence all sectors; this is obviously not true of
any other unit. Furthermore, the federal budget can be dovetailed with
the Reserve's monetary policy; this is obviously unrealistic when we
have fifty state budgets and thousands of municipal ones. And finally, a
high proportion of any local government unit's spending would spill
over to suppliers outside its borders, whereas most of the federal government's spending would accrue to sectors within the United States
economy; very little would be lost to foreign suppliers. Hence, the loss
of purchasing power to the spending unit would be exceedingly high
for any governmental unit other than the federal.

In aggregate, all these lesser governmental units spend billions, and
should be considered in a more detailed study. To some extent they are
implicitly included, for much of their spending is based on grants from
the federal government. Also, their spending tends to be less manage-
able in terms of variations to influence the economy. It is simply impossible to coordinate such a variety of units, particularly when they
have so many rigid items, such as debt service, education, and welfare.
In contrast, there is a much greater scope for change in the federal
government's budget, and so it can be manipulated more easily, although all such moves are subject to the legislative process. Since this
last qualification is a subject in itself, we shall ignore it, although this
does not mean that it is of lesser importance; anyone watching the
1963–64 tax-bill proceedings is well aware of this legislative factor.

The Cash Budget

In order to understand more clearly the economic impact of government activities, an explanation of the concept of the cash budget is
in order. We are interested here in the impact of receipts and expenditures. Hence, activities that do not affect these two items would be
better excluded from the analysis. Other items that might otherwise be
ignored, but which do affect these two flows, should be added. A
distinction must be drawn between the administrative budget (the one
voted on annually by Congress) and the cash budget, which makes the
necessary adjustments to this legislated budget, in order to arrive at the
one that is meaningful for our purposes. The difference between the
two can be explained by a few illustrative examples.

To holders of the so-called "baby bonds" interest accrues regularly. A provision is made for this charge in the annual budget. But the holders may not get the interest regularly, for it is paid only when the bond is cashed in. If *A* bought such a bond in 1943, he would accrue the interest in each year until 1953, when he decided to cash the bond at its maturity. Each year the budget would contain the accrued interest as a government expense. But the actual cash disbursement was in 1953, when all ten years' interest was paid to *A*, plus, of course, the capital value. The cash budget would therefore reduce the annual expenses for 1943 through 1952, increasing it in 1953 by the total interest payment. Here we have an illustration of an administrative expense exceeding the cash outlay in nine years, the latter being in excess in the tenth.

Perhaps the major adjustment involves Social Security funds. These are not budgeted for by Congress. The receipts vary with employment; if *A* works and is covered by Social Security, both *A* and his employer contribute to the fund. If more people work in covered employment, Social Security receipts rise; if employment declines, receipts fall off. Once the rates are set, inflow depends on employment, and no further taxation laws are necessary. But these assessments subtract purchasing power from the payers as would any other payments, and so they must be included in our analysis of inflows of purchasing power to the government. (True, the contributor may get funds back when he is out of work or reaches retirement age, but this is a separate operation.) Here, cash budgetary receipts exceed the administrative budget's receipts.

Outpayments reflect variations in unemployment and the growing number of retired persons. These payments, too, need not be provided for in specific expenditure legislation. The terms of payments are laid down; after that, the actual outflow of funds reflects the variations in these conditions. Hence, to the other streams of government spending must be added the various Social Security disbursements.

But even after we acknowledge the necessity for such adjustments, we have some knotty problems. For example, when does a government disbursement become a disbursement? Is it when the government contracts for some item, such as a ship? Is it when the money is being paid out by the shipyard? Is it when the shipyard is reimbursed by the government? Now, the actual additional spending occurs when the ship is being built. But the expectation of such a rise, which could also stimulate activity, is at contract time. And the recording of the expenditure on the government's books is when the bill is *actually* paid.

Let us take the problem of corporate income taxes. As profits are made, a tax liability is incurred. The actual money for the taxes may be set aside after the profits have been earned. And the payment to the government may be at still a later time. At what point does this tax flow to the government reduce purchasing power? When it is anticipated—at the time the tax liability was incurred? When the funds were isolated, to be held for eventual payment? Or when they are finally handed over to the tax collector? Will the anticipation of the tax affect the corporation's decisions? If so, at which of these three stages?

These timing problems are not merely technical quibbles. Much of the time lag between the various stages is a gap that can be calculated in advance. Hence, it can be taken into the corporation's plans, because of this definiteness. Yet, its length may be quite a few months. If the lag between contract and final payment is nine months, then a step-up in government spending will raise the actual cash flow to the economy three-quarters of a year later. The stimulus, if anticipated, will pick up activity well before it is actually experienced. Similar problems surround changes in the tax laws, especially where there is not the immediacy associated with the withholding device. A reduction in the corporate income tax may thus not actually change the cash remaining to the taxable unit until a year later, yet its expected benefit could stimulate corporate planning now. And then, if we add the time lag superimposed by the legislative process, we can really stretch out our analysis. The 1964 tax cut, first seriously proposed two years earlier, was reflected for many months before its actual enactment, and may have accounted for much of the improvement in business activity in 1962–63.

Built-in Stabilizers

Part of the government's economic impact is its variability as the level of business activity changes. Ideally, as the upswing becomes too great, withdrawals of purchasing power by the government should mount faster, thereby dampening the cycle sufficiently to remove any excess that threatens to spill over into inflation. In the downswing, the government should become a net contributor to purchasing power, thereby offsetting the declines in the private economy, and so stopping the recession. In practice, this shift of the government's influence could be through new legislation; in the boom, Congress could reduce outlays or step up tax levies, while in the recession it could step up expenditures and reduce tax rates. But this requires specific action and is subject to all the whims of the political process.

Alternatively, government spending and receipts could be so structured as to alter automatically in the desired direction. And in practice this has been achieved to quite a remarkable degree. We have not as yet reached the ideal; the rising government receipts in the boom cannot be counted on to remove enough excess demand to ward off inflation, nor can the increase in the government's contribution in the recession completely offset the loss of the private economy's purchasing power. But these swings in the private sector have been mitigated appreciably, and as the relative importance of the government in the total spending-receipts picture rises—as it has over the past three decades—this ability to implement the automatic stabilizers is correspondingly enhanced. Incidentally, the current trend toward tax reductions would reduce the impact of the built-in stabilizers.

Rather than analyze the entire government cash budget, we shall merely cite a few illustrations. Most notable are the Social Security programs and the personal income tax. As business activity rises and jobs increase, more people become subject to the Social Security tax, and so collections rise. Simultaneously, fewer people are unemployed, and so government outpayments decline. Net result: less purchasing power in the hands of the private economy. (The disposition of this money is discussed later in this chapter.) Furthermore, incomes are rising, and so the income tax take is increasing; as a consequence, the amount paid out as incomes is greater than the disposable purchasing power of the recipients by the amount subtracted for taxes. Once again we have curtailed purchasing power. Finally, the rise in incomes is raising spending and thus increasing tax revenues from the various excise charges on the purchase and sale of commodities. In brief, all along the line we are either removing purchasing power or reducing the disbursements of the government. However, we have not removed all the rise; what has been accomplishment is a diminution in the amount of the rise. The aforementioned taxes only take a percentage of the increase, so that there is still a substantial addition to purchasing power remaining in the economy.

On the way down the reverse of this operation gets into motion. As employment declines, there is less paid into the Social Security fund; as unemployment rises, more is paid out. As incomes decline, income-tax payments fall off. As activity declines, there is reduction in spending and so a decline in the amount collected from excise taxes. Once again we see a decline in the removal of purchasing power by the government and a rise in the outpayments. But, as before, the amount influenced is only a fraction of the aggregate decline in incomes. The declines in income paid out are greater than the declines in disposable income because of these various government flows, but there is still going to be a sizeable net decline in the economy's purchasing power, although not as great as would be if there were no such stabilizers to cushion the drop.

A simple illustration may show why these stabilizers are only partial contributors. If a man earns (net) $20,000, and his income rises by $1,000, his income-tax burden would rise some $300 to $400, depending on the state in which he lives and the numerous income-tax deductions he decides on. Net rise in disposable purchasing power is $600 to $700, or less than the income rise, but still a rise. If next year his income falls back by $1,000, his tax bill drops by $300 to $400, so that his purchasing power drops by only $600 to $700—again less of a drop than in income, but still a healthy proportionate decline.

But there is a feeling that these removals of purchasing power act too quickly in the American economy, especially in the upswing. As soon as there is even a mild boom—well before there is any fear of an inflationary explosion—the government becomes a net withdrawer, a net dampener. Hence, the recovery slows down well before we reach full employment. In fact, many observers feel that if the American economy were to operate at full employment, the cash budget would show quite a sizeable surplus, so much so that it would require a prodigious boom to offset this removal of purchasing power.

This depressing possibility shows up even more clearly if we think in terms of the longer run with its growth objectives. As our economy expands, average incomes rise because of the improvement in productivity per person, and also because of the tendency for prices to rise over any lengthy period. Incomes follow suit. If, for example, a hypothetical employee earned $4,000 ten years ago, the normal rise in real income because of production improvements might push his income to $5,000 today. But if, in addition, prices have risen by 15 per cent, he may have received offsetting cost-of-living raises of an equal proportion, so that his income would be $5,750, 44 per cent higher in money terms than ten years ago, though only 25 per cent more in purchasing power.

But our tax structure tends to be fairly rigid. Its various exemptions and rates continue for many years. Its progressive nature results in the proportionate income tax rising more rapidly than income itself. For example, very low-income groups may pay no tax. But as inflation raises their nominal income, they may move above the exemption limit and thus be liable for tax. Despite the fact that their real income is no greater, their tax liability now must be figured in, so that they are actually worse off. Further up the income line the same process occurs. Each inflationary rise boosts nominal income without altering real income. But the higher the nominal income, the more the proportionate tax bite. A low-income bracket may pay only 14 per cent, but as inflation raises this amount, the tax goes up to 16 per cent, 18 per cent, and so on. As a result, inflation raises the government's income-tax receipts more rapidly than the corresponding rise in real income. Theoretically, if all prices and incomes were to double, there would be no change in the community's real position. But the tax payments would more than double, so that after-tax purchasing power (in real terms) would actually be less. In brief, the progressive nature of our tax legislation makes it a deflationary influence in an inflationary economy because of this more rapid rise in the loss of purchasing power to the progressively rising rate structure.

This more rapid rise in government receipts, either in the boom or over the longer run, means that the depressing influence of this loss of purchasing power grows more and more as we improve our economic activity, and so the dampening effect gets even stronger. If the expansionary forces are not sufficiently strong to offset this, then the rising restraining actions of the government finally offset the economy's strength, and the boom ends. And it is felt that in the past few years this has been the case—that the boom was stopped before the full employment level—and thus the economy can never reach full employment because of this too rapidly operating, automatic stabilizing structure—the too rapid withdrawal of purchasing power well before we want its tightening to come into effect. Not only do we thereby reduce the cyclical upswing, but we also reduce the longer-run growth, as less than full employment generates a lower volume of savings and investment and thus a shrunken capital structure compared to what it might be. Expressed another way, our recessions are longer, our recoveries are weaker, and the longer-run average standard of living is below its potential. (It is this argument that was the justification for the 1964 tax reductions—to slow down the tax take as recovery began.)

Changes in Total Outstanding Debt

If the cash budget runs a surplus, the government is experiencing an excess of receipts over disbursements; if a deficit, the excess is in disbursements. The means by which this difference is bridged can also be used as an element to support fiscal-policy objectives.

SURPLUS. If there is a surplus, the government could use these funds either to maximize or minimize the intended deflationary effect. (Note that the achievement of an intended surplus is evidence that it wants some deflation.) The maximum would be if the funds were held idle at the Federal Reserve; receipt would drain the member banks of their reserves, thereby exercising a multiple restriction on the ability of the banks to hold assets and deposits. Not only is the surplus draining purchasing power from those who are paying funds into the Treasury, but, in addition, there is the multiplier deflation because of the drain on bank reserves and consequent reduction of deposits.

If the government did not want this multiplier element, then it could simply hold the funds idle in its member-bank deposit accounts. The payments would reduce the public's (active) deposits and raise the government's (inactive) deposits, so that the volume of deposits would be as before, but the average velocity would be lower.

A third, still less restrictive effect would return the funds to the economy through the repayment of some of the outstanding debt. We have here four possibilities: repayment of Federal Reserve holdings, member-bank holdings, other financial intermediaries, or the public. Each has differing effects on economic activity.

It should be remarked that the government cannot proceed as this last paragraph implies. It cannot say arbitrarily that only those bonds held by such-and-such a group will be paid off. Rather, it tends to concentrate on the redemption of the issues held by the group it prefers. For example, we have seen that Treasury bills tend to be held by banks, long-term bonds by insurance companies and pension funds, intermediate notes by still others, and so on. Moreover, if the Reserve was the one to be paid off, it could engage in open-market operations, buying a specific issue—to be redeemed later—and selling others not marked for redemption. Such switches in the Reserve's portfolio would not alter reserves, but would concentrate Reserve holdings. Then the Treasury would redeem that particular issue. If it wished to pay off mainly the commercial banks, it could redeem bills. If it was the nonfinancial intermediaries, then it would call in longer-term bonds. While each of these may also be held by other sectors, it would be the bulk of the holders that would determine which issue were called.

In preparation for redemption of any of these, the Treasury would first transfer the funds to its Reserve account. This tends to drain member banks of reserves, of course. If it is a Reserve-held issue that is redeemed, then we get a reduction in Reserve liabilities, as the Treasury deposits are cancelled against Reserve securities, and thus a freeing of the gold-certificate requirement (by one-fourth the cancelled deposits). This last freeing of required reserves is usually of little significance, since the Reserve normally has more than enough in required reserves. But the net effect, as can be seen, is virtually as restrictive as the Treasury holding the funds idle at the Reserve. Either way, we reduce member-bank reserves and, of course, the deposit multiple.

If it is commercial-bank securities that are redeemed, then we get a replenishment of reserves offsetting the loss when the Treasury transferred the funds to the Reserve. The net effect is therefore a reduction of aggregate deposits outstanding—the funds paid into the Treasury—and a freeing of required reserves against these deposits, plus the loss of the bonds that were redeemed. The only decline in purchasing power is the amount cancelled against the bonds. But in so doing, reserves were released, and the banking system can now make more loans and acquire other assets—create more deposits—and so offset the original decline in deposits. In summary, such redemption may at most only reduce the total money supply by the amount of the redemption, and it is possible that ultimately there would be no change in deposits; the decline in government bonds held by the banks being replaced by a rise in their holdings of other assets. Note that the active deposits paid over to the Treasury disappear when the bonds are redeemed, but that new active deposits are created if the banks then use the released reserves to acquire other assets. Note further that there would be some downward impact on yields as the banks tried to put their newly released reserves to work.

Finally, suppose the remainder of the economy receives the funds in payment for the redeemed bonds. The Treasury draws a check on its Reserve account and pays off the holder, who then presumably—initially—deposits the check with his bank, thereby swelling its deposits and reserves. Thus, the reserves lost when the funds were transferred by the Treasury to the Reserve are now replenished. The deposit decline caused by the payments to the Treasury are now offset by the inflow of deposits from those whose bonds were redeemed. The net effect on banks is nil; there is the same volume of deposits outstanding, although the ownership is somewhat different. The taxpayers have less in deposits; the bondholders now have more.

However, the public's holding of securities has decreased. Hence, the question then arises regarding their reactions. If they are liquidity-conscious, they may simply hold on to these funds. In that case the active deposits of the taxpayers have been replaced by inactive deposits. Alternatively, if the public wants to continue holding income-earning securities, it would now relend these funds, and so the deposits would once again be active. What has happened in the longer run is a decline in the public's holding of government bonds and a rise in its ownership of other debt. (Note that this logic applies whether the public in question were a financial intermediary other than a commercial bank, or simply an individual investor.) And, perhaps, as these funds are reloaned to the private sector, there is a decline in yields as a result of the pressure of this new supply, in which there would be further adjustments to reflect this shift.

If we were to pursue these alternatives in detail, we would also have to discriminate between demand and time deposits. For example, taxpayers may elect to pay their taxes by holding less in time deposits, while the released reserves might then be used to expand demand deposits. Or the funds might come out of demand deposits, so that the same amount of taxes would release a greater volume of reserves. All of these possible further complications would have to be taken ito consideration in any detailed study of the debt impact. But in view of the numerous ramifications these more detailed points would bring up, we have had to limit our comment to these few remarks.

DEFICIT. Our analysis of the possible sources of financing the deficit will be brief, since to a large extent it would be opposite to the analysis concerning the surplus. However, some points merit special attention. For example, the maximum expansionary effect—presumably the objective when we have a deficit—is to add to both money supply and bank reserves, thereby allowing for a multiple expansion in loans and deposits. To accomplish this, the Treasury could draw on any previous excess balances it might have had at the Federal Reserve, the outpayments flowing to the member banks and so transferring the deposit liability owed by the Reserve from the Treasury to the banks as increases in their balances. Alternatively, if the Reserve would purchase government bonds, it would also add to member-bank reserves. While it is restricted from subscribing directly, it could buy an amount in the open market equal to that being newly issued by the Treasury. This way it would feed into the economy the same amount being withdrawn by the public offering of the new debt.

A less expansionary influence would arise if the Treasury had balances at the commercial banks that had not been used. By paying these out, it transfers idle money to active deposits, though leaving the money supply unchanged. In our previous case we had also added to the total money supply, especially if the multiplying possibilities were realized.

The Treasury could also hope to have the commercial banks purchase the new issue. This would raise demand deposits, and so would require excess reserves being present to be used as the required backing. Otherwise, the banks would have to offset this rise in liabilities by a reduction elsewhere, so that the total deposit volume would be the same—that is, less going to the private sector, more to the government. Here the expansionary influences arising from the government deficit would be countered by the loss of funds no longer available to the other sectors. Whether one or the other was a more potent influence for business would depend on the many uncertainties surrounding such changes in the flows. Of course, if we did not wish to hinder private borrowers, and if reserves were inadequate, the Reserve could always relieve the situation through open-market purchases.

The minimum expansionary effect would occur if the issues were to other than the banking community. Here purchasing power would be given up by the subscriber and spent by the government. The money supply would be unchanged, but the velocity impact would depend on the relative activity of the two sectors. Presumably, in a recession the public investor's funds would be less active, so that its transfer to the government would probably result in some net rise in turnover. In addition, it is possible that these funds would otherwise have been (*a*) held idle or (*b*) lent to other borrowers. In the first possibility we not only get the rise in velocity as these idle funds become active, but also the investor now has more assets in nonliquid form. Will he reduce his other holdings to reestablish some desired liquidity? Will he reduce savings so that his accumulation of assets slows down, to offset the rise in government bond holdings? Obviously, we cannot answer these questions, yet these do raise important questions about the effects of such a government issue on the spending pattern of the investor. Similar questions could be raised with regard to the alternative possibility—if the funds lent to the government would have gone otherwise to a private borrower. The investor now has more in high-grade (government) assets, less in riskier (private) securities. Will he now react to reestablish some set distribution of risks among the assets in his portfolio? Will the thwarted borrower reduce his borrowings? Will he offer the market a higher interest rate to attract other sources of funds? Will this alter relative yields within the bond-market structure? As can be seen, any detailed pursuing of the implications would get us into an endless series of further inquiries, and so once again we must stop, having limited our discussion to the hints along which paths for further investigations would have to be conducted.

We have not differentiated very much between the individual public investor and the nonfinancial intermediary. Yet each has his own pattern of reactions. The latter may have to maintain a mix of securities, so that the addition of a new government issue could call for some of the adjustments we hinted at in the previous paragraphs. The individual, in contrast, may simply be buying another security, and may not have to worry about any particular constellation of types, yields, and risks. Hence, for him the new government bond may simply be a new opportunity, whereas for the institutional investor it is a change in the pattern of opportunities, altering the relative importance of government to other offerings. Since, in all probability, the bulk of the subscribers will be institutions, we can assume that the numerous adjustments that would arise from this altered composition of available assets will give rise to a whole series of changes in the relationships prevailing in the market. And just to add still further problems, if this does alter yield patterns, will it change the liquidity schedule? Savings plans? Risk spreads among securities? So complications increase.

Fiscal Influences on Investment

While the government can influence aggregate incomes and, through its taxation and spending, alter the distribution from what it would otherwise have been, it has a special influence on the savings-investment process. Most obviously, the level of the income tax affects the take-home pay, which, in turn, will affect the disposition of this amount between consumption and savings. Presumably, the less the tax, the greater will be the disposable remainder, and so the greater will be savings; but it will tend to rise more, proportionately, because of the diminishing marginal propensity to consume. Furthermore, the greater the absolute amount spent on consumption, the greater the volume of sales and thus output, and so the greater the demand for funds for capital outlays.

If, however, we assume that a dollar spent through the government has the same value as a dollar spent by the private sector—although the specific recipient may differ—then the sales volume will be the same, and so the incentive to invest. However, it is possible that the changed distribution in incomes, from taxpayer to government beneficiary, may alter average income levels, and so savings. Transfer from a high-income taxpayer to a lower-income recipient may reduce savings and increase consumption, and vice versa, if the shift is to a higher-bracket receiver.

But depending on the way they are levied, the tax rates themselves may affect savings. For example, suppose there is (a) a straight income tax of 10 per cent, or (b) a graduated rate, starting at zero for the first $2,000 and rising in 4-per-cent jumps for each additional $2,000. For a $12,000 income, the tax by either calculation will come to $1,200. Now, suppose further that this individual has an opportunity to earn $2,000 more income through additional work. Under plan (a), the extra income will net him $1,800 after taxes; under plan (b), because of the rising marginal rate, he will net only $1,520. This lower amount may not be worth the added effort and loss of leisure, whereas the former might. This differential becomes most evident when we get into the really higher brackets, such as occur in the United States income-tax structure. Note that for the $12,000 income in our illustration, the government revenue is the same under either method, but one is more discouraging. Hence, the lower this marginal rate, the more incentive to produce, the greater the volume of output, or the greater the willingness to risk a new investment, since the corresponding prospect of gain is greater. Under too graduated a tax structure, we penalize this willingness to risk more for a higher profit, since the tax mounts so sharply, biting into marginally additional income.

By various tax allowances or penalties we can thus encourage or discourage savings and investment. A high depletion allowance, which thus reduces taxable income, is an incentive to invest in petroleum rather than textiles, where no such bonus is present. If we wish to encourage the former, we have succeeded; if the latter, we have failed. An excise tax, by raising costs and selling prices, reduces sales, output, and so investment capacity. If we wish to discourage investment, an excise tax helps in that direction; if we wish to encourage investment, we would minimize such levies.

If savings are too low, we should keep income taxes on the high brackets low, for the higher the take-home, the more will be saved. Taxes on consumption purchases, by raising prices, will reduce consumption spending, and perhaps some people will thereby save rather than pay the higher price. This would probably be more true of luxuries that involve large amounts—motor boats, expensive automobiles, and the like.

Rather than go into the myriad details that can serve to influence these income components, we can generalize by saying that different tax structures can alter the volume of investment and distribution of income. Changes in investment levels, in turn, will alter the longer-run stock of capital equipment in the country. Changes in this stock thus alter the country's long-run productive ability. And this change, in turn, will vary the long-run income and output, and thus the long-run standard of living. As can be seen, the tax structure thus has both immediate and far-reaching repercussions. Again, many details and ramifications are beyond the scope of this text, but the reader should keep them in mind in assessing any specific fiscal policy.

Summary

The government, through its fund-raising and disbursing activities, can also influence the economy and so reinforce monetary policy. As a collector of money, it withdraws purchasing power from the public, and then, through its various spending functions, these funds are returned. Differences between these two flows thus alter net purchasing power. These activities also alter the distribution of ownership of purchasing power, which in turn can change spending, saving, and investment levels. In the analysis, however, we must correct the stated budgetary data for non-cash items, and estimate the effects of the timing differences between the *intention* to raise or spend money and the subsequent *action*.

To a certain extent, the government acts automatically to brake the swings in the business cycle. On the way up, tax receipts rise and some (Social Security) spending drops. The rise in income is thus muted somewhat in the resulting impact on additional spending power. Conversely, in the downturn, take-home tends to drop less than total income because of the more rapid decline in tax payments and the rise in Social Security spending. However, there is a feeling that these automatic stabilizers act too quickly in the upswing, and so the 1964 tax reductions were designed to reduce this force.

Through varying the source of new debt money or the redemption of maturing issues, the government also is an influence. Not only is it reshuffling purchasing power, but it can also, through proper direction, affect member-bank reserves and the community's total liquidity, and thus perhaps alter the total money supply and velocity in the desired direction. It must, however, be watchful that it does not overstep the mark and, in particular, not discourage incentives at the wrong time.

Chapter 23

THE INFLATION PROBLEM

Virtually all modern governments are committed to a policy of full employment. This does not mean that at all times everyone seeking a job must have one. But it does indicate a goal toward which economic measures and their implementation should be striving. While the precise level that constitutes full employment is a matter of some dispute, the intention, nevertheless, is quite clear; certainly the widespread unemployment of the 1930's would no longer be acceptable. Yet, as we also shall see, there may be an inherent contradiction between this full-employment hope and another often implicit objective—namely, monetary stability, or, more usually, price stability. In summary form, what the present-day American economy faces is the conflict between full employment and inflation. Are the two objectives compatible?

The Objectives

The desire for reasonably full employment needs almost no explanation. A person without a job must depend on some form of charity to meet his need for food and shelter. Often this is inadequate for a decent standard of living. Furthermore, if he has any skills, the lack of a job means lack of continued use, and so a gradual loss of his ability to perform at a higher-paying occupation. Society thus loses through the consequent downgrading of his productivity. Income deterioration forces cutbacks on spending for his family, thereby reducing their well-being and often their ability and desire to obtain an education. Their future productivity is lowered, and so the general worsening of productivity is perpetuated.

Some qualifications are necessary here. Some unemployment is inevitable—even desirable—in a dynamic society. Old products decline in appeal, such as buggy whips, while new ones rise that can better satisfy the economy's wants. People must move from industries of the former to those of the latter in order to meet these shifting tastes, and in the process of change some unemployment will arise. Unsuccessful firms, even in growing industries, could still fail, and once again, through unemployment, we transfer the resources from the less competent to the more successful. People get dissatisfied with their present employment and seek new work; again the transition spells unemployment. And finally, since as yet we have not eliminated the ups and downs of the business cycle completely, there will be variations in aggregate output and thus in aggregate employment. It is within these dynamic confines that the full-employment objective is pursued—to minimize these disturbances without halting the dynamic processes.

The opposition to inflation, however, is less obvious, and indeed, as we shall see, there is a significant minority of economists who even favor it within a limited degree. It may be worthwhile to spell out in more detail the pros and cons in this continuing argument.

The orthodox opposition to inflation—here to be understood as a general rise in prices at both the wholesale and retail level—comes in part from the impact on the fixed-income groups. Their expenses are rising, their receipts are fixed, and so inflation means a decline in their real standard of living. Usually these are the aged and retired people, who can no longer raise their income. Inflation thus dooms them to an ever-declining prospect with no hope of an alternative, the fruits of a lifetime's work being slowly dissipated.

Furthermore, inflation distorts economic activity. As prices rise, producers gain a windfall, since they see selling prices rising faster than costs. Profit margins widen, and so the incentive to expand increases. But the impetus from inflation is uneven; it benefits those groups whose costs are relatively most rigid. For example, suppose we have two competitors selling virtually identical products at the same price. One is very efficient, so that his costs are 90 per cent of selling price, and his profit margin is 10 per cent. The other is inefficient, and is heavily in debt; he has the 90-per-cent costs that the first one has, plus 3 per cent extra cost for inefficiency, plus 3 per cent interest charges on his debt; his profit margin is 4 per cent. Suppose prices now rise by 5 per cent, and the basic (90 per cent) costs move to 94 per cent. Our efficient producer now has an 11-per-cent profit margin, or one-tenth more. Our inefficient producer has 94 plus 3 plus 3, or 100 in costs, raising his profit to 5 per cent, or one-fourth more. While the inefficient producer still has a smaller profit than his more efficient competitor, relatively it has improved much more. He has thus a greater incentive to expand, and so resources flow to the inefficient sector.

Another distortion arises from speculation in anticipation of price rises. If we expect inflation, we wish to buy now (before prices rise) and sell later (after prices rise). As more and more buy now, we push up prices and thus bring into reality the expected price rise. The mere expectation of inflation can thus create real inflation; it is very likely that without the action on this expectation, there would not have been this price rise—if the expectation had been erroneous. But thanks to this speculative force, the price rise is created even if otherwise there would not have been this change. Hence, resources are diverted to such speculative activities, away from more productive channels.

Mention was made earlier of the possibility of inventory hoarding financed through bank loans. M rises, but the marketable supply does not, being put into storage instead. Such a possibility is heightened in times of inflation, for there is a feeling of virtual certainty that the passage of time will boost prices and so make such an operation profitable. Furthermore, if on a large enough scale, the rise in M (as a result of the financing) contributes to the added demand that pushes up P and so produces the expected outcome. To combat this tendency, the Federal Reserve must apply a tight-money policy, and often within a relatively short time it can see success. By restraining the banks, it dampens down the rise in the money supply, thus cutting off the extra purchasing power that might fuel the inflation. And, as time goes on, the interest cost on the borrowed funds puts more and more pressure on the speculator to sell out and thus cut his loss. Once he is convinced that the price rise is illusory, he then unloads his warehouses, adding to the marketable supply, pressing down prices, and so inducing still other hoarders to unload. Now the Reserve can ease up, for there is this additional supply to offset any rise in demand as a result of the resumption of bank lending. In capsule version, we have summarized much of the inventory developments that followed the outbreak of hostilities in Korea in June of 1950. At first there was inventory hoarding through bank borrowing, but later the Reserve applied enough pressure to end this movement, and early in 1951 the bubble burst.

An additional objection involves the international sector. If there is inflation in the United States and it threatens to get out of hand, so that foreigners with funds invested here fear that we may run into financial difficulties—specifically, an adverse balance of payments— then they may sell their holdings for dollars, convert the dollars into gold, and thus strip us of our reserves.

A more involved consideration concerns the effects on our capital structure. If a company purchases a capital good, it is expected to wear out over a period of time. To replace this loss of value, it sets aside as a deduction from income a depreciation allowance; this latter builds up in value as the machine is declining in usefulness, so that the combination of the two tend to maintain a stable value. Most companies tend to set aside the same amount regularly, usually arrived at by dividing the cost by the expected life. Thus, a $10,000 machine with an expected life of ten years would result in an annual depreciation charge of $1,000, so that after ten years the machine would probably have a zero value, but the depreciation reserve would now contain $10,000.

But with inflation, the end of this cycle would see such a machine selling for more than $10,000—perhaps twice as much. Hence, although the dollar value of the firm's assets remained the same, the real value of the depreciation reserve had declined, for now it would have to get an additional $10,000 to replace the worn-out equipment with its equivalent. Inflation thus results in a decline in the real value of the company's capital, because of the reduced impact of depreciation. What the company should have done was set aside an average of $2,000 annually—thereby reducing profits in the process—and then it would have the necessary funds for the replacement purchase. Instead, with the lower depreciation charge, profits were at a higher level, thus misleading the management, for they had not realized that the machine, in real terms, was declining in value faster than the depreciation fund was rising.

Critics contend that this is an exaggeration. Management, in a time of inflation, is fully aware of this problem, and so in addition to the depreciation allowance it sets aside an extra to offset this price rise. However, there is a tax aspect to this. Depreciation reduces stated profits and therefore reduces the tax liability. This extra that is set aside is not allowable as an expense, and so profits for tax purposes are not reduced and taxes are not affected. If this extra were allowable, then the added expense of this fund would be partly offset by a savings on taxes. The ramifications of this controversy would get us into some rather involved accounting and tax theory, and so, as we have done in other contexts, we shall stop after this simple presentation of the problem. However, this stopping short is in no way intended to minimize the seriousness of the issue, since, if there is a deterioration in our capital stock as a result of inflation, there is a deterioration of our long-run production potential, and thus a further hindrance to growth in our standard of living.

Another aspect of this capital problem concerns the "mix" effect. If more funds are diverted to speculating in commodities, in order to make the expected profits after prices rise, we have less available for fixed capital. Expressed another way, the economy has more invested in inventories—goods being held for the expected price rise—and less converted into machinery. The copper that could become part of our electrical equipment and so add to electricity output is now simply copper resting idly in a warehouse as its owner waits for the market price of copper to rise. In effect, if we rephrase this in liquidity terms, people have moved out of cash into goods; the latter has a higher liquidity than money, because it is felt that whenever the owner wishes to dispose of the commodity, he will get at least what he paid for it, probably more, whereas with money he gets no less, but no more either. Anticipating inflation means that he feels fairly certain that his goods will yield more in money *terms* than if he had held his assets in money *form*.

The Case for Inflation

As can be deduced from these various objections, a redistribution of income as a result of inflation results. Those with fixed incomes find a decline in real purchasing power. Those who owe fixed amounts find profits rising faster, so that more is left over after paying these fixed charges; their real income rises. (Recall our previous example of the inefficient producer: a 5-per-cent price rise increased his profits by one-quarter.) Speculators make more as prices rise, but the buyers of these commodities now face an increased cost. If they can pass on this cost rise, then their customers are the ones who bear the burden of the inflation. This may touch off an effort on the part of these people to raise their own incomes, to offset the price rise. Specifically, this means an attempt to raise wages. But if this succeeds, then costs rise still more, and so there is an inducement to put up prices again. And thus the cycle begins all over again. In short, once inflation gets under way, it becomes cumulative and is difficult to halt.

But inflation is not all bad. For one thing, the gradual rise in prices widens profits margins and so induces business to expand output and capacity. We thus get a step-up in the demand for goods and services, and it may be that only in this way would aggregate demand be sufficient to employ all our facilities. This constant stimulus also creates a need for more and more capacity, so that our long-run productive abilities are enhanced. In effect, we are transferring resources from consumption to capital formation, consumption being held back by rising prices. (Later we shall amplify this in our discussion of "forced savings.") A little inflation is therefore preferable to the alternative of a recession and underemployment of resources. The inflation merely redistributes the shares of total output; the recession is an actual loss of potential output.

Inflation also reduces the deadweight of the past. Business and individuals are constantly going into debt to expand their activities. Combined with compound interest, this debt can grow at amazing speeds. For example, if in 1800 an individual had lent $1,000 at 6 per cent, and if he had reinvested the interest at the same rate, his assets would now amount to more than $12 million! Hence, evolution of an economy tends to place an increasing burden on the productive facilities, as this rigid element of debt repayment and servicing (interest) mounts. If output and incomes should decline temporarily, we have this fixed obligation to pay out of a shrunken income, which means that the amount available for the remaining participants drops that much more. If 20 per cent of income goes for debt servicing, a 20-per-cent decline in income causes the remaining shares to drop by 25 per cent. But if inflation is constantly raising profit margins—reducing the real value of this debt—then we need not fear such pressures. The rising-income trend will make it that much easier to take on this burden.

Many people are so placed that they can offset inflation easily. Most workers who belong to well-organized unions can usually obtain wage increases to offset the price rise; their relative position is thus maintained. And since they are in the lower-income groups, they are more likely to be debtors than creditors; they owe either on their home or car or on other durables. As their wages rise, these payments form a smaller proportion of income, since they are fixed obligations, and so the share of income available for other uses rises. Their real standard of living may thus actually improve at the expense of those to whom these sums have been owed. There is a small offset to this gain, however. To obtain the increase in wages, they may have to strike; and during such periods, since they are out of work, their income is down. Hence, the cost of maintaining their position may entail some loss of output and income, for both the workers and the economy as a whole. Our logic is also modified as we go up in the income pyramid. The higher the income, the more likely will the earner have fixed assets, such as bank deposits and insurance, which are falling in real value. The middle executive class would be an illustration of the losers in this race.

Will inflation reduce the incentive to save? Why save if the money set aside will constantly decline in purchasing power? Or will the reaction be, "My money income is up, so I can afford to save more"? It is therefore possible for savings to react in any number of ways; so far in the United States it seems that savers' motives have not been influenced by these price-level shifts.

The Full-Employment Dilemma

What complicate the attainment of a full-employment economy are the contradictions it creates. For full employment to be attained, demand must be high, so high that capacity operations are approached and practically all the available labor is at work. But if such is the case, then we have two unwanted—or at least complex—by-products. Labor can now press for higher wages with greater assurance, since the high level of demand will make employers reluctant to allow a strike that would interrupt production and profits. Any resulting cost increase can be passed on easily through higher prices, since, with so high a demand, there will be little loss of sales resulting. Indeed, if this wage increase is widespread, then as prices rise to offset the increased wage costs, incomes go up as these higher wages are reflected in increased take-home pay. The latter, in turn, enables the consumer to pay the now higher price for his purchases. It is also possible for prices to rise even in the absence of a wage boost, since the strong demand will permit such action, with a resulting enhancement of profit margins. It would seem as though a full-employment policy has built inflation into the economy.

Suppose the Federal Reserve tried to hold the price line. To do so, it must stem an expansion in spending—MV must be a constant, since T is already the maximum attainable and since we do not want P to rise. But the cost and price actions are raising P. If we do not let spending rise—for the price rise means that the volume of sales now has a higher value (a higher P times the same T)—then T must drop to offset the rise in P. This means a decline in output and a cutback in operations. Employment would also be down. But then we would no longer have full employment. To stop inflation, we must give up this other objective. But to keep employment full, which means to keep T at its previous level, we must allow MV to rise to match the higher PT—actually, the higher P, which then raises PT.

We can look at this force from the individual company's point of view. Assume that it has been borrowing to pay for its wages and raw materials, the subsequent additional output then furnishing the funds to repay the loan. Now it must pay higher wages; its cost of production is higher. It must borrow a greater amount of money for the same volume of output. It therefore asks the bank for a larger loan. If this is granted, then the deposits created are greater now than before the wage rise. Before, it may have borrowed $10,000—adding that much to deposits—and then after the output is sold, the deposits are destroyed. With the increased wage bill, perhaps $11,000 must be borrowed— $1,000 more in deposits than if there had not been the wage rise—and so spending rises by the velocity of this addition during the period until the loan is repaid. In this way—if this reaction is typical of the economy—we expand M and thus provide the means for paying the higher PT. On the other hand, if the Reserve keeps a tight rein on bank reserves, so that the loan can be no more than before—only $10,000—then the firm cannot finance as large a volume of production. One offset is to produce only nine-tenths as much, the 10-per-cent drop[1] in volume offsetting the 10-per-cent rise in costs; this is our employment-decline alternative. The other is to try to operate with smaller cash balances through better funds management—to speed up V—and once again we sustain the inflation, the rise in V supporting the higher P. In this latter possibility the Reserve would then have to take steps to cut M, as an offset to the increased V. But to adopt so restrictive a policy—which again would produce the undesired decline in employment—might incur the wrath of both Congress and the public. And so the Reserve must choose, realizing that either way it has an unpleasant outcome—either too little employment or too much inflation.

Our inflationary illustration in this section has so far been a "cost push" example. But there can also be a "demand pull," if bank loans are expanded too rapidly, raising MV faster than output can rise. This, too, can occur. Suppose bank A is asked by borrower A for a loan to buy materials wanted for further production. This is a perfectly legitimate loan—supply will rise to balance the added money supply—so A gets the money. But at the same time, unknown to bank A and borrower A, bank B has been asked by borrower B for a similar loan for a similar purpose—to buy these same raw materials. Both, in other words, need these raw materials for their output, but there is only a limited quantity available. Both get the loan, both bid for these items, and so the pressure of demand forces up the price. Each may now buy only a part of the supply, costing more than anticipated; each thus turns out less in quantity, but at a higher cost. And so their selling prices must be higher to reflect this factor. Both banks have expanded the money supply, thus furnishing the means to make the demand

---

[1] More precisely, 9.1 per cent.

excessive and the price of the raw materials higher, as well as the wherewithal to purchase at this exorbitant price. Only if someone could check on both transactions could we have avoided this excessive expansion in loans and thus the resulting excess of demand. Such cases would be multiplied at full employment, when demand could outrun the ability of full-capacity operations to add to supply.

The problem is further complicated by many rigidities that have come to characterize the American economy. Corporations have been obtaining an increased ability to fix prices; the decline in price competition associated with oligopoly has reduced the probability that excess supply will be followed by price reductions, and has increased the likelihood that output will be cut back. Furthermore, prices are often set somewhat below what the demand would accept, so that in some form an unsatisfied demand at the going price is present—a waiting list, so to speak. With this type of pressure, any cost increase can then be passed on through higher prices, since sales would not drop off. Rather the size of the waiting list would shrink, some buyers dropping out because of the increased price, although not enough to cause unsold goods. As a consequence, any cost increase can then be used as the justification for a rise in prices; the corporation does not have to appear as a profiteer, but simply the victim of a labor or raw-materials squeeze.

Labor, too, has its rigidities. The tendency has been for the lower levels of manual workers to press for a narrowing of differentials. If they succeed, then the more skilled workers try to reestablish the differential. Wages bounce up—not because of increased productivity, but simply because the demand for the unskilled enables them to narrow these spreads, the demand for the skilled enables them to widen them. The wage structure drifts up over a period of time faster than per-capita productivity, so that wage costs per unit of output are made to climb faster, and thus another boost is given to prices. Or the oligopoly has an excuse for boosting prices.

Growth and Inflation

We have already indicated that inflation, by widening profit margins, gives an extra incentive to expand capacity, to increase the capital structure of the economy. In this way, the long-run productive potential is raised. But we have seen that such growth could be distorted if funds flow to the less efficient, whose profit margins tend to expand proportionately more quickly, or if there is a stimulus to the strictly speculative actions. Hence, many advocates of more rapid growth—whether in a country as developed as the United States or among the poorer peoples of the world who are anxious to raise living standards quickly—have advocated inflationary policies as a means of forcing growth, hoping that administrative measures could also be implemented to minimize the unwanted side effects. The achievement of such a goal therefore depends, in part, on the effectiveness of the controls that curb the less desirable repercussions.

The increase in capital formation arises from several forces. One is the rise in profit margins, and so an increase in profits flowing to business firms. Since these tend to save a higher proportion of such income than if profits had been lower and more was paid to workers, we get, through this shift, a rise in the community's propensity to save. Similar shifts occur if higher profits result in increased dividends, since the bulk of such payments go to the upper-income, higher-savings individuals. In addition, widened profit margins increase the incentive to borrow, and so the resulting ability to pay higher interest rates may entice more funds from the liquidity-conscious groups. Combined, we get a sharp increase in the demand for capital equipment.

With this rise in demand, the capital-goods producers can now afford to bid for any factors of production they need in order to expand output and thus come through with increased sales. They can thus bid away resources from other sectors, if the economy is fully employed, or attract unemployed resources, if present, diverting them from the other bidders. Here we get an increase in the importance, within total output, of this capital-goods component. This, of course, is simply a reflection of the changed flow of funds. On the money side, as we have seen, we have increased savings and loanable funds. On the demand side, an increase in capital-goods production now results. Our economy has shifted on both the funds-flows view and the real (output) form toward more capital goods. Correspondingly, the proportion going to the consumers'-goods sector (the proportion spent on consumption or the relative output of consumers' goods) has declined. The upward shift in the economy's propensity to save—the downward shift in the propensity to consume—is thus matched by the accompanying rise in real investment, proportionately (decline in consumption in proportionate terms). We use the modifying term *proportionate* since, if sufficient unemployed resources are present, both consumption and capital-goods production would rise, but the latter would rise more.

The income shifts towards the high savers mean relative shifts from the high-consumption-function groups. These latter are forced to reduce their purchases as prices outrun incomes. By compelling them to consume less, we thereby release resources that enable the economy to step up investment. Viewed in its aggregate form, inflation has forced the reduction in consumption (by the lower-saving components) and raised savings and investment. In a sense, therefore, inflation has forced the community to save more than it otherwise would have; hence, the concept of "forced savings." This concept also helps to explain how a new equilibrium may emerge even in an inflationary situation.

Equilibrium in Inflation

At first glance it would seem that inflation is not only a disequilibrium manifestation, but that it must continue in such imbalance. Each price rise calls forth a demand for higher wages. As costs go up, incomes go up. The price rise, if it is able to keep ahead of costs, raises profits and therefore the income of proprietors. Either way, we find inflating incomes, which then enable the recipients to buy at higher prices. Or if demand exceeds supply and so sets off a price rise, the resulting increased cost of this supply is matched by a rise in demand as incomes respond, and so we still have excess demand, although the monetary value of both supply and demand has risen. It would seem that such a process would lead to an unending spiral upwards. This could happen, of course, and the next section, hyperinflation, discusses such an outcome. But the spiral is not inevitable. If forced savings are sufficiently large, they could break the chain of reactions and so produce a new stability, but at a higher price level.

The major source of this possible stabilizing influence is the rise in the share of incomes accruing to the high savers. This, as we have already seen, is lowering the aggregate consumption. At the same time, it is stepping up the demand for capital goods. If the latter increase is less than the decrease in the former area, we have a net decline in demand. The drop in demand for factors of production to produce the consumers' goods is greater than the rise in demand for factors to produce the additional capital goods now being sought. We have reduced the pressure on the productive factors as a result of inflation and the accompanying income shift. Before, there had been excess demand; the productive factors could not meet the demand. Now we have reduced this demand, and if it is down by enough, we no longer have an upward pressure.

This would show up through the price rises for consumers' goods reducing demand by the high-consumption function groups. This must be sharp enough not only to eliminate the excess demand that started our inflation, but also by enough to release capacity to satisfy the now increased demand for capital goods. For example, if the demand for cars exceeds available capacity, prices could be raised and demand would decline. We could reduce demand back to existing capacity to supply. Meanwhile, investment in trucks may have risen, and so some of the car capacity must now turn out these additional trucks. Hence, the auto-demand decline must be that much greater, to release enough car capacity to be shifted to this added truck production. The inflation must therefore be greater in order to reduce consumer demand that much more; had the rise in investment been absent, we would not have had to reduce demand for consumers' goods so much, since more capacity would be available for their output. Consequently, the inflation would not have to be as intense.

A minor consideration that might enforce the trends discussed arises from the effect on real standards of living. As prices rise, a given income buys less. In real terms, the individual is poorer. Being poorer, he would cut savings more (proportionately) than he would reduce consumption. Hence, if those groups who are lagging in the inflation cycle—those whose incomes rise more slowly than prices—are also savers to any significant degree, they could offset the effect of rising prices to some extent by reducing savings, thus sustaining consumption. That is, in monetary terms they raise the proportion of income going to consumption. They now spend a greater number of dollars on consumers' goods. These goods have risen in price, so that the same volume of goods requires more dollars. If there is enough leeway through the savings shift, the number of dollars freed for consumption might equal the added number of dollars that their purchases now require, and so they need not reduce the real volume of their consumption. Or if savings are not quite that much, they can at least cushion the impact. We thus get less of a reduction in consumption, less of a decline in demand, and more of a drop in savings (in loanable funds). This could mean a shift from less active (savings) to more active (spending) flows, or a rise in velocity. And so the rise in V pushes up P even more.

Hyperinflation

We can now see how narrow the difference is between an emergence of a new equilibrium from inflation or the alternative of a cumulatively reinforcing spiral. Each price rise steps up profits and therefore the demand for capital goods. Then workers and suppliers try to restore their position by getting higher wages or prices, thus boosting their incomes and thus their monetary demand. If the forced-savings effect is weak—if there is enough slack in savings to sustain demand for consumers' goods on the part of those lagging in the inflation cycle—then the decline in demand is much less than the rise in demand for capital goods. We do not free enough productive factors to meet this new pattern, and so the demand for both consumers' and capital goods exceeds the ability to produce. And so both sectors can raise prices, thereby enabling them to bid up the price they must pay for the productive factors, and each, through such bidding, minimizes the shift of factors to the other sector. Each such bid raises incomes and thus sustains demand; each rise in demand allows a further hike in prices and an increased ability to bid for the productive factors. Any restraint, as already remarked, only provokes unemployment, presumably a greater evil.

Meanwhile, the rising cost of production is compelling businessmen to borrow more to finance the rising costs, so M increases. Less funds are now held idle, as people see commodities as a better liquidity hedge. Savers in the lower brackets save less—reduce their inactive funds—and so velocity speeds up. Business firms that cannot borrow as much as they need try to manage cash flows better in order to operate with less money, and so velocity gets another boost. We see both M and V rising, and although the temptation to expand output is there, the resources are not available. Overtime may add somewhat to the total produced, but overtime is at sharply higher costs—time-and-a-half plus the inefficiencies associated with excess utilization—and to offset these cost burdens, prices must go up still more. And as prices rise, people see still more inflation on the way, so they hurry to buy before things become even more expensive. Funds are drawn down to finance these extra expenditures, and velocity rises still further. The time between the receipt and disbursement of funds must be shortened, for the longer we hold money, the greater the price rise and the less its purchasing power. Idle time for money must thus be minimized. This, of course, means a step-up in velocity, as holders struggle to reduce k. And as this fans out through the economy, people buy more and more quickly; others are selling more and more quickly, getting funds more and more quickly. But they, too, wish to hold this money only for the minimum time. So they speed up their replacement ordering. Their suppliers, in turn, get money more quickly, but they, too, are similarly motivated. So they spend as quickly as possible. And so the volume of purchases soars; velocity rises more and more.

In the extreme possibility, such as occurs in a defeated country whose productive capacity and morale have been shattered—Germany after World War I, Hungary and China after World War II—this take-off of velocity finally leads to a complete collapse of confidence in the currency. Prices start to rise so fast that money loses its value too rapidly. It does not pay to sell for money, for by the time the seller goes to buy something with these funds he finds that the further price rise has made the paper worth much less. And so the use of money in transactions begins to drop off. Where possible, people start to fall back on the clumsy barter techniques. Or some more stable item is used instead of the rapidly depreciating money—for example, cigarettes. This commodity performed some of the monetary functions in post–World War II Europe. Or a foreign, more stable currency is used if sufficient supplies can be obtained—for example, by diverting sales to this other country and thus receiving its currency in payment.

However, we should not exaggerate such a possibility. Not every inflation spills over to such extremes. In fact, other than in countries whose productive capacity has been crippled by such disasters as war and earthquakes, in modern times there has not been an inflation that did not, at some point, either slow down or actually stop. True, for some Latin American countries there has been a slow continual erosion, but rarely has there been so drastic a decline in purchasing power as to result in an end to the use of money for transactions purposes. Certainly, no developed economy untouched by war has ever had inflation that carried over to the wild stages of hyperinflation.

Earlier in the chapter we did mention the arguments in favor of inflation—its stimulus to output and plant expansion, its reduction of the dead weight of past debt, and its substitution of full employment for an underemployed price stability. While agreeing that hyperinflation is to be avoided, proponents favor a "creeping inflation"—a price rise averaging no more than 2 per cent per annum. But if we know that this is to happen, critics answer, won't such a built-in inflation create forces that lead us into hyperinflation? At present, there is always the feeling that the monetary and fiscal authorities will try to check price rises; hence, enough people feel confident that these checks will occur so that they retain their confidence in the money and do not switch into goods. But if a positive policy of inflation is instituted, then all groups will try to protect themselves against the certainty of a decline in money's purchasing power.

The 2 per cent rate postulated for creeping inflation is so low in order to continue the incentive to save. Currently, rates on fixed investments like savings accounts pay about 4 per cent annually. If prices rise by 2 per cent, then the real value of the savings at the end of the year will have risen by only 2 per cent, despite the nominal rise of 4 per cent. Inflation has eaten up half the nominal income. However, the net (real) rise of 2 per cent is still better than nothing, and so the cautious saver still has some incentive to continue to utilize fixed investments, rather than switch to less familiar and more risky alternatives. We thus avoid any sharp change in the current flow of savings and loanable funds.

Specifically, labor would press for cost-of-living clauses. Each time prices rose, wages would be raised proportionately, regardless of productivity changes. Creditors would want index loans, in which the money paid back would be the original amount loaned, corrected for price-level increases; a doubling of prices between the date of the original loan and the current payment would thus call for twice the number of dollars from the debtor. Or fewer people would invest in fixed-yield assets—bonds, savings deposits, mortgages—and more money would flow into common stocks, the expected rise in profits thus swelling dividends and the market value of the stocks. We would see each price rise call forth an equivalent rise in costs and incomes, which would then boost prices still further. The 2-per-cent inflation would then become 4 per cent, 6 per cent, 10 per cent, and so forth. After enough groups had built in enough safeguards, the rate of increase would become larger and the speed of such adjustments more rapid. Soon we would have hyperinflation.

Monetary Policy and Inflation

We have seen that any monetary policy that succeeds in restraining any expansion in spending in face of a general rise in prices would probably result in a cutback in output and employment. Once too much of such idle resources emerged, authorities would come under pressure to let up on the brakes, expand the money supply, and so allow the price rise to be supported by the rise in output and incomes. It would seem that there is not much choice for the Reserve in such a situation.

Perhaps its best hope is to create enough of an uncertainty to keep enough confidence among the people so that many would still be willing to keep their assets either liquid or in fixed-yield assets. So long as they feel that there will not be a sustained, uninterrupted price rise, enough people may be induced *not* to switch into goods, and so the more extreme inflation can be avoided. The only way we can have a creeping inflation is if people think there will not be continuous price rises; if they think we will have a creeping inflation, then hyperinflation will result.

To enforce such doubts, the Reserve must, at times, introduce enough of a tight-money policy to produce the very unemployment we wish to avoid. A few such experiences may stop inflation temporarily, and so renew confidence on the part of the creditor class so that they can continue to stay in money and fixed debt. Over the long run, as a consequence, the economy would have alternations between price stability and full employment. When this becomes too great, there would be a decline in unemployment and creeping inflation. When the latter rise became too great, there would come a tightening and a return to unemployment and price stability. Thus, over any lengthy period there would be inflation, but not in each year, so that there would be many periods of doubt concerning the possibility of a price rise. These doubts would curb the speculative move into commodities, and thus reduce the upward pressure on prices. The recurring unemployment would similarly restrain wage demands. All combined would keep the liquidity holder satisfied with his monetary asset, and also keep the fixed-debt group satisfied with its position.

What would also help as a supplement would be a more vigorous use of fiscal policy. With better built-in stabilizers, any inflation would push up incomes, but it would also push up government receipts even more rapidly. Thus, an offset to the expansion would be the increased diversion of purchasing power from the economy to the government. Properly handled, as we have seen in Chapter 22, this could restrain much of the excess arising from such a situation. Then, in the reverse phase of the cycle, the stabilizers, by reducing government receipts more rapidly than the decline in income, would cushion the decline and thereby minimize the impact on output and employment. Note that there would still be some fluctuation in employment and prices. But what we have done is to reduce the swings and so reinforce the general feeling that inflation will not be continuous, and that it will not be allowed to get out of hand.

Summary

The American economy faces an important dilemma today—that is, full employment or price stability? The former, because of the tight demand situation resulting, tends to spill over into a rising price level. But, to maintain the latter, we must keep demand below capacity points, and so produce unemployment. Ideally, we want to avoid both extremes, for the social and economic losses arising from these unpleasant alternatives are grave. Income is redistributed, activities are diverted to less desirable ends, and perhaps over-all output suffers, both in the short and the long run. On the other hand, there are arguments in favor of a little unemployment and also a little inflation. But if we build into our policy this modification, there is always the danger that various groups will react to protect themselves, and so each will become more extreme. As a result, if we pretend that we wish to maintain stability of both employment and price levels, we may be able to keep the disequilibria to a moderate amount of joblessness and a small and slowly upward trend in the general purchasing power of our currency. Much of the difficulty is the result of numerous rigidities in modern society—wages, prices, factor immobility. But since these are with us, we must act within the framework, rather than as though we were a perfectly flexible economy. In this way we may avoid the extreme misery of the 1930's, with its shocking waste of idle resources, and the extreme of hyperinflation, a situation in which society abandons the use of money. The former will no longer be tolerated. The latter need not happen in a modern, industrialized, peaceful society.

Chapter 24

THE INTERNATIONAL
SECTOR

In this chapter we shall limit our discussion of the international sector to those aspects that influence the money-and-banking operations. Our exposition is necessarily compact, and to some extent it even distorts the true picture. The reader is therefore referred to standard works in the field, especially those that stress financial ties and transactions.

The Balance of Payments

The balance of payments records transactions between residents of a country and foreigners. Receipts cover sales of goods and services, interest, dividends and profits from overseas investments, and foreigners' capital invested in the country. Payments are for purchases of goods and services from foreigners, interest, dividends and profits on foreigners' investments in the country, and outflows of capital to purchase foreign assets. Among receipts would be short-term capital inflows—that is, either foreign capital coming in, or domestic capital previously sent abroad and now returning. Among payments would be outflows of short-term capital—both foreign capital being repatriated by its owners, and domestic capital going abroad. Gold sales to foreigners are regarded as receipts, since the Treasury receives dollars in payment; gold acquisitions are payments, since dollars are issued against the gold received. Foreign aid extended abroad is a payment, since money is given to the recipient, which then may or may not be used to purchase the aid-giving country's goods and services.

If we total all the payments and all the receipts the two must equal. This arises from the accounting concept of balance. If, for example, we sold $20 billion worth of goods, services, and securities to foreigners and purchased $19 billion, they would have received $1 billion less from us than they paid us. The difference would then probably be made up through the sale of gold to our Treasury—thus adding $1 billion in dollars paid out—and so we now get a $20-billion figure for both sides. Or American banks might decide to invest short-term assets abroad, lending $1 billion to the foreign debtor, and once again balance receipts and payments. Or foreigners might get the funds from their banks, which in turn would meet the dollar demand by withdrawing short-term funds from this country, the money taken out by these foreign banks returning as payment for the excess of foreign purchases. Regardless of alternatives, we get a balance of $20 billion for both sides.

Now it may be asked why the $1-billion deficiency in foreign payments was not effected through the sale of pounds, francs, marks, or other currencies for dollars. For this to happen, someone else must have been willing to buy pounds, francs, and marks and to sell dollars. But we have already said that Americans were offering only $19 billion for sale, to get the foreign currencies required for their purchases, while foreigners were offering $20 billion of their (foreign) currencies for dollars to meet their obligation. The foreign-exchange market, in other words, handles only the $19-billion part: Americans sell the $19 billion for foreign currencies, the amount they must pay for their purchases of goods, services, and foreign securities. Foreigners can sell $19 billion in foreign currencies—needed by the Americans to discharge their requirements—and receive the $19 billion (in dollars) in exchange, thus being enabled to pay for most of what they owe the Americans. There remains $1 billion owed to Americans that cannot be acquired in exchange; consequently, the resort to gold or short-term capital movements. In a sense, this last amount thus measures *the* United States balance-of-payments deficit or surplus. Expressed another way, a surplus could be interpreted as the sum of dollars paid out for (a) gold purchases, (b) liquidation of foreign short-term assets in the United States, and (c) acquisition of short-term balances (or other assets) abroad. A deficit would be measured by dollars received for (a) gold sales, (b) foreigners' acquisition of short-term assets in the United States, and (c) liquidation of United States short-term assets abroad. (The reader should be alerted that this is not the only definition; in more specialized works the problem of short-term capital flows and their relation to the payments deficit would be discussed in greater detail, but for our purposes this general summary suffices.) Note that our definition of the payments surplus or deficit insures that the overall payments account balances, since these three are the residual differences of all other transactions, assuming that the data are all accurate. (Again we must insert a parenthetical aside: balance-of-payments data collection often errs in accuracy, producing errors of $1 billion or more. Treatment of this errors-and-omissions item is also left to the more specialized works, although its magnitude is enough to give us pause.)

The Adjustment Mechanism

In summary, if we have a surplus, we either acquire foreign short-term assets, reduce our short-term liabilities to foreigners, or add to our gold stock. If we have a deficit, we either reduce our foreign short-term assets, add to our short-term liabilities to foreigners, or reduce our gold stock. These alternatives are of great significance for monetary and economic adjustments.

If we have a surplus, this means that foreigners owe to us. If we decide to add to our short-term assets abroad, we accept their currencies and then do not convert them to dollars. For example, if the British owe us (net) $14 million, equal to about 5 million pounds, our banks would accept the British money and use it to buy British Treasury bills or other short-term assets in Great Britain. The British payer, such as an importer, has turned over his pounds to an American bank. The bank then credits the American seller with the dollars in the United States, and this would probably mean a rise in deposit liabilities in the United States. The offsetting factor, as already mentioned, is the British asset. Hence, if a surplus is settled through an addition to our holdings of short-term assets, there would be a rise in deposits in the United States and a rise in foreign short-term liabilities to the United States—here, an American bank.

If the settlement had been through a foreign liquidation of American assets, the process would have been somewhat as follows. The British payer goes to his bank for dollars. There are not enough dollars arising from current sales in the United States market—hence our surplus—so the British bank sells some of its American assets. For example, it might have held United States Treasury bills, and the sale of these would give it dollars. These dollars could then be turned over to the American creditor, who would then deposit them in his bank in the United States. Offsetting this would be the decline in deposits by the American who bought the Treasury bills from the British bank. On the American side, therefore, there is a decline in foreign owner-ship of United States assets, but no change in total deposits (although there is a shift from the bill buyer to the American owed by the Briton). On the British side, the dollars used to settle the payment are paid for by the British debtor out of his (pound) deposit account. That is, the British banks now have fewer (United States) assets, but correspondingly fewer deposit liabilities in England.

Alternatively, the British bank may have had funds on deposit with other United States banks. It could have liquidated the British debt by drawing on these funds, charging the British debtor. The funds, when paid to the American creditor, would then go into his bank account. Net result: total deposits with United States banks are unchanged, but more is owed to Americans, less to the British. In Britain there is a decline in American-held assets and in deposit liabili-ties to the British. Note that in both these possible liquidations of British-owned American assets, there is no change in total United States deposit liabilities, although there is a shift in ownership. This could affect velocity, depending on the activity of the respective holders. Probably, the deposit held by the Treasury-bill buyer in the first alternative, or the British bank in the second, would be less active than after its transfer into the account of the American creditor. The latter is in all likelihood a business firm that has sold goods or services, and thus intends to use the funds received for further spending on output and income disbursements.

Finally, foreigners may ship gold into the United States, selling it to the Treasury and getting dollars in return, which then liquidate the debt. The dollars are an addition to the money supply, and when deposited, we get (a) a rise in deposits due the American creditor, (b) a rise in member-bank balances, offset in part by the fraction required as reserves against this new deposit, and (c) a rise in gold certificates, the reserve of the Federal Reserve.

We can thus summarize the effect of a balance-of-payments sur-plus by saying that if it is settled by foreigners liquidating United States short-term assets, the American money supply is unchanged, but there may be an effect on velocity. If either gold or foreign assets are acquired by the United States (the former by the Treasury,[1] the latter by the banks), then deposits in United States banks rise, and, in addi-

---

[1] If either the Treasury or the Federal Reserve acquired or sold foreign assets, the accounting would be similar to that for gold.

tion, their reserves rise if gold is the medium of settlement. In this last possibility, excess reserves rise, whereas if the addition is foreign assets, excess reserves decline, the rise in deposit liabilities not being matched by an increase in reserves.

In the gold-settlement illustration we omitted the foreign accounting. Here there are many possibilities, depending on the existence of central banks, exchange stabilization funds, monetary area balances (sterling, franc, escudo, and so on), plus a host of other possibilities. In all probability, however, the result will be a decline in deposits in the foreign banks, the payer giving up this asset, and probably a decline in the reserves of foreign banks, offset in part by the reduction in reserve requirements now that deposits are down.

If the United States has a deficit, then, as would be expected, there would be the opposite alternatives to those already covered. Deposits due Americans decline; the payments come out of our debtors' accounts. Foreigners may leave the funds here in our banks, thus keeping deposits unchanged—less owed to Americans, more to foreigners. Or they may buy other United States assets, in which case less is owed to the Americans making the original payment to the foreigners, more is owed to Americans who sold the asset, and more United States assets are owned by foreigners. Here, too, the change in deposit ownership may have a velocity effect. Alternatively, the payment may be through the sale of gold to foreigners, which means that the dollars received in payment from the original American debtor are drawn out of the banks and presented to the Treasury for the gold. Not only do the banks' deposit liabilities drop, but their reserves drop also, offset in part by the drop in required reserves now that deposits are less. In addition, the Reserve's gold certificates are less. Or, as a final possibility, United States banks might liquidate foreign assets, thereby leaving total reserves unchanged. Here the decline in deposits due Americans releases required reserves and adds to excess reserves, unlike the gold outflow. In all four types of settlement, foreign deposits in foreign banks would rise—the amounts being paid to those owed by the Americans. In the gold alternative there would also be a rise in the foreign banks' reserves. If foreign regulations permit the counting of short-term assets in the United States as reserves, in this case, too, such an acquisition adds to foreign bank reserves. In all four possibilities, foreign required reserves would have been increased. Excess reserves would rise where the settlement added to foreign bank reserves (gold and, where permitted, United States asset acquisitions), or declined where total reserves were unchanged.

For simplicity we have limited payments and receipts to demand deposits at reserve city banks. Actually, as previous chapters have indi-

cated, any deposit account could be affected, and so reserve requirements would vary, depending on whether the impact were on time or
demand deposits, and whether located in country or reserve city
banks. The reader can make the necessary adjustments for these possible qualifications; for ease of exposition we shall continue with our use
of checking accounts at the large city banks.

But even with this simplification, the method of settlement of a
balance-of-payments surplus or deficit can give rise to differing monetary impacts. For example, a United States surplus would raise deposits
held by Americans. It would also reduce deposits held by foreigners—
and so keep total deposits unchanged—if the settlement were through
the liquidation by the foreigner. But it would add to total deposits if
settlement were through our acquiring gold or foreign assets, since
there is no offsetting drop in foreign-owned deposits. Moreover, the
gold acquisition adds to total member-bank (and Federal Reserve)
reserves; the foreign-asset acquisition does not. The gold inflow would
be most expansionary of these four alternatives. The settlement
through the addition to United States bank holdings of foreign assets
might also be expansionary, since total deposits have risen, although
this also draws down excess reserves, since required reserves would
now be higher. The settlement through foreign liquidation of American assets has mainly a velocity impact.

Similarly, until we know the method of settlement, we cannot say
what the effect of a United States payments deficit would be. A gold
outflow would reduce deposits with United States banks, reduce required reserves, but also reduce total and excess reserves. This is the
most deflationary of the possibilities. Liquidation of our foreign assets
would leave total reserves unchanged, but the accompanying decline in
deposits—the payment by the American who owes the foreigner—
would reduce M; on the other hand, this reduction reduces required
reserves, adds to excess reserves, and so could be offset. Settlement
through the foreign banks' acquisition of United States assets would
have mainly a velocity impact.

Furthermore, where the settlement is through changes in foreign
ownership of United States assets, there would be a money-market
effect through yield alterations. A United States surplus might lead to
the sale of foreign-owned United States assets, depressing our yields,
and a United States deficit might lead to the purchase of United States
assets, lowering yields. Settlement through a shift in American bank
holdings of foreign assets could also have repercussions. An American
surplus entrenches on free reserves, but adds to the money supply.
Will our banks sell bills to regain reserves, thus depressing bill prices?
Will the initial expansion in M add to consumption? To investment?

Analogously, a United States deficit financed through the sale of foreign assets reduces our money supply, but raises free reserves. Will the banks then buy bills and lower yields? Will the initial cutback in M depress consumption? Or investment?

Simultaneously, all we have said regarding the United States would apply in reverse for foreign countries. Our surplus is their deficit, our deficit their surplus. So whatever adjustment is posed for the United States has its accompanying repercussions abroad.

We thus see that the balance-of-payments surplus or deficit sets up different reactions in the countries concerned, depending on the method of settlement. And the selection of the various payments alternatives often lies with the foreigner. That is, a United States deficit settlement would depend on foreign decisions, a foreign deficit (American surplus) settlement on United States decisions. (A foreign deficit settlement that is determined by Americans means that to the countries abroad it is the foreigner—the American—who made the decision.) If we have a deficit, the foreigners are net gainers of dollars. Will they leave them here, either as a deposit with an American bank or as the purchase of an American asset? Will they demand gold? This is up to them. We might make it attractive enough to influence the decision. If the interest paid on their deposit is high enough, it might induce them to leave their dollars with a United States bank. But it is still the foreigner who must decide. Similarly, if we have a surplus, we make the decision regarding the disposition of the foreign currencies. Do we use them to acquire foreign assets or gold?

The exception is if the debtor nation, the one with the balance-of-payments deficit, also has foreign assets. If, for example, the United States has a deficit, we might sell foreign assets. Or a United States surplus might be bridged through the sale of foreign-owned American assets. Here we enter into a complicated banking problem, to be discussed more extensively later in the chapter. Briefly, what we are asking is this: if we have a deficit, will foreign banks accept dollars, to be left here, or will our banks liquidate assets abroad? If we have a surplus, will foreigners liquidate assets here, or will our banks add to assets abroad? The answers will be determined by the relative attractiveness regarding the place to hold assets. Expressed differently, where will income (yields) be higher—in the United States or abroad?

If it is more attractive to hold funds here, foreign banks would be less likely to liquidate United States assets if we have a surplus, and our banks would be less likely to acquire foreign assets. Therefore, gold would probably flow to the United States. If it is less attractive to hold funds in the United States, then an American surplus would be more likely to be bridged by the sale of foreign assets here, or the acquisition of American assets abroad. If the United States had a deficit, and it was more attractive to hold funds here, then settlement would be through the acquisition of American assets by foreign banks and the sale of American foreign assets abroad. If it were less attractive to hold funds here, then our deficit would be met through a gold outflow, for now the foreign banks are not interested in acquiring more American assets, and our banks are not induced to sell foreign assets. In brief, higher short-term yields here would lessen the possibility of a gold outflow if we have a deficit (and increase the likelihood of a gold inflow if we have a surplus). Lower United States yields would increase the possibility of a gold outflow if we have a deficit (and lessen the likelihood of a gold inflow if we have a surplus). It is for this reason that we must also study the relative yield structure to see when and how we can influence the various methods of settling the payments imbalances.

To the extent that a surplus does set in force an expansion, incomes will rise, prices may also rise, and so goods and services become more expensive. This may reduce our sales to foreigners, thereby reducing receipts, and may stimulate purchases from foreigners, thereby adding to payments. These two shifts could eliminate the surplus, and thus bring about an equality of the two flows. A deficit that leads to a deflation reduces incomes and spending, and the resulting oversupply may cut prices. Our goods and services are now more attractive to foreigners, stimulating sales and receipts, and we can compete more effectively against incoming supplies, reducing our purchases of foreign items and thereby our payments. Once again we may have eliminated the difference between the two flows. Simultaneously, our surplus means a deficit abroad, which curtails incomes and spending abroad, and thus payments, and additions to receipts as price declines there stimulate sales; our deficit means a surplus abroad, thus expanding incomes and spending abroad, stepping up their payments and perhaps reducing their receipts if their prices also rise.[2] Both sides, in other words, are eliminating the differences between payments and receipts, and if the reaction is sufficiently strong, a new equality emerges, ending further adjustment.

From another viewpoint, the net purchases of goods and services represents the foreign aspect of the propensity to consume—the community's spending on consumption of products that happen to be supplied by factors outside the country. The long-term capital flows reflect the international comparison of the various marginal efficiencies. Where a foreign area has a greater marginal efficiency, capital flows from the United States to that country; and where a sector of the

---

[2] The reduced competitiveness of their more expensive exports could curtail sales abroad.

American economy has a greater marginal efficiency, capital flows in from abroad. This marginal efficiency is after correction for risk differentials. Thus, Castro's Cuba may have a superior profit opportunity, but in view of the confiscation danger, the yield is not enough to overcome this danger. The short-term capital flows reflect relative interest rates, again corrected for risk; if yields abroad are higher, United States short-term funds flow out; if our yields are higher, foreign funds flow in (or our funds flow back). This last statement must also be corrected for liquidity considerations; banks, for example, would not want to tie up too much of their funds in any particular foreign center, so that even if the yield there were higher, it might not draw any more money. Or if too much of the banking assets were tied up in foreign holdings, this might impair domestic secondary-reserve positions, since the liquidity of foreign assets is still not as good as with United States Treasury bills. In effect, the capital account—the combination of long- and short-term flows—thus represents the movement of liquid, loanable funds, either out of or into a country, except where the movement is tied to a specific project, such as construction of a plant abroad.[3] An outflow reduces the available supply of funds within the country and so tends to raise yields; an inflow, by increasing the available supply, tends to lower yields. Alternatively, an ouflow of funds indicates that there is an effective (foreign) demand for such funds in addition to the demand from domestic borrowers. This additional demand raises the yield, thereby attracting some of our liquid funds. This is also true conversely if the foreign demand declines.

The International Monetary Fund

Since World War II the International Monetary Fund (IMF) became an addition to the payments mechanism. To join, member countries pay in both gold and their own currencies, thus building up a fund of all important monies. Countries with balance-of-payments deficits can draw on this pool (within limits), paying in their own currency to get the particular currency needed to bridge the payments gap. These drawings must be repaid, since they are regarded as a loan, which, incidentally, draws interest. However, such drawings are mainly for transient deficits, where there is a reasonable prospect of its

---

[3] The one exception in which a capital flow is not in the form of liquid funds is a *direct investment*. Here, quite often, the company setting up a plant abroad often ships the capital equipment as its contribution to the new plant. Ownership and management are thus much closer than they would be with a portfolio investment—wherein the investor subscribes money for a bond or common stock, and is then satisfied merely to collect the interest or dividends, without having a voice in the operation of the foreign entity.

elimination, thereby producing a surplus subsequently; the receipts of foreign currency from this surplus can then be paid to the IMF to liquidate the loan. The IMF pays out and receives currencies as its resources are drawn on and replenished. If the country's deficit is relatively long-term, then more fundamental steps must be taken, perhaps including resort to the companion organization, the International Bank for Reconstruction and Development (IBRD, or World Bank), which makes long-term loans to improve fundamental economic strength. Among its other functions, the IMF has policed payments restrictions, to see that these are eliminated as soon as feasible. It has also restrained currency manipulations, to prevent a country's using this device to gain an international competitive advantage. It also acts as a meeting place for the world's monetary authorities, where they can make decisions reflecting current problems and policies.

Key Currencies

Countries that have balance-of-payments deficits meet these demands in two ways: if the creditor nations wish—in effect, if they have sufficient confidence in the debtor—they will simply accumulate balances held in various short-term assets of the debtor country. Alternatively, the debtor must have some satisfactory payments means to discharge its obligations; in practice, this means either gold or short-term assets held abroad. The concentration of such externally held reserves in a few countries has given rise to the key-currency concept; today these are mainly the United States dollar and the British pound. To meet possible external deficits, countries now hold gold and either dollars or pounds, the latter being liquidated when needed.

The rise of a country's currency to this key position is a reflection of past and present economic strength. As a country's trade expands— and the United States and Great Britain are two enormous traders in the world picture—more and more countries either make payments to these traders for purchases, or receive funds from sales of goods and services to them, or they get new investments from these economically powerful nations. As a result, there is a constant need to have dollars to discharge payments due to Americans, and there is a constant influx of dollars from American purchasers and investors. To facilitate such flows, foreign banks accumulate balances in the United States, thus having a pool of dollars to meet their own citizens' dollar requirements, this pool being replenished through the various receipts. Similar trends happen for those countries that do more of their transactions with the British, leading to balances in London.

As this concentration of balances grows, these other countries find a broader market for the purchase and sales of currencies in the key country. In New York there is a broad dollar-pound, dollar-franc, dollar-mark market, along with other foreign currencies. This broadness would also apply to the dollar against Japanese yen, Brazilian cruzeiro, and others. Hence, Brazilian traders with Japan soon discover that it is easier to sell cruzeiros for dollars and then dollars for yen in New York than to try to buy yen for cruzeiros in Brazil. There is not enough of a market in their own country for trades with these other currencies. Similar remarks would apply for a yen-cruzeiro transaction; it is easier to sell yen for dollars and then dollars for cruzeiros in New York than yen for cruzeiros in Japan. And so in the Japanese-Brazilian trade, payment is made in dollars instead of their own currency. Thus, the Japanese sell for dollars, not yen; the Brazilians for dollars, not cruzeiros. To make payments, one need only transfer dollars held in the balances built up in the United States. Brazilians have built up dollar balances because of receipts from Americans. Similarly for the Japanese. Then, these balances are used for payments due Americans. But they can also be used for payments to anybody who accepts dollars. Thus, the Brazilians who import from an American get their bank to give them a dollar draft drawn on their balances in New York; this reduces the Brazilian balance there, and the funds are transferred to the United States exporter. In effect, balances due Brazilian banks are now due United States exporters. Our money supply is unchanged, but the ownership has changed. Had the Brazilian imported from Japan, he would still get the Brazilian bank to draw a draft on its New York account, but now it is paid to a Japanese exporter. The latter deposits it with his bank—expanding deposits in Japan—and the Japanese bank forwards the draft for deposit in its New York account. From the United States point of view, all that has happened is that bank deposits owed the Brazilian bank are down, and those owed the Japanese bank are up, but the total owed foreign banks is the same. In both cases, the Brazilian importer's deposits with his bank in Brazil would be reduced as he paid for the draft. And it is probable that both foreign banks would be allowed to count these New York balances as reserves. If so, the loss of balances in New York would reduce Brazilian bank reserves, and these would be offset somewhat by the decline in deposits due the importer. Japanese bank balances in New York have risen, thereby raising their reserves. These are offset in part by the requirements to be held against the Japanese exporter's additional deposit balance.

From the American point of view, transfers between countries using dollar balances have virtually no effect. In contrast, American receipts from such countries reduce foreign dollar balances and raise deposits due Americans; United States payments to such countries reduce the deposits of the American payer, but raise foreign balances here. So long as all such balances are carried as demand deposits, the total volume of such deposits and the accompanying reserve requirement thus remains unchanged, and we see shifts in ownership and perhaps a differing velocity, since different owners may show different deposit activity.

Problems of a Key Currency—External

One problem facing a key currency is that it must maintain the foreign creditors' confidence in its balances. If rumors spread that a key currency is to be devalued, which means that in terms of foreign currencies the key currency will be worth less, then foreigners will hasten to convert their balances to gold to ward off such a loss. Neither the United States nor Great Britain has enough gold to meet 100-percent conversion. So each must always make certain that its policies do not disturb this feeling of faith. As we shall see later, this complicates cyclical control efforts.

Even if the system runs smoothly, there can be difficulties. Suppose Brazil holds its balances in dollars, but France does not. If a Brazilian owes a Frenchman, he goes to his bank and gets a draft drawn on the Brazilian balance in New York. The Frenchman turns this draft into his bank in Paris, but French banks do not want dollar balances. So they may turn the dollars into the United States Treasury for gold. As a result, United States bank reserves and the gold stock decline because of a deficit between two foreign countries, one of whom happened to use dollars and one of whom did not. Unless this loss of reserves is countered by the Federal Reserve, we get a deflation here because of transactions in which the United States was not a party.

Similar but opposite forces are at work if the payment is the other way. If the French owe the Brazilians, they may turn francs over to the Brazilian banks. The latter do not hold francs, but dollars. So they may turn the francs in for gold and then sell the gold to the United States Treasury, depositing the dollars received in their New York account. Result: a transaction to which the United States was not a party swells our gold stock and member-bank reserves, thus enabling our banks to expand. Again the Reserve must intervene if this is unwanted. In short, the Reserve must be on the alert constantly for such movements of gold to minimize the effects on our own economy.

We can also see that a flow of gold need not reflect any basic imbalance in the United States payments accounts. Earlier we had limited such flows to one of two possibilities. If we had a deficit and the payment was not made through a change in international short-term assets, then gold would flow out; if we had a surplus and the payment was not made through changes in such short-term assets, gold would flow in. In addition, gold may flow out if countries lose faith in our currency, or if dollar-balance countries have deficits with non-dollar-balance countries. Gold may also flow in, in addition to a possible surplus in our payments account, if countries renew their confidence in our currency, or if dollar-balance countries have a surplus with non-dollar-balance countries.

We can also reinterpret the alternative—the use of international balances. If we have a deficit with a country that keeps its balances in the United States, the likelihood is that gold will not flow out, but that our balances due foreigners will rise. If we have a surplus with such a country, there will not be a gold inflow, but a reduction in foreign-owned United States balances. (This assumes no change in foreign confidence in the dollar.) Gold would flow if the country in question did not hold balances here. In practice, however, virtually all countries hold some balances here. Hence, when we said "non-dollar-balance country," we meant this: a payment to such a country would raise their dollar balances if they were too low to finance current transactions, but it would also result in an outflow of gold if their dollar balances were already regarded as adequate. A payment from a country using relatively small dollar balances would reduce our liabilities to this country's banks if their balances were high enough to sustain such a drain, but would draw in gold if those balances in dollars had already declined too greatly.

We have intimated that the size of these dollar balances reflects the volume of transactions that must be serviced. If there is a lot of trade and many purchases and sales of securities, there will be a large volume of transactions. Just as for any individual, the larger the volume of such transactions, the greater the balance that should be maintained in case of differing flows of payments and receipts. But this balance may be enlarged for other reasons. For example, a foreign bank may wish to have liquid assets. The yield in its own country is appreciably lower than in the United States. So it deposits its funds in a time deposit with a United States bank to get this higher income. This deposit can be drawn on when needed, and so is no different from its balance for transactions purposes. Essentially, the deposit is in excess of such needs, and will be withdrawn if yields elsewhere should rise above the United States return. We thus see a role for interest rates; to pull in balances when desired, or to repel them if unwanted. We are now merging our *external* and *internal* forces.

Problems of a Key Currency—Internal

In the management of dollar balances, foreign countries tend to keep their demand deposits, on which they earn nothing, at the working minimum. The remainder is invested in short-term assets that can be quickly liquidated if their working balances drop too low. Hence, the variable is the *invested* portion, the day-to-day management keeping the *working* portion within narrow ranges, selling assets as the lower range is approached, buying assets as the upper range is reached.

This means that there is a constant influx and outflow of funds from the other sectors of the money market reflecting the net change in the payments position of these various foreign countries. A rise in aggregate (net) American payments tends to swell foreign (net) receipts, and conversely for an American surplus. The money-market reactions vary, depending on the specific assets involved. While we cannot exhaust the many possibilities, some indication of the complexities of such shifts is worth mentioning.

Assume that we have a United States deficit. Demand deposits are being drawn on to pay foreigners, so, initially, foreign demand deposits with United States banks increase. If this activity is within the range that such balances are normally kept, there is no further reaction other than the velocity consideration arising from such an ownership shift.

If the balances are excessive, the surplus portion might be switched into time deposits or certificates of deposit. This would free member-bank reserves and thus permit them to expand loans and deposits. Thus, the United States payments deficit, which could lead to a gold outflow and deflation if it is with countries that do not maintain large balances here, turns out to be expansionary in this alternative. And, such expansion might push up incomes and spending in the United States, thereby stepping up other purchases and imports, actually increasing our payments deficit. We could even see a decline in yields, if the member banks decide to use the surplus reserves by attracting more borrowers through such a concession. This lower yield might spread to other short-term assets, and thus induce some foreign creditors to sell their United States assets and shift them to another country where yields have not come down. Alternatively, if the banks used the excess reserves to buy Treasury bills, we would get a yield decline and perhaps, again, the loss of foreign funds. Such an outflow drains us of gold and brings down member-bank reserves, thus reversing the previous expansionary forces.

Suppose the foreign excess balance is invested in Treasury bills. This would lower yields here, and might again induce other foreigners to sell out and take their funds to another country. If not, the somewhat lower yield could lead to more borrowing as a result of an American deficit, and, as before, expansion rather than contraction would ensue. Perhaps the sellers of the bills will lend them at short-term elsewhere, and thus generalize the yield decline to other sectors of the short-term market.

Now a relatively new outlet appears—the Euro-Dollar market. These are dollar balances loaned to foreigners for a short term—in effect, a short-term loan by one foreigner owning dollar balances to another desiring such funds (perhaps to liquidate a dollar obligation). Such a loan might replace a loan from an American bank; in such a case the greater utilization of the demand deposit replaces the creation of a new demand deposit. Or the foreign borrower may be a bank wishing to maintain a larger balance here; in this case the deposit so transferred may be held idle, with a zero or low velocity. If this loan of foreign-owned balances replaces a loan by an American bank, does the latter then relend elsewhere? Does it carry on with somewhat larger excess reserves? Perhaps it now lowers its rate to other borrowers to absorb these idle funds. The possibilities here are endless.

Suppose, instead, that the United States has a surplus with countries that carry balances here. If these countries have adequate demand deposits, they would be drawn down, raising the deposits of the American creditor, and, except for the effect on velocity as a result of this change in ownership, this would be final. If, however, the working balances are inadequate, the foreign banks would then have to dispose of some of their other short-term United States assets. As we would expect, our reasoning would be similar, but opposite, to that for a payments deficit. Funds could come from the liquidation of a time deposit, certificate of deposit, Treasury bill, or recall from the Euro-Dollar market. Each of these would have varying money-market effects, although on balance they would probably be deflationary. The first two transfer low reserve-requirement liabilities to high reserve-requirement liabilities (demand deposits) while the bill sale would raise yields there. Calling in funds from the Euro-Dollar market might switch the borrower back to a United States bank, thus raising the demand for funds and thus, perhaps, our yield structure. Note that a surplus with a gold-using country, by drawing in gold and adding to member-bank excess reserves, is definitely expansionary, in contrast to the surplus outcome discussed in this paragraph.

So far, it has been assumed that the Federal Reserve did not interfere. If any of the reactions were contrary to those desired, it would have to intervene in an offsetting operation. If our payments surplus tightened bill yields just when an easy-money policy was called for, the Reserve would have to go in for open-market purchases to counter the deflationary possibilities. Fortunately much of the foreign assets in Treasury bills are in the custody of the Federal Reserve. It is always aware of any shifts of funds into, or out of, this part of the market.

The United States Dilemma

The role of the key-currency country has some painful implications for monetary policy, especially if the country has had sizeable payments deficits during a business recession, such as the United States has experienced since 1957. Stated simply, there is a basic conflict between domestic and foreign policy objectives.

Stimulating the economy calls for a cheap-money policy. But if it succeeds, lower yields will induce foreigners holding short-term assets here to sell out, convert their dollars to gold, then invest the funds in another country where yields are more attractive. The gold outflow would drain member-bank reserves and thus curtail their lending—the very opposite of what we are trying to instigate. Moreover, if we do succeed in stimulating the economy, we step up spending, including spending on imports, and so add to the payments to foreigners. This enables them to pull out still more gold. A high yield here would stop these unwanted reactions, but then monetary policy would no longer be able to help push the economy toward recovery and full employment.

A similar dilemma may occur in a boom. The Reserve may tighten money, pushing up yields, and thus restrain lending and borrowing. But this higher yield may attract foreign funds; gold flows in, flooding the banks with reserves, and thus ends tight money. Moreover, the check on domestic activity, if it reduces spending, would cut our imports, and our payments to foreigners, perhaps compelling them to send in still more gold to settle their payments.

There may be other unwanted reactions from domestic capital. A low yield to fight a recession might step up lending to foreigners; the lower cost of borrowing here would attract droves of such seekers after funds. The dollars turned over may then be spent abroad, thus draining us of gold, reinforcing the loss arising from the outflow of foreign balances. American corporations with large cash balances might switch their funds from the lower-yield American assets to the higher-income foreign assets. Once again gold might flow out. In short, easy money could precipitate a wholesale outflow of all types of funds, thus reducing our gold stock and member-bank reserves.

Conversely, a tight-money policy (raising yields here) would draw back American corporate funds invested abroad, which would also tend to make gold flow in. United States bank lending to foreigners would also decline as borrowing costs for the foreigner rose. The resultant decline in dollars loaned to foreigners, including inflows to pay off past borrowings, would reduce their use of our currency to make payments to other countries. Assuming that the loans were not to finance purchases in the United States, or that the decline in loans did not reduce such purchases here, the reaction of the banking sector's activity would also work to add to the gold inflow. The combined impact of these shifts in corporate and bank funds flows, by attracting gold, would thus boost member-bank reserves and thereby ease the tight-money pressure.

Yield Variations and Capital Flows

Unfortunately, we cannot say just what the dimensions of yield variations on long-term capital flows would be, especially considering the diverse nature of the latter. The feeling prevails that a rise in yields would postpone, not reduce, foreign long-term borrowing in the United States. Yield declines would speed up such borrowing. In other words, yield shifts affect the timing rather than the total amount borrowed. American short-term corporate funds invested abroad are especially sensitive to yield shifts in the British and Euro-Dollar market. Foreign private holders—mainly West European—are similarly sensitive to yield shifts.

There is also some evidence that balances held by European central banks may also be influenced by yield changes, although this is not too certain. The higher the rate here, the more likely such balances will be kept in United States assets. The lower the rate, the more likely such balances would be withdrawn. Alternatively, a rise in dollar receipts might go into assets in the United States if yields are attractive, into gold if not. A rise in payments to the United States might be made in gold if yields here are attractive, or met through liquidation of United States assets if yields are low. This latter alternative implies that shifts between dollars and gold affect only current flows, and that any previous balances built up tend to remain unchanged, regardless of the yield.

We need not repeat that the Reserve must also worry about the continuance of confidence in the dollar. If a cheap-money policy implies inflation, perhaps a loss of the dollar's value in the foreign-exchange market, then there would be a wholesale conversion of foreign-owned dollar assets into gold to avoid the possibility of loss. Since such possible claims on our gold exceed our total supply, we would face the threat of a complete loss of our international reserves. Hence, the Reserve tends to be more cautious when it comes to lowering domestic yields, and thus a little less effective in combatting a recession. The foreign sector thus impedes its ability to influence the domestic sector.

To some extent, this dilemma can be faced, though the degree of success is still in doubt. For example, in a recession the major stimulating influence could be through the long-term rate of interest, the rate of most concern to the corporate borrower. Short-term yields could be kept relatively high, to hold foreign funds, while the long-term rate is lowered through open-market purchases. This is simply another aspect of "Operation Twist," discussed in Chapter 19. Its success depends not only on the strength of the ties between the short- and long-term rates, but also on the amount of borrowing that would be affected. Operating only on the long-term rate still ignores the large bulk of loans that tend to reflect the shorter yields; many small business firms look to their banks for assistance, and a high Treasury-bill rate will tend to maintain high loan charges. Hence, the stimulus will be limited to the larger company that raises its finance in the securities market.

In addition, fiscal policy could be employed as a weapon in conjunction with the Fed's aims. While the Fed keeps short-term yields up, the government could embark on a vigorous spending program, coupled, if necessary, with a planned deficit. This step-up in spending could supply the push that monetary policy is inhibited from doing. But for the United States to plan for a deficit is still strange talk for many in this country, and implementation of such a recommendation must await further education of the electorate.

Conversely, opposite policies could be instituted if we are faced with a domestic boom and a balance-of-payments surplus. To raise yields would only attract more foreign funds and thus nullify efforts to tighten the banks' reserve position. But a Treasury surplus could put the necessary damper on the economy. But here, too, politics must be considered; any sizeable excess of revenues might just as easily set off a move to cut taxes and minimize the taxpayers' burden, although such a move would only further stimulate an already overextended economy.

These contradictions do not arise, it should be recalled, if a boom is accompanied by a payments deficit, or a recession by a surplus on foreign account. Normally, the boom would boost prices (thus reducing exports) and raise spending (thus increasing imports). This would produce a deficit. Tightening the home economy would also work to correct this external imbalance by reversing the upward price push and spending boom, thereby aiding exports and reducing imports. Only if in the boom the profits outlook were so good that large inflows of foreign funds were present, coming in to participate in the widening opportunities, would capital flows complicate the policy. Then we would have a payments surplus, and raising yields would only attract still more foreign capital, and enlarge the surplus still more.

Similarly, a recession cuts spending (thereby reducing imports) and tends to depress prices (thus aiding exports). Thus, a payments surplus would normally emerge. A reduction of yields to fight the recession would reverse these tendencies, and the consequent rise in spending and imports, and perhaps decline in exports if prices rose, would simply erase the payments surplus. But this assumes that foreign funds held here would not flow out. They may not, if the decline in yields is matched by a rise in profits expectations in the hope that the stimuli will lift the economic outlook. Foreign funds might then shift from bills to equities. But if the yield decline is more influential, then funds would move out, and the pressure on member-bank reserves could offset the Reserve's efforts. In all probability, any shift into equities would be relatively small, so that, net, there would be the outflow even with improved profits possibilities.

International Monetary Reform

One criticism of the key-currency set up is the contradictions inherent in it. As we have seen, countries using the dollars as reserves maintain balances in the United States. To obtain these dollars—to increase reserves—they must have a surplus with the United States. Our deficit is necessary for their reserves to remain adequate; if we run a surplus, we drain them of their dollars and so put them in a squeeze. But if our deficit continues, the other countries may wonder if we can sustain the burden. A rising deficit on our part means a rising volume of demand obligations owned by foreigners. This total already exceeds the entire United States gold stock. If these countries see these claims continuing to rise (as a result of our deficit), they may wonder whether all will be paid when needed. And so there could occur a wholesale conversion of these dollar balances. In other words, we must run a deficit for them to increase reserves, but if we run such a deficit, they may lose confidence!

To meet this problem, various reforms have been proposed. Their discussion is beyond the scope of this book, but one in particular merits attention—a World Central Bank. Essentially this means that the individual nations' central banks would carry their balances at this new World Central Bank. Surpluses and deficits would then be settled through transfers of such balances, just as member-bank payments are effected through transfers at the Federal Reserve. If world reserves are inadequate, the World Central Bank would engage in open-market purchases, buying individual government obligations and crediting the country's central bank with an increase in its balance, just as the Reserve operates with the member banks. If world liquidity is excessive, the new bank would go in for open-market sales.

If such a bank were to come into existence, would there be any need for gold? In principle, no. Just as within the United States there is no longer a use for gold, interbank settlements being effected through transfers of Federal Reserve balances, so intercountry transactions could be effected through shifts in the balances at the World Central Bank. The resources now devoted to the mining, handling, and storage of gold could then be released for more useful activities. (This might hurt the mining communities—especially in a country as dependent on gold as is South Africa—so that a transitional problem would have to be solved.) The world, in effect, would be on a completely credit arrangement.

Advocates on the side of gold have an answer, however. What safeguards would there be against over-issue—excessive creation of reserves? If, instead, we required a gold reserve against the liabilities of the World Central Bank, we impose a top limit on its credit, just as the Federal Reserve is limited now to demand liabilities (including currency) equal to four times its gold certificates. This need not hamper the World Central Bank, for the ratio could be so set up as to be well below the existing ratio, just as the Reserve has more than 25 per cent in gold certificates. But it would put a ceiling on too rapid an acquisition of securities, on too great a rise in credit extended the various central banks. The only growth in this total maximum would come through additional acquisitions of gold from newly mined production offered for sale to the Bank. Incidentally, if there were a fear of excessive creation of credit, more gold would be hoarded and less sold to the World Central Bank, and so the maximum credit possible would be correspondingly limited, thus putting some check on inflation. (For the basis of this logic, the reader is referred to the opening section in the next chapter.)

Summary

The foreign sector concerns the relationship between payments to foreigners and receipts from abroad. The difference then shows up as a change either in our assets abroad, in our liabilities to foreigners, or in gold flows. A deficit thus could reduce our foreign assets, increase our liabilities to foreigners, or lower our gold stock; a surplus could have the reverse effects. If gold flows, then bank reserves change, thus causing a multiple repercussion on the money supply. Gold outflows thus tend to reduce the money supply and spending, and so work to remove the initiating deficit; gold inflows tend to expand the money supply and spending, and so remove the surplus. Changes in assets and liabilities, on the other hand, have a much weaker impact, working mainly on velocity, as deposit ownership is altered. This holds particularly for a key currency such as the dollar, which is the basis for many foreign countries' reserves.

For a key-currency country, many additional problems are present. We must maintain confidence in the currency; otherwise balances would be converted and so strip us of our gold. Yields are no longer free to be varied to influence only the domestic sector, for a lower yield will tend to cause balances to flow out to higher-income centers, and a higher yield would attract balances. These flows, in turn, affect bank reserves and the money supply by a multiple. Yet all these shifts, as foreigners receive and make payments, may so alter their balances here as to influence our money market, and perhaps in ways contrary to what we desire for the domestic sector. We thus have a genuine problem for the Federal Reserve: which sector's interest is paramount in determining monetary policy? Because of these difficulties, many have urged that the entire system be reformed, and that the world go over to some sort of global central bank. In particular, they point out that there is an inherent inconsistency in the present payments arrangements. Other countries can gain dollars mainly through only one source—a United States excess of payments. But such an excess gives rise to doubts about the dollar's stability. Hence, we should remove the burden of providing reserves from the shoulders of any one country.

Chapter 25

MONETARY REFORMS

At the end of the preceding chapter, a brief summary was made of the use of gold as a regulator for the suggested World Central Bank. The rationale for this proposal is based on the supposed workings of the international gold standard in the years before World War I. While many specialists on the subject are inclined to doubt this alleged automaticity, the popular interpretation, especially among the financial communities, attributes to this system a device which, without intervention by any monetary authority, works so as to prevent both excessive inflation and depression. This has given rise to a nostalgic longing for a return to the "good old days," whereby reforms in our present banking arrangements would restore the "rule of laws" rather than of men.

The Idealized Gold Standard

Our description of the gold standard will be the popular presentation, not modified by the more questioning findings of economic specialists. It is representative of views prominent in banking circles both in the United States and in Continental Western Europe. We shall abbreviate it somewhat, omitting unnecessary details.

Every country was expected to adhere to the rules. This included free conversion of the country's currency into gold or acceptance of gold at a fixed price; the inflow thus expanded the money supply, and the outflow contracted it. In developed countries, this worked through the banking system, so that a gold outflow reduced bank reserves, thus compelling a multiple contraction of bank assets and deposits, and an inflow raised bank reserves, thus raising bank assets and deposits by a multiple. The inflow thus generated an expansion of spending, including spending on imports, and an outflow contracted spending, thus decreasing purchases of imports. In addition, the expansion boosted prices, thus making it harder to sell exports; a contraction put pressure on producers and stimulated their sales of exports. In brief, therefore, a gold inflow led to an expansion which stepped up payments to foreigners and reduced receipts, and thus ended the gold inflow, while an outflow raised receipts and reduced payments, thus eliminating the gold loss. Put another way, the excess of receipts which initiated the gold inflow set in motion forces that ended the receipts excess—the cause of the gold acquisitions—while the excess of payments, which caused the gold to flow out, set in motion forces which ended the payments excess and thus the gold loss.

If any country inflated, therefore, its prices rose, its exports became more costly, and so receipts fell off. In addition, foreigners found it a more attractive market, imports flowed in, and so payments rose. The net rise in payments drew off gold, cut bank reserves, and thus cut back spending, thereby ending the inflation. Conversely, if a country were in a recession, incomes dropped, and spending, including spending on imports, declined, thereby reducing payments to foreigners. Unemployment led to price declines, making its goods cheaper and enabling producers to sell abroad more easily, thereby boosting exports and receipts. The result was a net rise in receipts, an inflow of gold, and thus a rise in bank reserves, which in turn led to expansion and the end of the recession. Thus the gold flows reduced the extent of the country's cyclical fluctuations, braking inflations and mitigating recessions.

But suppose that all countries are inflating. Then all prices are rising, so there is no additional advantage to buy abroad, since foreign goods are spiralling just as much as home goods. And since prices abroad are rising, there is no reason for exports to fall off, since their competitiveness is unchanged. Or if all countries are in a recession, then the decline in business activity everywhere is cutting spending, including spending on other countries' goods, so that everyone's imports *and* exports are falling, both in price and quantity. There is thus no way for foreign trade to stimulate an economy.

Not so, reply the gold-standard advocates. In an inflation, costs everywhere are rising, including the cost of mining gold. But the selling price of gold is fixed. So, as inflation continues, mining costs rise and reduce the profit margin in producing gold. Gold output falls off. Less gold flows into the various banks, and bank reserves stop increasing as greatly. This slows down the expansion of loans and deposits, and finally the inflation comes to an end. If there is a worldwide recession, prices everywhere are dropping, including the cost of mining. Profit margins in the gold-mining industry are thus rising. More gold will then be produced, and bank reserves will be rising. This, in turn, will lead to a rise in bank loans and deposits, and so the revival is now under way. Once again, automaticity will iron out these swings.

If the system works so efficiently, why did it fail? In part, the answer is that it was not that efficient. The volume of newly produced gold is a small part of the total supply, so that shifts in the volume produced have miniscule effects on bank reserves. It would take years before the change in gold output showed up significantly in bank reserves, and meanwhile the world would have endured too much inflation or unemployment. Furthermore, the economies are not as flexible as postulated. Labor and corporate rigidities have reduced price movements, especially wage and price declines, so that one of the methods of adjusting to changed cyclical and payments patterns has been ended. Also, the swings of the economies produce enormous numbers of unemployed, or threaten to create tremendous inflations; democracies are no longer willing to submit to these hardships. True, the disequilibria may be transient, but several years can be a long transition to bear without work and income, or to see one's purchasing power decline as prices soar.

Perhaps the death knell was the Great Depression of the 1930's. If the business outlook is really bad, then nothing will induce companies to step up spending. Increasing gold production may raise bank reserves, but there are no borrowers to add to loans and deposits. Indeed, quite the opposite occurred. People with money rushed in to convert their currency into gold, thus depleting the banks of their reserves. By 1933 even the United States dollar could not meet this demand, and not a single developed land could weather this gold-hoard rush. Since the gold standard includes this free conversion, monetary authorities were exposed to the constant threat of a loss of reserves for purely panicky, emotional reactions.

What the gold-standard advocates really seek is a system that can be run according to the rule book, with a minimum of human discretion. But, charge their opponents, that is simply impossible. Modern man has learned to control his environment. Why should he not also try to control his economy? True, our tools are not as tested and certain as those of the scientist. But even if they are only halfway successful—even if we fail to eliminate the swings, but do manage to moderate them—we will have gone a long way toward removing the hardships of the business cycles. And even much of this can be mitigated in a wealthy country through various government relief and recovery aids. However, the desire for automaticity still recurs, partly because of the questionable success of our monetary managers. Those favoring automatic devices feel that intervention has actually increased, rather than decreased, the swings in our economy, and that the more automatically we can make our monetary adjustments, the less chance there is for human error.

Money-Supply Operations

One group of reforms concerns itself with regulating the supply of money—generally demand deposits. It is felt that the currency component simply reflects people's spending habits, that any rise in the total outstanding in excess of these day-to-day requirements would flow to the banks, and thus expand deposits, and any curtailment of the supply would force people to draw down their balances with the banks. Hence, effective regulation of the money supply amounts to, essentially, working on the banking component. Many of these specific suggestions originate with members of the University of Chicago faculty, and so interested readers can obtain a more complete statement of their philosophy and proposals from their various writings. The monetary reforms discussed here are really only part of a larger package for changing the working of the entire economic system.

By introducing automaticity, the reformers hope to reduce or eliminate the lags between recognition of the need for action and its final implementation. They feel that the lag arising from the reliance on individual judgments has resulted in a consistent delaying response, so much so that often the change is instituted after the need for it has passed. Furthermore, they feel that the existing organizations have biases which also lead them to slow or erroneous responses. The Treasury wishes to ease its debt-management cost and handling, and so prefers easy money. Indeed, so it is charged, when a strong Treasury influence has been evident, there has also been a more inflationary tendency in the economy. The Federal Reserve is banker-oriented, and so tends to view many economic problems from the narrower point of the financial sector. It thus has exaggerated fears of inflation, and bends over backward; the result, so it is charged, is that the times when Reserve policy has been more evident have been times of relative deflation.

100-PER-CENT MONEY. One reform would end the ability of the banking system to create or destroy demand deposits, the main variable in our money supply. The reserve requirement would be raised to, and kept at, 100 per cent. Every dollar in demand deposits would have a dollar in currency behind it. In this way, a deposit of currency would reduce the amount in the public's hands and raise demand deposits by the same amount, the currency paid in serving as the reserve for the additional deposit. The total money supply—currency in the public's hands plus demand deposits—would be the same, although the composition would have changed. No longer would an inflow of currency result in excess reserves and thus tend to raise demand deposits by a multiple, and thereby total purchasing power. We will have fixed the money supply.

An outflow of currency from the banks would also leave the total money supply unchanged. The bank would simply give up the currency serving as backing, the decline in demand deposits being offset by the rise in currency in the hands of the public. Once again there would be no multiple reaction. And so we have stabilized M although V is still uncontrolled.

The demand-deposit banks, of course, would no longer have income-earning assets other than what funds they received through the issue of stock. Demand deposits would be matched by non-income-earning currency. To operate without their customary income sources would thus require appreciable increases in service charges. Income would arise only if the banks issued stock, against which no reserves need be kept; the funds so obtained could be invested or loaned out, and would thus add to income, from which dividends could be paid. Note that at present the entire bank asset holdings, other than required reserves, provide income for expenses and dividends; with 100-per-cent reserves, very little of the bank assets would be in this category.

No longer could a borrower go to a bank and receive a loan through a simple entry in his deposit account. A bank could only lend out its excess reserves; but with 100-per-cent required reserves, how would this excess arise?—only through the issuance of stock or retained profits from service charges and other operations. In other

words, only if some saver gave up currency for stock could a borrower get currency as a loan. Loans would thus be matched by genuine savings, and not by the creation of additional purchasing power.
Would the return from such a loan be enough to pay a dividend high
enough to induce the saver to purchase stock? This question cannot be
answered, but if the reply is "no," then we may have cut down on
potential lending, and, thus, potential capital acquisitions and growth.

How would the total money supply expand? Only if the Federal
Reserve or Treasury bought in the open market some of the government debt, thus adding to the money supply by printing currency in
payment. If this addition were more than the public wanted to carry, it
could deposit the funds in a demand deposit, and so the rise in money
outstanding is in the form of a deposit expansion, rather than a currency increase. In this way, as the economy grew and more money was
needed for transactions purposes, the government or Federal Reserve
would meet this increased need through such open-market purchases.
Conversely, if spending were too high and it was desired to reduce the
money supply, the Reserve could sell bonds and thus withdraw money
from the public. Unlike the present arrangements, though, the multiple
repercussions through the change in excess bank reserves would be
absent. Incidentally, we would not have to be concerned any longer
with differing ratios against demand deposits in country and reserve
city banks; shifts would have no effect, since both would be required
to maintain the same 100 per cent in currency as backing for the
deposit.

If we were to go over to the 100-per-cent reserve system, we
would have a transition problem. The Treasury could issue currency
and redeem all bank-held government bonds, and the Federal Reserve
could acquire the other income-earning assets. This would reduce the
cost of the debt, since interest would no longer be paid on the part
acquired by the Treasury. The issue of currency would not be inflationary, since it would all be immobilized in the banks as part of the
100-per-cent reserve requirement. In other words, we would have replaced bank holdings of income-earning assets with idle (zero velocity) non-income-earning currency.

COMMODITY RESERVE CURRENCY. Benjamin Graham[1] proposed a new
backing for currency—commodities. A bundle of commodities would
be selected as a basic unit, and all purchases and sales would be based
on this unit. For example, if a bundle consisted of a pound of copper, a
bushel of wheat, two pounds of cotton, and a half-pound of iron ore,

---

[1] *World Commodities and World Currencies.* New York: McGraw-Hill,
1944.

then all purchases and sales would be multiples of each of these; a sale of ten basic units would thus call for selling ten pounds of copper, ten bushels of wheat, twenty pounds of cotton, and five pounds of iron ore. A purchase of four basic units would call for buying four pounds of copper, four bushels of wheat, eight pounds of cotton, and two pounds of iron ore. Purchases thus expand the demand for all commodities in the basic unit in the same proportion; sales result in a supply expansion of all commodities in the basic unit in fixed proportions.

The basic unit would then be calculated at some "equilibrium" period, and a cost per unit established with, perhaps, a 5-per-cent range either way. Whenever the composite value of this unit dropped by more than 5 per cent below the equilibrium price, the authority would buy basic units, thus pushing up the prices of the component commodities until the composite value was raised to the equilibrium price (plus or minus 5 per cent). Whenever the basic unit exceeded the equilibrium amount by more than 5 per cent, the authorities would sell commodities, thus lowering their prices, until the basic unit's value returned to the accepted range. Note that this would stabilize the value of the basic unit, but not the individual commodities; these would still be free to move so long as the over-all group did not change beyond the accepted amounts. If wheat rose 5 per cent and cotton declined 5 per cent, the basic unit would remain unchanged, and so no corrective action would be necessary. Thus, we would have stabilized prices in general without freezing individual prices, as is the problem facing the United States agricultural program.

Payment for purchases would be through the issue of currency, with the commodities as backing. There would thus be no financial restriction on the authority. Sales of the commodities—when prices rose too far—would deplete the backing for the currency, but simultaneously reduce the currency outstanding. In effect, low prices would lead to the authority's issuing currency and taking in commodities; high prices would result in the authority's issuing commodities and taking back currency. Inflation would automatically lead to commodity sales, thus adding to supplies and also withdrawing purchasing power. Deflation would lead to commodity purchases, thus adding to demand and increasing the supply of purchasing power. We would thus have an automatic countercyclical policy. The authority could operate on a national level, buying and selling commodities produced in that country, or at the international level, buying a worldwide selection of items.

In our discussion of 100-per-cent reserves, the monetary authorities still had to intervene if spending was too much or too little; judgment was still required regarding the timing of such a move. With the commodity reserve, the price-level shifts in the basic unit would be the automatic indicators for such intervention; judgment would be minimal.

QUALIFICATIONS. In fixing the money supply, we have implicitly assumed that the price level should be stable, or at least we have assumed that some desired price level is possible. But just what is a desirable price trend? Rising prices help businessmen through improved profit margins. Workers also tend to benefit, for the higher profit margins lead to increased output and employment. But fixed-income groups suffer, through a decline in purchasing power. Declining prices have the opposite effects, aiding the fixed-income groups, but hindering business and employment. Even a stable price level, which would seem to imply that we hope we are not helping either group unduly, can be a misleading guide. For example, if technological advances are reducing costs of production, a stable price level would cause a profits inflation. If we allow, say, wage costs to rise to eliminate this danger, then we upset wage relationships; those in this progressive industry gain relative to their not so lucky brothers, even though both may be doing the same work with equal skills and training.

Indeed, maybe we should—perhaps we must—give thought to the need to give some push to business if we want full employment. If so, then we really must prefer the rising price level. Or maybe we want to encourage savings and perhaps thereby aid capital formation; in that case, perhaps a slowly falling price level would be better. Whichever guide we select means we have decided to influence the income distribution pattern in some way. And this decision, by influencing such patterns of incomes, may then affect future savings and capital increases, future incomes, the demand for labor and commodities, and so forth. In short, even the decision to stabilize still requires judgment; we cannot automatically select a price trend as our guide for the automatic regulator to achieve that objective. Judgment cannot be banished. And if we cannot automatically select our objective, have we really gained through selecting an automatic regulator to achieve that objective? Aren't we really fooling ourselves regarding the impartiality of our reform?

Velocity

The various proposals to fix the money supply all ignore velocity. But this is a defect in all such reforms. For as we change the money supply, we change the available balances. If this change is not desired by the public, there may be unwanted adjustments. For example, if we reduce the money supply to stop excessive expansion, the drain on the public's liquidity may induce it to economize on the utilization of remaining balances by stepping up velocity. Or a rise in the money supply may not flow into demand deposits, as assumed in the 100-percent reserve suggestion. Perhaps this will flow to the other financial intermediaries, who then relend it and thus speed up its velocity. Clearly, by operating on M, we reduce only one disturbing source, and may even aggravate the reactions in V.

To meet this problem, various proposals try to vary the money supply opposite to the change in velocity. For example, the required reserve against a demand deposit would vary with its velocity, as measured by the ratio of checks drawn to the average balance in the account. The more active the deposits, the higher the amount of required reserves, and thus the less money available to expand the deposit volume.

To illustrate, assume that a velocity of 1 per month requires a 10-per-cent reserve, and that a velocity of 2 per month a 20-per-cent reserve. If we have $10 billion in reserves and the average velocity is 1, then total deposits could amount to $100 billion. If velocity is 2, then total deposits could be only $50 billion. Note that, for either alternative, MV is constant at $100 billion.

Suppose a person with an account showing a velocity of 2 paid money to a person whose account had only a velocity of 1. The decline in activity would release reserves, and so more deposits could be created. Hence, as V dropped, M would rise. Conversely, if the lower-velocity account paid funds to the higher-velocity account, required reserves would rise, and so some of the outstanding deposit volume would have to be reduced; the rise in V would be matched by a decline in M. In this way MV would be constant, rather than just M, and so PT would be constant. Presumably, if T rose, the authorities would take steps to expand M, so that prices would not drop, the higher PT equaling the higher MV. Presumably, too, the month-to-month shifts in V would not be so drastic as to cause too wide a swing in M in the opposite and offsetting direction. If velocity did change in large proportions, thus calling for opposite large changes in demand deposits, this would require volatile changes in the volume of bank assets, which could be upsetting to both business and the money markets. For example, a 10-per-cent jump in average velocity could call for a cutback in bank deposits of $15 billion—quite a large chunk to subtract in a short period. Hopefully, the monthly alterations in the totals would be confined within the range of normal ups and downs in bank activity. And the problems involved in assessing velocity would also have to be solved, resulting in a working degree of exactness.

Selective or General Credit Controls?

Within the group that continues to favor discretionary monetary policies, there is a division between those who advocate general controls and those who prefer selective controls. General controls affect the price and availability of credit, but do not attempt to determine just which channels are to be influenced. Selective controls try to affect specific sectors of the economy while leaving the remainder untouched. General controls include use of the Federal Reserve discount rate, open-market operations, and variations in required-reserve ratios. Selective controls include stock-market credit, mortgage terms, and installment-loan regulations. At present, the Federal Reserve has only one selective control—the proportion that a securities purchaser must put up in cash (his margin); in the past it has also had mortgage and consumer-credit powers, but these have been allowed to lapse.

The general controls are usually quite flexible and easy to modify or reverse. They are simple, impartial, and require little policing. A rise in the discount rate is easy to enforce; any time a member bank comes to borrow, the new rate is applied. Or an open-market sale requires a call to a bond dealer and then a check in payment. A policy of open-market sales can be turned into one for purchases by a simple change in instructions to the traders. There is no distinction made among the money-market members; all are treated equally.

Selective controls must be policed. Margin requirements are applied by hundreds of brokers, while mortgage and consumer loans are handled by the thousands. Promulgating a regulation does not mean that it will be observed; changing one requires that it be understood by all those affected. Policing and explanations take time, and so changes are difficult to make. Each change affects a specific borrower very obviously, and he is likely to complain of discrimination if the change is contrary to his desires. Indeed, he may even try to bring political pressure to bear to get a more favorable ruling.

And yet, selective controls have their appeal, mainly because monetary policies are not as widely influential as in past periods. Many companies are immune to shifts in interest rates. Either their internally generated funds are sufficient, so that they do not borrow, or the profits prospects are so good that changes in interest costs are not significant enough to change their plans. People who want to buy a house or automobile are not going to change their plans merely because the interest charge has varied; often a slight stretch-out in the life of the loan can more than offset the added interest, thus maintaining the monthly charge, although it must now be paid over a somewhat longer period. Similarly, declining interest rates may not stimulate borrowing; all that may happen is a shortening of the life of the loan. As a consequence, manipulation of the interest rate may not change the volume of such loans, and thus the ultimate impact on spending will stay the same.

Often we do not want to restrict or boost the entire economy, but just one or two sectors. A general tightening or loosening of credit would probably cause wide declines or increases in the volume of borrowing and spending. But perhaps the depressed or overextended economy is in only the steel and auto sectors, the high (or low) demand for autos causing an excess (or insufficient) demand for steel. If we tighten credit, all buyers of steel are affected; if we ease credit, all buyers are helped. But in addition, those affected change their spending on many other items, too, and these we do not want to affect. By changing our controls over consumer credit, we can directly affect auto sales and thereby the demand for steel. We avoid compelling other borrowers to cut back their spending (or increase it, if expansionary) and thus avoid generalizing the shift. The effect on the entire economy is thus limited to the repercussions from the auto (and steel) sectors.

The Canadian Discount-Rate Experiment

During the 1950's, the Bank of Canada experimented with a novel approach for improving the effectiveness of the discount rate. As the Federal Reserve—and most central banks—employ this instrument, the rate is set and remains fixed until a decision is made to change it. As a result, any change becomes an indicator of great significance, a guide to central-bank policy. Yet, as we have already seen, all that may be resulting is a technical change, with little or no monetary significance.

The Canadians, therefore, tried a new approach. They felt that the discount rate should be a penalty rate—that whenever a bank was forced to borrow, the cost of such funds should always exceed the possible additional income that would be obtained. Since it was felt that the secondary reserves—government short-term paper—were the logical quality equivalent to this borrowing, the discount rate was now to be a constantly varying figure ($\frac{1}{4}$ per cent above the Canadian Treasury-bill rate). Hence, it would always pay a bank from the profit-and-loss computation to sell such bills, rather than borrow. If it felt that it could not sell, either because it did not have such bills or because such a sale would impair its liquidity position, it could borrow, and the

cost would be this extra ¼ per cent. Henceforth, changes in the discount rate would occur each week as the general market forces
changed the bill rate. No longer would each shift be endowed with
immense policy significance.

Critics, however, feel that such a rigid discount-rate policy for-
feits some of the advantages that the Federal Reserve has in being more
flexible. For one thing, the change makes the discount rate only a
restrictive instrument; with the Canadian approach, there is no way to
implement an easy-money policy by reducing the discount rate below
the bill rate. Further, there is no assurance that the ¼ per cent will be as
inhibiting as appears at first glance. By borrowing, the bank may be
relending at much higher rates, and so the ¼-per-cent extra cost can be
absorbed. No longer would the high discount rate be regarded as a
caution to go slow; rather, it would become simply a dollar-and-cents
matter, depending on the use to which the borrowed funds were put.
The moral pressure against borrowing would disappear, since the rate
would no longer be regarded as a tool for central-bank policy.

Securities as Reserves

Another suggested reform that still works within the framework
of the generalist approach is the requirement that government securities be kept as reserves against deposits, or as a proportion of assets.
(Some Continental European countries have tried variants of this approach.) Just as member banks in this country must keep a certain
percentage of non-income-earning reserves against deposits, so this
suggestion would add the requirement that a proportion of the income-
earning assets be in government securities. Hence, any expansion in
deposits would require an increase in the banks' ownership of government securities; not all the expansion could be for business loans.

Depending on circumstances, this suggestion has various objectives. Where it is feared that the business boom is very strong, so that
the demand for new financing is threatening to spill over into inflation,
such a policy might slow down the willingness of the banks to extend
such financial assistance. As it is now, the efforts of the Reserve to
tighten monetary conditions could be thwarted, if the banks have a
portfolio of government securities; all the banks need do is sell these
off and use the funds so obtained (or reserves freed as deposits decline)
to add to business loans. In the reform, adding to business loans would
require adding to the bank holdings of governments. If reserves were
already at the minimum, then no further expansion would be possible,
since the switching from governments to business loans has been
stopped. Or if excess reserves did exist, only a part could be used to

acquire business firms' obligations, the remainder being required for the additional government securities in this reserve sector.

Whether the restrictiveness would be as here outlined, however, is open to question. As it works now, a bank could sell governments and use the funds for business loans. But this means that someone must have bought the governments sold by the banks. If our reform prevents the bank sale of governments, it also stops the buyer from acquiring these securities and the business firm from borrowing from the bank. It is possible that the potential bond buyer will then simply acquire a security issued by the frustrated corporation, and so the same volume of lending goes on, except that the individual who would have bought the government bond sold by the bank now becomes the direct financing source for the corporation. The lender has changed, but the results are the same.

On the other hand, if excess reserves are present, then, under our present setup, the bank can lend to the business borrower without liquidating securities, and thereby add to the money supply. Under the reform discussed, here it would also be buying government securities. If it has a lot of excess reserves, it could make both acquisitions, and thus, in order to make the business loan, it has to create still more deposits—the portion going for the added government securities. If its reserves are inadequate, then the reform stops it from making as much in business loans as it would like to—because of the companion need to buy Government securities—and it still uses all its reserves to create deposits, except that not all of this newly created money goes to business (some having been diverted to the government securities market). In other words, the reform does not really stop the creation of purchasing power, but simply diverts some of it to the nonbusiness sector.

However, the advocates of this reform often have a different situation in mind—a business boom accompanied by a Government budgetary deficit. This was especially likely in the reconstruction years following World War II. Both business and the government wanted excess funds to rebuild and expand. The combined demand exceeded the available resources of the banking system. Since there was the acute shortage characteristic of such a situation, profit margins were high, and business could afford to pay high interest rates to get the money desired. To compete, the government would also have had to make loans at high yields, thus adding to the budgetary-taxation problem. But if such a new reserve requirement were instituted, then the government would be certain that a desired volume of bank assets had to go into government securities. It would not have to raise the interest paid to get these funds, since it had an assured market. This would reduce the cost of the debt, and thus the budget worry, and at the same time assure the government that its financing problems were taken care of. Note that we do not reduce bank lending, but only divert funds to the government.

There are some dangers inherent in such a prospect. For one thing, by setting the securities-reserve requirement sufficiently high, the government can virtually guarantee itself a market for as large a volume of debt as it wishes. It could thus pre-empt an excessive portion of the loanable funds, and so starve legitimate business borrowing, thereby holding back conversion and growth of the private sector. This, in turn, would create shortages, which the government could then employ as a justification for still further expansion of its activities, to make up for the shortages arising from the lagging business response. And so a vicious circle leading to more and more state-run activity could emerge.

Another ill effect is the possible splintering of the money market. As it functions now, lenders and investors can freely move back and forth among the various issues, depending on the relative attractiveness of these. If, for example, a business boom emerges, there also would result a heightened demand for loanable funds. For these to be obtained, the rates on corporate bonds would rise and thus attract funds from the other sectors. But with this reform a large portion of the possible shift of funds is stopped; the banks that own governments could not freely shift out of this sector because of the securities-reserve requirement. We have thus reduced the fluidity of the money market, walling off the government sector.

Moreover, since there is an assured demand for governments, as already remarked, the yield on these issues could be kept artificially low. If this yield is so low that the rate on alternative securities exceeds this level by more than the risk premium—as would probably occur, since the government rate has been unduly depressed—there would be few buyers for these governments. Only the banks would buy—and only because they have to. We would thus have a market in governments limited to this one group of investors. And if business activity should decline, reducing bank activity, it would also release some of the government securities from the required reserve. The banks might then try to sell this excess, and where would the buyers be? Only by offering a very sharp price concession would purchasers now come in from the other sectors. Hence, we might see even greater swings in the government bond market as a result of this more narrow trading result.

Suppose the government were running a surplus, and redeemed some of its bonds. Then, to meet the reserve requirement, the banks would have to go out into the open market and buy government assets. But this new demand in the face of a declining supply might cause a sharp rise in bond prices and a sharp decline in yields. Once again, we get a greater instability in the government bond market, this time on the up side. Combined with what was said in the preceding paragraph, we may even discourage dealers from operating in so widely fluctuating and uncertain a market. The trading activity would thus be narrowed even further, and the resulting fluctuations would become even wider. In short, we may well destroy one of the main advantages of owning government assets—the stability of price and a facility for making transactions without disturbances.

An alternative approach to limiting bank lending has been the suggestion of marginally higher reserve requirements. A base period is selected, and, for deposits equal to or lower than the amount in this base period, the required-reserve ratio is the one already in being. But for deposits above this amount, the required-reserve ratio is higher. In this way, expansion in excess of this base figure is slowed down. By adjusting the base to the amount that is considered acceptable (that would not produce excess expansion), the additions which might tend to produce an inflation are correspondingly reduced. Put another way, the multiplying power of excess reserves is lower when aggregate deposits exceed a certain amount (the one in the base period). Note that the banks are still free to lend to whomever they wish; all that is curbed is the amount of such lending. And as the economy grows, the base-period amount can be adjusted upward; the higher requirement would always be against the additional expansion which, it is feared, might trigger the inflation.

There is a minor drawback to this proposal, however. We might have two banks, one at the basic limit and one below it. A dollar of excess reserves at the former would support less of an expansion than a dollar at the latter. The chance distribution of excess reserves would thus give rise to different amounts of deposits. Yet, for the community as a whole, if we wish to curb expansion, we want the smaller amount, regardless of which bank has these reserves.

Selective Controls

The preceding group of reforms—the discount rate at ¼-per-cent premium, the securities reserve, the marginally higher required ratio—all allow the banks freedom to lend to whomever they please and at the rates they wish, so long as they stay within these new requirements. Even the securities reserve left the banks free to lend, although the amount that could be loanable was reduced by the portion tied up in additional holdings of government securities. In practice, as we have already remarked, we may wish to restrict the banks further—limiting the amount going to a particular sector or the amount spent by consumers on special items.

STOCK MARGINS. The excesses of the 1929 stock-market speculation on borrowed funds led to the imposition of the first selective controls—the amount of money that securities buyers could borrow to carry such acquisitions. Generally speaking, when activity in the stock market threatens to become too hectic, the Federal Reserve raises the margin, thus lowering the proportion that can be borrowed. This gradually reduces aggregate purchases, since speculators now have less funds to operate with, and so presumably reduces the upward pressures. When market activity subsides, the margin is reduced, thus enabling borrowers to expand the scale of the operations. At the same time, by reducing lending in the boom, more of the available loanable funds remain for other borrowers; presumably a boom is accompanied by excess demands for such funds, and so the pressure on lenders is reduced as well. In the recession, when funds are ample, the reduction in margins may step up borrowing, but since there is this excess supply, no other "legitimate" borrower is denied funds as a consequence.

CONSUMER CREDIT. Most consumer credit (installment paper) is for the purchase of durable goods, especially automobiles. In an upswing, as incomes rise, the buyers' credit standing improves, and so they can borrow more for such purchases. Demand thus swells for two reasons: the income rise, and the increase in borrowing. In the downturn, as lenders become more cautious, loans are less readily made. Hence, demand declines because of the lower income and the reduction in lending. In practice there may still be net lending in the latter period, but at a much lower rate. For example, in a boom, the rise in incomes may produce a total demand for automobiles of $15 billion; in addition, installment lending might add $4 billion. In a recession, the income drop might cut auto purchases to $10 billion, plus lending of only $2 billion. Result: a total demand of $19 billion in the boom becomes only $12 billion in the recession. If, instead, we tightened installment lending terms in the boom and eased them in the recession, we might have a prosperity demand, as before, of $15 billion plus, say, $2 billion of installment loans, and a recession demand of $10 billion plus $4 billion in loans. Result: a total demand in the boom of $17 billion becomes $14 billion in the recession, a decline of $3 billion, less than half that experienced in the other illustration. We have thus used consumer credit to cushion the decline.

One objection to this control is the discrimination inherent in its objective. We do influence the auto buyer, but only the one who must buy on credit. The man who can pay cash for the auto is unaffected. Indeed, he is helped, because the pressure on supplies in the boom has been reduced, and so the cash buyer finds it easier to get his car. In the recession, the additional purchases by the credit group do not bother him, for automobiles are in ample supply anyway. It is the poorer buyer—the one who must borrow—who feels the impact of the controls. He cannot buy as easily in the boom, and must wait for the recession to get easier access to installment funds.

The industries selling on installment credit are similarly discriminated against. When controls are tightened, only they suffer the decline in sales; all other industries continue unaffected. Hence, if we wish to check a boom through less installment selling, we curtail the operations of only a portion of the economy. Similarly, if we use this type of credit to stimulate the economy, by easing up on the terms, these particular sectors are the main ones to enjoy the benefit.

Some observers contend that installment buying may actually step up savings. If there were no such borrowing, some buyers would spend all their money on consumers' nondurables. By borrowing to buy a durable, they must cut down their spending on these other items in order to produce the surplus to repay the loan. If this durable is, say, a home, then if the buyer resorts to a mortgage—which is akin to installment buying—he may have a greater asset total, for the loan repayment will gradually give him an equity, the difference between the depreciated value of the home or other durable and the remaining balance on his loan. Since loan and mortgage payments usually are scheduled to make the remaining outstanding balance decline faster than the depreciation of the durable, the result is this favorable impact on equity.

If a person would save anyway in order to make a purchase of a durable, but instead prefers to buy on the installment plan, he thus accelerates the timing of his purchase. Now he can buy before he has saved. Instead of saving and then buying, he can now buy, and the saving then pays off the loan. Of course, he pays more this way because of the interest charge. But in return he gets the services of the product that much sooner. In a sense, we can regard the cost of the installment loan as the price for speedier enjoyment of the use of the durable.

An arithmetic note should be added here. For any one installment loan there is the eventual repayment unless the borrower defaults. Thus, every additional loan is eventually repaid. If new loans are made more quickly than old ones are paid off, then aggregate, outstanding installment credit rises. If new loans are made in smaller amounts than are being paid off on the old loans, then installment credit outstanding declines. In our discussion of the automobile alternatives, the lending figures were really net—gross (new) installment loans less repayments. The decline in such loans could be simply a sufficient reduction in new loans, so that the continuance of repayments on the older loans thus reduced the net figure.

MORTGAGE CREDIT. The arguments surrounding the use of mortgage-credit controls are similar to those for consumer credit, except that the transactions are larger and the loans longer. Houses usually sell for ten times as much as an auto, and mortgages may run for thirty years or more. But the logic would be the same, although the magnitudes are larger. Of course, virtually no one could buy a house for cash; here, tightening would mean that more of the purchase price would be for cash, less through borrowing. Or the life of the mortgage would be less, thus making the monthly payments more. Conversely for an easing of credit.

Deposit Insurance

During the late 1920's, and more so from 1930 to 1933, there were areas that were hard-hit, and so borrowers found it difficult to repay bank loans. Depositors feared for the safety of their funds, and rushed to withdraw their deposits. The banks could not realize on all their assets, and so they failed. This shrank the money supply, making the bad times even worse. So more borrowers found repayment difficult. And more people wanted their money from the banks. And more banks failed.

To prevent this from recurring, the government set up the Federal Deposit Insurance Corporation (FDIC) in 1933 to guarantee deposits up to a certain amount (currently $10,000 per account). Thus reassured, there would be no need for the public to withdraw funds from the banks. And so banks would not fail. And so the money supply would not shrink. And so a recession would not worsen.

To finance this contingency, the FDIC has built up a fund from assessments on the insured banks. At present, its fund equals about 1 to 2 per cent of insured deposits, and, if necessary, it could borrow about an equal amount from the Treasury. Such a fund has thus proved more than adequate for the rare failure that still occasionally takes place.

But suppose people do panic again. Suppose they worry about whether a wholesale run of failures might exhaust the FDIC; then what protection would there be? If such a panicky feeling were to emerge, obviously there would not be enough funds to meet the drain. There just is not enough currency outstanding to service a 100-per-cent withdrawal of deposits. In such a situation there would probably be only one way out, if widespread insolvencies were to be averted. Either the Treasury or Federal Reserve would have to buy up the banks' assets, supplying newly printed currency in return. This the banks could then use to meet depositors' demands.

Would this be inflationary? Probably not, for the depositors do not wish to spend their funds; their concern is safety. Hence, they would probably hoard it at home, and so the zero velocity would remove any impact on the spending stream. Once the panic passed, the money would probably be redeposited, and then the banks could return the cash, receiving back the assets turned over previously. Suppose the depositors tried to send their funds out of the country? This could create an enormous supply of dollars on the world's foreign-exchange markets, and so drive down its value. If this were to happen, the government would have to restrict such attempts, to preserve the external value of the currency. Since our gold stock is far too small to meet such a situation, the only alternative would be to control the international sector, and so stop the flight from the country. Actually, if such controls were entirely effective, we would not have to sacrifice any of our gold; the Treasury would not have to redeem the currency for gold. All it need do is sell gold for foreign currencies, if that is necessary to maintain the external value of the dollar. But if we prevent the panic selling of the dollar, we prevent the need for gold sales.

Summary

Monetary reformers yearn for a probably nonexistent past, when the system worked automatically and when no human decisions, from which error could arise, were part of our control mechanism. Such was attributed to the gold standard, wherein production and costs were so interrelated that inflation, by raising costs, braked the gold supply, thus reducing the inflow to bank reserves, and so expansion gradually ended. The recession was brought to an end when costs fell low enough to stimulate gold production and the inflow to bank reserves. But the modern world does not have the price and cost flexibility necessary for this type of adjusting mechanism, and instead the experience has been inflation or widespread unemployment. This is the case for intervention.

Suggestions include general control over the money supply, velocity, bank assets, deposits in excess of certain limits, and the discount rate. These operate on the total volume of credit, generally disregarding the specific borrower. Selective controls go further, preferring to influence special sectors which threaten to get out of line, or whose activity it is felt is particularly influential on economic operations as a whole. These are frankly discriminatory, and, as such, call for much more policing, inviting political repercussions.

Chapter 26

THE CONTRIBUTION OF THE CREDIT SYSTEM

In this, our concluding chapter, we shall assess the contribution of the credit system. Is the credit system simply the "grease" that lubricates the exchange mechanism, thus essentially duplicating what we would have in a barter economy, though more efficiently? Or are there fundamental alterations in the economy that make the presence or absence of a smoothly working credit mechanism of extreme importance? Because credit is so intangible, its assessment is not as obvious as might be true for inventions of new machines; yet its contribution may be equally important for society's welfare.

Capital Formation

Raising productivity and living standards requires additional capital, either as machinery or as public works such as roads and schools. To attain this capital, we must produce more than we consume, the excess going into the formation of these projects. From the income point of view, this difference is savings; from the productive point of view, the excess is investment. Note that we need both the savings and the investment; output in excess of consumption need not lead to capital formation; it could be left as idle accumulations of commodities.

In a barter economy, theoretically, we could evolve a pattern of behavior that does lead to capital formation. For example, if I can catch three large fish daily, but need only two for the satisfaction of my hunger, I have several choices of action. I could eat more, consuming all three fish each day. I could work two days and catch six fish, but limit my daily consumption to two. Assuming that the fish will not spoil, I could thus loaf every third day and still not starve. A third choice would be that of the miser: each day I could catch three fish, consume two, and save the third. Each day my stockpile of fish would rise by one, but neither I nor anyone else would be touching it. In the modern sense I am saving, but it is not being matched by investment; it is not being put into any productive activity.

There is a final possibility that we may quickly realize. Suppose I limit my daily consumption to two fish, and catch fish only two out of every three days. Every third day I eat the excess from the preceding two days and work at building a boat. After several such cycles I will have finished my task. Once again I have a choice. Every third day I can go out in my new boat for pleasure; I have acquired a consumers' durable. This is analogous to saving for a pleasure automobile. Or I could use the boat to reach better waters and so step up my daily catch of fish. The resulting increase in my product per day would be a measure of the contribution of this boat.

Having stepped up my daily productivity, I could use the extra fish for several purposes, as before. I could have more leisure, since now fewer days' work will satisfy my needs. I could consume more. I could stockpile more fish. Or I could use the leisure to work on still other capital goods—for example, a net—and thus eventually step up productivity even more. Or, of course, I could choose from each of these possibilities. Note that if I choose net-making, the added productivity of my first capital item has made it that much easier to create still more capital; it has increased my surplus production still more, and so made it that much easier to stop fishing for a while and devote my efforts to still further capital formation.

An alternative is also present if I desire the boat or net. If someone else has already made such an item, I could trade the fish for the capital item. Or perhaps I make the boat, and then trade it with someone else who has saved fish. In other words, by specializing on boat-building or net-making, I could then trade these finished products for fish, and thus not have to go fishing myself. In effect, we have here a division of labor. Some members of a society catch more fish than they consume, and the excess is swapped with others who do not catch any fish, but make implements that enable the fishermen to catch enough excess fish to make such trades feasible. The fishermen would be similar to modern-day consumers'-goods producers; the implement-makers would be the capital-goods producers.

What we have illustrated here is akin to the modern corporation's generating its own funds from operations and then investing them in its own activities. The decision to save and the decision to put this excess into capital goods are both made by the same group. No credit enters into the picture, and so all that really differs is the ease with which specific capital acquisitions can be effected. In our barter example, the saver did not have to do the work himself. In the corporate alternative, the saving corporation did not have to make the equipment either; it could make a straight cash purchase of a machine.

Credit and Capital Formation

Suppose we alter one of our barter examples somewhat. Let us assume that not every member of the society can make nets or boats, or go fishing. At the moment all of them fish, and each catches three per day. Everyone so far has used this catch for his daily consumption. One now decides to live on only two fish, using the excess fish to acquire a boat. But unfortunately he does not have the skill to make such a capital good. So he must find someone who can. But for this latter person to quit fishing in order to make the boat means that during his working (or in-process) period he must get the fish from somewhere. This our saver can provide. Every second day he has caught two fish in excess of his own restricted consumption. This means that every second day he can give the boatbuilder one day's food, and thus free him for this new task. But the saver must have faith in the builder; he must trust him to spend his time working and not idling. In other words, there must be an assurance that the obligation will be fulfilled—the essential element in any credit transaction. Note that our boatbuilder could not have taken the time out to build the boat in advance of the purchase, for he has not reduced his consumption by enough to produce the fish surplus to free him from his daily chores. Because the saver and the producer of the capital goods are different, there emerges this need for credit.

Credit could emerge in another form in this barter economy. Suppose that *A* is not too skillful a fisherman, and barely catches his two fish per day. However, with a boat he could double his daily catch.

Since he must consume all his own catch now, he cannot produce a surplus with which to finance a boatbuilder. Suppose further that *B* is saving one fish per day, keeping it stored against future uncertainties, when he might be ill and thus unable to catch fish. *A* could go to *B* and borrow the surplus fish, using them to feed *C* while *C* builds a boat. Out of the resulting increased catch, *A* could then repay *B*, giving him the number of fish borrowed plus extra fish as a return for the favor. This last "extra," of course, is our modern-day interest.

Here we see the necessary faith in another form. *B* must trust *A*—that he will repay the fish, that he will give him the extra, and that the fish will come back when scheduled. For if *A* returns the fish, but much later than agreed upon, *B* may have taken ill in the interim. For example, suppose *B* is getting old and feels that in another year he will be unable to fish any longer. He has agreed to lend *A* the fish now, provided he gets it all back (plus interest) before the end of the year. If *A* delays—pays back the agreed sum, but three years later—*B* may be dead! *B* needed the fish next year, not in later years. On the other hand, if *A* must delay repayment, it is also possible that *B* is still healthy enough to fish, and so does not need the repayment yet. He may then agree to let *A* postpone repayment, but perhaps demand a somewhat increased "extra"—the equivalent of additional interest for the longer period of time, plus, perhaps, a penalty for (in effect) renewing a loan. And, of course, *B* must trust *A* that he will fulfill this new arrangement as per agreement. Incidentally, *A* also has a credit arrangement with *C* that *C* will produce the boat, thus enabling *A* to catch the extra fish to repay *B*.

It is quite obvious that we have the same transactions in a money society—the saver (*B*) who does not want to acquire the capital equipment, the man who wants the capital but does not have the savings for its purchase (*A*), and the actual producer of the capital equipment (*C*). Put another way, we have here three specializations—a division of labor, so to speak. There are those who specialize in producing savings, those who specialize in using capital equipment, and those who specialize in producing capital equipment. It is possible to combine them; we have illustrated this in the example of the corporation that both saves and utilizes capital equipment. But in our modern society this specialization has been carried very far, so that much of our savings comes from units that do not utilize them, being lent to others whose needs exceed their own funds.

Because of the complexity of modern-day society, we have even produced a new specialist—the intermediary who brings saver and borrower together—banks and other financial institutions. They could also be present in a barter economy, of course. *D*, for example, may know both *A* and *B*, whereas *A* may not be acquainted with *B*. Without *D*, *A* would not get *B's* fish. With *D*, the two can be matched. However, in the large and complex modern world, the possibility that lender and borrower are unaware of each other becomes a probability. Indeed, it is the rare saver who ever meets the final borrower! And, of course, the addition of this intermediary adds still further to the credit apparatus: now the saver must trust the intermediary, the intermediary must trust the borrower, and the borrower must trust the capital-goods producer. We thus see that credit—whether in a barter or a money economy—enables us to match divergences between the excess of income over consumption and the excess of spending over receipts. The latter, to repeat, cannot operate on this basis unless there is someone else who can supply him with the funds to close that gap. Put another way, the borrower, whose operations would produce a gap in which spending exceeds income, must be "married" to a saver whose gap is an excess of receipts over spending. Otherwise, the saver's gap would end up in idle hoards, while the borrower's needs would go unsatisfied. (Presumably the saver cannot use the excess himself, for if he could, he would have done so and thus removed his savings from the market.)

A minor comment might be added regarding "abstinence." In one sense the saver can produce savings only if he restricts consumption—if he abstains from spending. Savings are thus the result of abstinence. But it is also true that a man with a weekly income of $25,000 can easily save without denying himself anything. Yet he, too, has abstained, even though it has been much easier for him than his poorer relative earning $80 a week. He has held back his spending; abstinence was there, but easier to practice.

The Financial Intermediary

As can be seen from the discussion so far, there is one possible major sector where our savings could go to waste—where the saver is not the one who wishes to use the funds to acquire capital goods. In that event, not only do we need some other borrower who does have such an intent, but also we must find the means whereby the two can be brought together. In a society as large as ours, this is no easy task, and so the financial intermediary serves this purpose. We can therefore conclude that credit enables the saver and borrower to effect a greater use of savings, and this is further supplemented by the efforts of the financial intermediaries. Hence, to the extent that savings would otherwise go to waste, we have here a specific contribution of both our credit mechanism and the financial institutions that serve it.

The financial intermediary often serves another function—greater efficiency in the use of savings. For example, suppose there are two projects, one which could raise aggregate output by 10 per cent per annum and the other by 20 per cent per annum. Each requires the same amount of (borrowed) capital, but the saver knows of only the first, the less productive one. In the absence of a financial intermediary, he would thus lend his funds to the 10-per-cent project, since he has no alternative. But a financial intermediary whose job it is to seek out borrowers may, through its superior organization, also unearth the second borrower. More probably, the mere existence of a financial intermediary will attract to it more borrowers than are likely to discover any lone individual lender. Thus we can finance the more productive project. Presumably, since it is so much more productive, it can pay a higher price for the borrowed funds, not only covering the cost of the intermediary, but also returning a greater income to the lender. Furthermore, since its addition to output is greater, the aggregate output for society is enhanced more than if our 10-per-cent project had gotten the funds. We thus see a general improvement in benefits as a result of this superior allocation of loanable funds.

The financial intermediaries may also increase the incentive to save. A person who saves cannot, by merely setting aside such savings, raise his aggregate income. At best he reduces spending now, and the funds so saved can be spent later. He thus merely rearranges the time pattern of his spending. This may still be a benefit, of course. If his income is high now and is expected to decline later, this means that he reduces spending on less necessary items now in order to raise his spending on more necessary items later. But with the existence of intermediaries, he will probably be able to get a return (interest) for his savings, thus producing an actual increase. We thus see a possible incentive to save money, since this extra gain is possible. If so, then the aggregate volume of the community's savings would be more than if it did not have such intermediaries, and so the volume of capital formation and future levels of output are thereby increased. Once again we would have here a direct measure of the contribution of our credit mechanism.

In sum, therefore, we can measure the "real" contribution of the credit mechanism by its final effects on the volume of capital formation and the resultant impact on output and living standards. On the other hand, we must also put down a debit against the credit system. As we discussed earlier, the presence of a monetary system leads to the phenomenon of liquidity, with its unsettling effects. Shifts in liquidity can alter the supply-demand equilibrium, and so generate cumulative spirals either upward into inflation or downward into a recession. Such multiple reactions would be virtually absent in a barter economy.

While on balance the pros for credit outweigh the cons, we must realize that there is not a pure gain. Furthermore, at the individual level there is always the possibility of a borrower going into default, and so the lender loses his savings. Again this would be absent in the barter economy without credit, where everyone used only his own savings. Such losses of past income—such losses on consumption foregone—are possible only where we have introduced the credit pattern of lending and borrowing.

Growth and the Money Supply

Since in the modern world we do use money, we can for all practical purposes ignore the alternative of a barter economy. The economy today cannot change over to such a system. Hence, we must work within the framework of a money system, and our objective today is to increase its efficiency and contribution to our objectives of growth and stability.

In this section, we shall assume that we do achieve growth, that over the years the volume of goods and services is being expanded and that living standards are tending to rise. What should the money-supply reaction be to smooth this long-run trend?

What we are saying, essentially, is that there is a long-run tendency for output and the volume of saleable goods and services to rise—the T in our money equation. If we keep M constant, then either V must rise or P must drop. The former may occur, but if not, the latter must. But if prices decline, profit margins shrink, and unless costs are resilient—specifically, unless wages per unit of output can be reduced—then output will be cut back. We thus defeat our growth objective, of course, for if we decrease T sufficiently, then P no longer need fall. But the growth goal means a rising T.

Is it possible to rely on a rise in V? Probably some rise would occur, under the pressure of increased output, but there is no certainty that it will rise sufficiently to support an unchanged P. As the volume of production expands, and if M is kept constant, then borrowing is not being stepped up, and so the volume of demand deposits is the same. Then business firms to finance the added volume may manage their balances more efficiently, which, as we have seen, results in a higher V. But this rise is limited by their ability to economize. There are limits to such efficiencies, which means that there are limits to the extent to which we can increase velocity. When we consider the enormous rise in T over the past two centuries in the United States, it would be heroic indeed to have expected V to rise correspondingly and thus avoid any price deflation.

Hence our conclusion that the money supply must rise if growth is to be supported. We have already seen that the exact amount of this increase in M could still influence P; too little would mitigate, but not eliminate, a decline, and too much would actually cause a price rise. And these alternatives, in turn, would have their repercussions on the distribution of income. Here again we have a difference from the barter economy. Growth there would add to the supply of commodities, but also to the demand as the producers offered more in exchange. Both supply and demand would thus expand in step, and so the danger of a disequilibrium situation is lessened. If demand did not expand the marketable supply could not rise; any added output would then simply be stored for future use.

In the money economy, what growth produces is an increasing supply offered for money, and thus the money supply (MV) must expand. If not, then by simple division a larger volume of goods offered for the same volume of money produces a lower average amount of money per physical unit—in other words, a price decline. Growth also will raise demand, more money being offered for the goods. But if we have reached the limits of our economizing on money, we cannot get this added demand through a rise in V. Then either M rises, or aggregate demand in money terms remains unchanged. And, as our earlier liquidity discussion brought out, growth may also change the volume of idle funds that people wish to hold— the desire to be liquid. This can further alter the variations between the amount of money in the community and the amount that becomes effective demand through changes in the velocity component. Maximum growth without price instability thus becomes quite a delicate objective, for the changes in the volume of goods being offered on the market must be balanced with the shifts in the average velocity of the money supply.

Stability and Growth

Ideally, as we have remarked from time to time, the monetary system should be so controlled as to result in maximum growth with minimum instability. We have seen how many disrupting influences there are in a modern economy which make such a goal difficult to achieve. Yet it is the task of the Federal Reserve and the Treasury, using their monetary and fiscal powers, to strive toward this ideal as best they can.

But often there may be a conflict between what the monetary and fiscal authorities deem most advisable and what the public desires. This shows up especially in times of a boom, when there is the danger that the upswing may overflow into inflation. At such a point, the authorities are interested in restraining spending. But obviously, this will reduce the demand for specific commodities and services, which will irk the businesses and workers affected. Borrowers who are denied funds —or whose demands are met only in part—will complain of the inequities of monetary policy. Perhaps the public prefers a little inflation to a little less employment, whereas the authorities are striving for price stability at the expense of some joblessness.

Hence, an additional task for the authorities is one of educating the public. If the public is in error—if it desires both full employment and price stability when the two are incompatible—then clearly the opposition between these two goals should be discussed. We cannot oppose inflation and at the same time refrain from taking steps to reduce spending and lending. Such contradictions are the product of ignorance.

But it could also be possible that the goals desired by the public are different from those the authorities are striving to implement. For example, as our earlier case illustrated, the public might prefer a little more inflation if the alternative is a little less employment, whereas the authorities have the reverse priorities. Then the situation is more difficult. The authorities could try to educate the public and convert them to their own priorities, but are they correct in so trying? Perhaps it would be just as desirable for the public to register its demands more strongly, and bring to bear the necessary influences that would induce the authorities to implement policies more in line with what the public desires. In our preceding paragraph it was a problem of ignorance on the part of the public. But here there is a genuine difference in objectives; which of the two sets of views is to prevail may be simply a matter of relative strength in the political process.

In practice, especially in the United States, it would appear that both problems are present. There is ample evidence that the public does not realize that what it wants is often an incompatible set of objectives. But there is also ample evidence to make the outsider suspect that the Federal Reserve has often pursued policies which, even if rightly comprehended by the public, would not be desirable to the populace. In particular, the tendency of the Reserve to be excessively anti-inflation-minded has been commented on all too frequently. The sorry employment record that this country has experienced in the past half-dozen years may make us wonder just where the right answers can be obtained.

On the other hand, we should not go to so great an extreme in our criticism as to become unfair. The Federal Reserve System is charged with an awesome responsibility, and its operations can easily have far-reaching and perhaps catastrophic effects. Its members must make decisions based on incomplete information, much of it the reflection of economic activities that have already passed perhaps one or two months prior to the receipt of the data. These men must act on their interpretation of this information. In effect, they must take facts that are several months old and then read into them not only how this already stale picture of the economy indicates where the state of operations is currently, but also where it is tending in the near future. It is quite obvious that misinterpretations can easily arise in such circumstances.

Furthermore, as watchdogs for our monetary system, it is natural that their primary worry is the preservation of the currency's value. It is easy for outsiders not charged with any of these responsibilities to say that the Federal Reserve Board has been too worried about inflation. But the Board can point to the fact that although the United States has experienced inflation over the past two decades, it has been among the mildest that any of the other countries have had to suffer. We have not had to go through the searing hardships associated with the gradual decline to worthlessness that the German, Hungarian, Chinese, and other currencies went through. We have not seen our purchasing power go down by some 99%, as has occurred in many of the countries of Continental Europe and Latin America. The amount of unemployment that has been the price paid is to a large extent not the result of insufficient purchasing power—the major tool to halt inflation —but the consequence of numerous structural and technological influences that are reflective of our dynamic economy. It is asking too much to expect the Federal Reserve to stop the loss of jobs resulting from automation, the decline of old industries, the insufficient training of school "drop-outs," and the immobility of unwanted labor in the coal, textile, and agricultural sections of our country. Monetary measures simply are not adequate to cope with these tasks, and so should not be criticized for failing to do so.

Furthermore, our knowledge of the relationships between specific monetary policies and their repercussions on economic activity is still quite limited. In earlier chapters we have referred repeatedly to alternative outcomes arising from various moves that could be made by the Board. Expectations and uncertainties are still a tricky unknown in our equations, and, as we have seen, the same move at one moment of time may trigger reactions quite different if undertaken in a different economic environment. Of course, the many unsolved problems implied in this paragraph are the subjects for further study on the part of monetary economists and practitioners. It is along such paths that future research must be conducted, and many of our compatriots are even now working toward a better understanding of the complex interrelationships. The tools that the Federal Reserve was given at its formation on the eve of World War I were far better understood than when the Civil War's financial problems faced this country. Today we are still better able to cope with the many economic difficulties than we were half a century ago. And, hopefully, we shall close the gap even further in the next generations. It is these very unknowns, in short, that add the zest of adventure to the worker in the field of monetary economics.

Summary

The major contribution of the credit system is to enable specialization to take place in the savings-and-investment process. No longer must a saver also have an outlet for his funds in his own activity; he can turn the funds over to someone else to use. No longer must the man who wants to acquire capital goods also produce the savings; he can borrow. And the producer of capital goods need not be either a saver or an investor. Furthermore, we also have specialists, known as financial intermediaries, whose task it is to bring lender and borrower together, actually taking on the lending functions for the saver.

As a consequence, our main concern today is that the money supply expand in step with the growth in output capabilities. Too rapid a rise in the money supply breeds inflation; too slow an increase brings unemployment. The closer we get to our ideal, the less the disturbances from instability, and the greater our long-run productive capacity and living standards. To achieve this kind of monetary system is the job of the Federal Reserve; how well the members discharge their duty is a compound of their own abilities, their correct assessment of the desired objectives, and the general knowledge of monetary actions as they influence the economy. We are still a long way from paradise, but the passage of years has refined our tools and increased our know-how. The increasing precision of the mechanism is the task for the contemporary monetary student.

Bibliography

General Texts

Barger, H. *Money, Banking and Public Policy*. Chicago: Rand McNally & Co., 1962.

Chandler, L. V. *Economics of Money and Banking*, 3rd ed. New York: Harper and Brothers, 1959.

Day, A. C. L., and S. T. Beza. *Money and Income*. New York: Oxford University Press, 1960.

Halm, G. N. *Economics of Money and Banking*. Homewood, Ill.: Richard D. Irwin, 1956.

Harriss, C. L. *Money and Banking*. Boston: Allyn and Bacon, 1961.

Hart, A. G., and P. B. Kenen. *Money, Debt and Economic Activity*, 3rd ed. New York: Prentice-Hall, 1961.

Kreps, C. H., Jr. *Money, Banking and Monetary Policy*. New York: Ronald Press, 1962.

Ritter, L. S. (ed.). *Money and Economic Activity*, 2nd ed. Boston: Houghton Mifflin Co., 1961.

Shaw, E. S. *Money, Income and Monetary Policy*. Homewood, Ill.: Richard D. Irwin, 1950.

Smith, L. *Money, Credit, and Public Policy*. Boston: Houghton Mifflin Co., 1959.

Steiner, W. H.; E. Shapiro; and E. Solomon. *Money and Banking*, 4th ed. New York: Holt, Rinehart & Winston, 1958.

Whittlesey, C. R. *Money and Banking*, 3rd ed. New York: Macmillan Co., 1963.

Economic Instability

Ackley, G. *Macroeconomic Theory*. New York: Macmillan Co., 1961.

American Economic Association. *Readings in Business Cycle Theory*. Philadelphia: Blakiston Co., 1944.

Bronfenbrenner, M., and F. D. Holzman. "Survey of Inflation Theory," *American Economic Review*, September 1963.

Haberler, G. *Prosperity and Depression*, 4th ed. Cambridge, Mass.: Harvard University Press, 1958.

Hansen, A. H. *Business Cycles and National Income*, expanded ed. New York: W. W. Norton and Co., 1964.

Hayek, F. A. *Prices and Production*. Baltimore, Md.: G. Routledge & Sons, 1934.

Hicks, J. R. *A Contribution to the Theory of the Trade Cycle*. New York: Oxford University Press, 1950.

Klein, L. R. *The Keynesian Revolution*. New York: Macmillan Co., 1947.

Knorr, K., and W. J. Baumol. *What Price Economic Growth?* Englewood Cliffs, N.J.: Prentice-Hall, 1961.

Shaalan, A. S. "The Impact of Inflation on the Composition of Private Domestic Investment," International Monetary Fund *Staff Papers*, July 1962.

Money and Banking Development

Beckhart, B. H. (ed.) *Banking Systems*. New York: Columbia University Press, 1954.

Carothers, N. *Fractional Money*. New York: John Wiley & Sons, 1930.

Carson, D. (ed.). *Banking and Monetary Studies*. Homewood, Ill.: Richard D. Irwin, 1963.

Clapham, Sir John. *The Bank of England*, 2 vols. New York: Cambridge University Press, 1944.

Federal Reserve Board. "The Monetary System of the United States," *Federal Reserve Bulletin*, February 1953.

Hammond, B. *Banks and Politics in America from the Revolution to the Civil War*. Princeton, N.J.: Princeton University Press, 1957.

King, W. T. C. *History of the London Discount Market*. Baltimore, Md.: G. Routledge & Sons, 1936.

Mints, L. W. *History of Banking Theory in Great Britain and the United States*. Chicago: University of Chicago Press, 1945.

Myers, M. G.; B. H. Beckhart; J. G. Smith; and W. A. Brown, Jr. *The New York Money Market*, 4 vols. New York: Columbia University Press, 1931–2.

Netzer, D., and A. D. Goldstine. "Types of Money Use in the 1950's," *Journal of Finance*, December 1962.

Nussbaum, A. *A History of the Dollar*. New York: Columbia University Press, 1957.

Banking Institutions and Operations

Alhadeff, D. A. "The Market Structure of Commercial Banking in the United States," *Quarterly Journal of Economics*, February 1951.

Federal Reserve Bank of Kansas City. *Essays on Commercial Banking*. Kansas City, Mo.: 1962.

Federal Reserve Bank of New York. *Essays in Money and Credit*. New York: 1964.

Federal Reserve Board. *Banking Studies*. Baltimore, Md.: The Waverly Press, 1941.

Federal Reserve Board. *The Federal Funds Market*. Washington, D.C.: 1959.

Garvey, G. *Debits and Clearings Statistics and Their Use*, 2nd ed. Washington, D.C.: Federal Reserve System, 1959.

Luckett, D. G. "Compensatory Cyclical Bank Asset Adjustments," *Journal of Finance*, March 1962.

Orr, D., and W. G. Mellon. "Stochastic Reserve Losses and Expansion of Bank Credit," *American Economic Review*, September 1961.

Robinson, R. I. *The Management of Bank Funds*. New York: McGraw-Hill Co., 1951.

Smith, W. L. "The Instruments of General Monetary Control," *National Banking Review*, September 1963.

Tobin, J. "Monetary Policy and the Management of the Public Debt: the Patman Inquiry," *The Review of Economics and Statistics*, May 1953.

Federal Reserve System

Aschheim, J. "Open-Market Operations Versus Reserve Requirement Variation," *Economic Journal*, December 1959.

———. *Techniques of Monetary Control*. Baltimore, Md.: Johns Hopkins University Press, 1961.

Bach, G. L. *Federal Reserve Policy-Making*. New York: Alfred A. Knopf, 1950.

Carr, H. C. "Why and How to Read the Federal Reserve Statement," *Journal of Finance*, December 1959.

Federal Reserve Board. *The Federal Reserve System—Purposes and Functions*, 5th ed. Washington, D.C.: 1963.

Gaines, T. C. *Techniques of Treasury Debt Management*. New York: The Free Press, 1962.

Johnson, H. G. *Alternative Guiding Principles for the Use of Monetary Policy*. Princeton, N.J.: International Finance Section, 1963.

———. "Monetary Theory and Policy," *American Economic Review*, June 1962.

Meigs, A. J. *Free Reserves and the Monetary Supply*. Chicago: University of Chicago Press, 1962.

Miller, E. "Monetary Policies in the U.S. Since 1950," *Canadian Journal of Economics and Political Science*, May 1961.

Prochnow, H. V. (ed.). *The Federal Reserve System.* New York: Harper & Bros., 1960.

Roosa, R. V. *Federal Reserve Operations in the Money and Government Securities Market.* New York: Federal Reserve Bank of New York, 1956.

Smith, P. F. "Optimum Rate on Time Deposits," *Journal of Finance*, December 1962.

Smith, W. L. *Debt Management in the United States*, Joint Economic Committee Study Paper no. 19, 86th Congress, 2nd Session. Washington, D.C.: 1960.

Monetary Theory

Baumol, W. J. *Economic Theory and Operations Analysis.* Englewood Cliffs, N.J.: Prentice-Hall, 1961, ch. 12.

Hart, A. G. *Anticipations, Uncertainty and Dynamic Planning.* New York: Kelley, 1940.

Keynes, J. M. *The General Theory of Employment, Interest and Money.* New York: Harcourt, Brace, 1936.

———. *Treatise on Money*, 2 vols. New York: Harcourt, Brace, 1930.

Lange, O. "The Rate of Interest and the Optimum Propensity to Consume," *Economica*, February 1938.

Marget, A. W. *The Theory of Prices*, 2 vols. New York: Prentice-Hall, 1938, 1942.

McGouldrick, P. F. "A Sectoral Analysis of Velocity," *Federal Reserve Bulletin*, December 1962.

Modigliani, F. "Liquidity Preference and the Theory of Interest and Money," *Econometrica*, January 1944.

Robertson, D. H. *Money.* New York: Pitman, 1948.

Savings-Investment

Böhm von Bawerk, E. *Capital and Interest.* New York: Macmillan Co., 1890.

Dorfman, R.; P. A. Samuelson; and R. M. Solow. *Linear Programming and Economic Analysis.* New York: McGraw-Hill Co., 1958, chs. 11–13.

Duesenberry, J. F. *Income, Saving, and the Theory of Consumer Behavior.* Cambridge, Mass.: Harvard University Press, 1949.

Federal Reserve Board. *Flow of Funds in the United States, 1939–53.* Washington, D.C.: 1955.

Macaulay, F. R. *Some Theoretical Problems Suggested by the Movements of Interest Rates, Bond Yields and Stock Prices.* Princeton, N.J.: National Bureau of Economic Research, 1938.

Marcus, E. "The Interest-Rate Structure," *Review of Economics and Statistics*, August 1948.

Ohlin, B. "Some Notes on the Stockholm Theory of Savings and Investment," *Economic Journal*, March and June 1937.

Robinson, R. I. *Money and Capital Markets*. New York: McGraw-Hill Co., 1964.

Selden, R. T. *Trends and Cycles in the Commercial Paper Market*. New York: National Bureau of Economic Research Occasional Paper 85, 1963.

Wicksell, K. *Interest and Prices*. New York: Macmillan Co., 1936.

Non-Banking Intermediaries

Bloch, E. "Short Cycles in Corporate Demand for Government Securities and Cash," *American Economic Review*, December 1963.

Clayton, G. "British Financial Intermediaries in Theory and Practice," *Economic Journal*, December 1962.

Goldsmith, R. W. *Financial Intermediaries in the United States since 1900*. New York: National Bureau of Economic Research, 1958.

Gurley, J. G., and E. S. Shaw. "Financial Aspect of Economic Development," *American Economic Review*, September 1955.

Kreps, C. H., Jr., and D. T. Lapkin. "Public Regulation and Operating Conventions Affecting Sources of Funds of Commercial Banks and Thrift Institutions," *Journal of Finance*, May 1962.

Rieser, C. "The Great Credit Pump," *Fortune*, February 1963.

Tobin, J., and W. C. Brainard. "Financial Intermediaries and the Effectiveness of Monetary Controls," American Economic Association *Proceedings*, May 1963.

International Influences

Angell, J. W., "The Reorganisation of the International Monetary System: An Alternative Proposal," *Economic Journal*, December 1961.

Bloomfield, A. I. *Monetary Policy under the International Gold Standard: 1880–1914*. New York: Federal Reserve Bank of New York, 1959.

Brown, W. A., Jr. *The International Gold Standard Reinterpreted, 1914–1934*. New York: National Bureau of Economic Research, 1940.

Holmes, A. R. *The New York Foreign Exchange Market*. New York: Federal Reserve Bank of New York, 1959.

Holtrop, M. W. *Monetary Policy in an Open Economy: Its Objectives, Instruments, Limitations, and Dilemmas*. Princeton, N.J.: International Finance Section, 1963.

Machlup, F. *International Payments, Debts, and Gold*. New York: Charles Scribner's Sons, 1964.

Marcus, E., and M. R. Marcus. *International Trade and Finance*. New York: Pitman, 1965.

Morgenstern, O. *International Financial Transactions and Business Cycles*. Princeton, N.J.: Princeton University Press, 1959.

Mundell, R. A. "Capital Mobility and Stabilization Policy under Fixed and Flexible Exchange Rates," *Canadian Journal of Economics and Political Science*, November 1963.

Index